Books by James Thomas Flexner

American Painting

I. FIRST FLOWERS OF OUR WILDERNESS

II. THE LIGHT OF DISTANT SKIES

III. THAT WILDER IMAGE

AMERICA'S OLD MASTERS

THE POCKET HISTORY OF AMERICAN PAINTING
(also published as *A Short History of American Painting*)

JOHN SINGLETON COPLEY

GILBERT STUART

THE WORLD OF WINSLOW HOMER
(with the editors of Time-Life Books)

NINETEENTH CENTURY AMERICAN PAINTING

History and Biography

DOCTORS ON HORSEBACK
Pioneers of American Medicine

STEAMBOATS COME TRUE
(also published as *Inventors in Action*)

THE TRAITOR AND THE SPY
(also published as *The Benedict Arnold Case*)

MOHAWK BARONET
Sir William Johnson of New York

WILLIAM HENRY WELCH AND THE HEROIC AGE OF AMERICAN MEDICINE
(with Simon Flexner)

GEORGE WASHINGTON
I. *The Forge of Experience* (1732–1775)
II. *In the American Revolution* (1775–1783)
III. *And the New Nation* (1783–1793)
IV. *Anguish and Farewell* (1793–1799)

GEORGE WASHINGTON

Anguish and Farewell
(1793–1799)

George Washington, by Charles Balthazar Julien Fevret de Saint-Mémin. This was the last portrait of Washington, drawn when the ex-President was in Philadelphia during November 1789, organizing plans for an army to defend the United States from the French. Original lost. Reproduction courtesy of the New York Public Library. Astor, Lenox and Tilden Foundations

GEORGE WASHINGTON

Anguish and Farewell

(1793–1799)

by JAMES THOMAS FLEXNER

with photographs

LITTLE, BROWN AND COMPANY • BOSTON • TORONTO

FIRST EDITION

Library of Congress Cataloging in Publication Data

Flexner, James Thomas, 1908-
  George Washington: anguish and farewell (1793-1799).

  (His George Washington, v. 4)
  Bibliography: p.
  1. Washington, George, Pres. U. S., 1732-1799.
I. Title.
E312.29.F56   973.4'3'0924   72- 6875
ISBN 0-316-28602-8

Published simultaneously in Canada
by Little, Brown & Company (Canada) Limited

PRINTED IN THE UNITED STATES OF AMERICA

In Gratitude,
to the cultural force in the United States
that underlies all others:
the libraries

Contents

CONTENTS

List of Illustrations

[xi]

GEORGE WASHINGTON

Anguish and Farewell

(*1793–1799*)

Introduction

TO an extent which under examination becomes shocking, the passage of years has buried in historical memory the living Washington. The charm and splendor of his character, the greatness of his contribution to the United States and to human freedom everywhere, have been distorted into various caricatures, which are now regarded as the true man.

Even as it would be ridiculous to attribute a volcanic eruption to a molehill, so it is ridiculous to define Washington as a man incapable of achieving what Washington achieved. The cold hero who never smiled or loved or told a lie; the comic figure characterized by wooden false teeth; the hypocritical crook who refused any salary as Commander in Chief and then forged his expense account; the autocrat chuckling as he undermined the republican aspirations of American people; the self-congratulatory stuffed shirt — none of these could possibly have done what the record reveals Washington did. Not one of these would as a stripling have been entrusted with a dangerous and vital diplomatic mission through a frozen wilderness; not one could have kept, year after year, an unfed and naked army in the field to win a seemingly hopeless war against the might of Great Britain; not one would have repelled the possibility opened to him of being dictator or king; not one could have led a far-flung nation into a stronger constitutional union and then steered to solidity the first major republican government in the modern world; not one could have directed a mercantile nation torn by ideological disputes on the path of peace through the wars of the French Revolution; not one would have, in a position of perhaps unassailable power, always put first what he considered the welfare of the people.

Washington had to have the fierceness necessary to a successful soldier, the self-will necessary for a leader of men, the self-interest essential to the amassing of a large estate. He exploded sometimes into actions of which his best judgment disapproved. He could be very overbearing to his subordinates, even to fellow statesmen of such stature as Jefferson and Hamilton. In his private life as in his public, he was not always understanding, not always kind. Yet Washington wished to be wise and good.

Which of the triumphant generals, which of the great rulers in all time have so willingly relinquished power, have inspired so little fear among their contemporaries, so much love? Only after Washington's death could Jefferson have been correctly styled "The Man of the People." While Washington lived, even in his last unhappy years, the majority of the people followed, often in opposition to the expressed convictions of the Jeffersonians, wherever Washington led.

Washington's character comprised that pull of opposites which give color and depth. His heart was warm; his emotions fierce; his gentleness both deep and the result of control; his prudence due as much to self-education as to temperament; his intentions (although he sometimes slipped) altruistic; his force tremendous; his feelings oversensitive; his charm usually overwhelming. His motions were graceful although he had the physical strength of a giant. Conscious of an inadequate education, he was always slow of speech, seeking the right word. If he became sometimes self-righteous, he was always self-demanding. Although he was an aristocrat by temperament and achievement, his kindness knew no class or economic bounds.

This fourth volume in my life of Washington tells how the first President, although apprehensive because of the symptoms he felt within him of approaching old age, was forced to remain in power as his grasp did in fact weaken. By accepting a second term, he had laid open his fame, the reward for which he had so long labored, to attackers who gleefully charged that the weaknesses he now revealed had been characteristic of his whole career. He became deeply hurt, haunted by feelings of failure. Yet his last major services to the nation were as vitally important as his previous services had been.

Had Washington refused a second term or been unable to serve, the United States would quite probably have slipped into the wars touched off by the French Revolution, which wrecked much of Europe. Such involvement abroad might well have incited at home civil dissension that could have broken the union into two or more mutually hostile nations. The area now covered by the United States might well have become, in its political divisions, another Europe. Not even historians now most strongly interventionist believe that the newly formed republic would have been better off had it been caught up, while still weak and coalescing, in foreign politics.

The helm Washington held was at the opening of his second term tugged at from opposite sides by leaders who, while agreeing that peace was important to the United States, were greatly frightened by what they believed would be the effect in American farms and cities of victory achieved by one European camp or the other. The pro-French Jeffersonians saw British success lifting an aristocracy over the American people, while the pro-British Hamiltonians envisioned, should the French win, revolutionaries dominating the United States and perhaps setting up guillotines in American squares. Washington feared no tidal wave from Europe. He feared only the conflict between factions at home.

Avoiding, as best he could, the pro-French "brinkmanship" urged by Secretary of State Jefferson, the pro-British "brinkmanship" urged by Secretary of the Treasury Hamilton, Washington for a time persuaded the two rivals to work together, however acrimoniously, under his leadership. However, Jefferson became more and more unhappy and finally, disregarding Washington's importunings, resigned from the Cabinet.

Jefferson's resignation was for Washington the most destructive event in his entire career. The aging President was deprived of an invaluable counterweight in his administration to the able, grasping, and much younger Hamilton. And, no longer held down by executive responsibility, Jefferson went completely into the opposition, fanning the flames of what Washington considered irresponsible faction. Washington's acts and reputation became the target for clouds of envenomed darts. Although the mass of the people still loved and trusted him, he ceased, to his deep dismay, to be what he felt it was his duty to be: the accepted leader of all the people, everyman's President.

It had been assumed (even by Jefferson, who did not then object) that Washington would, like the kings who ruled around him, stay in power until death required a new President. Washington himself believed that the American experiment needed, to complete its demonstration that humanity could rule itself, the orderly relinquishment of power by one elected representative to his elected successor. This would be a prodigy in a world of kings. Although he might well have sought vindication from attacks in the overwhelming suffrage he would undoubtedly have received had he run again, Washington made his last major gift to the nation and the world by returning of his own free will to the private life for which part of his nature had always hankered. The republican system was thus sent rolling down its own road.

Washington longed for tranquillity, but carried bitterness back with him to his fields. He believed increasingly that he had been maligned from the worst motives, and betrayed by Jefferson. He finally became the partisan anti-French Federalist that he was to be wrongly accused of having previously been. Although periods of senility permitted him to engage in outrageous and unreasonable acts, he recognized, when urged by Federalists to run again for the Presidency in 1799, that for a man in his condition to agree would be "imbecility."

According to modern ideas, Washington was not at sixty-seven a truly old man. Yet his thread had been spun and he knew it. As soon as his final illness came upon him, he was sure — and not altogether regretfully — that this was the end.

Introductions being commonly written last, these paragraphs end twelve years' labor. Since this is the only extensive biography of Washington in more than a century which the author has lived to finish, my reaction should probably be relief that I am here alive to write these words and ready for future projects. Yet the completion of such a task as this brings sadness as well as jubilation.

In seeking imaginary intimacy with Washington, I have tried from the very beginning of my task to view the world over my protagonist's shoulder, attentive from day to day to his words as they were recorded in thousands of documents. I did, of course, step back sometimes to view Washington in the perspective offered by a distance of years. I would have been stupid to throw away the possibilities of clarifying the behavior of Washington's associates through documents not available to him but available to me. Although determined to prevent anything that has happened or been written during the intervening two centuries from dropping veils between me and my protagonist, I have profited from the researches and insights of my biographical and historical predecessors. But always my object has been to return to my stance at my protagonist's side, closer to the man who actually lived.

One of the advantages a biographer has over a novelist is that, while the novelist cannot spin out of his imagination a character whose dimensions are larger than his own, the biographer may stretch towards comprehension of an individual much greater than he. Although in this task the biographer cannot hope altogether to succeed, he need not altogether fail, and it is a fascinating adventure. During twelve years, I have on most mornings waked up anticipating association with an endlessly complicated and various individual who, so I became convinced, was one of the greatest men in all history. This is a privilege hard to relinquish.

When I started on this biography, I was asked again and again how I could expect to discover anything significant about a man whose life had been for two centuries examined and re-examined. My optimistic answers were based in part on faith — but only in part. Having written many books about the American eighteenth century, I had often run into Washington. The contexts were various, but on every occasion the person I met did not resemble accepted images. The one impressive and extensive modern life of Washington — that by Douglas Southhall Freeman and his successors — was only secondarily concerned with Washington as a man. It seemed to me that I would achieve something worth doing even if I did not go beyond extracting from the vast Washington archive those indications of character which had never been recognized and which might, through the alchemy of the biographer's art, be transmuted into the image of a living man. In this labor, as it turned out, I was assisted by the spirit of modern times that enabled me to present without creating any scandal such a frank character portrait as would have seemed shocking in any previous generation. I was thus protected not only from any personal inhibitions, but also from that temptation to defiance which must afflict a writer who knows that he is violating the inhibitions of others. The Washington who has appeared on my canvas gains in stature, I believe, from the demonstration that he was not cold and perfect, but was possessed with the same hungers as the rest of us, which he was by no means always successful in controlling. This is indeed the story of the education of a man who, out of an inner conviction of what he wished to be, created through his own intelligence and will the person he became.

Moving outside the realm of character study, I was amazed to discover how valuable a clarification of Washington's historical role could be achieved by pulling off, as does the restorer of a rebuilt mansion, later additions to get back to the original structure. This was true in relation to Washington's entire career, but particularly so in reference to the Presidency.

Many influential writers have studied Washington's governmental thoughts and actions less to discover what really happened, than to make their findings relevant to their own ideas concerning their own particular times. Still conspicuous in the Washington story are the theories that developed in the 1930's and 1940's when it was the historical fashion to view history, in the Marxist manner, as conflict between economic classes. Such class warfare was diagnosed (however anachronistically) in the federal period by pitting Hamilton, as the father of uncontrolled business enterprise, against Jefferson, who was viewed as the champion of the little man. Washington would have fitted in comfortably if accusations of fascist ambitions could have been made to stick. As it was, much use was made of the charge that he demonstrated rightist leanings by bowing too stiffly and entertaining too grandly — but this hardly served to make the first President a true class warrior. Since a noncombatant can be no more than a clog in a battle narrative, it became common to write about Washington's Presidency as if he had hardly been there. Page after page describes Hamilton's machinations and Jefferson's countermoves, Washington's name being thrown in occasionally to round out a sentence. This ignoring of the President was justified on the contention, which I believe this biography disproves, that Washington was no more than a shadow thrown by Hamilton.

My investigations have confirmed Washington in the position he held in the minds of his own contemporaries — even those who came to distrust him — as the towering figure in the Revolution and in the establishment of the government of the United States: the individual who did more than any other one man to create and preserve the republic.

An opportunity I had not foreseen was given me by the fact that the often surveyed panorama of Washington's career included a haunted forest which no historian or biographer had ever dared explore. This fourth volume of my *Washington* contains the first serious and nonpartisan examination of Washington's attitudes and behavior in relation to slavery. Cutting my own paths through the virgin forest, I found under the obscuring branches an historical discovery which seems to me of wide-ranging importance.

Starting from the conventional southern position, Washington found as

[8]

he grew older slavery more and more repugnant, while the Jeffersonian leadership, on the contrary, increasingly stilled those qualms which they had felt in the first burst of the American battle for freedom. Long before his Presidency, Washington saw advantages in the northern institutions which offered an alternate economic system to the slavery of his own native environment. His support of Hamilton's financial measures included this recognition, as did his unwillingness to accept Jefferson's contention that the future virtue and happiness of the United States depended on stamping out economic developments that menaced the hegemony of Virginian agrarianism.

Significantly, the nexus of opposition to the Virginian first President of the United States was in Virginia. As documents copiously demonstrate, fear of endangering the unity of the nation by further inflaming this opposition held Washington back, in the political sphere, from strongly advocating emancipation, and, in the personal sphere, impeded his efforts to bring justice to his own human possessions. A paragraph in a hitherto unnoticed letter, of which Washington kept no copy in his files, reveals what has remained unknown for almost two centuries: before returning to Mount Vernon from the Presidency, Washington secretly slipped into freedom some of his house slaves. His desire to free all his slaves during his lifetime has been lightly passed over or suppressed in the history books, nor has there been adequate recognition of the political significance of his doing what the Jeffersonian leaders did not do: free all his slaves in his will.

Washington, indeed, saw in the battle between Jefferson and Hamilton, the Republicans and the Federalists, the seeds of what became the civil war. And his own convictions were strongly on the side of emancipation.

The dozen years during which I have worked on this biography have seen violent shifts in the American attitude towards America. A wave of national self-abasement has viewed everything that had seemed noble in our history as suspect, hypocritical, probably evil. This biography was started before the self-disgust arose, and is, I believe, being completed when Americans are reaching out again to find aspects of their civilization of which they can be proud. Although not written with the intention of being particularly apposite to the present moment or any other, this biography may, I hope, serve the current need, since it describes the career of a man who, through the storms of personal temperament and outside circumstance, labored to keep virtue his guiding star.

I

The French Menace

C H A P T E R

1

An Angry Inauguration

IT was George Washington's sixty-second birthday, and ten days before his inauguration to his second term as President of the United States. Through the windows of his Philadelphia house he heard many feet strike the earth in unison. The sound brought back military memories, exciting, sad — and yet joyful, since the war in which he had commanded had been won. The nation that war had created prospered in physical peace. But there was no mental peace.

During that February of 1793, the footsteps were bringing Washington a delicate problem, since the soldiers were manifestly on their way to do him honor. He knew that the cannon shots and church bells which had greeted the dawn of his birthday and the later military displays were enraging good people who suspected that his government was inching towards monarchy.

Washington could not doubt that he could gratify many citizens by ignoring the Philadelphia militia now coming to attention in front of his house. But the plaudits of his compatriots were high among the satisfactions for which he had labored and it was not in his nature to rebuff men who wished to do him courtesy. He stepped to the window and, as the conservative *Gazette of the United States* reported, to the outrage of the radicals, "graciously" returned the military salute.[1]

That evening, in almost every town across the United States there were "birthnight balls." In most communities, these were considered the year's most glamorous social occasions. At Philadelphia the belles wove into their hair bandeaux embroidered "in language ancient or modern" with the legend "Long live the President." (We can visualize the mutual disdain between the fair pedants who sported Latin or Greek and the more cosmopolitan sisterhood who showed off their French.)[2] The diplomatic corps came out in their utmost splendor — how the ladies' necklines plunged; how the men's swords and medals rattled! That all these festivities followed the ancient tradition of birthday celebrations for kings seemed plain to those who cared to draw the conclusion. Washington thought it silly to draw the conclusion. He himself had demonstrated again and again his utter invulnerability to lures of royalty or dictatorial government. He was convinced that the United States was too solidly republican to be endangered by any aristocratic dreams or plots.

Following the old tradition, the Philadelphia birthnight ball could not begin until the guest of honor appeared. But this created no issue since it was a fetish with George Washington to keep no person waiting. The instant the hour struck, the band began "The President's March," ° and in came the tall General, still as erect as he had been on the Indian trails, and beside him his plump, diminutive wife.

It being not then the custom for the old to continue, as best they could, the behavior of youth, Washington, although once a passionate dancer, did not dance. However, he was too gregarious to remain seated beside Martha. Walking through the crowd, he greeted numerous people. If he paused to converse, the subject was never political tactics: disapproving of political parties, he considered himself allied to none. However, he was always eager to receive reports of the popular reactions in various regions to governmental decisions. Discussions of matters still pending were brushed aside. He talked of Revolutionary campaigns only to fellow veterans who would otherwise have felt cast down. If the President joined in a burst of mirth it would not be the result of some elaborately rehearsed anecdote. His taste was for unpremeditated sallies or a comic description of some events that had actually taken place. His humor could be macabre, as when he was amused that a politician had been killed in a duel despite the fact that the size of his opponent's nose had presented so perfect a target.[4]

At exactly the moment when the ball was scheduled to end, Washington, who had rejoined Martha, rose by her side. The band struck up a reprise of "The President's March," and the couple went out, unattended, but to prolonged cheers.

° Written in 1798 by an immigrant German bandmaster named Philip Phile, this tune was given continuing currency when, during the undeclared war with France, Joseph Hopkinson put new words to it beginning, "Hail Columbia, happy land!"[3]

[14]

The cheers were not echoed in the press of the emerging Republican party. Thus *The National Gazette,* edited by Jefferson's protégé and employee Philip Freneau, stated that the "monarchical farce of the birthday" had been promoted "with *great exertions*" by sinister persons for sinister purposes. Hitherto, the people "have passed over the absurdities of *levees* [Washington's official afternoon receptions] *and every species of royal pomp and parade* because they were associated with the man of their affections . . . but their own interest has at length conquered the delicacy of their attachment and they begin to express the abhorrence of the geegaws of a court with the manliness of freemen who are resolved not to erect a funeral pyre for their liberties." Washington was cherishing "a set of vipers . . . who, animated by too indulgent warmth, have struck their poisonous fangs into the placid bosom of peace and virtue."[5]

Although Washington knew that his official entertaining was not conspicuous for camaraderie he did not accuse himself of aristocratic haughtiness. He accused himself of ineptitude. Nurtured in the relaxed atmosphere of Virginia hospitality, he found grating to his sensibilities the formal receptions which he believed were forced upon him by his personal celebrity and his governmental position. Such routine hospitality, grounded not on friendship but on necessity and policy, brought out the shyness, the sense of personal awkwardness, that was part of his complex character.[6]

When Washington was setting out on a journey, his secretary wrote, "I must repeat what I have observed in a former letter, that as little ceremony and parade be made as possible, for the President wishes to command his own time, which these things always forbid in a greater or lesser degree, and they are to him fatiguing and oftentimes painful. He wishes not to exclude himself from the sight or conversation of his fellow citizens, but their eagerness to show their affection frequently imposes a heavy tax on him." As Washington's second term opened, he begged his brother-in-law, Burgess Ball, for help in finding a socially accomplished young man to "aid me in attentions to company."[7]

Washington found the rising tempo of the attacks on his personal behavior particularly upsetting because he had been persuaded to lock the door to escape. Not so long ago, he had believed that at this very moment he would be packing for his return to permanent retirement at Mount Vernon. But the leaders of the opposing political factions — Hamilton on one side, Jefferson and Madison on the other — had proved in complete agreement on one matter: unless Washington accepted the second term, which was almost upon him, the nation might pull apart. "Perhaps in no instance in my life," Washington wrote his close friend David Humphreys, "have I been more sensible of the sacrifice than in the present." However, "A Farmer" warned from the pages of *The National Gazette* that if the public continued to set Washington up as an "idol" he might well, over the prostrate body of the people, perpetuate himself in office as another Cromwell.[8]

Washington's first inaugural had featured great pomp, and elicited public rejoicing which Washington had considered unpleasantly hysterical. Now he asked his Cabinet° to decide, at a conference which he pointedly did not himself attend, what should be the nature of his second inaugural. Should it be conducted privately or in public? And how should the ceremonies be tuned so as best to please the majority of the people?

Jefferson, the tall, lanky Secretary of State; Edmund Randolph, the plump Attorney General; and Henry Knox, the fat Secretary of War, met at Knox's residence. One member of the Cabinet was missing. However, the lean Secretary of the Treasury, Alexander Hamilton, had submitted a written opinion.

Convinced that Hamilton wished to establish a monarchy, Jefferson surely expected that his rival would argue for great pomp. But Hamilton urged that Washington take the oath, in the presence only of the department heads, at his own house. Although Jefferson hated to agree with Hamilton, he could not disagree. However, Knox was vociferous in his opposition. Knox insisted that "parade" was required to emphasize Washington's conspicuous eminence, which was the only force that held the nation together. Randolph agreed with Knox. In this impasse, Hamilton was again consulted. At his suggestion, it was agreed that there be a simple swearing-in ceremony at the Senate chamber.

Washington's advisers suggested that he go from his residence to the Senate "without form, attended by such gentlemen as he choose." He chose to ride in his own coach, unattended, alone.

Although on March 4, 1793, crowds lined the streets and cheered the hero as he passed, the thoughts of the aging man who rocked by himself in his small, upholstered room were resentful. After he had entered with as little ceremony as possible, he delivered a curt speech. Here is George Washington's Second Inaugural Address in its entirety:[9]

° The word "Cabinet," although too convenient not to be used here, was only partially current in 1793: Washington preferred such phrases as "the Heads of the Departments and the Attorney General."

"Fellow Citizens: I am again called upon by the voice of my country to execute the functions of its chief magistrate. When the occasion proper for it shall arrive, I shall endeavor to express the high sense I entertain of this distinguished honor, and of the confidence which has been reposed in me by the people of the United States.

"Previous to the execution of any official act of the President, the Constitution requires an oath of office. This oath I am now about to take and in your presence, that if it shall be found during my administration of the government I have in any instance violated willingly or knowingly the injunction thereof, I may (besides incurring Constitutional punishment) be subject to the upbraidings of all who are now witnesses of the present solemn ceremony."[10]

Having spoken soberly of duty and punishment, Washington took the oath and returned as quickly and unobtrusively as possible to his residence. He was committed to four more years of what he angrily described as "slavery."[11]

As Washington sat in his study, many of his thoughts and worries flew overseas. After years of accelerating rumble, the French Revolution had exploded. Revolutionary France was at war with several of her aristocratic neighbors; the King had been deposed and imprisoned; the guillotine was active; and a republic had been declared. And the issues that were dividing peoples and nations abroad were crossing the ocean to heighten previously existing divisions at home. For the first time since America had won her independence, Europe was impinging seriously on the United States.

It had been in the middle of Washington's first term that conflicting factions had arisen within and without his administration. Led by Jefferson and Madison, a group who called themselves Republicans* had insisted that a "corrupt squadron," nurtured in the legislature by Hamilton's financial policies, were creating a monetary system which favored upstart urban speculators over the agrarians who, as they stood upright in their fields, supplied — so the Republicans insisted — the moral and philosophical base on which anti-monarchical institutions were grounded. Although fulminations and warnings had poured from the Jeffersonian press, the issue had failed to catch fire with the people: the Republican party still had hardly any existence outside Virginia.

---

* The more radical term "Democrat" then carried with it such implications of unbridled mob rule that, although it was applied to them by their opponents, it was repudiated by the Jeffersonians until a considerably later date.

But when in the fall of 1792 the top blew off the French Revolution, a situation was created which, as Jefferson put it, "kindled and brought forward the two parties with an ardor which our own interests merely could never excite."[12] The Republicans regarded the French explosion as a revival of the American revolutionary spirit, and saw it as the beginning of a universal re-creation of European institutions on American republican principles.

The Federalists had been limited during the previous controversy to accusing their opponents of wishing to subvert the Constitution by weakening the federal government and the nation's finances to a point of chaos, which demagogues could use for ends surely sinister but yet not clearly definable. The French Revolution supplied definitions. It was now argued that should the French cause triumph abroad, at home no American's property and life would be safe from mobs led by incendiaries. To this, the Republicans answered that if "freedom" were stamped out in France it would also be stamped out in the United States, where a king would then rule.

During the controversies of his first term, Washington had done his best to be neutral, and the situation he now found himself in, as a unanimously re-elected President, was one measure of his success. Another was the fact that he had held both Jefferson and Hamilton in his Cabinet. Yet, because the Hamiltonian program had been passed by Congress and not vetoed by Washington, the Republicans had found themselves drifting into the position of an opposition.

Since the fighting in Europe was still altogether landlocked — Prussia and Austria against France — there was no way that Americans could take governmental action either to encourage or to suppress the French revolutionaries. Local controversy found its outlet in squabbles over symbolism and manners. A movement was started in the House of Representatives to melt down, as "a useless bauble," the silver mace of that House which mingled Roman with native iconography: thirteen arrows tied together like fasces with an eagle on top. Any formal behavior was regarded as a confession of monarchical principles. It was in this context that Washington's way of life and method of entertaining were attacked as viruses infecting the purity of American institutions.

Jefferson was enchanted with this new development that could be counted on to increase the power of the Republicans since he was convinced that the majority of the people sympathized with the revolution in France. Hamilton, who agreed with Jefferson's estimate of the public mood, was worried. Lying low was clearly the order of the moment for the Hamiltonians.[13]

When on March 17, 1793, word came in that Louis XVI had made a one-way journey to the guillotine, Jefferson became all ears. He was determined to make political capital from the reactions of the leaders of Philadelphia society, whom he had dubbed with the damaging phrase "monocrats."* The males, he reported to Madison, were being more discreet than he had expected. However, the ladies "of the first circle are all open-mouthed against the murderers of a sovereign, and they generally speak those sentiments which the more cautious husband smothers."[14]

As long as Louis XVI had remained, at least titularly, on the throne, Washington faced no problem as to whether the shifting French governments were in fact legitimate. However, the declaration by the National Convention of a republic set up dangerous alternatives. Obviously, the aristocratic powers of Europe would not recognize the republican government. A government in exile, under a regent, might easily be established, recognized by France's neighbors, and assisted, perhaps successfully, in a counterrevolutionary takeover of power. The decision whether the United States should make the bold step of recognizing the revolutionary French government lay in the final analysis on Washington's shoulders. Not to do so would outrage the existing rulers of France and their American supporters. To do so would outrage the aristocratic powers and displease the American Federalists. Yet some decision had to be reached.

In this first major response to the new crisis, Washington plumped for the Jeffersonians and revolutionary France. The letter Jefferson drafted with the President's approval put the issue on a high plane of principle. "We surely cannot deny to any nation that right whereon our own government is founded, that every nation may govern itself according to whatever form it pleases. . . . The will of the nation is the only thing essential to be regarded." This letter accorded recognition on the assumption, which the Hamiltonians and aristocrats denied, that the existing French government reflected the will of the people.

In the same document Jefferson offered to pay the French republic more than was currently due as an installment on the war debt the United States had incurred to Louis XVI during her own revolution. The money was to be expended in the United States for provisions that would assist France in a period of famine. This had been a Cabinet decision,

---

* This word, implying both monarchy and aristocracy, had become Jefferson's favorite appellation for the Hamiltonians.

reached unanimously, since Hamilton had been unwilling to take the onus of voting to let the French people starve.[15]

Nature had not given Washington a son, but he loved, almost as a son, the Marquis de Lafayette. Lafayette had for a while led France, trying to keep the revolution there moderate, as the American Revolution had been. He had finally been forced to flee from the extremists to Austria, where the aristocrats threw him into prison. Now Washington held in his hand a letter from Mme de Lafayette imploring him to use his international prestige to secure the release of his dearest friend. How rapidly, had he been a private citizen, would Washington have hurried to his writing table! But now he did not trust himself to answer Mme de Lafayette. He asked Jefferson to draft a reply which would convey "all the consolation I can with propriety give her consistent with my public character and the national policy."[16]

Jefferson's letter expressed equal affection for Lafayette and for the nation that had banished him. It went on to say that, although Washington could not take the steps Mme de Lafayette desired, he was not "contenting myself with inactive wishes." Washington copied out the letter verbatim, perhaps with tears in his eyes, for he was not ashamed to weep. Then he took the longest step he thought he legitimately could. He had Jefferson instruct Gouverneur Morris, the American minister to France, "to neglect no favorable opportunity to express *informally* the sentiments and wishes" of the United States concerning Lafayette.[17]

When Lafayette's brother-in-law, the Comte de Noailles, appeared in Philadelphia, Washington was forced into behavior that could only make him feel even more bitter concerning the official entertaining for which he was so criticized and which he so disliked. Noailles had been Washington's fellow soldier and friend during the Revolution. Had Washington been at Mount Vernon, he would have ridden miles to greet Noailles enthusiastically on the road. But the aristocrat had come to the United States at the head of a delegation of émigrés from France; it was reported that he had a petition to present to Washington. The President felt forced to ask Hamilton to "intimate to him gently, and delicately," that the need to preserve the government's impartiality made it impossible for Washington to show his old friend any special courtesies.[18] However, Washington's unhappy, prudent self-sacrifice was wasted. Finding a sinister plot in the lack of any public Presidential gestures towards Noailles, the opposition published in the newspapers a report that Washington had, in the depth of the night, held a clandestine rendezvous with the aristocratic

Frenchman. They had been closeted for hours, poring together over papers. It was horrifying to imagine what dark, unworthy, antirepublican deeds those secret documents portended![19]

Another effort at discretion that boomeranged was Washington's refusal to receive Talleyrand, the French revolutionary who had been exiled from his own country and then from Great Britain. Later, when Talleyrand, as the result of a shift in French politics, became Minister of Foreign Affairs, his resentment at having been slighted by Washington helped draw the United States to the brink of war with France.[20]

Washington's favorite relaxation was to take, of a Sunday, the weekly report he received of activity on his farms, make a list of problems and opportunities, and then answer each point in great detail, scratching it off the list after he had done so. Thus in his imagination he was carried to the embellishment of his estate, the construction of barns, the planting routine on every field, the operation of his mill and his fisheries, the fertility of his herds, and a thousand other considerations both entertaining and absorbing. But this occupation was suddenly taken away from him. Word came that his estate manager, Anthony Whiting, was spitting blood with tuberculosis, and then there was silence. The mails from Virginia, which Washington so eagerly awaited, brought no news from Mount Vernon.[21]

Dislocation at the estate that supplied most of Washington's private income could be a very serious matter, since Washington was living beyond his salary as President, and intended, as soon as he could, to return to his life as a planter. It was essential that he get home and find out what the situation was.

After Congress had adjourned until fall, Washington labored to clear away all outstanding business. And he turned some of his leisure thoughts to a subject that had fascinated him ever since he was a young man: the breeding of horses.

Washington's only departure from strict propriety as Commander in Chief had been induced by an irresistible yearning to buy fifty or a hundred cavalry mares too worn down for military service yet still attractive to stallions. After the war, he had accepted from the King of Spain a majestic jackass whom he put to mares in a desire to breed supermules. Since mules ate less and pulled more strongly than horses, he hoped to develop varieties suitable for all the needs of Virginia.* Despite ridicule

---

* Historians of the subject date the "significant" introduction of mules into the United States from Washington's efforts.

and setbacks, he still intended to ride out in his carriage behind a team of mules. He had written his manager earlier in 1793, "When I consented to give up the first set of mules that were chosen for my carriage [was Martha one of the protesters?], it was because I was told they did not match well, or promise much, but that others were coming on, from which *a very good set* could be drawn." He was all eagerness to see how they were maturing.[22]

One problem raised by the production of mules was that not all mares would accept a jackass. If, being thus finicky, they remained not "satisfied," the foals they could bear would be lost for that season. Washington therefore wished to procure and have waiting for him at Mount Vernon a stallion capable of taking over when necessary. Washington was less interested in the horse's pedigree than his appearance. He wished the stallion to be fifteen and a half to sixteen hands high, "of a handsome carriage," and having "a small well-formed head and neck as constituting essential parts in the beauty of a horse."[23]

When he reached Mount Vernon in early April, Washington found his manager somewhat recovered. However, he himself lacked the strength to ride the circuit of his farms as he had in earlier years done daily. During his stay, he traversed the miles to his River Plantation "not more than once or twice."[24]

As Washington meditated on the situation in which he and the nation now found themselves, his conclusions differed from both Jefferson's and Hamilton's because he felt that the European ideological battle had no great relevancy to the United States. Neither a Hamiltonian nor a Jeffersonian,* neither an Anglophile nor a Francophile, he believed that the United States was quite capable of going her own republican way however the cat jumped abroad. The best summary of his attitude at this time was contained in a letter to David Humphreys:

"If it can be esteemed a happiness to live in an age productive of great and interesting events, we of the present age are very highly favored. The rapidity of national revolutions appear no less astonishing, than their magnitude. In what they will terminate, is known only to the great ruler of events; and confiding in his wisdom and goodness, we may safely trust

---

* The fallacy of the often expressed opinion that Washington was, during his first term, a repudiator of Jefferson's and a follower of Hamilton's policies, has been demonstrated in volume III of this biography. The most obvious proof is that Jefferson was just as anxious as Hamilton to have Washington accept a second term.

the issue to him, without perplexing ourselves to seek for that, which is beyond human ken; only taking care to perform the parts assigned us, in a way that reason and our own consciences approve of.

"All our late accounts from Europe hold up the expectation of a general war in that quarter. . . . I trust that we shall have too just a sense of our own interest to originate any cause, that may involve us in it; and I ardently wish we may not be forced into it by the conduct of other nations. If we are permitted to improve without interruption, the great advantages which nature and circumstances have placed within our reach, many years will not revolve before we may be ranked not only among the most respectable, but among the happiest people on this globe. Our advances to these points are more rapid than the most sanguine among us ever predicted. A spirit of improvement displays itself in every quarter, and principally in objects of the greatest public utility, such as opening the inland navigation . . . improving the old roads and making new ones; building bridges and houses, and in short pursuing those things which seem eminently calculated to promote the advantage and accommodation of the people at large. Besides these, the enterprises of individuals show at once what are the happy effects of personal exertions in a country, where equal laws and equal rights prevail."[25]

Before he left the capital, Washington had heard an unsubstantiated rumor, brought by a ship from Portugal, that France had declared war on England, Holland, and Russia.[26] Since such a war would involve major naval powers, the infection would no longer be limited to the continent of Europe. England would certainly use her control of the seas to try to blockade France. American boats running the blockade would be in peril of attacks, the repercussions from which might, in the present state of public opinion, carry the United States into war. Furthermore, aggressive American sailors and shipowners would see an opportunity to line their pockets and help France by setting their vessels up as privateers* and

---

* A privateer was a vessel belonging to a private owner which had been commissioned by a belligerent state to carry on the operations of war. Typically, privateers, avoiding warships and battles, fell on merchant shipping. After a captured vessel was brought to shore, some authority of the nation that had commissioned the privateer set up a "prize court" which determined whether the ship had actually been vulnerable to capture. If so, the "prize" was declared legal, which meant that the vessel and its cargo could be sold for the benefit of the captors. The earnings were divided according to a previously arranged formula between the owners of the privateer and the members of the crew, whose share was assessed according to their rank. There was no quicker way of getting rich than through this piracy, the legality of which was in the eighteenth century generally accepted.

pouncing on British shipping. Add that the United States had left over from the alliance during the Revolutionary War treaties with France which, if honored to the full, could by themselves create war with England.

On April 4, 1793, after he had been at Mount Vernon for two days, Washington received a letter from Jefferson doubting the war rumors and stating that a revolution in England was more likely. However, a paper soon came from Hamilton stating, "There seems to be no room for doubt of the existence of war." By the seventh, Jefferson had changed his tune, saying war was "extremely probable," and in a letter dated the eighth Hamilton expressed certainty that France had declared war on the three maritime powers.[27]

On April 12, Washington wrote both Jefferson and Hamilton that he was hurrying to Philadelphia. The United States was, he continued, in the most extreme danger of being drawn into war. Immediate action was necessary, since American vessels were already "designated [by French representatives in the United States] as privateers and are preparing accordingly." His ministers should work out, in preparation for his arrival, plans for governmental measures that would prevent American citizens from embroiling the United States with either England or France.[28]

2

The Neutrality Proclamation

W HEN the United States was struck by the danger of being drawn into a world conflict, the federal government was hardly more than four years old. The Constitution presented only general principles that required in practice much interpretation. During its brief existence, the government had had enough to do in drawing the conclusions that were demanded from day to day. Thus, when a brand-new problem like the European war came roaring in, Washington could find no American precedents to guide him. As for Old World precedents, were they applicable to a republican government?

The situation was parallel to that Washington had faced when, as a very young man during the French and Indian War, he had been concerned with building the roads that first crossed the Alleghenies. The difficult task of improvising a way around the obstacles ahead was further complicated by the significance cast on the labor by its uniqueness: the only road across the mountains would go far to determine future lines of trade.

Later Presidents have been well supplied with precedents, and the very existence of these signposts makes any new decision less significant. If the President ignores the signs, they nonetheless remain to be consulted on future occasions. But Washington's efforts to deal most effectively with an immediate problem were confused because his decision would throw so long a shadow. "Few who are not philosophical spectators," he wrote, "can realize the difficult and delicate part which a man in my situation has to act. . . . I walk on untrodden ground. There is scarcely any part of my conduct which may not hereafter be drawn into precedent."[1]

Only three years before the current crisis, when Congress had set up the "great departments," they had considered relations with the nations across the broad Atlantic of too little importance to occupy the full time of a Secretary. The official who had been known under the Confederation as Secretary of Foreign Affairs was given a broader title, Secretary of State, and all domestic matters not specifically assigned to other departments were added to his duties.

The issues between the United States and her continental neighbors, Spain and England, being during Washington's first term only potentially lethal, there had been no need to deal seriously with the question of authority in foreign relations. The Constitution had divided responsibility by providing that the President was to act with the "advice and consent" of the Senate. Although Washington had sensed the existence of a problem, no one had really worried over the fact (which of course still persists in the twentieth century) that awaiting the decisions of a legislative body, which must move slowly and argumentatively, is incompatible with situations that demand a speedy and forceful decision. Washington would undoubtedly have consulted the Senate in the current crisis had Congress been in session. But it was not. This created a dilemma for which the Constitution gave no hint of a solution.

At the moment, immediate need shouted down any recourse to theory. To delay a decision would be to make one by default, since in a few weeks so many American citizens would set up pro-French privateers that the United States would become, willy-nilly, a belligerent. Yet the size of the nation and the slowness of movement made impossible the convening of a special legislative session in less than six weeks or two months.

Washington remembered that "from the moment" news of war between England and France penetrated to Mount Vernon, he had recognized that the executive would have to act on its own, fast and hard. It would be necessary for him, as President, to issue a proclamation "restraining . . . our citizens from taking part in the contest."[2]

Did this mean that for the first time in the history of the government the executive would do what Washington had so strenuously sought to avoid doing: encroach on the legislature's prerogative of making law? There were many legal niceties that could be applied to answering this disturbing question. However, as Washington dashed in his carriage for Philadelphia, the question which impinged most urgently upon him was whether his Cabinet would be practical enough to abandon their squabbling in the face of imminent disaster, whether they would be bold enough to support the constitutionally dangerous decision that the dangerous moment required.

The crisis had found Hamilton busy at the capital. For more than a year he had engaged in clandestine foreign policy discussions with the British minister to the United States, George Hammond. While everyone was waiting for word of the outbreak of the war, Hammond reported twice to his government that Hamilton had given "most secret assurances" that he would "exert his influence" to keep the United States from being drawn into the conflict on the side of France. Hammond explained that "any event which might endanger the external tranquillity of the United States" would be "fatal" not only to Hamilton's financial system, but to "his personal reputation and to his future prospects of ambition."[3]

As soon as Hamilton knew that war existed, before the news had reached Mount Vernon, he wrote John Jay, the Chief Justice of the Supreme Court and his own close collaborator, to ask whether, under the circumstances, the United States should receive the new French minister — his name was Edmond Charles Genêt — who was on his way across the ocean to replace the minister who had represented the former French government. The ferment in which Hamilton found himself was revealed by his sending on the same day a second letter to Jay. This time he asked, "Would not a proclamation prohibiting our citizens from taking comm[issions] etc. on either side be proper?" Then Hamilton raised a politically shrewd question: In deference to the national pro-French sentiment, should the proclamation avoid actually stating that the United States was neutral in the war? He hoped that Jay would prepare a draft.[4]

As Jay well realized, Hamilton feared that receiving the representative of the new government might be construed as an acknowledgment that the treaties the United States had made with Louis XVI were still binding. Two provisions in particular seemed to contain seeds of war with England. The Treaty of Alliance committed the United States — this became known as "the guarantee" — to protect the French West Indies if they should be attacked and France should ask for aid. The Commercial Treaty provided that French privateers could bring their prizes to American ports, and that powers hostile to France might not fit out privateers in the United States.[5]

Jay replied to Hamilton that he considered it impolitic to try to bar the French minister or, for the time being, even discuss treaty provisions. He favored a proclamation with no mention of neutrality. "It is happy for us,"

Jay wrote, "that we have a Presid. who will do nothing rashly, and who regards his own interest as inseparable from the public good."

The draft of a proclamation which Jay enclosed stated that the United States would have "political intercourse" with any government actually in power, and required all citizens not to take any action against any belligerent. Jay then launched into a passage which presaged the Alien and Sedition acts that were to create such outrage when passed during John Adams's administration in 1798: Washington was to "recommend" that citizens refrain from public discussions that might cause controversy at home or might irritate foreign powers. Furthermore, the President should admonish printers to be impartial, publishing nothing that would offend either belligerent.[6]

There is no way of knowing whether Jay's draft was handed on to Washington. If it was, the President proved immune to the suggestions that he interfere with freedom of speech and the press.

Before the crisis actually struck, Jefferson wrote his collaborator Congressman Madison (who was home in Virginia during the recess of Congress) that if the British made an effort to blockade France, "I suppose Congress would be called, because it is a justifiable cause of war, and, as the Executive cannot decide the question of war on the affirmative side, neither ought it to do so on the negative side, by preventing the competent body from deliberation on the question." Jefferson foresaw a commercial boycott of the aggressor which would reveal "that nations may be brought to do justice" without fighting.[7]

However, when the war was actually declared, France seemed to have made the declaration, which could be construed as showing her the aggressor — and the last thing Jefferson wanted was an anti-French boycott. His eagerness not to submit to a British blockade remained unabated, but he wrote to Washington at Mount Vernon, without on this occasion avoiding the dangerous word neutrality: "We [must] take every justifiable measure for preserving our neutrality."[8]

Jefferson was at the gates of a dilemma which was to throw him (so his biographer Malone wrote) into an "agony" of nervous tension. He was already plagued by several unavoidable contradictions. How was America to preserve her neutrality without accepting a British blockade? And how could Jefferson's conviction that only Congress was competent to decide on war and peace be reconciled with the speedy action that was necessary if planned decisions were to be at all possible? To make matters worse from Jefferson's pro-French point of view, American neutrality would be to the disadvantage of France. Since the British navy kept most French merchant vessels off the seas, the ships available for American raiders to harass were mostly British.[9]

The problem of what to do lay, of course, in the particular province of the Secretary of State, but Washington habitually used his Cabinet as a whole and as he pleased. In this crisis, he had asked both Jefferson and Hamilton for suggestions. Jefferson was too torn to draw up a plan. Being pro-British and favoring executive power. Hamilton suffered from no confusions.

Having dashed into town. Washington examined what papers awaited him and then sent out a series of questions to serve as the agenda for a Cabinet meeting. Jefferson read them with horror. They seemed designed to lead, step by step, to repudiation of the treaties with France. Although the document was in Washington's autograph, Jefferson angrily concluded that it had been drawn up by Hamilton.[10]

Washington had renewed reason to be thankful that he had managed, despite increasing conflicts, to hold the leaders of the opposing factions in double harness. With Jefferson and Hamilton both present, the meeting he called for April 19, 1793, would be a good indication of problems ahead. If the Cabinet could be made to act with adequate unanimity, there was hope that the United States would be spared grave internal discord and a disastrous leap into foreign war. But if the meeting descended into angry quarrels — Washington's heart quailed at what might be the result. He must have been apprehensive as he waited for his Cabinet to assemble. Hamilton was commonly late, to Washington's perpetual irritation; if he was so on this occasion, he undoubtedly saw an unusually dark frown on the President's face.

As had been presaged in Hamilton's correspondence with Jay, the first question had been carefully phrased to give pro-French sentiment an out: the issue of whether the President should ban "interference" by American citizens in the war was carefully separated from whether the proclamation should "contain a declaration of neutrality." Jefferson eagerly seized this opportunity. Although he had urged "neutrality" in writing to Washington, he insisted that a declaration of neutrality would be an encroachment on the right of the legislature to establish policy. However, since a state of peace existed, the President could promulgate its continuance until the Senate came to a different conclusion. After a sharp debate, in which Hamilton insisted that to lay down a line of foreign policy was a necessary prerogative of an adequately strong executive, the word "neutrality" was banned.

Washington felt no need to take part in this argument. The verbal issue, however useful it might be in letting off steam, was in the present context irrelevant since, whatever wording was used, the proclamation would have to declare what was in effect neutrality. And it soon became clear, to Washington's relief, that, after the fireworks, the necessary decision would be reached. And so it was: the Cabinet agreed unanimously to issue a proclamation.

Washington assigned drafting the text, not to the Secretary of State but to Attorney General Randolph. This was not a slight to Jefferson but a kindness: unhappy about the whole situation, the Secretary of State was glad to be let off the hook, not forced to be the prime mover. He was later, when under attack from his own friends and supporters, to claim that he had voted for the Proclamation only because "it was not expedient to oppose it altogether, lest it should prejudice what was the next question, the boldest and greatest that ever was hazarded."

The next question was, Shall a minister of the republic of France be received? There is no indication in the notes Jefferson took at the time that the subject elicited any real disagreement. Hamilton, it is true, expressed regret that Genêt's arrival in the United States (he was at Charleston) made necessary an immediate facing of the issue. However, he voted with his colleagues to make unanimous the unavoidable decision to receive.[11]

So far so good, and on to question three: Should Genêt be received "absolutely or with qualifications"? Hamilton was instantly off on one of those long speeches in which he reveled. Even Americans who did not share his convictions that the present French government was illegal, bloodthirsty, and a menace to order everywhere, should realize that there might be further shifts in France, creating a different setup — perhaps a military despotism — with which they would not wish to be allied. But receiving Genêt without reservations would reaffirm the old treaties in perpetuity. This would wreck American neutrality. However, such an act was, fortunately, unnecessary. The actual circumstances gave the United States the right under international law either to denounce the treaties or to declare them suspended until the government in France took a final form.

Washington (as he later admitted) did not agree with Hamilton, but he listened without comment or telltale facial expression. Jefferson seethed. He was later to write that Hamilton "is panic-struck if we refuse our breach [behind] to every kick which Great Britain may choose to give it. He is for proclaiming at once the most abject principles, such as would invite and merit habitual insults."

When Hamilton finally ceased, Knox (so read Jefferson's notes on the meeting) agreed with Hamilton, "acknowledging at the same time, like a fool that he is, that he knew nothing about it."

Now it was Jefferson's turn. A letter he later sent Washington reveals that he was too upset to attempt an answer to Hamilton. He merely said that he considered it "clear" that the treaty remained "valid." Randolph chimed in with Jefferson. But then Hamilton (who had prepared himself better than had his colleagues) produced a quotation from a famous book on international law published in 1758 by the Swiss diplomat Emerich de Vattel. The burden was that treaties did not automatically continue when governments changed.

Since the infant United States had herself made no precedents, and no one in the room had anything else to quote, the passage that Jefferson referred to as "a scrap in Vattel" had a profound effect. Appealed to as the lawyer of the group, Randolph said "that in so great a question" he should choose to give a written opinion.

Washington leapt on the opportunity to stop the angry discussion by asking that everyone send in written opinions. He then passed over the issues remaining on the agenda, which dealt with future relations with France, moving to the thirteenth and last question. It required an immediate answer: Should Congress be called into a special session?

Involved was a head-on collision — at least as far as Jefferson was concerned — between constitutional theory and practical necessity. Jefferson accepted necessity, making unanimous the vote not to call Congress.[12]

Washington then adjourned the meeting. He could look back on it with satisfaction. He had long believed that, if men agreed on their ultimate objective, it made little difference on what path towards it they traveled. And, although conflict had been rife and tempers short, his Cabinet Secretaries had revealed a unanimous desire to keep the United States at peace. For his own part, he had not descended from his position as umpire by taking visible sides with anyone. He had allowed the debates to go on whenever there had been any possibility of unanimous decision, and then had managed, without appearing high-handed, to switch the procedure to the least inflammatory type of argument: the presentation of written statements. After he had studied those, he would make up his own mind concerning how the problems raised by the treaties with France could best be handled.

Washington was careful to exclude all other issues from the Cabinet meeting that considered the draft of the Proclamation which Randolph had drawn up under his own supervision. Approval being unanimous, Washington published the Proclamation on April 22.[13]

It stated that "the duty and interest of the United States require, that they should with sincerity and good faith adopt and pursue a conduct friendly and impartial towards the belligerent powers." All citizens were warned "carefully to avoid all acts and proceedings whatsoever, which may in any manner tend to contravene such disposition." Citizens who abetted hostilities on the ocean or loaded what was deemed "contraband by the modern usages of nations," would receive no protection from the United States, and those who engaged in belligerency within the jurisdiction of American courts would be prosecuted.[14]

The most important of the written arguments on how Genêt should be received were, of course, from Hamilton and Jefferson. Hamilton had a clear road down which he traveled energetically and at his usual great length. The French revolutionary regime, having been created in horror and continued with the bloodshed of the Terror, did not deserve American support. Various authorities on international law demonstrated that the United States need not apply treaties made with one government to another, the legitimacy of which was dubious and which had not demonstrated its ability to rule. To receive Genêt without qualifications would, however, reaffirm the treaties. This might be regarded by England as a cause for war and, in any case, would put the peace of the United States at the mercy of France.

Jefferson wove a complicated web. He introduced philosophical arguments to demonstrate the legitimacy of the French government, which he praised as serving the rights of man, and he found his own quotations in the recognized authorities which stated that treaties were not made with governments that changed but with peoples that remained constant. Then he came to the practical side of his argument. That was undoubtedly what impressed Washington.

When Jefferson acknowledged that in the last analysis "the law of self-preservation overrules obligations to others," he was stating what Washington had on a previous occasion expressed in his comment that it was useless for one nation to try to overreach another in diplomacy, since in all cases treaties would only be observed so long as they were advantageous to both parties. Jefferson's further contention that a treaty could not be legitimately denounced unless the danger it contained was "great, inevitable, and imminent," fitted in with the belief of the former general (who had become so adept at guerrilla warfare) that the longer you could postpone a confrontation the better. Washington agreed with Jefferson that receiving Genêt without comment concerning the treaties in no way reconfirmed them, and also in the conclusion that France might never try to draw the United States into the war by invoking "the guarantee." If she did so, the matter could be handled then. Washington was surely pleased to note that Jefferson, despite his prejudices, suggested a way to get around one of the more bothersome treaty provisions. The Secretary of State pointed out that, although it had been agreed that the enemies of France might not fit out privateers or sell prizes in the United States, it had not been specifically stated that the French themselves had this privilege. Neutrality could be furthered by applying the same rule to both belligerents.[15]

In telling Jefferson that the government would receive Genêt without any reservations, Washington added that he had never doubted that this was the correct course, but "since the question had been suggested, he thought it ought to be considered."[16]

Although the Proclamation had been against the French interest and the decision concerning Genêt and the French treaties against the British, on the domestic front the balance had not been even. Jefferson had gone along on the Proclamation but Washington had been forced to override Hamilton on Genêt. As the time of the French minister's arrival in Philadelphia came closer, Washington told Jefferson that he wished the French representative to be received politely, yet without enthusiasm. Jefferson was taken aback, but soon decided that this was the result of a conversation with Hamilton and intended as a sop to the pro-British party.[17]

The next ticklish issue involved how the Proclamation would be enforced. Bureaucracy had burgeoned so little that the only federal officials spread across the land were the representatives of the Treasury who collected customs duties. Hamilton suggested that these collectors report to him, as their normal superior, acts of American citizens contrary to the Proclamation. Jefferson concluded that Hamilton intended to set up a system of espionage that would enable him to blackmail his political opponents. However, the State Department had no equal facilities to offer. Jefferson could make no better suggestion than that enforcement be entrusted to regional grand juries. This would have placed the peace of the entire United States in the hands of any local group that, swayed by French sentiment or the greed of shipowners, condoned actions that would be considered, in the international theatre, a cause for war. Yet Jefferson was enraged when, as he put it, Randolph "found a hair to split," and when Washington thankfully accepted Randolph's compromise: the collectors of customs should report violations to the federal district attorneys, who would notify the Attorney General.[18]

According to Hamilton's original suggestion, the customs officers were to report the building of ships pierced for guns. To this Washington objected on the grounds that "I am not disposed to adopt any measures which may check shipbuilding in this country." And then he stated what was to remain his basic conception in the entire crisis: "To take a *fair* and *supportable* ground I conceive to be our best policy, and is all that can be required of us by the powers at war: leaving the rest to be managed according to circumstances and the advantages which may be derived from them."[19]

The publication of the Proclamation elicited howls of rage from the republican press, which clamored that the executive had finally betrayed its true predilections by unfurling the flag of monarchy. These attacks worried, discouraged, and angered Washington, but Jefferson's feelings were mixed. He exulted to Senator James Monroe, "All the old Spirit of '76 is rekindling! The newspapers from Boston to Charleston prove this, and even the monocrat papers are obliged to publish the most furious philippics against England."[20] But the fact remained that Jefferson had voted for the Proclamation.

The mails brought Jefferson reproachful letters from his closest collaborator, Madison. Vacationing in Virginia during the recess of Congress, Madison was temporarily free of all responsibility for keeping the United States (as he agreed she should be kept) out of the war. He expatiated to Jefferson that the Proclamation wounded "the national honor by seeming to disregard the stipulated duties to France. It wounds the popular feelings by a seeming indifference to the cause of liberty." Through expanding executive power beyond constitutional limits, it pointed to monarchy. "I regret extremely the position in which the President has been thrown.

The unpopular cause of Anglomania is openly laying claim to him. His enemies, masking themselves under the popular cause of France, are playing off their most tremendous batteries on him." Madison feared that Washington "may not be sufficiently aware of the snares that may be laid for his good intentions by men whose politics at the bottom are different from his own." If France were to triumph (as Madison hoped), "the ill-fated Proclamation will be a millstone which would sink any other character except Washington, and will force a struggle even in his."[21]

Jefferson expressed in his replies to Madison that opposition to the Proclamation which he would have expressed in action had he too been free of executive responsibility. The "premature declaration," he wrote, had been "officious and improper" and motivated by "such arguments as timidity would readily suggest." To keep worse things from happening, he had voted for it against his will. When Randolph had showed him the text, he had, in his disgust, merely glanced at it to make sure that the word "neutrality" was not included. He thus had no responsibility for the text as it stood.

Jefferson was soon contending that if his suggestions had been followed, America's decision to control her privateers would have been made to seem so tentative that Britain would have paid for a continuation of such protection with major concessions concerning the neutral rights of American merchant ships.[22] Historians have usually accepted this contention and praised its acumen. It may be wondered, however, whether the experienced British diplomats would have been as moved by subtle wording as by their appraisal of the great value to the United States of keeping out of the war. And certainly wording that implied the Proclamation was an irresolute measure that could any day be recalled would have made it much more difficult (if not impossible) to enforce in the United States, where so much pro-French sentiment and personal economic interest favored privateering.

The need for a truly firm stand may well have been brought home to Washington by his own guilty memories. In 1763 George III had proclaimed a boundary beyond which all the territory was guaranteed to the Indians. As a youthful land speculator, Washington had ordered his surveyor secretly to locate for him in the forbidden area valuable tracts. He regarded, he explained, the King's proclamation as "a temporary expedient," which meant that those who obeyed it would lose a head start they would never regain.[23]

As it was, the Proclamation was interpreted across the land as a basic announcement of foreign policy. This is clearly demonstrated by the fact that the politic omission of the word "neutrality" did not prevent the document from being commonly referred to as "the Neutrality Proclamation." Washington was soon using the phrase, and even Jefferson sometimes slipped into it.

Poor Jefferson was being tossed on the horns of a dilemma. In letter after letter to his querulous and critical supporters, he cast himself as a lonely champion fighting to the best of his possibilities in hostile lists against pro-British reaction. If the executive did not support France, that was not his fault! Hamilton and Knox always voted on the wrong side, while Randolph vacillated.

This analysis discounted Washington. Jefferson could, on occasion, admit that if the government did not completely go over to Britain "we shall be indebted for it to the President and not his councillors." However, so he would continue, more credit went to "the ardent spirit of our constituents." And this "ardent spirit" owed much to the public attacks on the President.[24]

It was May 21, 1793, when Freneau published a report that Washington had signed the Neutrality Proclamation because the Anglophiles had threatened that otherwise they would cut off his head. This, Jefferson noted, made Washington "sore and warm." He expostulated to Jefferson that "he despised all their attacks on him personally, but that there had never been an act of government, not meaning in the executive line only but in any line" which Freneau's *National Gazette* had not abused.

Jefferson's comment in his diary was that Washington had been duped by the monocrats into forgetting the importance of a free press: "I took his intention to be that I should interpose in some way with Freneau, perhaps withdraw his appointment of translating clerk in my office. But I will not do it! His paper has saved our Constitution which was galloping fast into monarchy."[25]

Jefferson was rather frightened than reassured by Washington's continuing insistence that the United States was in no danger of fostering a king. The Secretary of State took it seriously enough to record in his journal a rumor that "an old militia general up the North [Hudson] River" possessed a circular letter in Hamilton's handwriting proposing a plan for an American monarchy. Realizing the desperateness of his schemes, the Secretary of the Treasury, so Jefferson further noted, had prepared for himself an asylum in England lest failure forced him to flee the United

States. Did not these shocking rumors° make it all the more clear that the only hope for the future of the United States was to have the forces of darkness extinguished by the triumph of France in her war with "the conspirators against human liberty"?[26]

No such hysterical forebodings bothered Washington, nor was he so sure that France, that present habitat of the Terror, was a burgeoning haven of human liberty. On May 6, 1793, he prophesied Napoleon: "The affairs of [France] seem to me to be in the highest paroxysm of disorder; not so much from the pressure of foreign enemies (for in the cause of liberty this ought to be fuel to the fire of a patriot soldier, and to increase his ardor) but because those in whose hands the g[overnmen]t is entrusted are ready to tear each other to pieces, and will, more than probably, prove the worst foes the country has." He foresaw "a crisis of sad confusion and possibly of entire change in the political system."[27]

Washington's skepticism about the future of France did not mean that he shared Hamilton's sympathy with the British aristocratic power which he had fought during the Revolution. Far from it. There is no doubt that he felt emotionally closer to his former French allies. Yet such preferences, one way or the other, seemed to him irrelevant to the basic determination of American policy. The people of the United States, he believed, should show themselves "true friends of mankind" not by throwing their weight in the balance of European power politics, but "by making their country not only the asylum for the oppressed of every nation, but a desirable residence for the virtuous and industrious of every country."[28]

° These reports concerning Hamilton have never been substantiated.

Edmond Charles Genêt, the ebullient French minister to the United States, who tried to turn the American people against President Washington. Portrait by Ezra Ames. Courtesy of the Albany Institute of History and Art, gift of Mrs. George Clinton Genêt

Citizen Genêt

O N April 8, 1793, the new French minister, Edmond Charles Genêt, stepped onto the quay at Charleston, South Carolina, from the French frigate *Embuscade*. The pro-French citizens who turned out to cheer saw a bulky man of thirty with a thick neck. The lower part of his face, with its nobbed chin and thick lips, rose in a perpendicular line up to his extensive nostrils, but from the tip of his nostrils upward his head receded, the long nose arching backwards to a bald forehead which angled back even more steeply to a high hairline. His reddish hair,° making up with luxuriance for lack of area, curled down his cheeks in sideburns and, flowing over his collar, finished off the geometry of his head with a second, though wavy, perpendicular. In response to the ovation he received, he was all motion, bowing and gesticulating, and smiling. His English was fluent, and when he spoke it was with such glint of eye and passion of enunciation that he exerted on all around him the infectious hypnotism of a zealot.

Had Genêt been constitutionally able to control himself, his head would undoubtedly have no longer been on his shoulders. As a diplomat who had once represented the French crown, he would under normal circumstances have taken a last ride to the guillotine. His family had been (although not noble) close to the French royal family: one of his sisters was Marie Antoinette's favorite lady-in-waiting. His father had headed the bureau of information at the foreign office, and Genêt himself had startled the tight society at Versailles as an infant linguist. When he was

---

° All the principals in the ensuing drama — Genêt, Washington, Jefferson, Hamilton — were (or had been) redheads.

fifteen, he had helped compile the manual on English that was supposed to enable De Grasse's fleet to communicate with Washington's army. At that time, when a suicidal enthusiasm flourished among the French aristocrats for the American rebels, Genêt dined with Franklin and embibed the revolutionary enthusiasm that was later so wildly to flow. His imagination was always inflamed: he urged the French general staff to power a murderous flotilla of balloons with steam engines.

The Queen's patronage brought Genêt a series of diplomatic posts, but he always quarreled with his superiors. On being recalled from St. Petersburg because of the usual insubordination, he found a changed France. The King had been dethroned, and a new, amateur government, that of the Girondists, was trying to discover its way through the ancient tangles of diplomacy. As an experienced diplomat who had been a rebel in the royal service, the man who reveled in being called "Citizen Genêt" seemed a godsend. Given his choice of posts, he selected the United States.[1]

Genêt's mission was, of course, to the federal government in Philadelphia. Yet he landed at Charleston. The newspapers announced that he would set out the next day to present his credentials to President Washington. However, he did not. He had been greeted by an enthusiasm for the French Revolution and himself as its representative which he found not only heartening but intoxicating. Many sailors and shipowners expressed eagerness to receive French commissions that would give legal color to piratical attacks on British shipping. Genêt commissioned and sent to sea four corsairs.[2]

Spain had now joined the coalition against France, and Charleston was the city in the United States closest to Spain's American possessions. Was this the reason Genêt had chosen to land there? Hotheads, wishing to open the navigation of the Mississippi and gain title to new land, expressed a willingness Genêt found enchanting to accept French commissions and funds for attacks on Louisiana and the Floridas.

Although the Neutrality Proclamation had not yet appeared, Genêt seems to have been warned that Washington's government might not be too pleased by his activities. However, the Girondists, conscious of hostility from the rulers of most nations, encouraged appeals to the peoples against their governments. They had merely warned Genêt not to move in that direction too quickly or openly: "The cold character of Americans warms up only by degrees."[*3] But Genêt was convinced that could his su-

---

* During the American Revolution, Washington warned an officer who had to get on with the French expeditionary force that the French should be handled in a gingerly manner, since they were "apt to take fire when others scarcely seem warmed."[4]

periors stand beside him in Charleston, hear the plaudits to which he continually moved, they would realize that there was no need for caution with a people so red-hot for France. If the federal government were, indeed, cold, that was surely because Washington was a friend of that counterrevolutionary Lafayette and (so Genêt had been informed by the staunchest democrats) anxious to open his own path to a crown by espousing the British system.

Genêt's strategy seemed obvious: he would frighten "*le vieillard*" Washington and his evil advisers by demonstrating, through the popularity of his own person, the determination of the American people to do everything — even fight, if necessary — for France. The executive would have to listen since, as Genêt understood it, Washington was accountable to a popularly elected legislature.

Fishes being unable to cheer or vote, Genêt did not sail with the *Embuscade* for Philadelphia. After ten triumphant days in Charleston, he set out overland by coach. He proceeded slowly, in a glow of mass meetings and praises and self-satisfaction until at Richmond, Virginia, he received news of Washington's Neutrality Proclamation. He could only hope that the Proclamation was "a harmless little pleasantry designed to throw dust in the eyes of the British." But surely the matter needed looking into! More than a month after his arrival in the United States, Genêt decided to hurry to the capital and deal with the government to which he had been accredited.[5]

That Genêt was dawdling in Charleston was the first bothersome aspect of his behavior that came to Washington's attention. Soon even the newspapers had information that Genêt was commissioning privateers.[6]

On May 2, 1793, the very day that Washington issued the Neutrality Proclamation, provocative sounds came in through his windows: rushing feet, cheers, cannon shots which he was told (the President obviously could not run out to see for himself) were being fired in joy. The word was that the *Grange*, an English ship which had been captured by the *Embuscade*, had been sent ahead and was entering Philadelphia harbor with the British flag flying reversed under the flag of France.

Jefferson, less inhibited by rank, went to the waterfront. He wrote Madison that the fashionable people and the money men avoided witnessing the British humiliation while "the *yeomanry* of the city" flocked until "thousands and thousands . . . covered the wharfs. Never before was such a crowd seen there. . . . They burst into peals of exultation." Jefferson's own emotions were mixed. He was pleased by the French triumph and the cheering crowd — but it remained his duty to help preserve the peace by enforcing the Neutrality Proclamation. "I wish," so he commented to Monroe, "we may be able to repress the spirit of the people within the limits of a fair neutrality."[7]

Less enthusiastic than Jefferson about the French cause, so much more concerned with the deepening division among the American people, Washington would hardly have been human had he not been relieved when the disturbing sounds of jubilation finally shredded into silence. But then there was a knocking on his door, and in came Jefferson bearing papers and with a worried look on his face.

The document proved to be a protest from the British minister. Hammond stated — could the French possibly have so high-handedly violated American neutrality? — that the *Grange* had been captured not on the high seas but in Delaware Bay with the American pilot on board. Hammond demanded that the ship be returned to her British owners.[8]

How would the "thousands and thousands" of citizens who had so recently exulted on the waterfront react, if their own government hauled down the French flag and turned the British flag upright? No matter, Washington had no choice. He instructed Jefferson to inform Hammond that the President had ordered an investigation. The United States "will not see with indifference its territory or jurisdiction violated."[9]

Hammond's next protest, which Jefferson brought to Washington a few days later, pressed for an immediate decision on the *Grange* and indignantly submitted information received from the British consul at Charleston. Not only had Genêt been commissioning and fitting out privateers mostly manned by Americans, but the French consul, assuming judicial jurisdiction on American soil, had condemned (i.e., granted to the captors) two British brigantines. A quantity of ammunition was being gathered for export to France.[10]

Washington called a Cabinet meeting to draft a reply. It was obvious that no foreign court of law could be allowed legal weight in the United States. Although the Cabinet, not wishing to curb American industry, decided that Americans could not be forbidden to export arms, it was agreed that the United States would not violate neutrality by protecting such exports on the high seas. Since it had now been ascertained that the *Grange* was actually captured in American waters, measures would have to be taken to return her to her British owners. But in connection with the next question that Washington raised, the ministers' control broke. Recriminations flew. Washington requested written opinions and adjourned the meeting.[11]

The debated matter concerned what should be done about the privateers that had already been commissioned and the prizes that had been
captured before the Neutrality Proclamation became the law of the land.
Hamilton and Knox, as was to be expected, urged that the prizes be returned to the British and the privateers ordered away. It was Jefferson's
stand that was surprising (Malone, indeed, considers it the most pro-
French act of Jefferson's entire career as Secretary of State). He not only
urged that the French be allowed to sell the prizes on American soil, but
wished to perpetuate the early violations of neutrality by allowing the
pre-Proclamation privateers to continue to operate freely from American
bases. If the United States allowed the British to win the war, he warned
in explanation, her reward would be "the Cyclops' boon to Ulysses: last
devoured."

Randolph suggested a compromise solution which Jefferson suspected
was the President's "own": the prizes should not be returned to the British but future trouble should be avoided by ordering the privateers away.
Despite Jefferson's protests, Washington made this national policy.[12]

Washington certainly knew, since it was common gossip, that the opponents of all curbs not to the French advantage intended to use Genêt's arrival in Philadelphia as the springboard for mass demonstrations against
the government's policies. But Jefferson's role in this plan could not have
been clear to the President. It has remained for historians to determine
that Jefferson took no active part in organizing the mass demonstrations.
However, he did approve the idea, writing Madison that Genêt's arrival
would "furnish occasion for the *people* to testify their affections without
respect to the cold caution of their government."[13]

The speed with which Genêt had taken off when he heard of the Neutrality Proclamation brought him to Philadelphia on the same coach that
carried his letter announcing when he would arrive. However, the pro-
French party made up for this contretemps, which had prevented a lavish
reception, by adopting at a mass meeting an address to the French minister urging that, up to the very brink of "partaking in the war," the United
States should afford "every useful assistance to her sister republic." The
address was carried to Genêt's lodgings by "a vast body of citizens." In-
terpreting the paper as "an avowal of the principles of the revolution in
France" by "the citizens of Philadelphia," Citizen Genêt announced that
he was as much a delegate to the American people as to their government. Since "the ministers of a republic have no secrets, no intrigues," he
would confide to the crowd what he had not yet told the President: he

[43]

was empowered to negotiate a new treaty establishing closer relations between France and the United States.

Different reports concerning the effect of Genêt's announcement undoubtedly reached Washington. The Hamiltonians scoffed at a gathering of riffraff. The Jeffersonians exulted. Dunlap's *Daily American Advertiser* stated, "It is impossible to describe with adequate energy the scene that succeeded. Shouts and salutations were not unaccompanied with other evidence of the effect which this interesting interview had upon the passions of the parties." Washington knew that any true passions which had been aroused pointed, however much this was disavowed or even not actually desired, to the embroilment of the United States in war.[14]

As an effort to counteract the Republican resolution, some three hundred merchants voted an endorsement of the Neutrality Proclamation. Jefferson admitted that their statement contained "much wisdom," but added that it showed "no affection." Washington drafted a grateful reply.[15]

At two in the afternoon on May 18, Washington was scheduled to receive the French prodigal who had been roaming the nation for five weeks and three days. Although Gouverneur Morris had in his reports from France made light of Genêt — he had "more genius than ability," was an "upstart" and so "indiscreet" that he could easily be maneuvered into a corner if that proved "convenient" — Washington had heard enough to suspect that the Frenchman he was about to meet would prove a dangerous adversary. That Jefferson, who had talked to Genêt, was bubbling with enthusiasm, signaled the new envoy's magnetism.[16]

However, after the heavy envoy had danced ebulliently into his presence, Washington said no word and made no gesture which Jefferson found it necessary to criticize. Jefferson's eyes, indeed, were fastened with almost loving admiration on the French minister. "It is impossible," Jefferson burst out to Madison, "for anything to be more affectionate, more magnanimous than the purport of his mission."

Jefferson's letter then recounted Genêt's speech to Washington: "We know that under present circumstances we have a right to call upon you for the guarantee of our islands. But we do not desire it! We wish you to do nothing but what is for your own good, and we will do all in our power to promote it. Cherish your own peace and prosperity! You have expressed a willingness to enter into a more liberal treaty of commerce with us. I bring full powers to form such a treaty, and a preliminary decree of the National Convention to lay open our country and its colonies

[44]

to you for every purpose of utility, without your participating in the burdens of maintaining and defending them. We see in you the only person on earth who can love us sincerely and merit to be so loved." Jefferson summarized ecstatically, "he offers everything, and asks nothing."[17]

Genêt seems to have assessed the effect of his speech on the President according to his own sense of the brilliance of his performance. He left Washington's room on the same high horse that had borne him in. It was only later, when his plans had gone awry, that he decided that Washington had rebuffed him and his glorious cause. He then concluded that the President had been "profoundly wounded" by the contrast between the host of Genêt's American supporters and the handful of merchants — "mostly Englishmen" — who had endorsed the Neutrality Proclamation. Because Washington resented the fact that Genêt was more popular with his own people than he himself was, Washington "did not answer my frank and loyal overtures except in diplomatic language from which nothing resulted. . . . He only spoke to me of the desire which the United States had among themselves to live in peace and harmony with all the powers, and particularly France, and he avoided touching on anything that could have connection with our revolution or with the war which we were sustaining alone against the enemies of the liberty of peoples."[18]

We can only guess at what were Washington's reactions. Not listened to through ears as adoring as Jefferson's, Genêt's speech could well have sounded both unctuous and condescending towards the United States. Nor were the concessions Genêt put forward necessarily magnanimous. For France to envoke the guarantee would serve no useful end since the United States had no navy while the British so obviously and painfully did. Better for the French for the United States to skirt rather than actually engage in the war. The United States could then, under the protective cloak of presumed nonbelligerency, nurture privateers and supply the French West Indian islands that were cut off from the homeland. Not affection but necessity made France willing to open her colonies freely to American shipping.

After Genêt had departed, Washington felt the need of some reassuring company. In the evening, he put on his hat and walked through the city to call on the one member of his Cabinet who was not a zealot for one side or another. Attorney General Randolph was out. As Washington made his lonely way back to the Executive Mansion, he heard fusillades of cannon. They were salutes to Citizen Genêt, who was being tended a sumptuous banquet at Oeller's Hotel.[19]

A Darkling Plain

W ASHINGTON'S nervous tension was revealing itself in minor acts. Although his manager at Mount Vernon, Anthony Whiting, was a simple farmer trying to fill in and was furthermore ill with tuberculosis, Washington could not check his irritation at minor failures on his plantation. He fired off angry letters reiterating that his orders were being disobeyed. No one cared, he complained, "to what cost I am run for carpenters' tools." As for the Virginia under-sheriffs who were assessing taxes on Mount Vernon, they were "amongst the greatest rascals in the world." He wanted their claims examined to the bottom "because I am resolved not to submit to the impositions of such sort of people." Although he had habitually avoided court actions, he now wished to sue a debtor.[1]

Most amazingly, Washington slipped from the determination, which he had so rigidly pursued for so many years, never to take personal advantage of his public position. To his letter appointing one John Fitzgerald Collector of Customs of the Port of Alexandria, he added, "I am now about [to] give you a little trouble on my private account." He wished help in selling flour and tobacco stored in Alexandria warehouses.[2]

On June 9, 1793, Jefferson wrote Madison, "The President is not well. Little lingering fevers have been hanging about him for a week or ten days, and have affected his looks most remarkably. He is also extremely affected by the attacks made and kept on him in the public papers. I think he feels those things more than any person I ever yet met with. I am extremely sorry to see them." However, so Jefferson continued, Washington had brought the attacks on himself. "Naked he would have been sanctimoniously reverenced, but enveloped in the rags of royalty, they can hardly be torn off without laceration. It is the more unfortunate that this attack is planted on popular ground, on the love of the people to France and its cause, which is universal."[3]

Washington, of course, could have no conceivable objection to his Secretary of State's being in daily contact with the French minister: he had no way of knowing that Jefferson was being charmed into pouring out to the persuasive French representative his anxieties and self-defenses in a manner that was bound to influence future events. Writing to his own government, Genêt reported, "Mr. Jefferson gave me some useful hints regarding the men in office, and did not conceal from me that Senator [Robert] Morris and the Secretary of the Treasury Hamilton, attached to the British interest, exerted the greatest influence on the mind of the President, and it was only with the greatest difficulty that he counteracted their efforts." Furthermore, Jefferson, if Genêt's dispatches are to be believed, took back in conversation the official communications he signed: "He avowed to me that we should consider him in these transactions only the passive instrument of the President." Thus encouraged to feel that he could cooperate with his ally in the State Department by doing everything he could to undermine the President, Genêt wrote home that Washington "impedes my course in a thousand ways and forces me to urge secretly the calling of Congress."[4]

When it became clear to Jefferson what interpretations Genêt was putting on his confidences (and on more extreme sentiments expressed to him by less official pro-French lips), the Secretary of State was disturbed. He wrote Monroe that he was doing his best to "moderate" Genêt's "impetuosity." He was trying to dissuade the Frenchman from the "dangerous opinion" that the American people would disavow Washington's government, "that he had an appeal from the executive to Congress and from both to the people."[5]

Genêt was now insisting that his own interpretations of the Franco-American treaty were more valid than Washington's. He extended the provision that French privateers could bring prizes into American ports by concluding that the French were altogether free to do what they pleased with the prizes. Overriding Washington's protests, he continued to establish on American soil French courts which awarded British vessels to the privateers that had captured them. Genêt insisted furthermore that the Neutrality Proclamation was invalid because it was contrary to the French treaty. Thus privateers could be armed under French auspices in

American ports and manned by American citizens. Jefferson complained that Genêt's excesses would, unless curbed, damage the cause of France in American public opinion. He admitted that they might even pull the United States into the war.[6]

All of Washington's major worries did not, of course, involve the ocean. There were the forests. Even before the conflict exploded in Europe, uncomfortable and sometimes dangerous confrontations had arisen with the three alien forces that impinged on the western frontiers of the United States: the English in Canada to the north; the Indians along more than a thousand miles in the center; and the Spanish to the south.

At the peace conference at which they had acknowledged the independence of the United States, the British negotiators, who were ignorant of American geography and conditions, had accepted two provisions greatly to the disadvantage of Canada. They had ceded the forts that controlled a main highway for the fur trade: the route along the Great Lakes. And they had relinquished to the United States a huge area of fur-producing wilderness below the Great Lakes and west of the Ohio.

When the British realized the damage that had been done to their interests, they took steps. On the ground that the United States had violated the peace treaty by not paying, as had been stipulated, pre-Revolutionary debts to Englishmen, the British refused to relinquish the forts. And they took advantage of the fact that the Anglo-American treaty which had extinguished the British claim to the territory west of the Ohio had not extinguished the claims of the Indian tribes. The United States, it is true, insisted that they had bought the land from the Indians, but British agents encouraged the Indians to claim that the sales had been (as was often actually the case) negotiated fraudulently with tribesmen who had no authority to sell. Indian war parties carrying British arms prevented American settlers from crossing the Ohio, and themselves sometimes crossed for hit-and-run raids. The British hoped that, having demonstrated to Washington's government their power with the Indians, they would be allowed to act as mediators. They would then reserve to the tribes a major area that would supply their own fur trade and serve as a buffer between the United States and Canada.

Concerning the nonsurrender of the forts, Washington sent protest after ignored protest to the British government. But he was unwilling to allow the British any part in negotiations with Indians on territory claimed by the United States. He tried to win around the tribes themselves by a combination of military force and diplomacy. So far, military force had failed abysmally, pulling diplomacy down. Bolstered by the British, the Indians had defeated two American armies. And the triumphant tribes saw no reason for even talking to Washington's ambassadors.

That summer of 1793, Washington had a new and more powerful army gathering at Fort Washington (Cincinnati) under General Anthony Wayne. But Wayne was not to march unless a final effort at diplomacy collapsed. Using as mediators supposedly friendly Indian chiefs, Washington was trying to stage a conference with the defiant tribes at Lower Sandusky on Lake Erie.

"Delicacy and embarrassment," so Washington complained, were added to his position by "the different views which our citizens entertain." Endangered settlers were all for military action, but citizens safe in the back country saw no reason to expend blood and treasure to add to a nation that already had land enough more land that would only serve to draw more population away from the centers. Furthermore, most Americans were opposed to the establishment of any considerable military force. They regarded standing armies as the cause of ruinous taxation and the backbone of tyranny. Congress had kept the American military so weak that Washington could not, without crippling Wayne's little army that was stationed farther north, send any regulars to help Georgia protect her frontiers.[7]

Washington believed that the Indians had equal rights with frontiersmen. It was furthermore obvious that no peace could be negotiated with the tribes unless they could be assured of protection by United States law in their peaceful possession of the territories reserved to them. However, the application of equal laws to Indians was the last thing the frontiersmen wanted. Imagine being hauled in for murder merely because you had shot a passing Indian who might, had he seen you first and thought of it, have shot you! Imagine being unseated from the clearing you had painfully established just because the land had not been bought from the Indians at all — or had been fraudently bought! And communities which had suffered from scalpings could have little sympathy with Washington's holding back of the military until the results of the Sandusky conference were known.

At Cabinet meetings, Jefferson espoused the western point of view. He was so suspicious that Washington was sacrificing preparedness to negotiation that the President felt called on to state that he was hereby, in the presence of the whole Cabinet, ordering the Secretary of War "not to slacken the preparations for the [Wayne's] campaign in the least, but to exert every nerve in preparing for it."[8]

It was part of Washington's policy to determine what purchases from the Indians had been in fact fraudulent — and then either repurchase the land or return it to the tribes. However, Jefferson argued in the Cabinet for a conclusion that would, by legitimizing even the most notorious land-grabs, hamstring all efforts to achieve peace by negotiation. The government, Jefferson insisted, would be exceeding its constitutional powers if it alienated any land that had ever been annexed to the United States. Hamilton, Knox, and Randolph all disagreed. "The President," Jefferson noted, "discovered no opinion, but he made some efforts to get us to join in some terms which could unite us all, and he seemed to direct those efforts more towards me — but the thing could not be done."[9]

As Washington admitted to his confidant Governor Lee — "though perhaps it is best for me to be silent on this head" — he did not, under all the circumstances, expect any solid results from the conference about to convene at Lower Sandusky. However, he was determined to make it completely clear to the citizens of the well-populated areas "that the executive has left nothing unassayed" to avoid Indian warfare. He added a hope that, "if the sword is to decide . . . the arm of the government may be enabled to strike home."[10]

It seemed essential to limit to the greatest degree possible the enemies who would have to be coped with if Wayne did march against the Indians northwest of the Ohio. The operation should not stir up active British intervention or other Indian tribes or belligerence by Spain on the southern frontier.

Along the southern frontier, the basic problem was that the Mississippi, the natural commercial outlet of the central valley, was blocked to American trade by Spain, which controlled its mouth. Ever since the emigration across the mountains that had followed the Revolution, there had been a continual danger that the western settlers would take some violent action that would embroil the United States with Spain. The situation was complicated by the fact that there was a considerable overlap in the boundary claims of the two nations. To protect her lands and her valuable fur trade, Spain had made allies of the Indians in the area, particularly the powerful Creeks.*

---

* As a group, the tribes naturally preferred the enemies of the United States, since, having no excess population hungry for Indian land, the authorities of Canada and New Spain preferred to maintain wildernesses where Indian hunters could harvest for the fur trade.

Throughout most of Washington's first term, Spain's underpopulated North American possessions had been in so weak a position militarily that Spain had been as anxious as Washington to avoid warfare in the forests. Part of the weakness had lain in the fact that Spain, being in the opposite European political camp from England, could expect from Canada not aid but hostility. But now the British and Spanish kings had been drawn by their mutual fear of the French Revolution into an alliance which might find expression in North America.

During June 1793 Washington was notified that Spain had sent a reinforcement of 1500 men to Louisiana, a large force in relation to the tiny standing army of the United States. It was terrifying to contemplate what would happen if troops, each well supported by Indian allies, marched simultaneously south from Canada and north from Louisiana. Jefferson ordered the activating of spies in New Orleans, and asked the American minister in London to keep an eye out for troop movements to Canada.[11]

At Philadelphia, a diplomatic offensive, joined in by both the British and Spanish representatives, seemed under way. Ignoring American protests concerning the unsurrendered western forts, Hammond was presenting, concerning the American efforts to handle the problems raised by French privateers, a barrage of protests that were mounting in belligerence. And on the southern frontier, Spain's allies, the Creeks, had entered on a new militancy. As they lifted scalps, Georgia threatened to fight on her own if the federal government did not come to her rescue.[12] Yet every defensive step which forest rumor reported the United States had taken — including an alliance with the Chickasaws, who were unfriendly to the Creeks — brought to Washington's desk statements from the Spanish commissioners in Philadelphia that Spain would not sit idly by as the United States acted with hostility towards beloved allies of his Most Christian Majesty. Late in June 1793 Washington burst out to Jefferson, "It would seem that neither he [the British minister] nor the Spanish commissioners were to be satisfied with anything this government can do, but on the contrary are resolved to drive matters to extremity." Washington and his Cabinet decided, as a last hope to avoid war with Spain, to appeal over the heads of the commissioners to their government at Madrid.[13] Never had every effort to hold the lid down seemed more necessary, but Genêt did not want to hold the lid down.

Jefferson noted that, on July 5, the French minister called on him and "read to me very rapidly" instructions he had prepared for André Michaud, a French botanist who was going to Kentucky on what purported to be a scientific mission. Genêt also read proclamations he had prepared for the citizens of Louisiana and Canada (many of whom were French) urging them to revolt.

"In these papers it appears," so Jefferson's diary note continues, "that besides encouraging those inhabitants to insurrection, he speaks of two generals at Kentucky who have promised to him to go and take New Orleans," if the French met their expenses. Genêt made it clear that he intended to commission officers in both Kentucky and Louisiana, who would "rendezvous outside the *territories of the U.S.*" and, collecting what Indians they could, capture Louisiana, which would then be "established into an independent state connected in commerce with France and the U.S. That two frigates shall go into the river Mississippi and cooperate against New Orleans. . . . He said he communicated these things to me not as Secretary of State but as Mr. Jeff."

In whichever capacity, Jefferson replied that American citizens "would assuredly be hung if they commenced hostilities against a nation at peace with the United States. That leaving out that article, I did not care what insurrections should be excited in Louisiana."[14]

Genêt had already secured from the Secretary of State a letter of introduction for Michaud to Governor Shelby of Kentucky, which included the statement that Jefferson recommended the botanist to Shelby's attention as a confidant of Genêt. Now that he knew the true purport of Michaud's mission, the Secretary of State did not recall the letter. Indeed, he sent Michaud off with an introduction to a second major political figure across the mountains: Senator John Brown.

Genêt wrote his government that Jefferson had stated that the United States, being engaged in delicate negotiations at Madrid, could not officially join in the French operations, but "he seemed to me to sense vividly the utility of this project. . . . He gave me to understand that a little spontaneous eruption of the inhabitants of Kentucky in New Orleans would advance those things. He put me in connection with many deputies of Kentucky."[15]

Jefferson's behavior was all the more remarkable because by the time he cooperated with Genêt's freebooting schemes he had already lost confidence in the discretion of the French minister. And he must have known that he was acting contrary to the policies of his government. In addition to supporting a flagrant breach of neutrality, he was encouraging the establishment in the west of the very sort of independent nation, linked to a

European power as well as to the United States, which Washington had always dreaded and labored to prevent.° The explanation seems to have been that Jefferson considered the situation with Spain in any case "desperate," and war "an absolute certainty." He probably concluded that Genêt's freebooters would help to fight it. However, he did not disclose to Washington what Genêt was doing and what he himself had done.[16]

Some seven weeks later, Washington received a protest from the Spanish commissioners which stated that efforts were being made "to excite the inhabitants of Kentucky to join in an enterprise against the Spanish dominions of the Mississippi." Washington thereupon ordered Jefferson to communicate to Governor Shelby his command that the Governor investigate to determine if there was any truth in this charge, and to take legal measures to stop any activity that he might discover. In his resulting letter to Shelby, Jefferson stated piously that "nothing could be more inauspicious" to the interests of Kentucky "than such a movement at the very moment when those interests are under negotiation between Spain and the United States."

Shelby replied equally piously that nothing was going on.[17]

Although Washington could not know that his two chief Cabinet officers were operating behind his back, one in collusion with the British minister and the other in collusion with the French minister, he found plenty to be apprehensive about: "What with the current affairs of the government, the unpleasant aspect of matters on our Indian frontiers, and the momentous occurrences in Europe, I am not only pressed with the quantity of business but that the nature of a great part of it is particularly [he again used a phrase that was becoming a favorite with him] delicate and embarrassing."[18]

Over the objections of Jefferson, who suspected that Hamilton wanted the money so that he could corrupt the incoming legislature, Washington empowered the Treasury to swing a loan (already authorized by Congress) in Holland. The President explained that it would be well to have the money in hand, since at any moment a crisis might arise which would make it impossible for the United States to secure such a loan.[19]

Staving off the ominous shadows cast from every quarter necessitated innumerable decisions, large and small. Washington continued to work

---

° Had the scheme with which Jefferson was now cooperating succeeded, the Louisiana Purchase, over which Jefferson later presided, would have been impossible.

for unanimity in his Cabinet. When unanimity could not be reached, he postponed if possible, and otherwise, as tactfully and unobtrusively as he could, ruled on the matter himself. Although Jefferson cried out that he was being perpetually overruled, Jefferson's biographer Malone has concluded that Washington decided more often according to Jefferson's ideas than Hamilton's.[20] Nonetheless, the Secretary of State not only found the friction in the Cabinet meetings extremely unpleasant, but was bitter at losing in as many cases as he did.

What were Hamilton's emotions at being defeated even more often? He did not spread his feelings over sheets of paper as did Jefferson: although on political matters extremely prolix, concerning his personal reactions he held his cards close against his chest. However, a letter to him from his follower Edward Carrington indicates that he found it unpleasant "to continue in office and to stem the storms which envy, malice, or ambition can generate against you." Hamilton's father-in-law, Philip Schuyler, was to comment to him on "the chagrin you experience from the weakness or wickedness of those you have to contend with." It is further clear that Hamilton, who (unlike Jefferson) had no patrimony of his own,* and who, despite Jefferson's suspicions, was not using the opportunities for private gain presented by his office, was suffering financially from his government service.[21]

Jefferson's desire to resign had long been one of Washington's problems. Hamilton had also spoken of retiring, but so far only in general terms. It was late June 1793 when he sent the President a brief letter which indicated anger.

"Considerations relative both to the public interest and to my own delicacy," Hamilton wrote, "have brought me, after mature reflection, to a resolution to resign the office I hold towards the close of the ensuing session of Congress." He explained that he would stay that long because some propositions remained before Congress which were necessary to the full development of his "original plan" (undoubtedly of finance) and which were "as I suppose, of some consequence to my reputation." He wished, furthermore, to give "an opportunity, while I shall be still in office, to the revival and more deliberate prosecution of the inquiry into my conduct which was instituted [by his enemies] during the last session." He was giving Washington so much notice in order to "afford full time to investigate and weigh all the considerations which ought to guide the

---

* Schuyler was, of course, rich, but no proud man enjoys living indefinitely off his father-in-law.

appointment of my successor." Hamilton's closing was altogether formal: "With the most perfect respect, I have the honor to be, sir, your most obedient and most humble servant, Alexander Hamilton."[22]

That Washington tried to dissuade Hamilton from withdrawing may be assumed, but no record tells what arguments he used and what Hamilton replied. It is however clear that in late July Washington was still giving serious credence to the possibility that Hamilton would resign towards the end of the Congressional session, which would mean in the beginning of the following year.[23]

Anthony Whiting had become incapacitated by his tuberculosis, leaving Mount Vernon with no one at the helm — and just at the time of the June harvest. Washington felt required to make a flying trip home. Leaving Martha behind (she now found it too tiring to travel), he set out on June 23 in a phaeton drawn by a pair, with two or three reserve horses under the supervision of a groom. He learned on the road that his manager was dead, and he was followed by a dispatch stating that the appearance of a British privateer in New York harbor was eliciting French protests and creating a whole new set of problems. But as he tried to improvise some way to keep his managerless estate running, he remained temporarily uninformed of the truly gargantuan storm Genêt was blowing up in Philadelphia.[24]

5

The *Little Sarah*

WASHINGTON'S inability, after he reached Mount Vernon, to find "a confidential character" who could replace his dead estate manager, made his presence "at this important season almost indispensable." But, so he continued to Jefferson, "I know the urgency and delicacy of our public affairs at present will not permit me to be longer absent." Submitting "with the best grace I can to the loss and inconvenience which my private affairs will sustain," Washington set out again for Philadelphia after only some ten days at home.[1]

When he reached Philadelphia on the morning of July 11, 1793, weary from the long journey, he found awaiting him a packet of papers marked in Jefferson's handwriting, "instant attention."[2] A glance showed that the documents concerned the *Little Sarah* (renamed *La Petite Démocrate*), a brigantine which had been captured before the Neutrality Proclamation and awarded to the French. The small, fast vessel would, if armed and manned to extreme capacity, prove a very effective raider. Genêt, so Washington read, had been increasing her armament, as she lay in a Philadelphia dock, with guns secured in the United States, and also recruiting Americans for the crew — a double violation of the now operative Proclamation. Although the government of Pennsylvania was highly sympathetic to the French cause, the officials had felt it necessary to intervene. The Secretary of the Commonwealth, Alexander Dallas, called on Genêt. He was defied.

Jefferson made the next effort. He was kept waiting in Genêt's anteroom. When the French minister appeared, the Secretary of State asked for assurances that the *Little Sarah* would not put to sea until the facts could be finally ascertained and the matter laid before the President, who was expected back in three days.

Genêt, so the document Washington was reading continued, launched "into an immense field of declamation and complaint," orating on such "a very high tone" that Jefferson could not interpose a word. The United States was violating her treaty obligations to France. The United States allowed her flag to be insulted by the British, who stopped her vessels and took off provisions intended for the French Indies. If the United States lacked the spirit to protect her shipping, she should allow the French to do so. Genêt had, he continued, "been thwarted and opposed in everything he had had to do with the government." Since the President had illegally shunned the friendly propositions he had brought from France, "on the return of the President, he would certainly press him to convene Congress."

Having finally talked himself "into perfect good humor and coolness," Genêt allowed Jefferson to tell him that it was his diplomatic function to abide by the decisions of the American government while reporting his disagreements to his own government for their action. "He was silent at this, and I thought was sensible it was right."

But on the specific issue of the *Little Sarah*, Genêt still insisted "he should not be justified in detaining her." Jefferson replied that it "would be a very serious offense indeed if she should go; that the government was determined on that point and, thinking it was right, would go through with it."

Genêt then said the boat was not ready to sail. He implied, although he did not actually commit himself, that she would not leave until Washington returned. However, she would, for convenience in completing preparations, leave Philadelphia harbor for a new anchorage down the Delaware. "Let me beseech you," Genêt continued, "not to permit any attempt to put men on board of her. She is filled with high-spirited patriots, and they will unquestionably resist."

One can imagine how Washington's brow darkened at this threat to fight the United States in her own waters. It may well have been at this point in his perusal of Jefferson's long account that Washington, recognizing a truly major crisis, sent off a messenger to summon Jefferson.

The papers Washington held went on to state that Jefferson had told Genêt he took it for granted that the *Little Sarah* would not sail till the President returned. On this note, the interview ended. Jefferson departed to report to the Pennsylvania authorities: "I was satisfied that, though the vessel was to fall somewhere down river, she would not sail." Governor Mifflin "thereupon ordered the militia be dismissed."

In his report to Washington, Jefferson conscientiously repeated something Dallas had told him. During Dallas's interview with Genêt, the French envoy had said "that he would appeal from the President to the people."[3]

Washington's anger boiled. How dared a foreign representative "threaten the executive"![4]

As if foreseeing Washington's reaction, Jefferson tried, as he continued his written account, to soothe the President. Genêt, he admitted, "did in some part of his declamation to me, drop the idea of publishing a narrative or statement of transactions, but he did not on that, nor ever did on any other occasion in my presence, use disrespectful expressions of the President. He from a very early period showed that he believed there existed here an English party, and ascribed to their misinformations, industry, and maneuvers some of the decisions of the executive. He is not reserved on this subject. He complains of the partiality of the information of those employed by government,* who never let a single movement of a French vessel pass unnoticed, nor ever inform of an English one arming, or not till it is too late to stop her."

"The next day, Monday," so Jefferson's communication continued, "I met the Secretaries of Treasury and War in the Governor's office. They proposed our ordering a battery to be erected on Mud Island immediately, guns to be mounted, to fire on the vessel and even to sink her if she attempted to pass. I refused to concur in this order, for reasons assigned in another paper."

Reading on, Washington learned that before any effective action could be taken at Mud Island, the *Little Sarah* had passed that strategic spot in the middle of the Delaware River. She was anchored off Chester. Since the United States had no frigate available, the raider could not now be stopped except by such a boarding party as Genêt had threatened to resist.[5]

The messenger Washington had sent to Jefferson returned with amazing information. Jefferson was not available. He had left the city for his country retreat at Gray's Ferry, some miles above Philadelphia on the Schuylkill.

The President took up a pen and wrote angrily. "After I had read the

---

* Jefferson was referring to the Treasury Department's customs officials. These, although under the command of Hamilton, had been appointed by Washington.

papers put into my hands by you, requiring 'instant attention,' and before a messenger could reach your office, you had left town.

"What is to be done in the case of the *Little Sarah,* now at Chester? Is the minister of the French republic to set the acts of this government at defiance, *with impunity,* and then threaten the executive with an appeal to the people? What must the world think of such conduct, and of the government of the United States for submitting to it?

"These are serious questions. Circumstances press for decision, and, as you have had time to consider them (upon me they come unexpected), I wish to know your opinion upon them even before tomorrow, for the vessel may then be gone."[6]

Eventually a reply, written formally in the third person, came back from Jefferson's country retreat. He was sending more documents, but was not on his own way to town: "T. J. has had a fever the last two nights which has held him till the morning. Something of the same is now coming on him, but nothing but absolute inability will *prevent* his *being in town* early tomorrow morning."[*][7]

Washington quickly discovered that the documents Jefferson had enclosed were the opinions of the various Cabinet ministers on whether the *Little Sarah* should actually be fired at from Mud Island. That question was in itself obsolete, but the arguments were of interest since the basic issue was whether the United States should submit to French violations of her neutrality or should use force. The papers presented Washington with no surprises. Hamilton and Knox argued that if the United States allowed the *Little Sarah* to escape, the prestige of the government would be undermined and England would have a cause for war. Jefferson believed

---

[*] Jefferson's excuse for his absence — that he was not well — has usually been taken at face value, yet nagging questions remain. The whole sequence of events indicates that the Secretary was more unpleasantly than seriously ill: he was at his desk the following morning. Should he have considered this a crisis of such magnitude that it was his duty, even at his own considerable discomfort, to stand by his chief? Washington had, it is true, arrived the morning after he was expected. But Jefferson was, so Washington's letter indicates, still in town. Was Jefferson justified in leaving town without attending on the President, and then refusing, when summoned, immediately to return?

Perhaps Jefferson was motivated by a desire not to give Washington an opportunity to pass on to him the onus of reaching a decision. A paragraph in his private notes, suggestive although admittedly referring to an earlier moment in the crisis, reads, "It appears to me that the President wished the *Little Sarah* had been stopped by military coercion, that is by firing on her. Yet I do not believe that he would have ordered it himself had he been here, though he would be glad if we had ordered it." Some time later Jefferson (as we shall see) spelled out to Madison his desire to escape, as far as he could, executive responsibility.[8]

that violent action would exaggerate a minor infraction and give France a cause for war.[9]

The situation soon became completely clear to the President. There could be no doubt that Genêt was defying the government of the United States. On the other hand, a resort to force might escalate into serious fighting, all the more because Genêt claimed that he momentarily expected in American waters three — or maybe twenty — French ships of the line. Washington's conclusion was to limit his action to continued diplomatic protest. This would have to satisfy American honor and (as it actually proved to do) the British government.

When Jefferson reappeared and the Cabinet met, Washington revealed that his emotions were too excited to find release in wrath directed only at Genêt. He expressed anger with Mifflin (who had led a cabal against him during the Revolution) for having failed to detect the project "in embryo" and stop it "when no force was requisite, or a very small party of militia would suffice." He expressed anger with Knox (who had been during the Revolution his staunch supporter) for having committed federal cannon to a fortification on Mud Island which Mifflin wished still to raise in preparation for future emergencies. The result would be that every port in the United States would want to raid the limited federal arsenal. If Washington was still angry with Jefferson for having left him in the lurch, he did not say so.[10]

Genêt was vastly pleased with himself. He sent the *Little Sarah* out to sea — "when treaties speak," he explained sententiously, "the agents of nations have but to obey" — where she became one of the most effective of French raiders.[11] As for the pique of "Old Man Washington," Genêt felt that could be extinguished by a copious application of his own charm and powers of persuasion. He told Jefferson that he intended to call on the President and open his heart to him frankly. Jefferson warned that Washington probably would not receive him, but Genêt was an impossible man to stop.[12]

Washington was certainly surprised when, as he gossiped in his drawing room with Martha and Robert Morris, a servant announced that the French minister was in an antichamber. The President ordered that the caller be ushered in. Genêt made a graceful entrance. Martha greeted him, as he remembered, with "some very polite and obliging remarks." The two men sat silent. Finally, Genêt asked the President for a private interview.

Washington replied that the communications of diplomatic representatives should come to him through the Secretary of State.

What he wished to communicate, Genêt insisted, was "of the highest importance" — and perhaps they misunderstood each other.

Washington led Genêt into the adjoining room. After they were both seated, Genêt began. He explained to the President that he was not responsible for the protests of the American people "which appeared to alarm the government." He had "received not produced the movement" which was, Washington should not forget, an expression of "the honesty and integrity of the people." Genêt went on to admit that his own correspondence with the American government had been "lively." However, if Washington should "put himself in my place and consider" that the Neutrality Proclamation "had anulled the most sacred treaties," he would agree that "unless I were a traitor, I could not act otherwise."

Holding his face expressionless, Washington made no effort to interrupt or stop the Frenchman's flow of words. Genêt was now inspired to announce that France was emerging from the existing conflict with glory. However, as France's representative, he would show himself "generous." If the United States wished to destroy "at the feet of liberty" the old treaties made with Louis XVI in order to conclude new ones, whatever terms Washington wished to request would be considered with magnanimity.

After Genêt had concluded his presentation, Washington, so the envoy noted, "said to me simply that he did not read the gazettes and it was of very slight importance to him whether his administration was talked about." He accompanied Genêt to the head of the stairs, where he shook hands.

Washington's behavior had been so controlled that Genêt departed with "flattering thoughts" that he had won the President around. The next morning, he hurried to Jefferson's office to boast of his triumph. He had hardly begun his exposition when a door opened and in walked a stony-faced Washington. Genêt made one of his best bows and then noticed that Jefferson was now as stony-faced as the President. Genêt looked from one to the other for "an invitation to remain for which I would willingly have given part of my life." The two men just stood there silently. Then Jefferson made "an imperative sign" which, so Genêt later complained to him, "forced me to retire."[13]

6

The Genêt Harvest

JEFFERSON cried out to Madison concerning Genêt, "Never in my opinion was so calamitous an appointment made. . . . Hotheaded, all imagination, no judgment, passionate, disrespectful and even indecent towards the P[resident]! . . . If it ever should become necessary to lay his communications before Congress or the public, they will excite universal indignation. He renders my position immensely difficult. . . . I am on a footing to advise him freely, and he respects it, but he breaks out again on the very first occasion, so as to show that he is incapable of correcting himself.[1]

To Washington, Jefferson argued that Genêt's indiscretions were the random result of an unfortunate appointment, but Hamilton insisted that Genêt was applying to the United States an official French policy of trying to subvert all governments. For his part, Washington assumed that every nation would do its best to promote its own interests. However, he believed that Genêt's specific actions were too indiscreet to be blamed on France. He suspected, as he confided to Governor Lee, that Genêt had been egged on by malcontents in the United States: "As a man of penetration" he would, if "left to himself" certainly have pursued a more sound policy. "But mum on this head. Time may unfold more than prudence ought to disclose at present."[2]

Washington was deeply worried, not only by the violence of the opposition gazettes, by reports of widespread discontents in Virginia, by the threats in New York of physical violence against Federalists, but by what he himself saw on the Philadelphia streets. The climate there was thus described by that eloquent pro-Jeffersonian writer Claude Bowers: "The summer of 1793 was one of utter madness. Mechanics were reading the speeches of Mirabeau; clerks were poring over the reports of revolutionary chiefs . . . and even the women were reading with flushed cheeks Barlow's *Conspiracy of Kings*. Others too illiterate to read were stalking the streets like conquerors, jostling the important men of the community with intent, and sneering at the great. Men were equal. The people's day had dawned. Down the streets swaggered the mob looking for lingering relics of royalty to tear or order down. A medallion enclosing a bas-relief of George III with his crown, on the eastern front of Christ's Church, caught its eye. Down with it! The church officials did not hesitate, but tore it down. On swept the mob in search of other worlds to conquer. Occasionally the lower element, drinking itself drunk, staggered out of the beer houses to shout imprecations on a government that would not war with England."[3]

As a very old man, John Adams reminisced about "the terrorism excited by Genêt in 1793, when ten thousand people in the streets of Philadelphia, day after day threatened to drag Washington out of his house." They would start a revolution and declare war on England. The Vice President, so his account continued, had felt it necessary to order that chests of arms be brought him from the war office — "through by-lanes and back doors" — so that he could "defend my house."[4]

"That there are in this as well as in all other countries," Washington wrote, "discontented characters, I well knew, and also that these characters are actuated by very different views: some good, from an opinion that the measures of the general government are impure; some bad, and (if I might be allowed to use so harsh an expression) diabolical, inasmuch as they are not only meant to impede the measures of that government generally, but more especially (as a great means towards the accomplishment of it) to destroy the confidence which it is necessary for the people to place (until they have unequivocal proof of demerit) in their public servants." Washington could not resist adding that he could better be called a slave than a servant.

"In what," Washington asked, "will this abuse terminate?" He stated bravely that, since he was confident that "neither ambitious nor interested motives have influenced my conduct, the arrows of malevolence . . . however barbed and well pointed, never can reach the most vulnerable part of me." Yet "the outrages on public decency" had a "tendency . . . too obvious to be mistaken by men of cool and dispassionate minds, and, in my opinion, ought to alarm them, because it is difficult to prescribe the bounds of their effect." One effect seemed to Washington already visible: the "Democratic Societies."[5]

The Pennsylvania Democratic Society was inaugurated in Philadelphia on July 4, 1793, by men who had been closely associated with Genêt. The avowed object was to sponsor across the nation an interconnected network of clubs that would rouse and bring to bear pro-French and anti-administration sentiment. The Hamiltonians claimed that this movement was an importation, engineered by Genêt under the orders of his government, of the Jacobin Clubs which had led the French Revolution to its bloodiest phase. Some modern historians find the roots of the societies more in the Sons of Liberty, which had fostered the American Revolution. Neither theory could be reassuring to those who did not consider the United States in need of a new revolution.

A year after the Pennsylvania Society had emerged, Washington was to write, "I early gave it as my opinion to the confidential characters around me that if these societies were not counteracted (not by prosecutions, the ready way to make them grow stronger); or did not fall into disesteem from the knowledge of their origin and the views for which they had been instituted by their father, Genêt, for purposes well known to the government, that they would shake the government to its foundations."[6]

The *Little Sarah* incident brought home to Washington the need to determine in detail and announce what acts were permissible, what banned under the Neutrality Proclamation. A Cabinet meeting roused the usual disagreements, Jefferson being for interpretations useful to the French, Knox and Hamilton wishing to serve the British interest. The mediator, Randolph, was in Virginia. Finally frazzled beyond endurance, Washington told his ministers to meet without him and come to a conclusion among themselves.[7]

Jefferson volunteered that the way out was to ask the Supreme Court to codify the law. He persuaded his fellow ministers, who persuaded Washington to forward the request to Chief Justice Jay. After hesitating and being poked up by Washington, the court made a decision monumental in American legal history: "the lines of separation" drawn in the Constitution made it unsuitable for the court of last resort to give extralegal advice to the executive. In notifying Washington of this decision, Jay wrote in a manner which the President may not have found very soothing that the Justices "derive consolation from the reflection that your judgment will discern what is right and that your usual prudence, decision, and firmness will surmount every obstacle."[8]

Washington referred the whole matter back to his Cabinet. Faced with the inescapable need for getting together, the ministers succeeded in agreeing on eight basic "rules concerning belligerents," which Washington immediately promulgated.[9]

It was Jefferson's function to enforce the rules, and in so doing he applied the practical and balanced side of his complicated nature. However much he might in emotional moods fume, he did not want the United States to be involved in the European fighting, and, as a lawyer, he understood the importance of enforcing law. Furthermore, when he summoned his abilities in that direction, he was an excellent administrator. Jefferson wove a consistent and fair path through the hundreds of issues, each with its particular facts and complications, that the movements of foreign and American shipping brought to his desk. That during this day-to-day labor he managed to keep chained his predilections to France, made his actions above rational reproach, but added to the nervous strain of what was in any case a brain-rending task.

Genêt made nothing any easier. He insisted that "the opinions of the President" were contrary to the wishes of the American people, who were not "serfs" as Washington seemed to think. Genêt would do as he pleased.[10]

Hamilton, "sensible [as Jefferson put it] of the advantage they have got," wanted to lay an account of Genêt's actions before the people, a course which Jefferson believed would "danger a dissolution of the friendship" between the United States and France. Whenever Washington raised at a Cabinet meeting the question of what to do about Genêt, angry arguments made him further postpone the matter.[11] Finally, on July 23, 1793, he opened a meeting by himself putting forward a plan which accorded with ideas Jefferson had previously advocated. Washington suggested that the record should not be published in the United States, but sent to the French government, with "a temperate but strong" statement which, while making it clear that the United States did not blame France for what they regarded as the envoy's personal acts, asked for his recall. "In the meantime, we should desire him either to withdraw or cease his functions."

Although it was uncommon for Washington to start a discussion by stating his own opinion, Hamilton was not silenced. Jefferson reports that he made "a long speech," warning Washington that the government was in danger of being overthrown. However, it was not too late "to give the tone to the public mind" by publishing, with "proper explanations,"

Genêt's correspondence that was insulting to Washington and the United States.

Knox (so continued Jefferson) now tried to aggravate Washington by reporting that, according to rumor, the democrats were plotting to end the President's "tyranny" by chasing him out of Philadelphia. Washington did not rise to the bait. He adjourned the meeting that was going nowhere.[12]

However, since a decision on Genêt had to be found and Washington still did not despair of getting agreement, he called for August 1 a Cabinet session that was to start at nine in the morning and last until four in the afternoon, when all the ministers were invited to share in a "family" dinner.

The meeting opened with a complete review of all the relevant documents, as collected by Jefferson. Agreement was then reached on Washington's and Jefferson's suggestion that the record be sent to the French government. It was also agreed that the letter should ask for Genêt's recall. Knox found no supporters for his suggestion that the Frenchman be immediately expelled from the nation. It was decided that Genêt, having been notified that his recall had been requested, should be allowed to continue in office until his own government acted.

After Washington had listened to some bickering as to whether the letter to the French government should be worded in a peremptory or a delicate manner, he raised the explosive question: should the American public be informed of Genêt's misbehavior? Hamilton supported the affirmative in a speech which Jefferson clocked at three quarters of an hour and considered "as inflammatory and declamatory as if he had been speaking to a jury." Randolph opposed, and it was time for dinner.[13]

The next day, Hamilton led off by expressing dire forebodings: the Pennsylvania Democratic Society was spreading sedition across the continent. Jefferson replied (as it proved, inaccurately) that the society was altogether local in intention, and "if left alone," would die with the gubernatorial election. Turning to the avowed purpose of the conference, Jefferson stated that any publication of the official proceedings with Genêt would reveal that there were disagreements in the Cabinet. Furthermore, Genêt would surely release a reply; the President would get involved in controversy. Washington was undoubtedly disturbed by Jefferson's warning that he would be made to appear as the head of a party rather than the leader of the whole nation.

Jefferson was continuing: France would consider publication "unkind" since "friendly nations always negotiate little differences in private." France's efforts to subvert the royal governments in Europe were justifiable self-defense. To imply, as Hamilton wished to do, that France was also trying to undermine the republican government of the United States would strengthen the wicked princes. Surely the United States did not wish to "aim a fatal stroke at the cause of liberty!"

Knox, so Jefferson's account continues, intervened with a new attempt to enrage the President. In a "foolish, incoherent sort of a speech," he called attention to a lately printed satire, *The Funeral Dirge of George Washington and James Wilson* (an Associate Justice of the Supreme Court), which described Washington being placed, for his aristocratic crimes, on the guillotine. This time Washington reacted to Knox's incitation. He became, Jefferson remembered, "much inflamed, got into one of those passions when he cannot command himself, ran on much on the personal abuse which had been bestowed on him, defied any man on earth to produce one single act of his since he had been in the government which was not done on the purest motives." He stated "that he had never repented but once having slipped the moment of resigning his office, and that was every moment since, and that *by God* he had rather be in his grave than in his present situation. That he had rather be on his farm than to be made *emperor of the world*, and yet that they were charging him with wanting to be a king. That that *rascal Freneau* sent him three of his papers every day, as if he thought he would become the distributor of his papers, and that he could see in this nothing but an impudent design to insult him. He ended in this high tone."

When Washington had finally run down, none of his Cabinet knew what to say. There was a long constrained silence. Then Washington spoke quietly. He could see no reason to decide now whether or not the Genêt record should be published. Let the propositions agreed to at the previous day's meeting "be put into a train of execution, and perhaps events would show whether the appeal [to the public] would be necessary or not."

This was, of course, a victory — even if perhaps only temporary — for Jefferson's point of view. Washington also entrusted to Jefferson, who would make it as conciliatory as possible, the drafting of the letter that would be sent to France.[14]

At this Cabinet meeting, before rage had overwhelmed him, Washington had made what seemed to Jefferson a most damaging revelation. The

President had quoted Robert Morris as volunteering that, should he publish the Genêt correspondence, Morris would support the move "and engage for all his connections." Jefferson noted that "the President repeated this twice and with an air of importance." What raised Jefferson's hackles was the realization that "Mr. Morris has no family connections. He engaged then for his political friends. This shows that the President had not confidence enough in the virtue and good sense of mankind to confide in a government bottomed on them, and thinks other props necessary."*[15]

Personally, Jefferson found Morris's social circle repellent. In the same letter to Madison which stated that the "rags of royalty" must be torn off Washington, even at the expense of "laceration," Jefferson had complained that his own "rare" hours of relaxation were "sacrificed to the society of persons" who were "systematically undermining the public liberty and prosperity" and "of whose hatred I am conscious even in those moments of conviviality when the heart wishes most to open itself to the effusions of friendship and confidence."[16]

The Jeffersonians found it shocking that Washington was personally at home in the circles of which they disapproved. Even if it could be argued that the President's domestic staff and equipage were suited to keeping up the utility and dignity of his high office, no such an excuse could be made for Washington's friends who lived higher off the hog than he did.

Washington might write with admiration of "republican simplicity"[17] but the fact was that he enjoyed elegance. He often stated that men judge their position in the world not by its actuality but by comparison with those around them. As a boy, Washington had been, while in contact with Virginia's splendid aristocracy, a poor relation of a secondary family. He had worked hard, married well, and eventually placed himself in a position where he too could live in the manner of the leaders of the society in which he had been raised. To live thus did not seem to him ostentation, nor did it induce him to turn from his door poorly dressed men who had calls on his attention or sympathies. Many a ragged varlet shared as a guest in the luxuries of Mount Vernon.[18]

Had Washington stayed at Mount Vernon, Jefferson would not have been outraged, since the republican who was in Virginia terms better born than Washington — his mother was a Randolph — saw nothing to object to in the elegance of the plantation aristocracy. The trouble was that Washington had come to enjoy elegance in urban terms.

---

* That Jefferson was eager not to "confide" the record concerning Genêt to "the virtue and good sense of mankind," did not temper his suspicions of the President.

Where Virginia life was domestic, Philadelphia life was public: even private parlors seemed to adhere more to the outer than the inner world. Women had more freedom, were on display in eye-catching clothes, and quite possibly engaged in some of the immoralities to which their position seemed to open them. Men did not stay at each other's houses for days at a time, but perpetually popped in and out, talking first to this one and then to that one, in a maze of contacts and places. As for physical luxury, it seemed much more pervasive when great houses were not separated by hours of travel but were cheek by jowl. A new fashion spread like wildfire rather than with the slow flow of tidal rivers.

More profoundly upsetting than any surface manifestation was the difference in the source of wealth. It requires a major act of the imagination for twentieth-century Americans to realize how great a gulf separated in the eighteenth century wealth based on land from wealth based on trade. The social gap reflected, of course, a fundamental difference of interest between two economic systems whose political needs often seemed diametrically opposed. That wealth based on land was the old way allowed its proponents to add snobbery to economic rivalry: the Jeffersonians looked down on the Hamiltonians as pushing upstarts, while the Hamiltonians were indeed inclined to push too hard when it came to the splendor of their drawing rooms and the fashionable nakedness of their women.

It was natural for Madison to feel that the opinions expressed in cities were corrupt as compared to those expressed on farms; it was natural for Jefferson to exclude urban leaders from "the people." Since the vast majority of Americans were rural, and the urban proletariat (yet an infant force) was naturally resentful when splashed by carriages, attacks on the manners of the city rich had proved, during the fight over Hamilton's financial measures, a more effective propaganda line than erudite arguments concerning methods of funding and the utility of banks. That, when the European war broke out, the trading community considered it vital to their economic interest to support England, increased the polemics against their social behavior and against Washington for countenancing it.

Washington longed for Mount Vernon as much as Jefferson longed for Monticello, but he did not consider that he was engaging in treason to the agricultural way of life when he enjoyed the amenities of Robert Morris's (or Eliza Powel's) drawing room. Indeed, he believed that farmers and businessmen could live peaceably together: that a mixed economy would make for a stronger nation than pure agrarianism. As for the snobbish objections of the Jeffersonians to the Hamiltonians, they seem never to have entered Washington's head.

The problem of how he could maintain social contacts that would keep him in touch with all elements of the nation had worried Washington from the start of his Presidency. It was not in his nature to base friendship on political expediency. If Mrs. Morris rather than some Republican wife were Martha's best friend, so be it.° He did not feel ashamed that among the ladies of his acquaintance he was most fascinated by the rich urban charmer Eliza Powel. However much his levees were accused of smacking of monarchy, any decently dressed man was admitted. Washington did not blame himself if simpler citizens felt too embarrassed to come, if doctrinaire Republican leaders sneered and stayed away. He was using all the persuasion in his power to keep the critical Jefferson in his Cabinet. He was pleased that his secretary Lear had social connections among the Republicans. He wrote that he placed "great reliance" on information from his aide. "The opportunity you derive from mixing with people in different walks, high and low, of different descriptions, and of different political sentiments, much [must?] have afforded you an extensive range for observation and comparison; more so, by far, than can fall to the lot of a stationary character, who is always revolving in a particular circle."[20]

Jefferson expressed in personal letters to his Virginia supporters his dissatisfactions with the govermental policies which were contrary to his predilections but in which he had to share. Hamilton moved more directly, writing for the press letters the authorship of which was (at least in governmental circles) an open secret, although he signed them with various noms de plume.

° An anecdote, first published in 1855, has received wide currency. When Mrs. Washington went to see why Nelly was not practicing on her harpsichord, so the story goes, a strange man brushed by her in the corridor. She found Nelly looking embarrassed and then noticed a blemish behind a chair on the delicate cream-colored paint of the wall. "Ah!" she cried, "It was no Federalist! None but a filthy democrat would mark a place with his good-for-nothing head in that manner."

Washington Custis tells us that the relevant wall was papered not painted, and the story is self-discrediting because the words were said to have been spoken in private. We must postulate a servant with long ears and a long tongue, or that Nelly or Martha told the story in such a way that it reached Washington's enemies. In any case, if what mothers or grandmothers say to their female offspring when annoyed were taken seriously, civilization would be at an end.

There is no clear record that Mrs. Washington ever said anything offensive about anybody. Washington Custis remembered that he never heard his grandmother "*touch on the subject of politics at all.*"[19]

As "Pacificus," Hamilton presented to the public a line of interpretation and justification of the Neutrality Proclamation for which he had argued in the Cabinet and which Washington had refused to accept. The Presidential act, he insisted, went beyond a mere statement of the *status quo*. It had been a determination of foreign policy by the President. According to Hamilton the Constitution gave the President almost complete power over foreign affairs. Hamilton reduced the Senate's role to acquiescence after the event.[21]

Washington, so Jefferson wrote Madison, was made "uneasy" by Hamilton's claims. Jefferson was horrified. Unwilling himself to take up an answering pen, he recruited Madison, and sent him information on what had transpired at Cabinet meetings with which to counteract Hamilton's equally informed arguments.[22]

Concerning Genêt's misbehavior, Hamilton knew everything that the Cabinet knew. Although the President had decided not to publish the facts — at least for the time being — they presented much too valuable a weapon for Hamilton to let lie. Under another nom de plume, this time "No Jacobin," he accused Genêt of trying to subvert the government so that he could drag the United States, willy-nilly, into the war on the side of France.[23]

The French minister, entirely unabashed, had never flown higher. On August 1, the inhabitants of New York were wildly excited by a sea battle off Sandy Hook in which the *Embuscade* routed the British frigate *Boston* — and the next day the French West Indian fleet, fifteen warships, sailed into New York harbor.[24]

Washington thought it "proper" to warn Jefferson that Genêt was on the way to New York. The Frenchman claimed that he now had 1500 seamen at his command. He might use them to fit out new privateers "*in our ports.*"[25]

In New York, the Republicans were planning a mass meeting to hail Genêt and the cause of France, while the Federalists were finding their best defense in claiming that Genêt had maligned the President. On August 12, there appeared in the press a letter remarkable because it was signed not with one of the noms de plume then habitual, but with the real names of two important governmental figures: Chief Justice Jay and Senator Rufus King of New York. The letter stated succinctly: "Mr. Genêt, the French minister, had said he would appeal to the people from certain decisions of the President."[26]

Genêt responded with a public letter to Washington. He had, he stated, "demonstrated" to the President that the official policy was sacrificing French interests to those of the enemy. He had furthermore "represented without reserve that this conduct did not appear to correspond with the views of the people of America." Was Genêt to infer from Washington's behavior that "the slightest hint of an appeal, which a magistrate deserving of his high office would ardently desire, was to you the greatest offense I could offer"? Having in this public letter insulted Washington and both supported and made a direct appeal to the people, Genêt stated that he expected from the President "an explicit declaration" that he had never insulted him or expressed the intention of appealing directly to the people.[27]

Genêt's effusion must have reminded Washington of similarly insolent letters he had received some fifteen years before from another Frenchman (albeit of Irish extraction), General Thomas Conway.[28] Then the attack had been involved in the effort, which had seemed as if it might succeed, to unseat him as Commander in Chief. However, Conway's fulminations had proved a boomerang which struck Washington's opponents. The insolence of Genêt seemed to be having the same effect. A shout of outrage rose across the land.

The barometer most visible to Washington was supplied by the addresses to the President which were adopted by mass meetings held in various parts of the land. Ever since the promulgation of the Neutrality Proclamation, these had commonly denounced that act as unconstitutional, pro-aristocratic, and anti-French. But after Jay's and King's revelation, a wave of love for the insulted President and concern for the endangered peace of the United States became the dominant notes. Even citizens who continued to express sympathy for the French as "a people fighting against oppressors in defense of the Rights of Man," went on (as did the inhabitants of New London, Connecticut) to state that "the laws of neutrality ought unquestionably to be as sacredly observed as if the people of the United States were wholly indifferent in their attachment to the nations engaged in the war."[29]

This change of climate was, of course, grateful to Washington, yet he did not thank Jay and King for their effective propagandizing. Instead, he offended them by evenhanded behavior which they considered base ingratitude.

Officially as French minister, Genêt requested an inquiry into what he considered a libelous publication. Washington instructed Jefferson, as Secretary of State, to recommend to Randolph, as Attorney General, that he proceed in the case "according to the duties of your office, the laws of the land, and the privileges of the parties concerned."

In unison, Jay and King signed an angry letter to Washington. Ever since he had become famous, Washington had been familiar with their approach. Critics, not wishing to attack the powerful leader or not willing to admit that he could in his own right react unfavorably to them, had blamed his behavior on the influence of evil advisors. Now Jay and King "treated with much severity" Jefferson and Randolph, as being responsible for Washington's refusal to praise their revelation concerning Genêt.

King was informed that Washington was "deeply offended."

Desirous of "preventing the affair terminating in a rupture," Knox tried to persuade his fellow Federalists to seek a personal interview which would "heal all wounds." However, Jay and King were still too angry to honor the Federalist policy of cultivating Washington at all times.

Had the President met rancor with rancor, Jay would not have played his important role in the rest of Washington's administration. But the President sent for Jay, who could not refuse such a direct summons. To his long-time associate, Washington defended Jefferson and Randolph, and "also justified his own conduct." He complained of the "severity" of the Jay-King letter, "spoke of the difficulty of his situation and the necessity of his conducting with great caution."

Jay, so continues King's account of the affair, was voluble in his own defense, but calmed down when Washington expressed "friendship" for him, and also "respect and regard" for King. It developed that Washington had penned a justification of his own conduct which Jay could carry, with various explanatory papers, to King. Jay agreed to do so. After having studied the documents, King called on Washington to state that he and Jay were satisfied. Washington then gathered together all the relevant papers and threw them in the fire.[30]

7

Jefferson Seeks Escape

MARTHA WASHINGTON came home from a visit with Mrs. Samuel Powel — the conservative family friend whom Washington so particularly admired — fuming with outrage. Eliza Powel, so she repeated to her husband, had told her of a shocking happening at a charitable meeting held to supply the Philadelphia poor with firewood. A toast was proposed to the President as "the man of the people." At this, "a good deal of disapprobation appeared in the audience, and many put on their hats and went out." Washington was upset and hurt by this information, all the more because he found the story repeated in the newspapers.

Washington's secretary, Lear, whose sympathies were republican, tried to persuade his chief that the event had not actually taken place. The story was an "artifice" of the Federalists to work on Washington's emotions. Lear went on to argue that the most violent newspaper attacks on Washington, although ostensibly by Republicans, were actually devices of the Federalists to persuade Washington that the Republicans were his enemies. Lear was so little gratified by Washington's reception of these suggestions that he felt it necessary to lay the problem before Jefferson, who noted the matter in his diary.[1]

Washington could not doubt that a nexus of hysterical attacks on his government and slanders against his character was the newspaper edited by Jefferson's employee Freneau. Yet, as far as Washington could see, Jefferson was acting in his official capacity as the most faithful and valuable public servant. His expositions to the French as well as the British concerning neutral duties and rights, continued to be nonpartisan and brilliant.

Washington could not, of course, know that after Jefferson had joined with his fellow ministers in voting for a decision he found both necessary and distasteful, he would in letters to his followers deny or explain away his vote. Thus Washington saw more effectiveness than actually existed in managing a unanimity that included Jefferson's agreement. Yet had he been able to read Jefferson's letters, Washington would undoubtedly still have felt — for it was the fact — that Jefferson's continued service as Secretary of State was very valuable as a conspicuous demonstration that the government did not belong to any one party. Under existing circumstances, criticism bounced and roared: it would bounce higher and roar louder if Jefferson withdrew.

Pulling against each other, Jefferson and Hamilton, being men of commensurate power and intelligence, created an equilibrium in the center of which Washington stood. And since each minister was the ablest exponent of one of the dominant American points of view, Washington could, by listening to each, secure the most valuable intelligence possible towards his final decision. Both men had shown a desire to resign, but neither withdrawal seemed imminent until Washington received Jefferson's letter of July 31, 1793.

Jefferson began by reminding Washington that he had originally intended to retire at the end of the first Presidential term. However, "circumstances had arisen which, in the opinion of some of my friends, rendered it proper to postpone my purpose for awhile. These circumstances have now ceased in such a degree as to leave me free to think again of a day on which I may withdraw without its exciting disadvantageous opinions or conjectures of any kind." Confident that he would be able to get the affairs of his department in adequate order by the end of September, he wished at that date to shift to "scenes of greater tranquillity." This advance notice was given so that Washington would have time to select a successor. "That you may find one more able to lighten the burden of your labors, I most sincerely wish, for no man living more sincerely wishes that your administration could be rendered as pleasant to yourself as it is useful and necessary to our country, nor feels for you a more rational or cordial attachment and respect."[2]

Washington surely noticed that Jefferson, in stating why he had not resigned sooner, failed to mention Washington's importunings, or any sense of loyalty to the administration. As for the "circumstances" which had induced him to stay, these could hardly include, since Jefferson said they had abated, those domestic and international conflicts that Washington was convinced were more than ever endangering the United States. As Washington surely understood, Jefferson was referring to the newspaper attacks he had himself suffered which would have made him appear, had he then withdrawn, to be fleeing under fire. These attacks had indeed been modified, partly because Jefferson had pursued the executive policy of true neutrality, partly because Genêt had presented himself as so much more rewarding a target for Federalist polemics.[3] As for Jefferson's concluding statement of "rational and cordial attachment and respect," these were hardly warm words, but then it had been some time since Washington had signed his own letters to Jefferson "affectionately."

After mediating over Jefferson's letter for six days, Washington mounted his horse and rode out to the Secretary of State's country house at Gray's Ferry. He tried to appeal to his former friend's loyalty, stating that his regret at having accepted a second term had been greatly "increased by seeing that he was to be deserted by those on whose aid he had counted."

Washington then told Jefferson of Hamilton's letter in which the Secretary of the Treasury had asked to retire towards the close of the next Congressional session. Hamilton "had often before intimated dispositions to resign, but never as decisively before." Would not Jefferson postpone to the same date? If Washington could fill both vacancies at the same time, he could, without sacrificing talent, keep a geographic balance.

Washington, so Jefferson's notes continue, then "expressed great apprehensions at the fermentation which seemed to be working in the mind of the public; that many descriptions of persons, actuated by different causes, appeared to be uniting. What it would end in, he knew not." As a result of the recent census, the new House of Representatives would be larger than the old. Perhaps it would reveal "a different spirit. The first expression of their sentiments would be important." If Jefferson "would only stay to the end of that, it would relieve him considerably."

Jefferson replied by expatiating on his "excessive repugnance to public life" and the society he had to associate with in Philadelphia. He added that, "without knowing the views of what is called the Republican party here or having any communication with them. I could undertake to assure him, from my intimacy with that party in the late Congress," that there was no national political movement which opposed the government. The Republicans merely wished to re-establish the independence of Congress. Genêt "would be abandoned by the Republicans the moment they

[76]

knew the nature of his conduct; and, on the whole, no crisis existed which threatened anything."

Washington replied that he "believed the views of the Republican party were perfectly pure, but when men put a machine into motion, it is impossible for them to stop it exactly where they would choose."

It was now Jefferson's turn to bring up his standing worry: a monarchist party. Washington stated that there was none; Jefferson spoke of dark plottings; Washington replied "that if that was the case, he thought it was a proof of their insanity, for that the republican spirit of the Union was so manifest and solid."

Washington returned to the question of appointments to succeed Jefferson and Hamilton. He said that his first choice as Secretary of State would be Madison, but Madison had always expressed such an aversion to executive office that he had spoken to Jay. Jay had preferred his existing office as Chief Justice.

To a modern politician or political theorist, considering Madison and Jay as alternatives for the same foreign policy post would seem strictly out of *Alice in Wonderland,* since the two men espoused opposite international preferences from opposite ends of the political spectrum. But both men were able, and it was Washington's fear (which was to be painfully realized) that he would be unable to find, as replacements for the stars of his Cabinet, men with adequate experience and talent. Since it was the Cabinet as a whole that joined him in the crucial decisions, ministers of various opinions could be placed anywhere as long as there was balance in the whole. Washington could put in the Treasury — that present stronghold of the northeastern interest — a southerner, if he replaced the southern Republican Jefferson at State with a northern Federalist. He agreed in fact with Jefferson that Governor Johnson of Maryland would make the best successor to Hamilton since he was, as Washington opined, "a man of great good sense, an honest man, and he believed clear of speculations."

But how to replace Jefferson? After various names, including Randolph's, had been raised and objections found for each, Washington urged Jefferson to stay till December: "It would get us through the difficulties of this year, and he was satisfied that the affairs of Europe would be settled with this campaign, for that either France would be overwhelmed by it, or the Confederacy would give up the contest. By that time the Congress will have manifested its character and view."

Washington, whose own Mount Vernon was wallowing rudderless, listened to Jefferson's explanation that if he did not return at once to Monticello the loss would be "prejudicial beyond measure." Then Washington urged Jefferson not to make a final decision but to reserve his answer for two or three days. "Like a man going to the gallows," he explained, "he was willing to put it off as long as he could."[4]

Jefferson, who had assured Washington of his lack of "communication" with "what is called the Republican party here," took advantage of a private traveler to send to the Virginia Republican leader, Madison, a packet which "could never," he explained, "have been hazarded by post." The packet contained a complete transcript of the conversation he had just had with Washington. This "may enable you to shape your plan for the state of things which is actually to take place." Jefferson added a long letter outlining what he considered should be Republican strategy.

He would like to cut the ground out from under Hamilton by dividing the Treasury into two departments, one to collect customs and the other internal taxes. However, he feared that the Senate was so "unsound" that the proposition could not pass. Turning to the old issue of the bank, he wished the House to declare it unconstitutional, which would "suffice to divorce that from the government," even if the Senate did not concur. Then Jefferson urged a new policy in relation to the President.

Jefferson had regarded, even if regretfully, the personal attacks that hurt Washington deeply as valuable strategy. However, the misbehavior of Genêt had put so powerful a trump card in the hands of the Federalists that Jefferson had begun to wonder whether the policy of trying to erode Washington's prestige was not dangerous. He had been outraged — and had observed Washington's anger — when Knox had inserted into discussions as to whether the Genêt papers should be published mentions of publications that insulted the President. Lear's reports on the indignation Washington expressed in his domestic circle, and on the way Federalist callers "puffed . . . that party as the only friends to the government," had made Jefferson fear that abuse might "throw him entirely into the scale of the monocrats." Jefferson had, indeed, begun to agree with Lear in the suspicion that some of the most scurrilous attacks on Washington were planted in the Republican press by Hamilton's agents as "a detestable game . . . to place the President on their side."

In arguing to Madison that the Republicans should now cease hammering at Washington, Jefferson pointed out that the most present danger to the Republican cause was that Washington would allow the whole record of Genêt's behavior to be published in an appeal to the people. If the demonstrations of popular adherence to him should become as "general and warm as I believe they will, I think he will never again bring on the question." But, "if there is any appearance" of the people supporting Genêt against the President, "he will probably make the appeal."

The Republicans should furthermore cease their opposition to the Neutrality Proclamation lest they show themselves "in a very unfavorable point of view with the people" by "cavilling about small points of propriety" that would "betray a wish to find fault with the President. . . . The towns," so Jefferson explained to the plantation-bound Madison, "are beginning generally to make known their disapprobation of any such opposition to their government by a foreigner and declaring their firm adherence to the President, and the Proclamation is made the groundwork of their declarations." He deplored that "the popular leaders" did not have the good sense to abandon Genêt, since the only result of continued adherence would be to drive the people "to the other party."[5]

Madison's reply to Jefferson's suggestions would, had Washington seen it, have deeply wounded his feelings, since it revealed how far his once close friend and intimate adviser had become alienated from him. In conference with Monroe (who had long been suspicious of Washington) Madison had concluded that "over and above other motives," the President wished to hold Jefferson in his Cabinet as a "shield." Washington realized that "the departure of the only councillor possessing the confidence of the Republicans would be the signal for new and perhaps very disagreeable attacks."

The basis for this assessment of Washington's motives was spelled out in a separate letter to Jefferson from Monroe. Jefferson's two associates had taken at face value his often repeated complaints that he was fighting a lone battle in the Cabinet against a united opposition that included Washington. "If your opinions had more weight," so stated Monroe, it might be possible to conclude that Washington's "desire for your continuance was not dictated by self-love."

Madison and Monroe's conclusion was that Jefferson should not resign but rather take advantage of Washington's need to hide behind him. Jefferson should make "as few concessions as possible."[6]

The mails being slow, Jefferson had to make up his own mind long before advice came back from Virginia. As he later explained to Madison, he worked out a schedule which would enable him to accede to Washington's request in a manner that would not be politically or emotionally damaging. He would set it as a condition that he could handle his neglected affairs at Monticello by going home for six weeks in the autumn. It made sense that his absence would not overlap a three weeks' absence Washington was planning. "This got me rid of nine weeks." Of the remainder, four would be during the session of Congress, when presumably the executive would not be making decisions but waiting on the legislative. "My view in this was precisely to avoid being at any more councils as much as possible, that I might not be committed in anything further."[7]

After Jefferson had suggested (without of course stating his motives) this schedule to Washington, he became worried lest the President had not understood him. He sent a letter expressing "in writing more exactly what I meant to have said yesterday."[8]

Washington replied, "I clearly understood you on Saturday, and of what I conceive to be two evils, must prefer the least: that is to dispense with your temporary absence in autumn (in order to retain you in office till January) rather than part with you altogether at the close of September."[9]

8

A Rocky Road

JEFFERSON'S advice about abandoning Genêt was accepted only partially and then very reluctantly by his fellow Republicans. Freneau indicated his independence by continuing to cheer the French minister on in his battle with the President. Monroe wrote Jefferson that he was quite unwilling to make any concessions that admitted Genêt in the wrong, and Madison expressed a desire to sidestep the matter as far as possible. He drew up a model resolution which denounced (without mentioning Genêt) the interference of *all* outsiders in the American government; expressed loyalty to that government and veneration for Washington; praised the French cause; and lashed out against "the active zeal displayed by persons disaffected to the American Revolution and others of known monarchical principles in propagating prejudices against the French nation and revolution." Madison hoped that this address would be widely adopted in rural districts, although he feared the people there might have been too "misinformed" by "the language of the towns."[1]

As he waited to hear whether Jay and King were to be prosecuted,° Genêt was flying higher than ever. Genêt was perpetually in the press denouncing Washington and urging warlike preparation against England. Washington was forced to remove from office the French consul in Boston who, under Genêt's orders, had set up a French prize court on American soil. Yet the Frenchman's glory was over. In most American minds, he no longer wore a nimbus. He cast a shadow. That so many critics of the administration had given him enthusiastic support and often close coopera-

° It was December before Randolph wrote to Genêt declining to proceed against Jay and King.

tion, that a vocal minority was still marching by his side, placed the opposition much off balance. Now was the time for Washington, if he wished, to give his attackers a toppling push. Opportunities were copiously supplied by his duty to answer the addresses, expressing loyalty to him and disapproval of Genêt, which were being adopted (often under the eager leadership of Federalists) in all parts of the land.

Hamilton was, of course, making all the capital he could out of the Republican vulnerability. However, when Washington sent to Hamilton, for his suggestions, a draft of his answer to the resolution adopted in New London, he made it clear that he was not invoking the politician's controversial gifts. He asked for "such alterations in the expression of the draft . . . as in your opinion will make it palatable to all sides, or unexceptional."[2]

Eventually, the resolution Madison had drawn up came to Washington's desk as the sense of a meeting convened in Caroline County, Virginia. Although ignorant of the authorship of the address, Washington realized that it was a message from the opposition, since it was sent him (accompanied with a complaining letter) by that venerable leader Edmund Pendleton. Pendleton, who had befriended Washington as a young beginner and had helped lead Virginia into the Revolution, had proved suspicious (as was often the case with old patriots who had not moved with the times) of the Constitution and the federal government.

In his carefully worded reply to the resolution Washington assured "the citizens of Caroline of my fixed attachment to the free principles of our government, and of the confidence I have in the virtue and good sense of my fellow citizens, which, I trust, will always counteract any measures which might tend . . . to alienate them from the republican government they have established for themselves, and under which they have hitherto enjoyed unequalled prosperity and happiness." However, the part of his answer which most enchanted the opposition — they claimed it as a rebuke to the Anglophiles and circulated it widely — was this succinct paragraph: "The expressions of gratitude and affection by the citizens of Caroline towards the French nation for their generous aid and assistance extended to us in a time of need are truly laudable, and must meet the approbation of every grateful mind."[3]

Pendleton, in the personal letter with which he accompanied the resolution, had gone back to the older controversy, expressing doubts of Hamilton's honesty and suspicions that Hamilton's financial measures were intended to graft a British system on pure American institutions.[4]

Washington's reply began by expressing pleasure at being assured that he still held a place in Pendleton's "estimation," a matter which he had begun to doubt because it had been some four years since he had received the annual letter his former patron had promised. Then Washington mourned that the Virginia farmer had not listened to what Madison denounced as "the language of the towns." Washington wrote, "Sequestered you say you are from the world, and know little of what is transacted in it but from newspapers. I regret this exceedingly. I wish . . . that your means of information were coequal with your abilities . . . for be assured we have some infamous papers, calculated for disturbing, if not absolutely intended to disturb, the peace of the community."

Concerning Hamilton's "fiscal conduct . . . I will say nothing because an inquiry, more than probable, will be instituted next session of Congress . . . and because, if I mistake not, he will seek rather than shrink from an investigation. A fair opportunity will then be given to the impartial world to form a just estimate of his acts, and probably of his motives. No one, I will venture to say, wishes more devoutly than I do that they may be probed to the bottom, be the result what it will."

Washington added that he would always be glad to receive Pendleton's "unreserved opinion" on any important public measure and particularly on his own Presidential conduct, "for as I can conscientiously declare that I have no object in view incompatible with the Constitution and the obvious interests of this country, nor no earthly desire *half* as strong as that of returning to the walks of private life, so, of consequence, I only wish, whilst I am a servant of the public, to know the will of my masters, that I may govern myself accordingly. . . .

"Mrs. Washington enjoys tolerable good health and joins me most cordially in best wishes to you and Mrs. Pendleton. I wish you may live long, continue in good health, and end your days as you have been wearing them away, happily and respected. Always and most affectionately, I am, etc."[5]

Jefferson prepared for delivery to the French government the 8000-word statement requesting the recall of Genêt which John Quincy Adams was to consider "the most perfect model of diplomatic discussion and expostulation of modern times." It drew a careful line between Genêt's conduct and America's view of the intent of France. At a Cabinet meeting over which Washington presided, only one clause raised controversy: the comment that any falling out between France and the United States would be "liberty warring on herself." The phrase, Hamilton argued, would be offensive "to the combined powers," whom it accused in effect of warring on liberty. It was also objectionable because it would encourage Americans in "the idea that the cause of France was the cause of liberty in general, or could have either connection or influence on our affairs." Knox agreed.

Washington then spoke with (so Jefferson's note continues) "a good deal of positiveness." He "declared in favor of the expression; that he considered the pursuit of France to be that of liberty, however they might sometimes fail of the best means of obtaining it; that he had never at any time entertained a doubt of their ultimate success, if they hung well together, and that as to their dissensions, there were such contradictory accounts given that no one could tell what to believe."

Jefferson now took the floor. Asking the recall of a minister, he observed, was a harsh measure and Genêt would undoubtedly make out that his downfall had been due to an executive hostile to liberty. The people of the United States had heard suspicions that some parts of the executive were hankering for monarchy. Some specific statement was necessary to remove such misunderstandings.

After Randolph had voiced agreement with Hamilton and Knox, Washington expressed his agreement with Jefferson: the American people and also France should be reassured. There existed in the United States, so Washington continued, a "universal attachment" to France, which was "the only nation with whom our relations could be counted upon." He had "a strong attachment to the expression concerning liberty warring on herself" — but he would leave the decision to his advisers.[6]

When Washington thus delegated the decision, he knew (since all his ministers had expressed their views) that he would be (as he was) voted down. We can only guess at his motives. There was surely good reason to believe that the phrase was better omitted by a government aiming at neutrality. Was Washington indulging, as men in less responsible positions often did, in the pleasure of expressing, without influencing the result, indiscreet emotions? Or was he trying to sweeten the pill for Jefferson? Or was he becoming, as the years massed over his head, less resolute in his own opinions?

A few months before, Jefferson had expressed amazement when Washington allowed himself to be voted down.[7] But early in August 1793 Jefferson recorded a second instance when Washington gave in — or tried to please Jefferson by making out that he had done so. He had asked for a Cabinet discussion on calling a special legislative session when it seemed that a jury decision had thrown in doubt the executive's power to enforce the Neutrality Proclamation. By the time the Cabinet met, the legal situation had taken on a less grave aspect. Although Jefferson still favored the special session as a resort to the people, Hamilton, Knox, and Randolph voted no. In acceding to the majority decision, Washington commented to Jefferson that "he should have been for calling Congress himself, but he found the other gentlemen were against it."[8]

On Philadelphia's waterfront, a man turned yellow and died. Disease spread first among the sailors, grog sellers, and disreputable women of the stews, and then it began to reach out into other parts of the city. On August 19, Dr. Benjamin Rush warned of an epidemic of yellow fever. On August 25, Washington wrote, "We are all well at present, but the city is very sickly and numbers dying daily." On the 29th the newspapers published an official announcement that yellow fever was moving through the city, and added what preventive suggestions the medical art of that time could concoct. It is doubtful that Washington obediently sprinkled vinegar and camphor or set gunpowder afire. He had little use for the nostrums of medical faculties and was, in any case, surprisingly unalarmed.[9]

After Hamilton had announced with dark drama that he had the dread disease, Washington's note to the sufferer expressed the hope that his "apprehensions" were groundless and added reassuringly that, in any case, "the malignancy of the disorder is so much abated" that "not much is to be dreaded." He wondered whether Hamilton's condition had not made "a change so entirely favorable" that he could "bring Mrs. Hamilton with you to dine with us at three o'clock."[10]

Three days later, Hamilton seemed to be dying. This news coincided with a complete change in Washington's attitude toward the epidemic. He wrote Secretary of War Knox, "I think it would not be prudent either for you or the clerks in your office, or the office itself to be too much exposed to the malignant fever."[11]

By now, Washington's house was (as he later wrote) "in a manner blockaded by the disorder," that was "every day becoming more and more fatal."[12] When the President looked out the window, he saw the usually bustling street virtually deserted. Many Philadelphians had fled and those still in the city cowered behind locked doors. The occasional pedestrian flitted rapidly along in the very middle of the street, holding against his nose a wad of gauze. If he met another walker, he would maneuver to get to the windward, which could create a *danse macabre* should the other pedestrian attempt the same stratagem.° A sound of wheels would make both take to their heels, since the approaching vehicle might well be an open cart driven by a black (Negroes were immune to the disease) on which sprawled several corpses that had been unceremoniously dumped there for further dumping into the pits that had superseded graveyards.

Washington had long been planning to leave for Mount Vernon on September 10. As was usual with him at this time of year, he was publishing advertisements in the newspapers requesting "all persons having accounts upon the household of the President of the United States" to settle them before his departure. According to the historian of the epidemic, J. H. Powell, these advertisements struck terror into the hearts of the remaining inhabitants, since it seemed that, as long as the hero remained, the situation could not be truly desperate.[13]

For his own part, Washington felt uneasy about going away when Philadelphia was in such trouble. He confided to Lear that it had been "my wish" to stay longer, "but, as Mrs. Washington was unwilling to leave me surrounded by the malignant fever which prevailed, I could not think of hazarding her and the children." All he could do was to make it clear that he would not budge before the date he had originally set.[14]

Washington did not want to leave behind in the center of infection the moody, imperious, rich, intellectual, flirtatious, and handsome Eliza Powel, who was his closest female friend. In a private conversation, he asked her to join his family — she should bring her husband along — on their journey to Mount Vernon. Washington's "affectionate and friendly attention to me at this awful moment," she later confessed, "filled my heart with such sensibility as to render me incapable of expressing my feelings."

The letter that Eliza dispatched that evening was properly addressed to both Washingtons: "My dear friend and my very dear Madam." She stated that her husband, anxious to stay near his physicians and considering the danger exaggerated, had decided not to accept the invitation. He had, however, given Eliza permission to do as she pleased.

"This has thrown me into a dilemma most painful, the conflict between duty and inclination." She had in the end decided to stay: were her hus-

---

° Observation had revealed that the disease traveled through the air, although no one realized that it was carried by mosquitoes.

band to be taken ill when she could not give him "consolation and aid," that would "be to me a lasting source of affliction; and, God knows, I need not voluntarily add to the lot of sorrows. My life has been sufficiently embittered to make me very little anxious about protecting or preserving it. Death has robbed me of many friends, and time has abated the ardor of others, so that my life in my latter years has been little more than a sieve to let through some joy and some blessing."

Eliza added in a postscript that her husband (who may not have been altogether pleased to have the invitation tended in conversation between Washington and his wife) "would have done himself the pleasure of waiting upon you" to make his own explanations had he not felt that the Washingtons would be occupied in preparing for their journey.[15]

Washington seems to have got off in some confusion. Although he recognized, as he wrote Knox, that "the spreading and continuance of the disorder may render it inadvisable for me to return to this city as soon as I first intended," he did not (as he later regretted) take with him the papers that would enable him to conduct effectively the Presidential business from Mount Vernon. As an expedient to keep the government afloat, he requested Knox, "In case you should remain in the vicinity of it [Philadelphia], to write me a line by every Monday's post informing me concisely of the then state of matters." He also hoped that the Secretary of War would assist his steward and housekeeper "if by means of the disorder, my household affairs in this city should be involved in any delicacy. I sincerely wish and pray that you and yours may escape untouched, and when we meet again, it may be under circumstances more pleasing than the present."[16]

9

An Anxious Holiday

WASHINGTON had entrusted the parade to his fellow Masons, the only major organization in the United States given to pomp and regalia. They had done their utmost. Such was the order of march: "Surveying Department of the City of Washington, Mayor and Corporation of Georgetown, Virginia Artillery, Commissioners of the City and their attendants, stonecutters and mechanics, two sword bearers, Masons of the fifth degree, Bibles on grand cushions, deacons with staffs of office, stewards with wands, Masons of the third degree, wardens with truncheons, Secretaries with tools of office, paymasters with their regalia, treasurers with their jewels, band of music, Lodge number 22 of Alexandria, corn, wine, and oil, Grand Master *pro tem*, PRESIDENT WASHINGTON, and the grand sword bearer."

For the ceremony of laying the cornerstone of the Capitol of the United States, nature had provided a bright autumn day. "The President's House," where the parade started, was hardly more than a half-dug foundation. The procession advanced into what was a rough forest lane: stumps still in the middle of the road, tall enclosing trees. Sidelanes vanished into thick woodland. Washington could see only an occasional hint of the great city that glowed in his imagination. Here a surveyor's stake; there a half-cleared lot. The few completed houses sprawled at angles to the road: they had been built before Major L'Enfant had, with Washington's encouragement, laid out a capital city worthy of a nation many times larger and more powerful than the existing United States.

The procession moved with what solemn dignity the footing allowed until forced into an undignified halt. Ahead lay "Goose Creek," renamed "the Tiber." It lacked a bridge. The wardens with truncheons and the treasurers with jewels, and also the President of the United States, had to teeter across on a fallen log or go upstream where it was possible to leap from rock to rock.[1]

That the commissioners of the District of Columbia could not afford a bridge on their main avenue symbolized the situation which this ceremony was aimed at ameliorating. When Congress had empowered Washington to erect a new national capital near Mount Vernon, they had not opened their hearts to the extent of appropriating a penny. Washington had persuaded the local landowners to give half their acreage to the government in expectation of the great increase in value which a city would bring to the half they retained. Money for the public improvements and governmental buildings was to be raised by selling most of the government's holdings.

Although both Washington and Jefferson had given the project major attention, it had been haunted by a demon of discord. The brilliant L'Enfant had forced his own dismissal; the commissioners had fallen out with the local landowners; and, as inefficiency reigned, auctions aimed at selling lots found few bidders. Word circulated that the city would never rise. Pennsylvania, eager to change Philadelphia from the temporary to the permanent capital, announced plans to create at state expense such handsome public buildings as the infant city of Washington seemed unable to achieve.

It had thus become indispensable for the proponents of the new city to get moving at once on the public buildings — there were only two — that were considered necessary to the government. For the President's House, Washington approved a boxlike plan based on English architectural books which, if pedestrian, presented no particular architectural problems. But both Washington and Jefferson wished something more exciting for the Capitol: they fell in love with a design featuring a central dome and flanking wings, which had been drawn up by an amateur architect, the physician William Thornton. Since Thornton admitted to no knowledge of practical building, the execution was entrusted to a French professional architect, Stephen Hallett. Among the problems Washington had faced at the start of his second term, was Hallett's insistence that Thornton's plan could not be built except at murderous expense.[2]

To Jefferson, Washington wrote, "I do not hesitate to confess [that in choosing Thornton's design] I was governed by the beauty of the exterior and the distribution of the apartments, declaring then, as I do now, that I had no knowledge in the rules or principles of architecture and was equally unable to count the cost." He was mortified that more investigation had not preceded the choice, but speed had been made necessary by "the impatience" of everyone. Speed was still necessary. Jefferson should get the interested parties together and come to an immediate decision that would make it possible to lay such foundations as were already being laid for the President's House. Not one moment that could be avoided should be lost.[3]

Thornton proved amenable to editing, and it had become feasible to lay the cornerstone for the Capitol. The parade that was re-forming beyond the Tiber was intended to give impressiveness to this forward step. Washington had ridden over from Mount Vernon to throw his prestige into the scale. After everyone had been adequately dazzled, there was to be an auction of lots, which Washington hoped would be more successful than its predecessors. There would also be a continuing sale of a lottery for various pieces of real estate, the grand prize being a projected two-story hotel. Washington had bought a number of chances, including one for Lear's infant son, "our little favorite," to whom he sent, along with the ticket, his and Martha's "sincere love."*[4]

Having proceeded up a rise, the marchers reached the two sides of a large squared stone which protruded solitary from an otherwise unimproved hilltop. Washington advanced between the files. He was handed a silver plaque, verbosely engraved. As he ceremoniously laid it on the cornerstone of the Capitol of the United States, cannon sounded. The Masons then anointed the stone with corn, wine, and oil. After the Grand Master had delivered an oration, the crowd flocked to a booth containing a 500-pound barbecued ox.

Everyone having (it was hoped) become mellow and optimistic, the occasion moved to the business on which Washington's anticipations turned. The auctioneer mounted his rostrum, made his pitch, and began his chant. Building lot after building lot was put up for sale as Washington leaned forward in suspense. There were few raised hands, few shouting voices. Washington found himself — his act, he later explained, was "more the result of incident than premeditation" — breaking a silence to buy four lots on the East Branch. The next day, the sale continuing, he offered, lest there be jealousy, to buy four more lots at the opposite end of the city, but "little notice was taken of it." The atmosphere had, indeed, become utterly listless.[6]

---

* Washington was an inveterate purchaser of lottery tickets, taking chances on land, a necklace, the *Encyclopaedia Britannica*, a gun, a watch, etc.[5]

The financial crisis caused by the failure of the sale was deepened by the fact that purchasers at previous sales were failing to meet their installments. Since appeals to the public had not succeeded, Washington and the commissioners were forced to put the future capital of the United States into the hands of large speculators.

Before the cornerstone laying, Washington had met James Greenleaf, a Bostonian late resident in Holland, who claimed to have command of much money at home and abroad. Greenleaf had announced that he wanted to buy land in the capital on an "extensive scale," and the President had given him a cautiously worded letter of introduction to the commissioners.[7]

A few days after the failure of the auction, the commissioners agreed to sell Greenleaf 3000 lots, for which he was to pay in seven annual installments. He contracted to build ten houses a year for seven years. Furthermore, since the success of his speculation depended on the public buildings' being completed, Greenleaf would each month lend the commissioners $2200 at 6 percent interest. In sending his approval, Washington expressed the hope that the deal would bring in other "men of spirit with large capitals."

Greenleaf certainly did not lack spirit. He soon increased his holdings to 7234 lots, at the same time reaching his financial tentacles out among Washington's intimates.[8]

Lear had decided to go into business. Washington was not always cooperative with the efforts of his valued subordinates to find better opportunities elsewhere. However, Lear's young wife had just died, and his infant son Lincoln was to be shipped to New Hampshire to be raised by a relation. It was quite possible that Lear's mental state — he was eventually to commit suicide — left so much to be desired that a change was necessary.[9]

Anxious to be "a sincere friend" to the disciple who had lived with him so long, Washington endorsed Lear to the commissioners of the District of Columbia, and when the former secretary went abroad to purchase goods, gave him letters to the diplomatic representatives of the United States.[10] However, as the projected city languished, Lear found himself in need of more capital. Greenleaf became a partner. And, as he streaked like a meteor across the financial skies of Philadelphia, the plunger from Boston also drew into his orbit Washington's close friend, the elderly but forever optimistic financier Robert Morris.

Far from disapproving of this connection, Washington saw in it a fascinating opportunity for himself. His 30,000 acres on the Ohio and Kanawha rivers, which he had personally explored in 1770, had become a liability. Although too deep in the Indian country for effective settlement, they were now close enough to civilization to be taxed. Since Morris and Greenleaf were purchasing quantities of land in many places, Washington wondered why they did not take over his acres too.[11] He dangled the possibility before them, but they did not bite.

No sooner had Washington reached, from plague-ridden Philadelphia, what he hoped would be the quiet of Mount Vernon, than his slaves had crowded around him insisting that they had been deprived of their usual rations of dried fish. The overseer, Hyland Crow, was indignantly summoned. He said it was not his fault: the storehouse had been broken into and the fish stolen. In reply to this, the blacks brought forward "strong insinuations" that the reported robbery was a cover for Crow's having sold the fish. There was now no way of determining what had actually happened. Washington could only order that the slaves get their rations from then on.[12]

At least, Washington had his fine new barn to be proud of. It had been erected while he was in Philadelphia according to his plans, and it was intended to be "one of the most convenient barns in this or perhaps any other country." A favorite feature was an indoor threshing floor large enough to accommodate thirty hands. Washington had ordered that half the wheat from the entire plantation be gathered into the barn — and now was the time for the threshing. He rode out eager to see his agricultural improvement in triumphant action. But as he approached, he heard disturbing sounds — and, sure enough, he found that the wheat had been carried out of doors. Not thirty feet from the barn, on a flat place exposed to the weather, horses were treading the grain out in the old way. This additional "proof . . . of the almost impossibility of putting the overseers of the country out of the track they have been accustomed to walk in" made Washington order resignedly that a shelter be built under which the horses could trample out the wheat in the traditional manner.[13]

How desperately he needed the farm manager he had interviewed in Philadelphia and all but hired. Thomas Ringgold, of the Eastern Shore of Maryland, had recommended to Washington his own manager, William Pearce. Since Ringgold was known as "a loose and dissipated character," Washington had not been too moved by the recommendation — but one day Pearce had knocked on the President's Philadelphia door. The farmer was in a hurry — he had to catch a stage — yet Washington was impressed. The President was just concluding that his problem had been solved, when Pearce had announced that he expected one hundred guineas a year. This seemed to Washington "more than my Mount Vernon estate" would justify, but Pearce stuck to the sum. Washington said he would think it over.

Finally, Washington wrote Pearce that since he was sentenced to stay so far from Mount Vernon "under circumstances which does not allow much thought thereon," he could not deny himself the "satisfaction" of having "a person in whom confidence can be placed as a manager." But before the deal was closed, Pearce should meet him at Mount Vernon.[14]

When Pearce arrived, Washington was even more impressed. The farmer fascinated the President with an account of the improved ploughs they used on the Eastern Shore. Washington drew up a formal contract entrusting to Pearce "Mount Vernon and its dependencies, comprehending the several farms, mill, fishery, tradesmen of different kinds, ditchers, spinners, the person who has charge of the jacks, studhorses, mules, etc." In addition to raising crops and meat, Washington's principal objectives were improving rather than depleting the land by "judicious rotations" of crops; changing marshes into permanent meadows; introducing clover and other grasses where it could be done without too great expenditure for seed; and replacing — "timber being scarce," — wooden fences with hedges. The manager should gather weekly reports from the overseers, keep regular accounts for each farm and "every separate branch of the business." He should clothe "the people," etc., etc.

As Washington's pen ran over the paper, he tried to halt himself by stating that "to go into more detail would be tedious as it is unnecessary." But he was unable to resist piling detail on detail in his pleasure at the thought of a well-run estate. Certainly a man skillful enough to take over Mount Vernon did not need to be told to keep his ground well ploughed and his crop clear of grass and weeds, and his stock culled, and his cattle penned, and his overseers in good order, and — the list went on and on.[15]

Pearce could not take over until the first of the new year. As Washington wandered the Mount Vernon fields, he still had no effective assistance, while everywhere he looked there was something wrong. The carters and wagoners, desiring to catch their horses more easily in the mornings, were turning the animals loose in the clover lots, which were being eaten so bare that the frost would destroy the roots. The camp equipage which he had brought home from the Revolution was covered with mold in the

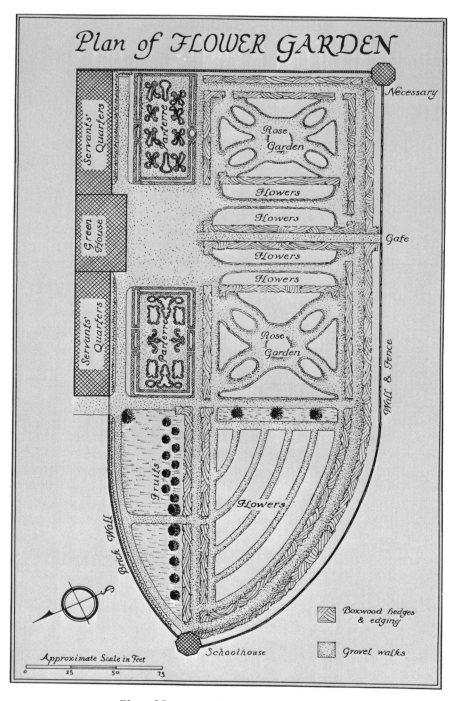

Plan of FLOWER GARDEN

Necessary

Servants' Quarters

Parterre

Rose Garden

Flowers

Flowers

Green House

Gate

Flowers

Flowers

Servants' Quarters

Parterre

Rose Garden

Wall & Fence

Fruits

Flowers

Brick Wall

Boxwood hedges & edging

Gravel walks

Schoolhouse

Approximate Scale in Feet

0   25   50   75

Plan of flower garden at Mount Vernon.
Courtesy of the Mount Vernon Ladies' Association

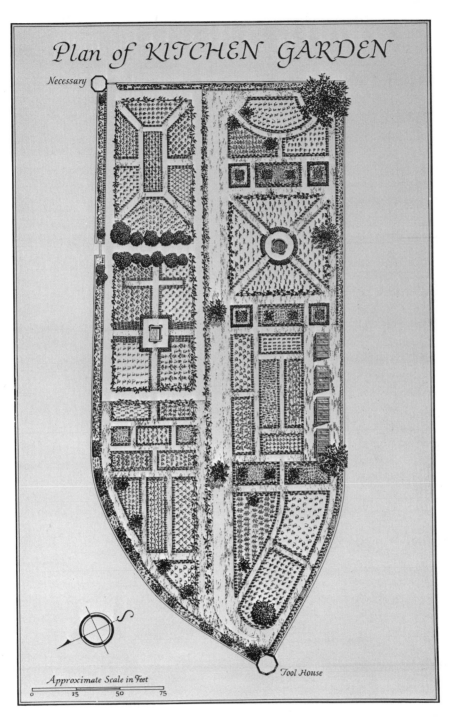

Plan of kitchen garden at Mount Vernon.
Courtesy of the Mount Vernon Ladies' Association

storeroom. If only he could remember to order that the marquee and trunks be cleaned and put out in the sun![16]

It had been Washington's role ever since he was made Commander in Chief to become, whenever the truly relevant official operation failed, in his own person the center of reliances. Now the government itself had disintegrated.

As the rest of the nation tried to isolate itself from Philadelphia lest the contagion spread, and post riders did not dare enter the stricken city, Washington had the greatest difficulty discovering what was the situation in the capital. Typical of his information was the testimony of two colonels who appeared at Mount Vernon. In New York they had conversed with a man who said that he had been told by Governor Mifflin that Philadelphia's Mayor Clarkson had stated that 3500 Philadelphians had died and that the fever was raging more fiercely than ever.[17]

Wishing to get a hundred dollars to a friend's son stranded in the pestilential city, Washington sent a note to Oliver Wolcott, Jr., the Controller of the Treasury, who was reported to be still at his post. But he wrote his friend, "such is the stagnation of business there, and so entirely changed is everything there by the retreat of the inhabitants . . . that it is always impossible from the little intercourse the people have with one another to promise anything on a certainty of having it complied with."[18]

Hamilton, Washington knew, had recovered at least partially from the fever, but he did not know how to reach the Secretary of the Treasury. Jefferson was at Monticello. Where was Knox? Randolph was lodged on the outskirts of Philadelphia, but did not consider it prudent to go to his office. "The heads of the departments being absent," Washington complained, "the disputes arising between the agents of the powers at war and other matters are transmitted immediately to me."[19]

Not only had Washington lacked the foresight to bring with him the governmental papers he needed for the effective transaction of business, but he had found no replacement for Lear. He was making do with the younger man who had been Lear's assistant. Although competent at his secretarial duties, Martha's nephew, Bartholomew Dandridge, did not have the maturity and experience to take, as Lear had done, considerable responsibility from the President's shoulders onto his own. Washington complained dismally, "I came here to look after my private concerns, but have no time allowed."[20]

10

First Reckoning

A CCORDING to the act of Congress which had authorized Washington to establish the future capital on the Potomac, Congress was to meet until 1800 in Philadelphia. However, Philadelphia would probably still be plague-stricken on the first Monday in December, when the next session was to begin. Washington, who always sought the practical, felt called on to designate some other spot, but feared he would be giving "food for scribblers." They might well charge that the executive was invading the prerogative of Congress. And sectionalism burned so brightly that wherever he chose a temporary capital, the north or the south would accuse him of bias. He broadcast requests for advice, one going to his former close associate Madison, with whom he had not communicated since the last Congress had adjourned.

All replies urged that he keep hands off: Congress would have to meet within the legal limits of Philadelphia if only in some open field for just long enough to select another place. Washington gave in to the extent of agreeing that for the time being he would take no action beyond establishing a place for the executive to meet. This would draw other members of the government there, and then all could thrash out, in terms of the situation then current, what to do about Congress.[1]

The mails from Mount Vernon bore letters summoning the Cabinet to meet Washington on November 1 at Germantown, six miles northwest of Philadelphia. He wrote Randolph, who was in residence nearby, to find him some place to stay. Since he knew that Germantown was crowded with refugees, the President would bring with him only his secretary, three servants, and five horses. He would not be the guest of any person. If Randolph could not find him "tolerably convenient lodging," rooms should be secured in a "decent" inn. He intended, Washington wrote Lear, to "move like a snail with everything on my back."[2]

Since communications with the Philadelphia area were still practically nonexistent, Washington had received no reply from Randolph when he set out from Mount Vernon. He was joined at Baltimore by a disgruntled Jefferson.

The Secretary of State was nursing two grievances. Because the usual stagecoaches were not running to the plague area, he was "fleeced" on the road of seventy dollars. Worse, the timetable he had carefully designed so as to avoid being further committed by executive decisions had been shattered when disease had forced him to be out of the capital at the same time as Washington. Now, his period of retirement to Monticello had been used up and he was returning to his duties at exactly the moment he had most wished to avoid: the period when, in preparation for the Congressional session, the executive would have to reach the most crucial decisions. How infuriating that (as he complained to Madison) "this fever" should "so far counteract my view"!

Having on the road experienced "the extremes of heat, cold, dust, and rain," Washington and Jefferson reached Germantown in a downpour to see hundreds of refugees from the stricken city tramping the streets through a deep mud. The Secretary of State could, as he complained, "obtain a bed in the corner of the public room of a tavern only . . . the other alternative being to sleep on the floor in my cloak by the fire."[3]

The President had been met at the outskirts of the village with a note from Randolph announcing that he had secured for Washington three rooms with two beds in the house of the Reverend Frederick Herman, the German teacher at the Germantown Academy. Breakfast and tea in the afternoon would be supplied, but dinner remained a problem, "for the clergyman cannot go so far as this meal." Randolph hoped that the keeper of the King of Prussia Tavern (where Jefferson was putting up) could get a cook "in which case he would send a dinner to your lodgings." This was achieved. Since there was a "charming and extensive prospect" in all directions, and Herman had "a beautiful garden and fruitful orchard" where Washington could sit, the President was not uncomfortable, but there was not space to transact business. He soon moved to the elegant two and half story mansion of Colonel David Franks.°[4]

From the room in which Washington now slept and perhaps from the

---

° Herman was paid $37.94 for ten days' board, lodgings, and candles for Washington, Dandridge, and Washington's body servant. Nearby board and lodgings for the other two servants cost $15.82. Franks later sent Washington a bill for $131.54 which the President protested so successfully that it was reduced to $75.56. Included were six shillings for "the damage done to a large Japanned waiter," 2/6 for a lost large fork, and 4/0 for four broken plates.[5]

very bed, the British commander in chief, Sir William Howe, had been awakened, almost exactly fifteen years before, by the news that the wild American rebels had, contrary to all expectations, poured at dawn into the Germantown streets. Then Washington had been on horseback, engaged in a desperate attempt to rally, with a surprising victory, a tottering cause. Now by his "propitious return to this state" he was again rallying his compatriots. A group of local inhabitants formally thanked him for "fortifying with your presence the good spirit of the Union, lately humbled by the calamity in Philadelphia."[6]

With the chill of early winter, the disease seemed, indeed, to have come to a halt. However, since the science of the time presented no explanation for this,° the break could well be only temporary. When Washington said that he intended to ride into the city, Randolph made violent objections: "You will hardly be at your door before . . . multitudes . . . will be induced by your example to crowd back and carry fresh and therefore vulnerable subjects into the bosom of the infection." Furthermore, the President would be endangering his own life: his friends had long been afraid that "your indifference about danger might push you too early into Philadelphia."[7]

Washington was not dissuaded. He was probably amazed to see that an epidemic left behind visual evidence exactly opposite from war. The houses were all whole. No refuse cluttered the silent streets. The city had never seemed so neat, so pure.

Although Washington continued to visit his office, he decided not to commit the government until enough Congressional leaders appeared to make their own decision. The executive would continue to meet in Germantown, which was becoming daily more agreeable as refugees returned to their city homes. The mails, so long suspended, began to move again, flooding Washington with correspondence, "and this too at a time when . . . I was immersed in the consideration of papers from the different departments after a separation" of "almost two months." He sometimes got involved with the smallest details, as when he accepted estimates for the mason's and carpenter's work on the Tiber lighthouse with the proviso that they erect "a plain staircase." However, he found time for a quick trip to survey the canal works being erected in western Pennsylvania at Reading.[8]

One of the casualties of the epidemic was Freneau's *National Gazette*, which was driven into bankruptcy by the dislocations attendant on the

---

° The disease-carrying mosquitoes had been killed off.

disease. Washington's relief was short-lived, however, since Benjamin Franklin Bache, the grandson of the philosopher, carried his *National Advertiser* (soon renamed the *Aurora*) into the breach, attacking Washington and the administration just as intemperately as Freneau had done. Washington preferred not to have his feelings lacerated by contact with Bache's columns. Dandridge was soon writing the publisher to send no more copies to the President. The President, Dandridge explained lamely, did not have time to read newspapers.[9]

When Washington re-established contact with Eliza Powel, he found her in a desperate state. Her husband had compromised with her fears by taking her to a house in the suburbs, but he *would* ride into Philadelphia, and on one trip he had been stricken with the fever. He went to bed in his town house and called in one of the physicians on whom he so relied: Dr. Benjamin Rush, whose cure for yellow fever was to bleed the sufferer until his body was almost devoid of blood.

Although Eliza had refused Washington's invitation to Mount Vernon on the grounds that it "would be to me a lasting source of affliction" if her husband should sicken deprived of her consolation and attention, she had failed to find the fortitude to risk death by visiting him in the city. She had sent in a servant twice a day to see how he was. One day he was no more.

The public extremity of her mourning did not impress the gossips of Philadelphia. Joshua Fisher commented that she had married for money, not love, and was probably relieved when Samuel died. However, Washington had never shared the views of those who found the voluble lady irritating and absurd. That she was now a widow made her friendship with the President even closer.[10]

Soon after his arrival at Germantown, Washington reached a decision that was to have its principal impact on American culture in the 1920's when, by aiding smuggling rumrunners, it alleviated the Sahara of prohibition. The question: At what distance from shore did American sovereignty protect ships from privateers? To Washington, Jefferson reported that the greatest extent which precedent authorized for territorial waters was the limit of sight, calculated at twenty miles. The least was the range of a cannon ball, calculated at three. Jefferson argued for the larger claim, although that would have been to the disadvantage of French raiders, but Washington sought the solution that would bring the fewest British complaints to his desk. He asserted that he intended his selection of the "three-mile limit" to be only temporary. However, it remained American law.[11]

To his Cabinet, Washington proposed "serious consideration" whether Genêt, who was still so actively trying to undermine the government, should not have his functions discontinued and be ordered out of the country. The President, Jefferson noted, "showed he felt the venom of Genêt's pen." Hamilton and Knox were, of course, for firm action. Jefferson was opposed. This time, Randolph agreed with Jefferson: he felt that making Genêt a martyr would revive sympathy that was fading. After the matter had been argued at two Cabinet meetings, Washington, so Jefferson reports, "lamented that there was not unanimity among us; that as it was we left him exactly where we found him." The matter of dismissal was dropped.[12]

Washington raised the question which Jefferson least wanted to take any responsibility for helping to answer: Should the official correspondence with Genêt be made public by being laid before Congress? The issue could no longer be postponed and the fact that all Genêt's continuing misbehavior had not disillusioned his more determined followers made it manifest that the executive would have to defend the request for his recall. As a practical politician, Jefferson felt compelled to vote for what he had hoped Washington would block and what he had written Madison was most to be avoided. To Washington's relief, the decision to publish was unanimous.[13]

The question was debated whether these revelations unfavorable to France should be balanced by revelations concerning England. The British had refused to take cognizance of American protests dating as far back as May 1792 concerning the occupation of the western posts. News was furthermore coming in that the British were engaged in destroying the American trade with the French West Indies by forcing into their own harbors provision-bearing ships. As these ships lay interned, the British were impressing the seamen into their own navy.

Hamilton and Knox objected to the publication of anything unfavorable to Great Britain. Randolph opined that, since negotiations with England were pending, English misbehavior should be only partially revealed. "I began to tremble now for the whole," Jefferson wrote, "lest all should be kept secret." But Washington intervened "with more vehemence than I have seen him show, and decided without reserve" that the British acts be revealed.

Jefferson was entrusted with drawing up the paper which would take the form of a report to Congress on foreign affairs.[14]

What Washington should say in his Fifth Annual Address was also a major ground for Cabinet discussion. That the President would have to explain the Neutrality Proclamation brought on the now familiar conflict between the Hamiltonian view that the President had exercised a right to lead foreign policy and the Jeffersonian attitude that the President had merely declared the *status quo* at a time when the country was actually at peace. Washington agreed with Jefferson, stating that "he had never had an idea that he could bind Congress against declaring war."[15]

When Washington spoke to Congress on December 3, 1793, he emphasized what the nation stood to gain by the Neutrality Proclamation: by declaring "the existing legal state of things" he had established "our rights to the immunities belonging to our situation." In enforcing the Proclamation, he had labored to "adopt general rules which would conform to the treaties and assert the privileges of the United States." He proceeded to a statement altogether respectful of the powers of the legislature: "It rests with Congress to correct, improve, or enforce this plan of procedure."[16]

Washington urged Congress to afford "an opportunity for the study of those branches of the military art which can scarcely ever be attained by practice alone." This vague wording of the need that was eventually (1802) to inspire the founding of West Point was a result of Cabinet disagreement. Washington's Revolutionary experience had persuaded him that preparedness required an institution to train artillerists and engineers, but Jefferson insisted that establishing a military academy was not authorized by the Constitution. Washington's comment was that "he would not choose to recommend anything contrary to the Constitution, but if it was *doubtful,* he was so impressed with the necessity of this measure that he would refer it to Congress and let them decide for themselves whether the Constitution authorized it or not."[17]

Washington reported to Congress that the proposed peace conference with the northwestern tribes at Lower Sandusky had come to nothing.* Negotiation having failed, Wayne's army had been ordered to march. This would, of course, delight the western settlers, but Washington had

---

* Washington left it for Jefferson to point out in his report on foreign affairs that the conference had been frustrated by the British authorities, who had demonstrated in the most high-handed manner that no such negotiations could succeed unless conducted with British sanction and on British terms.

no intention of encouraging the idea that force was the final solution to the Indian problem.

The basic need, Washington stated, was "to render tranquillity with the savages permanent by creating ties of interest." White "violators of the peace" must be brought to justice. Washington recommended that the government take over the fur trade so that it could be conducted equitably and without fraud. "Individuals will not pursue such a traffic unless they be allured by the hope of profit, but it will be enough for the United States to be reimbursed only."[18]

The passage in the address concerning newspapers in no way reflected Washington's own lacerated feelings. He urged "a repeal of the tax on the transportation of public prints. There is no resource so firm for the government of the United States as the affections of the people guided by an enlightened policy; and to this primary good, nothing can conduce more than a faithful representation of public proceedings diffused, without restraint, throughout the United States."[19]

Just before he delivered his address Washington had expressed satisfaction with the text, which he felt avoided "anything that could generate heat of ill humor." So it proved. The address pleased even the fire-eating Bache, who went to the almost incredible length of accepting Washington's justification of the Neutrality Proclamation. Bache wrote that "the whole style of the performance is replete with the energetic simplicity of expression that characterizes the Man of the People." And the conservative *Federal Gazette,* noting that Washington had indulged in "no unjust invective against the conduct of other nations, no swaggering rhapsody concerning the dignity, resources, and indignation of the United States," characterized the address as "distinguished by classical propriety of thought."[20]

11

Exit Jefferson

HAMILTON felt weak. The yellow fever had, he feared, undermined his constitution. In reply to a lost letter of his dated December 26, 1793, his father-in-law, Philip Schuyler, wrote Hamilton, "I fear much from the incessant application which you are under the necessity to give to the business of your department, increased as it of consequence must be, whilst Congress is in session. I have hitherto been much averse to the determination you mentioned to me, but when I reflect on the danger which your health is exposed to, and the incompetent reward for the most arduous and important services, and the chagrin you experience from the weakness or wickedness of those you have to contend with, I am reconciled [to your] intentions."[1]

These intentions were, of course, the determination to resign which he had expressed to Washington in his letter of June 21.[2] The time he had set in that letter — towards the end of the Congressional session — was coming nearer, but, despite what Hamilton had written to Schuyler, Washington no longer felt it necessary to seek a new Secretary of the Treasury. It was Jefferson who remained adamant about retiring with the new year.

Both possible successors with adequate experience in foreign affairs — Jay and Robert R. Livingston — seemed to Washington ineligible as long as Hamilton remained. To have the heads of two of the three great departments from New York would undoubtedly elicit outrage.

When Jefferson had suggested that he might be succeeded by Governor Thomas Johnson of Maryland, Washington had objected that "for want of familiarity with foreign affairs," Johnson would be "awkward in everything." But in the end, Washington, unable to unearth a better candidate, offered the post to Johnson. Johnson refused on the grounds of ill health.[3]

Not knowing where else to turn, Washington fixed his attention on Edmund Randolph.

Randolph's mature life had opened with a rending tear. His father, John Randolph, powerful as king's attorney, the ruling scion of Virginia's ruling family, had, at the outbreak of the Revolution, turned Tory and then fled Virginia with the Royal Governor. Young Randolph concluded that the best way he could clear himself was to serve as aide-de-camp to the Commander in Chief. Jefferson, Richard Henry Lee, and Patrick Henry jointly signed a letter of recommendation to Washington pointing out "how important a consideration it is that our country should be furnished with the security and strength derived from our young gentry being possessed of military knowledge."[4] The father had befriended Washington. Washington grasped the opportunity to befriend the son.

The twenty-two-year-old who joined Washington in Cambridge was tall and not yet "portly." "His features," a contemporary wrote, were "uncommonly fine; his dark eyes and whole countenance lit up with an expression of the most conciliatory sensibility; his attitudes dignified and commanding; his gesture was easy and graceful; his voice perfect harmony; and his whole manner that of an accomplished and engaging gentleman."[5] Washington was undoubtedly sorry to lose this paragon when, after Randolph had served four months, the death of an uncle called him back to Virginia to handle family affairs.

Virginia was delighted to have so attractive a Randolph to carry on that family's tradition of rule. Edmund became the youngest member of the Virginia Convention which urged independence on the Continental Congress. He became Governor at thirty-three. But always there was in his life a pull opposite to the public success he loved. His offices paid little, and he had inherited no considerable estate. He was forced to supplement his salaries by practicing law, "a profession which from the earliest moment of my life I abominated."[6]

During Washington's retirement after the Revolution, Randolph had served as his lawyer. Placing the gentleman over the businessman, he refused, as "a poor mode of acknowledging the repeated acts of friendship," to send Washington a bill. And Washington, although unwilling to accept anything free from a public body, saw no reason to rebuff this generosity of a young friend.[7]

[105]

Edmund Randolph, the beloved friend and favorite minister whom the elderly Washington tragically suspected of being a traitor. Private collection. Photograph, Frick Art Reference Library

In the preparation and ratification of the Constitution, Randolph played an equivocal role. Washington and his fellow Virginia delegates entrusted to him, because of his mellifluous voice and gracious manner, the presentation of the Virginia Plan on which the eventual Constitution was based. However, Randolph was one of the three delegates who refused to sign the finished document. The Virginia opposition was enchanted to rally behind so shining a champion, but in the end Randolph turned the tables by announcing that, persuaded by the arguments published since the convention, he had changed his mind. This switch did much to bring Virginia into the federal union.

When Congress established the attorney generalship, they envisioned a lawyer who would continue his private practice while on retainer to the President. The relative insignificance of the job made Washington feel that he could indulge himself by appointing to it a man with whom he had long been intimate.

During the first term, Randolph supplied Washington with various legal opinions. Yet he remained a secondary influence as compared with "the Heads of the Great Departments" until the war between England and France induced Washington to call frequent Cabinet meetings. In Washington's search for general agreement, Randolph proved extremely useful. The Whig son of a Tory father saw both sides of every question, and he shared Washington's determination to lean towards neither England nor France. Again and again, Randolph came up, after acrimonious controversy, with the compromise Washington adopted. Washington found this doubly valuable (he may indeed sometimes have suggested privately to Randolph what Randolph presented publicly) because he thought it politic to do as little visible imposing of his own opinions as he could manage.

When discussing in August 1793 with Jefferson who could be his successor, Washington had suggested Randolph. Jefferson had suppressed his hatred for the fellow Virginian who — although his own cousin — had, he felt, deserted him and the Virginia cause by finding compromises often satisfactory to Hamilton and the pro-British party.° However, Jefferson did confide: "I knew that the embarrassments in his private affairs had obliged him to use expedients which injured him with the merchants and shopkeepers and affected his character of independence; that these em-

---

° Modern historians have calculated that Randolph and Jefferson voted on the same side in sixteen of the nineteen major divisions from 1790 onwards, but in many cases Jefferson was dissatisfied with what he found it necessary to support.[8]

barrassments were serious and not likely to cease soon." Jefferson did not add that Randolph had just tried to borrow money from him.[9]

Randolph had never hidden from Washington the fact that he was perpetually strapped. Indeed, at the very time when the President was coming to a conclusion about the Secretaryship of State, Randolph warned Washington that, business in Philadelphia having been so stagnated by the yellow fever, he might well have to resign his Attorney Generalship and return to his Virginia practice. Later events were dramatically to reveal that worry concerning Randolph's financial vulnerability had sunk deep into Washington's mind. But for the moment Washington seems to have comforted himself with the thought that the Secretaryship of State would bring Randolph a larger salary than being Attorney General.

The best argument for Randolph's appointment was that, even if he had never specialized in foreign affairs, he was completely informed, having sat from day to day in the Cabinet. Believing that genius could quickly repair ignorance, Washington would probably have preferred a man of less experience and more transcendent ability, but he could not find one. The well of brilliant "founding fathers" had been emptied to the bottom.[*]

Even if Washington did not confide his current cogitations, Jefferson was well enough informed to suspect that Randolph, whom he considered the most "unfortunate" appointment Washington could make, might well step into his own shoes. However when Washington made a last effort to persuade Jefferson to stay, he turned the President's plea down so "decidedly" that, as Washington complained, "I can no longer hint this to him."[11]

Without hiding that he regarded the appointment as second best to Jefferson's remaining, Washington offered the Secretaryship of State to Randolph. Randolph accepted.[12]

On the last day of 1793, Washington received the expected letter which stated that Jefferson could no longer resist "my propensities to retirement. . . . With very sincere prayers for your life, health, and tranquillity, I

---

[*] Although enabled (as Washington was not) to examine future careers, the historian can suggest for the post no individual both available and superior to Randolph. That Washington had not lost his skill in recognizing ability is shown by his selecting at this time, as minister to Holland, John Quincy Adams, the twenty-six-year-old son of his long-time opponent John Adams.[10] Amazingly, Washington had now given important responsibilities to the four younger men who were in sequence to succeed his own successor, John Adams, as President of the United States, serving for another full generation, until 1828.

pray you to accept the homage of the great and constant respect and attachment with which I have the honor to be, dear sir, your most obedient, etc."[13]

Washington replied that he had received Jefferson's resignation with "sincere regret. . . . Since it has been impossible to prevail upon you to forgo any longer the indulgence of your desire for private life, the event, however anxious I am to avert it, must be submitted to. But I cannot suffer you to leave your station without assuring you that the opinion that I had formed of your integrity and talents, and which dictated your original nomination, has been confirmed by the fullest experience. . . . My earnest prayers for your happiness accompany you in your retirement."[14]

Washington felt that he had every right to be hurt by Jefferson's departure. With this many historians would not agree. They follow a misconception which has been so generally accepted that it is woven into the basic fabric of American historical thinking. They take at face value Jefferson's complaints and the greedy claims of the Hamiltonians that Washington had been a cat's-paw for (as one side would put it) or an admiring follower of (as the other side would boast) the Secretary of the Treasury. Jefferson, so the rubric runs, was so perpetually voted down in Cabinet meetings and so eternally frustrated by the President that the only surprising thing was that he did not resign sooner. He was being used as a front for policies with which he did not agree. He was *forced* to leave the Cabinet and go home.

The truth was that when a division in the Cabinet was not to be avoided, the President sided more often with Jefferson than Hamilton.[15] Washington was himself to remind Jefferson that there were as many instances within Jefferson's own knowledge "of my having decided *against* as in *favor*" of Hamilton's opinions. With this situation, Washington felt that Jefferson should have been satisfied. But Jefferson was not. He himself explained, "Were parties here divided merely by a greediness for office as in England, to take part with either would be unworthy of a reasonable and moral man, but where the principle of difference is as substantial and as strongly pronounced as between the republicans and the Monocrats of our country, I hold it honorable to take a firm and decided part, and as immoral to pursue a middle line as between the parties of honest men and rogues."[16]

Jeffersonian historians like to accuse Washington (as sometimes did Jefferson himself) of harboring at this time pro-British emotions. They are dead wrong. Washington had once, it is true, thought of England in the Colonial manner as "home," but that had been long long ago. His affections had not returned to the nation against which he had fought during eight painful years. The Revolution had left him without a single English friend.° Frenchmen had fought by his side both as allies and as members of his own army. With several of these he had preserved an intimacy, particularly with Chastellux and the man who of all men was closest to his heart, Lafayette. The avowed objective with which the French Revolution had started — the establishment of a republican government responsive to the people — was Washington's own objective. If he was more willing than Jefferson to admit that the objective was being mislaid during violent political convulsions, he had not abandoned the hope that it would be rediscovered. Whenever he felt he could without violating the basic neutrality of the United States, Washington slanted decisions the French way — but he did not feel that he could as often as Jefferson would have liked him to.

Jefferson's departure from the Cabinet, which turned out to be a complete break with Washington's government, was for the President a tragedy.

Among the many reasons why Washington needed Jefferson, there was a major one which he never stated. Whether it appeared in his conscious mind no one can tell. If so, it probably took the milder form of worry lest the information that came to his desk be lopsided, now that the principal champion of one cause had retired, leaving behind the champion of the other. Yet in some incoherent way the aging President may have sensed the possibility that he might now lack the strength to keep from being pushed off balance if the thrust of one much younger adviser of genius was no longer counteracted by a counterthrust exerted by another younger man equally determined and strong.

Almost two years before, Washington had said, in explaining to Madison why he wished to refuse a second term, that "he found himself also in the decline of life, his health becoming sensibly more infirm, and perhaps his faculties also." At about the same time he told Jefferson that his memory was failing him, and he feared he might be sinking into other inadequacies of which he was not aware.[17]

° The only friend who could possibly be considered an exception to this statement was George William Fairfax, who had been born in England and now lived there. However, Fairfax had been Washington's neighbor in Virginia for many years, and had married the Virginia-born Sally.

Jefferson noted concerning Washington at the time of his own retirement: "The firm tone of his mind, for which he had been remarkable, was beginning to relax; its energy was abated; a listlessness of labor, a desire for tranquillity had crept on him, and a willingness to let others act, or even think, for him."[18]

Washington was still holding on to his control of the executive but there arises from the mass of evidence on his behavior, an impression that cannot be exactly demonstrated but remains disturbing. The statements Jefferson several times made that Washington now invariably bowed to majority votes of his Cabinet are contradicted in other notations by Jefferson and seem, in part, reflections of the Secretary's own emotional desire to present himself as a champion fighting all by himself against a hostile majority.[19] Yet the President *did* appear to be depending, more than he had previously done, on the initiative and support of his advisers.

The man who had been so insistent on keeping all the reins in his own fingers was shunting even very important decisions to Cabinet meetings at which he was not present. Most worrisome was his failure to try to replace Lear with another altogether competent private secretary, or even to find Dandridge such an assistant as Dandridge had been to Lear.* Washington was now writing out much of his correspondence in his own hand. The number of communications emanating from the President's office was, as a result, much reduced, and a growing percentage of the letters that did get written were devoted to his private business: particularly lengthy instructions to his new manager at Mount Vernon.

At this time, when his powers seemed to be weakening, Washington was deserted by one of the two men on whose presence he relied to help him keep the vehicle of state on a central course. It would require tremendous strength to steer straight now that the right wheel was so much larger than the left.

---

* Lear's comment on Dandridge had been that he was "a young gentleman of an excellent mind, strong and natural parts, though but little acquainted with the world. His education has been very limited." The President's only secretary was in his early twenties.[20]

12

George Washington and Slavery

ETWEEN September 1 and December 12, 1793, probably during his
stay at Mount Vernon while the yellow fever was destroying lives in
Philadelphia, Washington reached what was for him an even more
revolutionary conclusion than when he had decided to raise his sword
against his King. The time is completely clear. In a letter of December 12
to the English agricultural reformer Arthur Young, Washington stated
that "the thoughts I am now about to disclose to you" were not "even in
embryo" when he had written Young on September first.

Washington now stated that he "entertained serious thoughts" of renting, if he could secure expert English farmers, all of the Mount Vernon
plantation except the Mansion House Farm, which he would hold "for my
own residence, occupation, and amusement in agriculture." Proceeding
with more emotion than seemed called for by the worry he expressed lest
in trying to lure cultivators from Great Britain he were violating some
British law, Washington wrote, "Whether in the opinion of others, there
be impropriety or not in communicating the object which has given birth
to them [his thoughts] is not for me to decide. My mind reproaches me
with none, but if you should view the matter differently, burn this letter."

Washington seems then to have thought better of communicating all
that he had in mind. He wrote that he wished to rent because he was
growing old, because he would like to live free from care, "and from
other causes which it is not necessary to detail."[1]

Washington, who believed that Lear was in Europe, sent him a copy of
his letter to Young in the hope that the former secretary could find ten-

ants for the four Mount Vernon farms — and also purchasers for western lands — "in the course of your peregrinations through England, Scotland, and elsewhere." In a covering letter he explained frankly to Lear why he was willing to dismember the Mount Vernon Plantation which he had for so long passionately amassed. In addition to the reasons he gave Young, he stated that he wished a certain income because he was "ashamed" to turn down, as beyond his means, charitable requests from people who believed that "I possess a good and clear estate." Then he stated, in a paragraph headed "private," that the motive which was "more powerful than all the rest" was "to liberate a certain species of property which I possess very repugnantly to my own feelings, but which imperious necessity compels, and until I can substitute some other expedient by which expenses not in my power to avoid (however well disposed I may be to do it) can be defrayed."[2]

Washington omitted from the copy of this letter he kept in his files the sentences that revealed his wish to free his slaves.[3]

For almost a century before George Washington was born, his ancestors had been practicing slavery in Virginia. Nothing seemed more naturally ordained by whatever force it was that created the world in which as a child he walked. Wherever the Washingtons moved domiciles, their slaves moved too; whenever they rode abroad, slaves worked in the fields they passed and tended the friends they visited. George's father, who died when the boy was eleven, left him only a small part of his middling estate, but that included ten slaves. As an aspect of his disastrous attempt to defend Fort Necessity, Washington lost a "valuable" slave attendant who died of wounds. When Washington took over Mount Vernon at the age of twenty-two, eighteen resident slaves were part of the deal. With his marriage to Martha came the management of several hundred Negroes, although most of them remained legally attached to the Custis estate. In his own right, he paid taxes in 1760 on 49, in 1765 on 78, in 1770 on 87, in 1775 on 135. By 1786, natural increase had raised the number of his blacks to 216.[4]

The most dramatic document revealing Washington as a cheerfully insensitive slaveholder is a communication he sent in 1766 to Captain Josiah Thompson of the Schooner *Swift*, concerning a slave he was consigning to the West Indies as punishment:

"Sir, with this letter comes a Negro (Tom) which I beg the favor of you to sell, in any of the Islands you may go to, for whatever he will fetch, and bring me in return from him:

    1 hogshead of best molasses
    1 ditto of best rum
    1 barrel of limes, if good and cheap
    1 pot of tamarinds containing about ten pounds
    2 small ditto of mixed sweetmeats, about five pounds each.
    And the residue, much or little, in good old spirits.

This fellow is both a rogue and a runaway (though he was by no means remarkable for the former and never practiced the latter until recently) I shall not pretend to deny." However, that "he is exceedingly strong and healthy, and good at the hoe, the whole neighborhood can testify." He had served as foreman of a work gang "which gives me reason to hope he may, with your good management, sell well if kept clean and trimmed up a little when offered for sale. . . . And must beg the favor of you (lest he should attempt his escape) to keep him handcuffed till you get to sea or in the bay, after which, I doubt not, but you may make him very useful to you.

"I wish you a pleasant and prosperous passage and a safe and speedy return."[5]

Eight years later, in 1774, Washington showed that a very different attitude towards slavery was moving in his mind. Concerning the rising British impositions, he wrote that if Americans submitted, "custom and use shall make us as tame and abject slaves as the blacks we rule over with such arbitrary sway."[6]

This passage is the more revealing because Washington had no conscious intention of expressing his opinion concerning slavery. He automatically drew a parallel between the rights for which he was willing to fight and the rights he and his compatriots denied their slaves. The phrase "we rule over with such arbitrary sway" implies disgust at that way he and his fellow planters used their usurped power. But most remarkable for his place and time was Washington's belief that "custom and use" could make white Americans as "tame and abject slaves as the blacks." Here was acceptance of the conception that the Negroes were debased not by their inherent nature (which could not be changed) but by the environment forced upon them (which could). Here was an instinctive repudiation of the conception that the Negroes might be, in fact, an inferior race. If the same causes could produce in white men the same characteristics that were most uncomplimentary to the blacks, there could be no fundamental division, in nature or in the eye of nature's god, between owner and slave, between George Washington and his human possessions.

In 1774, the "embryo" of emancipation was, as Washington tended his plantations, already growing in his mind.*

When Washington reached Massachusetts in July 1775 to take command of the Continental Army, he had hardly been (except for his periods in the wilderness) outside slaveholding Virginia and Maryland. Nurtured where slaves greatly outnumbered white men, he had been trained to fear the results should blacks be armed. He was horrified to find among his troops a considerable number of free Negroes. Although New England generals insisted that the blacks made good soldiers, Washington persuaded his Council of War, which was made up almost entirely of New Englanders, to ban them from the army. His argument, one gathers from a letter General John Thomas sent John Adams, was that any other course would damage the cooperation of the southern colonies.[9]

Early in November, Lord Dunmore, the British Governor of Virginia, declared all Negroes and indentured servants belonging to rebels to be free, and called on those who could bear arms to join the British forces. Washington wrote that Dunmore must "be instantly crushed," since, if he were allowed to seem formidable, Negroes would no longer be afraid to join him. The danger made Washington listen in his Cambridge headquarters to the warning "that the free Negroes who have served in this army are very much dissatisfied at being discarded." Lest they join the

---

* The movement of Washington's attitudes on slavery should be viewed in a world context. The institution was, of course, not invented for blacks from Africa; it was as old as the human race. Homer described slavery without indignation and yet with pity for the individuals enslaved. Christian doctrine absorbed slavery by seeing it as a condition of the body not the soul: all souls were equal before God but slavery was necessary in a world of sin. Popes practiced slavery; Thomas More included it in his Utopia; Martin Luther saw an appeal for freedom from the Swabian serfs as an effort to confuse Christ's spiritual kingdom with the world of affairs. John Locke, one of the theorists chiefly appealed to by the American revolutionaries, found slavery just.

An opening gun for emancipation was fired in 1772 when Lord Chief Justice Mansfield ruled that slavery was not supported by English law. The movement got going in the United States when, in 1776, the Quakers in Pennsylvania voted that their members should either be expelled or free their slaves. In 1777 the Vermont constitution prohibited slavery and shortly thereafter various northeastern states made various provisions for manumission.[7]

The movement led in the south by Virginia, to forbid the further importation of slaves, by no means implied emancipation. Thus Washington's neighbor and sometime mentor, George Mason, opposed importation, but urged that Virginia not ratify the Constitution lest the northern states use it to force emancipation. Nonimportation was to the economic advantage of Virginia as a slave-breeding state.[8]

British in Boston, Washington (without awaiting the approval of Congress) authorized the enlisting of former veterans. Congress's reaction was to agree, but only on condition that the Negro troops be limited to re-enlistments.[10]

By January 1778 Washington had reached the point of urging decisions in the Rhode Island legislature which brought many blacks into the regiments of that state. When the Rhode Island line was reorganized in 1780, he opposed segregation: the Negroes should be assigned in such a manner "as to abolish the name and appearance of a black corps."[11]

During October 1775 the mails brought into Washington's New England headquarters an ode in his praise by the slave poetess Phillis Wheately, who was celebrated among humanitarians as a demonstration of the possibility of black genius. Washington — he blamed a slip-up in his files — took two months to write an acknowledgment. He then compromised on the salutation, calling her not "Phillis," as a Negro would commonly be addressed, or "Miss Wheatley." His letter to "Miss Phillis" spoke of "the striking proof of your great poetical talents," and went on in a manner that seems to have been consciously intended as support of the black's claim to innate capacities: "If you should ever come to Cambridge or near headquarters, I shall be happy to see a person favored by the Muses and to whom nature has been so liberal and beneficent in her dispensations. I am with great respect, etc."[12] (A Virginia slaveholder expressing "great respect" to a slave!)

Among the brilliant young men Washington gathered around him as aides was John Laurens, a rich South Carolinian who had studied in France and developed there an abhorrence of the slavery practiced in his native state. Writing from Washington's headquarters, in January 1778, he asked his father to advance his patrimony altogether in able-bodied male slaves, whom he would embody as a batallion in the army, promising them freedom at the close. When the father asked what was Washington's opinion, young Laurens replied, "He is convinced that the numerous tribes of blacks in the southern part of the continent offer a resource to us which should not be neglected.° With respect to my particular plan, he only objects to it with the argument of pity for a man who should be less rich than he might be."[14]

More than a year later, in March 1779, the elder Laurens, a sometime

---

° At about this time, Washington urged on Congress hiring Negroes as wagoners in the Carolinas, Virginia, and Maryland. Only free blacks should be employed, as slaves would be tempted to seek freedom by deserting to the enemy. The recommendation did not include placing Negroes in a situation where they would have to be armed.[13]

president of Congress, wrote Washington, "Had we arms for three thousand such black men as I could select in Carolina, I should have no doubt in driving the British out of Georgia and subduing east Florida."[15]

Washington replied, "The policy of our arming slaves is in my opinion a moot point unless the enemy set the example." The enemy would certainly imitate the patriots, justifying "the measure upon our own ground. The upshot then must be, who can arm fastest — and where are our arms? Besides, I am not clear that a discrimination will not render slavery more irksome to those who remain in it. Most of the good and evil things of this life are judged of by comparison; and I fear comparison in this case will be productive of much discontent in those who are held in servitude." Washington then demonstrated his dissatisfaction with what he had written, by breaking out (although the subject was one concerning which he must often have worried), "As this is a subject that has never employed much of my thoughts, these are no more than the first crude ideas that have struck me upon the occasion."[16]

The situation in South Carolina became so grave — partly because slave unrest made men afraid to leave their plantations to fight the British — that Congress authorized — partly to reduce the danger of revolts — a force of 3000 slaves to be bought from Carolinian proprietors by Congress and formed into separate batallions under white officers. Those "who shall well and faithfully serve" to the end of the war were to be freed. This plan raised such consternation that the state government tried to get British agreement to South Carolina's sitting out the rest of the Revolution as a neutral. Only British refusal to accept anything but unconditional surrender kept the state in the war. The slave corps was not organized.

Young Laurens continued his agitations and by July 1782 Washington had come completely around, blaming the refusal of the southern states to enlist their Negroes — with an accompanying promise of manumission — on a subsiding of "that spirit of freedom which at the commencement of this contest would have gladly sacrificed everything to the attainment of its object."[17]

Serving, as Commander in Chief, year after year in regions of the United States where economic life was not grounded on slavery, Washington looked around him with envy. He came to consider that being dependent on slave labor was a *"misfortune."* By the fall of 1778, he had reached the point of writing his estate manager, "I every day long more to get clear of" his Negroes. However, since Virginia was almost completely devoid of free labor, Washington could see no alternative short of abandoning the agricultural way of life to which he had been raised.[18]

During the winter of 1778–1779 — he was trying to needle Congress into more effective support of the army — Washington lived in Philadelphia for a longer time than he had ever before been in any city. Surrounded with businessmen, he concluded that it would be to his financial advantage to sell his Negroes and invest the money in government obligations. "My scruples arise from a reluctance in offering these people at public vendue." However, so he argued with himself, "If these poor wretches are to be held in a state of slavery, I do not see that a change of masters will render it more irksome, provided husband and wife, and parents and children are not separated from each other, which is not my intention to do."

Washington went so far as to urge his estate manager to look into the prices which he could get for his slaves, but he was kept from taking the jump by three major considerations. He felt unsure (having no training in the matter) concerning the handling of free capital; he could not really bring himself to "traffic in the human species," and he could not bear the thought that, when the war was over, he would not be able to return to the world that he had always known.[19]

George Washington's forays into the future were balanced by a passionate concern with his own personal past. Mount Vernon, where he directed that his bones be laid, summed up much of Washington's past — and his life there had always been grounded in slavery.

As the war was ending, Lafayette wrote Washington from France, "Now my dear General, as you are going to enjoy some ease and quiet, permit me to propose a plan to you which might become greatly beneficial to the black part of mankind. Let us unite in purchasing a small estate, where we may try the experiment to free the Negroes, and use them only as tenants. Such an example as yours might render it a general practice; and if we succeed in America, I will cheerfully devote a part of my time to render the method fashionable in the West Indies. If it be a wild scheme, I had rather be mad in that way than to be thought wise on the other tack."[20]

Washington replied on April 5, 1783, "The scheme, my dear Marquis, which you propose as a precedent to encourage the emancipation of the black people . . . is a striking evidence of the benevolence of your heart.

I shall be happy to join you in so laudable a work; but will defer going into a detail of the business till I have the pleasure of seeing you."[21]

Late in 1784, Lafayette spent several weeks at Mount Vernon. However, no joint venture was undertaken to establish a plantation for free Negroes.

On May 16, 1785, Washington had as callers two British evangelists, the Reverend Thomas Coke and the Reverend Francis Asbury, who had been sent to the United States by John Wesley to help organize the Methodist movement. The fiery ministers had been traveling through Virginia preaching emancipation, despite threats from mobs, and also holding services for slaves. They brought to Mount Vernon a petition, which they had been circulating among the local Methodists, asking the Virginia General Assembly to legislate gradual emancipation.

Washington, Coke noted, "received us very politely and was very open to access." After dinner, the ministers requested a private interview and presented their petition, "entreating his signature if the eminence of his station did not render it inexpedient for him to sign any petition. He informed us that he was of our sentiments, and had signified his thoughts on the subject to most of the great men of the state; that he did not see it proper to sign the petition; but if the Assembly took it into consideration, would signify his sentiments to the Assembly by letter."[22]

Unanimously, the Virginia House of Delegates refused to consider the petition.[23]

Lafayette, having failed to concern Washington with his American scheme, turned in another direction, buying an estate in French Guiana and also blacks to free and put upon it. Washington's comment, written to Lafayette in May 1786, repeated exactly the phrase he had used three years before: his friend was revealing "the benevolence of your heart." Lafayette's action, Washington continued, was "a generous and noble proof of your humanity. Would to God a like spirit might diffuse itself generally into the minds of the people of this country! But I despair of seeing it. Some petitions were presented to the Assembly at its last session for the abolition of slavery, but they could scarce obtain a reading. To set them [the slaves] afloat at once would, I really believe, be productive of much inconvenience and mischief, but by degrees it certainly might and assuredly ought to be effected; and that too by legislative authority."[24]

Washington had resolved, at the close of the war, that he would live out the rest of his life as peacefully as possible on his plantation. He had promised the people that this would be the case. When he conferred with Lafayette in 1784, the Constitutional Convention, which was finally to draw him from his retirement, had not yet even quickened in the womb of history.

Being himself no fool, constantly reminded by his associates, Washington knew that as he rode his private acres, he carried a tremendous reservoir of power, potentially a major force in determining the future of the nation. If he ever brought this force to bear, he could, like the heir to a great estate, either expend it with effect or dissipate it. At what time and for what objective this accumulated prestige should be loosed was considered by American statesmen a matter of such moment that, when the Constitutional Convention was being organized, even its strongest supporters did not wish Washington to commit himself to attendance until it became clear that the recasting of the government was actually possible.[25]

Washington was willing to back publicly the Methodists' petition for gradual emancipation if the proposal showed the slightest possibility of being given consideration by the Virginia legislature. Lafayette's scheme involved brushing aside governmental channels. It was to be a revolutionary (if legal) act, undertaken by Washington and the French aristocrat as individuals but with the intention of creating, as Washington put it, "a precedent." In one breath, Lafayette admitted that the scheme was perhaps "mad"; in another, stated to Washington, "such an example as yours might render it general practice." Had Washington publicly engaged in such a venture, he would (however else it turned out) certainly so outrage public opinion in the south that he would lose his ability to lead the whole nation. He could not have presided over the Constitutional Convention; his national popularity could not have played its major role in securing ratification. There would probably have been, at least for the time being, no federal government.

Surrounded with frowning nobilities and kings, the United States was engaged in an experiment to demonstrate to all mankind that humanity was capable of governing itself by republican means. The implications of this experiment seemed to Washington stupendous, and he knew that ill-wishers prophesied gleefully that a government by the people could end in nothing but anarchy. He himself was only too conscious of forces that were leading the American people to pull not together but apart. And no issue was more divisive than slavery.

Furthermore, Washington was far from clear in his own mind how best

[120]

to tackle the problems which the flourishing existence of slavery raised for him personally, for the blacks whose destiny and role in society were involved, and for the United States as a nation.

Washington expressed resentment when in 1786, the year before the Constitutional Convention, a society organized by Quakers° for the purpose of freeing slaves tried — illegally he believed — to pry loose a Negro whom one of his Alexandria neighbors had taken into the free state of Pennsylvania. If the Quakers had acted according to law, Washington, so he stated, would not have objected "because from the penalties of promulgated law one may guard." But there was no avoiding "the snares of individuals and private societies." Illegal intervention was oppression rather than humanity because, by "begetting discontent on one side and resentment on the other," it induced more evils than it could cure.

Having gone that far in a letter of complaint to Robert Morris, Washington added that his objections to the activities of the Quaker society did not mean "that I wish to hold these unhappy people . . . in slavery. I can only say that no man living wishes more sincerely than I do to see the abolition of it." But that could, Washington repeated, only be done by legislative authority. Washington wished to see some plan adopted by which slavery was abolished "by slow, sure, and imperceptible degrees."[26]

The best summary of Washington's intimate attitude towards slavery before he entered the Presidency is found in a statement recorded by David Humphreys. "The unfortunate condition of the persons whose labors I in part employed has been the only unavoidable subject of regret. To make the adults among them as easy and comfortable as their actual state of ignorance and improvidence would admit; and to lay a foundation to prepare the rising generation for a destiny different from that in which they were born, afforded some satisfaction to my mind, and could not, I hoped, be displeasing to the justice of the Creator."[27]

During Washington's second year in the Presidency, the Quakers made another effort to upset the *status quo*. One of the compromises that had made possible the ratification of the Constitution in the deep south was provision that the slave trade could not be interfered with on the federal level until 1808. However, the Quakers petitioned that the trade be abolished at once. When instead of repudiating the petition as unconstitu-

---

° The Quakers were, in any case, no favorites with Washington, since they had made much trouble for him and his army during the Revolution because of a pacifism that was in its effect pro-British.

tional, the House referred it to a committee, delegates from the deep south threatened the very civil war that was to break out seventy-one years later.[28]

Although opposed to the slave trade, Washington characterized the Quaker petition as "very *mal à propos*" and was glad that, as a result of the report of the committee, the Quaker memorial "has at length been put to sleep, and will scarcely awake before the year 1808."[29]

In 1791, Pennsylvania cast a shadow in the direction of the President's property. He had lived in Philadelphia so long that, if his official service were considered to make him a resident, the household slaves he had with him might be automatically freed. He feared that, whatever was the letter of the law, those "who are in the practice of *enticing* slaves *even* when there is *no* color of law for it," might entice his. He did not think that the slaves who lived in his family "would be benefited by the change, yet the idea of freedom might be too great a temptation to resist." In any case, the belief that they had a right to be free might "make them insolent in a state of slavery." The situation was made worse by the fact that all the blacks involved, except Hercules and Paris, were "dower slaves" belonging to the Custis estate, which meant that if they were freed Washington might have to pay for them.

He urged Lear to get the involved blacks back to Mount Vernon before the issue arose. "I wish to have it accomplished under a pretext that may deceive both them and the public. . . . I request that these sentiments and this advice may be known to none but *yourself* and *Mrs. Washington*." Lear saw to it that Washington's control was not endangered.[30]

Such was Washington's record on abolition when, between September 1 and December 12, 1793, the dam suddenly went down.

Puzzled by the letter he had received offering for rent four Mount Vernon plantations. Arthur Young wrote asking what was Washington's intention concerning his slaves. Washington replied with an apology for "not being as explicit as I ought to have been." He did not intend to convey the Negroes with the land. "I have something better in view for them." The renters of the Mount Vernon farms could "hire them as they would do any other laborers."[31]

The plan Washington had finally formulated had two great virtues: it would enable him to support himself and would be more to the advantage of the blacks than setting them adrift at the instant that they were freed.

Manumitting Washington's slaves involved a tremendous financial re-nunciation. Even if he were principled against taking advantage through sale of their value, they were probably the greatest financial asset he pos-sessed and certainly (the rest of his valuable holdings being in real estate that might or might not sell) the most negotiable. One good field hand was worth as much as a small city lot, 3000 pounds of beef, or 300 gallons of whiskey. By selling a single slave Washington could have paid for two years all the taxes he so complained about.[32] He intended to free slaves by the hundreds.

In addition to renouncing forever the value of his slaves, Washington would, by freeing them, commit himself to a continual and considerable cash outlay. He would have to support the black children until they were old enough to support themselves. The old and infirm would have to be given pensions for the rest of their lives. Since longevity was not uncom-mon in his slave quarters and the birthrate was high, more than half of the blacks he freed would be, for a greater or a shorter time, dependent on his bounty.

These sacrifices seemed to Washington enough. He did not feel it nec-essary to reduce himself, after years of public service, to bankruptcy.° By renting his four Mount Vernon farms, he would secure the necessary in-come to pay the costs involved in freeing his slaves, to keep himself going, and he might, indeed, if all went well, be surer of earnings than he had been before.

For the welfare of the blacks, the scheme had a tremendous advantage. The only dictated immediate change in their situation would be that they were free. Now paid for their hire, those who wished could continue to pursue familiar tasks with their relations and old friends in familiar sur-roundings. This would help solve the extremely difficult problems of tran-sition.

The leap from slavery to freedom was so basic that (particularly in the cases of the most numerous blacks, the field hands) there sometimes seemed no way to prepare people in the first state for success (or even survival) in the second. A slave did not have any incentive to learn skills, become self-reliant, or in any way better himself; and, without stirring up chaos and even insurrections, a slave could not, Washington believed, be encouraged to have the psychology of a free man until he was actually

---

° This writer's great-great-grandfather, John Chew Thomas, did bankrupt himself in 1812 by manumitting more than a hundred slaves. He was reduced to writing stiff lit-tle letters to his sons-in-law asking for loans which they all knew could not be re-paid.[33]

freed. On one recorded occasion, Washington asked despairingly how "the mind of a slave [could] be educated to perceive what are the obligations of a state of freedom." The most that he hoped to do, as he told Humphreys, was not to prepare slaves for freedom but to lay a foundation on which they could be prepared.[34] According to the plan Washington had now conceived, the crucial preparation could take place after freedom but before it was necessary for the freedman to fly altogether away on his own wings.

What would happen at the Mansion House Farm, which he intended to keep "for my own residence, occupation, and amusement in agriculture," Washington did not state. He could not, of course, hold blacks in slavery there when the rest of his slaves were freed. Yet the inherent problems were, except perhaps economically, not serious. He had not for years raised any cash crop at the Mansion House, which meant that almost no field hands were involved. His flower and vegetable gardeners, his hostlers, his craftsmen, his domestic servants all possessed skills that would enable them to earn their support elsewhere if they pleased. Washington, who avoided as President visibly endorsing slavery, was employing in Philadelphia only white servants in positions where they would meet the public. Some would go with him to Virginia. He could employ others. And surely some of his house slaves were devoted enough to their masters to stay on as hirelings. The Mansion House Farm was the least of his worries.

Both of the difficult parts of his scheme, the protection of himself and the protection of his blacks, depended on his securing to rent his lands and hire his Negroes men who had the capital to get started and the skill to get going. Subdividing into small units would, he believed, create chaos and perhaps put his blacks into unworthy hands. Since, if the most destructive tensions were not to be raised, all the slaves would have to be freed in a single act, he could not carry out his scheme piecemeal. He wished one individual to rent each of his four farms, and the four individuals would all have to take possession at the same time. They would have, in all probability, because of the Virginian attitude towards slavery, to be immigrants. Washington's love of the land on which he had so long toiled, combined with his desire to have the venture succeed, made him insist that only farmers of demonstrated skill need apply.

Washington realized that to work all this out would (if it were, indeed, at all possible) take time. This was just as well. For Washington to free his slaves while he was still President would truly have upset the national applecart. As it was, the government was in serious trouble with the opposition. And the Virginians who led that opposition were not being drawn by their proclaimed position as custodians of the rights of man to open the gates of their slave quarters.° His hopes to free his slaves, Washington wrote, would have to be kept secret for "reasons of a political and indeed imperious nature."[36]

° Where Washington became as he grew older more and more concerned with manumission, Jefferson became less and less. Directly after the Declaration of Independence, Jefferson helped compose a plan (which he never presented) by which Virginia might gradually achieve emancipation. In his later years, Jefferson wrote, "On the subject of emancipation I have ceased to think, because it will not be the work of my day." In 1784 Jefferson urged that the western territories be closed to slavery, but as President he opened the Louisiana Territory and did not discourage attempts to open Indiana and Illinois.[35]

The French Menace Fades

A S the year 1794 began, Washington's most immediate worry (apart from the departure of Jefferson) was the southwest. His previous efforts had not killed the dangerous activities which had been encouraged by Genêt (with Jefferson's secret help). Reports came in that regiments, led by officers carrying Genêt's French commissions, were still being recruited in Georgia, South Carolina, and Kentucky to attack the Spanish possessions at the mouth of the Mississippi and in the Floridas. Defying Washington, Governor Shelby of Kentucky stated that he lacked the authority to prevent men from marching from his state.[1]

Hamilton was happy to take advantage of Genêt's incitations on the Spanish frontier. (How the Federalist would have loved to have known of Jefferson's!) Hamilton took it upon himself to draft, for submission to Washington, a Presidential message asking the Senate to advise the President that Genêt be separated, in response to his "heinous" violations of neutrality, from his official functions. Always eager to aggrandize the executive, Hamilton added that if Congress had not acted by a specific date (left blank by Hamilton), the President would take action on his own.

Washington was puzzled. "The critical state of things," he noted, "makes me more than usually anxious to decide right." He broke a long silence by asking advice from Vice President Adams. Then a comforting dispatch came from Morris in Paris. It stated that Genêt would be immediately recalled. Washington decided to wait.[2]

However, since Genêt had been throwing matches at powder kegs that existed independently of his incitation, his removal would not in itself quiet intrigue on the Spanish frontier. Washington prepared a stern proclamation, but kept it in his desk when the Federalists presented a bill in the Senate forbidding filibustering expeditions against powers at peace with the United States. So strong (and so dangerous) was the sentiment against such restraints that it took more than a month of sporadic debate and also the presentation by Washington of a documented complaint from the Spanish commissioners, to get the bill passed by the upper house. The lower house refused to follow. Then Washington felt forced to act against his theoretical principles. To achieve, despite Congress's unwillingness to act, what he considered essential for peace, he issued his executive proclamation. He went, indeed, further. Over the objections of Randolph, who feared that any such show of force would offend the west and south, Washington instructed Wayne to post troops where they could intercept any filibustering expedition that tried to float down the Ohio.[3]

Although no such expedition actually slipped the leash, the agitation in the west continued to upset Washington. He could not forget the resolution adopted during the previous December by the Kentucky Democratic Society, which was addressed to "all the inhabitants of the United States west of the Allegheny and Appalachian Mountains." Insistence that Spain should be attacked while her forces were occupied elsewhere, was only one part of the message. The document accused the federal government of desiring to keep the Mississippi blocked. This, plus the "odious and oppressive" excise tax which Congress had placed on whiskey, plus the effort to ban settlement on land not officially bought from the Indians, added up to a presumed demonstration that it was the policy of the east to bleed and contain the west. Remonstrance, so the resolution continued, might well fail to procure justice. Let the west prepare for self-defense by forming, in every area, Democratic Societies, which (like the Committees of Correspondence that fostered the Revolution of 1775) would keep in contact with each other.[4]

The west had, of course, huffed and puffed before, and Washington had shrugged off fears which had, indeed, proved in the upshot unfounded. But he was older now, and Democratic Societies had entered the situation. He knew by experience how effective the Committees of Correspondence had been. In response to alarmist views sent him from the Virginia state capital, Washington wrote that Governor Henry Lee had expressed "precisely my ideas of the conduct and views of those who are aiming at nothing short of the subversion of the government of these states, even at the expense of plunging this country into the horrors of a disastrous war."[5]

What a delightful change from Citizen Genêt! "He seems to be a plain, grave, and good man. . . . As far as we can judge from his looks and manners, he is a very agreeable man." So Martha Washington described the new French minister, Jean Antoine Joseph, Baron Fauchet, who presented his credentials on the President's sixty-third birthday. Fauchet argued about nothing and made plain the detestation of his government for the behavior of Genêt. There would be, he assured the President, no more flouting of American laws.[6]

Fauchet wanted Washington's permission to arrest Genêt and return him to France (where he would certainly be guillotined). This Washington could not countenance: he gave the man who had so violently fought and so grievously insulted him political asylum in the United States. Genêt was to marry a daughter of Governor Clinton and settle down as an upstate New York landowner who channeled his ebullience into a flood of inventions, most of them impractical.[7]

When Washington's interview with Fauchet was over, official Philadelphia swarmed in to felicitate the President on his birthday: "He was standing in the middle of the room and bowed politely to everyone as we entered. . . . After walking socially among the company and enquiring about the health of the individuals, he opened a door leading into another apartment, and, smiling, asked us if we were disposed for a little cake and wine by way of refreshment. The cake was round and nearly three feet [in] diameter and one in thickness. His wine was excellent and punch high-flavored. We all joined in the conviviality, the President mingling and partaking with the company."[8]

Washington could think back with pleasure to his talk with Fauchet: the French crisis seemed over. But this did not mean that the President could look ahead to relaxation. A British crisis which had arisen seemed likely to become even more grave.

II

The British Menace
and Conflict at Home

14

Rumblings of War with Britain

TO the sources of irritation with England which had existed ever since the Revolution, several had been added in 1793. Although the British Order-in-Council of June 8, 1793, which had instructed naval commanders to bring into British ports neutral ships bearing provisions for French possessions, provided that the British government would buy the cargoes at market value, there had appeared innumerable blocks and delays. The impressing of interned American seamen into the British navy continued.

Towards the end of the year, word came in of a treaty arranged by British diplomacy between the Bey of Algiers and Portugal, whose navy had been curbing the Algerian pirates. The treaty released the Portuguese navy to help the British fight France, but in the process loosed the Algerian pirates on American shipping.

This far, the actions of Great Britain had done no more (in Washington's words) than give "much discontent," but news which began to solidify late in February 1794 threw the nation "into flame."[1] The British had early in November ordered the capture and confiscation of all vessels laden with French goods or carrying goods to a French possession. However, the order was not announced publicly until late December. This gave British vessels — both naval ships and privateers — plenty of time to reach and attack without warning the American vessels that were crowding the shipping lanes to the French West Indies, where the ports had been opened to the United States by French war policy.

According to Samuel Flagg Bemis, the historian of Anglo-American relations, "the order was executed with the utmost thoroughness and under conditions which imposed great and unnecessary damage and hardship, not to speak of gross physical cruelty, on American navigators. Hundreds of American ships were soon lying idle in the harbors of the British West Indies awaiting the decision of local courts of admiralty, while their crews languished in fever-ridden prison hulks of those tropical ports."[2]

Further shocking news came in from the frontier. It was by now common knowledge that during the previous summer the British had frustrated Washington's efforts to conduct a peace conference with the northern Indians. Wayne had thereupon advanced with 3000 men to the southwest branch of the Maumee, where — it being too late in the season to proceed farther — he had erected a stockade in which to pass the winter. Convinced that war with the United States was inevitable (and welcoming the idea as perhaps eventuating in the return of New England to the British fold), the authorities in Canada refused to believe that Wayne did not intend to attack their territory as well as the Indians. Lord Dorchester, the Governor-General of Canada, announced to an Indian council that the United States and his King would soon be at war, with the result that the British and the Indians would divide up the northwest forests at their own pleasure. His words, supposedly secret, were leaked to Governor Clinton of New York, who sent the disturbing news on to Washington.[3]

The Federalists, who had been basking in the disgrace of Genêt, now found their own interests and policies severely menaced. Senator King diagnosed, even in the usually pro-Federalist and pro-British northern and middle states, "the most alarming irritation." Fisher Ames mourned, "The English are absolutely madmen. Order in this country is endangered by their hostility." The moderate Republican Robert R. Livingston expressed worry lest Washington, concluding that the people wanted war with England, go along with their desire.[4]

Washington wrote, "As there are those who affect to believe that Great Britain has no hostile intentions towards this country, it is not surprising that there should be found among them characters who pronounce the speech of Lord Dorchester to the Indians to be spurious." He himself did not doubt "the genuineness of the speech . . . nor of the intentions of the B [ritish] government to keep this country in a state of disquietude with the Indian nations, and also to alter the boundary between them and us if, by any means, they can effect it." He urged Clinton to make such inquiries concerning conditions in Canada "as might enable us, if matters should come to extremities, to act promptly and with vigor." How, for instance, would the inhabitants of Canada (most of whom were French) react if hostilities took place? What was the number and disposition of British troops, "especially about Niagara and Oswego?"[5]

During the opening months of the session of Congress, when British relations were still creating no more than "much discontent," Madison had introduced again the resolution for retaliation against the British mercantile laws — reciprocal restrictions down the line — which he had originally introduced in 1791. His new bill added that the additional tariff revenue paid by British shipping should be used to reimburse American shipowners for the damages they sustained at British hands.

The Hamiltonians had opposed Madison's recommendations before, and they opposed them again. Hamilton supplied the information that three quarters of America's trade was with Great Britain while only one seventh of British trade was with the United States. Who, Hamilton's spokesmen asked, had the most to lose from a trade war? And they pointed out that the revenues of the United States were vulnerable to British mercantile reprisals, being almost altogether dependent on customs duties.[6]

When in 1791 the Hamiltonians had pushed through their own tariff ideas, Washington had considered vetoing the bill because there was no counterdiscrimination against the British. Now he followed his policy of never intruding, with any statements of his own opinions, in legislative debates, but he did assist the Republicans by communicating to the House a dispatch from the American minister in London telling of an interview held the previous November with the British Foreign Secretary, Lord Grenville. Grenville had shown no willingness to discuss trade restrictions, and on the vexed matters of illegally held forts and Indian incitations he had only expressed disappointment that the United States would not allow Britain to rearrange the frontier as an arbiter in negotiations with the Indians.[7]

Congress had not acted when the new British violence threw the nation "into flame." Then Madison's proposals, so recently radical, seemed mere milk and water. New bills provided that the United States cut off all intercourse with the British until England had made complete restitution to every American merchant and had removed every soldier from soil claimed by the United States. It was also moved that the Treasury sequester all private debts due to British merchants as a guarantee to American shippers for indemnification.

On March 8, 1794, Hamilton sent Washington what he described tactfully as "some reveries" which had occupied his "imagination," but which were in fact the Federalist counterprogram. Congress should invest the President with the power to forbid by embargo all foreign trade. Furthermore, in order to preserve peace by strength and be prepared for war, the United States should fortify her principal seaports and raise an army of twenty thousand. The former aide-de-camp did not hesitate to outline to his former commander how the army should be organized. Nor did he hesitate to advise Washington on political behavior: "some executive impulse" ought to be exerted to put over his plan. "Many persons look to the President for the suggestion of measures corresponding with the exegency of affairs."[8]

Washington's deep objections to interfering with Congressional deliberations were not overcome by the memorandum; the Federalist legislators had to present their plan themselves.

As it turned out, a temporary embargo proved satisfactory to both parties. The Federalists reasoned that, if no American ships were on the water, no further British deprivations could further outrage American public opinion. The Republicans noted that the move would only damage Britain since trade with French possessions had in any case been stopped. And both sides saw in a refusal of the United States to supply the embattled British West Indian islands a lever to bring the British to reason.

On March 26, Congress voted by heavy majorities to bar all foreign trade for thirty days. Washington was soon deep in the problems of specific vessels whose situation under the embargo was equivocal, usually writing the necessary letters in his own hand. When Fauchet asked for some interpretations that would be favorable to France, Washington confided to Randolph, "I am *well disposed,* and think we *ought* to comply . . . if it can be done without involving unpleasant consequences."[9]

Congress quickly passed laws for fortifying seaports and for commissioning frigates to protect American shipping from the Algerian pirates — but the Federalist request for a military force placed many Republicans on the horns of a dilemma. It was indeed the very men who were most anxious to defy the British who were also most frightened of raising a standing army. Senator Monroe wrote Jefferson that the proposal was a Federalist plot "destructive to public happiness. . . . The order of Cincinnati will be placed in the command of it. . . . A particular character here [obviously, Hamilton]" was contemplated for generalissimo. The militia would be reduced to a cipher. "Thus we see this faction in our councils seizing with avidity every incident that may possibly tend to promote the great object of a change in government."

What a quandary! The "embarrassment" was increased, so Monroe continues, because "not the least confidence can be reposed in our executive council." To embark on a war under the leadership of the enemies of public liberty would be more dangerous than all British aggression. Yet taking no step would degrade the United States as a nation.[10]

The Republicans adopted as their policy extreme brinkmanship: twist the lion's tail hard enough to make him wince but not hard enough to make him pounce! As Madison explained it, the British wished to bar American trade with her own enemies but keep the branches of American trade that were useful to her. Since war with the United States would exactly reverse this pattern, England would go no further than she thought America would tolerate peacefully. She would stop any misbehavior that was made to her disadvantage.[11]

The Federalists did not cease to scent the breeze with the utmost alarm. Not only did they fear that the British might not be as patient as the Republicans postulated, but all interference with trade with Great Britain (including continuance of the embargo) would stagnate American economic life and destroy the customs revenues on which the solvency of the government relied. Sequestering private debts seemed to businessmen a horrifying proposal. However, unless the British could be persuaded radically to change their policy, which even Hamilton considered "atrocious,"[12] there could be no way of holding back extreme reprisals. Heated decisions of an emotionally aroused Congress were not likely to move London. The only hope seemed to be somehow to persuade Washington to overcome his scruples against acting in a matter that was before the legislature.

Washington was viewing the world scene with deep melancholy. He wrote the British philanthropist the Earl of Buchan, "If, instead of the provocations to war, bloodshed, and desolation (oftentimes unjustly given) the strife of nations and of individuals was to excel each other in acts of philanthropy, industry, and economy; in encouraging useful arts and manufactures, promoting thereby the comfort and happiness of our fellow men; and in exchanging on liberal terms the products of one country and clime for those of another, how much happier would mankind be! But providence, for purposes beyond the reach of mortal scan, has suffered the restless and malignant passions of man, the ambitious and sordid views of those who direct them, to keep the affairs of this world in a continual state of disquietude; and will, it is to be feared, place the prospects of peace too far off, and the promised millenium at an awful distance from our day.

"In the disturbed state at which most nations seem to have arrived," Washington continued to Buchan, "and from which it is my earnest wish to keep this country free (if it can be done consistently with honor and the respect which every nation owes to itself as well as to others), I shall avoid all details on political subjects."[13] To Richard Henry Lee, Washington said no more about the confusions in Congress than "what may be the final result of them, no mortal I believe can tell." Yet the idea of cutting through red tape by sending a special envoy to treat with the British must have entered his mind.[14]

Even if it trumped Congress's own deliberations, appointing such an envoy was within his Constitutional prerogatives, assuming that he could secure the Senate's consent. And Washington had taken similar steps twice before. When in 1781 the Continental Army seemed to be collapsing for lack of money and supplies, Washington had secured the consent of the Continental Congress to sending to France a special envoy, Colonel John Laurens, who, speaking for the army and personally for Washington, was to plead for more aid. Washington's second such effort had been when he was President and in relation to Britain: in 1788 he had personally commissioned Gouverneur Morris to try to straighten out with the British foreign office many of the problems that were still pending. It is thus highly improbable that Washington was surprised by Senator Oliver Ellsworth's suggestion.*

On March 10, 1794, Ellsworth of Connecticut had met with three other Federalist senators — King of New York, George Cabot and Caleb Strong of Massachusetts — at King's lodgings. The conference deputized Ellsworth to call on Washington with a series of recommendations, the most important being that "an envoy extraordinary" should be sent to Great Britain. Ellsworth should "insinuate" that the mission should be entrusted to an individual of the first talents, "enjoying the confidence of the friends of peace and of the government, and whose character was unexceptional in England." The President would, of course, agree that no other man could fill these qualifications as well as Hamilton.

---

* The idea was, indeed, in the air. Randolph claimed to have been "among the first, if not the first" to have suggested it to Washington.[15]

Ellsworth reported back to King that Washington was "at first reserved — finally more communicative and apparently impressed with Ellsworth's representation." However, he expressed disturbing doubts about appointing Hamilton. He himself had, of course, complete confidence in the Federalist leader, but did Hamilton possess "the general confidence of the country"?[16]

If Washington heard (as he undoubtedly did) that Republicans were expressing apprehension that the executive might take over,[17] this might help explain why he hesitated for a full month. Finally (Congress being no closer to a solution) he asked Senator Robert Morris for advice concerning a special envoy. Morris was already well primed by King. He favored the idea and urged the appointment of Hamilton. Washington's reply was from a Federalist point of view frightening. He was considering not only Hamilton and that other Federalist Jay, but the unpredictable John Adams, and the pro-French Jefferson. Morris was eloquent against Jefferson, and repeated his preference for Hamilton.[18]

When the word began to circulate that a special envoyship was now probable, King found "the conduct of the French or of anti-English party . . . somewhat extraordinary." Congress having demonstrated, while Washington waited, its inability to act, an executive appointment was now "called for from all quarters." Disagreement moved on to the question of who should be appointed. The Federalists believed that the Republicans wished to "embarrass" the mission by having one of their own number delegated, a possibility which could not be dismissed, since Washington had mentioned Jefferson to Morris, and rumor reported that Randolph had presented to Washington the dread name of Madison. The Republicans were chilled at the thought that Hamilton might be chosen: if he did not sell out the United States, he might achieve a treaty so successful that it would be a stepping-stone to the Presidency. Monroe composed a letter warning Washington that his appointment of Hamilton would be "not only injurious to the public interest but also especially to your own. . . . In case it is your wish I should explain to you more at large my reason for this opinion, I shall wait on you at any hour you may appoint."[19]

Although Washington had already talked with Federalist senators, his reaction to Monroe's offer was to wonder about the constitutionality of permitting individual senators to interfere in advance of the presentation of an appointment to the whole Senate for confirmation. He may also not have relished the idea of having to hold a noncommittal expression while the emotional Monroe blew off against Hamilton. In any case, he replied that if Monroe possessed "any facts or information which would disqualify Colonel Hamilton," they could be communicated in writing. Washington added that Hamilton was only one of the men under consideration. "I *alone* am responsible for proper nomination."[20]

Madison commented in a letter to Jefferson that, although appointing Hamilton would create a most unfavorable "sensation," Hamilton would feel "great mortification" if passed over.[21] Hamilton's friends were outraged by Washington's hesitation, and Hamilton himself, unable to credit that the President was not his passionate partisan, blamed Randolph who, he assumed, was acting as a cat's-paw for the Frenchman Fauchet.[22] As for Washington, he was undoubtedly held back by reluctance either to disgust the Republicans or to offend his ablest remaining minister, at the same time disgusting the Federalists.

Finally the Federalists became so nervous lest the whole project be dropped or fall into Republican hands that they decided to dynamite the logjam. King asked Jay if he would accept the appointment. Jay, who had previously expressed himself as shocked by the imminence of war, said he would prefer Hamilton but agreed to act if that seemed necessary. Then King noted in his journal, "Hamilton abandons the idea of the envoyship."[23]

In one of his long, didactic letters, Hamilton notified Washington that he was no longer a candidate. He was thus enabled to write freely: the President had "an indispensable obligation" to speak out publicly against the anti-British laws still pending before Congress, since they would, if passed, make a negotiated settlement impossible. He should also "nominate a person who will have the confidence of those who think peace still within our reach." Since he himself had withdrawn, the only suitable candidate was Jay.[24]

Washington again repudiated Hamilton's suggestion that he try to influence the legislation before Congress. But he knew that no man in the United States — except perhaps Jefferson, who had recently (as we shall see) refused the ministry to France — had as much and as varied an experience in foreign affairs as Jay. Washington decided to offer the special envoyship to the Chief Justice.[25] He could not know that this was to be the turning point of his career as President.

15

Two Envoys

JOHN JAY could be described as "the lost Founding Father." Although his niche in the American pantheon is not brightly lighted, he played, on many levels, a major role in the establishment of the nation.[1]

Originally Jay had been opposed to independence — but once it was declared, he did much to keep his native New York in the rebellion. He wrote the constitution of his state, interpreted it as the state's chief justice, and served two terms as governor.

On the national scene, Jay was equally important. During the Revolution he was president of the Continental Congress, minister to Spain, and one of the commissioners who negotiated the peace treaty with England. Under the Confederation, he was Secretary of Foreign Affairs. Influential in planning the Constitutional Convention (and in persuading Washington to attend), he was a co-author with Hamilton and Madison of the *Federalist*. For most of Washington's first Presidential year, he continued in charge of foreign affairs. Refusing the permanent appointment that then devolved on Jefferson, he became (as he still was) Chief Justice of the Supreme Court. He was now launching on a crucially important diplomatic mission. Why then does his name not reverberate louder in American annals?

Jay was tall and lank, with cold blue eyes and a long nose hooked over a tight, discontented mouth. In the 1790's, his still-dark hair, although thick on the sides, hardly interrupted the rise of his high, bald dome.[2] Although able, he was arid. He lacked that amiability and charm which many people found in Washington and Jefferson, and also that aura of

John Jay, the results of whose mission to England created the most painful problems Washington ever faced. Portrait by Joseph Wright. Courtesy of the New-York Historical Society

being a brilliant gambler, that inspirational glow (baleful if you disagreed with him) given off by Hamilton. When, after being prepared by private tutors, Jay got to college, his classmates considered him "serious," "grave," "sedate."

The scion of a ruling family in the most dynastically ruled of all states, Jay had no need to be ambitious: his characteristics were (as Bemis points out) self-assurance and self-satisfaction. Inherited social position barred him from wide personal contacts, and a puritanical streak encouraged his belief that he was always right. He had little of Washington's respect for public opinion. Thus, while Secretary of Foreign Affairs during the Confederation, he twice took stands that outraged wide segments of the nation. He agreed that the British had much right on their side in not honoring parts of the peace treaty, since the Americans had made little effort to honor their obligation to pay their prewar debts to British merchants. And he had been — until vetoed by a howl of frontier rage — willing to bargain away American insistence that Spain should at once open the navigation of the Mississippi.

Washington got to know Jay early in 1776, when the Continental Army was in New York. Since then a long if intermittent series of matters of state had brought them often into touch, but there is nothing in their correspondence to indicate that they were personally close.° Washington wrote Jay typically in 1779, "My friendship for you will always make me take pleasure in cultivating the esteem and confidence of which you so politely assure me."[4] Theirs was an association of mutual respect. Its even tenor was sharply cracked when Washington refused to repudiate out of hand the charges of the French minister against Jay and King. Since Washington was obviously following what he considered to be his duty, Jay's dudgeon could well be considered unjustifiably high. Perhaps an observation made by the British Foreign Secretary, after he had a chance to assess Jay, explains. Lord Grenville recorded that Jay was "unforgiving" if he thought his importance neglected.[5]

Jay's behavior after he had undertaken his mission raises the question as to whether he had altogether forgiven Washington.

No sooner had Washington offered the envoyship than a Federalist delegation trooped into Jay's lodgings. He greeted Hamilton, Strong, Cabot, Ellsworth, and King. They urged Jay to make it a condition of his accep-

---

° The most personal touch is Washington's offer to have his jackass serve Jay's jennies free of charge.[3]

tance that he not be charged with making any "complaint or menace" against the British. Jay agreed, called on Washington, and then reported back to the Federalist caucus that he had, "as far as he judged respectful, and in a decided manner," told Washington that the passage by Congress of any anti-British legislation would cripple his mission.[6]

Washington was not persuaded to break his rule against interfering with the legislature. The message he sent the Senate on April 16, 1794 — he considered it so crucial that "every word of it should undergo due consideration" — was brief and to the point. Peace with Great Britain "ought to be pursued with unremitted zeal, before the last resort, which has so often been the scourge of nations and cannot fail to check the advanced prosperity of the United States, is contemplated." He had nominated Jay as "envoy extraordinary." This did not indicate lack of faith in Pinckney, the present minister. "But a mission like this, while it corresponds with the solemnity of the occasion, will announce to the world a solicitude for a friendly adjustment. . . . Going immediately from the United States, such an envoy will carry with him a full knowledge of the existing temper and sensibility of our country, and will thus be taught to vindicate our rights with firmness, and to cultivate peace with sincerity."[7]

After a spirited but brief debate, with Monroe leading the opposition, Jay was confirmed eighteen to eight. That the old resentments against Jay were raked up surprised no one. But Washington was perturbed to have raised again (Randolph had already mentioned it to him) constitutional questions.[8] Should Supreme Court Justices be eligible for additional appointive office? Might not a President use the possibility to influence decisions of the court?

If Jay could be induced to resign as Chief Justice, the possibly unfortunate precedent would be avoided. Washington suggested, in a letter marked "secret and confidential," that Jay remain in London as regular American minister. This would also solve a second problem. A shift in the diplomatic corps had been dictated by a French request that Gouverneur Morris, who was suspected of royalist leanings, be recalled. With Jay taking over in London, Pinckney could be moved to Paris.[*] But Jay would have none of it. The judiciary, he insisted, had not been put on a solid enough footing for him to leave the court.[9]

---

[*] Having Pinckney in Paris would be satisfactory, Washington knew, to the Jeffersonians, since on a previous occasion, when the recall of Gouverneur Morris was under discussion, Jefferson had suggested it. The shift had been blocked at that time by the lack of a suitable replacement for Pinckney in London.[10]

According to established diplomatic practice, Jay should receive instructions that would limit him to proceeding within the boundaries of national policy. The Senate could not exercise its Constitutional right to take a hand in this matter without reviving the very debates which it was one object of the mission to ameliorate. They left the instructions to the executive.

Washington had long been opposed to tying the hands of men who were facing at a distance problems he could not foresee. His unwillingness during the Revolution to dictate to the commander of the northern army had been one reason that General Gates came to think of his command as equal if not superior to that of the Commander in Chief. As the Constitutional Convention was organizing, Washington's main fear had been that the delegates would be kept by rigid instructions from achieving in consultation the necessary self-education and compromises. Now Jay was going to a foreign country where the President had never been and to which communication was so slow that six months could pass between a request for a change in instructions and the receipt of a reply. It seemed to Washington that the envoy, in whose integrity he had the greatest trust, should be given the greatest possible latitude, and this premise was passionately endorsed by Hamilton and the other Federalist leaders, who intended to see that Jay decided things their way.

Jay's primary mission was to clear up all the political contentions between the United States and England. Some went back to the aftermath of the Revolutionary War: the nonsurrender of the northwestern posts, the nonpayment of American debts to British subjects, etc. Others were aspects of the new war: British raids on American shipping and indemnification therefor; the impressment of American seamen, etc.[11]

These issues, however, were not the only vexations to Anglo-American relations. There remained the British mercantile laws which had in peacetime as well as wartime placed American shipowners at a disadvantage. For years, the United States had been trying to persuade the British to negotiate a trade treaty. Supposing Jay should find the opportunity? Should he grasp it? Randolph later claimed, to Washington's outrage, that he had opposed giving Jay commercial powers, on the grounds that the Senate had, when it consented to the appointment, no such intention. Washington's Federalist ministers, desiring as inclusive a rapprochement with Great Britain as possible, were eager for commercial negotiations. The President's ruling was that it followed naturally that when the expense of such a mission was incurred the government would "embrace the

[143]

opportunity" to settle all matters. He knew the Francophiles would not be pleased. There was no need to announce now the scope of Jay's powers, since nothing could become binding until the Senate's consent was obtained.[12]

Washington and his Cabinet prepared a long list of the settlements which the United States would be glad to have achieved, but these were noted down as "amounting to recommendations only." There were items which the Republicans favored, including the contention, which had been pressed by Jefferson when he was Secretary of State, that according to international law "free ships make free goods." This meant that, except in the case of an actual impermeable naval blockade, American shippers could serve France and their own pocketbooks by ignoring British naval might as they carried French goods to market or took supplies into French ports. Hamilton made no ardent objections, probably because he saw how impossible it was that Great Britain would accept a contention which so negated the advantages she derived from her naval superiority.

There was a matter, however, on which Hamilton was vociferous. Randolph urged that Jay be empowered to consult, should the British prove obdurate, with the Russian, Swedish, and Danish representatives in London concerning the possibility of the United States' joining a league of armed neutrality that would protect neutral shipping against British aggression. Hamilton screamed that this would entangle the United States in European politics, and the remaining members of the Cabinet agreed. Although Washington seems to have felt that entering such an alliance would be unwise, he ruled that the instruction should be included so that Jay could use it to keep the British guessing, or as a threat.[13]

Jay's instructions contained only two hard and fast orders, the first legally necessary, the second reflecting a very basic American interest. He might accept nothing that would "denigrate our treaties and engagements with France"; and he might not agree to any commercial treaty which did not, to some extent at least, open the British West Indies to American shipping. According to Bemis, "Perhaps never in the history of the United States has a plenipotentiary been vested with more unfettered discretion."[14]

Jay's refusal to leave the Supreme Court had left Washington with the need to find a new minister to France. The embassy was the more important since the French, not wishing their enemy to have any advantage which they could prevent, had responded to the British orders about American shipping carrying French goods by promulgating their own orders that any American boat carrying British goods was fair prey for their own privateers and naval vessels. This was a flat violation of the French treaties with the United States. When the French heard that the Jay mission was contemplated, they scurried back, lest they lose an arguing point, to their old contention that free ships make free goods; but American shipowners were not paid for the vessels that had been confiscated in the interim.[15]

Among Washington's possibilities for the French appointment, there remained only one man who had adequate experience in foreign affairs, Robert R. Livingston. Although Livingston was at least as much a patrician as Jay, the infighting among the great New York families had pushed him onto the Republican side, which meant that his appointment could be regarded as a balance to Jay's. However, despite some arm wringing by Washington, Livingston refused the post.[16]

Washington sounded out Madison, who was not himself tempted but suggested Aaron Burr. Having too clear a view of Burr's character to be seriously interested, Washington offered the post to Senator Monroe. Conscious of how violently he had attacked the President, Monroe was amazed by the offer, writing, "I really thought I was the last man to whom it would be made."[17]

Washington was scraping the bottom of the barrel — and he probably did not realize the extent of Monroe's distrust for him. His memory traveled back to when the future senator had been an eager, ambitious, and determined youth of eighteen, who had been among the first Virginians (other than riflemen from the frontier) to join the Continental Army. Monroe shone in combat, particularly at the Battle of Trenton, where he was wounded. The Commander in Chief then unintentionally damaged the youth's military career by involving him in what was Washington's first experiment in true continental cooperation: he tried to strengthen the army by establishing "additional regiments" that were not organized by states but would mix men from all over the continent. Selecting to lead this venture some of his best officers, Washington included Monroe. But the project was ahead of its time. The sense of national union was not strong enough in the Congress or in the state legislatures to support regiments that were not the specific responsibility of particular states. Monroe's regiment collapsed.[18] He was not happy as a volunteer aide to General Stirling. But Virginia would not take him back into their ladder of command despite an impassioned plea Washington wrote on his behalf: "He has in every instance maintained the reputation of a brave, active, and sensible officer. . . . The esteem I have for him and a regard for

James Monroe, who, as official Minister to France, felt less responsible to Washington and the government than to Jefferson and the opposition. Portrait by Gilbert Stuart. Courtesy of the Pennsylvania Academy of the Fine Arts

merit conspire to make me earnestly wish to see him provided for in some handsome way."[19] Washington's effort having failed, Monroe took the step that determined his future career: he studied law with Jefferson, who became his permanent patron and friend.

The contretemps that had forced Monroe out of the army may well have soured him on Washington and convinced him that to an ambitious man state ties were of primary importance. In any case, he opposed the ratification of the Constitution on the grounds that Virginia might be prevented from pursuing her own interests.

President Washington, of course, knew that this had been Monroe's stand, and also that he had as senator been a leader of the opposition, but it was now Washington's object to please the opposition, and he had no basis for knowing that in disapproval of him personally and of his administration, in enthusiasm for the French Revolution, Monroe was more extreme than his friends Madison and Jefferson. In social intercourse, Monroe gave no fiery impression. He had the ingratiating manners of a Virginia gentleman, and his sallow, lined face, which received no light from his watery gray eyes, seemed mild and unpretentious.[20]

On being proffered the ministry to France, Monroe "desired Madison, in conference with a few of our friends, to determine what answer should be given." His advisers concluded "that I should accept upon the necessity of cultivating France."[21]

Although the nomination created "great surprise" in the Senate, Washington's prestige assured confirmation.

Still desirous to represent not a faction but the whole nation, Washington had been glad to balance an appointment satisfactory to one party with an appointment satisfactory to the other. And in his eagerness to preserve American friendliness with both major belligerents, he happily sent to each a man who would be well received and sympathetic there. The safety, for American policy, of this course depended on two assumptions: first, that the recipient of such high appointment would, on acceptance, lay his political prejudices on one side, acting with his colleagues as part of a unified team to achieve what was best for the commonwealth; second, that the President would be kept informed and would be obeyed as the final arbiter.

Monroe saw the situation exactly the other way around. Since his policies were well known, he regarded his appointment as an assurance to the American and the French people that these policies were approved by the government.[22] It would be chicanery to himself personally, to his constituents, and to France if Jay had been authorized to make any agreement with Great Britain of which he would not approve. Entrusted, as he saw it, to act in his own right, he paid little attention to those parts of his instructions which did not agree with his own predilections. That he should declare American friendship with France seemed to him correct, but he was not eager to ask the French to compensate for their spoliations on American commerce, and how could he, when he did not believe it himself, assure his Gallic friends that the citizens of the United States were not divided into a pro-French and a pro-English party? All in all, it seemed to him to make sense to rely for advice concerning his mission less on the President and the Secretary of State than on men in whom he had more confidence. Although he expressed to Washington fulsome thanks "for this very distinguished mark of your confidence," he arranged with Jefferson for a cipher so that he could communicate secretly with the leader of the opposition.[23]

Jay, although theoretically closer to Washington than was Monroe, also turned to personal advisers. He discussed with the inner Federalist group which of his instructions he should push for, which jettison. Hamilton wrote him a long letter which Bemis considered more influential on his conduct than all official communications, and, after Jay reached England, he sent to Hamilton information on his reception which, so he explained, he thought it wiser to keep from Mr. Randolph or others. The situation might be misunderstood by them, "but not you."[24]

Hamilton justified his writing the envoy behind the back of the Secretary of State by suggesting that perhaps Randolph was not taking the time to keep Jay adequately informed. And the Secretary of the Treasury took it upon himself to intervene directly in the negotiation. He told the British minister, Hammond, that the United States was willing to settle for very watered-down neutral rights and would not, in any case, entangle herself by entering an armed alliance with the European neutrals. Many historians contend that this information, which Hammond rushed to London, had a major effect on the outcome of Jay's mission.[25]

However, Washington was feeling no misgivings. Good-humoredly, he wrote, "The affairs of this country *cannot go amiss*. There are *so many watchful guardians of them* and such *infallible guides* that one is at no loss for a director at every turn."[26] It did not occur to him that perhaps he was dealing with men who were determined to be more than "guides," that, indeed, he might be losing the freedom to turn as he thought best.

16

Extreme Sensibility

WASHINGTON was suffering from an "irritable spot on my right cheek which had for years been increasing in pricking and disagreeable sensations." During June 1794 it "assumed the decided character of a cancer." (His mother had died of cancer.) He called in Dr. James Tate, who prescribed "an easy course." In two months, the trouble disappeared. Washington was impressed into recommending Tate, when the doctor sailed for England, to the countenance of the American minister there as a man "possessed of the valuable secret of curing cancerous complaints."[1]

Early one June morning, an English traveler, Henry Waney, rang the Presidential doorbell. Dandridge received him. Washington appeared, read his letters of introduction, and invited him to breakfast.

"The President," Waney wrote, "is tall and thin, but erect, rather of an engaging than a dignified presence. He appears very thoughtful, is slow in delivering himself, which occasions some to conclude him reserved, but it is rather, I apprehend, the effect of much thinking and reflection, for there was a great appearance to me of affability and accommodation. . . . There is a certain anxiety on his countenance which marks extreme sensibility."

Waney noted that Martha looked older than her husband. She was "short in stature, rather robust, very plain in her dress, wearing a very plain cap with her gray hair turned up under it." The caller had difficulty not staring at Nelly Custis, who was now sixteen and "a very pleasing young lady."

When the party went into the breakfast room, Waney found laid out on

Martha Washington, a silhouette cut by her granddaughter, Nelly Custis, in 1796. Courtesy of the Mount Vernon Ladies' Association

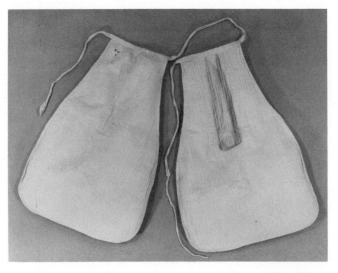

Martha Washington's pockets. Made of dimity and attached to a twill tape. The absence of decoration indicates that they were worn beneath her skirt. Courtesy of the Mount Vernon Ladies' Association

Nelly Custis, Washington's step-granddaughter and semi-adopted child, who as a secretly impish young lady persuaded visitors to Mount Vernon or the Presidential Mansion that she was the perfection of feminine beauty, gentleness, and soul. Courtesy of Woodlawn Plantation, National Trust for Historic Preservation

the table "small plates of sliced tongue, dry toast, bread and butter, etc., but no fish." Martha made the tea and coffee herself. "There was little appearance of form. Only one servant attended, who had no livery. The silver urn of hot water was the only article of expense on the table."[2]

Relaxing at Monticello unrestrained by any executive responsibility, Jefferson enjoyed the luxury of eating fire. He wrote Monroe, "Some few very quiet people, not suffering themselves to be inflamed as others are by the kicks and cuffs Great Britain has been giving us, express a wish to remain at peace. But the mass of thinking men seem to be of opinion that we have borne as much as to invite eternal insults in the future should not a very spirited conduct be now assumed." He then added, "For myself, I wish for peace, if it can be preserved *salve fide et honore*."[3]

Although Secretary of State Jefferson had urged postponing, as an issue that might never arise, American obligations under "the guarantee," planter Jefferson wrote Madison that the United States should voluntarily declare that she would make "common cause" with France to make sure that the British did not — as they were now trying to do — capture the French West Indies. To another correspondent he expressed the hope that a complete French triumph would bring "at length kings, nobles, and priests to the scaffolds which they have been so long deluging with human blood."[4]

During that passionate spring, the President sent his former Secretary of State one letter. The subject: fertilizer. True, there was a reference to the current crisis, but it was hardly what Jefferson expected. "We are going on in the old way, 'and slow.' I hope events will justify me in adding 'sure,' that the proverb may be fulfilled: 'slow and sure.' "[5]

To Gouverneur Morris Washington wrote concerning Jay's mission, "If he succeeds, well. If he does not, why, knowing the worst, we must take measures accordingly."[6]

Washington felt that it became a former Commander in Chief to urge military preparedness on Congress (although only in the most general terms), but he remained deaf to the importunings of Hamilton and his rout that he admonish Congress not to upset Jay's mission by establishing non-intercourse with Britain. In the Senate the vote was a tie, which John Adams, as presiding officer, broke in the negative. Washington commented that Adams, it was "generally believed," had acted not because he was opposed "to the ulterior expediency of the measure, but from a desire to try the effect of negotiation previous thereto. Sequestration of British property (exclusive of that in the funds) and other expedients of a similar kind have been agitated in the House of Representatives; but seem, I think, to be talked off the stage."[7]

And so it was. The British committed another violent overt act — they marched over the Canadian border and established a fort at the forks of the Miami. The Republican press, in full voice against the Jay mission, implied that Washington was guilty of an "atrocious crime" and had sent the Chief Justice out of the United States so that he could not be constitutionally tried. Yet the embargo, after being extended to a second month, was voted down. The more violent anti-British measures were voted down. Congressional action remained in suspense, awaiting the report of Washington's special envoy to France.[8]

Madison and Monroe (before he sailed on his mission) wrote angry letters to Jefferson. Said Madison, "The influence of the ex[ecutive] on events, the use made of them, and the public confidence in the P[resident] are an overmatch for all the efforts Republicanism can make. The party of that sentiment in the Senate is completely wrecked; that in the H[ouse] of Rep[resentatives] in a much worse condition than at an earlier period in the session." Said Monroe, "Through the influence of the Executive, aided by the personal weight of the President, the Republican party, notwithstanding its systematic and laborious efforts, has been able to accomplish nothing."[9]

There was some compensation for the Republicans in the fact that their congressmen had succeeded in drawing some blood from Hamilton. To make this all the more delightful, when Hamilton had tried to hide under the President's coattails, Washington had shooed him away.

Although Hamilton had been exonerated of misbehavior by the previous Congress, rumors to his discredit had continued to move across the country, and so Hamilton had asked for another investigation, "the more comprehensive, the more agreeable will it be to me."[10] Coming up with nothing new, his opponents pointed with heightened enthusiasm at a chink in Hamilton's armor already discovered. In the fall of 1790, he had applied to domestic purposes funds which Congress had appropriated to pay the European debt.[11] Hamilton defended himself by asserting that his act had been approved by Washington. On being told of this, Washington expressed to Randolph "surprise and passion."[12]

Onto Washington's desk came Hamilton's insistence to the Committee of Congress that he had indeed received the President's "sanction," although, so he admitted, he could find no firm evidence: "the communication and sanction were for the most part verbal." In any case, the basic consideration was his relationship with Washington: "The sanctions of the President were sometimes expressly and always, as I conceived, in their spirit founded in a material degree in the confidence that the measures proposed were guided by a just estimate of any part of circumstances which, from situation, must have been best known to me, and that they would always be in conformity to the law." In other words, Hamilton assumed that Washington had such confidence in him that he would always endorse his acts.[13]

Washington's reply was far from an expression of such confidence. "I cannot charge my memory with all the particulars which have passed between us." He was "satisfied" that "verbal communications . . . were made by you to me on the subject." He had no doubt that he had approved, but not unequivocally, because convinced that whatever Hamilton suggested must be legal. He had, in approving, laid down the "condition that what was to be done by you should be agreeable to the laws."[14]

Hamilton's reply was incandescent with outrage and hurt feelings. Since it would be assumed that the President's sense of "justice would have led him to rescue the officer concerned from even suspicions on this point," Hamilton's enemies would interpret Washington's "reserve" as a denial of Hamilton's veracity. It was being said that "you never know anything of the operation while it was going on." Hamilton feared that "false and insidious men, whom you may one day understand," would take advantage of Washington's want of recollection "by artful suggestions to infuse doubts and distrusts very injurious to me. . . .

"The situation is, indeed, an unpleasant one. Having conducted an important piece of public business in a spirit of confidence, dictated by an unqualified reliance, on the one hand, upon the rectitude, candor, and delicacy of the person under whom I was acting; on the other, by a persuasion that the experience of years had secured to me a reciprocal sentiment"; and acting also in the belief that the "general course of proceeding in so important an affair could not but be remembered, I did not look for a difficulty like that which now seems to press me."

Hamilton asked Washington to revise his letter or, if "the affair does not stand *well* in your mind," to accord Hamilton an interview. (That Hamilton found it necessary to make this request, reveals that the President's door was by no means always opened to the Secretary of the Treasury.) Hamilton wished to recall "to your memory what may have escaped it. . . . In the freedom of these remarks, I flatter myself, sir, that you will perceive nothing but that just sensibility which a man of honor, who thinks his veracity exposed to question, ought to feel; and that you will be persuaded I continue yet to retain, undiminished, all that respect which a long-established conviction of the existence of an upright and virtuous character ought to inspire."[15]

Washington refused in any way to change his statement.

Madison crowed to Jefferson that "The letter from the President is inexpressibly mortifying to his [Hamilton's] friends."[16] The Hamiltonians were, indeed, unwilling to believe that Washington would of himself be so unloyal to their idol. They decided to blame the insidious influence of Randolph. So great and vocal was their wrath that Randolph, who had indeed advised the President, took (as later events were to show he had every right to do) alarm. He wrote Washington that his having been by birth and upbringing connected with Republicans inspired suspicions. The truth was that "your character is the real object of affection to me." Randolph's basic political principle was "that no danger can attend us as long as the persuasion continues that you are not and cannot become, the head of a party."[17]

Jefferson commented that Washington's disavowal demonstrated that "the business of the Treasury has got beyond the limits of his comprehension."[18] An uneasy sense on the part of many legislators that no action should be taken that might even by implication point to the President's failing memory,* helped Hamilton achieve another vindication. As for Washington, he was determined not to be caught in the same box again.

On April 24, 1794, less than two weeks after Washington had refused to share responsibility for Hamilton's illegal shifting of funds, Hamilton asked his approval of applying one million florins out of three million borrowed in Amsterdam to the Dutch debt, and the other two million to paying off the national debt in the United States. Washington scurried through his files and found that he had already instructed Hamilton to apply the whole three million to the national debt. Notified of this, Ham-

---

* Washington's correspondence with Morris concerning the recall of that minister reveals a truly frightening failure of memory. In February 1793 it had been so strongly stated to Washington that Morris was *persona non grata* with the French government that he had urged Jefferson to take his place and had only left Morris in Paris when he could find no adequate substitute. Although to mention this now would have revealed to his friend his forbearance, Washington wrote Morris that, until the new French ambassador had told him the contrary, he had always "supposed you stood well with the powers that were."[19]

ilton had to blame *his* memory: he had forgotten, probably because he subsequently came down with yellow fever. But it was all of no matter: Washington could revise his orders since they had not yet been officially entered in the Treasury books. After a further exchange of letters, Washington stated that he could not "satisfy himself" that he was at liberty to alter an order he had "expressly" given. However, if Hamilton wished to bring the matter before Congress, Washington would have no objection to recommending that they endorse what Hamilton wanted. Hamilton quickly replied that he would prefer not to consult Congress, "as, under the circumstances of that body at this moment, much debate would probably ensue and perhaps no decision."[20]

Although Washington had come to ignore the matter, Hamilton had never taken back the statement made in his letter of almost a year before, that he intended to resign towards the close of the legislative session. Now it seemed wise to clear the matter up. On May 27, he wrote Washington that, since the prospects of the United States remaining at peace were "in a considerable degree precarious," he could not "voluntarily quit my post." He would stay on unless Washington had made other arrangements.[21]

Washington replied, "Of course, nothing has been done by me to render your continuance in office inconvenient or ineligible. On the contrary, I am pleased to have you determined to remain at your post until the clouds over our affairs, which have come on so fast of late, shall be dispersed."[22]

Congress finally adjourned on June 9, 1794. Although his conscience dictated that he could only stay away eighteen days, Washington set out with relief for Mount Vernon. He feared that his trip home would be slow, "as the weather is warm and my horses fat and out of exercise."[23]

On the road, Washington had a look at how the federal city was progressing (never a cheerful experience) and then decided to examine a lock that was building on that older project of his, the ever slowly advancing Potomac Canal. Since his horse's feet had become very tender on the roads, when he cantered out onto rough ground, the horse "blundered and continued blundering, until by violent exertions on my part to save him and myself from falling among the rocks, I got such a wrench in my back" that he had to dismount as soon as the danger was past. When he tried to mount again, he found he could not do so "without great pain."[24]

Nothing could have been more personally discouraging. Although he had often been ill, this was the first injury he had in his long and dangerous career ever suffered. He had galloped to hounds and on battlefields; he had grappled with ice roaring down wilderness rivers; he had weathered the hardships of an eight years' war. And now, on a routine ride, his aging bones had betrayed him.

After Washington had got somehow to Mount Vernon, he was frustrated in his major purpose, which was to discover how his farms had fared under the superintendency of his new manager. He could only hobble around his house. When he was not worrying about the state of the nation, he worried about his own finances. "If my receipts and expenditures are balanced at the year's end," he ruminated, "it is full as much as they have been competent to for years back." He was living on his salary as President, but he could hardly wait for the moment when that salary, with the duties it entailed, would cease. How would he pay his expenses then? Nothing had come of his effort to sell four of the Mount Vernon farms and free the Negroes. And quantities of his western lands were proving as immune to making money, or even paying their own way, as a group of drunken prodigals.[25]

Washington was becoming more careless about mixing his private business with his official position. He supplied the commissioners of the District of Columbia with rocks from a quarry he owned, and he elicited the help of the senator from western Pennsylvania, James Ross, towards selling his lands in the vicinity of Pittsburgh.*[26]

Washington informed Randolph that as soon as "I can ride with ease and safety," he would return to Philadelphia "whether I accomplish my own business or not." As it turned out, his back continued to refuse to let him ride. He embarked in a carriage the instant he considered himself "able to bear the jolting over the infamous roads I have to travel," arriving in Philadelphia on July 7, "made rather worse by my journey and a wetting I got on the road." He soon had to sit up as straight as he could to impress some Chickasaw warriors who were visiting Philadelphia and would have scorned a crippled warrior. He "delivered a short speech to them, smoked the peace pipe, eat, drank, and then retired."[28]

Washington had received at Mount Vernon a packet from the Democratic Society of Lexington, Kentucky. There was a letter to the society from a French inhabitant of Louisiana, which expressed regret that the

---

* A bit of the industrial history of the United States is summarized by reactions to the iron ore which surfaced on Washington's land around Simpson's Mill. When he had visited there in 1784, he deplored the outcroppings as reducing the fertility of the land. Now Ross notified him that the "show of iron ore within less than thirty yards of the mill door" actually increased the value of the land.[27]

projected army of "2000 brave Kentuckians" had not marched against New Spain, and urged that Kentucky continue its efforts to hoist in Louisiana "the flag of liberty in the name of the French republic." And there was an answering resolution adopted at a mass meeting of the society. It was labeled a remonstrance to "the President and Congress of the United States." The text called for strong action to achieve satisfaction from both Great Britain and Spain, but was primarily concerned with opening the navigation of the Mississippi. Having accused the general government of failing to seek effective measures, "the Citizens of Kentucky" expressed their expectation that the government would "demand categorically of the Spanish King" whether or not he would unblock the Mississippi, his "answer to be the final period of all negotiations upon this subject." Although nothing was said concerning the next step, the implication was clear.[29]

After reaching Philadelphia, Washington described to Randolph frightening alternatives: "What if the government of Kentucky should force us either to support them in their hostilities against Spain or disavow and renounce them? War at this moment with Spain would not be war with Spain alone. The lopping off of Kentucky from the Union is dreadful to contemplate, even if it should not attach itself to some other power."[30]

Washington and Randolph knew that no man stood higher in the confidence of the Democrats of Kentucky than Jefferson. The ideal solution would therefore be to make Jefferson such a special envoy to Spain as Jay was to Britain.

As Washington was considering whether to offer the mission to his former Secretary of State, he received a disturbing letter from Henry Lee. Lee reported the testimony of "a very respectable gentleman" who had asked Jefferson whether Washington were really governed by the British interest. Jefferson, so Lee continued, had answered "that there was no danger of your being biased by considerations of that sort so long as you were influenced by the wise advisers or advice, which you at present had."[31]

In his reply to Lee Washington expressed disbelief that Jefferson could make such a statement since "there could not be the trace of doubt in his mind of predilection in mine towards Great Britain and her policies, unless (which I do not believe) he has set me down as one of the most deceitful and uncandid men living: because not only in private conversations between ourselves on the subject, but in many meetings with the confidential servants of the public, he has heard me often, when occasions presented themselves,° express very different sentiments with an energy that could not be mistaken by *anyone* present."[32]

Perhaps Washington realized that Jefferson's low opinion of his advisers made this piece of gossip even more suspect. In any case, he persevered in his desire to entrust a Spanish mission to Jefferson. A sense of embarrassment, of estrangement seems to have kept him from himself writing Jefferson. Or perhaps he did not wish to apply personal pressure, lest, as a man who wished to be obeyed, he be enraged if he were refused. Making it clear that he was acting for the President, Randolph wrote Jefferson, pointing out the dangers the nation faced and requesting Jefferson's services.[33]

Jefferson replied on September 7, 1794, that he was suffering "constant torment" with rheumatism. In any case, "no circumstances, my dear sir, will ever more tempt me to engage in anything public." He added, "It is a great pleasure to me to retain the esteem and the approbation of the President. . . . Pray convey these sentiments and a thousand more to him."[34]

Unwilling to abandon the international possibilities — and also the quieting effect in the United States — of a special mission to Spain, Washington delegated Pinckney. The minister to Great Britain could be away from London while Jay was there.

Washington might breathe easier about foreign affairs. The French menace was — at least temporarily — stilled. Negotiations were under way with England and on the way with Spain. However, no moment of relaxation was to be accorded the President. At home, there appeared truly frightening trouble. Opposition to federal law and law enforcement was mounting in western Pennsylvania into the armed revolt that has gone down in history as the Whiskey Rebellion.

° This clause could not be more indicative: Washington did not theorize in the abstract but responded "when occasions presented themselves."

17

The Whiskey Rebellion

THE immediate cause of the Whiskey Rebellion was resentment in the four Pennsylvania counties west of the Alleghenies against a federal excise tax on alcholic liquor. The tax had been part of a package prepared by Hamilton late in 1790 to pay for the assumption of state debts. As Madison and Jefferson had supported assumption in return for agreement to a southern national capital, they had felt bound to countenance the raising of the necessary revenue. Madison had voted for the whiskey excise as the least objectionable available internal tax, and Jefferson had agreed, although he expressed worry lest in his recommendations Hamilton was not paying enough attention to public opinion.

Since Congress had established a direct line, bypassing the President, between the Treasury and the House (where money bills originated), Washington felt only partial responsibility for Hamilton's recommendations. And during the Congressional debates he followed his policy of expressing no opinion. Thus he did not have to make up his mind until the whiskey excise arrived on his desk as part of a tax bill which he would have to approve or disapprove in its entirety.[1] To veto would have bankrupted the government, and, in any case, Washington felt justified in vetoing a bill only if he considered it unconstitutional.

As a private man, Washington was irritated by all taxes and tax collectors. He also believed "there never was a law *yet made* . . . that hit the taste *exactly* of every man or of every part of the community."[2] Whether he considered the whiskey excise more objectionable than other levies he never stated. However, as the official responsible for the enforcement of the law, he was worried because it was "vehemently affirmed by many" that it could not be enforced in the southern states, particularly in Virginia and North Carolina.[3]

The tax, collectable at the still head, was likely to make most trouble in the back country where pioneering farmers, with a congenital objection to officials snooping in their back yards, often had their own stills. The contention that the tax could be passed on to the consumer made no sense where the consumer was also often the manufacturer (one had to be prepared for snakebites). Money being scarce in the west, jugs of whiskey circulated as currency, which meant that since they were not sold for cash, the distiller was not supplied with cash to hand over to the revenuer. Beyond the mountains, there was an additional problem: farmers (the Mississippi being closed and canal building stalled) had no way to get loads of grain to market, but when the grain was reduced to whiskey it was transportable. The tax seemed thus to be on the frontiersmen's very means of livelihood.[4]

When in the spring of 1791, just after the passage of the excise law, Washington made a tour of the south, and then visited western Pennsylvania — Lancaster, Carlisle — one of his objectives was to find out how much resentment actually existed against the liquor tax. In the southern states, he did not get into the piedmont, the most westerly road proceeding along the fall line. However, he consulted presumably knowledgeable officials, and did his best to make the travelers he met in shabby taverns talk. He was generally assured that, once it was understood, the law would meet with "very general approbation in those very parts where it was foretold that it would never be submitted to by anyone." There might be a few angry petitions, but these would be stirred up by "demagogues."[5]

This was good news, but Washington was not completely convinced. In his Third Annual Address to Congress, delivered that October, Washington stated that if the tax law could be amended to remove "any well-intentioned objections . . . it will consist with a wise moderation to make the proper variations." Congress did make changes, including a very considerable lowering of the percentage basis of the tax and also provisions to reduce the hardship of making immediate payments in cash.[6]

This eased protest everywhere but in far western Pennsylvania, particularly Washington County.° Inspectors were prevented from opening of-

---

° This region had played a major part in the President's past. When he had first visited the site of the local metropolis, Pittsburgh, it had been a confluence of rivers so deep in the wilderness that the only traces of humanity were Indian trails. After

fices and were personally threatened, while a mass meeting resolved to set up Committees of Correspondence to organize widespread opposition to the law. In September 1792 Hamilton sent to Washington at Mount Vernon a draft of a Presidential proclamation calling for enforcement and an end to "unlawful combinations." Secretary of State Jefferson was also away from the seat of government and Hamilton suggested that it was unnecessary to consult him, but Washington sent a messenger to Jefferson. Jefferson approved the proclamation, suggesting only a deletion from Hamilton's draft of the statement that the excise was necessary. Washington made the change and issued the proclamation.[7]

Matters now simmered down, all the more because efforts at enforcement were allowed to proceed in western Pennsylvania with tactful slowness. Some prosecutions were started by the Attorney General, but the identification of culprits was difficult and the charges were dropped. When in his Fourth Annual Address Washington again called the excise to the attention of Congress, it was merely to straighten out some details.[8]

The leading historian of the Whiskey Rebellion, Leland D. Baldwin, and the leading historian of the Democratic Societies, Eugene P. Link, agree that the solidifying in 1794 of the crumbling opposition was due to the spread across the mountains of the Democratic Societies. The principal grievance now was that, because the nearest federal court was in Philadelphia, distillers who were to stand trial had to make an expensive journey and be a long time away from their farms. In June, Congress gave jurisdiction to the state courts if there was no federal court within fifty miles.[*][9]

Why this new concession did not quiet the storm is a matter of controversy. That indictments handed out before passage of the new law were still returnable in Philadelphia is regarded by some historians as a machination on the part of Hamilton to keep the trouble alive for his own evil purposes. Hamilton claimed that the Democratic Societies, afraid that the

---

French Fort Duquesne had been built on that spot, to destroy it had been Washington's particular objective for years. He had seen the soil flowing with blood during Braddock's defeat. After the winning of the French and Indian War, he had patented wilderness land in Washington County, and after the Revolution, started legal action to expel some squatters. He had been so sure that sentiment in the county that bore his name was pro-squatter that he was surprised when he won the suit. He had not visited the area since 1784.

[*] Before this bill was passed, Washington used his executive authority to squash charges against two men indicted for riot in York, Pennsylvania. They would otherwise, he explained officially, be put to a great deal of time and expense to prove what he assumed was the fact, their innocence.[10]

new concessions would bring about peace, stirred up more trouble to serve *their* evil purposes. Other theories probably cut deeper. One is that the whiskey law was only the most conspicuously displayed of many frontier grievances. Another is that what was developing was in part a civil conflict within the western counties themselves. The prosperous distillers would profit if the tax put their smaller competitors out of business, and men with property to lose felt themselves confronted with the leveling passions of violent frontier misfits. Certain it is that the inhabitants of the little metropolis of Pittsburgh — 200 houses, 150 built of logs — were in terror that their town would be sacked by the wild men of the forest.[11]

In any case, the lid blew off. The house of John Neville,* a wealthy resident who had agreed to be excise inspector, was attacked, nor did the arrival of a small army contingent stop the battle. Shots were fired, a man was killed, the soldiers were forced to surrender, and the house was burned. The stills of anyone who paid the excise were destroyed; the barns of anyone who dared say a word for the government were burned; government representatives were stripped, tarred and feathered, and even seared with hot irons; all enforcement of law ceased; a mail carrier was attacked, the mails rifled, and correspondents persecuted as a result of the letters that were found. Sober warnings that the acts of the insurgents could be considered treason were laughed down.[13]

A similar insurrection in western Massachusetts — Shay's Rebellion of 1786 — had been a turning point in the history of the United States and also in Washington's life. The general realization that the Confederation lacked the unified power to deal with such a menace to public tranquillity had contributed to the Constitutional Convention, and Washington's own dismay had created much of the fuel that had blasted him out of private life and back into the public orbit. Then Washington, who had been justifying his retirement on the assumption that the people would create for themselves the restraints needed for government, had been profoundly

---

* Neville's appointment was, according to Baldwin, "nicely calculated to wean away from the opposition the wealth and 'respectability' of the region." The appointee's son, Presley Neville, was one of the agents Washington selected to help sell off his land in the district.[12]

That Washington did have such land on the market, gave him, of course, a personal economic stake. On the one hand, anarchy would certainly scare away purchasers. But if, in enforcing the tax and putting down the rebellion, he bankrupted all but the wealthy and threw much other land on the market, he would equally damage his sales. His interest was quite obviously in a peaceful society that would allow both the small and the large farmer to prosper.

disillusioned, crying out, "What, gracious God, is man! that there should be such inconsistency and perfidiousness in his conduct!"

Now, eight years of public service later, his shoulders galled by the yoke of government, he expressed less surprise and disillusionment than apprehension: "What may be the consequence of such violent and outrageous proceedings is painful in a high degree even in contemplation. But if the laws are to be so trampled upon with impunity, and a minority (a small one too) is to dictate to the majority, there is an end put at one stroke to republican government, and nothing but anarchy and confusion is to be expected thereafter; for some other man or society may dislike another law and oppose it with equal propriety until all laws are prostrate, and everyone (the strongest), I presume will carve for himself."[14]

Washington put much blame on the Democratic Societies. Those in western Pennsylvania were making an active effort to draw in their Virginia neighbors. Next down the mountain line was Kentucky. The spirit which had already been exhibited by the Democratic Society of Kentucky seemed to Washington "a matter of great wonder." Considering the government's unwearying efforts to open the Mississippi, the Kentucky protesters must be predisposed "to be dissatisfied under any circumstance and under every exertion of government, short of war with Spain which must eventually involve one with Great Britain."[15]

What seemed to Washington the irrational intransigence of the societies increasingly made him susceptible to an idea he had once scouted: that they were a response to the efforts being made by revolutionary France to overthrow all governments not in her service. Although he considered that most members were "dupes," the organizations seemed to be led by "*artful* and *designing* men" pursuing, "under a display of popular and fascinating guises, the most diabolical attempts to destroy the best fabric of human government and happiness that has ever been presented for the acceptance of mankind."[16]

In connection with mutinies in the army, in connection with Shay's Rebellion, Washington had stated that the method of procedure should be to discover if there were any legitimate grievances, right the grievances, and then, if necessary, "employ the force of the government."[17] He believed that major efforts had been made to right the grievances of the whiskey rebels. They complained of taxation without representation, but they had three members in the House, although their actual population justified only two. While Congress had again and again revised the whiskey law, in none of the sessions had any serious effort been made to re-peal the law.° Congress was being defied.[18]

Washington was facing both a current problem and a principle ex-tremely important for the future of the United States. The current problem was, as he saw it, a dangerous effort to undermine the power of the government. During the Revolution, he had been glad when a small mutiny in the New Jersey line had given him an opportunity to snuff out effectively the tendency of the unpaid troops to revolt. Now he wrote that, as "the first *formidable* fruit" of the Democratic Societies, the Whis-key Rebellion had been "brought forth, I believe, too prematurely for their own views, which may contribute to the annihilation of them."[19]

More far-reaching were the questions, as yet untried and undetermined, concerning what the federal government could do to protect itself against anarchy and disunion. Would the citizenry spring to arms to enforce laws — even unpopular ones — legally enacted by their government? In-volved was the standing menace of sectionalism. One could hardly imag-ine a more perfect example than the Whiskey Rebellion of one section re-fusing, because of its special interests, to permit the enforcement of a law nationally legislated and enforced without serious protest in the rest of the nation. Lurking in the wings was the menace of secession. If regions were permitted to deny at will the federal authority, one step might lead to another (already Kentucky was threatening her own war with Spain), and the nation fall apart. Washington could thank Providence that the test case was a small one — supposing Virginia had called out her militia to block the federal courts! — but yet the issues cut very deep.†

Since what regular army the United States had was over the frontier marching under Wayne against the Indians, Washington would have to rely on state militias. He began by trying to duck the unresolved question

---

° If the whiskey tax is viewed by itself and altogether in its western context, that it was permitted to exist seems inconceivable. The facts were that the Constitution vir-tually forbade to the federal government any direct internal tax and left excise taxes free both to Congress and the states. Since the customs duties, on which the federal government had a monopoly, would not meet expenses, it seemed important, both in the immediate situation and in the long range, for the central government to claim its right to the excise. It was necessary to find, in those years before the true birth of American manufacturing, some industry that was widespread enough to produce effec-tive revenue, and there was a feeling (which of course still exists) that liquor was a luxury the consumption of which could well be curbed. In 1794, excises were also put on snuff, loaf sugar, and that panache of gentlemen, carriages. Despite the continuance of the whiskey excise, Washington (as we shall see) was to establish a large and pro-fitable commercial distillery at Mount Vernon.

† Washington was facing on a small scale what Lincoln was to face in 1861.

as to whether federal sentiment was now strong enough to permit the militia of one state to cross the border of another. Explaining to Governor Mifflin that speed was of the essence and a federal call for militia involved much red tape, he tried to persuade the Pennsylvania authorities to take on the whiskey rebels on their own authority with their own forces. But Mifflin was as old a fox as Washington (they had been adversaries for years): he replied that the state government could see nothing over the mountains which could not be handled by routine legal procedure. He begged Washington to forget the idea of military compulsion.[20]

One of the most active national bugaboos was fear of tyranny imposed on the American people by an army. Another fear — it had at the start of the Revolution contributed to the appointment of the Virginian Washington as Commander in Chief of a till then exclusively New England force — was that one section of the nation would impose its policies on the others. The more an individual distrusted the government, the more dangerous he considered the possibility — and Washington knew that distrust had for a long time characterized the Republican leaders and had been encouraged by their propagandists. Yet, since Pennsylvania would not take the lead, the President might well need to call into the federal service, for a march into Pennsylvania, the militia of several other states. The objective of the march would be other citizens; they could be lachrymosely depicted as virtuous farmers defending their fields against usurpation! How could the government make clear what Washington believed: that the campaign was not a leap towards tyranny but rather an effort to preserve the sanctity of the ballot box, the right of a republican government to govern?

Before force was employed, the government should surely demonstrate absolute necessity. And any military action should be as undamaging to life, liberty, and property as was conceivably possible. Punishments should be tuned as low as was commensurate with having the example stick. In this path, the Democratic Societies loomed as frightening impediments. Washington believed that the leaders would labor to misinterpret his acts to their followers. What use was it to proceed temperately if the people were prevented from seeing the record? However, he could only try.

Hamilton recommended immediate action: Washington should order the militia of four states to rendezvous at the near side of the Alleghenies on September 10. Washington could not deny that delay might permit the revolt to spread. And no man knew better than he the military arguments for haste, since he had fought over the very mountain passes an army would have to traverse to reach the insurgents. He realized that, even if the terrain was not defended, it would become with winter almost impassable to an organized army. But he decided that he would start by sending, as "one more experiment of a conciliatory appeal to the reason, virtue, and patriotism," three commissioners: William Bradford, who had become Attorney General when Randolph stepped up to State; James Ross, the senator from western Pennsylvania; and Jasper Yeates, a Mifflin appointee to the Pennsylvania Supreme Court. Not to be outdone, Mifflin added his own state delegation.[21]

The federal commissioners were instructed that the executive could not promise any changes in the laws, which were "consigned by the Constitution to the legislature," but that the President was "willing to grant an amnesty and perpetual oblivion for everything which has passed" to those who would no longer obstruct the execution of the laws.[22]

Hamilton frankly hoped that the conciliation would fail so that the greater precedent could be established. What of Washington? His intimate, Randolph, wrote, "It would place a thorn in the remainder of his path through life to employ force against his fellow citizens" in order to give "solidity and permanence to the blessings which it has been his greatest happiness to cooperate with them in procuring for a loved country." But Washington surely realized too that if the insurrection petered out without strong steps being taken, the "solidity and permanence" would not be so effectively rooted.[23]

Of course, there was always the possibility of a boomerang. Perhaps only the most conservative militiamen would serve on such a mission, facing Washington with what he least wanted, not a national army but a force representing one faction and thus pointing towards civil war; perhaps there would be an equally disastrous rushing of men towards the opposite standard; perhaps the frontiersmen, who were no mean operators with a rifle, would not cave in but fight back, creating a really bloody civil war; perhaps the west — thank destiny, there was no way they could get help from France! — would turn for assistance where they could and make some deal with the British authorities. These were all terrifying possibilities. Washington found more or less comfort in his belief in the fundamental sanity of the American people. Yet it was a nervous time.

To be ready for action before winter, Washington called into the federal service such militia forces as would be required. They were to pre-

[167]

pare themselves in their various communities. Washington set no date for any general rendezvous. However, he ordered the insurgents "to disperse and retire peacefully to their respective abodes" by September first.[24]

The 12,950 men to be supplied by New Jersey, Pennsylvania, Maryland, and Virginia amounted to almost exactly the force Hamilton had recommended as strong enough to put down, with a minimum of bloodshed, the 7000 men he calculated western Pennsylvania might raise. But the requisition Washington approved differed from Hamilton's ideas in one important particular. Hamilton had wished one quarter of the force to be mounted troops (i.e., elite corps of gentlemen). Washington reduced the proportion to a little over one tenth.[25]

Secretary of War Knox, who had speculated unwisely in real estate on the Maine frontier, regarded it as a matter of his personal economic life or death to get to Maine and try to bail his affairs out. Having dispatched the militia requisition, he wished to depart. However, frightening reports came: the rebels were mobilizing; they would refuse to receive the commissioners; they had no fear of eastern troops and it seemed probable that the western troops in the regular army would go over to their side. In an agony of apprehension, Washington stopped Knox, but then Randolph reported that the western tax collectors who had fled to Philadelphia and were completely familiar with the situation viewed it with much less alarm. Eager not to bankrupt his old friend, Washington let Knox go, concocting for him a face-saving mission to inspect arsenals. Hamilton would add to his Treasury duties supervision of the War Department.[26]

There can be no doubt that Washington made a political mistake when he placed the man most distrusted by the opposition so clearly in charge of the military effort. Rumors grew that this was the beginning of the standing army that would put an end to American liberties.

The commissioners found western Pennsylvania in chaos. Law enforcement had ceased and with it any political structure that could be brought to bear. Some leaders of the insurrection advocated declaring independence from the United States. The guillotine was publicly recommended for "stockholders or their subordinates." Local supporters of the government were terrorized into silence, while men of property found it advisable to appear at rallies and express sentiments which they later told the commissioners they did not mean. It was finally decided to stage a referendum on September 11 (ten days after the deadline in Washington's proclamation). This proved to be a complete fiasco, partly because supporters of the laws were required to sign a statement many of them found insulting; but more because the insurgents spread terror at the polls. In Elizabeth Township, for instance, a resolution that those who supported the government should not have their property burned was voted down at a town meeting, after which everyone was invited to cast his vote in public. Since Mifflin's commissioners had done no better than Washington's, it was clear that a month of negotiations had failed.[27]

On September 24, Washington's commissioners reported that, in their opinion, the majority of the citizens in western Pennsylvania were in favor of submission, but that they were intimidated by a violent minority. In any case, there was no possibility of enforcing the law without extrajudicial help.[28]

In preparation for an unfortunate result, Washington had on September 9 empowered Hamilton to order that the militia actually mobilize in their various states. After receiving the commissioners' official report, Washington issued another proclamation stating that, although every effort at conciliation not inconsistent with the continuance of government had been attempted, the government was still "set at defiance." He blamed the insurrection on the "misrepresentations" of "misguided or designing men," and implored his fellow citizens "to call to mind that, as the people of the United States have been permitted, under divine favor, in perfect freedom, after solemn deliberation, in an enlightened age, to elect their own government, so will their gratitude for this inestimable blessing be best distinguished by firm exertions to maintain the Constitution and the laws." The loyal army was already in motion.[29]

The insurgents had counted on Washington's being unable to raise an army against them. In exalted moments, they visualized forces of their own marching on Philadelphia, "accumulating in their course and swelling over the banks of the Susquehanna like a torrent — irresistible and devouring." Washington had been worried. On August 10, he asked his brother-in-law, Burgess Ball, for information ("under the rose, I ask it") on whether the militia from Virginia's counties on the Shenandoah would be willing to help coerce the western Pennsylvanians. Sixteen days later, he wrote Governor Henry Lee that it gave him "sincere consolation amidst the regret with which I am filled" to learn that "the good people of Virginia" were anxious to subdue the insurgents. "With equal pride and satisfaction I add that, as far as my information extends, this insurrection is viewed with universal indignation and abhorrence." Washington came to believe that he could have secured five times the troops desired. As it was, the army he had raised so easily contained more men than he had fought with during most of the Revolution.[30]

The Hamiltonians had visualized an elite army of their supporters, but what had happened was much more satisfactory to Washington. He was to comment, "It has been a spectacle displaying to the highest advantage the value of republican government to behold the most and least wealthy of our citizens standing in the same ranks as private soldiers."[31]

This consummation had been achieved by the fact that the Republicans swung into line. They rallied to support the President, the laws, and the Constitution, partly to keep from being put politically out on a limb, but also out of fundamental loyalty. Over everyone hung the realization that aristocrats prophesied the certain eventual end of popular government as anarchy. Thus the radical editor Bache stated that the question was not whether the excise was proper or improper. Since the law was constitutional, every citizen had a duty to aid in its execution. Bache added that Republicans should enlist to "give the lie to bawlers against the Democratic Societies." The parent Democratic Society — that of Pennsylvania — denounced "excise systems" as "oppressive, hostile to the liberties of this country, and a nurse of vice and sycophancy," but added, after a sharp internecine battle, that they disapproved of opposition "not warranted by the frame of government."[32]

Everything was going merrily as a marriage bell when Washington made a mistake so politically inept that it could be considered an epoch in his career. Hamilton, aflame with desire to go along on the expedition, had been waiting for the President to mention the matter to him. But all Washington did was to express concern about "the propriety and expediency" of the President himself leading the march. Finally, on September 19, Hamilton wrote Washington, "Upon full reflection, I entertain an opinion that it is advisable for me, on public ground . . . to go out upon the expedition against the insurgents. In a government like ours, it cannot but have a good effect for the person who is understood to be the adviser or proposer of a measure [the excise] which involves danger to his fellow citizens, to partake of that danger."

Washington should have realized how bad an effect it would have on public opinion to allow a prominent role in the expedition to the man who was suspected of having purposefully fomented the crisis as a step towards military dictatorship. "You will remember, sir," Randolph later wrote Washington, "that I represented to you how much Colonel Hamilton's accompanying you was talked of out of doors, and how much stress was laid upon the seeming necessity of the Commander in Chief having him always at his elbow." Yet Washington, who himself assumed the command, not only agreed to Hamilton's coming along but suggested that they set out together.[33]

18

The Whiskey Campaign

IT must have been strange to be setting out again to command an army. For one thing, Washington was older. Even as he rode in his phaeton, his bones ached: he could not stay on horseback long. For another, his task was so much less hazardous now. During the Revolution, he had welcomed every sign of support. Now he detoured around Germantown to escape a corps of cavalry determined to clatter along beside him. As on that last day of September he traversed the twenty-five miles to "a place called Trap" (Trappe), he passed businesslike troops on their way to the rendezvous. And at Trappe a messenger appeared bearing from another campaign the most favorable possible news.

General Wayne had completed a march up the Maumee. A few miles from where the British crouched illegally at Fort Miami, he had met the Indians whom the British had so long encouraged and mustered. The tribes had been decisively defeated (Battle of Fallen Timbers, August 20, 1794). Obeying Washington's orders, Wayne had created no transatlantic incident by driving off the British invaders who were now completely in his power. The general had concentrated on the Indian settlements, destroying, as Washington noted in his diary, all those on the Miami River "up to the Grand Glaize, the quantity not less than 5000 acres, and the stores, etc., of Colonel McGee, the British agent of Indian affairs," who had imprudently kept his supplies outside the British garrison.[1]

Washington had had enough experience with the Indians* to know that

---

* Things had worked exactly the opposite way when, as a raw stripling, Washington had allowed his Virginia regiment to be defeated at Fort Necessity. Then the encouraged tribes had fallen like swarms of angry bees on the frontier.

this military triumph would, as the news moved along the intricate web of trails, give wings to American forest diplomacy. And the victory would surely make Washington's current task easier by calming frontier unrest.

Washington's immediate objective was Carlisle, the town on the eastern side of the Alleghenies that was the rendezvous for the militia from New Jersey and Pennsylvania. His dream was that he would receive there information of so great an abatement of opposition in the western counties that he would be justified in leaving the army and setting his horses a-gallop for Mount Vernon. He wrote Pearce that if he were not home by mid-October ("of which I have very little hopes") he could not, since Congress would convene in November, reach his acres until the following spring. This would be doubly grievous since, on his last visit, his back injury had prevented him from really discovering how his farms were progressing under the new manager.[2]

Washington comforted himself as best he could by turning a farmer's eye on both sides of the road. He noted that from Norristown to Reading, the land was "reddish" and "tolerably well cultivated." From Reading to Lebanon he admired the rich soil and the "barns, which are large and fine, and for the most part of stone." He took the reins as his carriage made the long ford across the Susquehanna. The river, he was told, "abounds in rockfish of twelve or fifteen inches in length, and a fish which they call salmon."[3]

On October 4, 1794, Washington reached Carlisle to find "all the troops that could be mustered" awaiting him in their most martial array. As Washington inspected them, he held a look of benignity on his face but his heart sank. "I clearly see," he wrote Pearce, "that it will not be in my power to visit Mount Vernon."[4]

For the time being, the militia of each state was under the command of the governor. Pennsylvania's Mifflin (who regarded himself as a military genius and had during the Revolution tried to unseat Washington) had abandoned his previous disapproval and was now all the warrior. He celebrated his military prowess in so many bumpers of wine that he gave orders which resulted in Philadelphia's elite light horses (silver bridles and matched bay mounts) firing at some ragged New Jersey militiamen whom they mistook for deserters. Fortunately, the young gentlemen were such incompetent marksmen that no one was hurt. But the near tragedy was symbolic of the confusion that reigned. Washington needled Mifflin about organization and supply. He could not fire a governor from the command of his own militia, but he appointed General Edward Hand, who had been one of his adjutant generals during the Revolution, adjutant general of the new army.[5]

From over the mountains came two representatives from the Committee of Safety ("as it is designated," Washington noted) with the avowed objective of giving information that "would prevent the march of the army into them." Mifflin considered it politic to shun the resulting conference. Present were Washington, Governor Howell of New Jersey, Hamilton and Dandridge.

Washington's diary contains a long account of the meeting. The President opened by promising that he "would listen patiently and with candor to what they had to say." What they had to say was amazing in relation to their avowed objective. William Findley and William Redick were both prosperous local leaders who had infiltrated the radical movement. They stated that, although "the people of consequence" were in favor of submission, the simpler people were not. Findley said he could not take responsibility for the re-establishment of the tax offices without military protection. He stated that "the ignorance and general want of information among the people far exceeded anything he had any conception of. That it was not merely the excise law their opposition aimed at but to all law and government . . . and that the life he had led for some time was such that, rather than go through it again, he would prefer quitting the scene altogether."

Redick added that the people had believed the opposition to the excise law so general that no troops would march against them. They were now alarmed. The more convinced rebels, who "were men of little or no property, and cared but little where they resided," were in flight. There was not "the least intention in them to oppose the army." However, if an invading army raised "resentments," the situation might reverse itself. While admitting that force might in the end be necessary, he hoped that the army would not at this time risk a confrontation by crossing the mountains.

Washington replied, "As I considered the support of the laws an object of first magnitude, and [as] the greatest part of the expense had already been incurred, that nothing short of the most unequivocal *proofs* of absolute submission should retard the march." He warned that should the soldiers enter the western counties, no group should approach them armed. If a single shot were directed at them, "there could be no answering for the consequences. . . . The army, unless opposed, did not mean to be executioners, or bring offenders to a military tribunal, but merely to aid the civil magistrates, with whom offenses would lie."

Findley kept his own account of the interview which, although it shows the western delegates putting up more arguments that matters might right themselves if the army did not march, supplements rather than contradicts Washington's account. Findley reported that, having been alarmed by a "licentious and inflammatory spirit" among the troops at Carlisle, he begged the President to accompany any advance. Unless Washington were present to curb the troops, the innocent inhabitants would have to make "common cause with the guilty, for there is no law, divine or human, to oblige people tamely to submit to being skewered, hanged, or shot in cold blood, and this was for some time the declared object of such as made the most noise."

According to Findley, Washington stated that the disorderly corps were being reorganized and made orderly. Any who refused "would be discharged from the army."[6]

Many records reveal that the richer, more conservative troops were eager to punish the rabble. Findley observed that Washington "labored incessantly" to remove this spirit. Hamilton forwarded to Mifflin "a formal expression of the very poignant regret he [the President] felt at the unfortunate accidents which happened in two instances previous to his arrival at this place, having occasioned the death of two persons; and of his extreme solicitude that all possible pains be taken to avoid in the future not only accidents of a similar kind, but all unauthorized acts of injury to the persons or property of the inhabitants of the country through which the army may march." The troops could not render a more important service to the government than by "a conduct scrupulously regardful of the rights of their fellow citizens and exemplary for decorum, regularity and moderation."[7]

Alexander Dallas, one of the Pennsylvania officials who had been lukewarm about the military effort, wrote home that Washington expressed sentiments "so elevated, so firm, and yet so prudent and humane that I am charmed with his determination to join us."[8]

Washington was worried about his wife. When he had left Philadelphia, there had been rumors that the yellow fever was returning. If it did, what should Mrs. Washington do? Should she leave town, that would make all the Philadelphians in the army worry about their own families. Should she stay, that would be "a source of continual uneasiness to me." Soon a happy letter came from Randolph, stating that "the apprehensions on account of the yellow fever have vanished."[9]

Congress was scheduled to meet on November 3. Only "imperious necessity" could, in the President's opinion, justify his absence. He wrote Randolph that he intended to proceed to Fort Cumberland, the rendezvous of the Maryland and Virginia troops, and then over the Blue Ridge to the jumping-off place, Bedford. If fighting seemed likely, "the lesser must yield to the greater duties of my office": he would proceed with the troops. "If not, I shall place the command of the combined force under Governor Lee of Virginia and repair to the seat of government."[10]

Dandridge wrote Knox (who had reappeared in his office) to send on Washington's camp equipage. The President, Dandridge, and Hamilton would each need "a single mattress with blankets." Despite Washington's preference for rum and water, since he was going into the land of whiskey, "he proposes to make use of that liquor for his drink." Send some.[11]

In order to avoid the perpetual salutes and ceremonies involved in meeting troops on the march, Washington took a back road to Cumberland. After passing through much unimproved land, he came to a region that brought back many memories. At Bath, where he spent the night, he had brought to the medicinal springs both his half brother Lawrence and his stepdaughter Patsy in searches for health that in both cases proved vain. Here he had become involved with that inventor of mechanical boats, James Rumsey, who had raised in him hopes of vessels that would make his Potomac Canal work by climbing up against the current. These hopes had also been vain. Concerning the past, Washington made no comment, but he did note that the road to Old Town (when he had first passed that way it had been along a dim trail through total wilderness) was extremely bad. It made "a severe day's journey for the carriage horses. They performed it, however, well."[12]

Cumberland had been Washington's headquarters during much of the French and Indian War. Then he had commanded a few buckskinned troops. Now 3200 men stood at arms in a double line through which he rode. He was "well lodged and very civilly entertained" in the house of an old Continental officer. Doubtless the occasions were less hilarious than when, as a young Virginia colonel, he was accused of allowing his officer corps to gamble outrageously and sink into drunkenness.[13]

Intelligence from the western counties indicated that the people would return to their opposition if the army disbanded, but were "very much alarmed at the approach of the army." It became clear that the federal force would not have to fight their way through the mountain passes. Washington notified Randolph that he would return to Philadelphia for the opening of Congress. But first he would proceed to the final staging ground at Bedford.[14]

The goodness of the road finally made Washington comment on his past: he noted that it "was opened by troops under my command in the autumn of 1758."[15]

At Bedford, Washington prepared a farewell to his troops: "No citizens of the United States can ever be engaged in a service more important to the country. It is nothing less than to consolidate and to preserve the blessings of that Revolution which at much expense of blood and treasure constituted us a free and independent nation. It is to give the world an illustrious example of the utmost consequence to the cause of mankind. I experience a heartfelt satisfaction in the conviction that the conduct of the troops throughout will be in every respect answerable to the goodness of the cause and the magnitude of the stake." This required, he made clear, supporting rather than breaking the laws. "The essential principles of a free government confine the provinces of the military to these two objects: first, to combat and subdue all who may be found in arms in opposition to the national will and authority. Secondly, to aid and support the civil magistrate in bringing offenders to justice. The dispensation of this justice belongs to the civil magistrate, and let it ever be our pride and our glory to leave the sacred deposit there unviolated."[16]

In his journal of the expedition, Washington hardly ever mentioned Hamilton by name, usually including him anonymously in that old military word for a general's aides: his "family." Yet the supremely efficient Cabinet minister had been most active in reorganizing the troops and the supplies; he had not only drafted but himself signed many of the most important letters communicating Washington's orders. And now Washington, when he set out for Philadelphia, left Hamilton behind. Although the Secretary of the Treasury had (Knox having returned to the War Department) no official role in the expedition, Washington instructed him to "open all letters of a public nature which may come to the army addressed to me." Hamilton was to forward those that related to the campaign to "the commanding general." Washington even communicated his orders to General Lee through Hamilton. After he had reached Philadelphia, the President wrote Hamilton without further comment, "Bache (as I expected) has opened his batteries upon your motives for remaining with the army."[17]

Washington's motives can be guessed. Among the four governors who were eligible to be made commander in chief, Lee was militarily by far

Frederick Kemmelmeyer:
Washington reviewing the
whiskey army. Courtesy of
Hall Park McCullough

WASHINGTON. ✳

army at fort Cumberland septemb.ᵣ 19 1794

the best choice — he was a brilliant soldier — but Washington, who knew him well, could not have great faith in his judgment. He was a zealot who went off on wild tangents. Hamilton could be counted on to carry out as well as any man could whatever he intended to do, and Washington was convinced that he would apply the policy Washington had laid down of conciliation.

As the expedition marched (without meeting any opposition except bad weather), Hamilton was conspicuously present. The civil aspects of the pacification, he made altogether his own, although he would occasionally, after enunciating a decision, tell the petitioner that as a matter of politeness he might also ask General Lee. A certain number of rebels were arrested, and many citizens interrogated (to their resentment) by a gimlet-eyed Secretary of the Treasury. But overall the spirit of the absent Washington prevailed. Not a single person was hurt, virgins who were so inclined slept undisturbed, the army paid for everything it used. Findley summarized, "The President was happily successful in reducing the licentious part of the army into subordination to the laws, and in inspiring the people of the western counties with such a measure of confidence as prevented any conduct of their part that could give the army any just cause of irritation."[18]

Washington, who was eventually to pardon the two insurrectionists who were sentenced to death, boasted to Jay in mid-December that the whiskey rebels had been brought to "a *perfect* sense of their misconduct without spilling a drop of blood."[19]

That the federal government had moved against the whiskey rebels with overwhelming force seemed to Washington to have had two major advantages: the opposition had been overwhelmed beyond fighting, and the fact that so large an army had come together had furnished "an additional proof that my fellow citizens understand the true principles of government and liberty."[20]

He wrote Edward Pendleton, "The spirit with which the militia turned out in support of the constitution and the laws of our country, at the same time that it does them immortal honor, is the most conclusive refutation that could have been given to the assertions of Lord Sheffield and the prediction of others of his cast that without the protection of Great Britain we should be unable to govern ourselves; and would soon be involved in anarchy and confusion. They will see that republicanism is not the phantom of a deluded imagination; on the contrary, that under no form of

government will laws be better supported, liberty and property better secured, or happiness more effectually dispensed to mankind."*21

The charges still rife in history books that it was evil to raise so extensive a force for a campaign where no fighting ensued is a hangover from
the republican fear that the whole maneuver was an effort of the Federalists to demonstrate that a powerful standing army was needed not only to
protect the nation from foreign enemies but to keep order at home. This
idea was clearly in Hamilton's mind, and Madison believed that had
there been fighting, a standing army would surely have resulted. It
would, indeed, have been accepted in any case if "the President could
have been embarked in it." The President would not embark in it. Washington urged on Congress only that a small force of militia be for the time
being kept in the western counties to prevent backsliding, and that the
militia law be revised to make the citizens' arm more effective if faced
with future insurrections.23

However, Washington did feel that the Democratic Societies, on which
he blamed the rebellions, should not be allowed to escape unscathed. He
was on the verge of the most devisive of all the personal acts he engaged
in during his entire Presidential career.

---

* Simcoe, the Governor of Western Canada, had hoped that the Whiskey Rebellion
would so embroil the United States that he would be enabled to carry into effect the
British policy of establishing a buffer Indian territory between the Canadian frontier
and the western American settlements. Instead the affair, coming on top of Wayne's
victory, was so impressive a demonstration of federal power that the stage was set for
Jay to gain, by negotiation, control of the northwest forts.22

19

The Democratic Societies

URING his campaign with the whiskey army, Washington's mind was, as he wrote, "revolving on the expense and inconvenience of drawing so many men from their families and occupations." He, as he wrote, "asked myself where would be the impropriety of glancing" at the Democratic Societies in his upcoming Sixth Annual Address to Congress. Not only did Washington hold them responsible for the insurrection, but he was "perfectly convinced that if these self-created societies cannot be discountenanced, they will destroy the government of this country."[1]

At a halting place fifteen miles from Fort Cumberland, Washington received a letter from the most Republican of his Cabinet ministers. Randolph expressed regret that a Democratic Society in South Carolina had adopted the name "Madisonian." This would put Madison in an embarrassing position. He must either "seem to approve by silence what I am confident he must abhor, or affront those" who intended to pay him a compliment. Randolph, so he continued, had seen no opportunity, before the insurrection, to destroy the Democratic Societies. He now believed that they might be crushed. "The prospect ought not to be lost."[2]

Washington replied that "*well*-disposed" persons either disapproved already or would soon have their eyes opened to "the tendency if not the design of the leaders of these self-created societies. I should be extremely sorry, therefore, if Mr. M——n, *from any cause whatsoever* should get himself entangled with them or their politics."[3]

"The continued interruptions of a militia camp" were preventing him, Washington went on, from giving much thought to his address. Randolph should prepare a text. Perhaps it should state that the "spirit" with which the people had supported "law and government . . . is a happy presage that future attempts of a certain description of people will not, though accompanied with the same industry, sow the seeds of distrust and disturb the public tranquility will prove abortive." Noticing how confused was his sentence (it was already a second draft) Washington continued, "I have formed no precise idea of what is best to be done or said on this subject, nor have I time to express properly what has occurred to me, as I am writing now at an hour when I ought to be in bed."[4]

Another letter from Randolph reported that already, before any results of Jay's mission were known, opposition to whatever Jay agreed to was being prepared: "Some of the furious ones . . . are very absurdly offended that Mr. Jay, instead of negotiating, did not make a peremptory demand for satisfaction, and, if it was refused, come away." Newspapers, Washington learned, were making great capital out of the report that, at a reception, Jay had kissed the Queen's hand.[5]

Washington got back to Philadelphia eighteen days before he was scheduled to address Congress. He found, so he wrote Jay, that "the general opinion" was that the Whiskey Rebellion "having happened at the time it did was fortunate." The Democratic Societies had "precipitated a crisis for which they were not prepared." They were vulnerable to "annihilation."

Washington intended, so he continued, to be more "prolix" in his address concerning the Whiskey Rebellion than "is usual in such an instrument." Many people were uninformed about his efforts at conciliation. He would not let the matter "go naked into the world, to be dressed up according to the . . . policy of our enemies."[6]

In his Sixth Annual Address, delivered to Congress on November 15, Washington gave twenty minutes to explaining the whiskey march, but only a few to the Democratic Societies, which he never specifically identified. Here in their entirety are all the relevant passages:

"In the four western counties of Pennsylvania, a prejudice, fostered and embittered by the artifice of men who labored for ascendancy over the will of others by the guidance of their passions, produced symptoms of riot and violence." After referring to governmental efforts to relieve the causes for complaints, Washington returned to the societies: "Associations of men began to denounce threats against the officers employed. From a belief that, by a more formal concert, their operations might be defeated, certain self-created societies assumed the tone of condemnation. Hence, while the greater part of Pennsylvania itself were conforming themselves to the acts of excise, a few counties were resolved to frustrate them."

At a later point in the address, Washington said, "When in the calm moment of reflection they [the citizens of the United States] shall have retraced the origin and progress of the insurrection, let them determine whether it had not been fomented by combinations of men who, careless of consequences and disregarding the unerring truth that those who rouse cannot always appease a civil convulsion, have disseminated, from ignorance or perversion of facts, suspicions, jealousies, and accusations of the whole government."

In his peroration, Washington stated, "Let us unite therefore in imploring the Supreme Ruler of nations to spread his holy protection over these United States; to turn the machinations of the wicked to the confirming of our Constitution; to enable us at all times to root out internal sedition and put invasion to flight; to perpetuate to our country that prosperity which his goodness had already conferred, and to verify the anticipations of this government being a safeguard to human rights."[7]

In thus warning of sedition, Washington denounced nothing and nobody by name; he suggested no penalties legal or social; he urged no political reprisals. The assumption was that the American people, when alerted to danger, would voluntarily and individually look around them and beware. What they were to step back from was defined as no particular policy, either federalist or republican, either conservative or leveling, but organized use of lies to undermine the government and to raise "civil convulsion." Groups outside western Pennsylvania were only implicated if it were felt that they fitted Washington's description. The President gave no hint of his suspicion that the Democratic Societies were servants of French propaganda. Although he believed that a major cause of trouble had been the fact that so many inhabitants of western Pennsylvania were recent immigrants, unfamiliar with American institutions and still responsive to anti-governmental resentments imbibed abroad,[8] his only mention of aliens in the address was to point out that orderly republican institutions enabled menaced foreigners to find asylum in the United States.

As compared to what was then daily published in pamphlets and the press, Washington's address was vague and mild. Any believer in dictatorial government would consider it milk and water. Yet the beloved Washington had gone far beyond the limits he had previously set for himself, and the prestige he wielded was enormous. One of the twenty ladies in the gallery remembered, "It really seemed as though we were addressed by a far superior being than any here below."

Representative George Thacher of Maine noted that as Washington read his speech, "he made use of much more motion than has been usual with him." When he asked for national support, "I felt a strange mixture of passions which I cannot describe. Tears started into my eyes, and it was with difficulty that I could suppress an involuntary effort to swear that I would support him."[9]

The first official reactions were elicited by the practice of the Senate and the House to reply to the President's annual addresses. The Senate, dominated by Federalists, expressed concern that resistance to law had been increased by "certain self-created societies."[10]

Dominated by Republicans, the House was in a quandary. The Republicans did not wish to accept any odium for the insurrection — Madison thanked his lucky stars that many of his followers had enlisted to put it down — but they regarded the Democratic Societies, in the leadership of which some had been involved, as their allies. Washington had, it is true, limited his denunciations to organizations in the rebellious counties, which opened the way for insistence that other societies were not included in the charges. The catch lay in a single word Washington used: "self-created." All the Democratic Societies were self-created in the sense that they were groups trying to influence the government but not provided for in the Constitution or the laws. A committee appointed to draw up the House's reply tried to duck the whole issue, but the Federalist minority would not permit that. A compromise was finally found in substituting for the phrase "self-created societies" another phrase Washington had used. The House deplored that "combinations of men" had conspired against the government.[11]

From his hilltop, Jefferson wrote Madison that the Republicans in the House had been pusillanimous: they should have denounced the entire whiskey campaign — "an armament against people at their ploughs" — and also Washington's speech. Madison replied that the Republicans were in a dangerous position from which they had to extricate themselves. And Jefferson's own admonitions soon took on a melancholy tone: "The tide against our Constitution is unquestionably strong, but it will turn. . . . Hold on then, like good and faithful seamen, till our brother sailors can rouse from their intoxication and right the vessel."[12]

Political parties were still so far hidden in the wings of history that

Washington was by no means out of step with his times when he put forward the vision of a government that achieved policy not as the result of a tug-of-war but rather as a synthesis of opposing points of view. Resolutions endorsing Washington's stand came from every kind of meeting, from state legislatures, and even from Democratic Societies themselves. In 1794, twenty-four such societies had been founded, bringing the number up to thirty-five. In 1795, only three stragglers came in. Those that had existed either died or sank into innocuousness. The Democratic Society movement did not long survive Washington's attack.[13]

Jeffersonians then and now have regarded Washington's assault on the societies as an attack on popular participation in government. The organizations he drove out of existence were, it is contended, awakening the people to their potential power and educating them in how to use it. In Washington's mind, such claims were self-serving poppycock.

His own experience told him that the American people did not need in the 1790's to have called to their attention the fact that they had the vote. In 1755, Washington had first run for the Virginia House of Burgesses in a frontier district very like what western Pennsylvania was now. Despite silk-stocking influence from the other side of the Blue Ridge, he had been defeated. Two years later, when he was better known in the constituency (and supplied more liquor) he was elected. Since then the nation had gone through a long war to achieve the right to representation. It was a rare community that did not have Revolutionary veterans to lead the way to the polls. If the voters acted as individuals not as members of groups, or even stayed home when they did not care enough to mark ballots, that did not seem to Washington a denial of popular rule.*

As for educating the voters, Washington saw education as "the security of a free constitution," but he felt that the Democratic Societies were presenting, for partisan ends, a travesty of education. His favorite charity had long been the establishment of schools, which would give people as individuals bases for judgment. And he wished to supply them as individuals with the information on which judgment could be based. Towards this end, he saw two primary channels. One: The reports of the local representatives whom popular suffrage had sent to the capital. Two:

---

* Studies have been made to show that where the Democratic Societies existed, a higher percentage of the voters went to the polls. However, as any Tammany politician could testify, "getting out the vote" does not necessarily imply greater attention to the best interests of the people.[14]

newspapers. Although he was continually outraged by what he regarded as misrepresentations in the press, he considered its role so important that he continually urged government support for the dissemination of newspapers through the mails. Washington felt that the greatest impediment to popular education was "demagogues," men who, either for the worst motives or because they were themselves ill informed, misled the people. The Democratic Societies seemed to him to have been created as stamping grounds for demagogues.

Since the Democratic Societies were forerunners of the political parties that were eventually to flourish, many writers argue that Washington's opposition to them was opposition to popular government, which they identify with such parties. Washington himself would have argued according to different preconceptions.

His earliest and subsequently his happiest years had been lived as part of a neighborhood. It was not chance that his only formal intervention in the debates of the Constitutional Convention was to urge that the size of the districts represented by individual members of the House be reduced. Regarding the neighborhood as the natural political unit, Washington wished to establish as direct a line as he could between localities and the national government. All intervening combinations seemed to him to get in the way. This was true of the states. Their jealousies had made him almost as much trouble during the Revolution as had the British. And a consolidation of regional attitudes into hostile camps seemed to him a major menace hanging over the union.

But how were the neighborhoods, with their diverse and limited outlooks, their various economic imperatives and prejudices, to be brought together into a unified whole? Washington's answer was that the leaders from the neighborhoods, each carrying in his mind the needs and emotions of his region, should get together with men from other places and work out in consultation and friendship policies that would suit all. This possibility had first been brought home to Washington by his experience in the Continental Army, as he himself (to begin with, a provincial Virginian) learned from the men around him to visualize the whole nation, and as he saw many another soldier walk the same intellectual and social road. The process had been repeated in the Constitutional Convention, and Washington was to urge, as a permanent training ground, a national university which would gather in, during their formative years, able young men from every part of the nation. At the moment, the best opportunity was presented by the federal government itself. In the Senate, in the House, in the executive offices, in the cosmopolitan society of the national capital men debated and mingled, reaching (it was to be hoped) large decisions. But this method would only work if the delegates arrived in the centers free to make their own judgments.

As far back as 1786, in objecting to a "Patriotic Society" organized to instruct the delegates from tidewater Virginia, Washington had stated (although *this* society agreed with his own politics) many of his basic objections to the Democratic Societies: "To me it appears much wiser and more politic to choose able and honest representatives and leave them in all national questions to determine from the evidence of reason and the facts which shall be adduced, when internal and external information is given to them in a collective state. What certainty is there that societies in a corner or remote part of a state can possess that knowledge which is necessary for them to decide? . . . What figure then must a delegate make who comes there [to the capital] with his hands tied and his judgment forestalled? His very instructors, perhaps (if they had nothing sinister in view), were they present at all the information and arguments which would come forward, might be the first to change sentiments." Even at that early date he added that "a few members of this society, more sagacious and designing than the rest, [might] direct the measures of it to private views of their own."[15]

Washington's theory was government by consent. Although the people could not decide in advance how national problems would develop and how they could best be met, they should be informed of every act that affected them, fully supplied with the arguments on both sides and the considerations that had motivated the eventual decision. It was to be hoped that (as was the case with the Constitution) the people would read the arguments, discuss the matter with each other and their returned delegates, meditate, and come to agree with wise policies which, in a purely neighborhood dialogue, they would have opposed. If they could not be convinced, they could persuade their delegate to work for a change in the law, or they could elect someone else.

Washington also accepted a safety valve to be used in moments of crisis. In denouncing the Democratic Societies, he added to the adjective "self-created" the adjective "*permanent*," which he usually underlined. He approved of the voters' meeting regularly (as in town meetings) to deal with problems which affected only their localities and the understanding of which was within their experience, but he felt that similar meetings should, on the level of national policy, be convened only when the voters saw an emergency. The result of this deliberation would be incorporated in an address to the President. Washington felt it his duty to respond to every such address he received with an individual, carefully considered reply. The process was thus direct personal communication between the neighborhood and the President.

The Democratic Societies in western Pennsylvania had constituted, as Washington saw it, a classic case of overpassionate concern with local interests. The movement as a whole presented another danger which Washington regarded as perhaps even more grave. The societies were attempting to establish a national network that would in many ways parallel the government itself. Washington saw this as the effort of a faction, engaged in proceedings "which arrogate the direction of our affairs without any degree of authority from the people," to interpose themselves between the government and the nation.[16] Their object, he believed, was to support special interests, foreign as well as American, and the methods they employed seemed to him destructive in the extreme.

The United States had been established for hardly a dozen years and the federal government for hardly six. Since the nation and its government had no legitimacy based on tradition, Washington regarded as the only cement that held the nation together the will and confidence of the current generation.* A major object of government was to earn and keep that confidence, but how could this be done if a nationally organized conspiracy misrepresented every act? Washington wrote Jay, "Against the malignancy of the discontented, the turbulent and the vicious, no abilities, no exertions, nor the most unshaken integrity are any safeguard."[17]

Functioning as a national group, the societies, Washington believed, were following French inspiration in an effort to undermine the government by destroying public confidence.[18] Should they succeed in bringing the government down, what would follow? Who could doubt that the result would be such a dictatorship as Washington might well, at several points in his career, have established, and which he had always spurned with loathing? Was it not then a republican rather than a tyrannical act to warn the people before it was too late?

---

* Hardly any of the apparatus of federal jurisdiction with which Americans are now so familiar was visible outside the national capital. In the 1790's, many citizens lived out long lives without ever seeing a federal office, paying a federal tax, collecting a federal payment, filling out a federal form, or meeting a federal bureaucrat.

Washington was convinced that the administration over which he presided had followed the Constitution that had been ratified by the people. He had himself been elected President twice, each time unanimously, with the support of all factions. If his Cabinet no longer completely represented what had become the opposition, this was because Jefferson had, despite his pleading, resigned. The Congress, whose laws Washington dutifully enforced, had been freely elected. Washington thus felt that what was under attack was not a faction in power, but the very government of the United States.

Since Washington's prestige was an invaluable asset to the prestige of the government, to make him out a villain, to attribute to him every sinister and insulting characteristic with which the government was to be labeled, seemed to many of the opposition an essential policy. Washington regarded such personal attacks as part of the effort to bring down the government. And he was not just a political power. He was a man, passionately desirous of the love of his fellow citizens and capable of being deeply hurt.

Down the years, Washington had succeeded in curbing, except on rare occasions, his proclivity to rage. He had practically never permitted anger to affect his public actions. The most conspicuous previous exception had been in relation to the Conway Cabal, when he had even gone so far as to encourage his aides to challenge his opponents to duels. That such anger entered into his attack on the Democratic Societies is revealed by a letter he wrote his brother-in-law, Burgess Ball. The emotional jumble of ideas allows us almost to hear Washington's voice in rage:

"Can anything be more absurd, more arrogant, or more pernicious to the peace of society than for self-created bodies, forming themselves into *permanent* censors and under the shade of night, in a conclave, resolving that acts of Congress, which have undergone the most deliberate and solemn discussion by the representatives of the people chosen for the express purpose and bringing with them from the different parts of the union the sense of their constituents, endeavoring as far as the nature of the thing will admit to form *that will* into laws for the government of the whole; I say, under these circumstances for a self-created, *permanent* body (for no one denies the right of the people to meet occasionally to petition for or to remonstrate against any act of the legislature, etc.) to declare that *this act* is unconstitutional and *that* act is pregnant with mischief; and that all who vote contrary to their dogmas are actuated by selfish motives or under foreign influence — nay, in plain terms are traitors to their country — is such a stretch of arrogant presumption as is not to be reconciled with laudable motives; especially when we see the same set of men endeavoring to destroy all confidence in the administration by arraigning all its acts without knowing on what ground or with what information it proceeds — and this without regard to decency or truth."[19]

When Jefferson had been a member of the Cabinet, he had warned Washington that an attack on the Democratic Societies would be "calculated to make the President assume the station of the head of a party instead of the head of the nation."[20] Had Jefferson still been at Washington's side, Washington might have been stopped again. Had Washington not been forced to prepare his address with such speed after having just returned from an exhausting and emotionally upsetting military campaign, he might have had second thoughts. As it was, Madison mourned that the President's attack "was perhaps the greatest error of his political life." It put him "ostentatiously at the head of the other party," and when the newspapers took up the matter, "the result could not fail to wound the President's popularity more than anything that has yet happened."[21]

Madison reported to Monticello that, during the debates in the House in reply to Washington's address, the Federalists had used Washington's disapproval of the societies as a springboard to help them leap far beyond anything Washington had himself said. They denounced "the press and every mode of animadversions on public men and measures." The "most sacred principle" of the Constitution was, Madison continued, under attack. For his part, Jefferson read into Washington's speech what the most rabid Federalists wished had been there: "It is wonderful, indeed, that the President should have permitted himself to be the organ of such an attack on the freedom of discussion, the freedom of writing, printing, and publishing."[22]

Washington, Jefferson continued, had been so "dazzled by the glittering of crowns and coronets" that he had set out "to suppress the friends of general freedom while those who wish to confine that freedom to the few are permitted to go on in their principles and practices." He referred to the fact that Washington had said nothing unfavorable that seemed applicable to the other two "permanent" and "self-created" national societies then prominent: the Society of the Cincinnati and the Chambers of Commerce.[23] It could be pointed out that Washington had already staged a major fight (which he lost) to make the Cincinnati completely nonpolitical, and that, although most were Federalist, some chapters of this organization of Revolutionary officers followed the politics of their regions to Jeffersonian conclusions.* It could be argued that the Chambers of Commerce, even if solidly Federalist, were pressure groups that, while trying to influence the officers of the government, made no effort to come between the government and the people. Yet Washington's theoretical case was surely weakened by his failure even to "glance" at these organizations in his diatribe. No man objects as much to his friends as to his enemies.

Even if for the moment he seemed to have triumphed, even if the adverse effects were slow to come to light, Washington had not behaved with his old surefootedness. All the more because he did not bring forward the general reasoning behind his denunciation of "self-created societies," he had, for the first time in his career, allowed himself to seem (what he desperately did not want to be) the head of a party. He had stepped down to engage in polemics against one segment of the nation. He should have realized that, however carefully he limited his attack, more rabid individuals would expand it, and that the expansion would be attributed to him.

Washington was not one to confess mistakes or take back anything he had said. Yet he gave the most convincing proof of his realization that he had set out on a wrong road. As President of the United States, he never again engaged in any public denunciation of any aspect of the opposition. Nor did he ever again make any public statement which could be rationally interpreted as limiting in any way the basic freedoms of the people.

---

* The society at Wilmington, Delaware, refused in 1796 to drink a toast to the President on the grounds that he had gone over to the Tories.[24]

20

Weatherbreeder

LATE in January 1795, John Adams wrote his wife, "In the Senate we have no feelings this session; no passions; no animation in debate. I never sat in any public assembly so serenely. What storm may be preparing I know not. A great calm at sea or an uncommonly fine day at land is called a weatherbreeder. But if Jay's dispatches don't arrive, we shall have no tempestuous weather this session."[1]

As the Republicans continued to lie low and Congress dawdled, Washington's Cabinet went through a great change. Both Knox and Hamilton retired. The Secretary of War would be ruined if he did not attend to his land speculations in Maine. Hamilton explained to his sister-in-law, Mrs. Church, "Public office in this country has few attractions. . . . The opportunity of doing good, from the jealousy of power and the spirit of faction, is too small to warrant a long continuance of private sacrifices. . . . The prospect is even bad for gratifying in future the love of fame."[2]

Hamilton's "private sacrifice" had been real. He had suffered innumerable "vexations" as a public target. Despite the suspicions of his enemies, he had so little lined his own nest that he needed to borrow in order to set up a law practice in New York. And new situations had arisen to block his road to future fame. The Republicans had finally found, in the Swiss immigrant Albert Gallatin, a financial expert whose stern eye, turned on the Treasury from the House of Representatives, curtailed Hamilton's freedom. In any case, the time for policy-making financial innovations had passed. As much of Hamilton's program as could be got through had gone through, and national attention had turned elsewhere.[3]

Knox departed carrying Washington's affections, and Hamilton sent the

President the warmest of letters: "Whatever may be my destination here-after, I entreat you to be persuaded . . . that you will always have my fervent wishes for your public and personal felicity, and that it will be my pride to cultivate a continuance of that esteem, regard, and friendship of which you do me the honor to assure me."[4]

Washington sent Hamilton a testimonial which made clear that he felt his retiring aide needed defense. "After so long an experience of your public services, I am naturally led, at this moment of your departure, which it has always been my wish to prevent, to review them. In every relation you have borne with me, I have found that my confidence in your talents, exertions, and integrity has been well placed." Hamilton had ample "title to public regard."[5]

In replacing Knox, Washington gave major consideration to the fact that, in the absence of any considerable standing army, the Secretary of War was principally engaged in Indian affairs. He selected a man with whom his own relations during the Revolution had been bad. Timothy Pickering had been implicated in the Conway Cabal and had opposed Washington's efforts, at the time of the Newburgh Resolves, to dissuade the unpaid army from terrorizing the governments. Although Pickering was an expert Indian negotiator, who agreed with Washington's humanitarian policy towards the tribes, it was hardly an improvement to see across a conference table not the rotund Knox's smiling sunlike face but Pickering's fierce hooked nose and bulletlike eyes.

To carry out the routine duties now desired of the Treasury, Hamilton procured the appointment of his first assistant, Oliver Wolcott, Jr., whose humorous, easygoing appearance was in marked contrast with Pickering's fierceness. However, behind Wolcott's soft, smiling features there lurked a passion for intrigue.°

Both of Washington's new appointees believed that Hamilton had a far greater intellect than the President and should, despite his retirement, be consulted on all matters. For his part, Washington felt that when Hamilton had left, he had left. Thus, without consulting the former Secretary, Washington gave serious consideration to appointing Tench Coxe, whom Jefferson had once recommended for the office,† to the second post in the Treasury. Wolcott ran bleating to Hamilton, who wrote Washington a let-

---

° Pickering and Wolcott — this may have influenced their appointment — were the only high government officials (Pickering was then Postmaster General) who had found the courage to stay in Philadelphia during the yellow fever.

† See volume III, pages 401–402.

ter of protest. His own reputation, Hamilton insisted reproachfully, was involved since everyone would suppose that Washington had consulted him. Coxe "would first perplex and embarrass and afterwards misrepresent and calumniate."[6] Washington made no appointment, temporarily entrusting the post to the auditor, who was satisfactory to Wolcott (and Hamilton).

The diplomat William Vans Murray wrote that the President was "in fine health and spirits." However, he *would* serve "*sweet* cake with wine."[7]

Washington frequented the theater, finding more variety there than we would today. One performance he attended presented first "a comedy called *The Young Quaker,* — or The Fair Philadelphian. . . . End of the play (by particular desire) the pantomime ballet of the TWO PHILOSOPHERS — to which will be added, a new musical piece called The CHILDREN in the Wood. . . . End of the farce, Mr. Martin will recite Dr. Goldsmith's celebrated epilogue in the character of Harlequin. The whole to conclude with a LEAP through a barrel of FIRE."[8]

Charlotte Chambers came to the capital to stay with the wife of the new Secretary of the Treasury. She wrote home that she wore to one of Martha's teas "my dress with white brocade silk, trimmed with silver and white silk, high-heeled shoes embroidered with silver, and a light blue sash, with silver cord and tassel tied at the left side. My watch was suspended at the right, and my hair was in its natural curls. Surmounting all was a small white hat and white ostrich feather, confined by brilliant band and buckle. . . .

"The hall, stairs, and drawing room of the President's house were well lighted by lamps and chandeliers. Mrs. Washington with Mrs. Knox sat near the fireplace. Other ladies were seated on sofas, and gentlemen stood in the center of the room conversing. On our approach, Mrs. Washington arose and made a curtsy — the gentlemen bowed most profoundly — and I calculated my declension to her own with critical exactness. The President soon after, with that benignity peculiarly his own, advanced, and I arose to receive and return his compliments." The President then sat down beside the pretty girl.[9]

Since Washington's stepdaughter had been an epileptic and died young, he had, until his step-granddaughters came in flower, little opportunity to play the paternal role to young ladies.

[195]

Eleanor Parke Custis (Nelly), who lived with the Washingtons, was at sixteen the youngest of the three sisters. Surrounded with Presidential etiquette, held tightly to her grandmother's apron strings, she was judged by John Adams to have enjoyed little liberty or exercise. Yet she was the most charming of the three, the one who was to leave a legend behind her for beauty.[10]

The divided state of the Custis family did not make for cheer among those who had been left in the outer darkness. Martha's daughter-in-law, remarried to the dour and unglamorous Stuart, longed for the splendors and gaiety of the Presidential mansion. The two older children envied the life lived with their grandparents by their younger sister and brother. The second daughter, Martha (Patsy), described Mount Vernon so glowingly to her own daughter that the child, when finally taken there, was disappointed to find it made up of nothing rarer than "trees, and house, and land." The oldest girl, Elizabeth (Betcy), was to claim, "I was the darling of my Grandmother Washington. . . . My heart," she wrote, "was almost broke when she was obliged to go to the General." During a visit of the President with aides to the Stuart household, Betcy was so overcome with shyness that she could not walk out to greet her step-grandfather or eat anything at dinner. "The General said that although he thought a young girl looked best when blushing, yet he was concerned to see me suffer so much."[11]

At the age of seventeen, Patsy became engaged to Thomas Peter, the son of a successful merchant in Georgetown. This betrothal of her younger sister induced Betcy to write her step-grandfather that she scorned love. The only wish of her heart was to have a miniature of Washington to wear on her breast.

"Respect," Washington answered, was all very well, but "there are emotions of a softer kind to which the heart of a girl turned of eighteen is susceptible, that must have generated much warmer ideas, although the fruition of them may, apparently, be more distant than those of your sister's."

He then advised her "in your contemplation of the marriage state" not to "look for perfect felicity before you consent to wed. Nor conceive, from the fine tales the poets and lovers of old have told us of the transports of mutual love, that heaven has taken its abode on earth: Nor do not deceive yourself in supposing that the only means by which these are to be obtained is to drink deep of the cup, and revel in an ocean of love. Love is a mighty pretty thing, but like all other delicious things, it is cloying; and when the first transports of the passion begins to subside, which it assuredly will do, and yield, oftentimes too late, to more sober reflections, it serves to evince that love is too dainty a food to live upon alone, and ought not to be considered farther than as a necessary ingredient for that matrimonial happiness which results from a combination of causes; none of which are of greater importance, than that the object on whom it is placed should possess good sense, good dispositions, and the means of supporting you in the way you have been brought up. Such qualifications cannot fail to attract (after marriage) your esteem and regard, into which or into disgust, sooner or later, love naturally resolves itself. . . . Be assured, and experience will convince you, that there is no truth more certain than that all our enjoyments fall short of our expectations; and to none does it apply with more force than to the gratification of the passions."[12]

Hardly had Betcy received this letter than she wrote her step-grandfather that *she* had become engaged to Thomas Law, a high-born English widower almost twice her age. Law had entered the British East India Company when seventeen and served there for eighteen years, rising to a high rank which did not seem to him high enough. He resigned in a rage and he had come to the United States to become a speculator in District of Columbia real estate. Washington was familiar with his flat face, so imbued with an aristocratic conviction of command that his expression was almost blank, although the eyes were wary and the long mouth pulled nervously tight.*[13] Washington was far from happy about the match (which, indeed, turned out to be a disaster).

To Betcy, the President expressed hurt feelings that she had not confided in him — "you know how much I love you" — but he gave reluctant approval, since she had found "after a careful examination of your heart you cannot be happy without him." He wrote Law that, although it was "*no immediate* concern of mine," he assumed that Betcy's mother and her guardian had made suitable legal arrangements to protect the bride. He expressed the hope he shared with Mrs. Washington that Law would stay in the United States, "for it would be a heart-rending circumstance" if the groom should separate his bride "from her friends in this country."[15]

Nelly went to the wedding and subsequently to the Alexandria ball. In

---

*In an effort to ingratiate himself with Washington, Law boasted that he had been "countenanced" by General Cornwallis (who had been too mean-spirited to attend his own surrender at Yorktown). Washington replied smoothly, "To stand high in the estimation of so respectable a character as Lord Cornwallis is a circumstance which must be as pleasing as it is honorable to you."[14]

reply to what she reported, Washington expressed his relief that the men at the ball had outnumbered the girls, if only by one. However, Nelly had now, in turn, expressed her disdain for men. Washington's answer was, "The passions of your sex are easier raised than allayed. . . . In the composition of the human frame there is a good deal of inflammable matter, however dormant it may lie for a time." Launching, as he commented, into "a lecture drawn from this text," Washington continued, "Love is said to be an involuntary passion and it is, therefore, contended that it cannot be resisted." However, when a "beautiful and accomplished" woman, who has "set the circle in which she moves on fire," finally marries, "the madness *ceases* and all is quiet again." This demonstrated that "love may and therefore ought to be under the guidance of reason. . . . When the fire is beginning to kindle and your heart growing warm, propound these questions to it. Who is this invader?" Having listed the qualities to be considered — Nelly should remember that "a sensible woman can never be happy with a fool" — Washington went on to regret that "delicacy, custom, or call it what epithet you will" precluded the ladies from themselves making any advances. But, so he continued half banteringly, he was not advising the young beauty to be a coquette. Although it was difficult to "draw the line between prudery and coquetry, it would be no great departure from the truth to say that it rarely happens otherwise than that a thorough-paced coquette dies in celibacy, as a punishment for her attempts to mislead others by encouraging looks, words, or actions, given for no other purpose than to draw men on to make overtures that they may be rejected." Washington ended by wishing his dear Nelly "a good husband when you want and deserve one."[*][16]

While the government dawdled, Washington devoted much attention to deals concerning his western acres which were becoming increasingly embedded in settlements.[†] "The disturbed state of Europe," he noted, was sending to the United States "full-handed immigrants." Consummating

---

[*] Washington's niece Harriot, the orphaned daughter of his alcoholic brother Samuel, who had long been in his charge, announced in 1796 that she wished to marry one Andrew Parks. Washington was worried because Parks only possessed £3000, "a precarious dependence . . . when applied to a man in trade." He admitted that Harriot, having very little fortune herself, could hardly expect a great one in her husband, yet he regretted that she had waited until he had escaped from the Presidency, so that he could have introduced her to some man more "respectable."[17]

[†] As he gradually reduced the small force of militia occupying western Pennsylvania, he raised the prices on his land there, which the consolidation of order made more valuable.[18]

deal after deal, he amazingly found himself, for one of the few times in his career, not short of cash. What a luxury to be able to write concerning some tobacco in an Alexandria warehouse, "I am in no hurry, nor under any necessity to precipitate the sale"! He had, indeed, capital to invest: he bought for more than six thousand dollars stock of the banks in Alexandria and the federal city.[19]

He would be willing, he wrote, to lease western acres for re-renting if he could count on a profit of 6 percent, "the legal interest of the U. States." He realized that businessmen often expected a greater return: "I have no inclination, however, to fall into those practices."[20]

Washington wished to establish "some system of American education. . . . It has always been a source of regret with me to see" American students sent to Europe before their minds were formed and they had "correct ideas of the blessing of the country they leave."° Not that he objected to foreign learning. He visualized importing to the United States "the best European professors." But he feared that young Americans might acquire in Europe (where he himself had never been) "habits of dissipation and extravagance," and also "principles unfriendly to the rights of man."[21]

Washington possessed fifty shares in the Potomac Canal Company and one hundred in the James River Canal Company, given him after the Revolution by the state of Virginia. He had accepted the shares on the condition that he could apply them to "objects of public nature."[22] At some unidentified date, but before 1795, he had drawn up a will in which he left the shares "towards the endowment of a university to be established in the Federal District provided that some well-digested plan be achieved before 1800."

The will stated that his intention was to have "young men from *all parts* of the United States" complete, under distinguished professors, their studies "in the different branches of literature, arts, and sciences." In addition to preparation for the professions they intended to pursue, they should "get fixed in the principles of the Constitution, understand the laws and the true interests and policy of their country." Furthermore, the students from the various regions would, "by forming acquaintances with each other early in life," be cured of "those local prejudices and habitual jealousies which, when carried to excess, are never failing sources of disquietude."[23]

° Washington had forgotten that, as a boy, he had yearned to follow his father and two older half brothers to school in the England that he then referred to as "home."

In a later exposition of his plan (his final address to Congress) Washington stated, "True it is that our country, much to its honor, contains many seminaries of learning highly respectable and useful, but the funds upon which they rest are too narrow to command the ablest professors in the different departments of liberal knowledge."* Such schools should be considered "excellent auxiliaries" for the national university.

Being in the national capital, the students at the university would be able to watch the government operating, becoming proficient "in the science of *government*." This would create "the future guardians of the liberties of the country."[24] If Washington's scheme, which so delightfully combined learning, national union, and advantage to the federal city, also contained seeds of an oligarchy, Washington remained unconscious of the danger.

An alternate possibility for a major American university was opened by the dislocations in Europe. When revolution hit Geneva, the famous faculty there, being both conservative and dependent on governmental support, found itself stranded. The professors decided it would be expedient to move their institution lock, stock, and barrel to the United States.

When the idea was proposed to Washington by John Adams, the President expressed no enthusiasm for trying to assimilate "an *entire* seminary of *foreigners,* who may not understand our language."[25]

Jefferson, so much more European-minded than Washington, was fascinated with the possibility, but, being so much less concerned with national unity, he visualized not a national but a Virginian institution. He queried members of the Virginia legislature, but found no enthusiasm.[26]

It may have been word of this activity that spurred Washington into making public his own scheme. He sent the relevant extract of his will to Randolph, suggesting that he show it to Madison in the hope that Virginia could be persuaded to back a national institution. And he wrote the commissioners of the District of Columbia saying that the time had now come to strike a blow for a university in their city. He would be glad to have the provision from his will publicized in any way that would help.

From Monticello, so long silent in communication with Washington, came a letter. Jefferson reminded Washington that when first offered the canal shares by Virginia, Washington had asked his advice. He now advised that the shares be applied to importing the University of Geneva.

---

* In planning the site for such a university in the national capital Washington sought space to include a botanical garden.

Had the two men still been on intimate terms, Jefferson's long exposition of the worldwide importance of that university might have sounded less like a cosmopolitan lecturing a provincial. Washington's support, so Jefferson continued, would undoubtedly overcome the reluctance of the Virginia legislature. Of course, since Virginia would contribute funds, the institution would have to be in that state. Being as suspicious of cities as Washington was of Europe, Jefferson felt that "moral" reasons further precluded location in the federal city. But, so he added soothingly, the site could be near enough to the District of Columbia that "the splendor of the two objects would reflect usefully on each other."[27]

Washington could not resist a debater's reply. Jefferson having informed him that "the colleges of Geneva and Edinburgh were considered as the two eyes of Europe," Washington noted that an all-Genevan institution could exclude professors from Edinburgh, some of the most celebrated of whom he had heard could be obtained. Jefferson had suggested that the federal city might not be "moral." Washington wondered whether the Genevans "might not be all of good characters." Furthermore, since the Swiss university had "been at variance with the leveling party of their own country, the measure might be considered as an aristocratical movement by more than those who, without any just cause that I have been able to discover, are continually sounding the alarm bell of aristocracy." (We can visualize with what pleasure Washington wrote that sentence: he may even have read it out loud to his wife.) In any case, Washington had anticipated Jefferson's suggestions with his own plans for a federal university. He was definitely going to will his Potomac shares for that purpose. However, in deference to the legislature of Virginia, which had made the original donation, he would ask their advice on what to do with the James River shares.[28]

On the same date, March 16, 1795, Washington wrote Governor Robert Brooke of Virginia stating that he would like to leave all his canal shares to a national university but that, if Virginia wished to establish its own "seminary of learning upon an enlarged plan, but not coming up to the full idea of an university," he would comply. The legislature voted for a seminary to be established in "the upper country." Washington then changed his will, leaving the James River shares to Liberty Hall Academy (which eventually became Washington and Lee University).[29]

For traditional reasons that no longer impinge on our thinking — all the more because the young are now allowed to vote before they become twenty-one — Washington was profoundly depressed by his sixty-third birthday. According to an ancient belief, the years, known as "climacterics," that divided the ages of man were designated by multiplying the various odd numbers — three, five, seven, nine — by seven. At three times seven, you became an adult. Nine times seven was the "grand climacteric," the threshold of old age.

The fact that he was at the moment in good health did not reassure Washington, as he revealed in letter after letter. Alas, he had now crossed into "the wrong . . . side of my grand climacteric." And "the natural decline of men, after they have entered into or passed their grand climacteric, will make its appearance in a variety of ways, too prominently for figures in the background of the picture."

A man, as is said, is as old as he feels. And the record leaves no doubt that, having passed his grand climacteric, Washington felt markedly older when he was struck by what was to be the greatest dilemma of his long career.[30]

21

The Jay Treaty Arrives

IN August 1794 Washington sent to Jay, who was then in London, a blast that contrasted sharply with the pro-British purrs which that emissary received from Hamilton. Having stated that he had received from the Governor of Upper Canada a protest "against our occupying lands far from any of the posts which long ago they ought to have surrendered," Washington blamed directly on "the agents of Great Britain" the Indian "murders of helpless women and innocent children along our frontiers." He expressed suspicions that among the murdering braves were English soldiers disguised with paint and feathers.

"Can it be expected, I ask, so long as these things" were encouraged by the British government, "that there ever will or can be any cordiality between the two countries? I answer, 'No!'" A knowledge that such were "*my* sentiments would have little weight, I am persuaded, with the British administration," but the fact remained that unless the posts were surrendered — Jay had reported to Washington they probably would not be — "war will be inevitable."[1]

In December, word came that Washington's other newly appointed emissary, Monroe, had behaved in a most surprising manner. He had personally appeared before the National Convention to present that French legislative body with an American flag. Although he had just warned Washington that, despite the fall of Robespierre, the guillotine would probably continue its plunging, he publicly announced official American admiration not only for the valor of the French armies but for "the wisdom and firmness of her councils." To all the world as well as his cheering audience, he pronounced an identity of interests between "the American and French republics."[2]

Jay protested to Washington that Monroe's act had impeded his own negotiations by increasing British hostility to the United States. Washington replied that Monroe had certainly been indiscreet, but the implied warning of a possible Franco-American alliance, "by alarming as well as offending the B [ritish] Ministry, might have no unfavorable operation in bringing matters to a happy and speedy result."*[3]

In those years of sail, winter so interdicted communication across the ocean that England and France seemed to move away an immeasurable distance. However, on the last day of January 1795, a vessel brought in an exciting rumor: Jay had signed a treaty during the previous November. The seamen had no information on what the document contained.[5]

Although random transatlantic sails continued to furl in American harbors, there was no further word. Every morning Washington wondered whether that day would bring the dispatch case which, when opened, would prove either a gift from Providence or Pandora's box. As the suspense deepened, the situation came to resemble the time when he had waited, week after week, for confirmation of Burgoyne's surrender. Then he had wondered whether the victory had actually taken place. Now he wondered whether Jay had actually signed.[6]

The Congressional session was drowsing towards its close. A few days before adjournment on March 3, Washington, in anticipation of finally hearing from Jay, announced a special session to convene on June 8.[7] The congressmen were straggling home, when a mud-spattered rider appeared from Norfolk, Virginia. He carried not the Jay Treaty itself, but a third copy. Yet the seal was unbroken and the evidence firm.†[8]

After Washington had studied what Jay had negotiated, he was "not favorable to it."[9] The best thing that could be said for the treaty was that the British had agreed to it. Here were solutions, happy or unhappy, to the most dangerous problems that were embattling Great Britain and the United States. Here, even if often unsatisfactory, were rules which, if followed, would prevent a disastrous war.[10]

The British agreed to evacuate the western posts, although at a some-

---

* Randolph was instructed to warn Monroe to be more politic in the future.[4]

† By error the first copy and a duplicate were sent on the same British packet: they were thrown overboard when the vessel was overhauled by a French privateer. The copy Washington received, which had traveled for three months on an American ship, had been kept hidden when the vessel was searched for contraband by another French privateer.

what distant date, June 1, 1796. However, Washington frowned at a clause which permitted fur traders to cross boundaries, thus opening to the British the Northwest Territory and even the Mississippi River.[11]

Washington was in favor of arbitration and had always believed that Americans should pay their pre-Revolutionary debts to British merchants, and thus he could not object in principle to the mixed commissions which Jay had agreed should establish the extent of the debt. Other mixed commissions were to settle boundary disputes and — here the machinery seemed unnecessarily slow and cumbersome — determine what Great Britain owed for illegal confiscation of American ships and goods. Washington noted with displeasure that there was no provision for reimbursing the owners of slaves and other property carried off by the British during the Revolution.

A specific statement in the text that nothing would be binding which was contrary to the previous international obligations of the United States, combined with his faith in Jay's skill as a lawyer, seems to have reassured Washington that America's old treaties with France had probably not been violated. However, the pro-French party in the United States would surely be displeased because the treaty outlawed a method of retaliation which they considered valuable: Jay had agreed that the American government would not interfere with the assets of British subjects in the United States.

That Great Britain had not accepted the principle, which had been so determinedly argued for by Secretary of State Jefferson, that free ships made free goods, could not have come to Washington as a surprise. Great Britain could not be expected to sign away, when the United States had no navy with which to enforce her views, a major advantage given her by her own sea power. Jay had agreed to that alternate law of nations, the *Consolat de Mar,* which allowed the removal from neutral bottoms not only of those specific goods defined as contraband but of *all* goods belonging to belligerent nations. If in this matter Jay had had no choice, surely he need not have agreed to a definition of contraband so vague — things "of such a nature" as to enable the enemies of Great Britain "to carry on war" — that it could be interpreted to prevent most American exports from being safely shipped to France, even in American bottoms. Jay had furthermore stipulated nothing concerning the extremely complicated issue of the impressment of American seamen.*[12]

---

* A major aspect of the problem concerned how seamen were to establish, when questioned on the high seas, their American citizenship. Jefferson thought they would

Those commercial aspects of the treaty which would not be made obsolete by peace were limited to a period of fifteen years. Jay had honored in a manner hardly more than *pro forma* the requirement that he must open the British West Indies to American trade: the British would admit tiny American ships, those under seventy tons. In return for this small concession, Jay had agreed that American vessels would not carry to other nations or even export from the United States (this was to prevent transshipping) any products natural to the West Indies: the molasses, sugar, and cotton for which France would pay so handsomely. Jay had seemingly been ignorant of the fact that was clear to Washington, since he had himself encouraged the development, that cotton was becoming a major export from America's own deep south.[14] Another disturbing commercial concession was Jay's agreement that any favorable clauses contained in a treaty between the United States and another nation would automatically apply to Great Britain. This threw a complete block in Washington's long campaign to retaliate against Great Britain for her restrictive customs laws.

Whether a different emissary from Jay — less pro-British, abler, more audacious — could have made a better deal is one of those "road not taken" questions that can be answered only in part. It is clear that an emissary who, finding the British intractable, had packed up and gone home, would have promoted catastrophe. But might not certain clauses have been modified? Jeffersonians liked to blame Jay's results on his own prejudices, and Jeffersonian historians have subsequently blamed Hamilton for having thrown away a major bargaining point by telling Hammond that the United States would never enter into an alliance with the Scandinavian countries. Hamiltonians pointed darkly to Monroe's indiscretion in France as a cause of British hostility Jay could not overcome. But all such considerations were, once the treaty had come into Washington's hands, water under a perilous bridge that had somehow to be crossed.[15]

Washington admitted that he had "great difficulty" with many of the commercial provisions, since he lacked "intimate" knowledge of American commerce and could not visualize what changes the treaty would make,

---

be worse off if reliance were placed on their presenting governmental certificates: they would lose the papers "in a thousand ways" or have them stolen. Jefferson's suggestion had been that an American bottom serve as protection for a number of seamen in proportion to its tonnage.[13] Such a rule that, in effect, free ships make free sailors obviously could not be accepted by the British, since their sailors, who were badly treated and badly paid, could all slip in foreign ports to American boats, leaving the British ships unmanned.

or how it "may affect our present or restrain future treaties with other nations." He was to regret that "I had no means of acquiring the information without disclosing its [the treaty's] contents."[16]

Intimate knowledge could easily have been secured from an obvious source. However, Washington refrained from consulting Hamilton. (This is enough by itself utterly to refute the endlessly repeated contention that the former Secretary had, when he retired, only moved from Washington's right hand to behind the Presidential chair.) Having secured from his own sources information on what the treaty contained, Hamilton did not dare offer unasked his advice to Washington — and he was not asked.

Nor did Washington take into his confidence the new members of his Cabinet, not Pickering, nor Wolcott, nor Bradford. He consulted only one man — the old friend whom he had originally appointed as Attorney General, explaining that, since the duties of that office were so limited, he could indulge his desire to have near him a man with whom he had "habits of intimacy." Randolph had received the document in his present role as Secretary of State. He was ordered by the President "rigidly" to conceal the text "from every person on earth" until the papers should be delivered under seal to the Senate for its consideration. In the meanwhile, Washington chewed over the treaty in conversation with Randolph. "Scarcely a day," Randolph remembered, "passed on which he saw me that he did not enumerate many objections to it."[17]

Since the text had arrived on March 7 and Congress would not convene until June 8, the treaty would be kept secret for three months. Washington (who never explained) seems to have recognized that the document contained dynamite. *Any* accommodation with England would outrage the pro-French party, and what Jay had produced was in fact objectionable in many ways and to many interests, including groups by no means ordinarily pro-French. Yet a refusal to ratify would, by sinking the government's efforts to reach an accommodation with England, outrage the Federalists and quite possibly throw the United States into a war with the world's greatest naval power, which had bases and allies — Canada, New Spain, the Indian tribes — on the North American continent.

Washington saw no solution to this dilemma, and Randolph had no useful advice to offer. Perhaps the Senate would find a way out. Certain it was that if the text now became public, controversy would during the three-month interim reach such heights that the Senate might be prevented from achieving a dispassionate decision — or even any decision. The confusion would surely be heightened if the French got word of the treaty in time to set their organs of propaganda in the United States at work.*

Washington yearned for a brilliant Senatorial decision. He had always stated that the legislature was the mainspring of republican government. Let the mainspring act! He would rest altogether on the Constitutional provision of "advice and consent." He would act exactly as the Senate advised.[19]

Washington was an aging man who had sustained much suspense and lived through many crises. There is no indication in his writings as to how much anxiety tore at him as the weeks moved by. He was able to make a very quick trip to Mount Vernon — he left Philadelphia on April 14, 1795, and returned on May 2. His back having healed, he went part of the way on horseback.[20]

Jay, who had stated that his health would not stand an ocean crossing in winter, was still abroad when his treaty reached the United States. In his absence, the Federalists had elected him Governor of New York. Arriving in that port during May, he announced he was not well enough to travel to Philadelphia for a conference which Randolph felt would be very useful to the executive in elucidating the treaty. He mailed Washington his resignation as Chief Justice. Washington's acceptance of the resignation was cold and routine.[21]

From South Carolina came a request from a veteran patriot, John Rutledge, that he succeed Jay. The eagerness with which Washington leapt at the opportunity revealed that he was still trying to keep not only a geographic but a political balance. Rutledge was so strong an anti-Federalist that Wolcott considered his appointment would, if confirmed by the Senate, bring "ruin and disgrace" on the nation.[22]

Congress came back to Philadelphia. The message Washington sent on June 8 reads in its entirety: "Gentlemen of the Senate: In pursuance of my nomination of John Jay, as Envoy Extraordinary to his Britannic Majesty, on the 16th day of April, 1794, and of the advice and consent of the Senate thereto on the 19th, a negotiation was opened in London. On the 7th of March, 1795, the treaty resulting therefrom was delivered to the Secretary of State. I now transmit to the Senate that treaty, and other documents connected with it. They will therefore in their wisdom decide

---

*Monroe had fatuously promised to hand over a copy, as soon as he received it, to the French Directory, and he was furious when Jay refused to send him one. Had Jay done what Monroe wished, the French would have had the treaty before Washington.[18]

whether they will advise and consent that the said treaty be made between the United States and his Britannic Majesty."[23]

The documents Washington submitted to the Senate were more inclusive than Randolph thought wise.[24] And Washington brushed aside Randolph's suggestion that he should make up his own mind whether he would ratify if the Senate advised him to. He replied that, "although the treaty was so exceptional to him, yet he would not separate from the Senate."[25]

The Senate met behind closed doors and under a seal of secrecy. The greatest opposition rose against Article XII, which limited the size of American ships admitted to the British West Indies and prohibited American trade in West Indian products. The Federalist tacticians finally moved for approval of the other twenty-seven articles while recommending "further friendly negotiations" concerning Article XII. On June 24, after eighteen days of stormy debate, the Senate so advised the President by exactly the necessary two-thirds majority: twenty to ten.

The baby was now fairly on Washington's doorstep, and a misshapen baby it was! No procedure was suggested for achieving a new Article XII. Washington wondered whether he should prepare a text and, before sending it to England, submit it to the Senate for consent. When Randolph objected that this would, by revealing acceptance of the Senate's approach, be the equivalent of announcing that he would ratify the treaty, he allowed Congress to adjourn without taking any action concerning the new clause.[26]

Now, at long last, Washington consulted his Cabinet. Did the Senate intend their resolution to be their final act or must a new Article XII, if agreed on with the British, be submitted to them? Washington underlined that he wished the opinions to be communicated to him in *"writing,"* which meant that he desired no such personal conferences with Wolcott, Pickering, or Bradford as he was often conducting with Randolph. The ministers, who had been waiting for months to find out what the executive was up to and pull their weight, were still confined to answering a procedural question. Eager, as Federalists, to encourage no impediments, all replied that the Senate did not have to be again consulted.[27]

Before adjourning the Senate had advised that, although the nature of the provisions might be revealed, the text of the treaty should not be published until the President had decided whether or not to ratify. However, Washington concluded that the time for secrecy had passed. He expressed to Randolph "a wish that the public opinion could now be heard upon the subject." However, the previous security precautions — hardly more copies had been printed than were necessary to give each senator one — now tripped up the President. Randolph made arrangements with a printer, but could not supply him since the executive's one extra copy of the treaty had first to be given to the new French minister, Pierre Adet, who had just replaced Fauchet. Before Randolph could get his copy back, a republican senator from Virginia leaked the text to the violent anti-government editor Bache. The pamphlet Bache produced included the statement that he was now giving to the people what their government had tried to keep from them.[28]

Washington had hoped to pass the buck. He would hold forth on the glories of legislative leadership, and then do what the Senate advised. But now that the treaty lay on his desk with the recommendation that he ratify, he could not bring himself to shirk what he felt was his responsibility. On July 21, Randolph wrote Monroe, "The President has not yet decided upon the final measure to be adopted by himself."[29]

On July 3, almost four months after the treaty had arrived, Washington finally consulted Hamilton. In a letter written in his own hand and headed "private and perfectly confidential," the President stated that he now felt free to communicate with his former Cabinet officer since the treaty had "made its public entry into the gazettes." Washington went out of his way to make clear that he was not turning to Hamilton as the ultimate expert or with the intention of doing what Hamilton advised. He believed that Hamilton had given as much attention to commercial matters "as most men," and that his governmental experience had "afforded you more opportunities of deriving knowledge therein than most of them." He wished "to have the favorable and unfavorable side of *each* article stated and compared together, that I may see the tendency and bearing of them, and, ultimately, on which side the balance is to be found."

In another passage, Washington revealed that he was out of touch with Hamilton and also felt embarrassed at calling on his former aide: "I do not know how you may be occupied at present or how incompatible this request of mine may be to the business you have in hand. . . . It is not my intention to interrupt you in that business; or, if you are disinclined to go into the investigation I have requested, to press the matter upon you."[30]

On receiving Washington's request, Hamilton sat down and wrote and

wrote and wrote, producing a letter — he later added to it with two sup-
plementary mailings — which when printed runs to forty-one pages. He
agreed that Article XII should not be accepted, but stated that the rest of
the treaty closed, "upon the whole as reasonably as could be expected,
the contraverted points between the two countries"; gave "the prospect of
repossessing our western posts"; and offered the United States an escape
from being implicated in the European war. The continuation of peace
was much more important to American commerce than any commercial
advantages or disadvantages. The compensation of pre-Revolutionary
debts that Jay had agreed to would cost less than one military campaign.
"The terms are in no way inconsistent with national honor," and all the
immediate disadvantages were capable of revision in a few years. "The
calculation is therefore a simple and plain one."[31]

In his reply, Washington expressed gratitude, adding, "Although it was
my wish that your observations should be diffusive, yet I am really
ashamed when I behold the trouble it has given you to explore and to explain so fully." He then went on to indicate that he himself was greatly
concerned over the provision that, while British ships might use American
seaports, American might not use British. This, it was true, only perpetu-
ated an existing situation, yet it was hardly "marked with reciprocity." He
was worried lest allowing Indian traders to cross the boundaries and nav-
igate the Mississippi would make for "disputes which may terminate seriously" and also for British domination on both sides of the line because of
the Britons' influence with the Indians, which they had not hesitated to
use in an "overbearing" and "underhand" manner.[32]

Washington showed Hamilton's letter to Randolph. The Secretary of
State came up with his own list of reasons why Washington should ratify
the treaty. Peace would be secured. There was little chance that altogether new negotiations could produce a more favorable treaty. Indeed, if
internal upheavals further weakened France, Britain might be even more
demanding. Randolph then put forward an argument long employed by
the Federalists and repudiated by Washington, who had stated that the
cure would be worse than the disease. Opening the Mississippi to the
British, Randolph said, would make it to their interest to help the United
States get Spain to open the river's mouth. The forts would come to the
United States, even if after a short delay. And if he refused to ratify,
Washington would expose the twenty senators who had voted for the
treaty "to a general assault," while weakening their allegiance to the gov-
ernment. This would be a victory for the minority in the Senate and the

majority in the House, who would assume that the President was now their own and would never be satisfied if they could not continue to dictate to him.[33]

On July 7, Washington had received shocking news: British cruisers were again seizing American grain ships bound for France.[34] The action of the British government, which came to be known as "the Provision Order," could, it is true, be considered justified under the treaty's loose definition of contraband. Yet such behavior, initiated even before the treaty had been ratified, frighteningly presaged that the British, far from intending to interpret the document in a friendly and accommodating manner, would push it to the furthest extremes.[*]

The Provision Order, having been unknown when the Senate had acted, added to the situation a vitally important new element, dispelling whatever dreams the President may yet have cherished that he could duck behind the Senate's consent.

---

[*] The British had been impelled by the fact that the issue of who would get the American provisions was a very grave one. The British were frightened by the failure of their winter wheat crop, while actual famine was stalking in France.

22

Tempest Strikes

ALTHOUGH he still discussed his own hesitations and plans only with Randolph, Washington now invited opinions on what stand the executive should take. Three of the four Cabinet ministers, Pickering, Wolcott, and Bradford, urged that Washington at once ratify the Jay Treaty in accordance with the Senate recommendation, but add a memorandum stating that, in the President's opinion, the terms of the treaty did not justify the Provision Order. Hamilton urged that Washington ratify at once, but instruct the American representative in London not to exchange ratifications until the Provision Order had been rescinded. The President accepted Randolph's advice, the least favorable to the British: Washington should hold off ratification until the Provision Order was actually withdrawn.[1] Washington had, indeed, become more dependent on his much younger (forty-one) friend and disciple than he had ever before been on any one man during his long career.

Randolph suggested that, as a first step, he himself call on the British minister. He would state that any doubts as to the President's sincerity in desiring harmony with England would be dispelled when the minister was informed that although several parts of the treaty were "by no means coincident with his wishes and expectations," the President had determined to ratify it, in the manner advised by the Senate, without again submitting it to that body after the necessary insertion of a new Article XII. However, the government had been informed that "vessels, even American vessels, laden with provisions for France, may be captured and dealt with as carrying a kind of qualified contraband. If this be not true, you can correct me.

[213]

"Upon the supposition of its truth, the President cannot persuade himself that he ought to ratify during the existence of this order. . . . The order being removed, he will ratify without delay or further scruple."

Washington approved Randolph's suggestion. The Secretary of State than called on Hammond, while the President waited nervously to hear the result. Randolph "returned to the President's room," and told Washington, "Mr. Hammond asked me if it would not be sufficient to remove the order out of the way; and, after ratification, to renew it? I replied, perhaps with some warmth, that this would be a mere shift, as the principle was the important thing. He then asked me if the President was irrevocably determined not to ratify if the Provision Order was not removed? I answered that I was not instructed upon that point."

Washington broke in to say that Randolph "might have informed Mr. Hammond that he would never ratify if the Provision Order was not removed out of the way."

At the President's next levee, Hammond took the Secretary of State aside and asked whether Washington "was irrevocably determined not to ratify the treaty during the existence of the Provision Order?" Randolph, deciding to leave the matter in suspense, avoided an answer.[2]

To Washington, Randolph argued that the existence of the Provision Order could be turned to American advantage. Discussion of the issue would permit a favorable clarification of Jay's vague definition of contraband. And this negotiation, coupled with the need to evolve a new Article XII, opened up the whole situation in a way that would make it possible to raise further issues. A memorial should be sent through Hammond* to the British government, in which the King would be "*invited:* (1) to provide by some clear distinction against the impressment of our citizens; (2) to reconsider the compensation of [for] the Negroes; (3) to cause the execution of the seventh article [reimbursement for illegal maritime captures] to be expedited and the expense thereof lessened; (4) to give instructions against the vexations of privateers."[3]

Washington empowered Randolph to prepare such a memorial with the necessary supporting documents. He himself was finding "the intense heat of the city" almost unbearable. For the first time in his long public career he decided at a time of crisis to go home for an extended stay. He hoped

---

* Since Jay had come home and Pinckney was still in Spain, the United States had no representative in London capable of carrying out negotiations.

The Powel coach. Washington often rode in this vehicle, which belonged to Eliza Powel and her husband. Having been made by the same Philadelphia coach builders, David and Francis Clark, the vehicle undoubtedly resembled Washington's own coach, which was painted white, and which the President tried unsuccessfully to sell to Mrs. Powel for her nephew.

Courtesy of the Mount Vernon Ladies' Association

to remain at Mount Vernon from mid-July until the end of September. After Randolph had got all the papers in order, the Secretary would journey to Mount Vernon for a final consultation.[4]

Washington was almost on the wing when Hamilton sent him a disruptive opinion: the executive could not agree to a revised Article XII without again going to the Senate for consent. Washington replied wearily, "As I shall be absent, and Mr. Randolph has before him the bringing of this business to a close, I wish you to write to him your ideas." Washington had already signed his name when he succumbed to a worry. The text of the treaty was just then circulating through the land. What would be the public reaction? Washington added a postscript: "Notwithstanding one great object of my visit is relaxation," he would be glad to hear directly from Hamilton concerning "the sentiments entertained of the treaty" or "any other interesting subject with which the mind of the public is occupied."[5]

On July 15, 1795, Jacob Hiltzheimer noted in his diary, "President Washington about eight o'clock this morning set out for Mount Vernon in a two-horse phaeton for one person, his family in a coach and four horses, and two servants on horseback leading his saddle horse." In his own diary, Washington noted that on the 16th at Elkton (where the British had once landed), "one of my horses was overcome with the heat." During the 17th, he "brought on the sick horse led." When he breakfasted at Baltimore on the 18th, the horse was clearly dying, but that was soon pushed to the back of his mind.

Just as he was stepping into the coach, he was "overtaken by an express" bearing dispatches "of an unusual and disagreeable nature." A mass meeting held in Boston had enumerated twenty objections to the Jay Treaty and requested the President to refuse to ratify it. This was disturbing because Boston was a Federalist, pro-British town. If the treaty were opposed there, where would it be approved?

Writing in haste before he set his carriage in motion, Washington asked Randolph to consult with the other members of the Cabinet on what answer to send back to Boston.[6]

For the remaining two days on the road, Washington asked everyone he met what they thought of the treaty. He discovered that "endeavors are not wanting to place it in all the odious points of view of which it is susceptible."[7]

Only after he had reached Mount Vernon on the 20th did it occur to Washington that it had been pointless to request that Randolph consult the other Cabinet ministers, since they were still ignorant of what he and Randolph had decided to do. He dashed off a letter to the Secretary of State: "In my hurry, I did not signify the propriety of letting those gentlemen know." Indeed, Randolph might, "on all fit occasions," state what had been decided, unless some new event had taken place which might change the decision.[8]

Washington's stay at Mount Vernon — oh, how he needed to relax! — was from the first a rack of anxiety. Bad news followed bad news, and Washington's strain was increased because he had allowed the Presidential staff to deteriorate to a point where he had to write out all his letters himself. Perhaps as a sop to keep the young man from resigning completely (as he wished to do) Washington had allowed his only secretary, Dandridge, to go off on an extended leave.[9]

Mass meetings all over the land were not only denouncing the treaty but engaging in physical violence. When Hamilton tried to address a meeting in New York (where Jay had so recently been elected governor) he was driven off the platform with a shower of stones,° after which the mob joined with a group of French sailors to march under a French flag to Jay's house, on the steps of which they burned the treaty. In Philadelphia a mass meeting, addressed by leading members of Pennsylvania's Republican government, adopted an inflammatory resolution. Then the mob carried the treaty, ignominiously impaled on a pole, to the door of the French minister's residence. Adet had the discretion not to respond, but the mob moved on to the residence of the British minister, where the windows were broken with stones and the treaty burned on the doorstep. Other copies were burned in front of the houses of the British consul and the conservative Senator William Bingham. And so it went, with varying particulars, from city to city.

Foreseeing a crisis "the greatest in its consequences which had occurred under this government," Randolph wanted to hurry for consultation to Mount Vernon.[11] Washington replied that it would be better that he himself come, if necessary, to Philadelphia, which was the nexus of information. "Party disputes," he complained, "are now carried to the length and truth is so enveloped in mist and false representation, that it is

---

° A witty Federalist remarked that the mob had "tried to knock out Hamilton's brains to reduce him to equality with themselves."[10]

extremely difficult to know through what channel to seek it. This difficulty to one who is of no party and whose sole wish is to pursue with undeviating steps a path which leads this country to respectability, wealth, and happiness, is exceedingly to be lamented. But such (for wise purposes it is presumed) is the turbulence of human passions in party disputes, when victory more than truth is the palm contended for."[12]

To Hamilton, Washington commented, "The string which is most played on, because it strikes with the most force the popular ear, is the violation, as they term it, of our engagements with France; or, in other words, the predilection shown by that instrument [the Jay Treaty] to Great Britain at the expense of the French nation." How exactly Washington had hit the nail on the head is revealed by Jefferson's report to Monroe, which jubilantly stated that the treaty "has, in my opinion, completely demolished the monarchical party here." Jefferson explained that "those who understand the particular articles of it, condemn these articles. Those who do not understand them minutely, condemn it as wearing a hostile face to France. The last is the most numerous class, comprehending the whole body of the people."[13]

That the United States had treaties with France but none with Britain, had encouraged the view that, even if she labored to keep out of the war, the nation remained in the French orbit. But now there loomed a treaty with Britain. It even accepted maritime practices that Secretary of State Jefferson had (although he had been unable to do anything about it) protested. There was a wide outcry that a wickedly aristocratic government had reversed American foreign policy from pro-French to pro-British. Even today, historians pursue this line. Thus, a neo-Federalist writer calls the Jay Treaty America's second Declaration of Independence — this time from France—while a neo-Jeffersonian finds the treaty a crushing defeat for the French-oriented policy, which he assumes the United States had, under Jefferson's leadership, previously pursued.[14]

Washington himself saw no alteration in the overall policy of the administration. That policy, he stated, had been laid down once and for all by the Neutrality Proclamation.[15] It steadfastly pursued America's determination to stay out of the war no matter what effect her neutrality would have on the fortunes of the European belligerents. Although the old French alliance had never been formally denounced, he assumed that it had become obsolete and been superseded, a conclusion to which he was encouraged by the French themselves, who had violated the treaty when it seemed to their advantage.* And in any case, the acceptance of the *Consolat de Mar,* which most enraged the pro-French partisans, changed nothing practical: it was merely giving countenance to what was bound to exist anyway.

However, Washington was worried lest the American mass meetings encourage the French government to conclude "that the treaty is calculated to favor Great Britain at their expense." In any case, the French would certainly take what advantage they could of American disunion. Washington could not guess to what lengths the French would go,† but as the citizens of the United States adopted more and more angry resolutions that might encourage active French intervention, Washington wrote, "I have never, since I have been in the administration of the government, seen a crisis which, in my judgment, has been so pregnant of interesting events; nor one from which more is to be apprehended."[18]

The situation was made all the more frightening by the fact that the support the government usually could count on from the mercantile community was eroding. Washington complained to Hamilton that many men "well enough affected to the government, are of opinion that to have had *no* commercial treaty would have been better," inasmuch as the pressure of economics — England needed America's foodstuffs and America was the best market for British manufactures — would "have forced or led to a more adequate intercourse between the two nations without any of those shackles which the treaty has imposed." It was also reasonable to object "that in the settlement of *old* disputes a proper regard to reciprocal justice does not appear." However, reasonable objection was being left far behind. "At present the cry against the treaty is like that against a mad dog; and everyone, in a manner, seems engaged in running it down."[19]

Washington kept insisting that he would not change the decisions he had reached "unless circumstances more imperious than have yet come to my knowledge compel it." But he was beginning to wonder whether he had not counted too heavily on Randolph's wisdom. He wrote his intimate

---

* The conception that free ships made free goods had been written into the French treaty, but when the British refused to honor that conception, the French, unwilling to allow the enemy an advantage, had ordered their cruisers also to apply the *Consolat de Mar,* and remove British goods from American bottoms. On learning of the Jay negotiation, they had returned to the original conception, obviously in the hope that the Americans would somehow get the British to agree to it.[16]

† Adet, having tactfully expressed "in an amicable manner" his "uneasiness" over the treaty, had hired a fast ship to carry the text to France. Official French reaction could not develop until the ship landed.[17]

adviser that the memorial which would go to England and, of course, be published in the United States was so crucial "as not only to require great individual consideration but a solemn, conjunct revision." Instead of having Randolph come to him, he would go to Philadelphia, so that the entire Cabinet could be consulted.[20]

This resolution was depressing — "to leave home as soon will be inconvenient; a month hence would be otherwise" — and Washington soon concluded that he had better not set out until he heard that Randolph was not already on the road to Mount Vernon. Perhaps he need not go after all, if Randolph could, in conference with the other "confidential officers with you" (this phrase, of course, excluded Hamilton), achieve unanimous decisions. If they disagreed or felt they needed him, he would be under way in a flash.[21]

On the last day of July, a servant returned to Mount Vernon from the post office at Alexandria with the usual mail pouch. On opening it, Washington was taken aback to find there, returned by mistake, the last batch of letters he had written the government. He instantly wrote a new letter to Randolph, repeating that he would come the instant he was called. In the most emphatic terms, he repeated his dismay and sense of impending doom. "This government, in relation to France and England may be compared to a ship between the rocks of Scylla and Charybdis. If the treaty is ratified, the partisans of the French (or rather of war and confusion) will excite them to hostile measures or at least unfriendly sentiments; if it is not, there is no foreseeing *all* the consequences which may follow as respects G.B. [Great Britain]."[22]

Before Washington could get his letter off, a great and prophetic storm struck Virginia. Heavy rains not only further depressed Washington by flattening his crops and carrying topsoil from his fields where it always tended to go — into the Potomac — but, by washing away bridges, isolated from the rest of the world his part of Virginia. His servants battered their way daily to Alexandria, but returned to report that no post had been received there. Finally, after six days during which the pouch had come back empty, Washington saw, with eagerness and anxiety, that it bulged.[23]

There were two letters from the Cabinet, one clear, the other puzzling and disturbing. Randolph wrote that Hammond had been recalled to England: since time could be saved by sending the completed papers with him, Washington should come to Philadelphia at once. Pickering repeated the information about Hammond and then continued darkly, "For a *special reason* which can be communicated to you only in person, I entreat therefore that you will return." Washington should in the meantime "decide on no important political measure. . . . Mr. Wolcott and I (Mr. Bradford concurring) waited on Mr. Randolph and urged his writing to request your return. He wrote in our presence. . . . This letter is for your own eye alone."[24]

Washington had been taking advantage of the end of the storm to inspect the fields at his Dogue Run plantation and had come to various conclusions he intended to communicate to his overseer. "The suddenness of my departure" made him forget to do so. However, even the odor of heightened crisis did not prevent him from pausing at Alexandria for a meeting concerning that darling project of his earlier years, the Potomac Canal. He was further slowed by the fact that the storm had created even more damage in Maryland than in his part of Virginia: "The roads are miserably torn up, and the mills, dams, bridges, etc., almost universally carried away." He was, in all, six days on the road, arriving in Philadelphia on August 11, in time for dinner.[25]

Pickering recalled that, as he was finishing his own dinner, a servant appeared saying that Washington "desired to see me. . . . I hastened to the President's house where I found him at the table: and Randolph — cheerful and apparently in good spirits — also at the table. Very soon, after taking a glass of wine, the President rose, giving me a wink. I rose and followed him into another room.

" 'What,' said he, 'is the cause of your writing me such a letter?'

" 'That man,' said I, 'in the other room' — pointing towards the room in which we had left Randolph — 'is a traitor.' "[26]

23

The Cry of Treason

PICKERING, Wolcott, and Bradford had all known, when given their appointments, that Washington was in the habit of thrashing out executive decisions with his Cabinet. They believed that their hands had been placed on the tiller of state. But, with the retirement of Hamilton and Knox, Washington changed his procedure. The new Cabinet ministers were not consulted; even the arrival of Jay's treaty did not induce him to call them in. On the contrary, he kept them completely ignorant of what the document contained. When the time came to communicate the text to the Senate, Washington did not communicate it to them. They were placed in the humiliating position of having to beg a peep from some Federalist senator.

After the Senate had advised and the treaty been published, when the President would have to act, surely they would be consulted. Not so! Washington departed for what was intended to be a long stay at Mount Vernon without giving them a hint of his intentions.

This was all the more infuriating because from the first Randolph had been informed and was in almost daily contact with the President. The graceful Virginian had a gift for inspiring in fellow Cabinet ministers disdain. For one thing, he was perpetually appealing to his colleagues for loans: he even tried to borrow two hundred dollars from that self-righteous New Englander, Pickering. For another, he seemed to be facile, without personal convictions, a lightweight. When someone argued with him, he was likely to agree in his mellifluous southern voice. But a minute later you would hear from the opposite side of the room that same voice agreeing with an opposite opinion. This had (as Randolph sometimes querulously admitted) the reverse effect from what he intended. Instead of persuading everyone that he was sympathetic to their points of view, he inspired everyone with suspicion.[1] Both Jefferson (who referred to him as "a mere chameleon") and Hamilton hated him.

But the endless smiler *did* have Washington's ear. Although he sometimes let drop a hint that the President would ratify the treaty, Pickering, Wolcott, and Bradford, who suspected him of pro-French leanings, believed that he was urging Washington to repudiate the treaty in order to foment a war with England that would throw the United States into the hands of his fellow Jacobins.[2]

How deep were the Federalists' worries concerning the internal state of the nation was revealed when Hamilton wrote Wolcott from New York City on July 28, "Our Jacobins meditate serious mischief to certain individuals." The militia were so politically unsound that they could not be relied upon. Would Wolcott arrange with Pickering (as he did) to have some federal troops available?[3]

Also on July 28 Wolcott confided to Hamilton, "Everything is conducted in a mysterious and strange manner by a certain character here." Then, becoming himself mysterious, Wolcott stated, "Some curious facts . . . have recently come to my knowledge. I cannot but suspect foul play by persons not generally suspected."[4]

When Wolcott wrote Hamilton two days later, he had been informed concerning Washington's and Randolph's intentions. "What," he asked, "must the British government think of the United States, when they find the treaty clogged with one condition by the Senate, with another by the President, no answer given in a precise form after forty days, no minister in that country to take up negotiations proposed by ourselves, the country rising into a flame, their minister's house insulted by a mob, their flag dragged through the streets as in Charleston and burnt before the doors of their consul, a driveler and a fool [Rutledge] appointed chief justice? Can they believe that we desire peace? I shall take immediate measures with two of my colleagues this very day. They are firm and honest men. We will, if possible, to use a French phrase, 'Save our country.' You must not think *we* have been to blame for the delay. We have constantly been amused by R[andolph] who has said that the President was determined to ratify. . . . Feel no concern, however, for I see a clue which will conduct us through every labyrinth except that of war. On that point, we must take our chance. It would be well if you or Mr. King or Governor Jay could be here some time next week, provided too much speculation would not be excited."[5]

[223]

The drama had begun in mid-ocean when the English frigate *Cerebus* was overhauled by the French packet *Jean Bart*. There was a splash as the French threw something overboard; another splash as an English sailor dived: and then a dripping packet of papers was handed to the British captain. The recovered dispatches, which found their way to British Foreign Minister Grenville, included a letter, dated October 31, 1794, to his government from French Minister to the United States Fauchet. In forwarding the letter to his own minister in Philadelphia, Grenville commented that its disclosure "to well disposed persons in America may possibly be useful to the King's service."[6]

On Sunday, July 26, Hammond invited Wolcott to dine. He led Wolcott into a private room and read out loud an English translation of the dispatch which, so Wolcott noted, "could not fail to establish a belief that something highly improper had been proposed by Mr. Randolph. . . . I considered the information as highly interesting. . . . I remarked that a discovery of such magnitude could not be permitted to remain with me," but he would have to be "put in possession of the document necessary to support my allegations."

Hammond demurred, and it was two days before Wolcott got the document. He showed it to Pickering, who agreed that, "considering the absence of the President, the letter ought to be shown to the Attorney General as soon as possible." The next day, Wolcott and Pickering carried the evidence to Bradford, who was in the country. "It was agreed that a letter should be written to the President requesting him to return to Philadelphia."[7]

"That man in the other room," said Pickering, "is a traitor."

Washington's reaction is unrecorded. Pickering spent two or three minutes summarizing the situation, and then, so he remembered,[*] handed Washington a copy of the dispatch. The President said, "Let us return to the other room to prevent any suspicion of the cause of our withdrawing."[9]

It may be doubted that the occasion proceeded in its former cheerful vein. Eventually, the guests went home and Washington was left alone with the fateful documents. Once before, he had faced a similar crisis. He had been handed papers which demonstrated the treason of a general

---

[*] Like most reminiscences written in old age, Pickering's account gives the author the only spotlight. Yet Wolcott was clearly also present. There is contemporary evidence that it was he who handed Washington the dispatch.[8]

whom he had up till that moment trusted and greatly admired. The revelation of Benedict Arnold's treason had been among the blackest moments of his life. Then he had been surrounded with friends; Lafayette had been at his side, Hamilton, Knox, and many another trusted aide. Now, except for servants, he was alone in the Presidential Mansion. Mrs. Washington and the children were at Mount Vernon. Dandridge had not returned. He had no staff. His only intimate colleague was the man accused. The evening light waned on the dread papers. Who knows how long he hesitated before he unfolded the sheets and began to read? It would be a lengthy task, as there were twenty-nine quarto pages.[10]

The dispatch had, it became instantly clear, been written at the time of the Whiskey Rebellion. In the opening paragraph, Fauchet stated that he would report the "secret" views of the United States government. Then came a disturbing sentence: "The precious confessions of Mr. Randolph alone throw a satisfactory light upon everything that comes to pass."[11] Washington read on with a constricted heart. As he turned page after page, he came on nothing more "secret" than an account of American politics written from the conventional Republican angle. Yet it was not reassuring that these sentiments were attributed to the adviser he considered nonpartisan.

Page after page, and then Washington reached the fourteenth of the numbered sections. Here Fauchet expressed a suspicion that the government had "hastened" the Whiskey Rebellion "in order to make an advantageous diversion and lay the more general storm which it saw rising. Am I not authorized in forming this conjecture from the conversation which the Secretary of State had with me and Le Blanc alone, an account of which you had in my dispatch number three?"[12] Washington undoubtedly riffled through the papers to see if dispatch number three was there. He could find no part of it.

The next section (fifteen) stated that Hamilton was responsible for the military march against the whiskey rebels, while the previous sending of commissioners (an act of which Washington was proud) was "due to the influence of Mr. Randolph over the mind of the President."[13]

Section sixteen proved to contain what Washington had undoubtedly been told by Pickering he would find. The French minister explained to his government that the Democratic Society of Philadelphia, "which in its turn influenced those of other states," was "balancing" whether to support the march or oppose it. The Philadelphia Society was controlled by men often "unknown to me, all having without doubt Randolph at their

[225]

head." While the government was still undecided on what measures to take, "Mr. Randolph came to me with an air of great eagerness and made to me the overtures of which I have given you an account in my number six." Fauchet's sixth dispatch was not present, but the paper Washington was reading continued, "Thus, with some thousands of dollars the republic would have decided on civil war or on peace! Thus the consciences of the pretended patriots of America have already their prices." But the French republic was too noble to sink to bribery, and so the Democratic Societies emitted resolutions supporting the executive's army.[14]

The remaining pages were anticlimactic, containing nothing but the usual anti-government propaganda.

That was the record in its entirety. What did it prove?

Washington's mind strained painfully, trying to trace through darkness an all-important path. It was obvious that Randolph had been indiscreet to a foreign diplomat. How damagingly was not clear since dispatch number three was missing. Yet Washington (who did not know that Hamilton and Jefferson and Wolcott were given to similar or worse indiscretions)* must have found the simple fact enraging and worrisome. Did Randolph really express such strongly pro-republican and pro-French sentiments as Fauchet attributed to him? The proud old man could not have been pleased to learn that Randolph took credit for sending the peace mission over the mountains, and boasted of his "influence . . . over the mind of the President." But the real crux was the implication that Randolph had sought a French bribe.

Of course, Washington lacked dispatch six, which would have made clear what actually had taken place. However, the fact that Randolph was always scrounging for money gave suspicion ominous support. Randolph had recently written Washington a complaint that only by abstaining from company and giving up his carriage could he live on his salary as Secretary of State.[15] True, the French dispatch had said that the bribe had been refused. But the dispatch was more than a year old. What was the situation now?

If Randolph were in pay of the French that might explain matters otherwise hardly explicable. While still at Mount Vernon, Washington had wondered whether the spark kindled in the Boston meeting had spread so extensively as the result of a preconceived plan. Since Washington had

---

* Supposing the chances of privateering had carried to the French and through them to Washington in an intelligible form some of Hammond's dispatches which revealed Hamilton undermining governmental policy?

reached Philadelphia, Pickering and Wolcott had undoubtedly not omitted to inform him of rumors afloat there that Randolph was "at the bottom of the protest meetings," the leader of "a conspiracy . . . to destroy the popularity of the President."° Was the subversive mastermind in fact Washington's greatest intimate, clinking French gold?[16]

Such thoughts wounded Washington's personal emotions. Of all the President's colleagues, Randolph had always been the most effusive of affection, writing such phrases as "the fame of him who has long been my patron is more dear to me than any connection with any other man."[17] Washington had taken pleasure in these assurances, so different from the mounting hostility he had experienced in Madison and Jefferson, the impersonal if warm good will of Hamilton. He reciprocated Randolph's affections. He had known Randolph ever since his aide had been a boy. After Jefferson and Hamilton had left him, he had made Randolph his right hand. Had his trust been betrayed? Had he allowed himself to be hoodwinked? Washington had prided himself on his ability to judge men, and had always been "mortified" if proved wrong.[18] Had his faith in Randolph been a sign of what he so feared, a decline of his powers? Had his dependence been a sign? Had Randolph betrayed that faith and dependence?

As his thoughts grew more desperate, more bitter, Washington could remind himself that Randolph had not been proved guilty of anything. He had admonished himself at Mount Vernon: "To be wise and temperate as well as firm, the crisis most eminently calls for."[19] Indeed, he had never in his career needed more than he did that night to be wise and temperate and firm.

During the Revolution, Washington had often been accused of indecision. He had procrastinated because the pros and cons he was massing on the opposite plates of a mental scale had not yet tipped the beam decisively. In the current crisis, he had agreed with Randolph's plan and had instructed the Secretary of State to prepare the necessary papers. However, he had not hurried the Secretary of State. It may well have been that he had hoped that in the quiet of Mount Vernon things would become clearer to him. He was to have another conference with Randolph before any actual action was taken.

It seemed to him now that Randolph had encouraged the delay. He

---

° Randolph was to complain of these rumors, which he insisted were concocted by his enemies. Wolcott was to claim that, concerning one of the remonstrances sent to the President, he had definite proof that it had been instigated by Randolph.

had, when his ministers had been assembled earlier that evening, expressed surprise that the memorial to the British government had not been prepared and agreed to. He had "supposed that everything of this sort had been settled." Randolph had shrugged the matter off: preparation had been held up because Pickering had raised objections. To this Pickering had assented, saying that he objected to the plan because it would involve a "ruinous" postponement in the ratification of the treaty.[20] But should not Randolph have straightened out or reported the disagreement?*

And was not Pickering right that the delay would prove "ruinous"? Washington had gone to a great length of secrecy to avoid what he recognized might be shattering controversy during the three months before the Senate ruled on the treaty. But he had so hoped that the Senate decision would, as a solid and responsible act, dampen argument that he had been surprised and shocked when the publication of the treaty had whipped up a greater storm than had previously raged during his entire administration. The civil hurricane might well tear the nation apart, driving the shattered hulk onto the reefs of war. Yet the plan he had agreed to with Randolph postponed indefinitely any truly final act that could still the storm. A memorial would have to cross the ocean to London; the stipulations would need to be decided on by the British government (which was always dilatory on American matters); the result would have to come back across the ocean, be considered in the United States, and then perhaps returned again as unsatisfactory. Since at least one winter would intervene, closing the Atlantic, the matter could not be solved in less than a year.

Was this what Randolph wanted? If he were actually conspiring as charged to import the French Revolution into the United States, he might well be seeking time for the protest to reach such inextinguishable proportions that it would become impossible to ratify the treaty if the British proved amenable to Washington's objections, impossible to continue the negotiations if they did not. And in Washington's opinion, the alternatives were "negotiation or war."[22]

---

* It seems clear that Randolph for whatever reason — it could have been unwillingness to abandon his unique position of power — had both been slow in informing his fellow ministers and lied concerning the matter to Washington. On July 25, he wrote the President that, having "within the hour" received instructions to that effect, "I had communicated to the gentlemen fully your determination with respect to the ratification." However, Wolcott's correspondence with Hamilton demonstrates that three days later he was still uninformed. He received the information at some time between the 28th and the 30th.[21]

A particularly irritating aspect of the situation was that Washington had been outflanked by the pro-British interest. He by no means controlled the incriminating dispatch; it was in the hands of the British minister and of Federalist leaders. If Washington went along with Randolph's plan, the dispatch could be published — if not by the Federalists, by the British — with the statement that Washington had seen it and was nonetheless following the advice of an adviser whom he now had reason to suspect of being in the pay of France.

The decision Washington reached during the anguished dark hours, pacing his room by candlelight or turning restlessly in his bed, would have been a most unhappy one even in unemotional daylight. He realized (for he had pointed out the danger in conversations with Randolph)[23] that he was in danger of ending forever in the popular mind the position of being above party that he had so labored to occupy. Yet he felt he had to stop the uncertainty. If he faced the nation with a firm and irrevocable act, "the paroxysm of the fever" might well abate. There would be no more point in mass meetings aimed at influencing the government, and the prestige Washington had for so long hoarded might lead the thoughts of the people in a single, unequivocal direction.*[24]

Since Washington could no longer temporize, there was only one way he could go. War with England would be infinitely more dangerous than war with France. In the loneliness of the dark and silent house, he concluded that he would have to follow the advice of the Senate exactly as given. Making separately his protest against the Provision Order, not trying to reopen negotiations on other matters than Article XII, he would ratify the Jay Treaty.

The decision dictated a cruel sequel in relation to Randolph. To have the quieting effect for which Washington hoped, the ratification would have to be carried through as smoothly and definitely as possible. If the Secretary of State believed the situation still normal, he would certainly obey orders, execute, however reluctantly, his official functions in the ratification of a treaty. However, if Randolph knew he was suspected of treason, he might well, whether guilty or not guilty, explode into some action which would introduce confusion and controversy and doubt into the

---

* Republican orators were using Washington's prestige to stir up opposition by intoning that the old patriot would save the future of mankind by getting rid of the treaty.[25]

very act of palliation. Washington would have to play a hypocrite's part in daily relationship with the man he still loved. Only after the treaty had been signed and was on its way across the ocean could Washington confront Randolph with the evidence and try to determine whether his dear friend was in truth guilty.

24

Oh, What a Fall

THE next morning, August 12, 1795, the Cabinet met in Washington's rooms. Randolph brought the memorandum he had drawn for Hammond incorporating the strategy that Washington had agreed on. He assumed that the purpose of the meeting was to push the other Secretaries into line and he was therefore surprised when Washington reopened the whole question of how the executive should act.

Pickering was instantly on his feet, asserting — it seemed to Randolph "intemperately". — that efforts to delay the treaty represented a *"detestable and nefarious conspiracy."* The treaty, he argued, should be ratified at once in the form that the Senate had advised, and with this Wolcott agreed.

Randolph then argued that if the treaty were ratified while the Provision Order remained in force, the United States would abandon a position she had long held — and had assured France she would continue to hold — in relation to contraband. He told Washington, "You would run the hazard of a war with France by combining to starve" her. As an obvious thrust against Pickering and Wolcott, he explained that stirring up French discontents was "the only possible chance remaining to the British partisans of throwing us into the arms of Great Britain." As he talked with his usual fluency, Randolph noted a lack of response in Washington's expression which made him conclude, "to my unutterable astonishment," that Washington was receding from his often expressed *"determination."*

Washington listened to some more argument back and forth, during which Bradford came in on the side of Pickering, and then brought the discussion to a close by announcing, "I will ratify the treaty."

The President now gave orders. Hammond should immediately be notified that Washington was ready to sign. A new memorial should be prepared for Hammond to carry to London. It would repeat the Senate's refusal of Article XII but reduce the stipulation that the Provision Order be rescinded to a statement that the President did not agree with the interpretation of the treaty on which the order was based.* The American agent in London should be prepared to proceed at once with the exchange of ratifications. A suitable form of ratification should be drafted and duly executed.[1]

The next morning, Randolph called on Washington to persuade him back to the old course. In order to demonstrate that the government had committed itself to France not to accept the Provision Order, he produced three dispatches that he had sent to Monroe while Washington was at Mount Vernon. Washington expressed a desire to keep them for more careful study, and, after Randolph's departure, prepared in his own hand an abstract of the documents. Most puzzling was a long attack on Fauchet as a desperate schemer against the policies of the government, who, in his efforts to embroil the United States with France, was trying insidiously "to acquire information from members of the executive to whom he resorted. I was not one of them." Freeman's successors, Carroll and Ashworth, deduce that this passage encouraged Washington's suspicions of Randolph. Was he trying to cover his own tracks by excoriating Fauchet and implying that any leakage of executive information came not from him but from other officials? The whole passage was given a hallucinatory tone by the obvious fact that all members of the executive except Randolph were surely too anti-French to be pumped by Fauchet.[2]

Preparation of the new papers, signing them and having them countersigned by Randolph, involved daily and sometimes twice daily conferences between the President and the Secretary of State. Washington gave no hint that all was not well: indeed, he seemed more appreciative and affectionate than usual. During those six days, he had Randolph twice for dinner, seating him at the place of honor, and once he violated his usual practice by not summoning the minister to his office, but himself carrying papers to his old friend's house. After the denouement, Randolph de-

---

* This method proved as effective as a refusal otherwise to ratify the treaty could have been. The British withdrew the Provision Order with the passing of the crisis that had inspired it, and eventually so completely abandoned the interpretation of the treaty on which the order was grounded that American shippers were officially reimbursed for their losses.

scribed Washington's warmth as shameful hypocrisy, but a different explanation is plausible.[3]

Washington was not convinced that Randolph was guilty. While overriding responsibilities prevented him from seeking the truth, his heart went out to his old friend, the emotion made all the more poignant by the possibility of disaster.

By August 18, Hammond had departed with the memorial and the treaty had been signed. The time had come to face the possible treason. But how? Since the milder Bradford had come down with what was to prove a fatal illness, Washington had no advisers he could turn to except Wolcott and Pickering. As he consulted them, it became more clear than ever that they did not share his own affection for the accused.

Washington had at his back no secret service; there was no available way to get at Randolph's financial records; the evidence had not mentioned by name any accomplices to be checked on. As for the known organizers of the meetings Randolph was said to have suborned, queries addressed to them might not be truthfully answered and would surely stir up hornets' nests. The French minister could, of course, be asked for the two missing dispatches, but Washington agreed with Wolcott that, if a conspiracy actually existed, the minister would not be such a fool as to hand over undoctored papers.[4]

The best that Washington could envision was to reach a conclusion by studying Randolph's behavior. He kept his own eyes open as the two men conferred from day to day. In retrospect, Randolph decided that the President, with Pickering and Wolcott, "became sentinels on all my words, all my gestures."[5] But Washington saw as his major expedient a confrontation. The incriminating document would be sprung on Randolph without any prior warning. Whether he was guilty or innocent would be revealed by how he reacted.

Pickering and Wolcott had to be present, not only to add their judgments to Washington's own, but to satisfy these two officers of the government who possessed the evidence and had made the charges. Wolcott, coming all over bashful, expressed "my earnest wish to be excused," but Washington insisted on his attendance. Pickering, ever tougher than Wolcott, opposed Washington's scheme. Why bother? Randolph was obviously guilty. Fire him out of hand! To this Washington would not agree, but in setting up the confrontation, he showed no consideration for Randolph's feelings. It may, indeed, have been his conscious intention to exacerbate those feelings in order to break through any disguise with which the Secretary of State might attempt to mask the true situation. Washington may have comforted himself with the thought that the more grueling the test, the more complete would be the exoneration if his old friend and confidant survived it.[6]

The form Washington set up resembled a court-martial, although Randolph's ordeal would differ in that he would receive no prenotification of the charge or even of the fact that he was going to be judged. The court would consist of his peers: the President and Randolph's fellow Secretaries. After being interrogated, the accused would wait outside while the judges conferred. He would then be called back for further questioning or a verdict.

Randolph remembered that on August 19, he set out as usual for the President's at nine in the morning. He was intercepted by Washington's steward, who asked him to postpone his visit until half-past ten. Randolph assumed that Washington was occupied with the southern mail or intended to ride out, but, having a short question involving the day's business, he asked the steward whether Washington "was then occupied with any particular person." The steward replied that "the President was every moment expecting some gentlemen."

The gentlemen were Wolcott and Pickering. As Randolph finally came in, his mobile face expressed amazement that Washington should be found in discussion, when he was not present, with the other Secretaries whom he believed Washington regarded "as but successors in *form* to the deliberative talents of their predecessors." He opened his mouth to explain the misinformation which had made him late for the conference, but was stopped by "the great formality" with which Washington "rose from his chair." He noticed that "Wolcott and Pickering were also marked in their efforts to a like formality."

Washington attempted some easy small talk with Randolph but it sounded hollow. Abandoning the effort, he put his hand in his pocket and pulled out the packet of papers. "Mr. Randolph! here is a letter which I desire you to read, and make such explanations as you choose."

Washington gave Randolph, who was fluent in French, the original dispatch. As the accused read the document through — it must have taken more than half an hour — the room was in complete silence. Pickering remembered that Washington had "desired us to watch Randolph's countenance while he perused it. The President fixed his own eye upon him, and I never . . . saw it look so animated." Finally, Randolph looked up and said that he assumed that he had been reading a captured dispatch.

Washington nodded his head.

After stating that this had all come as a surprise to him; that he was not prepared as others at the interview seemed to be; that he noted the absence of two essential documents; that he could not, on the spur of the moment, remember the circumstances with any clarity, Randolph added that he could "rely only on two principles which were established in my mind: the first that, according to my sincere belief, I never made an improper communication to Mr. Fauchet; the second, that no money was ever received by me from him, nor any overture made to him by me for that purpose. . . . However, I had some recollections of Fauchet having told me of machinations against the French Republic, Governor Clinton, and myself." He thought it not improbable that the reference to French funds "might be, in some manner, connected with that business, and might relate to the obtaining of intelligence."

According to Pickering, Randolph then said, "If I may be permitted to retain this letter a short time, I shall be able to explain, in a satisfactory manner, everything in it which has reference to me."

"Very well," said Washington, "retain it."

Randolph offered to "throw my ideas on paper," to which the President again agreed. Then Washington asked Wolcott and Pickering if they had any questions.

Pickering had none. Wolcott wanted more specifics on the machinations Fauchet was said to have mentioned. Having struggled with his memory, Randolph finally said that he had told Washington about an ominous meeting held in New York by Hammond and others. He appealed "to the President's memory for communications which I had made to him on this subject."

Washington replied (as Randolph remembered, "with some warmth") that he would not conceal anything which he recollected. But he remembered nothing.

The President was then called out of the room on an irrelevant matter. When he returned, he desired Randolph "to step into another room, while he should converse with Messrs. Wolcott and Pickering upon what I had said."

If Washington followed his usual practice, he kept his own council while he sought the opinion of his subordinates. Wolcott thought that the accused had exhibited "embarrassment" at one moment in reading the document and that one of his smiles had been forced; that his explanation of the bribery passage had been a "foolish story that could make no impression"; but the Secretary of the Treasury had to admit that, for the most part, Randolph had read Fauchet's letter "with composure." Pickering's memory of this conference was that all had agreed that Randolph had exhibited no guilty emotion.

As Washington prepared to call Randolph back, he was undoubtedly congratulating himself that his beloved friend and close coadjutor had come through the ordeal so well. When Randolph had time to recollect and put his recollections in writing, he would probably clear himself completely.

But the Randolph who came back through the door was a very different man from the one who had gone out. His face had lost the calm and reassuring look of innocence. His features were working with emotion.

Washington took no advantage of Randolph's disarray by trying to probe further. He merely said that, as Randolph wished to put his remarks on paper, he desired that the Secretary would do so.

Randolph answered confusedly that yes, he would prepare a written statement. However, he could not expect to remember much detail. He had, in fact, no distinct conception of what the missing third and sixth dispatches might contain, "except that it seemed from the inference" in the document he had read "as if I had encouraged the insurrection."

Washington asked how soon Randolph could finish his written reply.

Randolph answered, "As soon as possible." Then, he shouted "that I could not continue in the office one second after such treatment." He ran from the room, down the stairs, and out of the Presidential Mansion.[7]

Washington stared after his departing friend in amazement and then in horror.[8] According to the principles by which Randolph's ordeal had been planned, he had revealed guilt. Surely Wolcott and Pickering, who had in the early part of the interview been frustrated, did not lose the opportunity to press this conclusion home. Washington must have listened to their insistent voices in dismay, an old man whose clear judgment of his fellow men seemed to have been so desperately disproved, a man with warm emotions whose intimate friend seemed to have demonstrated himself a traitor.

After making as sure as they could that the President would not change his conclusion, Wolcott and Pickering departed, rejoicing. If Washington behaved as he had done after the discovery of Arnold's treason, he sat huddled in a dejected stupor. After a long time, there were footsteps and a servant brought him a letter. It was in Randolph's familiar hand.

25

War with an Old Friend

THE letter Washington received from Randolph denied all guilt. Then his old friend launched into reproaches. Washington had consulted "*others* . . . before the slightest intimation to me. . . . I was desired to retire into another room until you could converse with them upon what I had said. . . . Your confidence in me, sir, has been unlimited, and I can truly affirm unabused. My sensations then cannot be concealed when I find that confidence so immediately withdrawn without a word or distant hint being previously dropped to me!"

Having reaffirmed his resignation, Randolph added that Washington should not therefore conclude "that I mean to relinquish the inquiry. No, sir, far from it!" Although Fauchet had been recalled by his government, Randolph believed that he had not yet left the country. Randolph intended to secure from Fauchet the texts of the missing dispatches. He hoped that, until he had done so, Washington would, "as one piece of justice due me," keep the suspicion under which he suffered "in secrecy under your injunction."[1] The request was a large one.

Before the confrontation which had ended with such bitter drama, Washington had foreseen that, in order to protect the government, the accusing dispatch might well have to be published. "If he is guilty of what is charged," Washington wrote *then*, "he merits *no* favor." And if explanation were not given, "*he* and his friends" would surely use his separation from the government to reinforce their charge that the administration was pro-British.[2]

But now Washington did not have the heart to proceed as policy indicated. He replied, "Whilst you are in pursuit of means to remove the strong suspicions arising from this [Fauchet's] letter," he would enjoin secrecy unless something happened which would make an explanation absolutely necessary. But Washington did not accompany this promise with any expression of friendship; any hope that Randolph would keep his resignation in abeyance; any good wishes for the stricken minister's pilgrimage in search of exonerating evidence. Not knowing with what salutation to conclude this letter, he concluded it with none, merely signing his name: "George Washington."[3]

After the first shock was over, Washington sent Randolph warm wishes for his effort at vindication. Washington seems to have concluded that if the accused minister could clear himself the matter need never come to public knowledge. It could be regarded as an unfortunate misunderstanding between temporarily separated friends. Washington would privately congratulate and publicly demonstrate his renewed confidence. There had already been talk of appointing Randolph to the Supreme Court.[4]

However, rumors, perhaps surreptitiously nurtured by Wolcott and Pickering, were soon circulating to Randolph's discredit, and in any case the emotions of the displaced favorite were lacerated. To Madison he wrote, "I feel happy at my emancipation from attachment to a man who has practiced on me the profound hypocrisy of a Tiberius and the injustice of an assassin." Randolph informed the newspapers that he would explain and justify his resignation in an "appeal to the people of the United States."[5]

This challenge to the government completely changed the situation. If Washington preserved silence concerning the Fauchet dispatch, he would be allowing a now announced opponent to choose the weapons, the time and place for a battle. It would be like giving a rattlesnake the first bite. As the correspondence between the two men became hotter, Washington wrote Randolph a warning to be careful lest he force the release of the damning dispatch. But on second thoughts, Washington did not mail the threat.[6] He permitted no public reply to the newspaper agitations of his former aide.

Washington was at Mount Vernon when Randolph demanded of Pickering a copy of a letter Washington had written him on July 22, 1795. Pickering refused. Randolph thereupon confided the refusal to the newspapers, adding that the document was essential to his defense. Since the letter of July 22 stated Washington's then agreement with Randolph's policy of withholding ratification of the treaty until the Provision Order was rescinded, it became clear that Randolph intended to link his resignation with Washington's change of policy concerning the treaty. The situation was now moving onto very sensitive ground. Randolph was familiar with many confidential matters which, as the controversy over the treaty continued to rage, it would be wiser not to have published. But by going this far with his former friend, Washington had allowed himself to be trapped. Sure that he had behaved throughout with integrity, Washington concluded that no revelation could be as damaging as the implication that he had matters of grave moment to hide.[7]

Washington sent Randolph his permission not only to inspect the letter of July 22, but "to publish, without reserve, *any* and *every* private and confidential letter I ever wrote you; nay more: every word I have ever uttered in your presence." Washington's one request was that this permission be quoted in whatever vindication Randolph placed before the citizenry. The public would, Washington hoped, "appreciate my motives even if it would condemn my prudence in allowing you the unlimited license herein contained."[8]

Randolph replied loftily that Washington could take comfort in his assurance that he would not "exhibit to public view *all* and *everything* which is known to me." Washington sat down and dashed off a riposte full of invective — but he filed his letter away without mailing it.[9]

Randolph had resigned on August 12, 1795. On October 2, Washington wrote that the "anxious curiosity" of the public was "not wonderful," but it was "wonderful that so much time should be required to give birth" to Randolph's explanation. Washington, who always hated suspense, had to wait over two months more with this sword of Damocles hanging over his head. It was December 18, when Randolph's *Vindication* finally appeared.[10]

The time had long passed when Washington could read the defense as an impartial judge. The closely printed 103-page pamphlet, much of it couched in the form of a letter to the President, was a weapon catapulted at him with the intention of wounding as deeply as possible.

The first reaction of the President, who always wrote briefly (and who knew how to make a few words into a bullet),* must have been relief that Randolph had gone on at such length and — as a glance made clear — in so mixed up a manner. Nonetheless, the closest study was required.

---

* As in the destructive forty-eight-word letter he wrote General Conway. See volume II, pages 249ff.

Washington sat down with pen in hand and made a detailed résumé of Randolph's work.[11]

The President faced three basic questions: (1) How far had Randolph exonerated himself? (2) How far had he damaged the administration? (3) How far had he damaged Washington personally?

Having published (as Washington must have been surprised to see) the entire text of Fauchet's incriminating dispatch, Randolph defended himself from its implications with material gained from French sources. Fauchet had given him an affidavit stating that he had never made indiscreet disclosures, had never asked for or received French money. Fauchet's successor, Adet, had supplied what were identified as the pertinent passages in the missing dispatches. The extract from number three indicated that Randolph's "precious confessions" did not go beyond general statements on American politics and assertions that Washington preferred France to England. Washington must have smiled grimly to read that Randolph hoped "by the ascendancy he daily acquired over the mind of the President" to prevent the Whiskey Rebellion from becoming a civil war.[12]

The crux of Randolph's defense, since it dealt with his request for French money, lay in what was presented as an extract from number six. Randolph was quoted as having told Fauchet that four men could prevent the Whiskey Rebellion from turning into a civil war, "but, debtors of English merchants, they will be deprived of their liberty if they take the smallest step. Could you lend them instantaneously funds sufficient to shelter them from English prosecution?" Fauchet refused, and "I have never since heard propositions of this nature."[13]

Randolph's own gloss was that he believed some merchants, who sold flour to both the British and the French, could, if freed from inhibiting debts, procure information to demonstrate that the Whiskey Rebellion was being inspired by the British for their own purpose. This, Randolph continued, had been just a passing thought, expressed after he had mounted his horse to ride away from Fauchet's house. It had been so lightly spoken that he had not remembered it when confronted by Washington.[14]

Randolph insisted that his angry resignation had not demonstrated guilt. He had reacted as he did because the confrontation Washington had staged in the presence of enemies he despised had been insufferable to a man of honor.

Washington remained unconvinced by Randolph's defense. He discounted the evidence supplied by Adet, since, if a French plot had existed, it stood to reason that no French evidence was to be believed. Randolph's gloss about the merchants who needed to have their debts covered had a fishy sound. And, having set up the confrontation as the best way he could think of to discover the truth, the President could not admit that it had automatically led to the opposite result. Washington ruled Randolph guilty.° He never again in his writings mentioned his one-time friend's name.[15]

The question of how far Randolph had damaged the administration was linked to the question of how far Washington had been damaged personally. The pamphlet made perfectly clear his thinking on the Jay Treaty, including his lack of enthusiasm and his eventual change of mind. Although this revealed vacillation, it demonstrated nothing disgraceful. Washington's habitual predilection for France was well documented, which might, indeed, help to calm the civil storm. However, the pamphlet charged that the President had become incompetent. He had allowed himself to be duped by dishonest schemers into sacrificing Randolph and the French cause to the Federalists and the British, "The *immediate* ratification of the treaty with Great Britain can be traced to no other source than a surrender of yourself to the first impressions from the [Fauchet] letter." And again, "You prejudged the question. . . . You ought to have withstood the impulse which hurried you to prejudication."[16]

Randolph described emotionally and in detail Washington's behavior towards him from the first view of the dispatch to the final ordeal. He accused Washington of hypocrisy and betrayal of friendship. That Washington had what he considered compelling reasons for his behavior did not prevent it from sounding, in this recital, small, irrational, unworthy.[17]

Although Randolph made no misstatement of fact, the picture of Washington that emerged from his pages carried a definite tone of weakness and indecision. This was partly because Randolph painted himself as exerting — until his fall — so great an influence on Washington, and also, by wallowing in self-praise and self-pity, involuntarily depicted himself as a lightweight and a fool. Washington now believed he was also a knave. And yet it was true that Washington had relied on this man as he never had on any other.

° Modern researches have revealed what Washington had no way of determining: the extracts supplied from Fauchet's dispatches accord with the originals in the official French archives. It is now generally believed that Randolph was not guilty.

Randolph deplored that the President had lost his memory and thus could not be appealed to for support of various allegations. He exclaimed, "Had you been yourself, such as you were," Washington would never have been so duped by the Federalist party.[18]

Washington may well have walked to the mirror as is done by so many old men in need of reassurance. But never has the mirror reassured. The more an old man stares, the more clear are the marks, irrevocable and indelible, of accumulated years. The pamphlet lay on the table behind him. Never in his long career had Washington been placed publicly by an old friend in so vexing and humiliating a position. An old friend! And where were his new friends? Where were the strong men who were willing to share with him the responsibilities of the government?

III

Faction Rampant

26

Better His Hand Had Been Cut Off

THE nightmare had, it seemed, become reality. When Washington, after the Revolution, allowed himself to be lured back into public life, he had feared that he was endangering the fame, the love and admiration of his fellow citizens, which were his cherished reward for eight desperate military years. Now a Massachusetts minister, Dr. Nathaniel Ames, expressed popular sentiment when he wrote concerning Washington: "Better his hand had been cut off." The hero had "blasted all his laurels."[1] Washington seemed to have totally failed to still the civil storm by ending suspense concerning the Jay Treaty. Representative John Beckley crowed to Madison that the public, which had formerly indignantly rejected attacks on the President, now received them with "avidity." Washington had marked himself indelibly "as the head of a British faction, and gratitude no longer blinds the public mind."[2]

Every aspect of Washington's public career was gone over insultingly. The press clamored that he had been elected Commander in Chief only because he was so pallid a character that he aroused no antagonisms, and that after an inept military career, he had been chosen President because "the insipid uniformity of his mind" had been assumed — it was now demonstrated wrongly — to reduce the dangers from his ambitions. He had retired to private life after the war because the best opportunity then available, the governorship of Virginia, had not offered scope to his ambitions — but note how eagerly he had jumped for the Presidency! Even the mounting infirmities of old age were used to prove him a tyrant. Why did he not walk abroad or ride horseback as he used to do? The carriage in which he rumbled down the street behind a superfluous number of horses expressed antirepublican disdain.[3]

Most rending perhaps to Washington were two charges, one shockingly false, the other embarrassingly true. During the Revolution, the British propaganda machine had attributed to Washington letters forged to demonstrate that the rebel commander knew in his heart that he owed allegiance to George III. The forgery had contained details which made it on first publication obviously fallacious, but with the passing of years the facts which had shown it incredible had been forgotten. The *New York Daily Gazette* published the letters as authentic proof that Washington had always been a Briton at heart. For Washington, the revival was given greater poignancy because he had always suspected that the author of the forgery, who had revealed familiarity with his private life, had been Randolph's Tory father.[4]

But the most telling blow was the charge, published in the *Aurora*, that Washington, who had made a point of wishing to be paid nothing as President but expenses, had consistently overdrawn the salary Congress had instead voted him. Washington, we may be sure, tremulously asked Dandridge (who was at long last back at his duties) for the account books his secretaries had kept. What he found left him shaken and miserable, all the more because a second article in the *Aurora* — Wolcott guessed the information had been supplied by Randolph — was specific. By April 30, 1791, the President had overdrawn $5150. A year later, he was still $4150 in arrears. On March 1, 1793, the day of his second inauguration, he was down to $1037. But during the first three months of his second term, he drew $11,200 although entitled to only $6250. And he was in debt to the government at the moment.[5]

Although Washington insisted (and Wolcott published) that he used his salary only to pay his official expenses (which it failed to meet); although it was made clear that only recently, in Dandridge's absence, had he made any application for money himself; although Hamilton publicly insisted that the Presidential salary had never been "exceeded," only "anticipated,"[6] Washington could not help realizing — even if the cry that he be impeached was extreme — that the spotless image which he wished to leave behind him had been besmirched.

However personally painful, the newspaper attacks on Washington were less dangerous than the national surge of mass meetings which, in denouncing the Jay Treaty, shouted for unity with the French cause. To add to the crisis, the British cruiser *Africa* hovered off Newport harbor, seeking to intercept (as she almost did) Fauchet on his way to France, and occupying her spare time impressing seamen off American merchant ships. When some of the *Africa's* seamen did not return from shore leave, the British vice consul impudently demanded that the Governor of Rhode Island have them seized and delivered. Although Washington removed the credentials of the vice consul and authorized Rhode Island to use force, if necessary, against the *Africa,* he could not catch up with the damage. He wrote to Jay a passionate complaint that "the domineering spirit of Great Britain should revive again, just at this crisis, and the outrageous and insulting conduct of some of her officers should combine therewith to play into the hands of the discontented, and sour the minds of those who are friends to peace, order, and friendship with all the world." Washington feared that the United States would be propelled into war with Great Britain.[7]

Since swallowing the distasteful Jay Treaty had been, he was convinced, dictated by the best interests of the United States, he could not believe that the scream of the mass meetings was actually "the voice of the people." He asked whether, if the yeomanry had a "plain and simple statement of facts, nine tenths of them would not advocate the measure. But with such abominable misrepresentations . . . it is not to be wondered at" that "uninformed minds should be affrighted."[8]

The wave of protest, so widely spread across city and farmland and including so many classes of people, could not be blamed on the "self-created" societies which Washington had effectively squashed. The "misrepresentations of party" seemed to have got control of those neighborhood gatherings, coming it seemed spontaneously together at a moment of stress, which Washington had always approved. Although he sometimes angrily denounced the meetings in his private correspondence, he made no public attack. And in a letter to his crony Knox he revealed a recognition that there were new forces at work: "As I have found no better guide hitherto than upright intention and close investigation, I shall adhere to these maxims while I keep the watch; leaving it to those who come after me to explore new ways if they like, or think them better."[9]

Washington managed to get off to Mount Vernon in early September for six weeks, but he had never felt less able to relax. His personal position was darker than it had been even during the darkest days of the Revolution. Then he had been surrounded with admiring colleagues to help him carry his burdens and make at his dinner table an agreeable sound. Now he was almost in the situation of Macbeth, who cried out, before the woods advanced on Dunsinane, "The thanes fly from me!"

Bradford had died, leaving a second vacancy in his Cabinet. Pickering had, it is true, been delighted to fill in as acting Secretary of State, but Washington had no intention of placing the lethal, self-righteous Puritan in the top office. Nor did he intend to take to his bosom the bland, viperish Wolcott. Washington longed to be surrounded with "the old and proved patriots of the country."[10]

He offered State to William Paterson, an Associate Justice of the Supreme Court from New Jersey, who had championed the small states in the Constitutional Convention, but had proved loyal to the federal administration. Paterson refused. Washington offered State to former Governor Thomas Johnson of Maryland. Johnson refused. In urging the post on Charles Cotesworth Pinckney of South Carolina, Washington pointed out that "the affairs of this country are in a violent paroxysm": he needed help in "piloting the vessel." Pinckney refused. As an obbligato to this chorus, the Virginia lawyer John Marshall refused the post of Attorney General.[11]

Dropping in at Mount Vernon, Henry Lee urged Washington to offer State to Patrick Henry. This seemed a wild suggestion, since Henry had opposed the Constitution and, as Virginia's prime local luminary, had had many a run-in with his fellow Virginian who operated by preference on a national scale. Lee insisted that Henry's attitudes had changed, and Washington realized that securing the cooperation of Virginia's favorite orator would do much to dampen the opposition.*

Confused on how to proceed, Washington delegated the decision to Edward Carrington, one of Virginia's few important Federalists and (whether Washington knew it or not) an intimate correspondent of Hamilton's. Carrington (who could consult John Marshall) would know whether Henry had indeed changed his mind on the Constitution and also whether he had opposed the Jay Treaty in any public way that would embarrass the government. Carrington should read the letter to Henry that Washington enclosed, and, if in his judgment it were wise to go ahead, seal and mail the letter.

Washington's letter to Henry contained a passionate denial of the charge that he had become pro-British or had "any wish that is incompatible with the dignity, happiness, and true interest of the people of this country." His ardent desire was "to comply strictly with *all* our engagements, foreign and domestic, but to keep the United States free from *political* connections with *every* other country. To see that they *may be* in-

---

* Jefferson could hardly believe his ears when told that Washington had offered the post to Henry.[12]

dependent of *all* and under the influence of *none.*" Establishing "an *American* character," convincing the European powers that "we act for *ourselves* and not for *others*" was "the only way to be respected abroad and happy at home." To become partisans of either Great Britain or France would "disturb public tranquillity and destroy, perhaps for ever, the cement which binds the union."[13]

Carrington forwarded the letter. Henry refused.

Washington had been trying to keep his Cabinet balance by securing a Secretary of State who was not from the northeast, not pro-British nor a strong partisan of the Jay Treaty. None had been willing to accept and the post had somehow to be filled. He wrote Hamilton, asking him to sound out an extreme Federalist, New York's Senator King.

Hamilton replied, "The disgust which a virtuous and independent mind" feels at making itself a target for "foul and venemous shafts of calumny" induced King to refuse the office. "I wish, sir," Hamilton continued, "I could present to you any useful ideas as a substitute, but the embarrassment is extreme as to Secretary of State. . . . In fact, a first-rate character is not attainable. A second-rate must be taken with good dispositions and barely decent qualifications. I wish I could throw more light. 'Tis a sad omen for the government."[14]

The elderly President was left naked among his enemies.

27

A Brilliant Stroke

SINCE it seemed essential to have the top Cabinet office filled when Congress convened in December 1795, Washington finally gave in to what he had struggled so hard to avoid: he offered the Secretaryship of State to the man who had been filling in, to the grim, inimical Pickering. Perhaps because so obviously passed over until there was no other recourse, Pickering refused (he explained that he lacked the necessary talents); then agreed to reconsider; kept Washington on tenterhooks; made Washington beg; made Washington ask Wolcott to plead with him; and then finally stated magnanimously that he wished to keep Washington "no longer in suspense." Although happy as Secretary of War, Pickering would move up if the President insisted.[1]

Announcing Pickering for State, Washington offered War to John Eager Howard of Baltimore. Howard refused. Then Washington heard from Henry Lee that Patrick Henry might, although he had refused State, accept War. Eagerly Washington commissioned Lee to ask Henry. Congress now convened and the Senate added to the confusion by turning down Rutledge — he was accused of insanity — as Chief Justice. Failing, in his desperation (so it seems), to consult the candidate, Washington nominated for Chief Justice a long-time Associate Justice, William Cushing. Cushing was confirmed by the Senate, but declined on the grounds that he was too old (he was ten days younger than Washington). And Associate Justice John Blair resigned, leaving Washington with two vacancies on the court.[2]

The downfall of Rutledge emphasized the lack of southerners in the government. Henry would have been a marvelous antidote, but he again declined. Then Washington caught two Marylanders in one swoop. He had received an affectionate letter from his former aide-de-camp and drinking companion James McHenry suggesting Thomas Chase to succeed Blair. Washington not only accepted Chase but appointed McHenry, who proved delighted, Secretary of War. Making Charles Lee (Henry Lee's brother, who practiced law near Mount Vernon) Attorney General raised the bag to three southerners. Washington then felt free to appoint as Chief Justice the Federalist Senator from Massachusetts, Oliver Ellsworth.[3]

"The offices are once more filled," John Adams noted, "but how differently than when Jefferson, Hamilton, Jay, etc., were here." With this judgment, Washington would not have disagreed. Pickering had been a last resort. Washington could not bring himself to write Wolcott's father (when congratulating him on becoming Governor of Connecticut) a more enthusiastic endorsement than "your son, as far as my knowledge of him extends, is a very deserving character. He discharges the duties of his office with integrity and ability." Washington had not expected much of McHenry — "the fact is, it was a Hobson's choice" — and he found no more than he had expected. Under Lee, the office of Attorney General sank to minimal importance.[4]

Although the posts were filled, Washington was still, for all practical purposes, alone. In his great need, he had given in to a possibility which he had avoided for the ten months during which he had used Randolph as his prime minister and then tried vainly to lure at least one able adviser into his Cabinet. In the same letter (October 29, 1795) in which he had asked whether King would be willing to serve as Secretary of State, Washington requested Hamilton to play a primary role in the activity of the executive. Would the retired Secretary of the Treasury, although now a private citizen, help the President draft his Seventh Annual Address?[5]

Washington sent Hamilton in a rough form his ideas for what he wished to say. Shortly thereafter, he wrote that he had received further information which had given him new ideas: "I pray you to suspend your superstructure until you receive a ground plan from me."[6]

Washington's Seventh Annual Address was to be delivered in the Senate Chamber on December 8, 1795. The statesmen and politicians and a few privileged ladies who were waiting for the President to appear surely wondered what Washington — how glad they were not to be in his shoes! — would say at this time when his policies seemed so unpopular and he was personally under such violent attack. Surely he would try to justify his ratification of the Jay Treaty as he had in his Fifth Annual Address defended the Neutrality Proclamation.° In all probability he would attack the mass meetings which had flooded him with angry resolutions, as he had in his Sixth Annual Address attacked the Democratic Societies. He might well express personal bitterness as he had in his second inaugural. And it would be only reasonable for him to paint the state of the nation in the darkest colors in order to frighten the people into rallying behind him.

When Washington entered at noon, he was met by two Republican leaders of the opposition: Henry Tazewell of Virginia, officiating for the Senate in the absence of John Adams, and Speaker Jonathan Dayton of the House.[7] They ushered him with due formality to the rostrum. He laid out his papers and began:

"Fellow citizens of the Senate and House of Representatives: I trust I do not deceive myself while I indulge the persuasion that I have never met you at any period when more than at present the situation of our public affairs has afforded just cause for mutual congratulation; and for inviting you to join with me in profound gratitude to the Author of all good for the numerous and extraordinary blessings we enjoy."

Washington then began enumerating blessings. General Wayne had followed up his military victory by negotiating a treaty with the tribes northwest of the Ohio which promised "the termination of the long, expensive, and distressing war." The Creeks and Cherokees, "who alone of the southern tribes had annoyed our frontier," had demonstrated their sincere desire to put pre-existing treaties into effect, by returning the prisoners and property they had taken. Unfortunately, some citizens of Georgia had clouded the situation with "wanton murders" perpetrated on hunting parties of the Creeks. Efforts were being taken to "mitigate the usual consequences of such outrages."†

Next Washington turned to piracy on the Mediterranean. The Emperor of Morocco had recognized the treaty made with his father, thus assuring "the continuance of peace with that power." Information received from the American agent to Algiers, the home of the Barbary pirates, autho-

---

° In his many replies to petitions protesting the treaty, Washington had never gone beyond stating that, in following his constitutional duty, he had done what he considered best for the nation.

† John Adams noted that on December 5 Washington had just entertained at dinner the widow and children of Hanging Maw, who had been basely murdered by the whites. The President had given four other sets of Indians dinner the previous week.[8]

rized the hope of peace there too, and also "the restoration of our unfortunate fellow citizens from a grievous captivity."

Furthermore, the American envoy in Madrid (Pinckney) had "received assurances of a speedy and satisfactory conclusion of his negotiation." Every hearer knew that this involved the crucial question of the opening of the Mississippi. So far so good, but what about Jay's Treaty? Ah, Washington was getting to it now!

Washington stated that, as everyone knew, the treaty had been approved by the Senate "upon a condition which excepts part of one article. Agreeably thereto and to the best judgment I was able to form of the public interest, after full and mature deliberation, I have added my sanction. The result on the part of his Britannic Majesty is unknown. When received, the subject will, without delay, be placed before Congress."

As Washington paused, his hearers wondered whether he was going to leave the Jay Treaty at that. Washington continued: "This interesting summary of our affairs with regard to the foreign powers between whom and the United States controversies have subsisted" and with regard to the Indians "opens a wide field for consoling and gratifying reflections. . . . Prudence and moderation on every side" could now extinguish all the causes of external discord "which have heretofore menaced our tranquillity."

The pro-French legislators, who were continually crying that the Jay Treaty was anti-French, could hardly believe that Washington would move on from foreign affairs without mentioning France. But even in their incredulity they may have recognized that the President had outflanked them: the discussion had been of nations "which have menaced our tranquillity." His omission of France could be taken as a recognition of common interest.

Washington was now launched on domestic affairs. The moment seemed to be approaching when he would denounce the mass meetings of his opponents and perhaps the press, which had been leveling at him so many poisoned darts.

"Contemplating the internal situation, as well as the external relations of the United States, we discover equal cause for contentment and satisfaction." While Europe was involved in destructive wars and domestic convulsions, her useful arts destroyed and her populations starving, her hopes of "peace and repose" alloyed by the realization that burdens were accumulating that would "clog the future springs of government, our favored country, in striking contrast, has enjoyed general tranquillity — a tranquillity the more satisfactory because maintained at the expense of no duty. Faithful to ourselves, we have violated no obligation to others."

Prosperity showered on the United States as never before. "The molestations of our trade" (which were being protested) were overbalanced by the benefits the nation derived from a neutral position. American population was growing with a rapidity that guaranteed future security. Internal improvements were rushing forward accompanied by tax burdens so light as scarcely to be perceived. "Is it too much to say that our country exhibits a spectacle of national happiness never surpassed if ever before equaled?" And should not Americans "unite our efforts to preserve, prolong, and improve our immense advantages? To cooperate with you in this desirable work is a fervent and favorite wish of my heart."

Now at long last, Washington moved on to internal disturbances — but he did not mention current ones. Since the region which had supported the Whiskey Rebellion "now enjoys the blessings of quiet and order," he had pardoned all the convicted rebels.

Washington then made specific recommendations: Congress should review, in relation to the current situation, the army, the militia, harbor fortifications, the lack of a navy, etc., etc. He then devoted the longest and most detailed part of his address to arguing for his humanitarian approach to the Indians. He again urged that they be protected by law. He again urged governmental control of an equitable fur trade. He added "with pleasure" that the experiments of the government had not reduced the probability that Indians could be "civilized. . . . This work, if practicable, will reflect undecayed luster on our national character, and administer the most grateful consolations that virtuous minds can know."*

Washington concluded by stating: "Temperate discussion of the important subjects which may arise in the course of the session, and mutual forbearance where there is a difference of opinion, are too obvious and necessary for the peace, happiness and welfare of our country to need any recommendation of mine."[9]

The Republicans were wound up to so high a pitch of controversy that they regarded the lack of counterattack from the President as a white flag of surrender. Senator Tazewell reported to Monroe, "The flattering picture which he presents of our affairs has by some been considered as a

---

* See volume III, pages 300–303, for Washington's hope that the Indians, instead of being driven forever westward, could be gathered into the society of the United States, happily occupying parts of their old hunting grounds as farmers.

prelude to his resignation." And Giles wrote Jefferson that the President, having "at length" realized that "the public temper" plus the Republican majority in the House "will not tolerate threats," had concluded that he could do better by presenting "the amiable solicitude of his heart" rather than "the wisdom of his head."[10]

However, the traditional replies of the two legislative houses revealed that Washington (with an assist from Hamilton) had used his head as well as his heart. For the Senate, with its Federalist majority, to be fulsome was expected. The important development was that it proved impossible to stir up much opposition in the House. Giles did succeed in having a reference to "the undiminished confidence of your fellow citizens" rewritten, but the version that was adopted was not very different: "In contemplating the spectacle of national happiness which our country exhibits . . . permit us to acknowledge and declare the very great share which your zealous and faithful services have contributed to it."° [11]

Resorting to a wine maker's metaphor, Washington thus described the situation, "I have little doubt of a perfect amelioration of sentiment after the present fermentation (which is not only subsiding but changing) has evaporated a little more. The dregs, however, will always remain, and the slightest motion will stir them up."[13]

As a matter of fact, the opposition had been weakening even during the months when no one would join Washington's Cabinet and he had seemed most exposed. Jefferson mourned that, although the Federalists had been "in a defile where they might be finished," they were escaping. He attributed this partly to the prestige of the President;† partly to the detailed defense Hamilton had published of every clause of the treaty; partly to the violence of the opposition, which had so alarmed the merchants that they no longer dared oppose the treaty lest the government be torn apart.[14]

Nationally, Washington's annual address was proving extremely effective. To the simplistic argument that the treaty was anti-French, he had

---

° Jefferson wrote Giles that he was glad that the House had "respected appearances in favor of the President, who errs as other men do, but errs with integrity." Then, Jefferson accused Washington of having in his acknowledgment of the House's reply misquoted to his own advantage. While the House had stated that he had "contributed" to the national happiness, he had made it seem as if they had thanked him for his "agency." "The former," Jefferson explained, "keeps in view the cooperation of others. . . . The latter presents to view his sole agency."[12]

† The violently Jeffersonian historian Bowers writes that the Republicans made a major tactical error by trying, when the Federalists put Washington's reputation forward as a shield, to tear that reputation down.

opposed an equally simplistic argument, which was more tangible, closer to home. An opposition that has to admit to a state "of national happiness" is in danger of having the rug pulled out from under its feet. Washington had, indeed, not been engaging in amiable platitudes, but had, as of old, cut through the layers of controversy down to the basic, unassailable truth. The nation was still free and, despite irritations on the ocean and at conference tables, more prosperous than it had ever been.° The nation was a growing colossus whose security rested not on the victory of one or another power in the European conflict but on the continuation of conditions that would allow it to achieve unhampered its maturity. If this were indeed the case — and every American who looked around dispassionately realized it was the case — why all this howling of faction, all these accusations that the government was selling out the country? Why all this hysteria about the details of a treaty that was serving the major end of permitting the United States to grow?

Washington himself philosophized, "The restless mind of man cannot be at peace." And, again, "By the second sight, extraordinary foresight, or some other sight attainable by a few only, evils afar off are discovered" by some uneasy spirits, "alarming to themselves and, as far as they are able to render them so, disquieting to others."[16]

Word had not yet come back across the ocean of French reaction to the Jay Treaty but the authorities in Paris, persuaded by their diplomatic representatives (and also by the American minister Monroe) that the American executive was anti-French, had thought up an amusing scheme to embarrass the President. Monroe (in a manner for which he had been scolded by his government) had presented an American flag to the French National Convention, which gave it a permanent place of honor in their meeting hall. Why not return the compliment?[17]

On New Year's Day, 1796, Adet delivered to Washington a present from the French government to the American legislature. It was a tricolor made of the richest silk and highly ornamented with allegorical paintings: in the center, a cock standing on a thunderbolt; at two corners, bombshells bursting. The edges were hirsute with fringes and tassels of gold. The flag was accompanied by two addresses which spoke in the most ecstatic terms of brotherhood between France and the United States.[18]

° In February 1796 Washington wrote his estate manager to hold on to his wheat, since he expected the European situation to raise the price "beyond anything ever known in this country."[15]

Washington frustrated the embarrassing part of the French intention by stating that, although he would announce the transaction to Congress, he would deposit the colors "in the archives of the United States." However, he took the opportunity to stress strongly, for Europe and the American people to hear, sympathy with revolutionary France: "Born, sir, in a land of liberty; having early learned its value; having engaged in a perilous conflict to defend it; having, in a word, devoted the best years of my life to secure its permanent establishment in my own country; my anxious recollections, my sympathetic feelings, and my best wishes are irresistibly excited whensoever, in any country, I see an oppressed nation unfurl the banners of freedom. But above all, the events of the French Revolution have produced the deepest solicitude as well as the highest admiration. To call your nation brave, were to pronounce but common praise. Wonderful people! Ages to come will read with astonishment the history of your brilliant exploits! . . . May the friendship of the two republics be commensurate with existence."[19]

Madison's comment was, "The harangue of the President must grate the pro-British party, but they are cunning enough to be silent."[20]

Washington had not only wished to demonstrate that he was not, as charged, a slave of the British faction. He was actually angry with the British, who were again making trouble for him as they had during most of his career. By rancor and misbehavior, they were encouraging the "torrent of abuse" that was being poured over the President because, in his determination to keep the peace, he had been forced to sign a treaty which it would have been to Britain's own advantage to make more liberal.[21]

Before his public gesture in relation to the French flag, he had sent a confidential communication which he hoped would rise to the highest British circles.

Gouverneur Morris, on being relieved of his ambassadorship to France, had stayed abroad and was now in England. He had once been Washington's unofficial representative there. During the continued absence of Pinckney, Morris was the most distinguished American in London who had had connections with the government. From him, Washington received a letter complaining of the anti-British tone of the American press. "I was struck forcibly with the idea, as well from the style and manner as from its being [confined] to a single subject, that it had or was intended to have pass under the eye of Lord Grenville, although no intimation thereof was given to me." Washington concluded that he could use his reply to inform Grenville "in what light the people of this country viewed the conduct of his towards it."[22]

Covering page after page (he was in the end to apologize for having written so briefly), Washington went way back to the beginnings of the nation's and his own anti-British feeling. The French had been America's friends when the British had been their enemies during the Revolution. After the Revolution, the British had been indifferent to offers of "friendly intercourse" and had appointed as their consuls "ungracious and obnoxious characters," "rancorous" Tory refugees. British officials in Canada had, without being removed or punished by the home government, incited Indian attacks and were at that very moment exerting every nerve to keep the treaty Wayne had signed from taking effect.

British naval officers had insulted American ports, searched American vessels, and impressed seamen within American jurisdiction. They had seized entire crews in the West Indies. The Bermudian pirates and the Admiralty courts in that island had committed the most atrocious depredations and violences. Although the British had withdrawn the Provision Order, they had not renounced "the *principle* which constituted the most obnoxious and objectionable part thereof" and which had placed the United States in her "predicament . . . in her relations with France."

The British government should realize that a liberal policy would be the best way to gain in the United States advantages for her trade and manufactures. In the meanwhile, Washington's government was having the greatest difficulty, "under such an accumulation of irritating circumstances, to maintain the ground of neutrality" by not being driven into the arms of France.[23]

28

Swords with Two Edges

T HE major storm that would rock the legislative session was being amply presaged. Whatever might have been the shift of public opinion — a matter on which no one had accurate information — the Republican leaders were just as strongly opposed to the Jay Treaty as ever. Their majority in the House of Representatives had been left to one side as the Federalist-controlled Senate had urged ratification. This was according to the provision of the Constitution that the Senate alone should give "advice and consent" to the President on foreign affairs. But in the implementing of the treaty, if it should come back signed by George III, the House was determined to play a role.

The treaty could not be put into effect without various appropriations, and the Constitution provided that all money bills originate in the House. The House could block the treaty by refusing to vote funds. Such action would be doubly justified, so the Republican argument ran, because the treaty had determined matters that lay within the legislative province. Throughout the short history of the federal government, Congress had debated and determined trade laws. But in the mercantile provisions of the treaty, Jay had laid down rules of trade with Great Britain. Was this not an effort of the Senate and the executive to usurp legislative powers of the House? The issue was given a deeper significance because the House, which was elected directly by the people in their own neighborhoods, was considered the palladium of the rights of the common man.* The people, it was argued, must protect themselves against privilege.

---

* In most states, senators were elected not directly by the people but by the state legislatures.

What would follow if the House torpedoed the treaty, no one knew, since the wound with England would be reopened without there being in the Constitution or the laws any provision for closing it again — or, indeed, for making any other treaty that the executive could in good conscience ratify or a foreign power accept. Jefferson admitted that a challenge from the House would "bring on an embarrassing and critical state in our government." However, the risk had to be taken since he regarded the creation of commercial law under the treaty-making power by the President and the Senate, "the boldest act ever ventured on to undermine the government."[1]

Washington could only view the impending controversy with dismay. Yet it may be that he did not speculate too much on what would take place. He had never been addicted to crossing bridges before he came to them, and he was becoming increasingly inclined to escape any troubles he could avoid. The fight could not begin until the bone of contention reappeared from England, and in the meantime Washington had a period of leisure to think about his own affairs.

On February 1, 1796, he completed writing out an advertisement which ran to many thousands of words. It offered his far western properties — four tracts on the Ohio, four on the Great Kanawha, three on the Little Miami, and one in Kentucky — for sale. It announced (for the first time publicly) that he would rent the four Mount Vernon farms and the mill. He no longer insisted that each farm be leased by a single prosperous proprietor: a group, who took possession in a single deal, might rent field by field. In detailed descriptions of each farm, he specified that "covering" existed for a certain number of "black laborers" with their children, but made no further mention of slaves. They were not included in the list of what he would sell the occupants on "just and reasonable terms": draught animals, stock, tools, etc.

Those interested could apply to Dandridge for more detailed terms. Not only did Washington not publish these terms, but he was hesitant about showing them around. The most interesting clause read: "Although the admission of slaves with the tenants will not be absolutely prohibited, it would nonetheless be a pleasing circumstance to exclude them, if not entirely, at least in a great degree. To do which is not among the least of the inducements for dividing the farms into small lots."

With his western lands in mind, Washington arranged for his advertisement to be published in what newspapers there were on the frontier, and also to be nailed on the doors of the taverns of most resort. For his Mount Vernon offer, he did everything he could to have the advertisement circulated in England, Scotland, and Ireland. He explained that he wished to get from Europe associations of farmers (preferably English-speaking) "who know how (from experience and necessity) to keep land in an improving state rather than the slovenly ones of this country, who think generally of nothing else but to work a field as long as it will bear anything and until it is run into gullies and ruined." Another advantage of foreigners was that the issue of slavery would be less involved.[2]

Washington seems to have despaired of finding four expert farmers with considerable capital, each to rent one of his Mount Vernon farms and hire his blacks after they had been freed. However, as he wrote Stuart, "the current of my wishes set" even more strongly for freeing the slaves than for renting the farms. Yet the one was involved in the other. Until the results from his advertisements became clear, he could not determine "how I shall support myself" without the services of his slaves. Supporting himself involved, of course, supporting the young blacks until they could take care of themselves, and pensioning until death those of his Negroes who were too decrepit to work. Still faced with a political opposition that did not wish slavery interfered with, he still warned that his plans must be shrouded in complete secrecy.

For almost six months Washington had been troubled by a situation which appealed particularly to his most intimate emotions. Early in September 1795, he had received letters from fourteen-year-old George Washington G. G. Motier Lafayette, and an elderly French tutor, Felix Frestal. The family of Washington's spiritual son, the Marquis de Lafayette, had finally been released from imprisonment in France, and the boy had been sent by Mme de Lafayette, incognito, to the United States to be received into the family of his father's dear friend. They were in Boston and had written of their arrival. No obligation could have appealed more to Washington — except his obligation to the United States. And, alas, the two seemed to be in conflict. The Marquis de Lafayette was considered by the existing French government as the personification of reaction. What would the French think, what would the American democrats charge, if the Marquis's son and the tutor, who had also brought up the father, became permanent residents of the American Presidential Mansion?[3]

Washington instantly wrote the Federalist senator George Cabot, who

[261]

was in Boston, stating that despite "all the sensibility which has been ex-cited in my breast," despite his determination to be *"father, friend, and protector"* to his friend's child, he could not beg the youth and tutor to hurry to him. The boy should remain incognito — any publicity would be disastrous; he should go to Harvard. Washington would pay all expenses while he tried to work out some better solution.[4]

Some six weeks later, Washington heard from Hamilton that young La-fayette and his tutor had not been satisfied to stay in Boston: they were in New York on the way to a house in New Jersey where they intended to wait "until they hear some direction from you." The boy "appears to me very advantageously: modest, of very good manners, and expressing him-self with intelligence and propriety." The tutor, "a very sedate, discreet man," reported that, although they had not been officially allowed to leave France, the Committee of Safety had closed their eyes as they de-parted under assumed names. Hamilton thought the President was being too cautious. Washington's enemies would be gratified if he allowed pol-icy to restrain his affection. Furthermore, it was possible that the elder Lafayette might return to power in France.[5]

Washington's reply indicated that he was still not sure. He had tried unofficially to sound out the French minister but had failed. However, if Cabot agreed with Hamilton that it would do no damage or that "conso-lation [would] flow therefrom to young Lafayette and his tutor," Wash-ington would receive them, incognito, "at all events."[6]

Hamilton's next letter was cruelly uncommunicative concerning young Lafayette. Washington repeated that he was willing "to receive him under any circumstances or in any manner you may conceive best; and wish to know what that is." Having two days later (November 18) still not heard from Hamilton, Washington wrote him that, unless powerful contrary reasons had appeared, he should send the boy along without delay. "The young gentleman must have experienced some unpleasant feeling already from being kept at a distance from me, and I feel as un-pleasantly as he can do."[7]

This letter crossed one from Hamilton saying he had changed his mind. "Judicious" friends of his felt that Washington would be pointed at "as a favorer of the anti-revolutionists of France," which would be dangerous at this crisis.[8]

Washington then wrote the boy to go to Hamilton. When Washington could himself "embrace you . . . I shall do it with fervency." In the meanwhile, the lad should study hard so that "the season of your youth may be improved to the utmost."[9]

Washington enclosed this letter in an unhappy letter to Hamilton. He could not doubt that the feelings of both the boy and his tutor "are alive to everything which may have the semblance of neglect or slight, and indeed expectant as they must have been . . . of an invitation to fly to me without delay; and distressing and forlorn as the situation of one of them is, it is necessary that every assurance and consolation be administered to them." He was taking Hamilton's advice because "I am distrustful of my own judgment in deciding on this business lest my feelings carry me further [than] prudence, while I am a public character, will warrent. . . . It has, however, like many other things in which I have been involved two edges, neither of which can be avoided without falling on the other." Washington said that Adet, having finally been reached, replied that France did not war on women and children, but how would the American people feel if the boy and the tutor — God knows what were the tutor's political connections! — were perpetually seen in the company of the President?[10]

Almost a month later, three days before Christmas, Washington asked Hamilton whether his letter had ever been given to young Lafayette. Why had the boy not replied? "His case gives me pain. . . . His sensibility, I fear, is hurt."[11]

Hamilton replied that he had given the boy Washington's letter "which much relieved him." And shortly after Christmas Day, satisfactory letters from the youth and his tutor arrived.[12]

Washington was still dithering. He considered putting the young man up secretly in Germantown; he wrote Madison (whom he had not for a long time consulted) for advice, and even invited the dangerous pair to visit Philadelphia. Then the opposition came (for once) to his rescue. On March 4, 1796, Edward Livingston moved in the House that a committee be appointed to discover whether Lafayette's son was in the United States and determine whether any provisions should be made for his support. Since Livingston was a leader of the pro-French anti-Federalist party, Washington had no further hesitations. An invitation was rushed off. However, long after Washington had hoped "to have embraced you under my roof," he was kept in the suspense he so hated. It was April 11, 1796, before he was able to write gleefully to Secretary of War McHenry, who had once served with the boy's father, "Young Fayette and his friend are with me. Come dine with them today at three o'clock if you are not otherwise engaged."[13]

As time dragged on while everyone waited for the arrival of the Jay Treaty to start hostilities going, the Republican majority in the House could not resist showing its teeth to Washington. On the President's sixty-fifth birthday they denied, by a vote of 50 to 38, a motion to adjourn the House for half an hour to enable the members to call on the President. Nonetheless, so Madison complained to Jefferson, the birthday was characterized by "unexampled splendor." Bells rang, cannon boomed, and the Presidential Mansion was besieged with visitors. An Englishman noted that Washington seemed considerably older than "his birthday accounted for."[14]

Towards nightfall Washington was handed the best birthday present he could possibly have received: a copy of a treaty Pinckney had negotiated with Spain. Washington must have read it in amazement. After all the tribulations on the Mississippi and the southwest frontier, after angry mass meetings in Kentucky and Indian scalpings on the Georgia frontier, this!* The Treaty of San Lorenzo not only opened the Mississippi to American shipping but granted that goods for export could be stored at New Orleans tax-free. In the vexing boundary dispute, the treaty acknowledged the claim of the United States to go down to the thirty-first parallel. Spain furthermore promised to use her influence to restrain her Indian allies. The triumph was complete! Washington hurried the treaty to the Senate, which jubilantly accepted it.[16]

Washington soon had another treaty to submit, this one less idyllic, yet, everything considered, satisfactory, The Barbary pirates, who had long held Americans in captivity, agreed to release them all in return for a ransom of $80,000. They would in the future spare American shipping in return for a yearly tribute of $24,000. The Senate again consented without controversy.[17]

Washington was in daily anticipation of a certified copy of the Jay Treaty as modified and approved in London. However, instead of receiving a dispatch case, he was handed a South Carolina newspaper which had printed an unofficial text of the treaty that had wandered into

---

* Spain knew that her withdrawal from the war with France would infuriate England, and feared that the result of Jay's negotiation would be an Anglo-American alliance. The rising strength of the American settlements across the mountains was another worry. Thus concession seemed the best way for Spain to keep her weak North American possessions from being wiped out.[15]

Charleston harbor. The leaders of the House, who had openly denied the right of the President and the Senate to ratify the commercial clauses, expected Washington not to act until they had been consulted. But without waiting for the official dispatch, on leap year day, 1796, Washington declared the treaty the law of the land. John Marshall remembered that the Republicans in the House were "not a little dissatisfied."[18]

They struck right back. On March 2, Edward Livingston presented a motion requesting the President to submit to the House every document in the executive archives — Jay's instructions, all relevant correspondence, etc. — which might "throw light" on the treaty and how it had been negotiated.[19]

During two and a half weeks of debate, the House agreed that Washington might hold back documents which existing negotiations rendered improper to disclose, but voted down another amendment, proposed by Madison, that Washington might in general use his judgment on what should, in the public interest, be reserved. Thus, the bill which was passed on March 24 by a vote of 62 to 37 claimed for the House not only the right to reconsider treaties which had constitutionally become the law of the land, but the right of unrestrained supervision of the acts of the executive. And the opposition had also taken a giant step towards destroying all the accommodation which had been achieved with Great Britain.

As its delegates to present the request to Washington, the House sent its two most extreme leaders of the opposition: Livingston and Albert Gallatin. Washington received the document with the laconic statement "that he would take the request of the House into consideration."[20]

29

The Brink of a Precipice

WASHINGTON'S old-time constitutional adviser Madison believed that he would give in to the request of the House. The politically active Virginia attorney John Marshall explained, "In an electoral government, the difficulty of resisting the popular branch of the legislature is at all times great, but it is particularly so when the passions of the public have been strongly and generally excited." Marshall pointed to the wide popularity of the House's demand, the overwhelming vote, the implication that if Washington refused he had something to hide, and the danger the President faced of separating himself from the people.[1]

Marshall's use of the phrase "the popular branch" casts on the controversy a clarifying historical light. During the long Colonial period, governments had commonly consisted of a governor appointed by the Crown, a council or upper house appointed by the governor, and an assembly elected by the people. Although the governor's councils were (being made up of Americans) capable of being skittish, it was usually the lower house, "the popular branch," which fought for the rights of his Majesty's American subjects. Reliance on a single chamber of the legislature became so deep-seated that during the Revolution and for several years thereafter national power was vested exclusively in the Continental Congress, while in the states radicals often achieved unicameral legislatures, elected for a short time, that appointed judges and, like the Continental Congress, carried out the executive function through committees of their members. This, it was contended, was the only way to bring purely to bear the will of the people. It was partly because such governments rarely looked beyond immediate local issues or paid much attention to minority rights that the Constitutional Convention was considered necessary and created an instrument based on various governmental institutions checking and balancing each other.

In addition to serving the immediate ends of the Republican majority there, the campaign of the House appealed to the older sentiment. It would, if successful, result in a major Constitutional revision, putting "the popular branch" to some degree back into the saddle from which the Constitutional Convention had displaced it.

When (after the matter had been settled) Washington felt he could express his personal opinion, he wrote that "the *real* question" was not whether the Jay Treaty "was a *good* or bad one, but whether there should be a *treaty at all* without the concurrence of that House." Because of the national partiality for France and the unfavorable interpretations that could be placed on aspects of the treaty, "it was conceived that no occasion more suitable might ever occur to establish the principle and enlarge the power." Washington's guess was corroborated by Jefferson's private comment to Monroe: "On the precedent now to be set will depend the future construction of our Constitution. . . . It is fortunate that the first decision is to be in a case so palpably atrocious as to have been predetermined by all America."[2]

The House was not only wrestling with the Senate. The House was trying to climb over the fence into Washington's yard. It has been postulated in these volumes that one reason Washington was, both as Commander in Chief and as President, so meticulous about not attempting to encroach beyond his granted powers was that he could not bear to move in an area where his authority could be questioned. He would stay in his own territory, but others must stay in theirs.[3]

On a previous occasion, the House had asked for executive documents. It was investigating St. Clair's defeat by the Indians. The Cabinet, which then included Jefferson as well as Hamilton, had voted unanimously that the President should use his "discretion" concerning what papers could be disclosed without injuring the public.[4] Following this precedent, Washington could seek a compromise; while refusing to accept the House's blanket demand he could submit some selected documents.° However, he did not consider the situations similar. The House had a constitutional right to investigate a military defeat, but in Washington's opinion, no authority concerning treaties.

° Hamilton warned Washington that the papers were "a crude mass that will do no credit to the administration." However, they could have been pruned.[5]

In 1792, in a Cabinet discussion of an earlier effort to buy off the Algerian pirates, Jefferson had raised the question whether the House, which would have to appropriate the funds, should not be consulted in advance. Washington had replied that if the House did not carry out its duty to support a treaty constitutionally ratified, "the government would be at an end and must then assume another form." According to Jefferson, Washington explained "that he did not like throwing too much into democratic hands."*6

There was, of course, an obvious contradiction in the Constitution. This had again been brought home to Washington when, as Jay was crossing the ocean towards the treaty negotiation, Hamilton had suggested what he admitted was a maneuver to circumvent the House. He wished the executive to notify Hammond that in the treaty, which would be voted on only by the Senate, Jay would agree to paying the British various indemnities to which the House might object. Washington replied with a lecture: "The powers of the executive of the United States are more definite and better understood than those of almost any other country; and my aim has been and will continue to be neither to stretch nor relax from them in any instance whatsoever, unless imperious circumstances render the measure indispensable."7 But the fact remained that Jay did have the power, which he used, to agree to pay the indemnities.

In 1795, Washington had found himself faced with a situation which he considered so dangerous that he had felt justified in using the treaty-making power to enforce a policy that could not be got through the House. Georgia had thrown open to settlement fifty million acres which the federal government had, at the Treaty of New York,† agreed belonged to the Creek Nation. The executive appealed to Congress. A bill restraining Georgia passed the Senate but was defeated by the House. In March, after Congress had adjourned, war with the Creeks, which might spread to war with Spain and England, seemed so imminent that Washington concluded that he would have to act. He appointed federal commissioners who, overriding the Georgia government, arbitrated the dispute with the Creeks. Considering this now a matter of foreign policy, he secured, after Congress had reconvened, the consent of the Senate to what he had done.8

Washington's attitude was that, under all but the most extraordinary

---

* As was pointed out in volume III, pages 357–358, this conversation was one of the earliest causes for Jefferson's doubts of Washington.

† See volume III, pages 264–265.

circumstances, neither the executive-Senate combination nor the House should intentionally take advantage of the constitutional confusion to impose on the other. However, if in the course of doing what seemed dictated by the situation — as in the need for a commercial treaty and the need to prevent an Indian war — the House got pushed aside, that was unavoidable. Washington was also willing to accord the House the right to veto a foreign policy decision because "apparent marks of fraud or corruption (which in equity would set aside any contract) accompanied the measure, or such striking evidence of national injury . . . as to make war or any other evil preferable." The immediate issue was, in Washington's view, whether the results of the Jay Treaty could be foreseen as overridingly disastrous. "Every unbiased mind," Washington believed, "will answer in the negative."

Since the situation was not truly extraordinary, then, for the House to establish the precedent it sought, "would render the treaty-making power not only a nullity but such an absolute absurdity as to reflect disgrace on the framers of it." How ridiculous to have empowered the President and the Senate to make treaties that became the supreme law of the land and yet to have vested the House with a general power of veto![9]

Admittedly, the House fitted Washington's political preconceptions more than the Senate in two particulars: its members represented what Washington regarded as the basic national subdivision, the neighborhood; and it was not organized according to states' rights, but on a national basis according to population. However, there were two serious considerations on the opposite side of the ledger: secrecy and consistency.

The House was a large body that turned over completely every two years. Among its members were tyros in government and wild men from wild districts. From so numerous, heterogeneous, and inexperienced a body, universal discretion could not be expected — and one mouth babbling to the newspapers could embarrass or even sink sensitive negotiations. Furthermore, a nation that hoped to achieve international agreements — and, indeed, safety — could not tack around in the sea of diplomacy to suit a legislative body purposely set up to reflect every domestic change of wind. Washington believed that it was only "after time has been given for cool and deliberate reflection that the *real* voice of the people can be heard."[10]

Washington, who never saw a problem shorn of its application, knew that the Republican-dominated House would, if permitted, sabotage the Jay Treaty. This would not only reopen and aggravate the wounds with

England, but would serve notice on the world that the United States government was not in a position to negotiate a treaty that could be relied on. Washington had several times described himself as trying to steer the United States between the Scylla of war with England and the Charybdis of war with France. How could he steer a ship without a rudder?

The House's thrust did not (as a Constitutional amendment would) include any machinery to take the place of what was being overthrown. The Senate, with its Federalist majority, would surely not abandon its prerogative without a struggle. As for the Federalist suggestions that Washington frustrate the clamping shut of the purse by soliciting private contributions from the affluent, or appointing to the Jay commissions men rich enough not to need pay — that would hardly appease the democrats.

A forewarning of the dislocations to be expected if the House persisted was what Washington called, in writing his estate manager, "a suspension in purchasing, shipping, and the insurance of all sorts of property."[11] Fear of the action threatened by the House was making American merchants keep their vessels home lest, before the voyages were over, British cruisers be induced to fall on American shipping. The value of farm products, being dependent to a considerable extent on export, plummeted. Prosperity was shifting towards depression.

Should the House actually block the Jay Treaty, not only would American vessels leave their anchors down but merchants would forfeit the indemnities promised for previous depredations. The frontier forts would not be surrendered, and the outraged Britons, their own treaty violated, would be even less willing to encourage the northwestern Indians to abide by the treaty they had signed with Wayne. More than ever, the frontier would flame.

Arguing that England would not risk war with the United States, her best customer, the Republicans concluded that a strong stand would make his Britannic Majesty back down. Yet the British lion had so far shown no symptoms of lowering her tail in response to any outrage expressed by her former colonies. And if she responded with violence, with how much heat would American public opinion react? Washington believed that civil confusions, once started, were very hard to stop. Even if the pro-French leadership tried to avoid going over the brink, war with Great Britain might result.

Although he never despaired, Washington was inclined, in moments of stress, to foresee and prepare for the worst. The conservative pro-British community would consider an actual or looming war to have been excited by the radicals to serve their domestic ends; while the pro-French might well conceive that their political enemies were potential traitors who should, like the Tories during the Revolution, be violently restrained. In addition to fighting on the ocean and the frontiers, there might well be civil war in the streets and fields of the United States. And, since the balance of the factions broke on geographic lines, the eventual result might well be that the United States would separate into two or more nations.*

Communications being what they then were, any hostilities with England induced by action in the House were not likely to boil up until after the next election. Could that election be used to establish a less hysterical situation at home? Alas, there was no way that the contests for senators and representatives could be kept, if the House upset the apple cart, from further exacerbating party passions.

But what of the Presidential race? Washington hated to ask himself the question. In a conversation he held with John Adams on March 24, he said over and over, as if he were repeating a magic spell, that whatever the result of the House's bid, it would be of no personal consequence to him. However, he received a letter from Jay: "Attachment to you as well as to our country urges me to hope and pray that you will not leave the work unfinished. Remain with us at least while the storm lasts, and until you can retire like the sun in a calm, unclouded evening."[12]

If Washington were willing to accept a third term, he might not receive, as twice before, a unanimous vote of the electoral college, but surely there would be no real contest.† And the old standard, around which the nation had so many times rallied, would still be waving as a rendezvous for those who wished to find a middle ground.

Quietly, without doing more than hinting his resolve to anyone, Washington had for some time been making it clear that he would serve no longer. Now he wrote Jay that "the trouble and perplexities" with which he had been inundated as President, "added to the weight of years which

---

* The Federal Union was only eight years old and had not been really tried in any crisis. When it was three times as old (1814) and its political forms had evolved considerably further, there was serious talk in New England of secession as a result of the final outbreak of the long-avoided war with Britain.

† It was John Marshall's opinion that no one would have dared oppose Washington and thus his electoral vote would again have been unanimous.[13]

have passed over me, have worn away my mind more than my body, and renders ease and retirement indispensably necessary to both." But he recognized the possibility that "such imperious circumstance as I hope and trust will not happen" might render his retirement "dishonorable."[14]

Floating like a buzzard over the dark landscape ahead was the possibility that, if Washington accepted a third term, he might die in office.° This would not only frustrate forever his yearning for renewed peace at Mount Vernon, but would damage both his own reputation and the American republican experiment.

When Washington was being urged to abandon his post-Revolutionary retirement, he had expressed worry lest it be assumed that he could not resist the lure of power. Madison had replied that he could extinguish any such suspicion by returning to retirement. If he were to die in office, his friends would make clear that he had been serving duty not ambition.[15] But he could no longer count on those old Virginia friends who knew with what reluctance he had left his farm. Was not Madison himself a leader of the party whose publicists were accusing him of monarchical desires?

More important still was the fact that republican government had not yet demonstrated that it could peacefully leap the hurdle of succession. What had happened in France, where the guillotine helped along change in office, pointed indeed in the opposite direction. It would crown Washington's political efforts if he could retire from office to the accompaniment of a free election choosing his successor. This would be the consumating precedent he would leave to his people, the final governmental achievement he would will to the world. As he himself put it, he wished to give "an early example of rotation in an office of so high and delicate a nature" to "accord with the republican spirit of our Constitution and the ideas of liberty and safety entertained by the people."[16] But if he died in office, succession would follow the monarchical form: "The President is dead: Long live the President!"

All in all, Washington concluded that the effort in the House was bringing "the Constitution to the brink of a precipice" and putting "the peace, happiness, and prosperity of the country into eminent danger." This was "one of those great occasions than which none more important has occurred or probably may occur again."[17]

° Even retirement did not enable Washington to live out the third Presidential term.

Washington delivered his answer to the House on March 30, 1796.° It stated that the House had no constitutional right to executive documents except in the case of "an impeachment which the resolution has not expressed." The need for caution and secrecy in foreign negotiations had made the Constitution entrust them to the legislative body that had "a small number of members." That treaties were obligatory if ratified by the President with the Senate's approval was understood by foreign nations and had never before been questioned by the House. The state conventions which had ratified the Constitution had, as various of their proceedings showed, understood that the treaty-making provision included commercial treaties. Following its spirit of amity and mutual concession, the Constitution had created a balance by giving special powers to the Senate as a protection for the small states. Washington reminded the House that the journals of the Constitutional Convention had been given him for safekeeping: they revealed that a proposition that no treaty should be binding until ratified by law had been specifically rejected. It being perfectly clear that the assent of the House was not necessary, and it being essential that the boundaries fixed between the different branches by the Constitution should be preserved, Washington's duty forbade his compliance with the House's request.[19]

The Republican leadership had been convinced that the President, who had always sought to occupy the center, would not "hazard a breach with the House." They had expected that, if he did not agree he would suggest a compromise. His flat refusal struck like a bombshell. The Federalist representative Fisher Ames noted that the majority "party seemed wild on its being read."[20]

It was now clear that the leaders of the House's effort had made a colossal tactical error. Although securing the executive papers would have increased the prestige of the House and probably have given an advantage in attacking the treaty, the documents were by no means necessary to the House's basic contention. The appropriation could be denied by refusing rather than passing a bill, which would have given the President no opportunity for a veto. If the President adhered to his so far invariable rule of not moving out of his province to comment on legislative action in

---

° Preparing a draft of his own, Washington had also asked Hamilton for a draft. "Notwithstanding the anxious solicitude which was visible in all quarters," he held back his version until Hamilton's arrived. The New Yorker had, as usual, been verbose. Washington wrote Hamilton that he was going ahead with his own draft since it embraced the "principles" and it would take too long to copy in Hamilton's "reasonings."[18]

which the executive was not involved, his convictions need never have been expressed. But now his prestige had been brought to bear against the claims of the House. How could he so grievously have let the Republican leaders down? Why, oh why, had they stirred the old man up as with a sharp stick?

The day after he had publicly refused the papers, Washington further defied the House's claims by asking the Senate's approval for the appointment of commissioners to carry out various provisions in the Jay Treaty. John Adams commented, "The old hero looks very grave of late." He expected from the House "a fresh demand with strictures," but the Republican leadership had no desire to provoke him into further statements.[21]

Having gone into a Committee of the Whole* to discuss the President's message, the House immediately passed by twenty votes a declaration that they had a constitutional right and duty to consider the expediency of the treaty. Further ballots revealed that the Republicans had the votes to wreck the treaty if they wished to. Unable to keep his mind on anything else, Washington failed to remind Pearce that the time had come to put his favorite jack up for stud.[22]

The issue, Washington believed, was "agitating the public mind in a higher degree than it has been at any period during the Revolution."[23] However, he adhered, even more rigorously than he had during the debate over ratifying the Constitution, to his rule of keeping out of controversy. Then he had written private letters. Now he wrote down no further opinion whatsoever. This was principle but it was also good tactics. His stand was completely clear. Let other men rant, and accuse, and wave their fists in the air!

The Federalists set out to flood the House with petitions. "We must," Hamilton wrote, "seize and carry along with us the public opinion."[24] Some months before, this would have seemed impossible. But now the very issue which Jefferson hoped would carry the Constitutional change was proving a boomerang. The extreme violence with which the treaty had been attacked had encouraged a backlash. It was as if the public had been warned of a man-eating tiger only to be confronted with an unattractive and disagreeable alley cat. How could one reconcile statements like Jefferson's that the agreement was "really nothing more than a treaty of alliance between England and the Anglomen of this country against

---

* This was a method of reaching a decision which would be automatically reconsidered when the report of the "committee" was considered by the House in its official capacity.

the legislature and the people of the United States"[25] with the facts that it secured the surrender of the western forts so desired for frontier peace; that it set up machinery, however cumbersome, by which American merchants could gain indemnity for their losses to British cruisers; that it promised in terms, however irritating to the United States and unsatisfactory to France, a continuance, now under the protection of the British navy, of the transatlantic commerce which had been bringing prosperity to the entire United States? Best of all, it warded away what seemed a very real danger of war with England.

At a time when there were no public sports, no playlets flying through the air; at a time when oratory was admired as the public today admires pitching or broken field running, the whole nation followed the debate in the House. After various small fry had spoken, the Republicans loosed their champion, the Swiss immigrant Albert Gallatin. That, as he advocated a pro-French policy, Gallatin spoke with a thick French accent was — despite cries of "Shame! Shame!" from his cohorts — pointed out by the Federalists. However, what he said was incisive and persuasive. He rehearsed the constitutional contradiction. He argued that the government would not collapse since the Federalists would obviously not permit the destruction of something in which they had so much power. Mocking the idea that England would fight, he stated that the House, by destroying the treaty, would force further concessions from the British.[26]

The Federalists brought on their champion with the maximum of drama. Fisher Ames was sick in his native Massachusetts. He was, so the report ran, perhaps dying, probably too weak to reach Philadelphia. Bravely, he set out on the painful journey, collapsing here and there in the presence of newspaper editors, and then tottering on again. At last he was in the capital city, but could he reach the House, could he talk loud enough to be heard? He did speak on April 28, pointing out in a tremulous voice that he had so little time to live that he could not be moved by selfish motives: none of his hearers were less likely to be affected by whatever decision the House would make.*

Tuning his voice up to its true magic, Ames argued that the treaty had been legally ratified, and no one claimed that it was truly fatal. Every criticism was on some small point. Would the public allow the faith of the United States to be broken on a small wheel? And should the United

---

* Ames lived until 1808.

States submit to the influence of France? Any foreign influence of American policy was too much and ought to be destroyed.

When Ames came to the consequences of breaking the treaty, he painted a horrible picture of war. The Indians would descend again on the frontier. "I would swell my voice to . . . reach every log house beyond the mountains!" cried the ailing man. "I would say . . . wake from your false security! Your cruel dangers . . . are soon to be renewed. The wounds, yet unhealed, are to be torn open again. In the daytime, your path through the woods will be ambushed. The darkness of midnight will glitter with the blaze of your dwellings. You are a father: the blood of your son shall fatten your cornfield! You are a mother, the war whoop shall wake the sleep of the cradle." And so on until Ames, his final peroration completed, collapsed into the arms of his supporters.[27]

Even Ames's opponents wept. As soon as he considered his lips unsealed, Washington commented, "In the opinion of most that heard it delivered or have read it since, his reasoning is unanswerable."* Romantic history attributes to Ames's great oratorical feat the fact that two days later the House abandoned its pretentions and appropriated $80,800 to implement the Jay Treaty. Washington's own comment was, "Nothing, I believe, but the torrent of petitions and remonstrances which were pouring in from all the eastern and middle states, and were beginning to come pretty strongly from that of Virginia . . . would have produced a division (fifty-one to forty-eight) in favor of the appropriation."[29]

Madison wrote Monroe, "A crisis which ought to have been managed as to fortify the republican cause has left it in a very crippled condition. . . . The name of the President and the alarm of war have had a greater effect than were apprehended on our side." Jefferson added, "Congress has risen. You will see by their proceedings the truth of what I have always observed to you: that one man outweighs them all in influence over the people, who have supported his judgment against their own and that of their representatives. Republicanism must lie on its oars, resign the vessel to its pilot, and themselves to the course he thinks best for them."[30]

---

* Washington was soon writing Pearce that if Ames dropped in at Mount Vernon on his travels for his health, he was to be served the best wine.[28]

30

Finis with Jefferson

ACCORDING to John Marshall, Washington's negative to the call for papers accompanied by his firm denial of the House's claim to a role in treaty making "appeared to break the last cord of that attachment which had theretofore bound some of the active leaders of the opposition to the person of the President. Amidst all the agitations and irritations of party, a sincere respect and real affection for the Chief Magistrate, the remnant of former friendship, had still lingered in the bosoms of some who had engaged with ardor in the political contests of the day. But, if the last spark of this affection was not now extinguished, it was at least concealed under the more active passions of the moment."[1]

The violence of the feelings engendered in some breasts was revealed in an open letter to the President printed by the radical publicist William Duane. From the fatal moment when Washington refused the demand of the House, he wrote, "the brightness of your countenance is said to have faded . . . and like our first parents, you have borne about you the visible evidence of internal regret." Duane went on to write of a "tyrannical act"; "fatal forms of state secrecy"; "privilege of office"; "Machiavellian policy"; "monarchical privilege"; etc., etc.[2]

In reporting to his wife that he had gone to the theater with Washington, John Adams stated, "The turpitude of the Jacobins touches him more nearly than he owns in words. All the studied efforts of the Federalists to counterbalance abuse by compliment don't answer the end."[3]

To Humphreys, Washington complained, "I am attacked for a steady opposition to every measure which has a tendency to disturb the peace and tranquillity" of the country. "But these attacks, unjust and unpleasant as they are, will occasion no change in my conduct, nor will they work any other effect in my mind than to increase the anxious desire . . . to enjoy in the shades of retirement the consolation of having rendered my country every service my abilities were competent to, uninfluenced by pecuniary or ambitious considerations. . . . Malignity therefore may dart her shafts, but no earthly power can deprive me of the consolation of knowing that I have not in the course of my administration been guilty of a *willful* error, however numerous they may have been from other causes."[4]

The truth was that Washington had suffered a major failure. He had intended to relinquish to his successor a unified nation, marching like a band of united friends along a smooth highway that, by mounting ever towards more national prosperity and strength, demonstrated to all the world the glories of free government. He had wished to bring together all rational points of view in his person, his Cabinet, his administration. He could, it is true, still command majority support for ends he considered essential, but in doing so he had to batter to one side a vocal and numerous group of his fellow citizens. This usually proved to be the group led by two of his once closest and most trusted coadjutors: Jefferson and Madison. Washington had fought against the spirit of party, but the spirit of party had won, opening up a fissure so wide that even he could no longer straddle it.

Early in July 1796, Washington received a long letter from a former intimate correspondent now usually silent, from Jefferson. It had been inspired by the leak of a confidential governmental document.

To the Cabinet meeting which had in 1793 agreed on the Neutrality Proclamation, Washington had presented an agenda (probably drawn up by Hamilton) which listed all the major questions raised by the newly declared war, including whether or not the French alliance should be denounced. As it turned out, Washington adjourned the meeting before it got to the matter of the French alliance (which, indeed, had never been denounced).° Copies of the agenda had been possessed by only five men: Washington, Jefferson, Hamilton, Knox, and Randolph. But, during the debates in the House on the Jay Treaty, a copy had been circulated by Republican leaders, to demonstrate that it had always been the intention

---

° See chapters 1 and 2 of this volume.

of the administration to cut all ties with France, and in the process, France's throat. The House effort having failed, the document was given to the editor of the *Aurora,* who published it on June 9, 1796.

Jefferson's letter proved to be a passionate denial — "I attest everything sacred and honorable" — that it was he who leaked the paper. Washington, who suspected Randolph, must have thought it interesting that Jefferson was so worked up for fear that the suspicion would fall on him. What Jefferson went on to say was even more interesting. He insisted that he had never written for the public press, nor had he, with one partial exception, ever corrected anyone else's contributions. He knew that "a miserable tergiversator"° had represented to Washington that he was now "engaged in the bustle of politics and in turbulence and intrigue against the government. I never believed for a moment that this could make any impression on you or that your knowledge of me would not overweigh the slander of an intriguer, dirtily employed in sifting the conversations of my table, where alone he could hear of me." Jefferson, he continued, disliked "political discussions," but when they could not be avoided without affectation, he expressed his sentiments "with the same independence here which I have practiced everywhere, and which is inseparable from my nature."

Having made his protestations of unconcern with politics and intrigue, Jefferson belied them. Would Washington please return to him a document in Hamilton's handwriting he had given the President at the time of the *Little Sarah* crisis: "One loves to possess arms though they hope never to have occasion for them. They possess my paper in my own handwriting. It is just I should possess theirs."

Then Jefferson turned to the nonpolitical interest he most shared with Washington: "I put away this disgusting dish of old fragments and talk to you of peas and clover."[5]

Washington's previous letter to Jefferson, now some eight months old, had been signed not "affectionately" as had once been the President's wont, but "with very great esteem, etc."[6] Now Jefferson sent "very affectionate compliments to Mrs. Washington," adding, "I have the honor to be, with great and sincere esteem and respect, dear sir, your most obedient and most humble servant."[7]

° Jefferson, probably at a later date, wrote in the margin of the copy he kept of this letter the name "General H. Lee."

Washington must have wondered why Jefferson wished to persuade him that he was taking no part in the opposition to the government.* Being no fool, Washington surely noted that, while denying that he wrote for the press, Jefferson made no mention of political letters. It is improbable that Washington could have realized how regularly Jefferson corresponded on political matters with Madison and Giles, leaders in the House, and with Monroe, the American minister to France, but Washington's reply reveals that he was far from soothed by Jefferson's protestations:

"As you have mentioned the subject yourself, it would not be frank, candid, or friendly to conceal that your conduct has been represented as derogatory from that opinion *I* had conceived you entertained for me." Jefferson was quoted as having "denounced me as a person under a dangerous influence." His answer had "invariably" been that he had never suspected Jefferson of "insincerity"; that if Jefferson "would retrace my public conduct while he was in the administration, abundant proofs would occur to him that truth and right decisions were the *sole* objects of my pursuit; that there were as many instances within his *own* knowledge of my having decided *against* as in *favor* of the opinions of the person evidently alluded to [Hamilton]; and moreover, that I was no believer in the infallibility of the politics or measures of *any man living*. In short, that I was no party man myself, and the first wish of my heart was, if parties did exist, to reconcile them.

"To this I may add, and very truly, that, until within the last year or two ago, I had no conception that parties would, or even could, go the length I have been witness to; nor did I believe until lately, that it was within the bounds of probability, hardly within those of possibility, that, while I was using my utmost exertions to establish a national character of our own, independent, as far as our obligations and justice would permit, of every nation of the earth; and wished, by steering a steady course, to preserve this country from the horrors of a desolating war, that I should be accused of being the enemy of one nation, and subject to the influence of another; and to prove it, that every act of my administration would be tortured, and the grossest and most insidious misrepresentations of them

---

* Jefferson's motivations, which were undoubtedly extremely complex, must be left for explanation to his biographers. It is worth noting, however, that, during the following January, Jefferson pointed out to one of his followers that the people would support the President in whatever he did. "I have long thought therefore it was for the Republican interest to soothe him" by flattering him when possible and otherwise keeping silent. It would be unwise for the Republicans to "render him desperate as to their affections or entirely indifferent to their wishes."[8]

be made (by giving one side *only* of a subject, and that too in such exaggerated and indecent terms as could scarcely be applied to a Nero, a notorious defaulter, or even to a common pickpocket). But enough of this; I have already gone farther in the expression of my feelings than I intended."

Washington could not remember the details of the *Little Sarah* matter to which Jefferson referred, but would examine his files.° Then he followed Jefferson into an agricultural dissertation. He concluded, "Mrs. Washington begs you to accept her best wishes, and with very great esteem, etc."[9]

This was the last written communication which was more than pure routine that ever passed between George Washington and Thomas Jefferson.

° Eventually Washington ordered that a copy (not the original as asked) of Hamilton's statement be sent to Jefferson.

Henrietta Liston, the charming Scottish wife of the British minister, whom Washington admired but who ruled that the President had "a cold heart." Portrait by Gilbert Stuart. (Present location undetermined)

31

Thunder on the Left

AFTER the House gave in on the Jay Treaty, the Congressional session proceeded without any more fireworks.* The British delighted Washington by quietly evacuating the frontier forts on schedule. He was personally gratified at the recall of the ever complaining and disagreeable British minister, Hammond (who did not hide his dislike for Washington). To take Hammond's place, the British sent Robert Liston, a middle-aged and middle-class Scot, who had risen to high responsibilities in the diplomatic service despite a lack of family connections. Liston was as conciliatory as Hammond had been cantankerous; he did not meddle in American politics; he shared with Washington a passion for farming; and he had a delightful wife. The Listons became close friends to the Washingtons.

Henrietta Liston's blond hair was turning white but she had preserved that fresh and delicate complexion for which Scottish beauties are famous. Gilbert Stuart, who so often painted handsome women as social war-horses or pompous fools, immortalized Henrietta's charm in one of his gentlest, warmest, most decorative portraits. She wrote down at some length her reminiscences of Washington. They reveal that he opened to her, as to almost no one else, his personal emotions and memories. She was impressed by the old hero and flattered by his friendship and yet found their relationship disappointing. She sought in him more visible fire

---

* The House agreed, with only the minimum of party splitting, to Washington's request for additional sums for the foreign service, and the Federalist majority in the Senate reluctantly gave the south more representation in the national councils by accepting Washington's recommendation that the Southwest Territory be reorganized as the State of Tennessee.[1]

that would explain his great career. Although on one occasion that she recorded he kissed her, she accused him of having a "cold heart."[2]

Most amazingly, Washington appealed to the sympathies of the handsome matron with tales of his early hardships. He had been "needy" in his childhood and forced to follow what Mrs. Liston regarded as the lowly profession of "land surveyor." To her, Washington admitted his early ambition to join the British regular army: "He studied the [military] profession as one by which he was to make his bread." Her reaction to these reminiscences was to wonder how a man from such a background had achieved such "perfect good breeding and a correct knowledge of even the etiquette of a court. . . .

"His education," so Mrs. Liston's memoir continued, "had been confined; he knew no language but his own, and he expressed himself in that rather forcibly than elegantly. . . . Letter writing seemed in him a peculiar talent. His style was plain, correct, and nervous. Ill-natured people said that Washington did not write his own public letters, answers to addresses, etc. This is not true. I have known him to write in his usual impressive manner when no person was near to aid him; and what may seem conclusive, he has always written better than the gentlemen to whom the merit of his letters was ascribed. . . .

"His first and last pleasure appeared to be farming; and on that theme he always talked freely, being on other topics extremely cautious not to commit himself, and never spoke on any subject of which he was not master."[3]

When Mrs. Liston objected to Washington concerning his determination to retire, "he smiling asked if I remembered Gil Blas's story of the Archbishop of Granada?* 'I feared,' he said, 'the same thing might happen to me.' "[5]

Although she was to weep so voluminously when Washington publicly stepped down from the Presidency that her behavior became a matter of gossip, Mrs. Liston noted that he did not deserve the credit for his voluntary relinquishment of power that he was commonly accorded. "He had for eight years sacrificed his natural taste, first habits, and early propensities — I believe we may truly say — solely to what he thought the good of his country. But he was become tired of his situation, fretted by the opposition often made to his measures, and his pride revolted by

---

* The Archbishop promises to reward his servant, Gil Blas, for warning him when his sermons showed that his powers were deteriorating. After Gil Blas had carried out this instruction, the furious Archbishop discharged him.[4]

[284]

the ingratitude he experienced, and he was also disgusted by the scurrilous abuse lavished upon him by his political enemies."[6]

The Federalists were anxious to have Washington put off committing
himself for as long as possible — "if a storm gather," Hamilton asked,
"how can you retreat?" — but the Republicans were eager to see him go.
On May 14, 1796, Madison wrote Monroe in cipher, "It is now generally
understood that the President will retire, and Jefferson is the object on
one side, Adams apparently on the other." As for Washington, he wrote
firmly to his nephew, Robert Lewis, that he would "close my public life
on March 4 [1797], after which no consideration under heaven that I can
foresee shall again draw me from the walks of private life."[7]

About the first of May, 1796, Washington showed Hamilton, who happened to be in Philadelphia, the draft he had prepared for an address in
which he would say farewell to the American people. He hoped that
Hamilton would help him revise it. There was no great hurry. "As there
will be another session of Congress before the political existence of the
present House of Representatives and my own will constitutionally ex-
pire," he did not intend to say anything to the legislature concerning his
determination to withdraw, but to hold the announcement until "it shall
become indispensably necessary for the information of the electors previous to the election, which this year will be delayed until the seventh
of December."[8]

Washington set out for Mount Vernon in mid-June for what he hoped
would be a peaceful stay of two and a half months. By late June, the political skies had so darkened with a new crisis that he regretted "exceedingly" (as he wrote Hamilton) that he had not published his "valedictory
address" the day after the adjournment of Congress. He would have been
only "announcing *publicly* what seems to be well understood and indus-
triously propagated *privately*." And, since the announcement would have
preceded "any unfavorable change in our foreign relations," he would
have headed off the charge that he had delayed until "the current was
turned against me." Now his retreat might prove "difficult and embarrassing."[9]

Monroe had promised the French government to show them the Jay
Treaty in time for them to advise whether the United States should ratify
or not, but he could secure no copy. That the American minister, whom
they considered their friend, was being thus kept in the dark did not pre-

dispose the French authorities in favor of the treaty, and when, after ratification, a copy finally arrived, both they and Monroe were horrified. Monroe, indeed, believed that he had been deceived; had been led by Washington to give false assurances to the French concerning American friendship and the extent of Jay's powers; had, in sum, been wickedly used as an instrument to keep the French passive while Washington's administration perfidiously entered into an alliance with Great Britain. Monroe was not one to keep his mouth shut, nor was his house guest, Thomas Paine.[10]

As Monroe sent anguished complaints to his fellow Republicans in the United States, the French delayed their official protest. It finally came on March 11 in a memorandum from Foreign Minister De La Croix to Monroe. The first section, "Inexecution of Treaties," dealt only with various particulars of enforcement under the Neutrality Proclamation. Most significantly, the French could not — despite the charges rife in the United States — find in the Jay Treaty any specific violations of the old treaties between the United States and France. But De La Croix nonetheless insisted, "It would be easy to prove that the United States in that treaty have sacrificed *knowingly* and *evidently* their connection with the [French] Republic, and the rights the most essential and least contested of neutrality."*

The French insisted that Jay's inclusion as contraband of materials necessary for building ships — which France, being denuded of forests, needed if she were to have a navy — was an evident departure from neutrality. By not restricting the seizure of foodstuffs to circumstances when a port was effectively blockaded, the treaty "tacitly acknowledges the pretentions of England to extend the blockade to our colonies and even to France by the force of proclamation alone." Jefferson's efforts when Secretary of State to support a more liberal interpretation of neutral rights had constituted a "tacit engagement" to France which the United States had no right to abandon. The French minister submitted it to "Mr. Monroe [not, it will be noted, to the President of the United States]† to

---

* In his subsequent open letter to Washington, Paine expressed the French attitude in his usual vivid style: "A man, such as the world calls a sharper and versed, as Jay must be supposed to be, in the quibbles of the law, may find a way to enter into engagements . . . in such a manner as to cheat some other party without that party being able, as the phrase is, *to take the law of him.*"[11]

† The French government liked to think of Monroe not as a representative of the American executive, which they were assured was pro-British, but of the American people, whom they considered their supporters. Beverley Bond, the leading historian of the Monroe mission, states that Monroe, having accepted this conception, felt justified in taking his own line apart from the government he was supposed to represent.[12]

judge in what point these concessions accord with the obligations by which the United States have contracted to defend our colonial possessions."[13]

Monroe reported home that the French intended to recall Adet, their present minister, sending a special representative who would express outrage and sever diplomatic relations with the United States. Washington's quiet at Mount Vernon was further violated by a letter from Gouverneur Morris repeating the report in London that the French representative would be accompanied by a fleet and "be directed to exact in the space of fifteen days a categorical answer to certain questions."[14]

Washington could hardly believe that the French would engage in such "folly and madness. . . . Yet as it seems to be an era of strange vicissitudes and unaccountable transactions attended with sort of irresistible fatality in many of them, I shall not be surprised at any event that may happen, however extraordinary it may be."

Washington wished that, should an ultimatum be given, his answer could be "short and decisive to this effect: We are an independent nation, and act for ourselves. Having fulfilled and being willing to fulfil (as far as we are able)* our engagements with other nations, and having decided on and strictly observed a neutral conduct towards belligerent powers, from an unwillingness to involve ourselves in war, we will not be dictated to by the politics of any nation under heaven, farther than treaties require of us." But Washington felt that a strong reply was made impractical by "the unhappy differences among ourselves."[15]

Madison was told that Washington had said, "If war comes, it originated here — not there. The people of this country, it would seem, will never be satisfied until they become a department of France. It shall be my business to prevent it."[16]

Viewing the situation in the lurid light of the "calumnies" circulated in the United States to demonstrate that his administration was under the influence of Great Britain, Washington was, indeed, inclined to blame French dissatisfaction on American propaganda. The threatened embassy and ultimatum, he wrote angrily, had been encouraged by the proceedings in the House and also "perhaps by communications of influential

---

* This phrase kept open a way out should the French representative demand (Washington thought he might) that the United States honor "the guarantee" to defend France's West Indian possessions that still pended as part of the old Treaty of Alliance. As Jefferson had suggested when he was Secretary of State, the United States could claim that with the best will in the world she could do nothing as she was not a naval power.

men in this *country* through a medium which ought to be the last to engage in it."[17]

That medium was Monroe.° Whether or not this was a basic cause of French dissatisfaction, the American minister to France and the Republican leaders were indeed in close communication. Madison and Jefferson kept Monroe informed of Republican suspicions and dissatisfactions, while Monroe sent his allies in the United States copies of the theoretically confidential communications he was receiving from his government. He wished, he explained, "to put in your possession facts which may be useful . . . perhaps to the public and certainly to myself."[18]

Monroe's Paris-inspired suggestions would have set on end what little hair of his own Washington had left. To Madison, Monroe had written in cipher that Great Britain's greatest dread was war with the United States. Having jettisoned the Jay Treaty, the United States could and should take the western posts by force, perhaps capturing Canada — with Bermuda for good measure — while the British lion cowered, afraid to strike back.[19]

These letters Washington did not, of course, see. However, Pickering showed him an intercepted essay prepared by Monroe for anonymous publication in the *Aurora*. It was to be the opener of a series of such communications that would inform the American people of the "actual state of things" in France. Monroe suggested that his contribution could be called a letter from "a gentleman from Paris to his friends in Philadelphia," subsequent installments being "occasionally varied as from some other quarter, as from Bordeaux, that it may not appear to be a regular thing." The installment Washington held in his hand told of dismay in France caused by the Jay Treaty.[20]

Wolcott informed Washington that "a gentleman worthy of confidence" had seen instructions in the hand of Adet ordering French agents to help elect Jefferson. Other Frenchmen were being sent through the west to create a new nation there politically connected with France.† Spain, so international rumor ran, was going to cede Louisiana back to France, which would be the signal for a march up the Mississippi Valley against Canada. Washington's advisers linked mysterious pro-French and anti-ad-

---

° From his post in Holland, John Quincy Adams wrote his father (who may well have shown the letter to Washington) that Americans in Paris, including Monroe and Paine, were misleading the French to believe that the United States was now actually an ally of Great Britain.

† French activity in the west was a fact, but, of course, nothing new. Jefferson referred to it and Monroe officially reported it.[21]

ministration letters received by western leaders to the circle around Monroe, and insisted that it was impossible that the American minister could have been ignorant of them. Gallatin was reported to be deep in French intrigue and in perpetual secret conference with Adet.[22]

Washington had once (as the development of Arnold's treason demonstrated) been dangerously unsuspicious of plots, but now he was perturbed by a sequence of newspaper reports which first stated that he would come from Mount Vernon to Philadelphia for the Fourth of July, and then that he had not appeared because of a carriage accident. Although he could not "fathom" the "scheme," he was sure that it served some "insidious purpose," as did "other reports, however unfounded. . . . Evidence enough has been given that truth or falsehood is equally used and indifferent to that class of men."[23]

The news Washington received was given a more ominous sound by the fact that the vessel involved had been named after his intended place of retirement. The *Mount Vernon* (American registry) had been captured by a French privateer. The President feared that this signaled a new hostile policy. He saw "strong ground to believe the French mean to continue the practice of seizing our vessels in their commerce with Great Britain. It is the buzz of the democrats, and the *Aurora* is evidently preparing the public mind for the event as the *natural* consequence of the British treaty." Washington wrote Pickering that he would abandon his own Mount Vernon for Philadelphia if necessary. In the meanwhile, would the Cabinet consider requesting an immediate explanation from Adet? And would they also consider whether it would be advisable to send "an extra character to France to explain the views of the government and to ascertain those of France"?[24]

The conception of a special envoy, which had already been discussed in Federalist circles, was an obvious one after the Jay and Pinckney missions. Washington wrote Hamilton for his opinion on whether he could initiate such a mission without securing the advice of the Senate. If not, was there sufficient ground for calling a special session? Should an envoy extraordinary be decided on, who "would not be obnoxious to one party or the other? . . . And what should be done with Mr. M — [Monroe]?" A final ominous thought: Would the French make matters worse by refusing to receive the President's representative? "Their reliance on a party in this country for support," Washington commented dourly, "would stimulate them to this conduct."

Washington was no longer apologizing for the Jay Treaty, and he had warmed up to its negotiator. He asked Hamilton to discuss the new problems with that veteran diplomat, "as I have great confidence in the ability and purity of Jay's views." Having gone this far, the President seems to have felt anxiety lest the two Federalists take too much on themselves. He explained, "I am anxious always to compare the opinions of those in whom I confide with one another, and again (without being bound by them) with my own, that I may extract what good I can."[25]

As Washington waited for a reply, the situation boiled confusedly. Reporting that the Directory was being dissuaded from sending a representative with an ultimatum, Monroe took the credit for himself and his party: he had represented to the Directory that such behavior would make more difficult the position of the American friends of France. Washington snorted at this vision of the pro-French party as an asset. The whole threat, he suspected, "may have originated in a contrivance of the opposers of the government [those in France, of course, which meant Monroe, Paine, etc.] to see what effect such threats would work, and finding none that could answer their purpose and no safe ground to stand on if they pushed matters to extremity, the matter may terminate in gasconade."[26]

Washington blamed French rage concerning the Jay Treaty on failure by Monroe to give "a just and timely representation of the fact [s], with accompanying explanations," which he "had it in his power and was instructed to make." The rage seemed to be finding expression on the ocean. Although the case of the *Mount Vernon* was proving inconclusive — the vessel might have been sold surreptitiously to British owners — Adet had been "mysterious" in his answers concerning French naval policy, and ships of undoubted American ownership were being captured.[27] Some positive new move in relation to France was still called for.

Washington's advisers agreed that he could not appoint an extraordinary representative during the recess of the Senate, but they ruled that he could replace, in anticipation of consent, one regular minister with another. And neither Washington nor any of his circle doubted that Franco-American relations would be improved by the recall of Monroe.[28]

The first step was to find a replacement. Marshall refused. Then, as a long shot, Washington offered the post to Charles Cotesworth Pinckney, the older brother of the former minister to London,° who had already

---

° Having completed his brilliant treaty with Spain, Thomas Pinckney had asked to come home. Washington had replaced him in London with the Federalist senator Rufus King.[29]

turned down appointments as Associate Justice, Secretary of War, and Secretary of State. Particularly anxious to secure the South Carolinian because he was *persona grata* with the Jeffersonians, Washington importuned Pinckney: "Unless the virtuous and independent men of this country will come forward," the nation would fall into the hands of men "who are more disposed to promote the views of another [country] than establish a national character of their own."[30]

To Washington's great relief, Pinckney accepted.

Washington recognized that the recall of Monroe would "set all the envenomed pens to work."* He urged Pickering to go over all the official correspondence concerning France, "from the period matters began to change from their ancient habits and to assume their new form . . . with as critical an eye as Mr. Bache or any of his numerous correspondents or communicants would do, that, if there is anything in them (not recollected by me) that can be tortured into an unfriendly disposition towards France and not required by the neutral policy adopted by the executive, approved by the people, and sanctioned by the legislature; or which the peace, honor, and safety of this country did not require, that I may be apprized of it, as my conviction of the contrary is strong."[32]

But even if the executive was above reproach, how, under Washington's policy of never fighting back, could it be arranged that "the enlightened public could have a clear and comprehensive view of the facts"? Washington mulled over the matter for almost a month, and then decided that the causes for Monroe's recall "should be spoken of *unofficially* by the officers of government."[33]

Among Washington's other innovations, he invented the executive news leak.

---

* Despite Washington's desire to protect himself from "scribblers," he had quite complacently allowed his farming passions to put him in a position which would, had it been found out, have given Bache the most extreme joy. The previous May, when Thomas Pinckney was still minister to London, Washington asked him to thank the British foreign minister "for his politeness in causing a special permit to be sent to Liverpool for the shipment of two sacks of the field peas and a like quantity of winter vetches, which I had requested our consul to send me for seed." It had not occurred to him that such a permit was needed, but he was grateful for it. Although without mentioning the special permit, Washington referred to this imported seed in his ultimate letter to Jefferson.[31]

32

Washington's Farewell Address

ASHINGTON'S Farewell Address ranks in popular acclaim with the Declaration of Independence and Lincoln's Gettysburg Address. Thus the rumor that it was written not by Washington but by Hamilton has shocked or delighted generations with a subversive or a debunking ring. Fortunately, the evidence exists to determine exactly what took place.

In the spring of 1796 Washington had felt that he resembled a warrior who must, as he withdraws, face his enemies with his sword held before him. He considered it proper, as he explained, to inform "the yeomanry of this country" of the abuse under which he had suffered, of the motives behind it, of the silence with which he had suffered under it, of "the consequences which would naturally flow from such unceasing and virulent attempts to destroy all confidence in the executive part of the government — and that it was best to do it in a language that was plain and intelligible to their understandings."[1]

Washington dug through his files and pulled out the draft of a farewell address which Madison had prepared to his specifications when he had intended to retire at the end of his first term. He resolved to include that text verbatim to show not only that "such *an address was written*," but that it was "*known also to one or two* of those characters" (Madison and Jefferson) who were now most vigorously attacking the government. The old address proved that he had not wanted a second term. The corollary, that he had no personal motive for wishing to extend the power of the executive, would serve "to lessen in the public estimation the pretentions of that party to the patriotic zeal and watchfulness on which they endeavor to build their own consequence at the expense of others." And the realization that his wish to retire was nothing new should "blunt if it does not turn aside" accusations that he was now withdrawing because of fallen popularity and despair of being re-elected.

Sitting down to write his new address, Washington specified that Madison had been "privy to the draft," and then cut out the name and phrase.[2] The draft he now copied out stated that he had done his best and hoped he would be forgiven any involuntary errors. He had arrived at a period of life when retirement was necessary, and, in any case, a rotation of offices was congenial to liberty. Since the great and essential interests of all Americans were the same, continued union would make the nation prosperous and one of the most independent in the world. The seeds of amendment engrafted in the Constitution could be used to bring it near perfection. While keeping a watchful eye on the government, the people should avoid undue suspicions.

The quotation completed, Washington wrote that changes at home and abroad required a further statement of "the most ardent wishes of my heart": he hoped that party disputes would subside; that, while the nation filled exactly all its engagements, the citizens would avoid undue affections for or alliances with foreign powers. As he liked to do, he pointed out that twenty years of peace and national unity would make the United States so strong she could defy all outside interference. The different branches of the government should not encroach on each other, and the public should not withdraw without just cause the confidence that was for public servants "the best incentive to a faithful discharge of their duty." Do not assume that acts not easily comprehended without special information are by definition wrong!

Then Washington wrote in anger one of those paragraphs which affirm what they deny: "As this address, fellow citizens, will be the last I shall ever make to you, and as some of the gazettes of the United States have teemed with all the invective that disappointment, ignorance of facts, and malicious falsehoods could invent, to misrepresent my politics and affections — to wound my reputation and feelings — and to weaken, if not entirely destroy, the confidence you have been pleased to repose in me; it might be expected at the parting scene of my public life that I should take some notice of such virulent abuse. But, as heretofore, I shall pass them over in utter silence."

His international policy had been "unconcealed — plain and direct" — to be found in the Neutrality Proclamation, which Congress and the people had approved.

He believed that the record of his administration would acquit him in the estimation of the people, but if it did not, he hoped, "as I did not seek the office with which you have honored me, that charity may throw her mantle over my want of abilities to do better; that the gray hairs of a man who has, excepting the interval between the close of the Revolutionary War and the organization of the new government, either in a civil or military character, spent five and forty years — *all the prime of his life* — in serving his country, be suffered to pass quietly to the grave, and that his errors, however numerous, if they are not criminal, may be consigned to the tomb of oblivion as he himself soon will be to the mansions of retirement."

Having stated that he did not claim infallibility, Washington defied malice to charge him with willful error, or the neglect of any public duty which in his opinion ought to have been performed. His administration, "the infancy of the government and all other circumstances considered," had been "as delicate, difficult, and trying as may occur again in any future period of our history," and through it all he had to the best of his judgment, with the best information and advice he could obtain, "consulted the true and permanent interest of my country, without regard to local considerations — to individuals — to parties, or to nations."

He had not, he was proud to declare, served his country "from ambitious views," or from ignorance of the hazards to which he was exposing his reputation, or from any expectation of pecuniary gain. His finances had received no addition from his services, "but," so he added and then scratched out, "the reverse." He had, his text continued, "restrained the bounty of several legislatures at the close of the war with Great Britain from adding considerably to my pecuniary resources. . . . I leave you with undefiled hands, an uncorrupted heart, and with ardent vows to heaven for the welfare and happiness of that country in which I and my forefathers to the third or fourth progenitor drew our first breath."[3]

Such was the angry and self-defensive "farewell address" Washington wrote in his dismay and desire for self-justification.

About the end of April 1796, Washington showed his yet incomplete draft to Hamilton. Hamilton said that so important a paper required serious consideration, and that he would be happy to help Washington revise it. Washington promised to mail the paper, when finished, to Hamilton in New York. On May 10, Hamilton wrote Washington, reminding him of his promise.

On the 15th Washington sent what he stated was his only copy: he had not even kept his preliminary notes. If Hamilton thought it best "to throw the *whole* into a different form," he should go ahead, but nonetheless return Washington's own draft with emendations. Showing that he himself had misgivings, Washington authorized Hamilton to discard the "egotisms (however just they may be) if you think them liable to fair criticism . . . notwithstanding some of them relate facts which are but little known to the community."[4]

More than a month and a half passed before Hamilton, whom Washington had poked up in the meanwhile, notified Washington that he was preparing an altogether new draft. There was no need for hurry, he explained, since Washington should, in view of the possibility of an overriding crisis, keep himself uncommitted as long as possible. Two months before the Electors cast their ballots in December would be soon enough to announce his decision. "The parties will in the meantime electioneer conditionally, that is to say, *if you decline*, for a serious opposition to you will, I think, hardly be risked."[*][5]

Twenty-five days later (July 30) Hamilton wrote Washington that he was sending "herewith a certain draft which I have endeavored to make as perfect as my time and engagements would permit. It has been my object to render this act *importantly* and *lastingly* useful." He had eschewed all immediate controversies "to embrace such reflections and sentiments as will wear well, progress in approbation with time, and redound to future reputation."[6]

This was an altogether new text. Hamilton had started on his other task of revising Washington's own text, but the longer he thought about it, the "less eligible" it seemed. It was "awkward," seemed to imply that Washington would not be believed unless he presented evidence, and "I think there are some ideas that will not wear well." When he had both speeches before him, the President could judge.[7]

Washington's first reaction to what has become known as "Hamilton's Main Draft" was, as he stated in acknowledging its receipt, dismay at its length. "All the columns of a large gazette would scarcely, I conceive, contain the present draft. But, having made no accurate calculation of this matter, I may be much mistaken." He would give the draft "the most attentive consideration."[8]

---

[*] In some states, the Electors were chosen by state legislatures that had been chosen months before. The possibility that Washington might be available would thus impede the campaigns of Jeffersonian legislators who might try to block his election as President.

Washington's letter crossed in the mails one from Hamilton enclosing his revision of the draft Washington had himself prepared. It excluded all Washington's self-justifications and attacks on his opponents. It was, indeed, an entire rewriting, which differed from his independent draft primarily in not taking the long-range view of an unruffled statesman, but being an appeal to the people at a time of crisis. Although shorter than Hamilton's Main Draft it covered much the same ground, sometimes, as Hamilton noted, expressing an idea in a way that pleased him more than the version in the earlier text.[9]

Concerning the two manuscripts he had now sent, Hamilton wrote, "Whichever you may prefer, if there be any part you wish to transfer from one to another; any part to be changed"; or if Washington wished that any idea in his own draft which had been omitted be replaced; "in short, if there be anything further in the matter in which I can be of any [use], I will with great pleasure obey your commands."[10]

After "several serious and attentive readings," Washington decided that he "greatly" preferred Hamilton's Main Draft to the other versions. It was "more copious on material points, more dignified on the whole, and with less egotism." He liked to think that it would please readers abroad "whose curiosity I have little doubt will lead them to inspect it attentively and to pronounce their opinions on the performance."[11]

Hamilton's Main Draft became the basis for what is known as Washington's Farewell Address.

Washington transcribed Hamilton's Main Draft in his own handwriting, making the innumerable verbal changes (see the example on the opposite page) involved in altering another man's style to suit his own taste. Part of his objective was obviously to get completely clear in his mind the text that lay before him. Only after he had made verbal revisions in Hamilton's entire manuscript did he scratch out the parts of which he did not approve. At some point, probably towards the end of his labor, he inserted what he considered superior passages from Hamilton's second manuscript and added some ideas entirely new.

To Hamilton, Washington expressed only one major objection. There was no mention of the importance to a free nation of education. The President wished to argue particularly for his project of a national university. Hamilton replied that the university project belonged rather in Washington's next address to Congress. Washington had to admit that so specific a

ROUTINE REVISIONS BY WASHINGTON OF
HAMILTON'S MAIN DRAFT OF THE
FAREWELL ADDRESS

Hamilton	Washington
To the duration and efficacy of your Union a Government extending over the whole is indispensable. ~~Without this~~ No alliances however strict between the parts could ~~have the necessary solidity or afford the necessarily~~ be an adequate substitute. These could not fail to be liable to the infractions and interruptions which all alliances in all times have suffered — Sensible of this important truth ~~and with a view to a more intimate Union~~ you have lately established a Constitution of General Government, better calculated than the former ~~one~~ for an intimate union and more adequate to the direction of your common concerns — This Government the offspring of your own choice uninfluenced and unawed, completely free in its principles, in the distribution & of its powers uniting energy with safety and containing in itself a provision for its own amendment is well entitled to your confidence and support.	To the efficacy and permanency of Your Union, a Government for the whole is indispensable. No Alliances however strict between the parts can be an adequate substitute. They must inevitably experience the infractions and interruptions which all Alliances in all times have experienced. Sensible of this momentous truth, you have improved upon your first essay, by the adoption of a Constitution of Government, better calculated than your former for an intimate Union, and for the efficacious management of your common concerns. This government, the offspring of our own choice uninfluenced and unawed, adopted upon full investigation and mature deliberation, completely free in its principles, in the distribution of its powers, uniting security with energy, and containing within itself a provision for its own amendment, has a just claim to your confidence and your support.

recommendation would violate the tone of his Farewell Address. He asked Hamilton to draft a general statement concerning education. When Hamilton failed to do so, Washington wrote a paragraph himself, by far the most succinct part of the address.°[12]

The ideas Washington found expressed in Hamilton's Main Draft proved to be, with very few exceptions, his own. No man was more familiar than Hamilton with Washington's way of thinking, and he had learned through an association that had begun nineteen years before that Washing-

---

° Having got his manuscript back from Washington for a few days of polishing, Hamilton regretted that he could not have "written it over, in which case I could both have improved and abridged."[13]

ton would not knowingly allow himself to be pushed in directions other than those his own judgment dictated. When he was himself unsure of his way (as in financial policy) he would, it is true, accept guidance. Otherwise, the way to influence him was to travel, with at least seeming deference, beside him; to be present when decisions were made, wait until you were consulted, and then put forward your ideas in a way that made them seem extensions of Washington's own thinking. Almost every time Hamilton had violated this formula, he had been slapped down. Had he drafted a farewell address according to conceptions with which Washington did not agree, Washington would have pushed the draft indignantly aside. Hamilton had dwelt on ideas which he knew the President would gladly accept, only inserting partisan statements that served the Federalist cause when he thought he could do it so skillfully that the old gentleman would not notice.

Hamilton's labors on the address may well reveal an emotional attachment to the older man who had played so major a role in his life since he had been twenty years old. He also had a large political stake in having Washington leave the Presidency with undiminished prestige. The Federalists had long claimed Washington as their own, and every month now the old hero's struggles to escape such identification were becoming less and less effectual.

The draft Washington revised with satisfaction began by traveling quickly over the personal considerations with which he had opened his own draft. His acceptance of the Presidency had been a sacrifice; he had wished to retire after his first term and had prepared an address for the occasion (no longer quoted); he was happy that the situation now permitted him to retire; he was getting older; he had been carried through his troubles by popular support (Hamilton's addition);[14] and he hoped from his retirement to observe a virtuous nation continuing the blessings that would encourage nations throughout the world to seek a similar liberty.

Clearly not wishing to omit altogether the mood of self-justification so prominent in Washington's first draft, Hamilton had inserted that Washington would find comfort in the thought that "the involuntary errors I have probably committed have been the sources of no serious or lasting mischief to our country." Now Washington scratched the sentence out "to avoid," as he noted in the margin, "the imputation of affected modesty."[15]

The next section of many pages dealt with the importance of permanent union. Since union was "the palladium of your political safety" the "internal and external enemies" of the country would direct at it their strongest batteries.* Americans had no major differences in religion and habits; regional economic interests could be keyed together to the prosperity of all; union was a protection against foreign influences that would involve the United States in European broils. Since the Constitution was the rock on which union rested, no branch of the government should encroach on any other. Only experience, the "surest standard," should inspire changes. The spirit of innovation should be avoided as a weapon in the hands of those who wished to tear the union apart. All these points existed elsewhere in Washington's writing. Hamilton added another matter which, although it worried many of his contemporaries, seems not to have bothered Washington: the question whether popular government could extend across an area as large as the United States. Hamilton, with Washington acquiescing, admitted that the doubt existed, but warned the people to "distrust the patriotism" of those who encouraged such doubts.16

Leaving in Hamilton's statement that the government must be strong enough to "withstand the enterprises of faction" and protect "rights of person or property," Washington scratched out a Federalist gloss: "Owing to you as I do a frank and free disclosure of my heart, I shall not conceal from you the belief I entertain that your government as at present constituted is far more likely to prove too feeble than too powerful."17

The next extensive section dealt with "the spirit of party." "Unfortunately . . . inseparable from our nature," this spirit was most dangerous in popular governments where it was not restrained by force. Undoubtedly with an eye on France, Hamilton wrote — and Washington went along — that the revenge of one faction triumphing over another "has perpetrated the most horrid enormities." It had led to despotism. Although the United States would probably not give in to such extremities ("which nonetheless ought not to be entirely out of sight"), parties did great mischief. They fostered geographic schisms and foreign intrigues; intervened between the people and their government; encouraged the rule of minorities and demagogues. To the contention that parties were useful in a free country as checks on the administration and to keep alive the spirit of liberty, the answer was, "there will always be enough of that spirit for every salutary purpose." Political contention was "a fire not to be quenched," but "it demands a uniform vigilance lest, instead of warming, it should consume."18

Hamilton, so Washington probably noted with appreciation, balanced

---

* Unless otherwise noted, quotations in this chapter are given in the wording actually promulgated.

objections to popular factions with warnings against the machinations of "a small but artful enterprising minority." But then Hamilton tried to undermine the balance in a passage which Washington scratched out. It stated that "the extraordinary influence" of "birth, riches, and other sources of distinction" was particularly dangerous in small countries that were liable to a coup d'etat, but in large countries like the United States popular factions were more to be feared. So far, so even, but then Hamilton went on at considerable length concerning the dangers of demagogues. Since Washington saw less danger in pressure groups which tried to manipulate government than in misleaders of the people who poisoned popular government at its source, he allowed to stand Hamilton's lack of proportion in the amount of space given to warnings.[19]

Hamilton's passage on religion expressed sentiments Washington had never put on paper. The President accepted, with only verbal changes, the statement that "whatever may be conceded to the influence of refined education on minds of a particular structure," it was too much to expect that national morality could prevail without religious principles. However, another of Hamilton's contentions was more than Washington, as a deist, could accept. He changed "nor ought we to flatter ourselves that morality can be separated from religion" to read "let us with caution indulge the supposition that morality can be maintained without religion."[20]

Washington went along with Hamilton, as he had many times before, on the importance of establishing public credit. Although Washington had, particularly before he became President, denounced luxury as unworthy of American patriots, he now scratched out Hamilton's paragraph on the subject with the comment "not sufficiently important." He changed Hamilton's description of the arts as the "ministers and the means of national opulence" to the "ministers and cause of national opulence."[21]

The section on foreign affairs was the longest in the address. It was to be the best remembered and most influential. In defining the basic American foreign policy of isolation from European struggles, which was to be observed (with minor breaches) for more than a century, Hamilton wrote down sentiments which he had many times heard Washington express.

A new declaration of independence, followed in politics long before it was followed in literature and the fine arts, was embedded in such sentences as these: "Europe has a set of primary interests which to us have none or a very remote relation. . . . Our detached and different situation invites and enables us to follow a different course. . . . Why forgo the advantages of so peculiar a situation? Why quit our own to stand upon foreign ground?"[22]

Since, when the address was being written, the interests of the United States were leading her automatically into a course which was in effect pro-British, the pro-British Hamilton could come out as strongly for a purely American policy as the President, who wished to favor neither belligerent. In asking why the United States should "entangle our peace and prosperity in the toils of European ambition, rivalship, interest, humor, or caprice,"* Hamilton's text pleased Washington by making no distinction between the European preferences of the rival American factions. All those who wished to take sides in European conflicts were denounced as "tools and dupes," usurping "the applause and confidence of the people to surrender their [the people's] interest."[23]

The distinction made in the address between political treaties (which should be avoided) and commercial treaties (which could be useful if limited in term) was more sharply drawn than was usual in Washington's writings. Hamilton penned and Washington followed what was both a statement of general principles and a defense of the Jay Treaty. Commercial policy should consult "the natural course of things," establishing, so that the rights of merchants could be defined and defended, "conventional rules of intercourse," the most favorable circumstances would permit.[24]

As he had often heard Washington insist, Hamilton wrote that the policy of the government had been established by the Neutrality Proclamation. He then put into Washington's mouth this answer to the nagging question whether the official policy violated the old alliance with France: "After deliberate consideration with the aid of the best lights I could obtain (and from men disagreeing in their impressions of the origin, progress, and nature of that war) I was well satisfied that our country, under all circumstances of the case, had a right to take and was bound in duty and interest to take a neutral position." Washington scratched out the parenthesis concerning men with different views, and then made several efforts to add a further passage that would justify the American position more clearly. On his second try, he came up with the statement that the government's acts appeared to him "warranted by well-established princi-

---

* This was the closest the address got to the phrase, usually attributed to it: "entangling alliances." It was President Jefferson who in his inaugural address most conspicuously used the phrase.

ples of the laws of nations, as applicable to the nature of alliance with France in connection with the circumstances of the war and the relative situations of the contracting parties." He discarded this complicated sentence, and wrote that some of the considerations, being "of a delicate nature, would improperly be the subject of explanation." This he scratched out.

Then he came up with: "The considerations with respect to the right to hold this conduct it is not necessary on this occasion to detail. I will only observe that, according to my understanding of the matter, that right, so far from being denied by any of the belligerent powers, has been virtually admitted by all." A note in the margin reveals that he was not really satisfied by this formulation, but, being unable to think of a better, he let it stand.[25]

Hamilton had preserved, in a revised form, the statements in Washington's original draft that Washington had not been moved by ambition or lust for power, and had not gained but lost money by his government service. All this Washington now scratched out, noting that it might have "the appearance of self-distrust and mere vanity."

As for the conclusion of Washington's peroration, a statement that his desire for the happiness of his country was "so natural to a citizen who sees in it the native soil of his progenitors and himself for four generations," this was by way of being an insult to Hamilton, who was an immigrant from the British Indies. Perhaps for that reason, Hamilton accepted Washington's last paragraph with only a few verbal changes. It was Washington's turn to move the nativist sentiment, slightly toned down, into the middle of the final paragraph, where it would be less emphatic. He concluded his Farewell Address: "I anticipate with pleasing expectation that retreat in which I promise myself to realize, without alloy, the sweet enjoyment of partaking, in the midst of my fellow citizens, the benign influence of good laws under a free government, the ever favorite object of my heart, and the happy reward, as I trust, of our mutual cares, labors, and dangers."[26]

When the text of his Farewell Address was finally completed, Washington was in Philadelphia, having come from Mount Vernon primarily to confer with C. C. Pinckney, the new minister to France. He was irritated to be held up by the slow arrival of Pinckney, which also postponed the publication of the address: Washington intended to be on his way back to Mount Vernon when the capital received his long, official announcement that he would not serve again.[27]

On September 15, Pinckney finally arrived. Washington then made the gesture of showing the document to his Cabinet. Pickering put his oar in, insisting on "going over it in detail," for which purpose he kept the manuscript without permission overnight. Washington paid little or no attention to whatever suggestions he made.[28]

Nowadays when the national payroll supports a multitude of propagandists and publicity men, it is hard to realize that Washington had no regular channel for getting his statement to the public. Deciding to release it to one Philadelphia newspaper "and suffer it to work its way afterwards," he summoned to his office David Claypoole, owner of the *American Daily Advertiser*.[29]

After Claypoole had put the address in type, he carried proofs two or three times — he could not remember which — to the President. Washington, he noted, "made but few alterations from the original, except in the punctuation, in which he was very minute." Eventually, the printer needed the manuscript no longer. In returning it to the President, Claypoole "expressed my regret at parting with it . . . upon which, in the most obliging manner, he handed it back, saying that if I wished for it, I might keep it."[30]

This act was the more remarkable because Washington had no other copy. The address had to be inscribed in his own archives from the newspaper columns. He instructed his secretary to record it "in the order of its date. Let it have a blank page before and after it, so as to stand distinct. Let it be written with a letter larger and fuller than the common recording hand."[31]

Washington was in his carriage rolling towards home when the *American Daily Advertiser* for September 19, 1796 appeared on the Philadelphia streets. Filled as usual with small advertising notices, the front page gave no indication that the four-page gazette contained a momentous news scoop. On the left of page two, the editor had run, in slightly enlarged type, a one-column head:

To the PEOPLE of the United States
Friends and fellow citizens:

Washington's text, introduced with no further preamble, filled all of that sheet plus two and a half columns of the next. At the end, indented and in type somewhat slightly enlarged were the words: "G. Washington, United States, September 7, 1796." That was all. The editor added no explanation or comment.[32]

There ensued a great scurrying in the offices of other newspapers, first in Philadelphia, then along the highroads, then down the byways, then in cities across the ocean, as the address was set up again and again.° Washington in the meanwhile was at Mount Vernon, listening for what the reaction would be.

He had asked McHenry for a report from Philadelphia that concealed nothing. Writing on the 25th, McHenry gave a discouraging report: he painted the address as a partisan triumph. The friends of the government shed tears and mourned Washington's determination to depart, while the enemies of the government "discovered a sullenness, silence, and uneasiness that marked a considerable proportion of chagrin and alarm at the impression which it was calculated to make on the public mind." Dandridge's report sent a day later was more pleasing. He had been unable to discover "a single instance of disapprobation of any part thereof."[34]

The occasion was, indeed, for most Americans a moving one. The regret — even fear — brought to many a heart by Washington's impending retirement was balanced in the brain by deep reassurance from the manner of his going. Jefferson had, while he still admired Washington, looked ahead with complacency to Washington's still being President in 1800 — which implied that he would die in office as kings do.† The Constitutional Convention had been unwilling to put any limit on how long the President might serve. Washington's decision to retire at the end of his second term was so climactic an act that the precedent he thus established was not violated for more than a century and then restored by a Constitutional amendment. Unless propagandists could whip into life — as the *Aurora* tried to do — the idea that Washington was retreating because he knew he could not be re-elected — which took *some* doing — the President had refuted the canard of his harboring monarchical conceptions. He was demonstrating the principle essential to a free government that succession should be determined as a matter of course by the people rather than by Father Time's scythe. He had gone against the precedents of history, which made his act the more remarkable, the more endearing.

That Washington's address was in fact a farewell gave it protection and emotional strength. Protection, since what Washington advised could not

---

° Victor Hugo Paltsits, who examined over a hundred immediate reprintings, could find only in the *Courier of New Hampshire* the heading "Washington's Farewell Address." That name came later.[33]

† See volume III, page 351.

be considered the self-seeking of ambition. Emotional strength, because the address resembled (as many a paragrapher pointed out) such a death-bed admonition of a dying patriarch as had carried a magical significance probably since the birth of man.

Furthermore, the address cut down through faction to basic American principles. Despite powerful and vocal advocates of what is today called "brinkmanship," Americans then agreed that a neutrality that fostered peace was the true path for the United States. Washington may have slurred over the matter of the French treaty, yet every rational man knew that the old "alliance" could not be truly honored if the nation were to keep out of the war. And in denouncing subservience to Europe, Washington had made no distinction between the pro-French and the pro-British. He had also managed to make strike in both directions in his denunciation of faction. Political parties had not yet truly developed; the behavior of factions in France was hardly reassuring; and many Americans had vivid enough memories of the dislocations attendant on their own revolution (however happy the outcome) not to seek a replay. As for Washington's insistence on the dangers of regionalism and the importance of national union, regionalists might huff and puff, but in 1796 no responsible individual wanted the nation torn apart.

Most newspapers that editorialized on the address glowed with praises: citizens' bodies and state legislatures passed resolutions of thanks. Although there were conspicuous exceptions,° the Republican opposition was silent about the address, preferring, as they pursued their efforts to win the election, to attack the administration and Washington in other contexts.

By 1810, the Farewell Address was so revered as a foundation on which the nation rested that one of Hamilton's executors was horrified when he found among the dead man's papers a draft in Hamilton's handwriting. Knowing that Mrs. Hamilton was claiming authorship for her husband, the executor entrusted the relevant papers to Rufus King so that, if asked, he could say that he did not have them. Rumors which leaked into informed circles created consternation among Federalists: Judge Richard

---

° William Duane published a forty-eight-page pamphlet, *A Letter to George Washington . . . containing Strictures of his Address,* which interpreted every passage in the baleful light cast by the assumption that Washington was a tyrannical monster plotting with an evil junto. The President's comments on parties were, for instance, described as "the loathings of a sick mind," spurred on by hatred and wounded pride.[35]

Peters mourned that he could not burn Hamilton's draft. Republicans too were upset: Madison wrote Jefferson that he regretted the possibility of the address being attributed to Hamilton, since the text would take on different meanings if associated with a man of such "political doctrines and party feelings."

Learning that King had the papers, the Hamilton family demanded them. King refused to give them up. The family sued and in 1826 got the documents back. Then they had second thoughts. Instead of making a sensational publication, they deposited the papers with the rest of the Hamilton archive in the Library of Congress. The evidence was finally published during 1859 as part of a general edition of Hamilton's papers.[36]

Scandal has an immortality of its own, and today, more than a century after the record has been available, it is still believed that a conspiracy of establishment fat cats is for sinister reasons preventing the American people from knowing that Hamilton wrote Washington's Farewell Address. How often has this biographer had the charge thrown in his face with a sneer!

What was the true situation? The facts are all before us. What conclusions shall we draw?

That Hamilton never claimed the authorship of the address has been regarded as conclusive, but proves nothing, since he must have realized, as his followers later did, that his by-line would confuse and fillet the effect of the document.

It is impossible to determine absolutely whether, if left to himself, Washington would have released the self-pitying draft which he wrote in anger months before he intended to publish anything. Certainly, doing so would have reduced his stature in the annals of history. His natural proclivity to rage had, of course, exploded on other occasions during his presidency. Yet he soon gained control of himself. To assume that on this occasion his better judgment would not in the end have intervened, is to assume that the aging man had, to a much greater extent than the record indicates, lost his habitual surefootedness.° Certainly, when first sending Hamilton his draft, he had expressed doubt concerning the "egotisms"; certainly, in revising Hamilton's Main Draft, he had cut out what dubious personal passages Hamilton had not already discarded.

° Washington's greatest indiscretion as President, the attack on the Democratic Societies, had been perpetrated in haste, when his service with the whiskey army almost overlapped the convening of Congress.

When Washington had retired from the army, he had prepared (without aid from Hamilton) a statement of advice for the nation which came to be known as Washington's Legacy. This paper's tone resembles that of the completed Farewell Address. Would not Washington, on leaving the Presidency, have followed his own precedent? We may guess that he would, but the fact remains that Hamilton's urging was the immediate cause of his discarding his own draft. And Hamilton not only recommended the elevated address but drafted it.

Washington made hundreds of verbal changes, yet much of Hamilton's literary style remained. This is most conspicuous in the prolixity. Washington's natural tendency was to be concise, to pack sentences with ideas until a dense, although usually clear, paragraph covers all phases of the problem. Hamilton was more inclined to argue things out, as in a legal brief. The Farewell Address is by far the most extensive paper Washington ever issued, being several times as long as Washington's Legacy.

The address could correctly be attributed to Hamilton if it expressed Hamilton's ideas. This it only did insofar as Hamilton's ideas coincided with Washington's. When he did try to slip in something of his own with which Washington did not agree, Washington almost always recognized the thought as alien and cut it out. Thus the Farewell Address was as much Washington's as any Presidential paper is likely to be that has been drafted by an intimate aide. If all such documents were attributed to the speech writers, American history, particularly that of recent times, would read very differently and surely less accurately.

That Washington's Farewell Address was conceived of in its existing form and largely composed by Hamilton is a fact. Yet it is also a fact that the famous document is correctly styled "Washington's Farewell Address."

33

False Teeth and Stuart's Washington

AS Washington prepared for his retirement from the Presidency, hoping to escape his enemies with his reputation untarnished, he remained happily ignorant that a painful physical disability was being grafted onto his legend until in the minds of future generations his attribute — like St. Catherine's wheel or St. Sebastian's arrows — would be a pair of ill-fitting false teeth. For this situation, the portrait painter Gilbert Stuart was most to blame.[1]

The disfigurement of Washington's mouth had, it is true, for some years troubled images by other portrait painters, but no other created such widely known or physically convincing likenesses, and only one — the semi-naïve William Williams, who had been specifically requested to produce a factual document — was so powerfully motivated to show the distortion of the aged face.

Washington was unhappy with the false teeth he wore when Stuart painted him. They had been made in 1789 by the New York dentist John Greenwood from hippopotamus ivory to which human teeth were attached with gold rivets.° There had been a hole through which Washington's one remaining natural tooth protruded.

In January 1797 these dentures collapsed. As Washington explained in a letter to Greenwood, the bars that, running along the sides and the front, held the teeth together, were too wide and projected too far, "which causes both upper and under lip to bulge out as if swelled. By filing these parts away (to remedy the evil), it has been one cause of the teeth giving

---

° See the illustration in volume III, page 207.

way." His own one remaining tooth had by now come out: Washington had hoped to find it to send Greenwood, but could not. However, the loss did not seem "material, as the one which supplies its place answers the purpose very well."

Greenwood, so Washington continued, was not to think that the bars were the only disfiguring aspects of the contraptions. He insisted that nothing be done with the teeth themselves "which will, in the *least* degree force the lips out more than *now* do, as it does this too much already; but if both upper and lower teeth were to incline inwards more, it would show the shape of the mouth better, and not be worse in any other respect."[2]

Washington also complained that the teeth had turned black. Greenwood replied that this was the effect of port wine, which, being sour, took all the polish and color from ivory. He urged Washington to take his dentures out after dinner and put them in clean water, while he wore another set. Or he could clean them with a brush and some chalk scraped fine. If the blackness remained, the President could make the teeth yellower by soaking them in broth or pot liquor or preferably porter (stout), being careful not to use tea as it was acid. Should acid nonetheless eat holes in the teeth, Washington should procure some wax and a hot nail: put the wax into the cavity and melt it there with the nail.[3]

The relationship between Stuart and Washington has its legend. The American born and raised Stuart, who had become one of the greatest portraitists in London, in those years the world capital of portraiture, is said to have returned to the United States out of a revered desire to devote his art to glorifying Washington. This is an extreme exaggeration. A profligate alcoholic, Stuart had been forced to flee the British Isles because of debts. Painting Washington was, it is true, one of the objects of his hegira, but only because he expected "to make a fortune" from producing and selling "a plurality of portraits" of the world's most famous man.[4]

Stuart was in no hurry. Landing in New York City late in 1792 or early in 1793, he stayed there for more than two years; every citizen with the price was proving eager to be immortalized by the most accomplished portraitist the United States had ever seen. Only when he had finally exhausted all business in New York, did Stuart set out for Philadelphia with a letter of introduction to Washington from John Jay.

Stuart was invited to appear at one of Washington's levees. Habituated to the aristocratic manners of Europe, he assumed, when admitted without ceremony into a room crowded with people, that he was in an antechamber waiting with other visitors to be ushered into the presence. Washington, seeing a stranger wandering confusedly about, separated from a group, walked over and introduced himself. Stuart was completely taken aback, a state of mind which he did not enjoy. For his part, Washington may well have been surprised to find this nervous man, with a tortured dissipated face, was the artist celebrated for creating such suave likenesses.[5]

In any case, sittings were eventually arranged, to begin in September 1795. Washington was embarrassed at being stared at and hated to keep his long body immobile: he considered posing one of the most irksome chores imposed on him by his eminence. However, he was always prompt. He appeared on the dot, aloof and ceremonious. Stuart had prepared as for a duel. The man who considered painters vastly more important than statesmen, could not forget that he had been put out of countenance on his first meeting with the General. He had surely dressed himself to the nines, and mustered all the sophistication he had acquired in the best London circles. He was prepared to make clear to Washington what a fine fellow he was.

Having sat down, Washington obediently assumed the pose commanded. Then, so Stuart remembered, "an apathy seemed to seize him, and a vacuity spread over his countenance most appalling to paint." Stuart had a ready solution to the problem. He was famous for being able to keep his sitters amused and their faces alive by his ability to converse with brilliance on any subject. However, to the urbane chitchat Stuart first brought forward, Washington responded not at all. Then the painter tried "to awaken the heroic spirit in him by talking of battles." Washington made noncommittal replies. Stuart then summoned his smatterings of ancient history: surely the modern Cincinnatus would be glad to talk about the old one. He was not.[6]

Washington seems (as Stuart's rival painter, John Trumbull claimed) to have been put off rather than interested by the painter's glib tongue and showy erudition. Although they were to spend many hours together, Stuart and Washington never established any personal rapport.[7]

The painter remembered that only once did he make the President smile. The anecdote was about the mayor of a rural English village, by trade a baker, who, when trying to greet James II, was so frightened that he could not enunciate a word. A friend jogged the mayor's arm and whispered, "Hold up your head and look like a man." When Stuart told how the flustered mayor repeated this admonition to the King, Washington's distorted lips grouped themselves around his false teeth in an expression of mirth. But the smile vanished as quickly as it came.

Stuart had other memories of moments of relaxation during the many sittings Washington gave him. The President's face lit up on one occasion when a fine horse galloped by outside the window. He could be drawn out to some extent on horses and farming. And, however wounding this was to Stuart's pride, if Washington were encouraged to bring a friend whose presence enabled him to forget the presence and activity of the painter, he would talk with considerable animation. By chance, Stuart discovered how to make Washington's rugged features take on all the grimness of a warrior commanding a battle. All the painter had to do was be late for a sitting and keep the General waiting.[8]

Stuart's long study of Washington's physiognomy made him comment, "There were features in his face totally different from what I had observed in any other human being. The sockets of the eyes, for instance, were larger than what I ever met with before, and the upper part of the nose broader. All his features were indicative of the strongest passions; yet like Socrates his judgment and self-command made him appear a man of different cast in the eyes of the world." And again, "Had he been born in the forests . . . he would have been the fiercest man among the savage tribes." Washington's body, however, gave a different impression. The old man had "aldermanic proportions. His shoulders were high and narrow, and his hands and feet remarkably large."[9]

Stuart was engaged in what was for him a difficult task. He wished his likeness of the popular hero to be popular. He wanted to sell many copies and have engravings made. However, reverence was not part of his character, and his personal feelings towards Washington were not warm. He could not forget that during an early sitting he had said, "Now, sir, you must let me forget that you are General Washington and that I am Stuart the painter."

Washington had replied (according to his own lights courteously), "Mr. Stuart need never feel the need of forgetting who he is or who General Washington is."[10]

An expression partly humorous, partly angry of Stuart's feelings is to be found in a portrait he did of a handsome poetess, Mrs. Perez Morton, who was one of his particular admirations. It amused him that the vain belle should express reverence for Washington, so he painted her buckling a bracelet on her shapely arm, while a bust of Washington observes her dourly. The sculptured head that Stuart imagined for his composition seems to have come from some other sphere: to have descended from Olympus or risen from hell. It is aloof and melancholy, more handsome than Washington was in life, but untouchable, inhuman, immune to propitiation. The false tooth–distorted mouth contributes a look of iron ferocity.

Stuart painted Washington from life three times, and made from each life portrait a flock of copies. The first group is known as the Vaughan type. The likenesses are serene but unsmiling, both fleshy (for Stuart was a great flesh painter) and craggy. The distortion of the mouth is minimal. Today, these are the most admired of Stuart's Washingtons, but, although he secured many orders for replicas, he abandoned this likeness after he had made others. One may only guess why the later versions were preferred: the Vaughan type was neither obviously grand nor was it charming and intimate.

In the Vaughan canvases Stuart honored the approach which he had developed in reaction to aristocratic portraiture. He believed that an artist should not organize his likenesses to indicate rank — automatically imbuing a nobleman with what society considered the correct attributes of nobility — but should treat artistocrat and commoner alike, putting down on canvas, frankly if suavely, the "animal" he saw before him. Towards this end, he liked to discard all accessories which showed a man's position in the world, placing a character study of the face against a flat background. The Vaughan portrait showed in addition to the head only enough body to give it position.

The social leaders of Philadelphia were far from satisfied. They wished a likeness of the President suited to their aristocratic pretensions. When the beautiful Mrs. Bingham promised to persuade Washington to pose again, and when Stuart came to realize that there would be a large international market for such an image, he decided to shelve his equalitarian ideals and create a royal likeness of the old President. Mrs. Bingham begged hard; Washington agreed to pose for a full length; and Stuart created what are called (because the original version was given by Mrs. Bingham to the British peer Lord Landsdowne) the Landsdowne type.[11] As Stuart, immersing the figure in a welter of fancy accessories, created the kind of picture he despised, he dwelt with great savagery on the distorted mouth. Stuart may well have sneered to himself when the society connoisseurs overlooked the blemish as they admired the gilt table and chair, the gleaming sword in Washington's hand, the imposing columns and the swooping curtains.

Gilbert Stuart's famous Athenaeum portrait of Washington, which he never finished, so that he would not have to deliver it to Mrs. Washington, who had commissioned it and persuaded her husband to pose. Courtesy of the Museum of Fine Arts, Boston

A fine example of Gilbert Stuart's Landsdowne-type full lengths of Washington. Courtesy of the Pennsylvania Academy of the Fine Arts

Gilbert Stuart's Vaughan portrait of Washington, a result of the first
sittings he secured, is neither so popular or famous as the later Athenaeum portrait, but is surely a better likeness. Courtesy of the National
Gallery of Art, Washington, D.C.

To tease the handsome poetess Mrs. Perez Morton, who professed a great admiration for Washington, Stuart painted her clasping a jewel on her wrist, while
an imaginary bust of Washington looked on grimly. This vision may well have
expressed, more than the formal likenesses, the great painter's feelings towards
his august sitter. Courtesy of the Henry Francis Du Pont Winterthur Museum,
Wintherthur, Delaware

Stuart's third opportunity came because Mrs. Washington yearned to have a life portrait for herself. The painter returned to his preferred approach of a head against a plain background, creating the likeness which has become so standard that (as has often been said) if Washington came back and did not resemble it, everyone would believe he was an imposter. What came to be known as the Athenaeum head lacks the power, the depth of character study in the Vaughan portrait, but it achieves a most satisfactory combination of impressiveness and intimate charm. Executed with an uninsistent virtuosity, it is handsome in color, monumental in shape, completely illusionistic. The lips are pulled into a tight line, but not to an extent that is clearly unnatural.

Realizing that he had at last hit the bull's-eye, Stuart resolved not to honor the intention which had induced Washington to sit. He would not deliver the canvas to Mrs. Washington, but keep it himself as the source of innumerable salable copies. He never finished the background so that, whenever Martha asked for the painting she had ordered, he could express regret that it was not finished. Stuart claimed that the President himself had whispered, when his wife's back was turned, that, since the picture was of such advantage to Stuart, the painter might keep it.[12] In view of Washington's generosity in giving Claypoole the manuscript of the Farewell Address, this seems possible, but Martha never forgave Stuart. Forced to put up with a copy of the Athenaeum portrait, she insisted it was not like. Stuart had in the version prepared for Washington's wife disfigured, more than in the Athenaeum original, Washington's mouth.

No one knows for sure how many times Stuart copied the Athenaeum head: he even put it on top of Landsdowne bodies. The labor was a financial necessity, since the painter was improvident, running up huge bills for liquor and snuff, but Stuart resented having so endlessly to copy himself, and the resentment was accompanied by angry distortions of the mouth. He himself defended his practice by stating, "I wanted him as he looked at the time."

The connection between Stuart and Washington was to prove damaging to them both. Many of Stuart's replicas of his life portraits are the worst pictures he ever painted — he used to run up two in two hours — but because of their subject they hang in prominent places, making the great portraitist seem in the eyes of the world an inferior artist. And they have encouraged the world to think of Washington as the hero with ill-fitting false teeth.

Darkness on the Ocean

THE extremity of the international difficulties Washington was to face during his final six months in office had been presaged before he released the Farewell Address by a strange message from Monroe, who was still serving in Paris. The text of a letter Washington had written Gouverneur Morris in England had somehow — although the missive had been dispatched on an American boat — got into the hands of the French Directory, where it had given great offense. Washington dug the letter out of his files and found it was the one in which he had lambasted British misbehavior, on the theory that Morris would have an opportunity to show it to Lord Grenville. The French, one would have thought, would have been pleased at Washington's denunciation of many British policies, including their seizing of provision ships. Washington could not comprehend what "the French government could take exception to unless the expression of an ardent wish that the United States may remain in peace with *all the world* . . . should have produced this effect." The conclusion was inescapable that nothing the United States could do short of denouncing the Jay Treaty and throwing overboard Washington's neutrality policy would placate France.*1

Pinckney, who was on his way to France, would surely have his troubles. However, when Washington was back at Mount Vernon after publishing his Farewell Address, he resolved to put such problems out of his mind. To the Secretary of State, he wrote that he supposed that French

---

* Concerning Washington's Farewell Address, Adet denounced to his government "the lies it contains, the insolent tone that governs it, the immorality which characterizes it."2

action awaited "circumstances which are not yet sufficiently developed." Until something momentous happened, he was not to be bothered. Reversing his onetime desire to supervise everything, he stated piously that making copies of papers to send him took time that should be devoted to more important business.[3]

After a six weeks' holiday, Washington returned to Philadelphia on October 31, 1796, to find that an international storm had indeed broken. The French minister, Adet, had presented a paper to the Secretary of State and at the same moment released it to the *Aurora*. The document stated that the Directory had on July 2 resolved: "The flag of the Republic will treat the flag of neutrals in the same manner as they suffered it to be treated by the English." This decision meant that the French would seize British goods in American bottoms. Doing so violated the old Franco-American treaty, but Adet laid the blame at the door of the American government, which, so he contended, had by accepting the Jay Treaty given preference to the British, thus shattering the former alliance with France. The United States had abandoned rights promised the French by Jefferson when he was Secretary of State. Furthermore, Washington's government had ignored French protests against her acquiescence in various British naval policies, including the impressment of American seamen. Unless the American executive agreed that the French might have the same advantages as Jay had permitted the British, the United States would become the enemy of France.[4]

The French action, Washington knew, spelt disaster for American shipping in West Indian waters, where there were many French ports from which privateers could operate before the British navy could intervene. Washington rushed off to Hamilton a letter freighted with problems. Considering the "indignity" offered the government by Adet's publication in the opposition press of an official dispatch, how should Adet be received if he appeared at the next Presidential levee? And in what way could the government defend itself from Adet's public attack? Unless the executive also had recourse to the newspapers, it would undoubtedly be assumed that the government had no defense. On the other hand, might not "the dignity of the government" be damaged by a newspaper contest with a foreign diplomat to gain the support of the American people? Might it not be proper "at the ensuing session [of Congress], which will close the political scene with me, to bring the French affairs since the controversy with Genêt fully before Congress"? However, if this were done, it might be necessary to include some papers which he had previously said the House had no right to see. What was one to make out of the contradictions between what Adet had announced and what Monroe had reported as official French policy? "But I am fatigued with this and other matters which crowd upon me, and shall only add that I am very affectionately yours. . . ."⁵

Hamilton replied that he had consulted Jay, who agreed that Washington's manner of noticing Adet's publication "ought to be *negative;* that is by the personal conduct of the President towards the minister." Adet should be received "with a *dignified reserve* holding an *exact medium* between an *offensive coldness* and *cordiality.* The point is a nice one to be hit, but no one will know better how to do it than the President." Eventually, there would have to be some more specific reply. Whatever the mode, it would "require much care and nicety to steer between *sufficient* and too *much justification,* between *self-respect* and *provocation.*" If Hamilton were not completely confident of Washington's discretion, "I should be afraid of Mr. Pickering's warmth. We must if possible avoid rupture with France," which could become "no less troublesome to us than to the rest of the world."⁶

But Washington had been too impatient to await Hamilton's advice. He allowed himself to be persuaded by "the gentlemen about me" to do what he had never done before: defend the administration in a newspaper release. When Hamilton saw what Washington had agreed to, he reacted with dismay. He urged Washington to get the executive out of the newspapers with all speed. The President must curb Pickering's "warm and angular" temper. Hamilton added the sobering news that the French consul in New York was asking around about medical facilities for an expected French fleet.⁷

The document which had been released to the press was the answer to Adet signed by Pickering as Secretary of State. A line was drawn between treaty obligations and the law of nations. The treaty with France established in Franco-American trade the principle that free ships made free goods. However, international law did not require Jay to insist on the same practice in Anglo-American trade. France therefore had no reason to complain and no excuse for violating her treaty with the United States. Pickering went on to say that all Adet's protests had been answered except when couched in "indecent" terms. He referred to the "singularity" of Adet's recourse to the American press.⁸

In approving this letter, which insisted that France was bound by her treaties however disadvantageous to her they had become, Washington for the first time accepted a contention which was illogical from his own point of view and inconsistent with his own previous actions. He had philosophized more than once that it was useless to try to overreach another nation in diplomatic negotiations since no nation could be expected to abide by any agreement that seriously damaged her interests. He had justified that cornerstone of his own foreign policy, the Neutrality Proclamation, on the grounds that it was so obviously to the advantage of the United States to keep out of the war that any steps necessary to that end were justified. Not only Washington and Hamilton but also Jefferson when in office had anticipated finding ways of evading "the guarantee" should France actually demand that the United States live up to that stipulation by helping to defend her West Indian possessions. Fortunately, France had never forced evasions by evoking the guarantee. As for the decisions of the administration in relation to privateers and prizes, ways had been found to skirt around such treaty provisions as would have given the French advantages which breached American neutrality.

It is significant that although Jay had been successful in not breaking the letter of the French treaties, Washington had failed in several attempts to write an explanation he found satisfactory of the relationship between the Jay Treaty and American obligations to France.[9] He was not truly impressed by Jay's niceties, yet he did not wish to state publicly that he considered the United States justified in following her interests whatever the treaties, still formally in force but obsolete, provided. He preferred to insist (as he had in his Farewell Address and elsewhere) that the United States had lived up scrupulously to all her international obligations.

It was altogether clear that by removing British goods from American bottoms, the French had done what the United States had, by fancy footwork, avoided doing: they had violated the letter of the old Treaty of Alliance. This gave the United States a debater's advantage. That the embattled administration should have used the advantage is not surprising. What is surprising is that Washington should increasingly and with more and more emotion insist that the French were not only totally unjustified but also perfidious in breaking their treaty obligations to the United States.

To this inconsistency Washington seems to have been, in the first instance, moved by his rage at renewed French interference in America's internal affairs, now specifically aimed at influencing the forthcoming election. Adet's next publication was clearly an effort to help reverse American policy through the elevation to the Presidency of France's friend Thomas Jefferson.°[10]

The publication was, although released to the newspapers and published as a pamphlet, a presumptive answer to Pickering. Adet damned in detail executive decisions all the way back to the first that Genêt had protested. Having insisted that the Jay Treaty was in effect a treaty of alliance with England, Adet announced that he had been recalled. France would send no other representative until "the executive of the United States returns to sentiments and measures conformable to the interests of the [French] alliance and the sworn friendship between the two nations."[12]

In his peroration, Adet tried to rekindle the emotions of the Revolution: "There yet exist men who can say, here a ferocious Englishman murdered my father; there my wife tore her bleeding daughter from the hands of a ruthless Briton! . . . Oh Americans . . . ye who have with French soldiers so often flown to victory and to death . . . your hearts have always beaten in union with those of your companions in the army! . . . Judge of their feelings! Remember at the same time that if generous minds are alive to injuries, they can also forgive. Let your executive return to a proper conduct, and still you will find the French faithful friends and generous allies."†[13]

Adet's pamphlet was soon reinforced by another, the work of the man whose *Common Sense* had, twenty-two years before, been so fertile a cause of George Washington's espousing the independence of the United States. Paine had aimed this barb directly at his old friend's heart: the title was *Letter to Washington*.

The epistle, which ran to many pages, was in part an enlargement of an abusive letter which Paine had sent to Washington personally in Septem-

---

° Adet had been so ordered by his government (which had been egged on by Monroe) and boasted that he was succeeding. Although Jefferson had long before (October 1795) sent Adet a violently pro-French letter which Malone considers indiscreet, he was not personally involved with Adet's agitations. On the whole, historians believe that Adet's efforts had little effect on the election, probably because they came too late.[11]

† A comment made by the English satirist then resident in Philadelphia, William Cobbett (Peter Porcupine), is irresistibly quotable: "Some imaginations are said to rush forward like a flood, others to flow like a stream, and others to glide like a current, but poor Citizen Adet's neither rushes, flows, nor glides; it trickles like the eyes of his masters, it drains, it dribbles, it drops. Dear Citizen, if you love me (of which I much doubt, bye the bye) never again employ your eloquence to rouse the passions, for it lays them as completely as the cold hand of death."[14]

ber 1795. This letter (which Washington had not answered) had upbraided the President for not having intervened officially to get Paine out of a French prison. Paine now put forward the ingenious argument that he had not sacrificed his American citizenship by serving as an official in a foreign government because the National Convention in which he had sat was (although it did incidentally rule France) dedicated to writing a constitution rather than acting under one, and was thus not a governmental body. Washington's failure to claim Paine as an American citizen was a deliberate act of treachery. Washington had conspired with Robespierre to have Paine guillotined for fear that Paine would otherwise expose his own monstrous behavior.*

Gouverneur Morris, Washington's Federalist minister to France, so Paine continued, had snickered to see Paine's life in danger, but the noble Monroe had got Paine out of jail and made him his house guest for a year and a half. "Now once more abroad in the world, I began to find I was not the only one who had conceived an unfavorable opinion of Mr. Washington."

In his many pages aimed at demonstrating that "almost the whole of your administration" was "deceitful if not perfidious," Paine assumed that any action that displeased French public opinion or did not further French interests was pro-British, contrary to treaty obligations, and damaging to the reputation of the United States. All Washington's professions of friendship for France were despicable lies.

Stating that "it is time the eyes of America be opened upon you," Paine traced Washington's whole career in a crimson fusillade of insults. He had, as a young man in the Jumonville Affair, murdered ambassadors. His "Fabian" tactics during the Revolution (which Paine had once praised) showed him a general of majestic incompetence and timidity. The Constitution he had supported (which Paine had once considered

---

* The charge that Washington wanted Paine put away as a radical, or had at least icily behaved with monstrous ingratitude, is still in the ammunition belts of those who wish to think the worst of the Father of their Country. The reader of these volumes does not need to be reminded that Washington had felt that he could not intervene officially even to save the man he most loved, Lafayette. He did, it is true, make personal representations concerning Lafayette, but not Paine, of whose actions during the French Revolution he less approved and who was less close to his heart.

Another complaint is that, in acknowledging copies of *The Rights of Man* which Paine had sent him, Washington had coldly sidestepped all comment. As a matter of fact, the President who wished to remain nonpartisan had used common sense. Paine would undoubtedly have published any compliment Washington sent him. Jefferson was, indeed, to get into hot water by having a letter *he* wrote to an American printer appear as an introduction and seeming endorsement of Paine's extremely controversial work.

"the admiration and wonder of the world") he now called "a copy, not quite so base as the original, of the British government." Washington's character was mean: "If you are not great enough to have ambition, you are little enough to have vanity." Paine's peroration read, "As to you, sir, treacherous in private friendship (for so you have been to me and that in the day of danger) and a hypocrite in public life, the world will be puzzled to decide whether you are an impostate or an imposter; whether you have abandoned good principles or whether you ever had any."[15]

Washington agreed with Peter Porcupine that Paine's attack was surely more than personal: it was inspired by the French government. He believed that the Gallic propaganda machine, having failed in subverting America to its taste, had concluded "that there was too much confidence and perhaps personal regard for the present chief magistrate and his politics. The batteries latterly have been leveled at him particularly and personally and, although he is soon to become a private citizen, his opinions are to be knocked down and his character reduced as low as they are capable of sinking it, even by reporting absolute falsehoods."[16]

The old British forgeries, made during the Revolution to demonstrate Washington at heart loyal to the Crown, were being, Washington complained, again "brought forward with the highest emblazoning of which they are susceptible with a view to attach principles to me which every action of my life have given lie to. But *that* is not a stumbling block with the editors of these papers and their supporters. And now, *perceiving* a disinclination on my part, perhaps *knowing* that I am determined not to take notice of such attacks, they are pressing this matter upon the public mind with more avidity than usual, urging that my silence is a proof of their genuineness." One of Washington's last acts before his retirement was to prepare, for permanent deposit at the Department of State, a denial of the authenticity of the letters.*[17] Concerning Bache, who was perpetrating the forgeries, Washington commented ruefully, "This man has a celebrity in a certain way, for his calumnies are to be exceeded only by his impudence, and both stand unrivaled."

Washington's final public appearance was to be his Eighth Annual Address, delivered on December 7, 1796, some three months before his term ended. How upset he was in anticipation is revealed by a letter from Eliza Powel written to Martha that morning. Eliza was, she stated, send-

---

* Pickering published the denial instantly after Washington had returned to private life.

ing a bottle of hard-to-get stomactic remedy, some "true Martinique noyan. . . . I think it would not be amiss if my good friend the President will take a glass on his return from the Congress. I know his sensibility, diffidence, and delicacy too well not to believe that his spirits will be not a little agitated on the solemn and I fear last occasion that he will take of addressing his fellow citizens. He appears to have an invincible diffidence of his own abilities."[18]

How right Eliza was in assuming that Washington would be upset is revealed by Henrietta Liston's account of his speech: "I happened to sit very near him, and as every person stood up at his entrance and again when he began to read, I had an opportunity to see the extreme agitation he felt when he mentioned the *French*. He is, I believe, much enraged; this is the second French minister who has insulted him to the people."[19]

In his address, Washington did not attempt, as he had always previously done, to keep a balance between his statements concerning the warring European nations. His reference to England showed the provisions of the Jay Treaty being smoothly applied towards future amity: the frontier forts had been delivered expeditiously; the commissions to settle boundaries with Canada and to establish compensation for British depredations on American commerce had met and in each case the fifth commissioner, chosen by the evenly divided other four, had been an American.

Very different the situation with France: "Our trade has suffered and is suffering extensive injuries in the West Indies from the cruisers and agents of the French republic, and communications have been received from its minister here which indicate the danger of a further disturbance of our commerce." The President kept "unabated" his "constant, sincere, and earnest wish" for harmony with France "to the utmost extent of what shall be consistent with a just and indispensable regard to the rights and honor of our country. . . . In pursuing this course, however, I cannot forget what is due to the character of our government and nation. . . . I reserve for a special message a more particular communication on this interesting subject."

Washington recommended the establishment of a navy. Although the specific immediate need he mentioned was to protect American shipping from pirates in the Mediterranean, he went on to say, "It is our own experience that the most sincere neutrality is not a sufficient guard against the deprivations of nations at war. To secure respect to a neutral flag, requires a naval force, organized and ready to vindicate it from insult or aggression. This may even prevent the necessity of going to war by discouraging belligerent powers."

Much of the rest of the message grew from the conclusion Washington had reached, in consultation with Hamilton, that, as his Farewell Address would deal only with general principles, this annual address would constitute his testament as far as specific proposals were concerned. In a passage that should have pleased his Republican hearers, Washington urged adequate pay for governmental officials, since "it would be repugnant to the vital principles of our government virtually to exclude from public trusts, talents and virtue unless accompanied by wealth." The President came down hard on that recommendation for a national university which Hamilton had persuaded him to omit from his Farewell Address and also repeated emphatically the recommendation he had previously more obliquely made for a military academy. Having gone this far, Washington went further, making other recommendations for federal action that would stretch the Constitution far beyond strict interpretation.

Agriculture should be "an object of public patronage." Congress should establish public boards to collect and diffuse information and to encourage, by premiums and small subsidies, agricultural discovery and improvement. The embryo of the welfare state could be found in Washington's question, "To what object" could "the public purse . . . be dedicated with greater propriety?"

The address also contained what could be considered a foretaste of socialism. The idea had been suggested by Hamilton, who may have drafted the paragraph, although the statement has an indefiniteness unusual for Hamilton. Washington stated that "as a general rule, manufactures on public account are inexpedient." However, when the condition of the American economy made it improbable that manufactures essential to equip an army in wartime could be got going in a reasonable time, might not the government take steps to make sure that the nation would not be helpless if supply from abroad were interrupted? Only goods that the nation could not otherwise produce would be manufactured by the government, and in peacetime the government's output would be limited *"to the extent of the ordinary demand for the public service."* Citizens would continue to import to supply their own needs. However, the proposal recognized that in wartime the government manufactures could expand "for the supply of our citizens at large, so as to mitigate the privations from interruptions of their trade." If Hamilton composed the paragraph, he was careful not to go into the question of what would happen when peace returned. As for Washington, he had traveled a long way in this as well as his agricultural proposals from his objections to Hamilton's Report on Manufactures. He had then felt that the Constitution would be illegally stretched if the federal government even offered premiums to encourage infant industries.°

Washington concluded, "The situation in which I now stand, for the last time in the midst of the representatives of the people of the United States, recalls the period when the administration of the present form of government was commenced; and I cannot omit to congratulate you and my country on the success of the experiment."[20]

° See volume III, pages 308–309.

You're In and I'm Out

WASHINGTON's preserved writings contain not one reference to the election of 1796; there is no record that he expressed his preference for anyone. Yet he must have observed developments, particularly in the Presidential race, with rapt interest.

Now that Washington was no longer offering a unanimous choice, the Electoral College was being given its first real try. The machinery proved extremely hard to manage. Each Elector had two votes, not differentiated between the Presidency and the Vice Presidency. Since the colleges of the different states met separately and at various times, adjustments on the national scale were almost impossible. In 1800, this was to create the famous contretemps when the Republican Vice Presidential candidate, Burr, got as many votes as the Presidential candidate, Jefferson, thus establishing a stalemate. In 1796, the Republican ticket was the same, but Jefferson was so much better known than Burr that he automatically got the larger vote.

It was the Federalists who were confused. In theory, they ran John Adams for President and Thomas Pinckney for Vice President. However, the south preferred Pinckney and so did Hamilton, who felt that he would be more amenable to control than the crusty old patriot from Massachusetts. Solid for Adams, New England viewed the Pinckney threat with alarm. The result was that some Federalist Electors of both persuasions threw away their second votes so as to secure a majority for their favorite. Although Adams got the top vote, Jefferson slipped into the second place and was designated Vice President.

Washington undoubtedly preferred Adams to Jefferson, as not in the

French interest. And he believed that "the candid part of my country-men," even those currently bedazzled by pro-French propaganda, would be brought to their senses by the summary of Gallic behavior which he had promised (in the Eighth Annual Address) that he would submit to Congress. However, he postponed the actual presentation until January 19, 1797, when there was no possible chance of its influencing the election.[1]

Although the document was in effect an answer to Adet, it was couched, to avoid all appearance of a propaganda war, in the form of instructions to C. C. Pinckney, who, as the minister to France, was to lay it before the Directory. Pickering prepared the text, having been admonished by Washington that it should be "full, fair, calm, and argumentive without asperity or anything more irritating in the comments than the narration of facts." Even if the document made no impression on the French, "much depends on it as it relates to ourselves and in the eyes of the world."[2] The lengthy statement, weighted with evidence, was to answer Adet's detailed charges in detail. The concluding summary should, so Washington instructed Pickering, state that the conduct of the United States had been "regulated by the strictest principles of neutrality," without any attempt to violate the treaty with France or any withholding of friendship. Although the government had felt no necessity to confide "the unpleasant details" to the French, all British violations of neutrality had been protested. "Conscious of its fair dealings towards all the belligerent powers, and wrapt up in its own integrity, it [the government] little expected . . . the upbraidings it has met with. . . . We have no doubt, after giving this candid exposition of facts, that the Directory will revoke the orders under which our trade is suffering, and will pay the damages it has sustained thereby."[3]

In fact, Washington had the most extreme doubts. "The conduct of the French," he wrote Hamilton, was "outrageous beyond conception, not to be warranted by her treaties with us, by the law of nations, by any principle of justice, or even by a regard to decent appearances." He asked Hamilton what could be "attempted" to preserve the peace "consistently with the respect which is due ourselves."[4]

The best idea any of his advisers could come up with was to supplement the ordinary diplomatic channels by reinforcing Pinckney with two extraordinary delegates, thus emphasizing the desire of the United States to achieve accommodation. But who should be sent? Hamilton suggested Madison as *persona grata* to the Directory and the French faction at home. The other appointee should be the Massachusetts Federalist George Cabot, who would act as "a salutary check upon too much Gallicism." However, Washington decided to wait until he knew how Pinckney was received. Late in February, Washington heard shocking rumors that the French had refused to take cognizance of the new American minister. But rumors were not official word, and in any case his retirement was so imminent that the whole mess could be left behind him with the best of conscience to his successor.[5]

Reverting to the theatrical metaphor which had been has favorite when he was leaving the army, Washington wrote his step-grandson, "As the curtain of my political life is about to drop, I am, as you may suppose, a great deal hurried in the closing scenes of it." At long last using the long-designated name "Washington" for the federal city, he labored to give construction there a conclusive push. (Would the New Englander Adams be interested?) Much other official business had to be cleared up; he felt impelled to a round of Herculean entertaining; and the endlessly complicated move to Mount Vernon needed to be organized.[6]

He had all the diplomatic corps for dinner; he dined the entire Pennsylvania Assembly on three successive days; all the military and naval officers in the city appeared on another day; and he had four dinner parties for visiting Indian chiefs. The drunken braves were not his only social hazards, since he scrupulously entertained even the most hostile of the opposition. Gallatin reported that on one such occasion "our most gracious queen" — as he sarcastically called Mrs. Washington — had asked after his wife, which made him refer to Martha as "a very good natured and amiable woman." Then the Republican leader added firmly, "Not so her husband." He noted that Washington was "more than usually grave, cool, reserved."[7]

Washington's last birthday in public office was celebrated with a general passion which moved some Republicans to surprising enthusiasm and others to even greater disgust. As this was his sixty-sixth anniversary and as certain heavy weights were then known as sixes, Washington evolved a pun that was considered lame even by the hearer who recorded it. "Gentlemen," the retiring President said, "I feel the weight of years. I take a pair of sixes on my shoulders this day." How often Washington brought out this witticism during a round of almost unbroken visits remains one of the mysteries of history.[8]

In the evening, the Washingtons attended a ball in their honor in Rick-

The ornament at the center of the Presidential table. Courtesy of the
Mount Vernon Ladies' Association

ett's Amphitheatre: twelve thousand persons were said to have squeezed in. That several were almost trampled to death in the rush for supper was not considered to have taken from the "splendor, taste, and elegance" of the occasion.

When the President-elect handed in Mrs. Washington and the President immediately followed, the applause was, according to one guest, "indescribable." Martha was "moved even to tears," and the President's "emotions were too powerful to be concealed. He could sometimes scarcely speak."[9]

If the crowd felt that such adulation was healing the wounds from which the President suffered, they were wrong. As one of his last acts as President, Washington wrote to his long-time companion General Knox: "To the wearied traveler who sees a resting place and is bending his body to lean thereon, I now compare myself, but to be suffered to do *this* in peace is, I perceive, too much to be endured by *some*. To misrepresent my motives, to reprobate my politics; and to weaken the confidence which has been reposed in my administration are objects which cannot be relinquished by those who will be satisfied with nothing short of a change in our political system." Washington added, "Although the prospect of retirement is most grateful to my soul, and I have not a wish to mix again in the great world or to partake in its politics, yet I am not without regret at parting with (perhaps never more to meet) the few intimates whom I love. Among these, be assured, you are one."[10]

In his eagerness to extricate himself, Washington was determined to set out for "more tranquil scenes at Mount Vernon" the instant he could get off, however inclement the March weather. This induced a search for horses "true and steady," capable of overcoming any amount of "mud and mire." To be delayed on the road would be "dreadful."[11]

President-elect John Adams was in all probability the man who had for the longest time been most deeply jealous of George Washington. He believed that he had personally created the hero when, seeking a southern candidate to unite the rebellion, he had suggested that the tall Virginian be made Commander in Chief. Since then, although Adams considered Washington uneducated and by no means as intelligent as he himself was, the spotlight had moved wherever Washington traveled, leaving Adams forever in comparative shadow. But now the situation was finally righting itself. Washington was stepping down from the Presidency and Adams was stepping up.

Elegant in a pearl-colored suit, wearing a sword and a cockade, Adams was seated by himself in the state carriage, moving to his inauguration through cheering crowds. Then the stocky figure advanced with ceremony to the House chamber. As he entered he saw that most of the eyes that turned to him were wet with tears. And in a moment, the eyes turned away again to dwell on a tall elderly man in an old-fashioned black coat, who had (as Adams later learned) walked to the ceremony unaccompanied, and was now sitting to one side of the dais.

Adams confided to his wife in two successive letters, "Your dearest friend never had a more trying day than yesterday. . . . Everybody talks of the tears, of the full eyes, the streaming eyes, the trickling eyes, etc., etc., but all is enigma beyond. No one descends to particulars to say why or wherefore. I am, therefore, left to suppose that it was all grief for the loss of their beloved."

What made the intended triumph over Washington the more equivocal was the expression in the retiring President's face. He seemed, Adams complained, "to enjoy a triumph over me. Methought I heard him say, 'Ay! I'm fairly out and you fairly in. See which of us will be happiest!' "[12]

Adams took the oath, made his speech to applause, and departed. Everyone's eyes turned back to the dais where Washington stood to the right of Jefferson. He motioned Jefferson to go out ahead of him. Jefferson politely refused. Washington motioned again, now imperiously. Vice President Thomas Jefferson walked down the aisle before that private citizen, George Washington.[13]

As soon as each individual could disentangle himself, the audience rushed after Washington to the street. They saw him walking towards Francis Hotel to congratulate the new President. As Washington went through the door and the door closed behind him, the crowd, seeing their hero pass away from them, made "a sound like thunder."[14]

IV

A Stormy Retirement

Friends and Strangers

AVING been away from home for eight years, believing that the dignity of the nation (to say nothing of his own feelings) would be hurt if the President lived in a tacky manner, Washington had used quantities of his own resources to furnish the Presidential Mansions first in New York and then in Philadelphia. What Congress had originally supplied him had been unable to stand up under daily official use. Washington noted that the linen and glassware were destroyed and replaced at his own expense over and over; the carpets having completely worn out, those now on the floor were his; the kitchen furniture was all a new dispensation, paid for from his purse. Washington had sold many thousands of western acres to keep the Presidential Mansions floating as he thought they should float.

After her husband had taken over, Abigail Adams complained that the "public furniture" Washington had left behind was in deplorable condition: "There is not a chair to sit in. The beds and bedding are in a woeful pickle." Washington had seen no reason why he should donate to the government what he had so expensively bought. Adams had been voted $14,000 to purchase furniture for the Presidential Mansion. Let him spend it! Washington was willing to let him have everything in the two main reception rooms at prices reduced because the furnishings were second-hand.[1]

Adams's $14,000 came to roughly £3500, and he could have the furnishings of the Green Room at a bargain: £663. Washington had reached this total item by item. The chandelier with eight lights was surely cheap at £76 13s. plus three pounds or so for the gilt chain on which it hung, the tassels and the gilt flower which dangled from it. The green silk window curtains of rich flowered satin came, with matching drapery, to only £78. A sofa, twenty-four arm chairs, and two stools, upholstered in the same satin, added up to £161. All these, with a carpet at £92 8s. were the basic furnishings Washington hoped Adams would buy. Also available, "although the sale of them is not desired," were various other items including two looking glasses "very cheap" at what they cost: exactly £92.[2]

Adams was so tempted by these fine things that Washington was to depart for Mount Vernon believing that his successor would buy them. But then New England thrift took over. Adams had already refused a pair of horses for which Washington had tried to pry from his pocket a thousand dollars although (as the President-elect noted indignantly) one was nine and the other ten years old. Commenting that "everyone asks and everyone cheats as much as he can," Adams added to his wife that Washington "says he must sell something in order to clear out."[3]

Washington offered the horses Adam had refused to Eliza Powel. As businesslike as you please, she wrote her friend, "I will give you one thousand dollars for your horses on delivery of them provided that I understand you clearly that they are only ten or eleven years old, that they are perfectly sound, well broke and gentle, and will drive with a postilion or in hand as may be most convenient."[4]

When the President responded to this note by pointing out that the horses would be heartbroken if separated from his old coach which was also for sale, Eliza replied that she personally found the coach comfortable, but she intended to give the horses to her young nephew who preferred "the moderns to the ancients." Thus Washington had to face the sad separation of the horses from "their espoused coach."[5]

After Adams had turned down the Green Room furnishings, Washington wrote Lear to ship most of them to Mount Vernon (where they may still be seen). He gave the chandelier to Mrs. Robert Morris, the brackets and mirror to Mrs. Powel. Eliza bought his private desk, for what he said it had cost him, ninety-six pounds. He expressed the hope that she would deduct for any damages that occurred while it was being moved, but did not think of the secret drawer where she was to find, to her great amusement, a packet of love letters addressed to the President.[6]

Despite the many objects he had sold, and those he had wanted to buy that he could not afford, Washington had no lack of possessions to transport from Philadelphia to Mount Vernon. He hired a sloop to carry by water everything but the most breakable, filled her full, and still had a superflux.[7] The invoice reveals that he sent "ninety-seven boxes, fourteen trunks, forty-three casks, thirteen packages, three hampers, one ton of iron, four bundles rod nails, twenty-four plough plates, four bundles leather, three bedsteads, two spits, one band for a kettle, four trivets, two gridirons, one rack spit, one heater, fourteen round iron rods, one pair kitchen andirons, one small grate, one pair of [fire] dogs, one iron chamber tub, three iron ash pails, one cage, two plate baskets, two wooden pillars, two plate warmers, one safe, one mangle, one marble slab, seven empty demijohns, one demijohn with honey, six fire buckets, one bundle fruit trees, three baskets, three green venetian blinds, four laths for venetian blinds, four folding screens, three chimney boards, two mahogany India blind frames, one bidet, one large carpet, seven bandboxes, one flag, four new window blinds, one tin shower bath, one toilet table, one floor mat."[8]

Before the sloop was fully loaded, Washington set out with his family, including young Lafayette and tutor, in a coach further crowded by innumerable fragile packages. From every stopping place, he wrote Lear afterthoughts on what should be done with this or that object left behind in Philadelphia. At Chester, he added high-spiritedly the postscript of a harassed family man, "On one side, I am called upon to remember the parrot; on the other, to remember the dog. For my own part, I should not pine if both were forgot."[9]

It was March 15, 1797, when the coach rumbled up one side of the bell-shaped driveway to what the ex-President called "my long forsaken residence at Mount Vernon." Nelly hurried off a note to a friend, "Grandpa is very well, and much pleased with being once more *Farmer Washington*."[10]

Washington was, indeed, promising himself "more real enjoyment than in all the business with which I have been occupied for upwards of forty years." As he watched the Potomac move majestically below his hillside as it had done since his boyhood, everything he had experienced out in the great world appeared to him "little more than vanity and vexation." Ceasing to be a doer, he would view life "in the calm lights of mild philosophy."*[11]

Before Washington could sink into the calm "indispensable for contemplation," he would have to prepare Mount Vernon to receive the furniture arriving on the sloop, which might any day be descried mounting the Po-

---

* This phrase, which Washington repeated in many letters, carried his memory back to the great love of his youth, Sally Fairfax, for it was a quotation from Addison's *Cato*, the play in which he would have been "doubly happy," as he wrote her, "in being the Juba to such a Marcia as you would make."[12]

tomac towards his wharf. He summoned his painters to freshen up the rooms, but soon discovered that he had "begun at the wrong end." His carpenters would have to prepare for the painters. Hardly had they begun than problems emerged that were beyond the skills of his slave artisans. He would have to import a joiner from some city. And then he wandered into the cellar carrying a bright light. "More by accident than design," he discovered that the great girder which supported the banquet hall was so decayed that "a company only moderately large would have sunk altogether into the celler."[13]

Further inspection revealed that there was hardly a structure on the Mount Vernon plantation that did not need repairs. Washington found himself surrounded by "joiners, masons, painters, etc., etc., and such is my anxiety to get out of their hands that I have scarcely a room to put a friend into or set in myself without the music of hammers or the odiferous smell of paint." So Washington wrote in early April. Seven months later: "Workmen in most countries, I believe, are necessary plagues. In this, where entreaties as well as money must be used to obtain their work and keep them to their duty, they baffle all calculation." He could fill several letters "with the perplexities I experience daily from workmen."[14]

The workmen had their problems too. Washington rose with the sun. "If my hirelings are not in their places at that time, I send them messages expressive of my sorrow for their indisposition. Then, having put these wheels in motion, I examine the state of things further," always finding more "wounds" in his structures that needed to be healed. By then, "breakfast (a little after seven o'clock) . . . is ready. This over, I mount my horse and ride round my farms, which employs me until it is time to dress for dinner, at which I rarely miss seeing strange faces, come, as they say, out of respect to me. Pray, would not the word curiosity answer as well? And how different this from having a few social friends at a cheerful board!

"The usual time of sitting at table, a walk, and tea, brings me within the dawn of candlelight, previous to which, if not prevented by company, I resolve that as soon as the glimmering taper supplies the place of the great luminary, I will retire to my writing table and acknowledge the letters I have received; but when the lights are brought, I feel tired and disinclined to engage in this work, conceiving that the next night will do as well. . . .

"Having given you the history of a day, it will serve for a year. . . . It may strike you that in this detail no mention is made . . . of reading. . . .

I have not looked into a book since I came home, nor shall I be able to do it until I have discharged my workmen . . . when possibly I may be looking in doomsday book."[15]

Doomsday book! Although Washington had been fearless in action, braving death to an unnecessary degree on many a battlefield, whenever his mind was not kept active, he was haunted by premonitions of death. During his earlier years, the specter had been an insubstantial bugaboo. But now the member of a short-lived family was sixty-five. Although his health seemed excellent, a sense of the imminence of death penetrated in a profusion of metaphors into his correspondence. His thread was nearly spun; his glass had almost run out; for only "a few years, perhaps days, I may be a sojourner here," may "remain on this terrestrial globe." He avoided the celebration of a family wedding as "better calculated for those who are *coming into* rather than *going out* of life." He hoped that the esteem of good men and the consciousness of having done the best for his country would "alleviate pain and soften any cares which are yet to be encountered, though hid from me at present."[16]

To his flirtatious Philadelphia friend, Mrs. Powel, Washington struck, at least until the last sentence of his message, a less lugubrious note. Having drafted a letter to Eliza for Martha to copy and sign, he wrote a postscript. "I am now, by desire of the General, to add a few words on his behalf. . . . Despairing of hearing what may be said of him if he should really go off in an apoplectic or any other fit (for he thinks all fits that issue in death are worse than a love fit, a fit of laughter, and many other kinds which he could name) he is glad to hear *beforehand* what will be said of him on that occasion, conceiving, that nothing extra will happen between *this* and *then* to make a change in his character for better or for worse.° And besides, as he has entered into an engagement with Mr. [Robert] Morris and several other gentlemen not to quit the theater of this world before the year 1800, it may be *relied upon* that no breach of contract shall be laid to him on that account, unless dire necessity should bring it about, maugre all his exertions to the contrary. In that case, he shall hope that they will do by him as he would by them: excuse it. At present, there seems to be no danger of his giving them the slip, as neither his health nor spirits were ever in greater flow, notwithstanding, he adds, he is descending and has almost reached the bottom of the hill or, in other words, the shades below."[17]

° How wrong he was, the reader will see.

President Washington is sassed by his dear friend Eliza Powel. Courtesy of the Mount Vernon Ladies' Association

Dear Sir
    Feeling myself incapable of nourishing an
Implacable Resentment; and in conformity with your letter & dispassionate Judgment — I have after maturely considering all that passed
Yesterday, determined to dine with you Tomorrow, when I will endeavor
to meet your Ideas with Fortitude.
                    With Sentiments of Respect & Affection
                        I am Sir
                            Your sincere Friend
                                Eliz[a] Powel

Wednesday 1st June 1796
President of the United States

Eliza Powel, who teased and admired President Washington, and was
his favorite female friend. Portrait by Thomas Sully. Collection unknown.
Photograph, Frick Art Reference Library

As Washington was leaving Philadelphia, he had, feeling that a personal leave-taking "is not among the most pleasant circumstances of one's life," said farewell to Eliza Powel in a letter. His family, he wrote, begged her to be assured "of the great esteem and affectionate regard we have for you. To add anything more particular as it respects myself, would be unnecessary."[18]

Shortly after he had got back to Mount Vernon, he received from the charmer a communication which ran as follows: "Like a true woman, so you will think, in the moment of exultation, and on the first impulse — for you know we are never supposed to act systematically or from attentive consideration — I take up my pen to address you, as you have given me a complete triumph on the subject of all others on which you have I suppose thought me most deficient, and most opposite to yourself; and what is still more charming, your candor shall preside as judge, nay you shall pass sentence on yourself, and I will not appeal from your decision. Suppose I should prove incontestably that you have without design put into my possession the love letters of a lady addressed to you under the most solemn sanction; and a large packet too. What will the goddess of prudence and circumspection say to her favorite son and votary for his dereliction of principles to which he has hitherto made such serious sacrifices? Was the taste of your sex predominant in your breast; — and did the love of variety so preponderate that, because you had never blundered as President, was you determined to try its delights as a private gentleman? But to keep you no longer in suspense, though I know that your nerves are not as irritable as a fine ladies' — yet I will with the generosity of my sex relieve you, by telling you that upon opening one of the drawers of your writing desk I found a large bundle of letters from Mrs. Washington, bound up and labled with your usual accuracy."

Lear, who was present at the discovery, was unwilling to be saddled with responsibility for the packet. Eliza then sealed it "with three seals bearing the impression of my blessed friend's arms such as I myself use." Mrs. Washington, she wrote, need have no fear that she had peaked. On second thoughts she added in a postscript that she had sworn Lear to secrecy: Washington did not need "unless you choose" to inform his wife concerning "the circumstance alluded to."[19]

Washington replied that, had it not been for the fact that he had no love letters to lose, the opening part of Eliza's letter "would have caused a serious alarm, and might have tried how far my nerves were able to sustain the shock of having betrayed the confidence of a lady." He was amazed to find that he had mislaid the letters and thanked Mrs. Powel for her "delicacy." Had she peeked, "the correspondence would, I am persuaded, have been found to be more fraught with expressions of friendship than of *enamoured* love." A reader of the *"romantic order,"* who wished to give the papers "the warmth," would have had to set them on fire.[20]

This description of Washington's relationship with Martha may, of course, have been influenced by his attitude towards his correspondent; no man sends to a lady in whom he is interested expressions of passionate affection for his wife.* However, what Washington wrote Eliza is our best information on the tenor of his correspondence with Martha, since, after the General's death, she burned the letters exchanged between them.†

The teasing contrast Eliza drew between Washington's behavior as President and as "private gentleman" implies (although somewhat ambiguously) that at least some of the letters from Martha, which Washington stated were so lacking in emotions of the "romantic order," dated from before his first inaugural. If so, how did they get into a desk he had acquired in New York during his Presidency? Had he, when, leaving Martha behind as he had set out to undertake the frightening task of presiding over the nation, carried his wife's letters along as a domestic talisman? We know that Martha had been, during his Revolutionary command, such a talisman; how eagerly he had anticipated, as every year the army collapsed into winter quarters, the arrival of his wife, who brought with her the comfort of his hearth! Washington, indeed, took marriage, which he equated with "domestic felicity," very seriously, writing that it was the most important event of a man's life.

No authentic evidence gives any indication that Washington was ever unfaithful to Martha,§ and Eliza's letter demonstrates that to her knowledge — which was surely considerable — Washington had not — it

---

* It will be remembered that years before, when Washington was engaged to Martha, he had responded to teasing from Sally Fairfax by stating that Sally was the only woman he really loved.[21]

† Martha was probably motivated by a desire to keep this intimate part of her relationship from the eyes of a world which had so perpetually intruded in her marriage. Only two letters, written just after Washington had accepted the post of Commander in Chief, have survived, and these because they had been (again) forgotten in the drawer of a desk. See also volume III, page 32.

§ Since Washington did not keep copies of his most personal correspondence — the most interesting communications with Eliza (as with Sally Fairfax) were preserved by the lady — the possibility exists that love letters by Washington may have been destroyed by prudish descendants of the recipient, or await, caressed by spiders, discovery in some attic.

seems to her own amusement and perhaps irritation — indulged "the taste of your sex" for "variety." However, this did not mean that he always found Martha's company exciting. After he had been back at Mount Vernon from the Presidency for months, he sent Lear this SOS: "I am alone at *present* and shall be glad to see you this evening. Unless someone pops in unexpectedly, Mrs. Washington and myself will do what I believe has not been done within the last twenty years by us, that is to set down to dinner by ourselves."*22

Martha, who was in fact a little older than her husband, had gone downhill more rapidly. She was glad to have him draft the letters she obediently copied. She was so "greatly distressed and fatigued" by the lack of an efficient housekeeper that high wages were no object in relation to the necessity of filling in the gap; although Washington did make it a reservation that, "be her appearance what it may," the housekeeper might not eat at the family table.24

To David Humphreys, then minister to Spain, Washington wrote that "when you shall think with the poet [again Addison in *Cato*] that 'the post of honor is a private station' and may be inclined to enjoy yourself in my shades," he would be welcome at Mount Vernon. After Humphreys had replied (in Washington's rueful paraphrase) that "every man who is in the vigor of life should serve his country," Washington mourned the disappointment of his "desire of a companion in my latter days." Humphrey's news that he was getting married "would of itself," Washington continued, "have annihilated every hope of having you as an intimate." The experience of living at Mount Vernon with Martha and her niece Fanny Bassett had taught the General what he expressed in another context: "I never again will have two women in my house when I am there myself."25

Finally Washington wrote his nephew Lawrence Lewis, "As both your aunt and I are in the decline of life and regular in our habits, especially in our hours of rising and going to bed, I require some person (fit and proper) to ease me of the trouble of entertaining company, particularly of nights. . . . In taking these duties (which hospitality obliges one to bestow on company) off my hands, it would render me a very acceptable service." Washington was already paying too many wages to offer any salary, but Lewis would have plenty of time to read "if you have any in-

---

* Lady Liston, who considered Washington "more a respectful than a tender husband certainly" was surprised to find Martha, after her husband's death, "grieving incessantly."23

clination for it . . . I have a great many instructive books on many subjects, as well as amusing ones, etc., etc., etc."[26]

Lewis came, and soon was spening much of his time with Nelly Custis,
now eighteen who, in the opinion of a visitor, Benjamin Henry Latrobe,
"has more perfection of form, of expression, of color, of softness, and of
firmness of mind than I have ever seen before or conceived as consistent
with mortality."[27]

A swing of Nelly's emotional pendulum had made her decide (a decision she was greatly to regret when it was too late) that she preferred the
quiet of the country to city gaieties, and wanted nothing more than to
spend the rest of her life on a plantation. She still enjoyed singing to her
playing on the harpsichord. A domestic vignette is hidden in Washington's apology to the Secretary of State for having inadvertently opened a
letter that should have been forwarded. His mind, he explained, was "by
the Ganges in the twilight."[28]

As an older woman, Nelly was to remember that the "grave dignity"
which her step-grandfather "usually wore" did not prevent him from
laughing heartily at her "saucy descriptions of any scene in which she
had taken part, or any one of the merry pranks she then often played."
When she and her youthful companions were amusing themselves, Washington would appear to share their hilarity, and then reluctantly withdraw
"because his presence created a reserve they could not overcome."[29]

Nelly's two married sisters — Washington expressed pleasure that their
husbands were both "rich men" — lived in the federal city, where Peters
and Law owned and operated real estate. There was much visiting back
and forth. Martha had great-granddaughters to spoil, and if the fissures
that were to shatter Eliza Law's marriage had begun to develop, this was
invisible to the Washingtons.[30]

The difficulties of the grandson, Washington Custis, were only too visible. Custis remembered how the General had shed tears when upbraiding
him for his "manifold errors and follies." The lad was not vicious the way
his father had been. As far as Washington knew, he had no vices, but he
seemed "inert," indolent and withal stubborn. After he had failed to
buckle down at the University of Pennsylvania and Princeton, his grandfather, "distressed to know what to do," brought him to Mount Vernon in
the hope that he himself could propel the boy with the power that had
propelled the nation. He wrote down instructions, pointing out that "sys-

tem in all things should be aimed at, for in execution it renders everything more easy." Custis might go out with his gun before breakfast but had to be back for that meal. From then to an hour before dinner, he would "confine yourself to diligent study." Since, while the afternoons were short (this was written in January) there was only a brief break between dinner and tea, during this time Custis could amuse himself. After tea, he should study until bedtime. Saturdays could be devoted to riding, gunning, etc. Sundays were not mentioned. The youth should always be on time for all meals: "It is not only disagreeable but it is also very inconvenient for servants to be running here and there and they know not where to summon you."[31]

The ex-President found that by eternal vigilance he could keep the boy in his room, but he could not make him study, and if he relaxed supervision for a moment, there would be the sounds of footsteps running up and down the stairs and the boy's voice talking to anyone who would talk to him. When Washington went out the front door, Custis went out the back. The hero finally decided that for him to attempt to control the lad was "as idle as the endeavor to stop a rivulet that is constantly running."[32]

On first reaching Cambridge, General Washington had ruled the New Englanders a "dirty, nasty people," but that was long ago. Now he believed that the attention of New Englanders "to morals and a more regular course of life" might reform Custis. He suggested to Martha that the boy be sent to Harvard. Sadly, the old lady agreed to submit, but it was clear that it would be "a heart-rending stroke to have him at that distance." Finally, Custis was sent to St. John's College, Annapolis.[33]

The boy failed to write home, driving his grandmother into agonies of anxiety. Gossip stated that he was spending much time with a young lady. Faced with the charge, the boy admitted that he had fallen in love, but affirmed that he had told his charmer that he was entirely dependent on "the absolute will" of his friends. Her parents had turned him down as too young, and there the matter had ended. Custis added to his stepgrandfather, "Let me once more, sir, on the shrine of gratitude plight my faith to you. Let me unclasp the sacred books of morality and lay my duty, nay my all, at your feet." But he did not want to stay at St. John's College, asking whether when he came home for vacation he could not come home for good. Washington's reply expressed astonishment: Had he not tried to impress "indelibly" on the youth's mind that he had been sent to Annapolis to finish his education? Washington wrote the president of

G. W. P. CUSTIS

SHARPLESS, ARTIST

"Little Washington," Washington's semi-adopted step-grandson, who, despite mutual tears, could not live up to the routines and tasks assigned him by his guardian. Pastel portrait by a member of the Sharples family of George Washington Parke Custis. Courtesy of Washington and Lee University

St. John's (as he had written to the officials of every one of the colleges the young man attended) a despairing letter which could hardly have increased the student's reputation with his teachers.[34]

Poor George Washington Parke Custis! All the boy wanted was to be allowed to grow up like his neighborhood playmates as a relaxed southern gentleman. By placing his tremendous personal strength behind another way of life, Washington cowed the boy, drove him into a cringing passive resistance that obscured his true gifts and energy. For in his later years, Custis was by no means a dullard. Without applying to his work any system, he was a successful playwright: he once wrote a producible drama in a nine-hour burst. He also earned celebrity as an orator. Interestingly enough, he dedicated much of his life to deifying in the national memory the step-grandfather who had so frowned on his youth.

What a contrast loomed, after Washington's retirement to Mount Vernon, between George Washington Parke Custis and George Washington Motier Lafayette. Mrs. Liston described young Lafayette as "a gentle, melancholy, interesting youth." A male visitor found that "his figure is rather awkward," but his manners were easy, his conversation alive with "wit and fluency." Washington considered him "aimiable and sensible." He enjoyed joking with young Lafayette at the dinner table, and was greatly impressed by his being a veritable paragon of filial piety.[35]

While Washington was still President, the French youth had importuned him into taking steps to procure the release of his father which Washington had considered indiscreet. Now, the boy was so upset at not receiving news that Washington wrote the Postmaster General asking that the deputy postmasters in all the seaport towns be asked to send any letters for young Lafayette, however addressed, to Mount Vernon. Then word came that the Marquis had been released and was joining his family in France. This was no more than a rumor, but young Lafayette was determined to be off across the ocean at once to join his father. Washington tried to dissuade him: the report could so easily be false, and the impetuous young aristocrat might not himself be safe in France. But nothing would suffice. Washington finally advanced the necessary money and rode with the youth as far as the federal city on his journey to transatlantic shipping at New York. It was an anxious parting. Washington, as his letters reveal, remained haunted with anxiety. How dreadful if the son's "filial and fraternal affection" were to be rewarded by "sore disappointment and regret!" Three months elapsed before word that the Marquis was safely in Hamburg calmed Washington with the conviction that the youth would actually reach his father.[36]

The reminiscences of the New England merchant Thomas Handasyd Perkins, who had felt entitled to call at Mount Vernon because he had befriended young Lafayette when the lad had first appeared in Boston, give us our only hint that the General could upon occasion indulge in the American frontier occupation of telling tall tales. (Or was it, in fact, an odd biological observation?) As Washington sat with his visitor on the piazza, a toad hopped by. Had Perkins, the ex-President asked, ever seen a toad swallow a firefly? Perkins having admitted that he had not, Washington said that *he* had, and that for some time thereafter the toad had periodically lighted up like a lantern.[37]

Although Washington complained of the endless coming and going at Mount Vernon, the gregarious retired statesman would have been lost without it. The human tides that surged along his driveway and from his river landing washed in not only the curious, the impertinent and the pompous, but relations and friends, and also strangers he found interesting. One of the latter was Benjamin Henry Latrobe. The brilliant young English engineer and architect described how Washington talked to him hungrily.

Latrobe had arrived at Mount Vernon during July 1796 in the early afternoon with a letter from Bushrod Washington. He was kept waiting only about ten minutes before the President appeared "in a plain blue coat, his hair dressed and powdered. There was a reserve but no hauteur in his manner. He shook me by the hand, said he was glad to see a friend of his nephew's, drew a chair, and desired me to sit down."

Learning that Latrobe was on his way to the Virginia town of Bath, Washington was prompted to reminisce, but not about those aspects of that health resort which recalled his ancient, tragic emotions. "He said he had known the place when there was scarce a house upon it fit to step in; that the accomodations there were, he believed, very good at present." A family who visited there regularly would do best to build a house, which could be done for £200. He himself had a house there which he supposed was going to ruins. However, he would not wish to stay at Bath unless forced by illness, since he understood that many persons went there who were not ill, and their "dissipations" disturbed the others. "This, he observed, must naturally be the case in every large collection of men whose minds were not occupied by pressing business or personal interest." Latrobe noted that in making such comments on "the rapidly increasing immorality" of the American citizenry, Washington showed no "moroseness" or any great concern. "They seemed the well-expressed remarks of a man who has seen and knows the world."

The conversation turned to Washington's effort to build a canal through the Dismal Swamp. Latrobe was flattered that, despite Washington's knowledge of the subject and passion for it, he listened with interest to the young man's comments, "taking the pains either to object to my deductions where he thought them ill-founded, or to confirm them by very strong opinions of his own."

Since, when Washington had first greeted Latrobe, he had said that he should be writing letters, after about an hour the young man got up to leave. Washington told him to "Keep my chair," and then drew him out on canal building in England.

The next subject was coal mines on the James River. Latrobe spoke of a silver mine. "He laughed most heartily upon the very mention of the thing." On being assured that it was practical, he said, "It would give him real uneasiness should any silver or gold mines be discovered that would tempt considerable capital into the prosecution of that object, and that he heartily wished for his country that it might contain no mines but such as the plough could reach, excepting only coal and iron."

After they had conversed for more than two hours, Washington got up and said, "we should meet again at dinner." Latrobe prowled about the lawn, and on his return found Mrs. Washington, to whom he introduced himself. "She immediately entered into a conversation upon the prospect from the lawn, and presently gave me an account of her family in a good-humored, free manner that was extremely pleasant and flattering." Latrobe concluded that she had once been a beauty, but could hardly take his eyes off Nelly Custis, who was a beauty now.

For an hour before dinner, which was delayed in hopes of the arrival of Lear, Washington "talked freely upon common topics with the family," which included young Lafayette and his tutor. At dinner, Latrobe "felt a little embarrassed at the silent, reserved air that prevailed. As I drink no wine and the President drank only three glasses, the party soon returned to the portico." Although Lear now arrived with his three sons and Dandridge, Washington retired in about three quarters of an hour.

Latrobe felt it "a point of delicacy" not to stay any longer. He was about to leave when Washington reappeared, asked if he had any pressing business, and then said, "Sir, you see I take my own way. If you can be content to take yours at my house, I shall be glad to see you here longer."

Coffee was served on the piazza about six o'clock. After it had been removed, Washington asked his guest about the state of the crops in the countryside through which he had come. "A long conversation upon farming ensued, during which it grew dark, and he then proposed going into the hall. He made me sit down by him, and continued the conversation for above an hour. During that time he gave me a very minute account of the Hessian fly, and its progress from Long Island, where it first appeared, through New York, Rhode Island, Connecticut, Delaware, part of Pennsylvania, and Maryland. It has not yet appeared in Virginia, but is daily dreaded." He then disucussed at length the advantages and disadvantages of growing Indian corn, and the different merits of a variety of ploughs he had tried. Latrobe promised to send him an improved plough, "which he accepted with pleasure." About eight o'clock, Washington retired to bed. "There was no hint of supper."

The next morning, "the President came to the company in the sitting room about one half hour past seven, where all the latest newspapers were laid out." He talked to Lear about the progress of the Potomac Canal and the federal city. Breakfast — tea, coffee, and cold broiled meat — was soon over. As Washington stepped out the west door, a group of people (unidentified) gathered around them. He stood there conversing for about an hour about the federal university which he had labored vainly to get started. "He spoke as if he felt a little hurt upon the subject." When at about ten Washington made a motion to retire, Latrobe called for his horses. After they had appeared, the ex-President went over to Latrobe's servant "and asked him if he had breakfasted. He then shook me by the hand, desired me to call if I came again into the neighborhood, and wished me a good morning.

"Washington," Latrobe summarized, "has something uncommonly majestic and commanding in his walk, his address, his figure, and his countenance. His face is characterized, however, more by intense and powerful thought than by quick and fiery conception. There is a mildness about its expression, and an air of reserve in his manner lowers its tone still more. . . . He was frequently entirely silent for many minutes, during which time an awkwardness seemed to prevail in everyone present. His answers were often short and sometimes approached to moroseness. He did not at any time speak with very remarkable fluency; perhaps the extreme correctness of his language, which almost seemed studied, prevented that effect. He appeared to enjoy a humorous observation, and made several himself. He laughed heartily several times in a very good-humored manner. On the morning of my departure he treated me as if I had lived for years in his house, with ease and attention." Yet Washington seemed to Latrobe to be fundamentally disgruntled, "as if something had vexed him."[38]

Other travelers' accounts reveal that Washington became silent, even resentful, at efforts to make him talk politics. Although he liked to reminisce about his fellow officers during the Revolution, he was less willing to discuss Revolutionary battles than his ancient experiences in the French and Indian War.° Perhaps because he had then passed through the home territories of so many of his visitors, he often talked about his tours as President to New England and the deep south. Arnariah Frost was impressed by his eagerness to know all about the marriage of a tavernkeeper's daughter whom he remembered as having "superior sense and knowledge for one in a country village."

At the end of every meal, Washington drank individually the health of everyone present and then always announced the same final toast, "To all our friends!"[40]

Alas, so many of Washington's old friends had vanished. Alexandria, that community for which the young Washington had surveyed and drawn the first town plan, had grown into a bustling commercial center, but in all the now numerous houses there lived not one family he and Martha had known when they were first married. In his own Virginia neighborhood, and across the river in that part of Maryland he had so often visited, almost every face he had seen ruddy with wine was now in another part of the world or moldering underground. When one of his few remaining ancient friends, the Reverend Bryan Fairfax, sailed on family business to England, Washington was enabled to reach out towards the dearest of all his onetime companions. For Bryan Fairfax was the brother-in-law of the incomparable Sally, whom the young Washington had so loved.

Washington composed for his wife a letter to Sally (which she obediently copied) expressing regret "at not having you as a neighbor and a

---

° Washington told one Arnariah Frost that Forbes's climactic capture of Fort Duquesne (which had grown from strategy he violently disapproved) had been achieved by luck. Forbes, who had not expected to advance, had received an unforeseen shipment of supplies, while the French, disappointed in the supplies they expected, had sent their Indians home.[39]

companion." To Bryan Fairfax, Washington wrote, "Mrs. Washington begs the favor of you to put her letter to her old neighbor and friend Mrs. Fairfax into a channel for safe delivery." Harking back to the discretions he had once had to practice, he did not disclose that the packet also contained a letter of his own.[41]

During the twenty-five years since he had been a permanent resident of Mount Vernon, so Washington wrote, "many important events have occurred and such changes in men and things have taken place as the compass of a letter would give you but an inadequate idea of. None of which events however, nor all of them together, have been able to eradicate from my mind the recollection of those happy moments, the happiest in my life, which I have enjoyed in your company.

"Worn out in a manner by the toils of my past labor, I am again seated under my vine and fig tree. . . . It is a matter of sore regret, when I cast my eyes towards Belvoir, which I often do, to reflect that the former inhabitants of it, with whom we lived in such harmony and friendship, no longer reside there; and that the ruins can only be viewed as the memento of former pleasures." He often wondered why Sally did not return, rebuild the house, and spend "the evening of your life" down the road from Mount Vernon.[42]

But Sally Fairfax did not come to help relieve the old hero's loneliness.

37

George Washington, Art Collector

WASHINGTON had bought many pictures during the eight years he spent as President in the cities of New York and Philadelphia. The lists he made to insure framing and shipping as he prepared to return to Mount Vernon, supplemented by other information, including the inventory of the objects at Mount Vernon at the time of his death, give a firm insight into Washington's artistic taste.[1]

The old hero is revealed as a resolute collector. The opinions of connoisseurs, the artistic shibboleths of his era, did not frighten him from his habitual mental attitude, which was not unconventional in the sense of desiring to be different but rather pursued its own ends independently of convention. Reflecting his own philosophy, interests, and experience, Washington's taste was usually ahead of his time and it anticipated a major development that lay several generations ahead, not only in the United States but on the continent of Europe.

During Washington's entire career, correct taste was neoclassical. The "highest" forms in the visual arts were "historical" painting or sculpture: depictions aimed at exemplifying the virtues and vices of humanity in exalted contexts. There were representations of great men out of the past and dramatic scenes enacted or imagined long ago. At its most correct, neoclassical art illustrated aspects of the ancient Greece or Rome that were considered to have more universal application than other civilizations.

Washington's first essay as an art collector, undertaken when he was twenty-eight years old and recently back from the French and Indian War, bowed to the historical taste, although it went beyond the purely

[356]

classical. He ordered from London small busts of famous generals: Alexander, Julius Caesar, the Duke of Marlborough, etc. His English factor sent what was more exactly in fashion: a group showing Aeneas carrying his father to safety as Troy burned, and two other groups, featuring Bacchus and Flora.[2] The mythological pieces, which included nymphs whose charms were partially revealed by parted draperies, appealed to Washington more than the depiction of Trojan filial piety. Washington owned at his death a print called *Cupid's Pastime,* another called *Diana Deceived by Venus,* and several visions of classical nymphs bathing. However, he ceased rapidly to be concerned with those aspects of neoclassical art which would have glorified his taste in the eyes of correct connoisseurs and seemed to them most suited to his position. When an admirer sent him six huge engravings of Alexander's victories, Washington was no longer interested in that Greek general. He deposited the sumptuous masterpieces of the mezzotinter's art in a portfolio (where they still languish today).[3]

In 1785, the great French neoclassical sculptor Jean Antoine Houdon appeared at Mount Vernon to collect studies and a life mask as materials from which he would create, after his return to France, a full-length statue of Washington. The General was soon writing Jefferson (who was in Paris) that, although he did not claim "sufficient knowledge of the art of sculpture to oppose my judgment to the taste of connoisseurs," he ventured to suggest that perhaps his figure should not be draped in a toga. Might not "some little deviation in favor of the modern costume" be permissible? This innovation, "which had been introduced in painting by Mr. West, I understand is received with applause and prevails extensively."[4]

Pennsylvania born and raised Benjamin West, world-famous inhabitant of London who was soon to succeed Sir Joshua Reynolds as president of the Royal Academy, was almost an exact contemporary of Washington's. Shaped by a world unknown to antiquity, he had, after at first following the most accepted taste, made a break which led the neoclassical mode away from ancient Greece and Rome, up through the medieval to modern times. Washington owned reproductions of four works by West.

Other American artists had gathered around West. Washington owned an engraving of Copley's *Death of Chatham,* which depicted the statesman collapsing in Parliament after a pro-American speech. This was as far as the American historical painters resident in London dared to go in glorifying the American Revolution and the British defeat at Washington's hands. West left this saga to one of his students who had doubled as a Revolutionary soldier and even served briefly as Washington's aide. John Trumbull undertook eight historical paintings, from *The Battle of Bunker Hill* to *Cornwallis' Surrender,* that he hoped to have engraved as "a national work" which would put the pictures in every prosperous American home and the considerable earnings in his pocket. Washington publicly and enthusiastically endorsed this effort. Only two of the prints were completed in Washington's lifetime, neither featuring the General himself. Washington bought four pairs and hung six of the engravings on the multiple walls of Mount Vernon.[5]

Also on those walls was *A Battle Fought by Cavalry* (described as being in a gilt frame and presented to him by an English admirer), *A Dead Soldier,* after the English painter Joseph Wright of Debry (also a gift), and two religious prints that were appraised at the low sum of fifteen dollars each: "one likeness of Saint John" and "ditto of Virgin Mary." This more or less completed Washington's observance of high taste.[6]

Washington's favorite art was, of course, architecture: he designed Mount Vernon himself. A letter he wrote in 1798 to the semi-professional architect William Thornton reveals that he regarded the classical orders as conveniences rather than infallible canons of taste, and that he did not care what the experts and critics thought: "Rules of architecture are calculated, I presume, to give symmetry and just proportion to all the orders and parts of building in order to please the eye. Small departures from *strict* rules are discoverable only by the skillful architects or by the eye of criticism; while ninety-nine of a hundred, deficient of their knowledge, might be pleased with things not quite orthodox. . . . These ideas, as you will readily perceive, proceed from a person who avows his ignorance of architectural principles, and has no other guide but his eye to direct his choice."[7]

Self-educated, Washington was entirely ignorant of Latin or Greek. He was, indeed, highly critical of a schoolmaster who taught two of his wards dead languages while omitting the mathematics that would enable the boys to survey land they might own or buy.[8] Although some of his admirers liked to think of Washington as a reincarnation of Cincinnatus, Washington saw himself as a reincarnation of nobody. Never once in his writings did he wonder how any dead hero would have dealt with the problems that he had to face. He hardly ever looked to the past. Precedents were not to be followed but made. Thus the backward view basic to

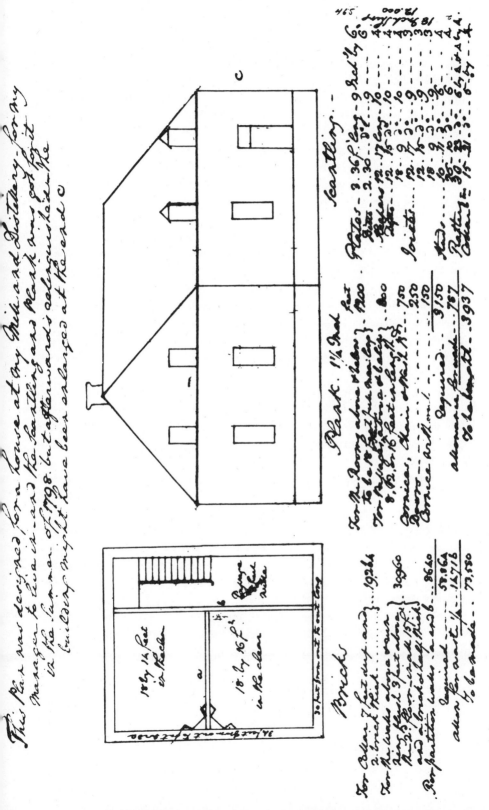

Washington's own plan for a home for his miller and distiller reveals the amateur architect's aesthetic pleasure in a well-designed page. Courtesy of the Mount Vernon Ladies' Association

true neoclassicism appealed to him not at all. He was sympathetic to the artistic revolution of his fellow Americans in London who were trying to bring historical painting up to date. Their efforts to combine artistic grandeur with factual truth exactly fitted Washington's preconceptions. In sponsoring Trumbull's series he wrote, "The greatness of the design and the masterly execution of the work equally interest the man of a capacious mind and the approving eye of the connoisseur. He has spared no pains in obtaining from the life the likenesses of those characters, French as well as American, who bore a conspicuous part in our Revolution; and the success with which his efforts have been crowned will form no small part of the value of his pieces."[9]

The paradox of English and American eighteenth-century neoclassicism was that, although reigning aesthetic theory scorned portraiture, portrait painting was the most prosperous and the liveliest of the arts. Even the great Sir Joshua Reynolds mourned that his practice could not help being inferior, because in achieving a likeness he had to deal with a specific personality rather than a universal truth of humankind. Yet an increasingly individualistic society demanded and was willing to pay for individual likenesses.

The theorizing that separated the universal from the specific could have meant nothing to Washington, who always saw the two together as a single entity. Yet Washington went naturally along with the conception that portraits were utilitarian objects, inherent parts (like chairs to sit in) of ordinary existence. He had acquired a likeness of his beloved half brother Lawrence. Martha brought with her to Mount Vernon pictures of herself and her two children painted by John Wollaston. Washington began himself commissioning portraits when in 1772 he called Charles Willson Peale to Mount Vernon. After that, more pictures of himself, his family, and his friends accreted. He would not accept objects of art as gifts from the creators, but he was glad to receive gifts from sitters. Thus he hung in his living room a family group showing the Marquis de Lafayette, his wife, and three children.[10]

Faces, engraved as well as painted, stared everywhere from the walls of Mount Vernon. Although he recognized differences in verisimilitude and pleasing effect,° Washington was primarily concerned with the likeness.

___

° In presenting his own portrait by the American painter Joseph Wright to the Comte de Solms, a distinguished officer in the Prussian service who was making a collection of "military heroes," Washington penned his one comment on a portrait

He thought of his many portraits not as an art collection but as a group of personal mementos. In this his attitude was typical of his time.

It was when Washington bought what he called "fancy pieces of my own choosing"[12] that he revealed taste far ahead of his time. The reigning neoclassicism regarded landscape painting as a lower form of art. Landscapes could express human emotion only indirectly and, before the rise of the romantic movement with its attendant pantheism, nature was not considered in her own right elevating to the spirit of man. Taste for landscape painting exploded into common acceptance in the United States in 1825, with the triumphant exhibition of three Hudson River scenes by Thomas Cole. In this move to what became the dominant nineteenth-century painting mode, America was behind England but ahead of France, where the mid-century conflict was between two schools of figure painting, one led by Ingres and the other by Delacroix.

The neoclassical taste that damned landscape was never truly indigenous to America. Local connoisseurs took it the more seriously for the very reason that it had been imported from the acknowledged centers of culture. However, Washington was too self-reliant to abandon, in order to be culturally correct, his natural predilections. He had been unenthusiastic about Jefferson's desire to have the buildings in the new national capital follow the most accepted European taste.[13] And his own taste for nature amounted to love. During his years of exile as a general and a statesman, his mind flew to Mount Vernon as a haven of peace. The metaphors that came automatically to his mind when he wrote referred to the woods and streams and fields. In the 1790's, he became a devotee of landscape art.

The most acceptable name in landscape painting was that of Claude Lorrain, whose nostalgic views of Italy were close in sentiment to the historical mode. Among fine landscape prints, those after Claude were easiest to come by. Washington bought and hung a good many, but he also collected numerous other landscape engravings which cannot be specifically identified from the titles that appear in the lists. Among his total holdings Washington owned were two pairs entitled *Morning* and *Evening*, a *Sun Rising* and a *Sun Setting*, several *Storms* on land and sea, a

---

that might be considered art criticism. Wright's "forte seems to be in giving the distinguishing characteristics with more boldness than delicacy. Although he commonly marks the features very strongly, yet I cannot flatter you that you will find the touches of his pencil extremely soft, or that the portrait will in any respect equal your expectations."[11]

The paintings on the following four pages

Nymphs Bathing. This engraving, which Washington had framed on his return from the Presidency to Mount Vernon, hung at the time of his death "in the first room on the second floor." Although the margins have been trimmed, the name Christian Wilhelm Ernest Dietrich remains visible in the lower left-hand corner. Courtesy of the Mount Vernon Ladies' Association

Morning (or Evening) on the Hudson River, by William Winstanley. This feebly poetic rendition in the conventional "Arcadian Mode," as descended from Claude Lorrain, represented Winstanley's typical style and was presumably already painted when purchased by Washington in 1793. Courtesy of the Mount Vernon Ladies' Association

Genessee Falls, New York. This canvas, also by William Winstanley, reveals how the artist's style changed in response to the passion of his exalted patron for realistic views of American scenery. Bought by Washington in 1794. Courtesy of the National Collection of Fine Arts, Smithsonian Institution

The Great Falls of the Potomac: the reach of river which most fiercely opposed Washington's determination to open the river to navigation with a canal. This literal rendering, so unconventional for the eighteenth century, was painted, presumably to Washington's order, during 1796 or 1797 by George Beck. Courtesy of the Mount Vernon Ladies' Association

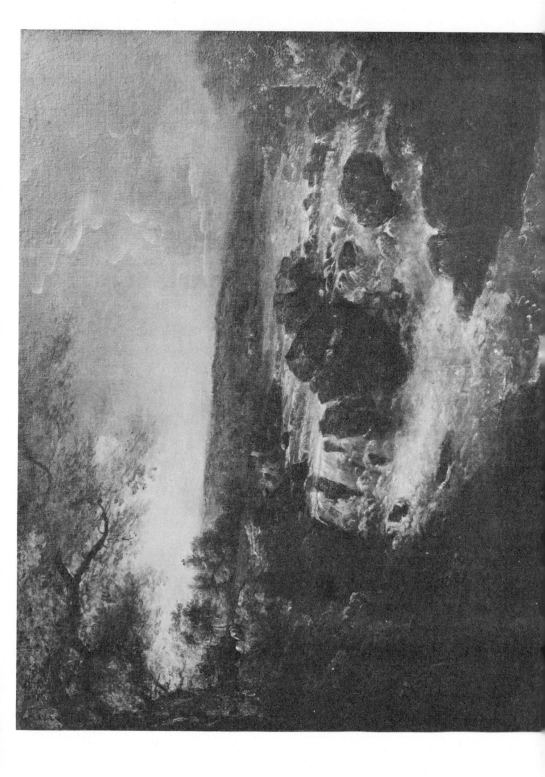

sea battle, a *Hobbema's Village* and a *Gainsborough's Forest*, a *View on the Po River*, a *Cottage*, and "a likeness of a deer." Other prints embellished landscape with genre or mythological figures. There were two depictions of herdsmen, views of whale fisheries, *The Dancing Shepherds, Musical Shepherds, Adonis Carried off by Venus*, etc., etc.

But it was the oil paintings Washington bought that really revealed the originality of his taste. Since engravings were cheap and unobtrusive, purchasing them was not considered a major cultural act, and thus connoisseurs who would have perished rather than buy a landscape in oil felt they could, without damaging their reputations, add some landscape prints to their portfolios. This was made the less reprehensible because the prints usually represented not nature in her crudity but places and times full of historical human associations. No prints of any quality then existed of the American land, it being understood that American scenery, as the least elevated by years of civilization, was the crudest of all. If taste could not contemplate an engraving of American nature, how much more shocking would an oil painting be! Yet the only paintings (other than portraits) that Washington bought were American views.

Because of the aesthetic objection to American scenery, almost all the landscapes that were produced in the United States were intended as decorations. Compositions that balanced natural elements, often European in reference and half imaginary, were run up to be nailed (for instance) in the paneling over a fireplace.° To secure at New York or Philadelphia (to say nothing of Mount Vernon) landscapes that truly evoked American scenery was by no means easy.

During 1792, there appeared in Philadelphia "a little pert young" Englishman called William Winstanley. According to the art chronicler William Dunlap, he "was understood to have come to New York on some business connected with the Episcopal Church. He was of a good family in England and had received a gentlemanly education." Partly because landscape was not considered a serious enough art to be much pursued by professionals, dabbling in it was regarded as an agreeable accomplishment for gentlemen amateurs as well as for young ladies. This probably was the basis of the agreeable proficiency in landscape Winstanley

° Washington's first purchase of a landscape fell in this category, although he followed the Virginia pattern by buying it not locally but abroad. On April 15, 1757, he ordered from his London factor "a neat landskip three feet by twenty-one and a half inches — one-inch margin for chimney." The factor sent him a scene, featuring a forest, shepherds with sheep, and a harbor with ships, which he described as being after the style of Claude and for which he charged £3 15s. 6d. Washington inserted it in the overmantle in his front parlor.[14]

brought with him to America. His Episcopal business (so it seems) failing him, he practiced in the colonies as a landscape painter.[15]

In 1793, Winstanley showed Washington two of his oil paintings that professed to depict scenery on the banks of the Hudson. True, the groves and glassy still water and foreground peasants revealed no observation of American nature. They followed a tepid diminution of the old Claudian tradition which had entered in England the artistic vernacular. However, they gave a sense of space and light which could spark in a strong imagination a feeling of the outdoors. In April 1793 Washington bought the two canvases for thirty guineas.[16]

Hamilton was delighted with the paintings, writing, "There are two views of situations on Hudson's River painted by Mr. Winstanley in the drawing room of Mrs. Washington which have great intrinsic merit, and considered with reference to his [Winstanley's] opportunities as related, announce a very supreme genius in the branch of painting, worthy of encouragement."[17] Washington remained fond of the pictures, but yearned for canvases more specific to the American land as he experienced it.

In September 1793 he wrote the commissioners of the District of Columbia, "Mr. Winstanley, a celebrated landskip painter, is disposed to take a view of the federal city or of the grounds in the vicinity of it. . . . His designs are more extensive, and I have suggested the Great and Little Falls, the passage of the River Potomac through the Blue Mountains, the natural bridge, etc., as grand objects."[18]

What happened to this scheme is not known, but Washington did buy another pair of canvases from Winstanley.[19] The example that remains, *View of the Genesee Falls, New York,* differs so greatly from the two Washington procured ready-made that it seems probable that Winstanley had tried to change his style to suit the desires of his illustrious patron. Gone are the Claudian overtones. The canvas is a crude stumbling towards those realistic views of untamed American scenery which were to come into their own in the days, almost a half century later, of the Hudson River School.

Washington had not lost his desire to own what Winstanley had, despite his suggestions, failed to deliver: paintings of the wild Potomac water through which he was promoting a canal. In January 1797 he procured from George Beck (1748 or 1750–1812) views of the river as it broke through the Blue Ridge and also as it roared along the Great Falls.[20]

Beck was an Englishman who, unlike his compatriot Winstanley, had left in his homeland a record of his artistic activity. The son of a Staffordshire farmer, he had become one of those craftsmen who, in the dawn of British landscape art, moved back and forth, as he also engaged in other activities, between teaching art to amateurs, creating topographical views, and exhibiting on the same walls with exalted professionals. Before he came to the United States in 1795, Beck had drawn maps for the military engineering corps, been tutor to the daughters of a marchioness, and exhibited fifteen landscapes, including views of gentlemen's country seats, at the Royal Academy and the Society of Artists. He had also made a sketching tour through the western counties of England and through Wales. His wife was to boast that in "the picturesque and romantic scenery of Wales," as he contemplated "the sublimity" of the Welsh mountains, he transferred to canvas nature's "mildest graces."[21]

The last thing Washington wanted in the landscapes he ordered from Beck was "nature's mildest graces." He wanted to have depicted the fierce grandeur of the savage impediments he intended somehow to traverse with his canal. As had probably been the situation with Winstanley's *Genesee Falls*, he imposed his own taste on the artist. The two canvases he bought from Beck reveal a literalness which is again so out of keeping with its time that the result is harsh, rough, discordant as compared with the conventional milk-and-water views of more civilized places that Beck painted for others.

How far (if at all) Washington realized the aesthetic inadequacy of what he had received is not clear. There seemed, indeed, to have been in existence no other literal renditions of wild American scenery to offer a gauge for judgment. Washington valued and enjoyed what he had. He was eager to carry, at his retirement, the paintings from Philadelphia to Mount Vernon, but yet worried lest it might be his duty to leave at least some of such important works on view at the Presidential Mansion.° He finally compromised by stating that he was willing to sell the two Winstanley Hudson River scenes to his successor. John Adams felt no inclination to buy.[23]

In a nation devoid of art museums, the President's House, then located in America's major city of Philadelphia, was indeed the most conspicuous

---

° "To encourage literature and the arts," Washington wrote, "is a duty which every good citizen owes to his country."[22]

place for the showing of works of art.° The pictures Washington collected attracted so much attention that, when the retiring President offered at auction the effects he did not wish to carry with him to Mount Vernon, the public was disappointed to find that "the paintings, prints, etc.," were not to be sold.[24] It is true that, despite this interest (attested to by Washington's secretary, Tobias Lear), the President's taste was too unconventional to send collectors scurrying out on their own in search of realistic American landscapes.[25] Yet the fact remains that the Father of his Country was, in his role as a patron, the grandfather (or perhaps the great-grandfather) of that most indigenous of American artistic movements, the Hudson River School.

° The Corsican sculptor Giuseppe Ceracchi tried to give Washington busts of Bacchus and Ariadne and, when the President adhered to his policy of refusing all such gifts, begged "with earnestness" that they be permitted to remain in the President's House. Washington had temporary pedestals made for them, "and always announced them as your workmanship and your property." He was duly outraged when Ceracchi (who was eventually to be executed for trying to assassinate Napoleon) some three years later demanded payment for the statues.

38

Income in Retirement

AMONG the reasons why Washington had not been more reluctant to become President was that he could not, in any case, have continued his existing life at Mount Vernon. The money he would earn would save him from the disagreeable necessity he foresaw of practicing "frugality and economy."[1]

As it turned out, his Presidential salary, put on top of the earnings from his farms and the rents collected on western acres, had not enabled him to meet his expenses. And now his salary had ceased. Of course, he no longer needed to keep up two establishments. However, that by no means saved the situation. In September 1799 he wrote that "were it not for occasional supplies of money in payment for lands sold within the last four or five years, to the amount of upwards of $50,000" (several hundred thousand dollars in modern currency), he would be "in debt and difficulties."[2]

Land speculation was, of course, a fundamental aspect of American economic life, but it had become in the last few years an extremely tricky one. General Knox was above the knees in financial trouble because of the new settlements he had started in Maine. The once richest man in America, Washington's onetime financial mentor Robert Morris, landed in debtor's prison, as did former Governor Henry Lee. However, Washington's far-flung land holdings did not rock but sustained his boat.

He had achieved his stability by avoiding those financial facilities which he had helped Hamilton create. Despite efforts by Morris to lure him into the North American Land Company, which briefly and then disastrously controlled six million acres of American soil, he did not increase his grasp with the slippery leverage supplied by credit. As Washington explained, "It has been a maxim with me from early life never to undertake anything without perceiving a door to the accomplishment in a reasonable time with my own resources."[3] Thus his unsold acres were (except for taxes never too burdensome) no drain on his assets but awaited sale as if they were jewels laid away in a strongbox.

Washington had unique possibilities, of which, in his later years, he took full advantage. Most land speculators were limited to buying huge tracts wholesale, or specializing in one or two regions they knew well, or buying specific properties in the dark. But Washington's name was known in every part of the United States, and people of influence were enchanted to have contact with him. A few years before, he had leaned over backwards not to presume on his eminence. Now he was shameless about demanding favors* He asked far-flung correspondents to give him on-the-spot reports on the fertility of land he owned or wished to acquire, to define position in relation to rivers how navigable and to rising communities how large? He asked what were the going prices in the neighborhood; what were the assets and probity of potential purchasers; and even wished his correspondents to supervise deals for him. Government officials were called on to determine what further legal steps were needed to enforce his patents; surely they would not wish to see injustice done him! For the services of gentlemen, he never offered payment, but asked permission to reimburse actual outlays. Only in matters too minor "to trouble my friends with" did he employ paid agents.[5]

Washington was also profiting from having started purchasing when a teen-ager. Almost a half century had passed since he had bought his first land in the Shenandoah Valley. His military experiences against the French and Indians on the way to Fort Duquesne (now Pittsburgh) had familiarized him with land in western Pennsylvania, for which he had paid, so he boasted, one hundredth part of what it was now worth.[6]

When in preparation for his last will Washington made a list of his evaluated land holdings, he reached the total of $488,137 (several millions in modern currency). This estimate was based on what he considered foreseeable increases in value. Concerning the present, he complained,

---

* This was the case not only with land speculation. He used the Secretary of the Treasury to handle his private funds. He asked Governor Robert Brooke of Massachusetts to arrange the itinerary from Boston to Mount Vernon of a housekeeper he had employed. When the Governor did not respond with alacrity, he wrote angrily that Brooke had proved himself "very ungenteel."[4]

"My estate, though it might sell on credit for a tolerable sum, has been and probably will continue to be an unproductive one."[7]

Washington was having difficulties with his sales that reflected trouble on and beyond the ocean. The influx of full-handed immigrants, who had fled Europe at the beginning of the war, had been increasingly choked off. Thus land could be disposed of in large units only to American speculators who, foreseeing future not present profits, wished extended credit.[8]

Because of French maritime blocks to American commerce, cash was in any case extremely scarce.* These same blocks made the prices of farm products plummet to a point where few cultivators wished to buy acreage.

Since Washington could not wait for the situation to right itself, every deal was complicated. Although unwilling to buy on credit, he could not hope to get, when he sold, more than some cash down. The more cash he required, the lower the price he could ask. And the prevailing lack of fluid assets made it difficult to distinguish between reliable offers to purchase and what Washington called "the vague, speculative, and unmeaning offers of men who have no wherewithall to fill an engagement and do not mean (more than probable) to do it."[10]

If what seemed a good opportunity swam into his ken, Washington became an eager salesman, extolling his land, which, he insisted, would instantly skyrocket in value. He usually set a price from which he could comfortably descend as he bargained. If there were problems of fact he urged arbitration: one man appointed by his own representative, one by the prospective purchaser, and a third by these two.[11] In the end, he specified exactly the size and dates of future payments. Having gone through all this, he regarded the sums due as assets he could count on, but only too often at the specified dates and long thereafter no money would appear.

In a moment of leniency or despair, Washington sold provisionally his farthest western holdings, the thousands of acres on the Kanawha, to a plausible man who he had been warned was unreliable. Not even the first payment came in. Washington fired at this delinquent some of his mightiest cannonades: "It would be uncandid, Mr. [James] Welch, not to inform you that I have heard too much of your character lately not to expect tale

---

* The ragtag and bobtail that served as specie is revealed by what Washington received from one of his agents in September 1795 as rents on western lands: bank notes, $98: silver coin, $293.94; 62½ French crowns; 15 ounces, 1 pennyweight, and 20 grains of gold at 5/3 pence a pennyweight; 12 ounces, 1 pennyweight, at 3/4 pence a pennyweight; the whole adding up to £475 10s. 1d.[9]

after tale, and relation after relation of your numerous disappointments by way of excuses for the noncompliance of your agreement with me; but this, I assure you, will not answer your purposes. . . . Be cautious therefore, how you provoke explanations that must inevitably end in your disgrace and entire loss of character. A character is valuable to all men, and not less so," Washington continued nastily, "to a Speculator." Washington took back the Kanawha land, which was at his death still part of his estate.[12]

(Amusingly enough, an unsuccessful bidder for these many wild acres was Washington's calamitous biographer "Parson Weems."[13])

In routine cases of nonpayment, Washington would threaten lawsuits, but would in the end agree to a postponement, on the understanding that there would be "no further indulgence." The postponed date would come round; often, no money; often, all to do over again. The worst delinquent was Governor Lee, who owed $20,000 for Washington's holdings at the Dismal Swamp.* Washington's emotions were kept harassed and his pen active but the results were not completely frustrating. There was an intermittent but considerable flow of cash, for rents as well as for sales.

Unattuned to a purely business attitude, Washington did not feel justified in pressing a debtor merely because the money was due him. He felt that he also had to demonstrate that he needed the money. Thus, the ex-President's correspondence is full of passages picturing him on the point of bankruptcy.

Often Washington allowed sentiment or simple kindness to carry him into very unbusinesslike deals. His nephew Samuel Washington, who already owed him money, built an expensive house, and then wrote piteously for more funds to prevent his property's being sold at half price: the General handed over another thousand dollars to the tunes of a scolding and a dark explanation that by doing so he was preventing himself from buying grain for his mill that was lying idle because of the lack of it.[14] In making personal loans, Washington exacted no interest, and he sometimes extended this privilege to complete strangers. He had never met Benjamin Smith Barton, but on hearing that this distinguished professor of botany was having difficulties, he provided the scientist with sixty dollars to be returned in a month. Two years later, Washington was still trying to procure payment.[15]

Washington showed starry-eyed enthusiasm in relation to two projects which had long been close to his heart: the Potomac Canal and the federal

---

* See volume I, pages 289–291.

city, which he was still too modest to call by the official name "Washington."

The canal staggered along from year to year, like an invalid occasionally half-recovered and never altogether past hope. Washington was forever optimistic. Long after many matters came back to his relaxing memory (as he complained) less like reality than a dream, he convinced a visitor that he had "a prodigious memory" by reciting all the rivers, creeks, and lakes from Maine southward that offered possible means of communication from the west to the ocean. He was convinced that, "maugre all the endeavors of Pennsylvania and New York to direct it [the commerce of the west] to other channels," the Potomac was the "great highway that nature has marked out," even for produce from the upper Ohio and the Great Lakes.[16]

Washington boasted in his letter to Sally Fairfax that the Potomac had been cleared to Fort Cumberland, upwards of 200 miles, and that efforts were being made to open the Shenandoah for 150 miles more. He did not point out that this would not extend the water route over the Alleghenies. Nor did he confide to his old love that before any produce could reach the ocean, it had to be carried around the Great Falls. There was, indeed, much more to be accomplished. In May 1798 Washington sold all his "six percent stock of the United States," and loaned the proceeds — $3494.31 — to the canal company. Four months later, he exerted his influence towards a loan from the state of Virginia, but there was now so great a proliferation of canal projects that the effort failed. It was agreed that each shareholder should be assessed $100 a share. Many reneged. Washington found the money. Till the day of his death he believed that his Potomac Canal stock would make a reasonable financial basis for the national university to which he willed it.°[17]

The year 1800, when the national government was to move to the new city of Washington, was approaching inexorably, but construction was lagging. Washington (as we have seen) † had been grateful when, after the failure of small investors to buy enough lots, large operators — James Greenleaf, Robert Morris, John Nicholson — had contracted to pay in installments for thousands of lots, to build a specified number of dwelling

---

° Nature had, in fact, "marked out" as her "great highway" not the mountainous Potomac route but the flattish terrain in northern New York that was eventually traversed by the Erie Canal. Although the Potomac Canal operated unprofitably for years as a local facility, it never got over the mountains.

† Chapter 9.

houses every year, and to lend the commissioners annual sums towards completing the public buildings. In the summer of 1794, the speculators met their obligations and all seemed to be going swimmingly. Then the French occupation of Holland laid a flattening hand on the rising capital of the United States. Having relied on Dutch loans, the speculators could not meet their second payment, due in May 1795. Washington, foreseeing a "vital wound" to his darling project, became angry with his old friend, Robert Morris, the collapse of whose affairs was not yet visible. Concerning the conduct of Morris and his associates, Washington wrote Randolph, "one can scarcely forbear thinking that these acts are part of a premeditated system to embarrass the executive government." However, Morris, blaming all on Greenleaf, explained how his hands were tied, and the friendship continued.[18]

There was some activity in the spring of 1796 — hammers reverberated again from houses the speculators were building — but the spurt proved abortive. As the money market tightened, the whole tribe of bold and extensive operators sank ever deeper in their mass of operations. By October 1797 Greenleaf was in debtors' prison. After maintaining sieges in their houses for several months against an army of constables, Morris and Nicholson finally joined him. The bubble had altogether burst.[19]

In the fall of 1795, President Washington had asked Maryland for a loan to assist construction of the city on her border. No go. Washington was eventually forced into what he had long avoided: an appeal that Congress assist financially in the erecting of the federal city. He feared that this would break open a hornet's nest of opposition from those regions which wanted the federal capital for themselves. The President cautiously asked for no appropriation: he merely wished Congress to agree that, if the government-owned property in the federal city were to prove inadequate security for a loan, "the United States will make good the deficiency." Despite the opposition of a vocal minority, led by Pennsylvania, Congress voted to authorize the President to borrow no more than $500,000. Washington turned first to Holland. The situation there was still too grievous. After several other attempts had failed, he again tried Maryland, which, now that the loan had been federally guaranteed, came up in December 1796 with $100,000.[20]

The size of the city plan which L'Enfant, envisioning the future, had prepared with Washington's approval was proving a hazard since it prevented the landowners from pulling together. Investors in different areas fought with each other for the few improvements that could be afforded.

The best solution Washington had been able to see was to have the three commissioners of the District of Columbia — or at least one of them — live in the district and thus be able to respond soothingly to difficulties from day to day. But hardly anyone worth appointing was willing to live in the embryo town that was little more than an alternation of forest and mud. Such was the situation when Washington retired.

From his retirement, Washington could comment in a gay mood concerning the imminent arrival of the government: "Oh well, they can camp out. The Representatives in the first line, the Senate in the second, the President and his suite in the middle." As a matter of fact, the Capitol and the President's House were so far along that they would be, at least partially, habitable. The really grievous problem was where the officers of the government would live. Washington, who had put up part of the funds for a hotel, decided, after his return to Mount Vernon, that he would erect as his personal project twin buildings, which he envisioned as having a facade that would make them resemble one large structure. Although he hoped that the rent he would secure from a boardinghouse keeper would yield him seven and a half percent on his investment, he insisted that his primary motivation was patriotic: to supply "accommodation for members of Congress."*[21]

Washington himself drew up the floor plan. Each house was to have three stories (he later added "garret rooms") and a kitchen building joined to it with a covered way. Each house had four rooms on a floor. Since the ground floor chambers, through which it was necessary to pass to reach the stairs, were designed to be for general use, there would be (not counting the garrets) a total of sixteen bedrooms. Washington calculated that this would accommodate twenty to thirty congressmen.

The whole was to be "not costly but elegantly plain." He asked Dr. William Thornton, who had produced the original plan for the Capitol, for advice, and was soon arguing that it was not necessary to adhere to rules of architecture as long as the eye was pleased. Washington wished Thornton to make the brick exterior walls look like stone by applying the method he had worked out for Mount Vernon. You dashed, "as long as any will stick," sand upon a thick coat of paint. The sand had to be perfectly white, made from the softest free stone, pounded and sifted, and

---

° Washington's example did give a considerable boost to the federal city. Other men erected dwelling houses, selecting lots as he had done near the Capitol. This outraged owners of land in what then seemed the widely separated area around the President's House.[22]

then the fine dust blown away by a soft breeze. If Thornton could not get suitable sand, Washington would have it prepared at Mount Vernon. "It must be dashed on hard, and as long as any place appears bare." [23]

Washington had started the buildings in a moment of financial optimism and with a specific boardinghouse keeper in mind, but the money he had expected to come in from his debtors (primarily Governor Lee) did not arrive, and the boardinghouse keeper did not even answer Washington's request when it came time to make a definite agreement. Furthermore, the man who was used to having all but the most skilled labor done by his own gangs was horrified at the bills he received. How could a well little more than thirty feet deep cost £70?[24]

On June 25, 1799, Washington entered what he called "a new scene" with such trepidation that his letter to the president of the Bank of Alexandria contains a major confusion: in the body of the letter, he asks to borrow $1500, but in the postcript speaks of borrowing $5000. Actually, he wanted only $1500, although eventually he added another $1000. The notes had to be renewed periodically, an operation which Washington described himself as being quite incapable of doing without having the bank president point out every step.[25]

Washington was worried and remained worried. Again and again he expressed horror at having been forced into "a measure I never in the course of my life had practiced." The luxury of his Mansion House, the spreading farms at Mount Vernon, the deeds to far-flung lands that were stowed away in his strongbox, all seemed, when the old farmer woke up in the nights, evanescent. He was terrified to think that he had been reduced to "a necessity of borrowing from the banks at a ruinous interest." [26]

The Retired Lion Roars

W HEN staying at Mount Vernon as President, Washington had sent to the post office in Alexandria every day, but now he often let two or three days pass. This was an act of will. Had he not "turned aside from the broad walks of political into the narrow paths of private life?" Although he regretted "many transactions which do not comport with my ideas," he remained persuaded, so he insisted, that "if any great crisis should occur to require it . . . the good sense and spirit of the major part of the people of this country will direct them properly." [1]

Confidence in the fundamental soundness of the people had been Washington's justification for his refusal to continue after the Revolution in the public service. Then military victory had created a sharp break — if he returned to the national stage it would be in a different play. Yet he had been drawn back. Now his age justified retirement. However, there had been no break. The drama in which he had so recently starred was still on the stage.

John Adams had inherited the French attacks on American shipping and the question of how the new American minister, Pinckney, would be received in Paris. On both scores, the news proved bad. The Directory announced that any American seamen found on British vessels would — even if they had been impressed against their wills — be hung as pirates. The Directory gave a hero's send-off to the recalled minister Monroe but refused to receive Pinckney.

Adams had kept all of Washington's Cabinet Secretaries. In corresponding with them, Washington began by laying down the principle that, although he would be glad to receive from them such information as

[379]

it "was not contrary to the rules of your official duty to disclose," he would not reciprocate by making any comment. However, he could not hold himself in when he read Adams's speech to a special session of Congress.[2]

The second President was more belligerent than the first had ever been. Adams labeled the French refusal to receive the American minister as a demonstration that they would continue to harass American shipping unless the American government changed its policies to suit France. Such behavior "ought to be repelled with a decision which shall convince France and the world that we are not a degraded people; humiliated under a colonial spirit of fear and a sense of inferiority, fitted to be the miserable instruments of foreign influence."[3] Adams stated that he desired peace, but urged that merchant vessels be armed for their own protection; that the navy be strengthened and the militia reorganized into a powerful military force.

This was regarded by the Republicans as a pro-British war speech; Madison expressed the wish that the more moderate Washington was back at the helm. Washington wrote Wolcott that the President had "placed matters upon their true ground. . . . The crisis calls for an unequivocal expression of the public mind, and the speech will mediately or immediately bring this about."[4]

Washington still saw as the major danger the belief of the Directory that the American people were so predominantly on the French side that the existing government of the United States could be defied or even overthrown. Conspicuous support for Adams's strong statement would, he believed, serve notice on the French that their judgment of the American situation was wrong. He denied that the existing American policy was pro-British. And it was hard for him to envision that the American people could, in an irrational passion for France, fail to realize that the neutrality which he had himself established and which Adams was doing his best to follow was the only road to peace. The people should compare "the most happy, flourishing, and prosperous train" of the United States with the situation of the European nations, which "appears so awful that nothing short of Omnipotence can predict the issue! . . . Our course is plain: they who run may read it. Theirs so bewildered and dark, so entangled and embarrassed, and so obviously under the influence of intrigue that one would suppose, if anything could open the eyes of our misled citizens, the deplorable situation of those people could not fail to accomplish it."[5]

However, the fact remained that it was "the right of the people" that

their will "should be carried into effect. Their sentiment *ought* to be unequivocally known that the principles on which the government has acted
and which from the President's speech are likely to be continued, may be
either changed or the opposition that is endeavoring to embarrass every
measure of the executive may meet effectual discountenance. Things cannot, ought not to remain in their present disagreeable state. Nor should
the idea that the government and people have different views be suffered
any longer to prevail at home or abroad, for it is not only injurious to us,
but disgraceful also that a government constituted as ours is should be
administered contrary to their interest and will, if the fact be so."[6]

Thus Washington believed that the people must be encouraged to
speak and must be obeyed even if, as a result, the nation were drawn into
a war "more bloody, more expensive, more calamitous, and more pregnant of events than modern or perhaps any other time can furnish an example."[7]

He waited with trepidation for news of what would be the first test: the
reaction of the House of Representatives to the President's address. When
the speech was approved by a vote of 60 to 40, he expressed no pleasure, but mourned that it had been opposed by "so great a minority."[8]

Carrying into execution what Washington had discussed with Hamilton
at the end of his Presidency, Adams appointed two more delegates to
serve with Pinckney as an enlarged special commission to deal on an
emergency basis with the French. The additional representatives were El-
bridge Gerry, to represent the Republicans, and Washington's protégé
John Marshall. On his way to the seacoast, Marshall spent two nights at
Mount Vernon. The ex-President could not resist putting his oar in. He
agreed with the envoy on what steps should be taken, and later wrote
Pinckney of his pleasure to learn of "the congeniality of sentiments which
prevail between you and General Marshall, having taken the liberty of introducing him to you as a gentleman in whom you might place entire
confidence."[9]

By means of a military coup d'etat, achieved through the assistance of
Napoleon's troops, the government of France was revolutionized on September 4, 1797. Washington did not wish to "pronounce" but he felt this
augered badly for the success of the American mission. It was, he added,
"laughable . . . to behold those men *amongst us* who were . . . sounding
the tocsin upon every occasion that a wild imagination could *torture* into

a stretch of power . . . in the executive of the United States all of a sudden become warm advocates of those high-handed measures in the French Directory which *succeeded* the arrestations on the fourth of September. . . . But so it always has been and I presume ever will always be with men who are governed more by passions and party views than by the dictates of justice, temperance, and sound policy."[10]

Washington was convinced that "*no* occurrence . . . will change the sentiments or (which perhaps would be more correct) the conduct of some characters amongst us." The French were counting on this. He himself would be "very much mistaken" if the mass of the people would not desert these intransigent leaders in a moment of crisis, but "I pray devoutly that the Directory may not bring the matter to a trial."[11]

Although Washington requested Freneau to desist from mailing to Mount Vernon copies of *The Timepiece,* a new journalistic venture of his old attacker,[12] the ex-President could not ignore the publication of a wounding letter by Jefferson and also of two pamphlets — one by a former French minister to the United States and the other by a former American minister to France — which were presented as eyewitness accounts of how his foreign policy had betrayed the French cause.

Jefferson's letter appeared in the *New York Minerva* for May 2, 1797, and was copiously reprinted across the nation. It had been written more than a year before to an Italian radical, Phillip Mazzei, who had once been a neighbor near Monticello. Jefferson described the political scene as opposition between "an anglican, monarchical and aristocratic party" on one hand, and "the main body of our citizens. . . . Against us are the executive, the judiciary, and two out of three branches of the legislature." He then launched into a denunciation that was popularly assumed to be an attack on Washington: "It would give you a fever were I to name to you the apostates who have gone over to these heresies, men who were Samsons in the field and Solomons in council, but who have had their heads shorn by the harlot of England."*[13]

The two pamphlets appeared during the winter. In that by the former French minister Fauchet Washington was particularly outraged by the

---

* Jefferson asserted privately that his reference to shorn Samsons and Solomons did not refer to Washington — it referred to the Society of the Cincinnati[14] — but if this disclaimer reached (which seems doubtful) Washington's ears, it would hardly have removed the sting: Jefferson had stated that the executive Washington had led was pro-British and in opposition to the people.

statement that he had received a M. Talon, on a confidential mission from
the French royal pretender, before he received Genêt. Washington had no
memory of Talon. If they had ever met, it must have been publicly at a
levee. No longer, as he saw it, prevented by his position from defending
himself, he asked Pickering to publish a denial.[15]

The screed of the former American minister Monroe was a long one —
507 pages — and mostly devoted to the reprinting of documents. Reading
it in the frozen stillness at Mount Vernon, Washington did what he had
never done before: he kept up a running argument with the author in
notes written on the margins. Monroe's contentions that he had been sent
to France in a dishonest effort to hoodwink the allies of the United States,
that the Jay Treaty had been a calculated surrender to Great Britain, etc.,
etc., filled Washington with sarcasm and rage. Concerning Monroe's insistence that he should have been allowed to do what he promised, show
the treaty to the French before it was ratified by the Senate, Washington
wrote, "None but a party man lost to all sense of propriety would have
asked such a thing; and no other would have brought himself into such a
predicament." In answer to Monroe's statement that if the United States
had stood firmly on ground favorable to France, the French would have
denied them nothing, Washington jotted, "That is to say, if we did not
press *them* to do us justice but had yielded to *their* violations, they would
have aided us in every measure which would have cost them *nothing*."
When Monroe commented sarcastically that he left it to others to determine what crisis made the United States turn from France to England,
Washington riposted, "As he has such a happy knack of determining, he
ought not to have let the opportunity escape him." Washington found a
"mischievous and dangerous tendency" in Monroe's "exposing to the public view his private instructions and correspondence with his own government."*[16]

Washington's total reaction was that "cowardly, illiberal, and assassin-
like" means were being employed to undermine the government. On
March 1, 1798, he wrote that he had "until lately" believed that France's
depredations against American commerce and the "indignity" with which
she had treated American peace overtures would have united all parties
and all men "except those who wish to see the waters troubled." But the

---

* Jefferson wrote Madison that Monroe's book was "masterly" and "deemed unanswerable." He wrote Monroe that Fauchet's publication "reinforced the views you
have presented of the duplicity of the administration here."[17]

[383]

reverse seemed to be the case. Whether the situation "can end at any point short of confusion and anarchy is *now* in my opinion more problematical than ever."[18]

Washington's anxieties were enhanced by one of the strangest incidents of his entire career. It all started with what seemed a silly letter from Albemarle County, Virginia (where Monticello was), signed John Langhorne. The presumptive author regretted the "unmerited calumny" which Washington suffered, but assured the ex-President that he was like a sun temporarily eclipsed only to be the more admired when the eclipse passed. Why then should he distress himself? "Too imprudently delicate! Is your peace to be broken because there are fools and knaves in the world? These observations have been made, sir, in the hope that they might possibly administer some comfort to a mind eminently great and virtuous."[19]

Washington assumed that Langhorne was "a pedant who was desirous of displaying the flowers of his pen." But the ex-President believed that every letter must be answered. He thanked Langhorne for his "favorable sentiments," and stated that he was unwounded by the envenomed darts. "Within me I have a consolation which proves an antidote against their utmost malignity, rendering my mind in the retirement I have long panted after perfectly tranquil."[20]

More than a month later, Washington received a letter, dated November 18, 1797, also from Albemarle and signed by another stranger: John Nicholas. Nicholas stated that Washington's reply to Langhorne had laid for a long time unclaimed in the local post office, and then had been sent for "by a *certain character* in this county closely connected with some of your greatest and bitterest enemies." Although his name was not Langhorne, this individual asserted the letter was an answer to one he had written. "The only conclusion," so continued Nicholas, "I can draw from this strange circumstance is that *certain men,* who are resolved to stick at nothing to promote their wicked and inglorious views, have fallen on this last miserable, deceptive means. . . . Living where I do, immediately in cannonshot of the very headquarters of *Jacobinism* [Monticello]," the writer realized "how much you have been deceived in the principles and *professions of friendship of certain characters in this quarter.*" Nicholas would say no more until he called at Mount Vernon, which he hoped soon to do.[21]

Washington knew that various members of the Nicholas family were

[384]

neighbors and important political allies of Jefferson. This particular Nicholas he could not exactly place, although he believed he was acquainted with his father. He wrote him, "I know not how to thank you sufficiently." Were the object of the anonymous author of the Langhorne letter what Nicholas suspected, it "fell far short of his mark," since Washington's reply had supplied no ammunition enemies could use. Washington enclosed copies of the correspondence. "If they should be the means of detecting any nefarious plan" against the government, he would be happy. He would be glad to receive the informant at Mount Vernon.[22]

Nicholas replied on December 9, "Mr. Langhorne . . . is a favorite nephew of *your very sincere friend* Mr. Jefferson, raised and educated directly by himself from a child, and a constant dependent and resident in his house." Washington undoubtedly recognized in this description Peter Carr.[23]

Holding onto himself, Washington did not answer Nicholas's letter. But Nicholas, a busybody and gossip and about the only Federalist of his name, had no intention of letting the matter die. On Washington's sixty-sixth birthday, he sent another letter, in which he denounced the "vile hypocrisy of *that man's* professions of friendship towards you" as revealed in the Mazzei letter. He had heard Jefferson say, "The destruction of Monroe was premeditated in his appointment [to France], as he was the *center* around which the *Republican* party rallied in the Senate." Nicholas knew that Jefferson, under the pretense of silence and indifference, was "one of the most artful, intriguing, industrious, and double-faced politicians" in existence.[24]

Nicholas's further statement that he was acquainted with the General's reliable nephew Bushrod opened to Washington a road along which to proceed. He would express his feelings in a letter to Nicholas, but would send it to Bushrod with instructions not to deliver it unless Nicholas's character and the actual situation warranted.[25]

The letter to Nicholas stated, "Nothing short of the evidence you have adduced, corroborative of intimations which I had received long before through another channel,* could have shaken my belief in the sincerity of a friendship, which I had conceived was possessed for me, by the person to whom you allude. But attempts to injure those who are supposed to stand well in the estimation of the people and are stumbling blocks in their way (by misrepresenting their political tenets), thereby to destroy

---

* Washington probably referred to the letter from Henry Lee here discussed on pp. 158.

all confidence in them, is one of the means by which the government is to be assailed, and the Constitution destroyed. The conduct of this party is systematized, and everything that is opposed to its execution, will be sacrificed, without hesitation or remorse, if the end can be answered by it.

"If the person whom you suspect, was really the author of the letter under the signature of John Langhorne, it is not at all surprising to me that the correspondence should have ended where it did; for the penetration of that man would have perceived at the first glance of the answer that nothing was to be drawn from that mode of attack. In what form, the next insidious attempts may appear, remains to be discovered. But as the attempts to explain away the Constitution, and weaken the government are now become so open; and the desire of placing the affairs of this country under the influence and control of a foreign nation is so apparent and strong, it is hardly to be expected that a resort to covert means to effect these objects will be longer regarded." Washington went on to say that, if "the gentleman you have alluded to" believed that the executive had been "premeditating the destruction of Mr. Monroe in his appointment . . . it is to be hoped he will give it credit for its lenity to that gentleman for having designated several others (not of the Senate) as victims to this office *before* the sacrifice of Mr. Monroe was ever had in contemplation. As this *must be some consolation* to him and his friends, I hope they will embrace it."[26]

Bushrod wrote Washington that, suspecting a "base and insidious plot," he was seeking "in complete secrecy . . . the real actors." However, he soon got the matter entangled in the petty personal animosities of Albemarle County. As a newspaper polemicist, he published Federalist blasts in the *Virginia Gazette and General Advertiser* under the pseudonym of "Americanus" (which everyone in the know recognized). He was commonly answered by "Spectator," who was Peter Carr. On July 3, Bushrod could not resist referring to "secret and underhand workings of the same Spectator's noble benefactor and near relation." This aroused one "Columbianus," who accused "Americanus" of assuming "the dignified character of an informer for the purpose of disturbing the tranquillity of the neighborhood."[27]

Bushrod thereupon wrote angrily to Washington that he had "no objection to being called an informer" when he was protecting "against a *villain* or *villains*" the man who had rendered the country the "greatest of services . . . I knew *John Longhorne* was a scoundrel, but did not suppose he would ever be so stupid as to provoke a publication of his own villainy." Bushrod wanted Washington's permission to bring out "the history of the whole affair . . . to show in what light I stand *as a dignified informer*." Or perhaps Washington would rather deputize the task to John Nicholas, who was "not in a very good temper with that party who is prosecuting him." In neither case would Washington's cognizance be mentioned.[28]

Bushrod's letter reached Washington in Philadelphia, where he was organizing an army against the threat of a war with France which he felt was partially the fault of the Jeffersonians. He answered that if Nicholas could demonstrate "indubitably" that the letter was a forgery written for "nefarious" purposes and that "the person he suspects [obviously Jefferson] is the *real* author or abetter, it would be a pity not to expose him to public execration, for attempting in so dishonorable a way to obtain a disclosure of sentiments of which some advantage could be taken." And again, "If a *trick* so dirty and shabby as this is supposed to be [can be] *clearly proved*, it would, in my opinion, be attended with a happy effect at this time; but, on the other hand, if it should be attempted and fail, the reverse would be the consequence." [29]

In August, Bushrod wrote that he would urge Nicholas to publish if he could "fix the fact." Having heard nothing definite by the last day of 1798, Washington wrote to find out what had happened. Nothing had happened, since all efforts to fix the fact on Jefferson had been unavailing.[30]

Historians, having exhumed the Langhorne letter and compared the handwriting with letters certainly written by Peter Carr, have demonstrated that the forgery was indeed written by Jefferson's favorite nephew. In answering one question, this raises a flood of others. Why did Carr address Washington under an assumed name but without disguising his handwriting? Why did he allow the reply, which was conspicuously from the ex-President (for Washington franked his letters with his signature), to lie for a long time uncalled-for, attracting attention, and then claim it in a note which he signed with his correct name?[31] Was there a sinister plot, and, if so, what could it hope to achieve? Was Jefferson privy to what took place?

The best guess of which this writer is capable is that the Langhorne letter was a bibulous prank. It seems to have been designed to make fun of Washington's pretentions to injured greatness and to elicit a pompous, self-righteous reply that would raise renewed mirth among drinking companions. No precautions were taken commensurate with a high intrigue fraught with possible great danger, and it is difficult to see what political capital could have been drawn from any reply called for by the Langhorne posturings.

Surely, whatever might have been his moral reactions, the politically astute Jefferson would never have countenanced something so silly which could become a lethal boomerang. If he is to be implicated by history, the only possible way would be to conclude that his intimate's extremely disrespectful behavior towards Washington — Carr's very carelessness concerning discovery added to the insult — reflected an attitude now rife at Monticello towards the old, beleaguered hero.

As for Washington, to modern hindsight he overreacted. That his able nephew Bushrod overreacted to an even greater extent reveals the hysteria of the times, but does not altogether explain away the frenetic behavior of a man who had been during so many years so notable (despite lapses) for withstanding hysteria, for striking the calm, the reasonable, the healing note.

It is natural for old men to be suspicious, to see plots. And it would require almost more than the fortitude of a saint not to be affected by the type of attacks which were made on Washington and his administration. Not only had his behavior been condemned because of entirely unfounded distrust of his motives, but what he did had been distorted; and not only had his acts been distorted, but he had been assailed by lies which the perpetrators often knew were total lies. The vilification to which he had been subjected in newspapers of national circulation that were semi-official party organs has no parallel in modern America except in those fly-by-night sheets in which extreme crackpots shout at each other.

As long as he had been in office he had tried, although towards the end with sometimes stumbling feet, to walk the path he had charted for himself: the path of complete neutrality between factions at home and belligerents abroad. Once he was out of office and intended to remain so for the rest of his earthly career, moderation ceased to be a matter of state. He permitted himself to espouse extremes. He became at last what he had for so long been accused of being: devotedly pro-Federalist. Since he doubted the intentions of all others, he communicated exclusively with Federalists. He could no longer palliate the efforts of the French government to interfere in American politics: he had become angrily anti-French. In his denunciations of French attacks on American commerce, he no longer pointed out that Britain was also guilty. He came to believe that the leaders of the opposition, patriots who had been his coadjutors and friends, were eager to make the United States a vassal of France: might indeed cooperate with a French invasion.

To Washington's view, the situation which had at the opening of the Revolution called him to arms was repeating itself. In December 1798 he wrote, "Having struggled for eight or nine years against the invasion of our rights by one power and to establish an independence of it, I cannot remain an unconcerned spectator of the attempt of another power to accomplish the same object, though in a different way, with less pretentions — indeed, without any at all."[32]

Mount Vernon in winter.
Courtesy of the Mount Vernon Ladies' Association

40

A New Call to Arms

THE winter of 1797–1798 was so extremely severe that Washington was often forced to stay in the Mansion House. By the hour, he propelled his long body back and forth, back and forth on his porch, which he measured at ninety-two feet, eight inches, but the exercise did not calm his nerves. Despite his long experience of how the wintry ocean stopped communication with Europe, he asked querulously on March 4, "Are our commissioners [to France] guillotined, or what else is the occasion of their silence?"[1]

On that very day, President Adams heard that the commissioners had been repulsed. He gave the bare news to Congress while the voluminous dispatches he had received were being decoded or translated. As the news piled up, Adams concluded that the national honor required a declaration of war.

The commissioners had been notified that the Directory had been "greatly exasperated" by Adams's inaugural address. Before the President's delegates could be received, the United States would have publicly to announce a change in policy. Soon the commissioners had callers: three mysterious agents who were designated as X, Y, and Z (which led the entire matter to become known as the XYZ affair). These persons stated that if the commissioners repudiated the policy of their government, gave foreign minister Talleyrand a large bribe, and promised the French government in advance a huge loan from the United States, the Directory might condescend to receive the mission.

It was Hamilton, acting behind the scenes, who persuaded Adams against war. The President finally decided not to excite the American people by giving Congress a full account of French behavior. However, the Republican majority in the House, concluding that the explanatory papers had been withheld because they justified the French, demanded publication. Early in April, Adams responded to their request. Shock waves ran across the land stirring up angry mass meetings that sent to Adams a flood of anti-French addresses.

However, the outrage was not universal enough to please Washington. He commented, "One would think that the measure of infamy was filled and profligacy of and corruption in the system pursued by the French Directory required no further disclosure . . . to open the eyes of the blindest." Yet the efforts of "the Demos," to rally their forces through the columns of the *Aurora* indicated that the pro-French leaders would not recant unless convinced that they would be deserted by their followers. And even if the leaders altered their "tactics," it could not be assumed that they had changed their "convictions."[2]

The previous Congress, while voting for coastal fortifications and strengthening the infant navy, had refused to augment the army of 3000 men. Now Congress authorized an "additional army" of 10,000 and the organization on paper of a 50,000-man "provisional army," which was to leap into form if an actual invasion took place. Carrying out the total plan was entrusted to the President.

Eager to be kept in touch, Washington made arrangements with members of Adams's Cabinet: Pickering, for instance, was to mark which of his communications were confidential. But Washington had no confidential communication with Hamilton, whom he had written only twice since his return to Mount Vernon. The first letter accompanied the gift of one of the wine coolers Washington was distributing after they had been inadvertently left behind in Philadelphia. The second letter asked Hamilton to help young Lafayette get off to France. Neither even mentioned national affairs.[3]

Although Hamilton knew that Washington did not like to have others make the first move, in mid-May he could no longer hold himself in. He wrote Washington, "At the present dangerous crisis of public affairs, I make no apology for troubling you with a political letter. . . . The powerful faction," Hamilton was convinced, wished "to make this country a province of France." Foreseeing "a serious struggle with France," Hamilton viewed the anti-administration forces as extremely dangerous, particularly because he believed that they controlled public opinion south of Maryland. Would not Washington "make a circuit through Virginia and

North Carolina under some pretence of health, etc."? Washington could take the opportunity to throw his weight behind the government's policies and also "revive enthusiasm for your person that may be turned into the right channel. . . . In the event of an open rupture with France, the public voice will again call you to command the armies of your country. . . . It is the opinion of all those with whom I converse that you will be compelled to make the sacrifice."[4]

Washington's reply dismissed the idea of a southern tour: his health "never was better," which would encourage his enemies to draw "malicious" conclusions. Furthermore, Washington did not agree that the south was ready for the yoke of France. Opinion in Georgia was reported sound. Mass meetings in the Carolinas and western Virginia supported the government. If the middle counties of Virginia were still silent, this was because they "wanted leaders."*

As Washington's letter to Hamilton continued, it revealed that his ideas were by no means identical with those held in the centers by many Federalists. Not even considering the possibility of an American declaration of war, Washington foresaw *"open war"* only if the French mounted "a formidable invasion." Nor did he hope (or half hope), as did such subtle Federalists as Hamilton, that French hostilities would make the Republican opposition seem traitors in wartime. Washington's hope was that American protest at the behavior of the French would mount so resoundingly that the French, convinced that any expeditionary force would not be welcomed by American democrats, would not risk major hostilities.

Did he not foresee that popular outrage would, indeed, "frown" the subversive leaders into silence, he would be "infinitely more disquieted" than he was. "If a crisis should arrive when a sense of duty or a call from my country should become so imperious as to leave me no choice, I should . . . go with as much reluctance from my present peaceful abode as I should do to the tombs of my ancestors.

"There is no conviction in my breast," Washington continued, that he was the best choice to lead a new army. If he were to serve, it would have "somehow or other" to be "unequivocally known" that the national preference "might not be given to a man more in his prime." He would also want to know in advance "who would be my coadjutors," and whether Hamilton would be disposed to take an active part.

In closing, Washington stated that Hamilton need not have apologized

---

* This was, of course, the region where Jefferson and Madison led most strongly.

for his "free communication on these political topics." Washington would be gratified by a continuation of the correspondence.[5]

Hamilton's reply backtracked on his proposal of a southern tour, "an undigested thought begotten by my anxiety." He was sure that Washington would not only be the popular choice as commander in chief, but would be needed to unite the country. As for Hamilton himself, he would have to be given a rank "proportionate to the sacrifice I am to make. . . . The public must judge for itself as to whom it will employ, but every individual must judge for himself as to the terms on which he will serve, and consequently must estimate his own pretensions." Hamilton saw himself both supervising the army and leading it into battle. He wished to be "inspector general with a command in the line."[6]

The letters Washington now wrote abounded with statements that, having envisioned no event that could possibly "turn my eyes from Mount Vernon," he would serve the nation again with great regret. He expressed a fear that his acceptance of a new command would be considered "a restless act, evincive of my discontent in retirement." Yet, when a long month had passed without his hearing anything official from the government, Washington called himself to the attention of the two officials most involved. A rumor that the Adamses were planning to visit the federal city enabled Washington to send the President a note approving his policies and suggesting that he and Abigail stay at Mount Vernon. As Secretary of War McHenry had not reported on a minor chore Washington had referred to him, Washington wrote him petulantly that he did not wish to "force my correspondence on you."[7]

Neither reply could ignore what Washington had most in mind. Adams regretted the improbability of his coming south, stated politely that he wished Washington was still President, and then penned five sentences on the military: "In forming an army, whenever I must come to that extremity, I am at an immense loss whether to call out all the old generals or to appoint a young set. If the French come here, we must learn to march with a quick step, and to attack, for in that way only they are said to be vulnerable. I must tax you sometimes for advice. We must have your name if you will, in any case, permit us to use it. There will be more efficacy in it than in many an army."[8]

McHenry's letter was more specific. Having reported on the chore, he stated that he thought American privateering and reprisal on French shipping would soon be authorized. "You will see how the storm thickens and that our vessel will soon require its ancient pilot. Will you? May we flatter ourselves that in a crisis so awful and important you will accept the command of all our armies? I hope you will, because you alone can unite all hearts and hands, if it is possible they can be united."[9]

Washington selected the Fourth of July to answer both these letters. To Adams, he stated, "In the case of an *actual* invasion by a formidable force, I certainly should not entrench myself under the cover of age and retirement." Although the French were "intoxicated and lawless," slaughtering their own citizens as well as disturbing the repose of the whole world, he could not foresee an invasion. If the government had reason to know differently, delay in preparation might be dangerous.

Despite the standing habit of triumphant generals to fight (and often lose) new wars in the manner that brought them success in the old, Washington wrote Adams, "The mode of carrying on the war against the foe that threatens must differ widely from that practiced in the contest for Independence": not only the quick step, but long marches and severe encounters.° Remembering how, during the first years of the Revolution, his command had been clogged by ancient militia generals who won from their troops such nicknames as "Granny," Washington urged the President to ignore seniority inherited from the Revolutionary army and choose as general officers able younger men. The commander in chief, "be he whom he will," should be extremely careful in selecting his general staff, since otherwise "his plans and movement, if not defeated altogether, may be so embarrassed and retarded as to amount nearly to the same thing."[10]

In his letter to McHenry, Washington was, as he pointed out, "frank, undisguised, and explicit" concerning whether he would accept appointment as commander in chief. He had discussed the matter with no one, lest his interest be misinterpreted, and thus he did not know whether "the sacrifice I should make" would really please his fellow citizens, "for as neither ambition, interest, or personal gratification of any sort could induce me to quit the walks of private life, to be disappointed in the *only* object I should have in view, would be mortifying beyond my powers of utterance." Then Washington held forth at much greater length than he had to Adams on the importance of good general officers who would not sink the reputation of the commander in chief and perhaps the country

---

° In a later letter to Adams, Washington was more specific. During the Revolution, "time, caution, and worrying the enemy until we could be better provided with arms and other means, and had better disciplined troops to carry on, was the plan for us." But now, "they ought to be attacked at every step, and, if possible, not suffered to make an establishment in the country, acquiring thereby strength from the disaffected and the slaves."[11]

with it. He would only accept if he were assured that the public supported him and that he would have such officers.[12]

After what may have well been a sleepless night, Washington wrote McHenry again the next day. Washington had reread the President's letter and concluded that, "though not so expressed in terms," it indicated not only that he should command the army but, "if I take his meaning right," he should also aid in the selection of the general officers. Washington now stated categorically, "if I am looked to as commander in chief," he must be allowed to choose such members of the general staff "as will be agreeable to me. . . .

"Although I make my stand at the general staff, I conceive that much will depend upon active and spirited officers for the brigades and divisions." The former Commander in Chief had surveyed in his mind his coadjutors during the Revolution: "Under the rose, I shall declare candidly" his doubts that "a desirable set could be formed from the old generals; some on account of their age or infirmities; some from never having displayed any talents for enterprise; and others from their general opposition to the government or their predilection to French measures." Washington added that he wanted in the high command no men who claimed recent conversion to the policy of defense against France: "Those who will come up with a flowing tide will descend with the ebb, and there can be no dependence upon them in moments of difficulty."

Washington was also worried about the timing of the role he would play. The President, "knowing that 10,000 men cannot be raised by the blowing of a trump," would want to get started, but Washington felt that he should do no more than allow his appointment to be announced, until "the emergency *becomes evident.*" For him to undertake active duty before then would be both bad policy and disagreeable to him.

McHenry, Washington hoped, would communicate these sentiments to Adams "*as from yourself.* . . . If you are at liberty and deem it expedient, communicate the responses which shall be made to it to me."

After he had read this letter, McHenry, that passionate admirer of Hamilton, must have felt a lack. Washington had not urged a high rank for Hamilton. Washington had not mentioned Hamilton. His only specific recommendation had been that the director of hospitals be his family doctor, James Craik, "who, from forty years of experience is better qualified than a dozen of them together."[13]

Adams recognized that America's greatest need at the moment was a navy, and preserved his old distrust of powerful armies led by powerful generals. Speeding the launching of frigates, he made no move towards raising the "additional army" Congress had authorized. He no longer, it is true, suspected Washington of dangerous ambitions — but what of Hamilton? Hamilton had, by intriguing for Pinckney, tried to stab Adams in the back during the last election, and if ever a man had a dictatorial glint in his eye, it surely was the endlessly efficient and aggressive upstart from the West Indies. There seemed, indeed, to be a plot in motion to give Hamilton control of the new army: Adams could hardly pass the time of day with one of his Cabinet ministers without being told that Hamilton was indispensable and could not be expected to serve except at an exalted rank. Similar messages flooded in from the Federalist leaders of Congress. Finally, Adams felt driven to acting as precipitously as if a French expeditionary force were actually coming up the Delaware. Without waiting to receive Washington's reply to his letter (the reply had, indeed, not yet been written), Adams faced the Hamiltonians with a *fait accompli*. On July 2, he nominated Washington to be lieutenant general and commander of all the military forces of the United States. Congress instantly and unanimously ratified the appointment.[14]

If Adams hoped that Hamilton would chew his fingers in wrath, he was wrong. Convinced that Washington would be a superannuated cipher, Hamilton believed that, should he secure the second rank (which was probably the most he could achieve), the army would eventually fall into his hands.

Washington was amazed to learn from the newspapers that he had been appointed. Part of his surprise was that he was not emotionally upset. "I expected," he wrote, "to pass the remnant of a life (worn down with cares) in ruminating on past scenes and contemplating the future grandeur of this rising empire. But we little know ourselves, much less the designs of Providence."[15]

His active worry was caused by the fact that, having been appointed without consultation, he had been unable to lay down any conditions for his acceptance. A letter from McHenry did not calm his agitation. The letter said that the Secretary expected to be sent to Mount Vernon to complete arrangements. But McHenry did not say what arrangements. Not knowing to what extent Adams (whom he did not trust) had predecided the command and organization of the army, Washington awaited the interview "with sensations easier to conceive than describe."[16]

Doggedly, Washington adhered to his determination not to send every day for the mail. The bags, when they appeared, were suddenly swelled to bursting: everyone seemed to be urging Washington in passionate terms not to refuse the appointment. A letter from Pickering separated itself from the mass. It stated that Adams was disinclined to make Hamilton "*second* to you and the *chief* in your absence." However, Hamilton had too much sense of his own worth to be second to anyone but Washington. Pickering considered high rank for Hamilton so essential that "I am willing to risk any consequences" to secure it.[17]

Washington replied that, although Hamilton's services "ought to be secured at *almost* any price," there were strong reasons for giving General C. C. Pinckney of South Carolina (who was on his way back from his abortive French mission) the post of second in command. If the French were so insane as to invade, they would undoubtedly strike the south because that was the weakest part of the nation; because they would expect to find most friends there; because "there can be no doubt of their arming our own Negroes against us"; and because the south was nearer their own islands and also Louisiana, which they would certainly take if they could. Pinckney, a spirited, active, and judicious officer fond of the military profession, would undoubtedly be unwilling to serve under Hamilton. (Pinckney had been a general during the Revolution and Hamilton, although in effect Washington's chief of staff, had never risen above colonel.) And if Pinckney refused to serve, distrust would follow among his connections, who were more influential than any other group in the three southernmost states.[18]

McHenry arrived at Mount Vernon on the evening of July 11, carrying two letters, one from Adams and one from Hamilton. The President was all conciliation.* "If it had been in my power to nominate you President of the United States, I should have done it with less hesitation and more pleasure." He owed Washington "all the apologies I can make," for having appointed him without first securing his agreement. Adams had been driven "by the urgent necessity I am in need of your advice and assistance."[20]

Hamilton's letter warned that Adams had "wrong preconceptions"

---

* Adams had warned McHenry that his mission called for "great delicacy. It will require all your address to communicate the subject in a manner that shall be inoffensive to his feelings and consistent with all the respect that is due from me to him."[19]

which would exclude "men of capacity and exertion" from the higher ranks. Washington should come to Philadelphia and cope. "It will be conceived that the arrangement is yours, and you will be responsible for it in reputation."21

Neither of these epistles riveted Washington's attention as much as McHenry's statement that the bill for setting up the army was before a Congress that was expected to adjourn in less than a week. All the high officers might well be irrevocably appointed before Washington could say a word! He considered galloping for Philadelphia. Better yet, he could send back his commission, asking that it be returned to him or annulled depending on whether his conditions as to appointments were met. McHenry persuaded him that this course would indicate "distrust." It was finally agreed that McHenry would dash for Philadelphia, and communicate Washington's ideas to Adams.

Washington was later to claim that he had laid down as a firm condition of his acceptance that the President would make no top appointments of which he did not approve. At the time, Washington recognized that this demand would be disrespectful of the office of President. It could not be included in his official letter to Adams, which would undoubtedly be published. In that letter, he agreed to serve "with the reserve only that I shall not be called into the field until the army is in a situation to require my presence."

On the two previous occasions when he was called into the national service, Washington had stated that he did not wish to be paid. Now he merely wished no "emoluments . . . before entering into a situation to incur expense."

Much of the letter was given over to what would, on publication, become a recruiting exhortation. Washington denounced the "insidious hostility" of the French, praised "the wise and prudent" pacific measures of the Adams administration. Having "exhausted to the last drop the cup of reconciliation, we can with pure hearts appeal to Heaven for the justice of our cause."22

Washington's prime reservation was relegated to a report McHenry mailed Adams. "To avoid misconception," as he later put it, Washington had McHenry add to the document, after it was otherwise completed, the statement that he would carry to Philadelphia the names of persons Washington considered "the best qualified for his confidential officers, without whom, I think, he would not serve."23

The new Lieutenant General and the Secretary of War agreed that the three major generals should be Pinckney, Hamilton, and Knox. In seniority, Knox was way ahead of the others, but the conferees wished him now to be last, since (although eighteen years younger than Washington and always fat) he had relaxed into considerable torpor. Washington explained to McHenry why he wished to put Pinckney over Hamilton. McHenry replied (as Washington remembered) "that Colonel Hamilton was designated second in command, and first if I should decline acceptance, by the Federal characters of Congress, where alone anything like a public sentiment relative thereto could be deduced." Since Hamilton had a large family, and no certain income except the law practice he would have to give up, he could not, McHenry continued, be expected to accept the financial sacrifice unless "the second rank was proposed." Washington remembered that Pickering had written him the same thing, and he did not, as Adams did, suspect collusion between the Hamilton supporters: "If there has been any management in the business," he wrote later, "it has been concealed from me."

Washington admitted that, although Hamilton had during the Revolution never reached the rank of general, "his opportunities and experiences could not be short of those who did," and that his subsequent offices had put him "upon as high ground as most of the men in the United States." Yet the geographical arguments for Pinckney could not be denied.[24]

The conferees finally concluded that the three generals would be listed for presentation to Congress in this order — Hamilton, Pinckney, Knox — but Washington would write Hamilton trying to persuade him that it was his patriotic duty to soothe public opinion in the south (about which he had expressed such great worry) by stepping down for Pinckney. Since Hamilton's reaction could not be determined before Congress adjourned, Washington and McHenry came to an agreement which Washington was later to deny. In approving the names of the generals, Congress should postpone decision on their relative ranks by leaving it to President Adams.[25]

Henry Lee was recommended to fill in if any of the three candidates for major general refused. Men were selected for brigadiers and the various staff positions. Individual regiments would be recruited by states, and thus Washington wracked his memory to prepare a geographically oriented list of "the most intelligent and active officers" in the fighting that had ended sixteen years before. Although when he had called out the whiskey army he had been particularly anxious not to have it an exclusively Federalist force, he now felt that the army about to be raised had "everything to be feared from treachery or neglect in his office" by the lukewarm. He thus tried to exclude from the total officer force known partisans of France. The result was full of holes — he could think of no suitable colonels from New Hampshire, Delaware, North Carolina, or Georgia — and he noted that he might have inadvertently included men "of bad political principles, and others whose true characters I have mistaken." The whole required further investigation.26

Washington also prepared a memorandum which stated that the lower officers who would recruit and discipline the troops locally should be appointed at once. Although selecting the higher officers was less urgent, the sooner they could be announced the better. However, they should not be called out or paid until circumstances actually required their services. The Lieutenant General was not urging a crash operation to meet an immediate menace.27

To the pile of papers McHenry was to carry to Philadelphia Washington added a letter to Hamilton which stated his prudential reasons why Pinckney should be next after the commander in chief. "My wish to put you first and my fear of losing him are not a little embarrassing," Washington mourned, and then he passed the buck in a manner he was soon to forget. "After all, it rests with the President to use his pleasure."28

McHenry's departure to dash for Philadelphia left Washington with the disagreeable task of writing Knox, who was, with the exception of Dr. Craik (and, of course, Martha), his very oldest close friend. Knox would surely be hurt at having his inferiors in seniority put over his head, but Washington regarded it as a matter of principle to make personal friendship subservient to the good of the nation. And he was convinced that Knox would be of little use to the commanding general. Admitting freely that he himself had sunk from the height of his powers, Washington surely realized that he would be much more dependent on his subordinates than he had been during his previous military commands. The increasing shrillness he was to display concerning the selection of those subordinates was undoubtedly caused by the sense of weakness which in turn induces fear.

Perhaps because of confusion as to exactly what he was doing, perhaps because Knox was such an admirer of Hamilton, Washington wrote Knox that, having been informed that "the public estimation" demanded Hamilton as second in command, he had agreed "with some fears, I confess, of the consequences." Pinckney had also to be preferred because of his southern connections. Knox would see that this only left open to him the third place among the major generals. Since they were forming a *new* army which, if called to duty, "is to fight for everything that ought to be dear and sacred to freemen," Washington hoped "that former rank would be forgot" and that the only contention would be "who shall be foremost in zeal at this crisis to serve his country in whatever situation circumstance may place him." Washington concluded, "With that esteem and regard which you know I feel for you, I remain your sincere friend and affectionate servant."[29]

On his arrival in Philadelphia, McHenry went at once to the President, without pausing to see his own family. He was told that Congress, having passed a bill to set up the army, had adjourned, but the Senate was waiting to act on the appointments to the offices created. He gave Adams the list of major generals on which he and Washington had agreed.

Adams sent it to the Senate on the understanding that the sequence in which the names were listed should not be binding. One look at that sequence had showed Adams that he had scotched the snake, not killed it. There was Hamilton at the top, and Adams realized, as well as Hamilton did, that the actual authority might drop down a level from Washington's aging hands. Adams stated that Hamilton had no right to stand so high, and he did not know what merits gave Pinckney preference over Knox.

To make Washington's reasoning clear, McHenry showed Adams Washington's "private" letter to Hamilton. The President was thus informed that Washington wanted Pinckney first and Hamilton second.[30] So far so good, but Knox was still last. Since it was a conception as old as American continental cooperation that the two top leaders of any communal endeavor should be one from the south — preferably Virginia — and one from New England — preferably Massachusetts — Adams could not accept a list that placed the only New Englander at the bottom.

If Adams had been willing to follow Washington's preferred sequence of generals, if he had not felt that Massachusetts was being insulted, the danger he saw (it was quite possibly an actual one) in making Hamilton second in command could at that point have been sidetracked. However, the President's determination to put Knox at Washington's right hand was to create an acrimonious controversy during which the old hero succumbed to his most irresponsible acts since he had been an unwhipped puppy during the French and Indian War.

41

A Sad Affair

O N August 4, 1798, the new Lieutenant General, who was perpetually sending for the mail and not finding the letters he wanted, angrily accused the postmaster at Alexandria of inattention to his duties.[1] George Washington could no longer even pretend that he was keeping his mind on his fields.

One of the questions that plagued him was what would happen if the invasion of England which Napoleon was projecting ended in a French triumph. The Republicans envisioned a blessed era of peace, but Washington believed that the Directory would have to "find employment for the troops or the troops will find employment for the Directory." There would furthermore be a good chance that France would repossess Louisiana and the Floridas, thus augmenting the menace to the United States.[2]

Washington decided that he should find, to carry him into possible active duty, a charger "equal to my weight, which, without saddle, may be estimated at 210 pounds.* Being long-legged and tall would be no recommendation, as it adds nothing to the strength but a good deal to the inconvenience of mounting."[3]

The Senate had confirmed the list of officers it had received from Adams. Hamilton's name still came first and Knox's last among the major generals, but there was no stipulation that this order determined seniority. Washington was far from pleased to learn that Adams had added two brigadiers on his own. "What in the name of military prudence," he burst out to Pickering, "could induce the appointments of [Anthony] White

---

* Washington was within one pound of his weight — 209 pounds — during the last year of the Revolution.[4]

and [John] Sevier? . . . The latter was never celebrated for anything (that ever came to my knowledge) except the murder of Indians, and the former for nothing but frivolity and empty show and something worse." Washington was more than indignant — "very much hurt on the *general ground* I took" — that nothing had been done to make Edward Carrington adjutant general. Without waiting for Adams, Washington had written Carrington, offering him the post.[5]

Washington wished to know whether his letter had persuaded Hamilton to serve under Pinckney. "I am," he complained to McHenry, "thrown entirely into the field of conjecture. . . . Will Colonel Hamilton accept? Have you heard from the other general officers?"[6]

The dearth of news did not mean there was any dearth of mail. Washington received such a flood of letters from men who wished commissions that he was forced to appeal through McHenry to Adams for money to pay a secretary. Lear returned to his employ° and helped him decide which applications should be forwarded, which brushed aside.[8]

Almost a month after his interview with McHenry, Washington received in the same mail answers from Knox and Hamilton. Knox's communication filled Washington with "disquietude and perplexity in the extreme." His old friend stated that he had opened Washington's letter "with all the delightful sensations of affection" only to learn with "astonishment" that "for more than twenty years I must have been acting under a perfect delusion." He had believed that his friendship for Washington was reciprocated. "Nay more: I flattered myself with your esteem and respect in a military point of view." His "feelings and happiness" had been "much wounded." He could not, without public disgrace, serve under officers so obviously his juniors in the Revolutionary service.[9]

Hamilton wrote that he believed he was the preference of "a real ma-

---

° During the five years since he had resigned as Washington's secretary, Lear had been much battered. He had married Fanny Bassett Washington, Martha's niece and the widow of Washington's nephew, only to have her die within the year. The business venture to which Washington had encouraged him in the federal city had, with the difficulties of his partner Greenleaf, come down around his ears: he was forced to scrounge. Washington lent him money. However, in leasing him some Mount Vernon acres, Washington made it firmly clear that in *this* relationship no favoritism was to be expected. It became necessary to scold Lear when, after entering correctly in his books some payments he had collected for Washington, he applied the money to his own needs. Although Washington saw to it that Lear was made president of the Potomac Canal Company, he expressed worry when Lear wished the deeds to funds lent to that company made out to him alone: Might it not, Washington asked a third party, be "more secure" to include the names of the directors? Despite all this, Washington resolved that, if he were called to arms, Lear would serve as his chief aide. His old secretary, he explained, had given him "fourteen years of proof of his integrity and abilities."[7]

jority of leading federal men," and that Pinckney's pretensions to seniority were illusory. However, "if the gentlemen concerned are dissatisfied and the service destined to suffer by the preference given to me, I am ready to submit our relative pretensions to an impartial decision. . . . It will never be said with any color of truth that my ambition or interest has stood in the way of public good."

Hamilton added a warning which seemed only too justified by what Washington was experiencing: "McHenry is wholly insufficient to his place, with the additional misfortune of not having the least suspicion of the fact." Hamilton had journied to Philadelphia to help get the army going, but had been rebuffed, and was returning to New York.[10]

After a flash of anger at being so reproached, Washington wrote Knox as soothing a letter as he could, in which he denied any doubt of Knox's continuing military abilities. The importance of pleasing the south through Pinckney and the Federalist leaders through Hamilton had forced his hand. He hoped that Knox's patriotism would induce him to reconsider.

Washington's reply to Hamilton is a shocking summation of how his powers were dwindling. It is the most confused paper that had ever come from his pen. It shows his mind in a complete whirl.

Having enclosed for Hamilton's perusal Knox's offended letter, Washington wrote that, if the Senate had not intended the sequence of generals they had approved to be binding and "the commissions are yet to issue," perhaps Knox could after all be put ahead of Pinckney. Since Knox's seniority was so obvious, Pinckney (who had not yet got back from France) could hardly object. Where this left Hamilton was not made clear. However, Washington hoped that Hamilton would fill in for the inadequacies of McHenry, devoting "a good deal of your time to the business of recruiting *good* men and the choice of *good* officers."

Most amazingly, Washington's letter to Hamilton made no reference to Hamilton's offer to accept rank below the other generals if the service required it.[11]

The next day, Washington wrote McHenry that if he were now "called to the army in the moment of danger," he would be as ignorant of "everything relating thereto as if I had just dropped from the clouds. . . . Having staked my life, my reputation, my fortune, my ease, my tranquillity and happiness," he would like to know what was going on.[12]

On August 18, 1798, Washington was "seized with a fever." He tried to shake it off by pursuing his usual rides and occupations, "but it continued to increase upon me." Dr. Craik was sent for in the middle of the night of the 21st. He called in consultants, and labored, according to the medicine of the time, to get the old man to the point where he could stand doses of "Jesuit's bark," a remedy for malaria. Washington wasted fast, losing in all twenty pounds, but on the 24th, he was able to take the bark. "Since which," he wrote on September 3, "I have been in a convalescent state, but too much debilitated to be permitted to attend much to business."[13]

While he was still shaky, Washington received a letter from Pickering stating that Adams was backing Knox's claim that he had a "legal right," because of his seniority in the Revolutionary army, to be the first of the major generals. This principle, Pickering pointed out, would raise to the top of the new army, over the heads of Hamilton and Pinckney, a whole crop of superannuated officers.[14]

Washington replied to Pickering, "The President ought to ponder well before he consents to a change of the arrangement."[15]

To McHenry, Washington wrote angrily that the law authorizing the army had been passed "before the middle of July and was positive; and the middle of September has produced no fruit from it." How would the executive account for this delay? It was "inconceivable" and a source of sore regret. Public resentment of the French treatment of the American commissioners was "evaporating fast, and the recruiting service which might have been successful (of the best men) a month ago may be found very difficult a month hence (of the worst kind.)"[16]

When finally notified that Adams was adamant about putting Hamilton last and that McHenry was writing the aggrieved officer urging him nonetheless to serve, Washington, who had not himself written Hamilton for more than a month, made no move to back McHenry's plea. He wrote the Secretary of War, "I will defer saying anything on the President's *new* arrangement of the three major generals until you shall have communicated the result of Colonel Hamilton's answer to me."[17]

Hamilton informed McHenry that he would not serve. McHenry sent this news to Washington along with a transcript of a letter he had received from Adams. Adams had written crustily that he regarded Hamilton primarily as inspector general, which gave him no rank in the line over any other major general, not excluding Edward Hand and Lee, who had been appointed to the "provisional army" that was for the time being to remain altogether on paper. Adams had been willing to mark time, so his letter continued, in the hope that the officers could straighten the matter out among themselves. They had not done so. The President could, of course, consult Washington. However, the only result would be that the problem would "come back to me at last after much altercation and exasperation of passions." He would determine it then just 'as he did now: Knox first, Pinckney second, Hamilton the very last. Adams added an angry comment: "There has been too much intrigue in this business with General Washington and me. If I shall ultimately be the dupe of it, I am much mistaken in myself."[18]

This was too much for Washington. He flew off the handle.

Notified by McHenry that he was joining Pickering and Wolcott in a Cabinet protest against the President's decision,[19] Washington rushed off a letter to McHenry labeled "private and confidential." Washington stated that, although he could not write directly to Adams "without betraying your confidential communication," he foresaw the alternatives of submitting to the President's "forgetfulness of what *I* considered a compact" or of publicly resigning as Commander in Chief of the army.

In girding himself for battle, Washington realized that he had no evidence of any "compact." He felt he had "a right" to ask for a copy of McHenry's letter to Adams from Mount Vernon in which the condition had been stated. And, unless McHenry saw some "impropriety," he would be glad to see the instructions the President had given McHenry in preparation for the interview, and also a copy of the Cabinet ministers' protest. Washington added pessimistically his doubt that Adams, having committed himself, would back down.

McHenry, ignoring Washington's heading "private and confidential," forwarded to Adams (who was in Massachusetts, attending the sickbed of his wife) the popular hero's statement that he foresaw the alternative of accepting Adams's "forgetfulness" or publicly resigning. When McHenry reported his indiscretion, Washington was not displeased. Instead, he decided to follow up McHenry's disclosure with a letter of his own to the President.[20]

But first he notified "Major General Alexander Hamilton" that he was intervening. "Until the result of this is known, I hope you will suspend a final decision."[21]

Washington's letter of September 25, 1798 to his successor began by stating that, if any expression should escape him which might appear to be incompatible with his regard for the President's public station and Adams's private character, "let the purity of my intentions, the candor of my declarations, and a due respect for my own character be received as an apology."

Had Adams given him an opportunity before appointing him, he would have made it clear that he would only accept if the general and staff officers were chosen with his concurrence. As it was, both he and the Secretary of War had entertained no doubt that this was intended, and McHenry had in his letter to Adams so stated. But his order of major generals had been reversed, and various appointments of which he did not approve had been made, "not only without the least consultation with me, but without the least intimation of the intention."

Washington then assured Adams that it was "most foreign from my heart" to try to increase the powers of the Commander in Chief or lessen those of the President. Adams would recognize that a man "who had staked everything which was dear and valuable upon the issue" would not "trust more to chance than could be avoided. It could not be supposed that I was insensible to the risk I was about to run, knowing that the chances of losing were at least equal to those of increasing that reputation which the partiality of the world had been pleased to bestow on me." And no person acquainted with "the sacrifices I was about to make and the impartiality of my conduct in the various walks of life could suppose that I had any object in view [in wishing to control appointments] than to obtain the best aides the country afforded."

Washington then launched into a passage which showed that his memory of recent events had completely blacked out. He forgot that he and McHenry, being unable to agree on whether Pinckney or Hamilton should come first, had decided that the list presented to the Senate should not be construed to indicate seniority. Washington had written Hamilton that it was up to the President to decide. But now Washington wrote the President that the list, on which Hamilton's name had been first, was understood by the Senate to indicate seniority and could not legitimately be changed by executive fiat.

Although he had hardly moved beyond the borders of Mount Vernon, Washington undertook — on the basis of information written him by Hamilton's supporters — to lecture the President on public opinion — even in Adams's own New England. Hamilton was generally desired as second in command. Washington now ardently backed this preference. During the Revolution, "as the principal and most confidential aide of the Commander in Chief," Hamilton had had more opportunity to survey the whole military scene than commanding generals. "By some he is considered as an ambitious man and therefore a dangerous one. That he is ambitious I shall readily grant, but it is of that laudable kind which prompts a man to excel in whatever he takes in hand. He is enterprising, quick in his perceptions, and his judgment intuitively great."

Concerning Knox, "there is no man in the United States with whom I have been in habits of greater intimacy; no one whom I have loved more sincerely, not any for whom I have had a greater friendship." But this could have no influence on his mind compared to the public good. Washington then skirted over his real reasons for skirting over Knox.

Washington apologized for his "prolixity," and then stated that there was "another subject not less interesting to the commander in chief of the armies (be him whom he may)." This ungrammatical parenthesis was the land mine in the letter. Having thus thrown in a hint that he might resign, Washington asked why no man had been recruited, no battalion officer appointed.

The closing paragraph read, "I have addressed you sir with openness and candor and I hope with respect, requesting to be informed whether your determination to reverse the order of the three major generals is final, and whether you mean to appoint another adjutant general without my concurrence? With the greatest respect and consideration, I have the honor, etc."[22]

Having completed this letter, Washington decided not to mail it until he had slept on it. By morning, he had concluded that he needed advice. But whose? It should be someone in the main flow of information. Hamilton was obviously excluded. Washington was not close to Pickering or Wolcott. He was personally close to McHenry, even if he regarded the Secretary of War as somewhat of a fool. In the end, he decided McHenry it would have to be. He decided to send McHenry a draft of the letter for advice as to whether Adams should receive it or not. "You will readily perceive that even the *rumor* of a misunderstanding between the President and me, while the breach can be repaired, would be attended with unpleasant consequences. If there is no disposition on his part to do this, the public must decide which of us is right and which of us is wrong."

Washington was too impatient to wait until he heard from McHenry: he mailed the letter to the President. There can be no doubt that hysteria was upon him. A few days after he had written Adams, the man who had once labored to lure into the Revolutionary fold lukewarm Tories, warned McHenry, "You could as soon scrub a blackamoor white as to change the principles of a professed Democrat."[23]

Throwing to the winds the scruples that had during the first year and a half of his retirement kept him from interfering in his successor's government, Washington moved to use Adams's Cabinet as if it were his own. On

October 1, he urged McHenry to discuss with "the gentlemen who act with you" whether he could "with propriety and due respect for my own character" keep his commission, and also what would be the national effect if he resigned. Having gone this far, he found his mind filling with worries. McHenry should ask for this advice *not as a matter required by me,*" but as "questions propounded by *yourself,* entirely and absolutely." Furthermore, Washington had begun to wonder whether McHenry and Pickering were *certain* that Adams was mistaken in believing that New England would be disgusted if Hamilton were put over Knox. He had some suspicions that Pickering "is not a friend to Knox, but cannot suppose that this would have any influence on the case." Washington ended by commanding McHenry to burn his letter "as soon as it is perused, as I will do your answer, that neither one nor the other shall appear hereafter. With much truth, etc."[24]

Adams was no more pleased than one would expect, to have trained on him the heavy artillery of the man who had topped him during most of his career. Yet he had no choice but surrender. Imagination could hardly conceive the chaos into which both political power and public opinion would be thrown if the angry old man at Mount Vernon carried out his angry threat. On the day after he received Washington's letter, Adams replied. Although he asserted the authority of the President to determine the rank of officers, he agreed to use that authority in backing whatever decisions Washington made concerning the major generals and (as far as remained possible) the adjutant general.

"I hope your own health and Mrs. Washington's remain perfect. Mine is very indifferent and Mrs. Adams' extremely low. Confined to the bed of sickness for two months, her destiny is still very precarious, and mine in consequence of it."[25]

Washington could not resist sending a copy of Adams's capitulation to McHenry, but he wished no whisper to come to the President that he had done so. "That the contents of my letters to and from him are in the possession of others may induce him to believe in good earnest that intrigues are carrying on in which I am an actor, than which nothing is more foreign from my heart."[26]

Washington's reply to the President was majestic. Adams's letter, he wrote, "demands my particular acknowledgments." He regretted Mrs. Adams's illness. He and Mrs. Washington were well. He made some comments on the appointment to adjutant general. He signed himself "with great consideration and respect." But he made no mention of the issue which had created his threat of resignation and on which he had driven the President into retreat.[27]

Washington had got his way. But it was because Adams (who was only three years his junior) was temperate when he was not that he achieved his ends without damage to the United States and his own fame. The more he believed that the nation was dangerously divided and there was treason afoot, the more irresponsible was his threat that he would openly attack the President and let the public decide "which of us is right and which of us is wrong." What had happened to his long-held belief that the safety of the nation depended on confidence in the executive, that only irresponsible demagogues sought to tear that confidence down?

There was certainly reason in Washington's belief that accepting Knox as his second in command would be trusting his weight on a crutch of lath. However, both Hamilton and Pinckney were able officers, and Washington had at the start wished to elevate the southerner over the New Yorker. His eventual willingness to pull the house down in order to secure the second post for Hamilton revealed that he no longer possessed the resolution to stand up against a concerted attack of his advisers, even if they were men he did not admire or even trust. Adams was right in suspecting that there was "too much intrigue in this business" and that it had influenced Washington.

Despite the effects of the years, Washington had viewed national events from Mount Vernon "in the mild light of calm philosophy" until he had been pulled back into official responsibility as Lieutenant General. However, once he had felt it necessary to protect himself from the appointment of Knox, he had slipped into the typical syndrome of retired functionaries in relation to their successors. And in failing to resist this temptation, he had revealed in other ways the weakening of his faculties. No other document the old hero ever wrote went so far in self-righteousness as did his angry letter to Adams. And the man who had characteristically moved directly and in the open had put himself in a position (as he himself realized) where he could be accused, if the facts came out, of carrying on "intrigues" behind the President's back.

Washington had blown up what was at its rational extreme no more than a medium-sized disagreement, into an issue that threatened to convulse the nation. And at various moments in the controversy the brilliant pragmatist seems to have lost contact with reality.

In many another man Washington's conduct might well seem no more than a heightened aberration. But for Washington it was a shocking violation. Those of us who have in these volumes (or elsewhere) followed his long career can only view his hysteria with deep sadness. We mourn not only that a great man should become so disfigured, but for all humanity. Not even the most resplendent hero is immune to the passing years.

42

Plateaus on a Descending Path

A S Washington moved from Mount Vernon over the winter roads towards Philadelphia, a worry pricked him. He remembered that the group which had waved good-bye from his doorway had not included his nephew Lawrence Lewis. Wrack his brains as he would, he could not remember whether Lewis had been at breakfast. If the nephew had breakfasted with the family, his subsequent absence indicated disrespect. But if he had not come downstairs at all, then he must have been unwell, and Washington had slighted *him* by not mounting to his room to say good-bye. Finally, Washington decided that he would rather apologize than accept the risk of having been discourteous. He wrote Lewis that "an appointment to·be in Alexandria at a certain hour, my anxiety to accomplish it, and the pressure of many things upon me until the moment I stepped into the carriage, was the cause of my not bidding you adieu the morning I left home." [1]

Washington, who had insisted that he would never again travel more than ten miles from Mount Vernon, had set out on November 5, 1798, attended by Lear, four servants, and six or seven horses. It took six days to traverse the snowy roads and cross the icy rivers. Despite "my extreme impatience" to get back to Mount Vernon and his perpetual concern lest with deepening winter some great storm block the roads, he was held in Philadelphia for five weeks. "Making selection of the officers for the twelve new regiments and arranging them to the different states is," he explained, "a work of infinitely more difficulty than I had any conception of." [2]

Washington confessed to Eliza Powel — "although of this you must not

[413]

be the informer" — that he conducted conferences even on the Sabbath.[3] The talks were first two-sided, between Washington and Hamilton, but Pinckney finally got back from France and materialized. McHenry, representing the executive as Secretary of War, hovered on the outskirts. President Adams kept aloof, although he entertained Washington at dinner.

The principal problem — to find officers in every community who had the prestige and popularity to draw into the service the troops they would command — was complicated by Washington's unwillingness to accept men recommended by opposition congressmen lest they "poison the army." If the old general was preparing a force that could in the wrong hands — and had he selected the wrong hands? — serve tyranny, the fears and suspicions that were now rolling in his brain made him unconscious of it.

Washington elicited from Pinckney's observations in France what information he could. In how many ranks, he asked, did the French form a line of battle? The answer being three, the conferees decided to follow suit. Did the French use pikes and should the Americans have them? Washington urged McHenry to get moving at once towards importing newly invented cannon from Scotland. The proportion of officers to men, the organization of supply, whether the cavalry should be recruited nationally or, like the infantry, by states in proportion to population, were among the subjects discussed. Throughout, the attitude was that what had been done during the Revolution was of importance as informing experience but not as precedent.

Although he still did not foresee a French invasion of the United States, Washington felt that, should France fall heir to Louisiana and the Floridas, the United States might well have to take the offensive. One of the questions he propounded was whether in such a crisis the commander of the army might, without delaying for further governmental sanction, order an invasion.[4]

Washington complained that he was so overwhelmed with duties "as scarcely to afford me time to look into a newspaper." Yet his gregariousness exploded in the presence of his many old friends. Hardly a night when he did not dine out. The most dramatic of the occasions surely was when the former President of the United States went through the doors of the debtors' prison to have dinner with Robert Morris.[5]

Washington dined with the Listons. Eliza Powel's parlor beckoned, and Washington wished he could get there more often. The General commissioned her to buy a handsome present for Nelly Custis: she could expend "thirty or sixty or more dollars" on "a handsome muslin or anything else that is not the whim of the day." The General added, "Is there anything not of much cost I could carry to Mrs. Washington as a memento that she has not been forgotten?" He had observed that if a lady felt overlooked, there would be "a contest regardless of right — no unusual thing — in which an innocent babe may become the victim of strife."6

Concerning an afternoon in Philadelphia, Washington, for one of the few times in his life, boasted of having been rude. He was writing at his desk when a servant appeared to announce the Reverend Blackwell. In a memorandum, Washington described his disgust when, on going downstairs, he found waiting in the parlor not only Blackwell but George Logan.

Logan had gone to France with the blessing of Republican leaders and, although a private citizen, entered into negotiations with Talleyrand.° This pleased the French, who preferred to deal not with American diplomats but with pro-French citizens who they claimed were the true representatives of the American people. Concessions concerning foreign trade were made at Logan's request, and he carried back to the United States the message that, since France would respond to a spirit of accommodation, American military and naval preparations were unnecessary and indeed harmful. Washington's Federalist correspondents had described to him Logan's actions as part of a subversive plot.7

Ignoring his unannounced caller, Washington shook hands with Blackwell. Logan stated his name and offered his hand. Washington shook it "with an air of much indifference." He asked Blackwell to be seated. Logan sat down unasked. Washington addressed all his remarks to Blackwell. Logan addressed all his to Washington. The unwelcome guest had the audacity to suggest that if the yellow fever returned to Philadelphia, Washington might stay at his house. "I thanked him slightly, observing there would be no call for it."

When Blackwell got up, Washington walked to the door, expecting Logan would go too. Logan stayed. He tried to interest Washington by an account of seeing Lafayette at Hamburg. Washington "remained standing and showed the utmost inattention to what he was saying." Eventually Logan volunteered that he had gone to France in the hope of ameliorating the crisis.

° The "Logan Law," which Congress passed to make illegal such unofficial foreign policy missions, is still on the statute books.

Washington could not resist hinting that there had been more behind Logan's mission than met the eye. The interloper "seemed a little confounded, but recovering said that not more than five persons had any knowledge of his going." Jefferson and another Republican leader had not gone beyond furnishing him with certificates of citizenship. And his mission had successfully established that the president of the Directory had "discovered the greatest desire that France and America should be on the best terms."

Washington and Logan now got into a hot argument. Washington stated that if the French wanted to be believed, they should cease their attacks on American commerce and make restitution for the injuries already received. Logan said that the Directory was "apprehensive" that the American government and its envoys were anti-French. Washington insisted that America had proved her good will by putting up with too much. Logan said that the French were modifying their policy, and went on to describe the French military successes and power as if to insinuate "that we should be involved in a dangerous situation if we persisted in our hostile appearances."

Washington now really let go. He asked Logan whether "the Directory look on us as worms, and not even be allowed to turn when tread upon?" The United States "had borne and forborne beyond what even common respect for ourselves required and I hoped the spirit of this country would never suffer itself to be injured with impunity by any nation under the sun."

Washington's memorandum came to an abrupt end without telling how the two men parted.[8]

Washington had always had a fascination with uniforms. As a stripling during the French and Indian War, he had designed the regalia for his Virginia Regiment. Now he recommended that the army adopt as an identifying cockade to be worn in every hat, "a small eagle, of pewter, tin, or in some instances [his own?] silver, fixed by way of button in the center of a rose cockade."

For himself as Commander in Chief Washington specified "a blue coat with yellow buttons and gold epaulettes (each having three silver stars); linings cape and cuffs of buff; in winter buff vest and breeches; in summer a white vest and breeches of nankeen. The coat to be without lapels, and embroidered on the cape, cuffs, and pockets. A white plume in the hat to be a further distinction." Having secured approval for this vision, Washington hurried the order off to the best tailor in Philadelphia.[9]

On December 13, Washington signed an extensive final report to the executive, which had been written in the first person. The text added to innumerable military details a lecture obviously aimed at the President: "The act augmenting the army is preemptory in its provisions." Whether the executive might forbear to execute such a law raised a "nice" argument "of a kind it is generally prudent to avoid." However, it was safe to contend that such suspension could only be justified by "considerations of decisive cogency. The existence of such considerations is unknown."

The existing symptoms of a "probable" accommodation with France, ascribable to the vigorous measures of the American government, could be destroyed by a relaxation of those measures. And it was impossible to foresee what further crisis might be created by the flux of European events. "There may be imagined situations of very great moment to the permanent interests of the country which would certainly require a disciplined force." The Secretary of Treasury reported no lack of necessary funds. It followed therefore that there should be no avoidable delay in raising the provisional army to the full force authorized by Congress.

The literary style of this document tells volumes. Among the many important papers Hamilton drafted for Washington, it is almost unique in exhibiting, without any recognizable emendations by Washington, Hamilton's legalistic prose. The old man seems to have added nothing but his signature.[10]

Hamilton must have been all eagerness to know with what authority Washington was going to entrust him. Whether or not he had already discussed the matter with his second in command, Washington took off for Mount Vernon on December 14 without officially divulging his intentions. Only while he was being prevented by contrary winds from crossing the Susquehanna, did he send McHenry his determination. He explained, "Close application to other matters, with which you charged me whilst I was in Philadelphia, and my extreme impatience (on account of the season and the weather) to leave it, must be my apology for not doing this sooner."

Washington was later to write Hamilton that "to engage partially in military arrangements" would be "unpleasant . . . as it incurs responsibility without proper means of decision." Now he wrote McHenry that he had decided that, unless crisis actually dictated, he would undertake no "direct agency" in the raising of the army. However, he by no means handed the authority over to Hamilton. Pinckney should be in charge of the three southernmost states and, if he agreed, Virginia. Although Hamilton was to be responsible for the rest of the troops, his "proximity to the seat of government" would enable him to act directly under the control of the executive.

Washington believed that the real danger lay at the mouth of the Mississippi, and he may well have heard that Hamilton's enemies suspected him of wishing to use the army to carve out an empire for himself as the Napoleon of the southwest. In any case, Washington stipulated that reports from the commander of the western army (General Wilkinson) to Hamilton should be relayed through McHenry. This, Washington explained, would enable the Secretary of War "to give immediate orders in cases which may be too urgent to wait for the agency of General Hamilton."[11]

Like a half-worn-out motor, Washington's mind sometimes failed to turn over, but it could still function with power.

Moving as rapidly as the weather would permit towards the peace of Mount Vernon, Washington became increasingly concerned lest his refuge prove not peaceful after all. He had arranged for a troop of cavalry to be commanded by his nephew Lawrence Lewis with another close protégé, George Washington Craik, as a lieutenant. And then he had gone rashly further: he had recommended Washington Custis for the lowest rank: cornet.

Now, in the narrow confines of the rocking carriage, Washington had horrifying visions of how Martha would react to a military appointment for "an only son, indeed, the only male of his family." He shot off to McHenry a letter praying that no mention of the appointment be made until the consent of the mother and grandmother had been secured.

On his arrival at Mount Vernon, Washington discovered that Lear had already let the cat out of the bag. The ex-President was soon making a speech to his wife. If real danger threatened the country, no young man ought to remain an idle spectator. If, on the other hand, American preparedness averted the evil, Custis would get credit without danger. Furthermore, military concerns might divert the youth's attention from the matrimonial ideas to which he was too prone. More impressed probably by her darling grandson's eagerness, which she did not wish to disappoint, Martha, after having listened meekly, made "not the least objection."[12]

Washington warned his family that, since the actual appointment was at the pleasure of the President, the matter should not be talked about. But he was soon writing McHenry that, as senior cornet, the nineteen-year-old innocent had a right to advance to a lieutenancy which the original appointee had refused. Washington added that he was not asking this as a favor. "I never have and never shall solicit anything for myself or my connections. I mean nothing more than the statement of a fact." (Custis, in fact, soon became a colonel as aide-de-camp to General Pinckney.)[13]

Custis's affairs had not, however, proved the greatest excitement of Washington's return. Lewis, as the General put it, had resolved that "before he enters the camp of Mars, he is to engage in that of Venus." And with whom? With the enchanting Nelly Custis.° Washington, who had not had "the smallest suspicion that such an affair was in agitation," was nonetheless very pleased, for he was fond of both lovers, and this linking of the Washington and Custis lines suited his frustrated dynastic conceptions.[15]

The couple had decided they would be married on his birthday, and after he described the new uniform that was being made for him in Philadelphia, Nelly threw her arms around his neck and drew from him the delighted promise that he would give the regalia its formal debut at her wedding.[16]

Off to McHenry went another letter: "On reconsidering the uniform for the commander in chief, it has become a matter of doubt with me (although as it respected myself *personally* I was against *all* embroidery) whether embroidery on the cape, cuffs, and pockets of the coat, and none on the *buff* waistcoat, would not have a disjointed and awkward appearance." He was also concerned about the design of the cuffs and pocket flaps. Let not McHenry regard these as trivial matters: "it being the commencement of a distinguishing dress for the commander in chief of the armies of the United States!" It was essential, Washington added, that the uniform be at Mount Vernon by February 22.

Twelve days before his birthday and the wedding, Washington reminded McHenry that the uniform should be "accompanied with cockades and stars for the epaulettes."

Eleven days before the wedding, Washington wrote the tailor that if

---

° After the wedding, Washington returned to his previous metaphor, but with a change. Lewis, "relinquishing the lap of Mars for the sports of Venus," had resigned from the army. Lewis proved so good at these sports that Nelly had a baby in the shortest respectable time.

A letter from Eliza Powel reveals that Martha had opposed the match until she "found the thing inevitable." No explanation is given. Perhaps Martha was foresighted enough to recognize that Nelly would become unhappy because Lewis was sickly and without enterprise.[14]

Bushrod Washington had not left Philadelphia, he would serve as a safe means for forwarding the uniform.[17]

Day after day passed. Finally a package arrived but it was discouragingly small. It proved to contain eagles for the cockade but, alas, no stars for the epaulettes. And nothing more arrived. When Nellie was married on the 22nd at "about candlelight," Washington wore his old uniform.[18]

Washington was notified that the tailor had been unable to find in the entire United States the necessary gold thread. However, some was expected in the spring shipments from Europe. As Washington meditated on this information, it suddenly occurred to him that the tailor might be stalling because he had forgotten to pay for a black satin robe he had had made while he was in Philadelphia. He hurried a note to Eliza Powel begging her to get in touch with the tailor and pay the bill. She replied that she had leapt, pocketbook in hand, into the breach.[19]

On May 2, Washington poked the tailor up again. On June 7, he expressed to McHenry the hope that he might have the uniform by "the anniversary of independence." Four days before the Fourth, Washington dashed off to McHenry this message: "I shall send up to Alexandria on Wednesday, but shall feel no disappointment if the uniform is not there." It was not there.[20]

A sartorial Icarus, Washington had tried to fly too close to the sun. In final despair, the tailor sent the uniform off to Europe to be finished. Washington never had the pleasure of wearing it. Before it returned, he was dead.[21]

43

A Passenger Only

IN all American history no legislation has a more obnoxious reputation than the Alien and Sedition acts passed by Congress during the XYZ hysteria in the same session that authorized the new army. The Alien Acts raised the residence requirement for naturalization from five years to fourteen (the maximum to date in all American history) and provided that the President might expel from the country any alien he ruled dangerous. The Sedition Act made punishable false, scandalous, and malicious writings intended to defame or bring into disrepute the government, Congress, or the President.

That Washington would, as President, have done what Adams did — sign the bills into law — seems improbable. He did not, it is true, expect as much loyalty to the United States in the foreign born as in the native born. When President, he had suffered from violent attacks on himself or his administration launched by recently arrived Europeans from Gallatin downward. One fertile source of pro-French feelings — it inspired William Duane, who had succeeded Balch (now deceased) as editor of the *Aurora* — was Irish hatred for the British. Although Washington sometimes expressed his misgivings in private letters — as when he blamed the Whiskey Rebellion on newcomers unpersuaded to American free institutions — he had never, even privately, advocated any discrimination against aliens.° Publicly, he had gone no further in drawing a distinction

---

° Washington's plans both as a real estate speculator and a landlord often involved the importation of aliens. He had made grateful use of European engineers, architects, craftsmen, often more skillful than any America could supply, in the army and at the Potomac Canal, the federal city, and Mount Vernon.

between new arrivals and old Americans than stating in his Farewell Address that he felt towards his country "the fervent love . . . so natural to a man who views in it the native soil of himself and his progenitors for several generations."[1]

Probably no man in American history suffered more than Washington from newspaper libels, from a reviving of old lies and the concoction of new ones with a wild irresponsibility that American mores would not possibly accept today. Yet the attitude of his prime was what he thus summarized in 1792: "These kinds of representations is an evil which must be placed in opposition to the infinite benefits resulting from a free press."[2]

But now Washington believed in the existence of a conspiracy. While taking no public stand, he wrote to Alexander Spotswood that Americans should "consider to what lengths a certain description of men in our country have already driven and even resolved to further drive matters, and then ask themselves if it is not time and expedient to resort to laws against aliens (for citizens you know are not affected by that law) who acknowledge no allegiance to this country, and in many instances are sent among us . . . for the express purposes of poisoning the minds of our people . . . in order to alienate their affections from the government of their choice, thereby endeavoring to dissolve the union and of course the fair and happy prospects which were enfolding to our view from the [American] Revolution. But, as I observed before, I have no time to enter the field of politics."[3]

The complicated legal considerations raised by the Sedition Act,* which would of necessity have concerned Washington when it would have been his duty to approve or veto the statute, did not concern him now. He now viewed the outcry against the law as a maneuver by the opposition to discredit the government. "Anything else would have done. Something there will always be for them to torture and to disturb the public mind with their unfounded and ill-favored forebodings."[4]

When late in July 1799 Duane charged in the *Aurora* that the officers of

---

* Some recent historians have tempered the traditional all-out blast against the Sedition Act by arguing that it toned down jurisdiction which American courts had inherited from British common law: the new law limited fines and terms of imprisonment for libel, made truth of the charges a defense, and substituted for judicial determination trial by jury. To this, other historians rebut that the common-law provisions might have proved inapplicable in the United States: the act changed a dubious legal contention into an enforceable statute.

It is, incidentally, a fallacy to state that Jefferson (who was in his own Presidency to prosecute newspaper attackers as Washington never did) was opposed in principle to punishing libel. His opposition was to federal rather than state jurisdiction.

the government were wallowing in British bribes, Washington wrote McHenry jocosely, "And pray, good sir, what part of the $800,000 have come to your share? As you are in high office, I hope you did not disgrace yourself in the acceptance of a paltry bribe. A $100,000 perhaps?" To Pickering, Washington wondered whether the government's decision to prosecute Duane had been wise. Suppression might well be less effective than allowing the journalist enough rope to "have hung himself up something worse." Should the true dimensions of the effort to promote "a disunion of the states" come clear to the people, the conspiracy "like untimely fruits and flowers forced in a hot bed will, I hope — whatever my expectation may be — soon whither and in principle die away like them."[5]

In another mood, Washington wrote that Duane's charges should be given a fair and impartial investigation. If they proved true, he would be "deserving of thanks and high reward for bringing to light conduct so abominable." However, "if it shall be found to be all calumny . . . punishment ought to be inflicted."[6]

While viewing with horror the excesses of the Republicans, Washington now failed to criticize those of the Federalists. He identified the party in power with sound government and, indeed, with freedom from French domination. He still delivered no speeches and made no public statements, but having completely abandoned the nonpartisan stance of his best years, he could no longer hold on to his determination never to interfere in elections.

He summoned John Marshall to Mount Vernon. The lawyer came with Washington's nephew Bushrod. The pair went upstairs to change; they reappeared chewing tobacco and decked out in hideously stained work clothes. Having secured their laugh, they wished sympathy because their own possessions had vanished in a mix-up of baggage. But Washington would only express concern for the wagoners who, on opening what they thought were their saddlebags, found in them the useless clothes of lawyers.

Washington's objective was to persuade Marshall to reconsider his decision that he could not afford to shelve his law practice in order to run as a Federalist for Congress. As the two men paced back and forth on Mount Vernon's long porch, Washington argued that Virginia was woefully in need of effective and not misguided leaders. When Marshall stuck to his guns, Washington (so it is said) moved from entreaty to "a peremptory and angrily expressed command." Marshall was so disturbed that he rose very early the next morning in the hope of getting off without another discussion. But you had to rise before dawn in order to be up before the General. Marshall encountered Washington on the piazza and finally accepted the decision that was to lead to his epoch-making career as Chief Justice of the Supreme Court.[7]

Washington importuned the retired old patriot Patrick Henry to run for the Virginia Assembly. Although Henry had been regularly refusing office and was so feeble he could hardly stand, he came out of his den still able to roar loud enough to be elected — but he died before he could serve.[8]

During February 1798, several months before Washington had got into his hassle with Adams over commissions, Philadelphians were preparing for the usual ball on Washington's birthnight. The invitation they sent to President and Mrs. Adams set fury surging through the Presidential Mansion. Abigail wrote that the Philadelphians lacked "the least feeling of real genuine politeness." Instead of celebrating the birthday of the President they celebrated the ex-President's birthday and asked the President to attend! "I do not know when my feelings of contempt have been more called forth." Adams considered that the very office of the Presidency had been insulted.[9]

As the summer unrolled, Washington conceived a plan for responding to the President's choler that could be counted on to please Adams, and yet had from Washington's own point of view its comic side.

The documentation begins with a letter written in July by Washington to McHenry: "The *graybeards* of Alexandria, pretty numerous it seems and composed of all the respectable old people of the place," had formed a company to defend the neighborhood from the French. It had been intimated that if Mrs. Washington would present them with a standard, "it would be flattering to them." He wished to have run up in Philadelphia something "handsome" but not "expensive."[10]

At a later moment, Washington decided that the presentation should be staged on Adams's birthday, and that the standard should be decorated with this in view. The "very elegant" flag that Martha ceremoniously handed to the chief graybeard revealed, worked in silk against azure blue, the golden eagle of America dangling a portrait of whom? Why, of course, of Adams. But, alas, the best laid plans sometimes go at least temporarily awry: Adams's first reaction was probably anger. In reporting the affair in Philadelphia, *Claypoole's American Daily Advertiser* identified the portrait the eagle had dangled on Adams's birthday as a likeness of

Washington. Eight days passed before Claypoole published a correction, making it clear that Adams had been complimented, not insulted.[11]

Although Adams had been frustrated concerning a noncommanding rank for Hamilton, he still held the final trump card. As long as no army was really needed, he could sit on his hands concerning mobilization — and the automatic inefficiency of his Secretary of War helped this strategy along.

Washington, apprised of the situation through the newspapers, through his mail, by callers at Mount Vernon, viewed it with a calm surprising after his recent explosion. It was Hamilton who, as he skimped his law practice in an effort to lead an army that failed to gather, chafed and chafed. But Washington did not write him, and he held off for two months before he finally presumed to communicate with the Lieutenant General. "I more and more discover cause," Hamilton mourned, "to apprehend that obstacles of a very peculiar kind stand in the way of efficient and successful management of our military concerns."[12]

Assuring Hamilton that he need not hesitate to communicate with him, Washington replied that, if the augmented force had been intended to be more than a threat, the delay in recruiting it "baffles all conjecture on reasonable grounds. . . . Far removed from the scene, I might ascribe these delays to wrong causes, and therefore will hazard no opinion respecting them, but I have no hesitation in pronouncing that, unless a material change takes place, our military theater affords but a gloomy prospect to those who are to perform the principal parts in the drama."[13]

Since Washington foresaw no military action except possibly on the southern frontier, where existing militia furnished an adequate military force, Washington had come to regard the situation as primarily a personal embarrassment. Late in March 1799 he sent McHenry what he stated was a "*private* communication." If it contained "more freedom and candor than are agreeable. . . . I will promise to offend no more by such conduct, but confine myself (if occasion should require it) to an official correspondence."

His mail, he wrote, was flooded with queries from appointed officers, many having quit their businesses in anticipation, who could not understand why they had not received their commissions. "Blame is in every mind, but it is not known where to fix it. Some attach it to the P [President]; some to the S of W [Secretary of War], and some, *fertile in inventions*, seek for other causes [i.e., Washington himself]. . . . What could I

[425]

say? I am kept in as much ignorance as they are themselves. . . . It is not unreasonable to suppose that if there be reasons of state operating the policy of these delays, that I was entitled to sufficient confidence to be let into the secret."

His mind running back to the Hessians, Washington wrote that he did not consider himself a "mercenary" officer. His service had been undertaken in "heartfelt sorrow" because he felt it was his duty. He regretted in particular being frustrated in his desire to leave his affairs, and those estates of which he was a trustee, "in such a clear and distinct form as that no reproach may attach itself to me when I have taken my departure for the land of spirits."* [14]

Back to Washington came a whole flood of explanations: uniforms were lacking; seniority could not be established because some appointees had never answered queries as to whether they would serve; etc., etc. But it seemed clear that the fundamental difficulty was executive indifference encouraged by the fact that the war scare which had followed the publication of the XYZ papers had abated.

McHenry, who was not notorious for imagination, undoubtedly saw no sarcasm in his sending Washington a war game he had imported from London. It was "a small box containing military figures for the practice of tactics. . . . Perhaps they may serve occasionally as a substitute for the chess board." [16]

Out of Washington's mailbag came a letter from Joel Barlow, a distinguished American resident in France, which stated that the differences between that nation and the United States were based on *"misunderstanding."* The Directory had declared that they would receive, without asking for money or "apologies for offensive speeches," any minister from the United States who came with good will. [17]

Despite his objection to private citizens' dabbling in foreign policy, this document seemed to Washington important enough to override his hesitation in communicating directly with his successor. Forwarding the letter, he stated that Adams could judge whether it was "written with a very

---

* Washington had intended to put his mind on paper work after the Revolution, and again on his retirement from the Presidency. He wished, he wrote, to devote "all my leisure hours" to straightening out personal records and "the arrangement and overhaul of" civil and military documents "that they may go into secure deposits and hereafter into hands that may be able to separate the grain from the chaff." However, because of "visits, my necessary rides, and other occurrences," his accounts had remained "in a jumble." He was glad to blame the breakdown on his military call. [15]

good or a very bad design." The message seemed to have been composed with the *"privity"* of the Directory. If Adams should conclude that the letter, was "calculated to bring negotiation upon open, fair, and honorable ground and merits a reply, and will instruct me as to the tenor of it, I shall with pleasure and alacrity obey your orders; more especially if there is reason to believe that it would become a mean, however small, of restoring peace and tranquillity to the United States upon just, and honorable, and dignified terms." Washington added that he was "persuaded" that this was "the ardent desire of all the friends of this rising empire."[18]

After a considerable wait for a reply, Washington received, on or near his sixty-sixth birthday, the most exciting letter that had come to Mount Vernon since it was first rumored that he would command a new army. Adams wrote that he had postponed answering Washington's communication "till I had deliberated on it . . . as well as a multitude of other letters and documents, official and inofficial, which relate to the same subject, and determined what part to act." He had determined to break the diplomatic stalemate with France by appointing the American minister to Holland, William Vans Murray, "minister plenipotentiary to the French republic." This had been done on the strength of a letter from Talleyrand stating that the American representative would be honorably received. However, lest there be chicanery, Murray was to stay in Holland until the French assurances were officially communicated. Washington could be sure that "no babyish and womanly blubbering for peace" would induce Adams to agree to anything dishonorable.[19]

Was this the break Washington yearned for? Or did Adams protest too much; had he been tricked by the French, or had he suddenly turned soft? The hurried letter repeating the news Washington received from Pickering expressed warm Federalist disapproval but was not particularly communicative.[20] And thus Washington greeted with anxiety a visitor who appeared from Philadelphia and was likely to be informed.

This visitor, who cannot be definitely identified, was certainly a Federalist since (and this is very important in assaying Washington's judgments) none other now came to Mount Vernon.° The General learned that Adams's announcement had exploded like a bomb in Philadelphia, since he had not consulted his Cabinet or any Federalist leaders before sending Murray's appointment to the Senate to be confirmed. More dis-

---

° In January 1798 Washington wrote Pickering that he had summarized an anti-Republican document "to some good Federal characters who were dining with me," who thought it "the best dessert I could have offered."[21]

turbing to Washington was his informant's statement "that there had been no *direct* overture from the government of France to that of the United States. . . . On the contrary," so Washington continued to Pickering, "Talleyrand was playing the same loose and roundabout game." * The ex-President believed that the United States, considering the "indignities" she had suffered, should have waited for the Directory "to come forward in an unequivocal manner, and prove it by their acts. . . . This would have been the course I should have pursued, keeping equally in view the horrors of war and the dignity of the government. But not being acquainted with all the information . . . I may have taken a wrong impression, and therefore shall say nothing further on the subject at this time."[22]

To President Adams, Washington wrote noncommittally that he hoped Adams's arduous duties were not impairing his health, and also that the United States would "pass this critical period in an honorable and dignified manner without being involved in the horrors and calamities of war."[23]

In order to get assent from the Senate for the appointment of Murray, Adams was forced to add two other commissioners and agree that, by holding these appointees in the United States, he would postpone the negotiation until official assurances had been received from the Directory. News and interpretations sent by Pickering and other Federalists made Washington conclude that Adams had gone off half-cocked. This conclusion was encouraged by the nonappearance of the desired confirmation from France. Washington was soon expressing the wish that some way could be found for the President to reverse himself without enabling the Republicans to charge that he was turning his back on negotiation. One thing was certain: as long as a peace mission loomed, the military preparedness for which the Lieutenant General certainly had some responsibility would continue to languish.[24]

In mid-July 1799, Washington's mailbag brought him a letter from Governor Trumbull of Connecticut which suggested that, in order to head off at the coming election "a French President," Washington might have to announce that he would again accept the office. In examining the letter, Washington noted that it had been more than a month in transit. Perhaps he guessed what Trumbull later admitted in reply to his query, that the

---

* Talleyrand's letter had not been to any American official but to a minor French diplomat who had given a copy to Murray.

letter had been handed around for approval to various Federalists, including disloyal members of Adams's Cabinet.[25]

Washington's reply was a tragic demonstration of how completely he had lost his belief that he could lead the whole nation; how utterly he had abandoned the conception that the United States could be governed by an administration which, transcending faction, represented all the people and pleased most of them. Washington felt that the personality, the abilities, of the candidate were now irrelevant. All that mattered was that he be the choice of a faction (or what we would today call a political party.)*

Let the opposition, Washington wrote Trumbull, "set up a broomstick and call it a true son of liberty, a democrat, or give it any other epithet that will suit their purpose, and it will command their votes in toto." The Federalists would have, in self-defense, to respond to whatever candidate was presented on their side with the same unanimity. "Wherein then would lie the difference between the present gentleman in office and myself? . . .

"Although I have abundant cause to be thankful for the good health with which I am blessed, yet I am not insensible to my declination in other respects. It would be criminal therefore in me, although it should be the wish of my countrymen and I could be elected, to accept an office under this conviction, which another would discharge with more ability; and this too at a time when I am thoroughly convinced I should not draw a single vote from the anti-Federal side." Were he to listen to persuasions, "I should be charged not only with irresolution, but with concealed ambition which waits only an occasion to blaze out; and, in short, with dotage and imbecility."[26]

Trumbull's reply agreed — perhaps in order to tie the ex-President closer to the Federalists — that Washington would not get a single anti-Federalist vote. The worrisome matter was that the Federalists would not be able to unite *their* voters behind Adams, who was still holding on to his efforts to find an accommodation with France. The Federalists would, however, unite behind Washington.[27]

Washington responded, "I must again express a strong and ardent wish and desire that no eye, no tongue, no thought may be turned towards" his return to the Presidency.[28]

---

* That this melancholy view of the effect of political parties was not altogether unfounded is revealed by the Presidencies of men like Warren G. Harding.

After Nelson's great naval victory at the Battle of the Nile, the pendulum of war swung so violently that by October Washington saw the possibility of a major military defeat in Europe of revolutionary France. He expressed his ardent wish, "on the principles of humanity and for the benevolent purpose of putting a stop to the further effusion of human blood, that the successful powers may know at what point to give cessation to the sword for the purpose of negotiation. It is not uncommon, however, in prosperous gales to forget that adverse winds may blow. Such *was* the case with France. Such *may* be the case of the coalesced powers against her."

On the principle that "a bystander sees more of the game generally than those who are playing it," Washington favored mediation by neutral powers. Did the old man sometimes envision himself, as the most famous neutral in the world, making his first trip across the Atlantic to help lay down "the best and surest foundation for the peace and happiness of mankind without regard to this, that, or the other nation"? If, ignoring for the moment the weight of his years, the old hero indulged such a dream, he never committed it to paper.[29]

Pointing gleefully to another upheaval in the French Directory, Federalists were rubbing their hands together in anticipation of a restoration of the French monarchy when, to their extreme horror, Adams decided at long last to unleash his embassy to the Directory. The Federalists regarded this as a disastrous measure which would encourage the Republicans in the United States and perhaps unite the nation as a military ally with the sinking French revolutionaries. Washington was shocked and puzzled. The governmental change in France had, it seemed to him, opened wide a door through which Adams could retreat from his unfortunate move towards negotiation. That Adams should have slammed shut the door was "to those of us who are not behind the curtain," in "the present state of European affairs, incomprehensible."[30]

Turning to the only force that could possibly stop Adams, the Federalists barraged Washington with importuning that he intervene. If the Father of his Country had agreed, he would have closed his career by opposing what was to turn out to be one of the happiest strokes in the whole history of American diplomacy. To McHenry, Washington wrote, "I have been stricken dumb, and I believe it is better that I should remain mute. . . . I have for some time past viewed the political concerns of the United States with an anxious and painful eye. They appear to me to be moving by hasty strides to some awful crisis, but in what they will result, that Being who sees, foresees, and directs all things alone can tell. The vessel is afloat or very nearly so, and considering myself as a passenger only, I shall trust to the mariners whose duty it is to watch, to steer it into a safe port."[31]

This statement was George Washington's last important political act.

44

Black Mount Vernon

I N 1791 Washington spirited a group of his blacks back from the Presidential Mansion to Mount Vernon lest his possession of them be undermined by a Pennsylvania law that automatically freed slaves kept in that state for a period of time.° Six years later, Washington, as he prepared to return home from the Presidency, saw in the same Pennsylvania law an opportunity secretly to free some of his slaves. By the simple expedient of leaving the blacks behind, he could manumit them so inconspicuously that the southern opposition to the government need never find out.

Washington, indeed, covered his tracks so well that his act remained hidden from history until this writer chanced upon it when making a routine check of a seemingly trivial correspondence.

Shortly after his return to Mount Vernon, Washington ordered from his Philadelphia tailor, James McAlpin, some clothes for his step-grandson: "1 dress coat, 1 common coatee, etc." After McAlpin had sent his bill, accompanied with some information, Washington replied from Mount Vernon on July 3, 1796. The money, the General stated, would be paid by his agent in Philadelphia. Then Washington continued, "I thank you for the information respecting John Cline, but shall give myself no further concern about him, for it was always my intention to have given him his freedom (as I did the other servants under similar circumstances) when I retired from public life, had he remained with me."[1]

Washington's cook Hercules, dreading a return from the city to Mount Vernon, ran away in Philadelphia before Washington could (if such was

---

° See chapter 12.

his intention) willingly let him go. The practical problem this created demonstrated that it was almost impossible to proceed in Virginia on anything but the meanest scale without slaves. All Washington's efforts to hire a free replacement for Hercules failed. After months had passed with the serving of inferior meals, Washington realized that he would either have to recover Hercules or buy another black chef. Since he had resolved never "to hold another slave by purchase," he was faced with a quandary: Which was worse, to buy a new slave or to reclaim an escaped one? Perhaps it was the claims of his pocketbook that made him try to have Hercules apprehended. However, all ended happily. Washington finally found a white housekeeper who could cook. Hercules remained free.[2]

The one occasion when Washington made truly major efforts to recover a slave involved heartache — but it was not the black's emotions that were lacerated. Martha, her maternal instincts frustrated by the deaths of all her four children, mothered not only her grandchildren but every white child who appeared at Mount Vernon. She brought up two black girls, Oney Judge and a companion, almost, so Washington was to write, as if they were her own children. Becoming perfect mistresses of the needle, the girls sat by Martha in her parlor, sewing day after day. That the girls were becoming young women went unobserved: no plans were made for their future. An eccentric Frenchman who called often at the Presidential Mansion was seen in conversation with Oney Judge, but this was not particularly noticed until the slave disappeared. As the Frenchman — he was now thought to be insane — ceased his visits, it was assumed that he had eloped with the girl, who was believed to have had no funds of her own. Martha's feelings were deeply hurt, and, since she feared that the Frenchman would get the girl pregnant and then abscond, her anxieties were greatly aroused.

During September 1796 Washington wrote Hamilton requesting that the collector of customs at Portsmouth, New Hampshire, where Oney Judge had been seen, should procure her return. "What will be the best method to effect it, is difficult for me to say. If inquiries are made openly, her seducer (for she is simple and inoffensive herself) would take alarm and adopt measures (if he is not tired of her) to secrete or remove her." It would be best to seize her by surprise and put her on a vessel bound for Alexandria. In one of those ungrammatical sentences which usually indicated some stress or emotion, Washington concluded, "I am sorry to give you or anyone else trouble on such a trifling occasion, but the ingratitude of the girl . . . (and Mrs. Washington's desire to recover her) ought not to escape with impunity, if it can be avoided."³

Joseph Whipple, the Portsmouth collector of customs, found Oney Judge and summoned her, pretending to offer employment. He reported that, "after a cautious examination," he concluded that she had been carried away not by any seducer but by "a thirst for freedom." When "uninfluenced by fear," she expressed great affection for her master and mistress, with a willingness to return and continue to be their slave for the rest of their lives. However, so continued Whipple, she would rather suffer death than be handed on to any other person. Whipple stated that he had persuaded her to trust the Washingtons, but the arguments of her friends in Portsmouth's free black community had made her change her mind. She wished definite assurances. The customs collector added that public opinion in Portsmouth was in favor of freeing all Negroes. Washington's only recourse would be to induce the United States Attorney in New Hampshire to invoke the Constitution in an effort to make that anti-slavery state return Oney.⁴

Washington refused to accept the idea that Martha's protégée had not been carried off by the Frenchman — he had lately received confirmation "through other channels." He would not be at all surprised if she were pregnant. He had heard that she had at one time expressed a desire to return to Mrs. Washington. If she would come home willingly, she would be forgiven by her mistress and all would be as before. Otherwise, he still hoped that "compulsory means" would be used. He added that he did not advocate "such violent measures . . . as would excite a mob or riot . . . or even uneasy sensations in the minds of well-disposed citizens. Rather than either of these should happen I would forgo her services altogether, and the example also which is of infinitely more importance."⁵

Whipple replied that the girl could not be spirited off without exciting a riot. Thus, Oney Judge had achieved her freedom.⁶

Washington intended, of course, to free all his slaves either before or after his death. He nonetheless felt that he could not give Oney Judge the assurance she desired. "It would," he explained, "neither be politic or just to reward *unfaithfulness* with a premature preference, and thereby discontent beforehand the minds of all her fellow servants who by their steady attachment are far more deserving than herself of favor."⁷

As he prepared to return from the Presidency to Mount Vernon, Washington wrote his overseer to encourage a young slave called Cyrus to fit himself "for a waiting man. . . . To be sober, attentive to his duty, honest, obliging and cleanly are the qualifications necessary." The President obviously fancied "afro" haircuts: Cyrus was to get a strong horn comb and use it so that his hair would grow long. If everything worked out, the young man would "become useful to me at the same time that he would exalt and benefit himself."[8]

In 1799, Washington enumerated his household slaves as two cooks, seven servants (three men and four women), and two postilions.[9] It was with these slaves, who participated to some extent in his own standard of living, that Washington was most personally concerned. Although on occasion he vented his rage upon them,* he was usually considerate of their feelings. He had indulged Hercules (before the cook ran away) by allowing him to keep his incompetent son around the kitchen as a useless helper; and his former body servant Will, now crippled and an alcoholic, was a constant presence around the Presidential Mansions and at Mount Vernon.[11]

Should a house slave sicken, he received the best medical attention. Consternation reigned in the Mansion House when a small dog belonging to one of the ladies bit Washington's body servant, Christopher, and shortly thereafter, as Washington wrote, "died (I do think) in a state of madness." Christopher was rushed "to a medical gentleman in Alexandria, who has cut out, as far as he could, the place bit, applying ointment to keep it open, and put the boy under a course of mercury." This, however, so little relieved the general anxiety that Christopher was rushed off to Dr. William Stoy of Lebanon, Pennsylvania, who had a reputation for curing hydrophobia. Washington begged Stoy to spare no expense and let him know as soon as possible what the chances were. Young Lafayette, who had departed from Mount Vernon in the middle of the crisis, asked in his letters for news of Christopher. Washington replied that not only had Christopher been cured but he had come back with such faith in the doctor that he would not object to being bitten by a dog at the height of hydrophobia.[12]

What was Washington's dismay some two years later, to discover by the chance of a note picked up in his yard, that Christopher was planning to flee with his wife (a mulatto belonging to a neighboring landowner) on a boat about to sail from Alexandria. The matter was somehow patched

---

* Mrs. Liston wrote that Washington had "acquired a uniform command over his passions on public occasions, but in private and particularly with his servants, its violence sometimes broke out."[10] The "servants" whom Mrs. Liston encountered at this time (in Philadelphia) were undoubtedly white, yet it is hard to believe that Washington would not have been equally free with his slaves.

up, and Christopher reappears in history standing, still a slave, hour after hour by his master's deathbed.[13]

Significant of the human thrust for freedom was the fact that the house slaves, who were less debased by their environment and usually had skills with which to support themselves, were, despite their privileged position and even the affection of their employers, most likely to run away.°

When Washington had been, between the Revolution and the Presidency, a settled resident of Mount Vernon, he had brought forward so many of his promising blacks that in 1788 the overseers of all his five farms were slaves who, even if they were not paid salaries, lived in snug houses on an elevated scale. Davey, he wrote, "carries on his business as well as the white overseers and with more quietness than any of them." During his absence as President, this effort collapsed; white overseers took over. And after his return, nervousness gripped him. In 1798, when Washington was one overseer short, the black foreman virtually managed Dogue Run plantation. Washington considered making the arrangement permanent, "but when I perceive but too clearly that the Negroes are growing more and more insolent and difficult to govern, I am more inclined to incur the expense of an overseer than to hazard the management and peace of the place to a Negro, provided I can get a good overseer on moderate terms."[15]

For his own sake as well as theirs, Washington had from the first done his best to train black artisans. He attempted nothing elaborate,† and even what he attempted did not go well. He felt that he could not, without utterly undermining discipline, communicate, until the moment came, his determination to free his slaves; and thus the black artisans saw no incentive to become skillful. Why should they labor to save money for their master? He specified in contracts with white artisans that they teach their skills to the blacks, but also relied on them to keep the slaves at work. Suffering with a head carpenter more interested in bottles than saws, Washington complained, "In the manner they conduct under his su-

---

° Field hands did, of course, on occasion abscond. Washington felt that efforts should be made to recover the fugitives and punish them by whipping lest there be a mass exodus from his slave quarters. Concerning Caesar, he wrote significantly that the slave would probably get completely away since he could read if not write. However, he hesitated to have the runaways advertised for in his name, and forbade it in papers north of Virginia.[14]

† In 1799, Washington enumerated his slave artisans as follows: two smiths; two bricklayers; six carpenters; three coopers; one lame shoemaker; two gardeners; two millers; five distillery workers; three wagoners and carters; nine spinners and knitters, two male (one lame) and seven female.[16]

perintendency, it would be for my interest to set them free rather than give them their victuals and clothes."[17]

After Washington's departure for the Presidency, he lost contact. Thus he wrote in 1795 that he did not know where "among my people" to find a black fit to be trained as a gardener: "The children of Daphne at the River Farm are among the best disposed Negroes I have, but I do not recollect whether there be any of a fit size."[18]

If the artisans could see no incentive, how much less the field hands! Washington had under his control, spread out over the five farms, the population of a large village: in 1799, 317 blacks. They staged no overt revolts, but they worked and obeyed orders only when they were forced to, and then to the least extent that was feasible. Knowing that they would be fed and clothed and housed in the same manner whether or not Washington made money, they were concerned with their own interests, which in no way paralleled his.

Although there may well have been Virginia estates on which slaves moved in lockstep to the bellowed commands of whip-wielding demonically efficient overseers, Mount Vernon was not one of them. Mount Vernon was a whirlpool of anarchy where all managerial efforts hardly sufficed to keep the confusion from overflowing the banks.

Slaves could not be imprisoned without giving them a vacation and penalizing the owner. Having little or no private property, they could not be fined. They were not permitted the self-respect that made them amenable to scoldings or disgrace.° Although house slaves could be demoted to the fields and field hands threatened with being sold to the deep south or the Indies, such punishments were extreme and rarely carried through. The only truly available means of correction — common then also for whites† — was corporal. However, much resort to the lash brutalized overseers, bothered Washington, and, as Washington pointed out, often engendered "evils worse than the disease" by making the victims even more sullen and uncooperative. When he was in residence, Washington ruled that no slave could be whipped until a written complaint had been submitted to and passed by him.[20]

° As Washington put it, "Blacks are capable of much labor but having (I am speaking generally) no ambition to establish a *good* name, they are too regardless of a *bad* one."[19]

† Whippings were, for instance, the standard punishment for common soldiers in all armies, including the American army during the Revolution. The younger Washington had less objection to whipping white soldiers than the elder Washington had to whipping slaves.

Washington's formula to achieve order and productive activity was for the overseers to be perpetually with their charges: in the daytime directing and presenting good examples in the fields; at night, home and sober, listening for suspicious sounds. In fact, the overseers were the most discouraging link in the plantation chain. The slaves suffered from their brutalities and were plenty clever enough to take advantage of their weaknesses. If an overseer absented himself from the fields, the slaves lolled in the shade; if he went off visiting, the slaves leapt onto the plough horses and rode all night, leaving the animals too fagged out for ploughing. If an overseer got drunk or stole, the slaves blackmailed him with threats that, unless he reduced tasks and discipline, they would report his derelictions to Washington.[21]

Complaints by the slaves of sickness presented a nexus of problems. Washington mourned that some overseers, regarding "these poor creatures" as scarcely more than "a draught horse or ox," heartlessly took no care of them if they were too ill to work. Or the sufferer would be equally heartlessly driven into the fields, where the sight of his hollow face and wavering body would anger and outrage Washington as he rode along. But if a slave were allowed to escape labor by pretended illness, the whole work crew would soon come down with mysterious diseases. Washington suspected that some of his chronic invalids, who ate and did nothing, were chronic malingerers, and there were certain mothers who insisted that their children were perpetually ill.[22]

Concerning one complaining slave whom Washington believed perfectly healthy, the General wrote, "He has had doctors enough already, of all colors and sexes, and to no effect." Washington's mainstay for medical crises, black as well as white, was his old friend Dr. Craik. It was not untypical of Washington to give cruel orders and then rescind them. Thus in 1792, he wrote his manager not to waste money on a doctor if a slave were clearly past help. But two weeks later he ordered that sick slaves should receive medical attention from the very start to the very end of all illnesses.[23]

When the slaves temporarily slipped the moorings that were supposed to keep them on their farms, they found innumerable ways of harassing their master to their own amusement or profit. If the doors were not sternly watched to prevent the entry of any offspring but those of the privileged house servants, the Mansion House would be awash with black children, running around and breaking things. The flowers in the gardens were picked and trampled; vegetables and fruit disappeared. A strict quota on dogs had to be established and then if possible enforced to keep the plantation from becoming a sea of canines, each trained by his black owner, or so Washington believed, to assist in clandestine hunting and keep watch during robberies: "It is astonishing," the master commented, "to see the command under which their dogs are." Robberies were the rule rather than the exception! Anything portable that was not locked up or nailed down or kept under constant surveillance tended to disappear. It would be eaten by a slave, or carried by a slave (or an overseer) either to a "tippling house" kept by a nearby poor white or into the emporium of a crooked merchant in Alexandria.[24]

Washington lived long before the six-hour day. Farmers commonly worked from dawn to sunset, and boys labored to the best of their strength beside them. (Our schools still honor the long summer holiday originally designed to make this possible.) When their kitchen chores gave them leisure or there was a harvest to bring in, white women and girls worked in the fields beside their males. It was thus not altogether tyrannical that Washington expected his slaves to waste no daylight. His presumption was "that every laborer (male or female) does as much in twenty-four hours as their strength, without endangering their health or constitution, will allow of."*[25]

From the age of fourteen, children were considered part of the regular work force; younger teen-agers did household chores. Cripples were, if possible, found work that would fit with their infirmities. The aged and the truly disabled were supported in idleness.

The men and women were separated into different work gangs. They labored on the farm where they were domiciled, except for roving gangs like the ditchers. In an effort to keep the overseers active, Washington established a system by which they had to account weekly for the number of work days assigned to their labor force. All lost hours had to be explained.[26]

In reporting on American agriculture to the British expert Arthur Young, Washington wrote that white labor was very expensive because of the ease with which a man could obtain land over the mountains, but high wages were not the worst expense; white laborers were "accustomed to better fare than I believe the laborers of almost any other country."

---

* Washington himself was usually at work before either the sun or his field hands had arisen. However, he took more time out for dinner.

Washington did not add that those white workingmen who remained in central Virginia were not the most progressive or the most honest.° He wrote in 1792 that he had "more white people about my house than are governed properly in my absence." It made little difference to him whether the thieves who stole his goods were white or black.[28]

While the wages and keep of a white farmhand cost from ten to fifteen pounds sterling a year, a black cost only eight to twelve. In 1790, he analyzed his expenses for a typical group of twenty-three slaves. Only ten were old enough to work. The ten laborers received annually for clothing "sixty ells of the best German Ozenburgs, fifty yards best cotton," ten pairs of plaid stockings and shoes. He calculated half or perhaps a third of this for the young. All twenty-three Negroes needed about five new blankets a year. They ate sixty-nine barrels of corn, ten barrels of pickled herring, "meat now and then, suppose 500 weight in all," receiving also "milk, fat, etc." Ground was often allotted them for gardening, and "the privelege given them to raise dunghill fowl for their own use." Corn husks were supplied to feed the fowl. For the twenty-three slaves, a doctor would ordinarily be called in six times a year and a midwife twice. When Washington totaled these costs against the value of what the slaves produced, he ended up with a loss.[29]

Washington never summarized how his field hands were housed, and modern efforts to determine this matter must at best be hazardous. The plantation was large, and various alterations took place with the passage of years, and the relevant structures were not placed on permanent foundations subject to archeological research. It seems that there were basically two kinds of buildings: cabins built by the slaves themselves and larger quarters put up by Washington's carpenters and masons. The cabins, often made of logs chinked with mud, with dirt floors, and chimneys of daubed laths, were not unlike those occupied by the troops at Valley Forge and by many a frontier family. The larger structures seem to have resembled the longhouses of northern Indians or (if you please) an old-fashioned railroad sleeping car, the accommodations being a series of double berths on both sides of a center aisle. One fireplace burned in the center of each unit. Washington did not pretend the quarters were comfortable, writing Arthur Young, "These buildings might not be thought good enough for the workmen or day laborers in your country."[30]

° Washington believed that the poor whites in his neighborhood lived in part off his blacks. They could not without encroaching on his property "and their connection with my Negroes . . . live upon the miserable land they occupy."[27]

The Polish revolutionary and writer Julian Ursyn Niemcewicz, who visited Mount Vernon in the late 1790's, described the cabins as "more miserable than the most miserable of the cottages of our peasants. The husband and wife sleep on a mean pallet, the children on the ground. A very bad fireplace, some utensils for cooking, but in the middle of the poverty some cups and a teapot. . . . A very small garden planted with vegetables was close by, and five or six hens, one leading ten to fifteen chickens. It is the only comfort that is permitted them, for they may not keep either ducks, geese, or pigs. They sell the poultry in Alexandria, and produce for themselves some amenities. . . .

"General Washington," Niemcewicz continued, "treats his slaves far more humanely than do his fellow citizens of Virginia. . . . Either from habit or from natural humor disposed to gaiety, I have never seen the blacks sad. Last Sunday, there were about thirty divided into two groups, and playing at prisoner's base. There were jumps and gambols as if they had rested all week."[31]

It was common for slave owners to discourage permanent marriages among blacks as creating complications in the mobility of individual slaves: a family was defined as a mother and her children. Washington adhered for a considerable time to this conventional attitude. When in 1786 he made a list of his slaves, wives were noted only for the four black overseers. Before the Presidency, Washington was inclined to be doubting and annoyed when a slave claimed to be married, although he usually based his actions on acceptance of the claim. Since the ownership of children descended down the female line, children were commonly identified through their mothers: Washington would, for instance, refer to a boy as "Doll's Will." For years, when slaves assumed last names — Oney Judge, Christopher Sheels, Will (Billy) Lee — Washington agreed to the appellations more to indulge the slaves than because he took them seriously. However, at about the time that he decided to make an effort to free his slaves, he became greatly concerned with slave marriages. He must have strongly encouraged them, since the list of slaves he made in 1799 recorded the great majority of the adult slaves as married to specific blacks.[32]

Taking slave marriages seriously greatly complicated the problems of manumission since almost exactly half of the slaves on the Mount Vernon plantations were legally bound in a manner that made freeing them impossible. These were the "dower" slaves who had come to Washington at the time of his marriage. Attached, with the progeny of the women, to the

Custis estate, they would automatically, on Martha's death, become the property of her grandchildren. They had copiously intermarried with the slaves Washington controlled.

While still in Philadelphia, he had expressed great concern over the dislocations that would flow from his ability to free some members of a family but not others: "To part will be affecting and trying events, happen when it will." He decided to shrug the matter off for the time being, since the problem was not an immediate one, but it kept bothering him to such an extent that he ordered his overseer to determine at once, by listing marriages, how many slave couples would have to be separated.*[33]

Although Washington worried about placing members of the same families on the opposite sides of the great divide of freedom, he did not feel it necessary to house husbands and wives on the same Mount Vernon farms. Nor did he, if slaves found partners on neighboring plantations, try to unite the couples by purchase or exchange. Saturday night is indicated as the standard time when couples could get together. Older children were not, if work patterns intervened, kept housed with their mothers. There seem to have been day nurseries that freed the mothers of small children for their labors. In the larger quarters, there were probably communal kitchens, since some females unconnected with the Mansion House were designated as cooks.[34]

Although emotional Christianity became a great outlet for slaves at a later date, Christianizing slaves was during Washington's lifetime neither prevalent nor encouraged. As a philosophical deist, Washington felt no duty to convert his slaves. In his 1799 listing, a sixty-year-old dower Negro seems to be identified as "Mint'r," but the writing is so blurred that the presumed abbreviation cannot be read with complete certainty.[35] This confused note remains the only indication that the blacks, although allowed holidays on Christmas, Easter, etc., had any Christian activity of their own. If tribal religions wove through the slave quarters — during his younger days many of Washington's blacks were born in Africa — the proprietor made no mention of them.

Washington, who had known slaves since his birth, acted on the belief that their greatest satisfaction came from living with old friends in a familiar atmosphere. Their greatest dread was of transplantation to strange places among strangers. Undoubtedly, this conviction was a major motive

---

* What he would do with the dower slaves if he relinquished his farms and freed the others was another matter on which he was glad to postpone decision. Perhaps he could find some reasonable way to hire them out.

for his professed unwillingness to buy or sell a slave. As far back as his Revolutionary service, he had ordered his manager not to move any of his blacks, even to one of his own distant plantations, unless they agreed. They almost never agreed. When he wrote that he wished to "gratify" a slave, he was sure to be explaining some uneconomic action that prevented the breaking of familiar ties. Occasionally he backslid. In 1786 he reluctantly accepted, lest he get no payment on a debt, "six or more slaves" belonging to John Francis Mercer. During 1787, his need for a bricklayer made him buy Neptune only to find that "he seems a great deal disconcerted on account of a wife which he says he has. . . . This also embarrasses me, as I am unwilling to hurt the feelings of anyone." Washington intended to keep him for a while "to see if I can reconcile him to the separation (seeing her now and then)." If Neptune could not be reconciled, Washington would send him back.[36]

Eyewitness accounts exist of blacks weeping when Martha departed, rejoicing when George Washington returned,[37] and these can be interpreted, as have been similar accounts concerning other celebrated slaveholders, to demonstrate that the proprietor was loved by his Negroes. Since the slaves left almost no written records, their emotions can only be fathomed through imaginations too easily colored by the preconceptions of the imaginers. Certain it is that a yearning for the proprietors' presence could be purely practical. The owners served as a court of appeal from often brutal overseers. Washington did his best to restrain his overseers, and when his attention could be caught, he applied, within his judgment of the slave's role, justice.

Since Washington left a plethora of written records, his attitudes to what he called "my people" can be defined. His emotions were warm towards some of his house slaves but he never expressed for his field hands the affection he had expressed for the common soldiers during the Revolution. Concerning his blacks as a group he felt anxiety, frustration, pity, and guilt.*

Anxiety was endemic in all regions where the slaves greatly outnumbered the whites. It can be traced as far back in Virginia history as slavery can. Washington inherited it from his forefathers along with the institution itself. His fears were sharpened in 1791 by the bloody slave revolt

---

* It should perhaps be reiterated that, despite the snickering rumors that circulate, not one shred of conceivably authentic evidence has been discovered which links Washington sexually with any slave.

in Santo Domingo (Haiti),[38] and he dreaded in the Revolution and again during the war scare involving France that the enemies of the United States would "arm our slaves against us."

Washington's frustration was grounded on the unwillingness and disability of the uneducated, unmotivated slaves (and their debased overseers) to cultivate the land neatly and intensively, to carry out any innovations or use any machinery that human ingenuity could break. The extent to which the blacks dominated farming at Mount Vernon is demonstrated by Washington's plaint that his English farmer, James Bloxham, having been unable to persuade the slaves of his methods, had slipped inadvertently into theirs.[39]

Pity and guilt made Washington determined to free his slaves, but did not induce him to attempt radical alterations in their lot while they remained in bondage. This was in keeping with the eighteenth-century philosophical conception that freedom was so basic a human need that without it one can achieve nothing.[40] As it would be useless to urge a chained man to run, the degradation inherent in slavery was only remediable by breaking the chains.* Although Washington was to provide that his slaves should, after freedom, be taught to read and write, he made no effort to establish literacy in his slave quarters.

Complaining all the while that his slaves loafed and wasted his substance because they knew that they would be supported however they behaved, Washington believed that the manner in which he supported them was justified as commensurate with what they in fact earned. Nature testified that their way of life was healthy. The group of twenty-three slaves concerning whom Washington had written a summary augmented in nine years to forty. Between 1786 and 1799, Washington's total holding rose, almost altogether by natural increase, from 216 to 317. Of this latter figure, about half, 42 percent, were either too young or too old to work. The most abundant product of the Mount Vernon plantation was, indeed, black children.[41]

In August 1799 Washington wrote that he was supporting at great expense more Negroes by a full half "than can be employed to any advantage in the farming system, and I shall never turn planter" again.† He could, of

---

* This conception justified a way out of a serious dilemma: educating slaves could only increase their dissatisfaction as long as they were held in bondage. Washington believed (as he often noted) that discipline — nay, even safety — required no major shake-ups until the whole complex was shattered.
† Planters grew tobacco, which had to be cultivated with a hoe, and this required much labor. Substituting a plough for hoes in the cultivation of corn, wheat, grass, etc., greatly reduced the need for farmhands.

course, have cut the Gordian knot, showering himself with wealth, had he been willing to sell the superflux. He was not even willing to hire them out. Slaves, he noted, could not be leased "in families to any advantage, and to disperse the families I have an utter aversion." His blacks might be maltreated by the renters, or, even if they were not, might bother Washington with "perpetual complaints" which would make him "uneasy" about problems that it was beyond his authority to solve.[42]

Washington continued sporadically, whenever opportunity offered, his efforts to rent the farms on terms that would not include the slaves, but, as his declining years passed, the end remained unachieved. When he drew up his will in July 1799, a final decision could no longer be postponed. The provisions he worked out reveal that the old man was unable to visualize any practical solution to the dilemmas involved in bringing freedom to black Mount Vernon.

To free, as he did, all the slaves he controlled was soothing to his conscience and an ultimate public testimony to the convictions he had for so long felt himself forced, by circumstance and political necessity, to keep secret. But what about Martha?

Surely his wife, who was not strong and was also older than he, should be spared, if she survived him, the dislocations inherent in so great a turnover for some hundred and fifty individuals, a situation further complicated by the unavoidable but painful separation between his own and the dower slaves. He decided not to free his slaves until "the decease of my wife." Then in the only turgid passage in the otherwise clear document, he explained, "To emancipate them during her life would, though earnestly wished by me, be attended with such insuperable difficulties on account of their intermixture by marriage with the dower Negroes, as to excite the most painful sensations, if not disagreeable consequences from the latter, while both descriptions are in the occupancy of the same proprietor."

Reasoning that the separation of the blacks would come more easily when the whole estate was broken up — the plantation was on Martha's death to be divided between three heirs — Washington, who had always seen a danger of convulsing his slave quarters with premature hints of manumission, chose to ignore the situation Martha would find herself in when some hundred and fifty individuals eagerly awaited her death to set them free.

What generosity could solve came easily. The old and infirm among Washington's freed slaves were to be "comfortably clothed and fed by my heirs while they live." Children whose parents could or would not take care of them were to be supported until they were old enough to be legally bound as if they were white apprentices. They were to serve until the age of twenty-five, "be taught to read and write, and brought up to some useful occupation agreeable to the laws of the Commonwealth of Virginia providing for the support of orphan and other poor children." In other words, they were not to be discriminated against, but gathered into the white world as if they were not black.

For helping the able-bodied to adjust to a new life and secure their livelihood Washington had no plan. His only provision for them was aimed at foiling the harpies who got possession of free blacks and sold them farther south or in the Indies: "I do hereby expressly forbid the sale or transportation out of the said Commonwealth [Virginia] of any slave I may die possessed of, under any pretext whatsoever." [43]

The upshot at Mount Vernon is best described in the words of Abigail Adams, who visited there in December 1800, almost exactly a year after Washington's death. The estate, she wrote her sister, "is now going into decay. Mrs. Washington with all her fortune finds it difficult to support her family, which consists of three hundred slaves. One hundred and fifty of them are now to be liberated, men with wives and young children who have never seen an acre beyond the farm are now about to quit it, and go adrift into the world without horse, home, or friend. Mrs. Washington is distressed for them. At her own expense she has cloaked them all, and very many of them are already miserable at the thought of their lot. The aged she retains at their request; but she is distressed for the fate of others. She feels a parent and a wife. Many of these who are liberated have married with what are called the dower Negroes, so that they quit all their connections — yet what could she do in the state in which they were left by the General, to be free at her death? She did not feel as though her life was safe in their hands, many of whom would be told that it was their interest to get rid of her. She therefore was advised to set them all free at the close of the year."

Mrs. Adams then launched into a passage denouncing "the baleful effects of slavery." [44]

Concerning the adult slaves Washington freed, Washington Custis remembered, "Although many of them, with a view to their liberation, had been instructed in the mechanic trades, yet they succeeded very badly as freemen: so true is the axiom 'that the hour that makes man a slave takes

[446]

half his worth away.'" The General's heirs did not limit their support to blacks who had been infirm at his death. Taking others back under the wing of his estate, they made their last pension payment in 1833. Washington's provisions for preparing the children for a white world could not be carried through before his Virginia neighbors passed laws against educating blacks.[45]

Washington's record in regard to slavery is obviously open to attack from those who have not had to walk the trails he walked (and who may not be traversing their own trails more successfully). Was his behavior unworthy? He certainly would not have defended what he did. He knew that he was inconsistent, confused, and not always altruistic. He knew that he had found no real solutions. Shortly after he had first launched on his imperfect efforts to find a practical way to free his slaves, he had cried out to an old friend, "With respect to the other species of property concerning which you ask my opinion, I shall frankly declare to you that I do not like even to think, much less talk of it." [46]

Perhaps Washington's record can be most fairly assessed in relation to other Virginians who faced the same problems in the same years. In this context, Washington shone. Modern historians have completely refuted the conception that during Washington's later years (before the wide dissemination of the cotton gin) slavery was weakening in Virginia. As Robert McColley states, "If an occasional Virginian abandoned the slave system, many more adopted it. The number of slaveholders was always increasing." In 1790, only 8 percent of the blacks in Virginia were free. William H. Freehling tells us, "Race prejudice made emancipationists rare in Virginia, and almost nonexistent in South Carolina."[47]

Compare Washington's record to Jefferson's: Jefferson, who urged practical steps against slavery as a younger man, limited himself after 1785 to expressing libertarian sentiments in letters. He lived high, and between 1783 and 1794 sold at various times some fifty slaves to meet his debts and expenses. In 1819, he instructed his manager, "I consider the labor of a breeding woman as no object, and that a child raised every two years is of more profit than the crop of the best laboring man. In this, as in all other cases, Providence has made our interests and our duties coincide perfectly. . . . I must pray you to inculcate upon the overseers that it is not their labor but their increase which is the first consideration with us." In his will, Jefferson, while freeing five slaves to whom he was related by blood, retained some 260 in bondage. It has been claimed that he had no other choice, since there was then a law that no newly emancipated slave could remain in Virginia. However, Virginia was not the only place in the world, and exemptions could be secured. Jefferson, indeed, asked in his will that the Virginia legislature make exceptions for the five slaves he did free.[48]

There can be no doubt that on the issue of slavery Washington was out of accord with the actions — if not the sometime professions — of his home state, the rest of the south, and the Virginians who led the opposition to his government.

45

Farmer Washington

THE approach of a small dome, bobbing over the crest of one of the Mount Vernon hills, set overseer and slaves into a frenzy of activity. Washington's blond, colorless skin had always been susceptible to sunlight, and now in his old age, after he had been kept indoors for so many years, his broad-brimmed white hat failed to give adequate protection. Attached to his saddlebow by a long stick, an umbrella swayed perpetually over his head.[1]

Now no pack of hounds fanned out ahead of him as they had done when he had hoped that his day's adventures would be varied by the starting of a fox. Hounds had been banned from Mount Vernon lest they molest the General's pet deer. He rode alone, in plain, drab clothes, dismounting to open and close gates.[2]

Mount Vernon had never in his lifetime been fertile: thin, depleted topsoil over clay that repelled moisture. As a younger man, he had labored to enrich the soil, to prevent and repair washouts. During his two retirements after his two wars, years had stretched ahead, and every year there had been some improvement. But during his virtual absence as President, everything had gone backward, and now there was no time; not for experiments, not for long-range plans, not for improving his stock by crossbreeding, perhaps not even for getting the farms decent again. The death of his brother, Charles Washington, brought him "awful and affecting emotions. . . . I was the *first* and am now the *last* of my father's children by the second marriage. . . . When the summons comes, I shall endeavor to obey it with a good grace."[3]

The man who had efficiently managed a nation found very irritating the evidence which he saw every day that he was failing to manage his estate efficiently. Tools lay helter-skelter, exposed to the weather. He ordered that less land be more intensively cultivated,⁴ but ride where he would, he could see no intensive cultivation. Only scraggly hedges where he had wanted impermeable "live fences"; only stunted corn and buckwheat so incompetently ploughed under that it would probably fail in its function of fertilizing the fields; only wispy ditches inadequate for drainage during any real downpour.

His manager, the elderly Scotch farmer James Anderson, bore the brunt of the executive power that had managed a nation. When Washington pointed out deficiencies here and there and everywhere, Anderson always promised that they would instantly be rectified, but as Washington rode grimly from trouble spot to trouble spot, he found nothing had been done. This, he commented, "is not at all pleasant to a man who has practiced himself, and been accustomed to meet as much regularity as I have from others."⁵

At the end of December 1787 Washington expressed his dissatisfaction in a long letter to Anderson: the manager was wasting time shifting workers unnecessarily from one task to another; he was allowing carts to wait empty half a day for their loads, etc., and so forth, and so on. The Scot responded by requesting to resign at the end of 1798. If he had not been so interfered with, Anderson growled, he could have done better.⁶

It would be "strange and singular indeed," Washington replied, if the proprietor, who had to pay all the expenses, could say nothing without hurting his manager's feelings. He would "never relinquish the right of judging in my own concerns (though I may be pleased always to hear opinions) to any man living while I have the health and strength to look into my own business." The trouble seemed to be that Anderson had too much to do. Why did he not, while receiving the same salary, accept a reduction of his responsibilities to the distillery, the mill, and some of the fisheries?⁷

The distillery, in which Anderson had persuaded Washington to engage, showed possibilities of turning into a big business. There were five stills, capable of producing 12,000 gallons a year, into which Anderson fed rye and corn "in a certain proportion." Washington's hogs lived nearby off the residue. This operation, combined with the "commercial mill" which incorporated the most modern automated equipment, could process much more grain than Washington's own farms produced. They were often idle because other purchasers moved faster than Anderson did in contracting for neighboring crops. However, unlike Washington's farms, the distillery, mill, and fisheries brought in a flow of cash. Washington regarded them as his best means of support.[8]

If Anderson agreed to limit his activities, Washington would be able to handle his own farms without interference, but Anderson preferred to continue as before supervising the whole estate. Washington accepted Anderson's predeliction. Mount Vernon staggered along as before.[9]

The proprietor's dissatisfaction was given edge by the surprise appearance at Mount Vernon of an English agricultural expert. In the fall of 1797, Richard Parkinson, author of *The Experienced Farmer,* had responded to Washington's advertisement by expressing interest in renting Mount Vernon's River farm. Washington had replied that he would be glad to show him the land if Parkinson came to America. After that there was silence, until almost a year later word came that Parkinson was crossing the ocean on his way to River farm, bringing with him the famous racehorses Phenomenon and Cardinal Puff, six stallions, ten brood mares, enough bulls and cows to get five breeds of cattle started in America, a variety of highly bred boars and sows. The cargo would be unloaded at the Mount Vernon dock, and Washington would surely be glad to pay the freightage: £850.

Washington, who was about to leave for his consultation in Philadelphia concerning the army, expressed surprise and dismay: "When measures *commence* badly they seldom *end* well. I have nothing to do with him or his property." He instructed Anderson to refuse to pay the freight, to show Parkinson around, and, if it seemed as if the Englishman would rent River farm, to house and board the menagerie except the stallions. Such horses and "especially their keepers" were "generally very troublesome."[10]

Parkinson was not a gentleman — Anderson believed that the visitor's real objective at Mount Vernon was to get his job — but Washington expressed himself as "much flattered" by the presence of so distinguished an agriculturist. However, so Parkinson's account continued with obvious satisfaction, the General was soon "not well pleased with my conversation." The English farmer told the American hero that the barrenness of Mount Vernon was "beyond description." If Washington were to offer him 1200 acres as a present, he would not accept them.

To justify this stricture Parkinson had, of course, to treat Washington "with a great deal of frankness. . . . I gave him strong proofs of his mistakes" by comparing Mount Vernon with English farms. Washington supposed that he had "fine sheep° and a great quantity of them," but in fact he had on 3000 acres only a hundred "and those in very poor condition." Parkinson's own father, he told the General, had 600 acres and yet clipped 1100 sheep. The father got ten pounds of wool per fleece, the American not three. The elder Parkinson grew ten times as much wheat per acre as the General did — and so on down through all Washington's farming activities and possessions, except in one item: mules. Parkinson admired Washington's mules.

After he had made perfectly clear his opinion of Washington's farms, Parkinson refused an invitation to spend the night and departed. Washington sent Lear after him to ask whether he needed some money. He replied that he did and was handed a purse, "which I gladly accepted."[11]

After Nelly Custis Lewis had "dropped" expressions that she and her husband would like to live near Mount Vernon, Washington wrote the husband that he intended to will the couple Dogue Run farm, the mill and the distillery. Would not Lewis like to take them over now, paying the adequate rent which Washington's circumstances forced him to require? This would give Lewis employment: "Idleness is disreputable under any circumstances." The area contained an excellent building site. Should Washington change his mind about willing the land, he would repay any expenses Lewis incurred. Although he had no distant idea of any such change, "nor any suspicion that you or Nelly would conduct yourselves in such a manner as to incur my serious displeasure; yet at the same time that I am inclined to do justice to others, it behooves me to take care of myself by keeping the staff in my own hands."[12]

Washington had hardly made this offer before he half took some of it back. He still wished to sidetrack Anderson by moving him over to the distillery and mill. He could, of course, have discharged the contentious Scot out of hand, but he was "unwilling," so he wrote Lewis, "by any act of mine to hurt his feelings or . . . to lessen his respectability in the eyes of the public." After some further vacillation and confusion, Washington was frustrated by his kindness of heart. Anderson considered himself in the first instance a farmer and wished to remain so. Lewis took over, in addition to Dogue Run farm, the distillery and mill, while Anderson con-

---

° Actually, Washington mourned that during his absence as President his sheep had deteriorated to a point where they were almost worthless.

tinued to function bumblingly between Washington and the control of his other acres.[13]

One of Washington's last projects was drawing up a plan for the rotation of crops, beginning in 1800 and continuing through 1803, after which the cycle would repeat. Dealing with, in detail, every field and pasture, the manuscript ran to between 30,000 and 40,000 words, a prodigious labor of visualization and concentration which must have filled many hours a day for many weeks. Washington's object was to make "everything move like clockwork," make everyone know what to do every minute, which "would be less harassing to those who labor and more beneficial to those who employ them." Those who employ them! The plural seems to imply that Washington had undertaken this task only partly to instruct his own employee Anderson. He wished his heirs to continue to farm his beloved acres as he would have done.[14]

Washington's will, dated July 9, 1799 (which superseded another), represented even more elaborate preparation. To get clear how he would go about freeing his slaves, he listed them all on countless tables which made clear where they were housed, what was the occupation and family status of each. Another manuscript that ran on for page after page was a schedule of his land holdings outside Mount Vernon: twelve separate tracts in Virginia, four on the Ohio, five on the Great Kanawha, two in Maryland, one in Pennsylvania (the ancient site of Fort Necessity, his first military defeat), one in New York, three in the Northwest Territory, and two in Kentucky. For each tract, he summarized the history of its accession, and its physical features, then estimating its worth. All this done, he was ready to start on the will itself.

For the finished document, he ordered elegant paper, approximately 8⅛ by 6¼ inches, the watermark in the center of each sheet showing a goddess of agriculture seated upon a plough, holding in one hand a staff

The watermark in the paper Washington had specially prepared so that he could carefully inscribe on it his last will and testament. A tracing from the original. Courtesy of the Mount Vernon Ladies' Association

rising to a liberty cap, and in the other a flowering twig; the whole encircled with a broad band within which was written "GEORGE WASHINGTON." Using his most carefully elegant hand, spacing the lines evenly, breaking words without regard to syllabic structure so that the right-hand margin would be as straight as the left, Washington covered 28⅓ pages.

Although Washington had always had a taste for neatly elegant manuscripts, there may have been some heartache hidden in this effort to give exterior grandeur to what was for a man of his upbringing an unsatisfactory task. If only he had had children of his own, a son or even a son-in-law to carry on at Mount Vernon, how different, how much shorter the document would have been! As it was, his approach remained dynastic. He spread memorabilia and cash gifts to old friends and dependents, faithful servants and the heirs of these; he provided for the support of incapable slaves after they were freed, and set up an annuity plus immediate freedom for his crippled body servant Will. But none of these provisions were more than dents in the main body of his estate. Bequeathing to Lear lifetime use of the farm his faithful dependent occupied, Washington stipulated that it should return to his own estate at Lear's death. In providing that all his property not specifically willed — mostly the lands outside Mount Vernon — be sold and the proceeds divided into twenty-three parts, he assigned all the parts to relations.

Martha was to have most of the estate for her lifetime. Then Mount Vernon was to be broken up into three farms. The Mansion House, nearby acres, and his own papers were willed to his nephew Bushrod Washington, partly because he had agreed with Bushrod's father, John Augustine Washington, "while we were both bachelors" that, if he fell during the French and Indian War, that favorite brother, who was managing the estate, could have it. The other two sections went one to the Lewises and the other to his and Martha's double nephews, the two sons of George Augustine Washington and Fanny Bassett. Washington Custis was so well off on the Custis side that it was unnecessary to provide for him handsomely.

Charitable bequests, other than the many provisions for individuals, went altogether to education, partly for the poor and partly for future national leaders. The will contained another of Washington's lectures on the importance to national union of a national university.

Washington boasted that in the preparation of the document "no professional character" had been consulted. He had, "although it has occupied many of my leisure hours to digest," drawn it up himself. He trusted it was "plain and explicit," but provided, in case of dispute, for arbitration.

A fascinating opportunity had been presented the devising Washington by a box, made of the oak that had sheltered Sir William Wallace after the Battle of Fallkirk, which the Earl of Buchan had given him with a request to pass it, at his death, to the American who should appear to merit it best. That Washington should hesitate what to do with the box must seem amazing to the millions of Americans who have down the years been indoctrinated with the idea that Washington had become little more than a puppet for Alexander Hamilton. Here, conveniently at hand, was a chance to designate Hamilton as his successor! Washington willed the box back to Lord Buchan.

"The family vault at Mount Vernon requiring repairs and being improperly situated besides, I desire that a new one of brick, and upon a larger scale, may be built at the foot of what is commonly called the vineyard enclosure, on the ground which is marked out,* in which my remains, with those of my deceased relatives (now in the old vault) and such others of my family as may choose to be entombed there, may be deposited. And it is my express desire that my corpse may be interred in a private manner, without parade or funeral oration." [15]

The old warrior, the old President, the great hero wanted no marching troops, no solemn dignitaries, no American Westminster Abbey. He wished to be buried quietly, beside his own relations, on a hillside of the childhood home he had always loved.

---

* This vault, the present one, was not actually built until 1830–1831.

46

Death of a Hero

O N December 12, 1799, Washington entered in his diary: "Morning cloudy. Wind to northeast and mercury 33. A large circle round the moon last night. At about ten o'clock it began to snow, soon after to hail, and then to a settled cold rain. Mercury 28 at night."[1]

His secretary, Tobias Lear, remembered that the storm started shortly after Washington had ridden out to inspect his farms. "As he never regarded the weather, he kept out from about ten (A.M.) till three o'clock." After his return, Lear carried him some letters to frank. Having franked them, Washington said the weather was too bad for a servant to go to the post office.[2]

"I observed to him," so Lear's account continues, "that I was afraid he had got wet. He said, No; his greatcoat had kept him dry — but his neck appeared wet and the snow was hanging on his hair. . . . He came to dinner without changing his dress. In the evening, he appeared as well as usual."[3]

Washington's journal note for December 13 reads, "Morning snowing and about three inches deep. Wind at northeast and mercury at 30. Continuing snowing till one o'clock, and about four it became perfectly clear. Wind in the same place but not hard. Mercury 28 at night."[4] These were probably the last words that George Washington ever wrote.

Washington[5] admitted to a sore throat, "but," so Lear wrote his mother, "considering it as a trifling matter he took no measures to relieve it; for he was always averse to nursing himself for any slight complaint." He did take the precaution of not riding out again in the storm. After the sky had cleared, he walked out on the lawn between the piazza and the river to mark some trees he wished to have cut down. His voice was hoarse, but he made light of it. During the evening, he sat in the parlor with Martha and Lear, reading some newspapers that had come from the post office. "He was very cheerful," Lear noted, "and, when he met with anything which he thought diverting or interesting, he would read it aloud, as well as his hoarseness would permit."

After Martha had retired, Washington asked Lear to read to him the report of some debates in the Virginia Assembly. When he heard that Madison had gone to the length of supporting Monroe for the Senate, he became upset. He "spoke with some degree of asperity," which Lear "endeavored to moderate, as I always did on such occasions." Eventually, Washington regained his cheerfulness and prepared to set off for bed. Lear urged him to use some medicine.

"No," said Washington. "You know I never take anything for a cold. Let it go as it came."

Between two and three in the morning, Washington awoke Martha to say that he had suffered an ague and was feeling extremely unwell. Observing that he could scarcely speak and was breathing with difficulty, Martha was alarmed. She wished to summon a servant, but Washington would not let her do so, lest by getting out of bed she should catch cold. It seems to have been at this point that the hero decided he was going to die. As two of his physicians later put it, "He was fully impressed at the beginning of his complaint . . . that its conclusion would be mortal; submitting to the several exertions made for his recovery, rather as a duty, than from any expectation of their efficacy."

At daybreak a maid came to make the fire. She was sent to get an overseer named Rawlins, who commonly ministered to sick slaves: Washington wished to be bled before the doctor (who had also been sent for) could get there. Lear was awakened. "A mixture of molasses, vinegar and butter was prepared, to try its effect in the throat; but he could not swallow a drop. Whenever he attempted it, he appeared to be distressed, convulsed and almost suffocated."

The sun was up by the time the overseer appeared. He had brought his lancet, but he was white and trembling. Washington bared his arm and, speaking with difficulty, said, "Don't be afraid." The incision having been made and the blood running pretty freely, Washington observed, "The orifice is not large enough."

At this, Martha, who was not sure that her husband was prescribing the right treatment, begged that too much blood should not be taken. She appealed to Lear "to stop it." Lear tried to intervene, but the General put out his hand in an arresting gesture. As soon as he could speak, he said, "More!" However, Martha continued to plead, and the bleeding was stopped after half a pint had been taken. While Lear applied various poultices and soaked Washington's feet in warm water, Martha sent for a second doctor.

The first physician to arrive was his lifelong friend Dr. Craik. Craik used Spanish fly to draw blood into a blister directly from Washington's throat; he also took more blood from Washington's arm. The patient obediently tried to use a gargle of sage tea and vinegar, but the only result was that he was again almost suffocated. Craik urged him to cough. He tried, but could not do so. Craik sent for a third doctor and bled the General for a third time. "No effect however was produced by it, and he continued in the same state, unable to swallow anything."

Between three and four in the afternoon, two horsemen galloped separately up the driveway to Mount Vernon: Dr. Elisha Cullen Dick of Alexandria and Dr. Gustavus Richard Brown of Port Tobacco. Recollections become a little contradictory at this point, but it seems that the two new physicians each in turn examined Washington. Then the three doctors withdrew for a conference.

The facts on the conference are more precise. Drs. Craik and Brown agreed on the diagnosis of quinsy (an extreme form of tonsillitis) and urged further debilitating treatment — more bleeding and blisters and also purges. Dr. Dick, who at thirty-seven was by far the youngest of the three, argued that Washington was suffering from "a violent inflammation of the membranes of the throat, which it had almost closed, and which, if not immediately arrested, would result in death." He urged an operation that would open the trachea below the infection so Washington could breathe.

At first Craik seemed convinced, but Brown persuaded him that the operation might be fatal. Suspecting that his colleagues were afraid to assume such responsibility in the case of a patient so famous, Dick said that he would take all blame for failure on himself. Still Craik and Brown would not agree. Then Dick urged that the patient be not bled again. He did not deny the therapeutic efficacy of bleeding, but felt that it should be applied to the elderly only sparingly. Concerning Washington, he said, "He needs all his strength — bleeding will diminish it."

Later, after he had had time to think calmly, Craik wrote Brown that they should have listened to Dick. Had they "taken no more blood from him, our good friend might have been alive now. But we were governed by the best light we had; we thought we were right, and so we are justified." (Down the years doctors have speculated on the nature of Washington's illness. One guess is diphtheria, another a virulent streptococcus infection of the throat. Either disease would, in the state of medicine at that time, have been fatal regardless of the treatment prescribed.)

As a result of the doctors' despairing conference, Washington was bled for the fourth time: "the blood ran very slowly — appeared very thick," but the operation "did not produce any symptoms of fainting." When, towards four in the afternoon, Washington proved able to swallow a little, the doctors took advantage of this situation by giving him calomel and other purges.

"About half past four o'clock," Lear recorded, "he desired me to ask Mrs. Washington to come to his bedside — when he requested her to go down into his room and take from his desk two wills which she would find there, and bring them to him, which she did. — Upon looking at them, he gave her one, which he observed was useless, as it was superseded by the other, and desired her to burn it, which she did, and then [she] took the other and put it away into her closet."

Lear wrote his mother, "To the last moment he wished to be useful. As often as he could speak, he mentioned to me something he wished to have done."

Later, as Lear sat by his bed holding his hand, Washington said, " 'I find I am going. My breath cannot continue long. I believed from the first attack it would be fatal. Do you arrange and record all my late military letters and papers — arrange my accounts and settle my books, as you know more about them than anyone else, and let Mr. Rawlins finish recording my other letters, which he has begun.'

"I told him this should be done. He then asked, if I recollected anything which it was essential for him to do, as he had but a very short time to continue with us. I told him, that I could recollect nothing, but that I hoped he was not so near his end. He observed, smiling, that he certainly was, and that, as it was the debt which we must all pay, he looked at the event with perfect resignation."

As the afternoon wore on, the pain in Washington's throat and his distress at his difficulty in breathing increased. He continually asked, "in so low and broken a voice as at times hardly to be understood," what time it was. He tried for a while sitting up by the fire, but, finding no relief, asked to be returned to his bed. Then he kept trying to shift his tall frame

[459]

into a more comfortable position. The smaller Lear would lie down on the bed beside him "to raise him, and turn him with as much ease as possible." Washington would mumble the hope that he was not giving too much trouble. To one of Lear's assurances of his eagerness to help, Washington replied, "Well, it is a debt we must pay to each other, and I hope when you want aid of this kind, you will find it."

He asked when his nephew Lawrence Lewis and his step-grandson George Washington Parke Custis would return from a trip. Lear said he believed about the twentieth of the month. "He made no reply to it."

Craik came in and approached the bedside. "Doctor," Washington managed to enunciate, "I die hard, but I am not afraid to go. . . . My breath cannot last long." Lear noted: "The doctor pressed his hand, but could not utter a word. He retired from the bedside, and sat by the fire absorbed in grief."

The other two physicians entered. They ordered that the sufferer be painfully pulled up into a sitting position. "After repeated efforts to be understood," so wrote Craik and Dick, he "succeeded in expressing a desire that he might be permitted to die without further interruption." As Lear quoted him, "I feel myself going. I thank you for your attention. You had better not take any more trouble about me; but let me go off quietly; I cannot last long." Medical science, however, cannot give up trying. The doctors, although they admitted they were "without a ray of hope," applied blisters and also poultices of wheat bran to Washington's legs and feet.

Everyone noted that at no point in his illness did Washington complain or refer to his agony. As the evening lengthened into night, he limited his convulsive efforts at speech to asking what time it was. His breathing became a little easier, and then a fear struck him — the fear of being buried alive. Summoning all his powers, he managed, after several false starts, to say to Lear, "I am just going. Have me decently buried, and do not let my body be put into the vault in less than three days after I am dead."*

Lear bowed assent, being too moved for words. Washington fixed his gaze. "Do you understand me?"

"Yes, sir."

" 'Tis well." These seem to have been the hero's last words.

---

* This quotation is from Lear's journal. To his mother, Lear quoted Washington somewhat differently. "My dear friend, I am just about to change my scene: my breath can continue for but a few moments. You will have me decently interred, and do not let my body be put in the tomb in less than two days after my death."

The place and bed where Washington died.
Courtesy of the Mount Vernon Ladies' Association

WASHINGTON'S BIER.

Washington's bier, from a woodcut by Benson J. Lossing.
Courtesy of the Mount Vernon Ladies' Association

The night dragged slowly on. The two younger doctors, not being intimates of the family, waited downstairs. From the windows of the second-floor room, lamplight threw glistening squares on meager snow. Within, Dr. Craik sat, as he had for hours, staring into the fire. Washington's body servant, Christopher, stood by the bed, a post he had not deserted since morning, although Washington had several times motioned him to sit down. A group of house servants — "Caroline, Molly and Charlotte," and some others — stood near the door. Lear was hovering around the head of the bed, intently trying to interpret every gesture and do what he could to ease the sufferer. Martha was sitting near the foot of the bed.

No one thought to look at a clock, so we only know for sure that it was approaching midnight when Washington withdrew his hand from Lear's and felt his own pulse. Lear called Craik, who came to the bedside. Washington lifted his arm and then his "hand fell from his wrist." As Lear reached out for the limp hand, Craik put his own hand over Washington's eyes. There was no struggle, not even a sigh.

In a calm, controlled voice, Martha asked, "Is he gone?"

Unable to speak, Lear held up his hand in a signal of assent.

Printed cotton kerchief mourning the death of Washington. Courtesy of
the New-York Historical Society, New York City

V

Conclusion

The Second Term Surveyed

WASHINGTON'S position in the historical memory of later generations — particularly during the twentieth century — would surely have been less troubled had he persevered in his determination not to accept a second Presidential term. However, such a refusal would have been for the evolving United States a misfortune, if not a disaster.

Most of the events which are cited by his critics as damaging to his reputation — and which also came close to breaking his heart — took place during Washington's second term. But he did succeed in keeping the United States at peace while all the surrounding world went up in flames, and he created the foreign policy which the nation was to pursue — with one major slip in 1812 — for more than a century, during which the nation grew, almost unmolested from abroad, into the great power which during 1916 moved again onto the European scene.

Although there was some overlapping, the phenomena Washington faced during his two terms were in essence different. During the first, he had been primarily concerned with translating the blueprint provided by the Constitution into an actual government serving a nation prosperous and reasonably united. In his second term, he had to cope with crises abroad that menaced the peace of the United States, and, by exacerbating disagreements at home, threatened (at least so it sometimes seemed) to tear the nation apart.

When Washington stepped down from the Presidency, he left behind him a still raging storm, but the government continued to steer according to the bearings he had insisted on, avoiding, for some years, the reefs he had avoided.

The desire for peace which was the lodestar of Washington's second term was shared by almost all responsible national leaders. Yet his neutrality policy suffered very serious attack. This was because "peace" and "neutrality" are capable of various definitions. A limited war (say, such an attack on Spanish Louisiana by American freebooters in French pay as Jefferson encouraged) can be considered not a war. And "neutrality" can be more or less neutral. Although the corollaries they drew were opposite, Jefferson and Hamilton, the Republicans and the Federalists, agreed that neutrality did not exclude helping your favorite side to the greatest extent possible without becoming an active belligerent. Washington disagreed: he wished to keep neutrality on an even keel without experimenting on how far you could tip it safely to either port or starboard.

Washington agreed with Jefferson and Hamilton that there was a point beyond which a nation cannot with safety and honor accept being pushed. The crux was where you found that point. Each faction palliated depredations and insults inflicted on the United States by what each considered the right side, and strongly resented those perpetrated by the side each considered wrong. Until the very end of his second term, when the situation had greatly deteriorated and his own powers had considerably weakened, Washington worked hard to react equally to provocations whether British or French. His object was always to handle the problem in such a way that provocations would cease.

Washington had fought the French as a young man and the British as he approached middle age. In his first war, he had served with Englishmen but always, as a colonial, in subordinate capacities he deeply resented. His second had been a fratricidal war, always more bitter than a foreign conflict, and he had been joined by French allies who, although they sometimes took the bit in their own teeth,* got on with him reasonably well. More important to his emotions had been the French volunteers in his own Continental Army, who had obeyed his orders and been vastly useful: the engineer, Duportail; his spiritual son, Lafayette. There can be no doubt that when the European war first exploded and for a considerable time thereafter his personal sympathies were pro-French. Yet as early as October 1789 he recognized, as Jefferson and the Republicans failed to do, that the French upheaval was traveling in directions unfavorable to the rights of man.[1] Since he considered tyranny the same mon-

---

* The occasion on which he had been most grievously overruled by Rochambeau eventuated in the victory at Yorktown, which surely kept the memory from bearing much sting.

ster from whatever direction it came, he could see no major gain for humanity in a victory of either the British or the French. And he did not believe that either victory would make much difference to the United States. America's best contribution to the future of mankind would not be, he believed, to serve as a makeweight in European squabbles, but rather to build behind her ocean moat a republican paradise that would in the present serve as a haven for refugees from the European burning, and in the future as a beacon spreading far the light of liberty.

The policies of the belligerents towards commerce, and also any moves (actual, projected, or suspected) affecting territory on the North American continent, had to be of major concern to Washington. However, he kept his policies so consistent in the face of the shifting military fortunes of the belligerents that most discussions of campaigns in Europe have proved irrelevant to this volume. Underneath his relative unconcern with the immediate pitches of history lay the bedrock of Washington's conviction that, whatever happened abroad, the United States could, if the people remained united, take care of herself.

Washington's total experience made him regard the United States as less dependent on Europe than did his advisers. The historical fashion that has seen him as a typical English Whig, the tendency of most Englishmen and a surprising number of Americans to believe that Washington was born in England, could not conceivably have been more off the true track. Except for a brief trip to the West Indies accompanying a dying brother, Washington never set foot outside what came to be or was the United States. Hamilton and Robert Morris had been born and raised as British subjects, Gallatin as a Swiss. John Adams, Jefferson, and Monroe spent much time abroad. Madison, it is true, had remained in America, but, like most of Washington's colleagues, he differed from the first President in two highly relevant particulars: he was more given to book learning and he was not importantly shaped by the frontier.

For many years, no other President had as little formal education as Washington. Even Andrew Jackson studied law. Our first President learned in school nothing (except for the practical art of surveying) that we would today consider beyond the elementary grades. He never undertook any advanced professional studies. Although he got together a considerable library, he was only a sporadic reader. His sources of information were experience and conversation.

During Washington's lifetime, almost all available books reflected

Europe. This was true of the works on political philosophy that fascinated theorists of the American Revolutionary debate, of the legal tomes that guided the innumerable lawyers who helped found the nation. Even light reading was almost certain to be imported. But for a man who never went abroad, experience was native.

Conversation often brought in foreign ideas. Yet the words Washington heard always moved through the American air. There is no indication that he was (after he had got over the English colonialism of his youth) particularly interested in accounts of European experiences. Philosophical discussions not applied to the problems with which he struggled did not appeal to him. As a thinker as well as a farmer, he had no use for exotics that would not root in the American soil.

Washington first supported himself as a surveyor on the fringes of settlement. He achieved celebrity when nineteen by accomplishing a perilous mission through the wilderness. During the French and Indian War, he was an Indian fighter. Although he became a successful planter and was a routine member of the House of Burgesses, his frontier achievements constituted, until the Revolution carried him in new directions, almost the total sum of his adventures, his reputation, his public service. More than a century before the historian Turner had evolved his theory of the expanding frontier, Washington saw the west as a continuing source for "incorruptible love of liberty."[2] A man thus shaped, with such memories and such convictions, could only listen with amazement and regret when those two lawyers who had hardly strayed from the safe settlements, Jefferson and Hamilton, insisted that the American future depended on who won the European war.

Through a large part of his second term, Washington adhered confidently to his belief that the mass of the American people stood too firmly on their own feet to be shaken by European quarrels and European propaganda. Before the end, it is true, he came to fear the French because he believed their American partisans were becoming a danger to the United States. French springs for French actions concerned him so little that he blamed outrage in Paris over the Jay Treaty on incitations by American Republicans at home and abroad.

The accusation that the President was under the thumb of Hamilton was by no means the only such charge leveled at Washington. Again and again throughout his major career complainers stated that Washington behaved in a manner which they did not like because he was dominated by the unfortunate influence of a third party. When Mifflin, outraged that General Washington did not regard the protection of Philadelphia as the be-all of strategy, hightailed from the Continental Army to foster the Conway Cabal, he blamed the malignant New England influence of Greene. When President Washington refused to praise Jay and King for signing a public attack on Genêt, they concluded that he had been corrupted by Jefferson and Randolph. When Washington did not come to Hamilton's defense after the Secretary of the Treasury had been discovered illegally shifting funds, Hamilton envisioned dirty work by Randolph. And when Washington did not do everything that Jefferson and the Republicans wanted, in loud voices that have reverberated down the corridors of history they commonly blamed Hamilton.

This succession of charges could be taken to demonstrate that Washington was like a chameleon, perpetually taking on the color of one man or another. Such a theory would, of course, contradict the conception of a perpetually dominant Hamilton. In any case, it has never been seriously put forward.

Part of the explanation undoubtedly lay in Washington's method of asking advice from the holders of various points of view. If the advice was given verbally, he usually listened without committing himself. He accepted written arguments without comment. He weighed the council he received, without revealing process or progress, in the privacy of his own brain. Should the decision he finally announced resemble the program suggested by one adviser, it was natural for those overruled to assume that Washington had deserted reason because he had been unduly swayed.

Paradoxically, such conclusions were fostered by the reverence in which Washington was held. Better to think him fooled than foolish! And, if you wished to attack the decisions of so popular a man, it seemed prudent to strike at him obliquely by attacking his advisers. Thus the Republican press excoriated the "vipers" who had gathered around Washington under the leadership of the king viper, Hamilton, before they found the fortitude to accuse the President himself.

Within the inner circle of Washington's associates there was a more personal and poignant phenomenon — jealousy. Those who work with a man they revere and through whose support they can gain great power, naturally wish him to follow their own advice, preferring them to colleagues whom they dislike and consider wrong-headed. Without accusing anyone of homosexuality it must be said — how ridiculous to deny that

[471]

normal males are physically attracted or repelled by other males! — that Washington exerted an almost hypnotic charm particularly on men. As a group ladies found him, despite his eminence and affability, withdrawn, austere. Men followed him to death in battle, rushed out to cheer as he passed by, and in small rooms fought for his favor.

The mutual hatred of Jefferson and Hamilton had many facets, all of them sharp. Both having grown up more or less fatherless, they vied for Washington's sanction as a substitute father.° And they stood on the opposite sides of one of the great watersheds of modern history. Jefferson represented the old conception of an agrarian aristocracy, Hamilton the business society being brought in by the industrial revolution. From Jefferson's point of view, the bastard from the West Indies was a vulgar upstart; from Hamilton's point of view Jefferson was a hypocrite: a social snob ranting about equality. Both men enjoyed extreme statement. Hamilton, when he exaggerated, expressed disdain for the people; Jefferson, when he exaggerated, expressed sympathy for the beheading of aristocrats. Temperamentally, the two men seem to have been born to grate on each other. Hamilton was all fire and ginger, obviously ambitious, martial in manner, impeccably dressed. Jefferson lounged in rumpled clothes; politics, he insisted, meant nothing to him; he wished only, so he said, to withdraw into the intellectual delights of philosophic speculation. That both men were extremely effective and transcendently able made it a battle of champions. In such battles, mediators do not come off unscathed. Among other wounds, Washington suffered the charge that he acted as a slave of Hamilton.

The reasons why Washington seemed to Jefferson (and even more to Jefferson's coadjutors and followers down to today) † to have favored Hamilton lay for the most part completely to one side of any personal in-

---

° Washington himself lost his father at an early age but became instantly, under the stern eye of his mother, substitute father to his younger brothers and sister. He attached himself to his older half brother Lawrence, and, when Lawrence died, to William Fairfax. Then from his early twenties onward, he followed in the wake of no man.

† Actually, the charge that Washington was dominated by Hamilton was only one of the charges which the Secretary of State, in office and retired, made against the President: Washington gave in to Cabinet majorities created by the vacillation of the despicable Randolph; he allowed himself to be misinformed about French developments by Gouverneur Morris, who was surely a royalist; he was swayed by the entire Federalist apparatus; he himself had aristocratic pretensions; he associated with the wrong circles in Philadelphia; he lacked faith in the people. In other moods, as we have seen, Jefferson sang the opposite tune and praised Washington for keeping American policy from being altogether aristocratic and pro-British.

fluence on him or any personal affections he felt. The situation opened with Jefferson lagging for months before he appeared for his Cabinet post. He arrived with no program, to find Hamilton going full blast with a program of his own. It took him a little time to find that he was opposed to what Hamilton was projecting, and then he discovered that Washington was not opposed. Since his fellow Virginian had been raised in the same agrarian slaveholding society as he himself had, Jefferson expected Washington to agree that the alternate economic system being fostered by Hamilton would undermine the republic. When Washington proved sympathetic to business enterprise, it seemed obvious that he had been corrupted by Jefferson's hated rival.

While all for plantation luxury, Jefferson hated city luxury, but Washington enjoyed the finely appointed drawing rooms of men like Robert Morris and women like Eliza Powel, urban sophisticates whose interests coincided with Hamilton's policies. Washington had always been (as Hamilton was) somewhat of a dandy. And the old President found it necessary — so he said — not to keep open house in Philadelphia as he did in Virginia, but to set up specific times and occasions when he would receive members of the public. Did not all this mean that Washington's ear was cocked to Hamilton's siren song?

Jefferson was already convinced that Hamilton was favored in their rivalry when the European war struck. Neither Washington nor any other American could change the fact that the only road to peace, neutrality, was in its effect pro-British. All that Hamilton had to do — although he was much too energetic a man to act that way — was to sit still and allow events to carry the executive (Jefferson included, as long as he remained in office) in the directions of which Hamilton approved.

In defending from the outrage of his supporters acts which he could not as a practical man avoid, Jefferson encouraged in the Republican thought of his time (and in subsequent historical writing) what might be called "the Shield Theory": Washington urged Jefferson to stay in the Cabinet, and gave other Republicans important assignments for the purpose of raising a shield that would protect the government from criticism and hide from the public its secret pursuit of a Hamiltonian pro-British policy. Although Washington was obviously glad to present as united a facade as possible to the public, the more serious aspects of the accusation fall to the ground when it is realized that Washington was in truth pursuing American neutrality without regard to the European outcome.

Malone summarized the situation by stating that, although they started from opposite points, Jefferson and Hamilton often "arrived at the same practical conclusion, for the simple reason that it was the most sensible one. The main difference at this stage was not in policies but in guiding principles." Malone adds that in those principles Washington was much closer to Jefferson than Hamilton.[3] However, Jefferson finally decided that he was being pushed too close to the wall: he resigned, leaving the field of battle to his rival.

While Madison vacillated, Jefferson had consistently been suspicious of federal power, and this suspicion increased when the central government seemed to be following the lead of his enemy. He tried to head off the Bank of the United States through strict interpretation of the Constitution. Feeling that Virginia's interests were being menaced, he plumped strongly for states' rights. Again, Washington found himself on the same side as Hamilton. He did not believe that the Constitution should be used as a noose around the neck of the federal government. Nor did he share Jefferson's reverence for the traditional culture of their common birth-state.

As Jefferson became more disapproving of Washington, he became increasingly worried by Washington's prestige with the American people. While still Secretary of State, he countenanced violent attacks on Washington in the Republican press. There can be no doubt that the President was, as long as he remained in office, more tolerant of Jefferson than Jefferson was of him. The President's position made forbearance in one sense easier — he *did* hold the ultimate power — but few holders of power are willing to seek unanimity not by attempting to smash down the opposition but by tolerating and encouraging a clearly disloyal subordinate who incited insult and attack.°

To demonstrate that Washington was as President little more than a puppet of Hamilton's, it is common to bring Hamilton himself forward as

---

° When Jefferson himself became President, he reversed himself on most of the issues over which he had fought Washington. He was persuaded by his own Secretary of the Treasury, Gallatin, to continue the Bank of the United States. In carrying through the Louisiana Purchase, he violated strict construction of the Constitution more than Washington ever did. After events had made clear that Washington's prophecies had been correct concerning the French Revolution, Jefferson became suspicious of the French, even considering an alliance with Great Britain. He applied legal controls to the freedom of the press in a way that Washington had never done. (He *did* adhere to his disapproval of formal restrictions on Presidential accessibility, but it is a question whether he could practically have done so had not the capital moved from the metropolis of Philadelphia to that then rural hamlet, Washington, D.C.)

a star witness. Again and again he is quoted as having written that Washington had been "an aegis very essential to me." But the circumstances under which Hamilton made this statement are not duly examined.

The quotation comes from the letter Hamilton wrote Lear in response to the news that Washington had died. Lear, for so many years a member of Washington's household, had been personally much closer to the General than Hamilton had ever been; he stood at the moment (Martha being presumably incapacitated by grief and shock) as the standard bearer of the little group gathered around Washington's bier. Hamilton, being no fool, must have divined that Lear disliked and distrusted him.* Yet in his letter, Hamilton not only described Washington as his "aegis," he also put in the claim that he himself had more reason to be upset than Lear: "Perhaps no man in this community has equal cause with myself to deplore the loss." [5]

The letter of condolence Hamilton sent Martha ten days later also included claims: "There can be few who equally with me participate in the loss you deplore. In expressing this sentiment, I may, without impropriety, allude to the numerous and distinguished marks of confidence and friendship of which you have yourself been a witness, but I cannot say in how many ways that confidence and friendship was necessary to me in future relations."[6]

If, when you were at a funeral, you heard a man insist to the chief mourners that no other men — or very few — had been as close as he to the deceased, would you conclude that he was stating a fact or that he was trying for psychological reasons of his own to elicit sanction for a contention of which he himself was not sure? And it is clear that Hamilton was thinking more of his own dependence on Washington than of any dependence by Washington on him.

The basic difference between Washington's relationships with Hamilton and Jefferson is symbolized by the fact that Hamilton (it is hard to believe!) never visited Mount Vernon. Washington and Jefferson shared a love of farming — and also concern with Washington's favorite secondary projects: the Potomac Canal and the federal city. On this level of shared personal interests, Washington had little more in common with Hamilton than a concern with sartorial elegance and the ability to enjoy urban luxury. All of Hamilton's paraphernalia of credit and banks seemed to Wash-

---

* Lear, for instance, wrote Humphreys in 1793 that Hamilton "puffed himself too high," creating unnecessary opposition to the government.[4]

ington, however valuable they might be for the nation, matters that he should himself keep away from. By the time he became President, Washington no longer felt the military enthusiasm which still burned in Hamilton.

Jefferson had joined Washington in the House of Burgesses in 1769; they had corresponded during the Revolution; they had become personally close during Washington's post-military retirement; but they had never collaborated intimately until Jefferson became Secretary of State. As men are brought together by daily association in a common labor, Washington had known Hamilton the longer. Having joined the General's military family in 1777, the twenty-six-year-old had quickly assumed the duties of chief of staff. After having served for four years, he resigned in anger. Hamilton then asserted that he had consistently repelled manifestations of friendship on Washington's part, preferring "to stand rather on a footing of military confidence than of private attachment."[7]

Although his relationship with Washington was certainly a great emotional as well as a great exterior force in Hamilton's life, it continued on a level of professional association rather than private friendship. When the two men had business together, they corresponded; when there was no business, they did not. During the three and a half years between the Revolution and the Constitutional Convention, Washington wrote Hamilton only one letter: it dealt with the Society of the Cincinnati. When Hamilton took it upon himself to urge Washington's acceptance of the Presidency, Washington pushed the interference aside with the statement that he was discussing the matter with "my best friends."

Hamilton was generally considered the obvious choice for Secretary of the Treasury, and Washington found no cause to regret the appointment. Hamilton handled recondite financial matters to the satisfaction of those who understood (Washington was hardly more of an initiate than Jefferson). He was furthermore a reservoir of efficient energy. Wherever the President was, wherever the other members of the Cabinet might be, Hamilton could usually be found at his desk. It is hard for us to realize now, when communication is quick and federal officials have so proliferated, what a comfort it was to have an able man usually on the scene. If Hamilton interfered in the Department of State, so did Jefferson (to the best of his ability) in the Treasury, and Washington disapproved of neither since he wished the government to function as a unit.*

---

* See volume III, pages 401–402.

Neither Hamilton [8] nor anyone else could call on President Washington at will or even send an unsolicited memorandum. At conferences, Washington would not accept the introduction of new business. Rather than attempt to "force [as Randolph put it] an opportunity,"[9] the best way to call an idea to Washington's attention was to hook it cleverly onto some matter concerning which discussion had already been requested. Any other method called for apologies plus a hint that such unusual action had been made necessary by crisis. Hamilton had down the years become expert at walking this tightrope, but it remained a tightrope rather than a free path to Washington's attention.

Naturally, after Jefferson's departure, Hamilton's voice became more persuasive in the conferences Washington called. This was certainly independent of the President's intention. Although Hamilton did play a partisan role in the preparation of Jay's instructions, Washington resisted Federalist pressure to entrust the mission itself to the Secretary of the Treasury. He deeply hurt Hamilton's pride by refusing to admit, in the matter of the misapplied appropriation, that he automatically approved what Hamilton did because of his great faith in his friend and colleague.

When Hamilton finally left the Cabinet in order to make a better living for his family, he clearly intended to do what historians claimed he did do: hold his position as principal adviser. But Washington's belief that the discussion of official business should only be with the relevant officials was strengthened by the long-standing bounds of his relationship with Hamilton. He turned passionately to Randolph. Only after Randolph had been shot out from beneath him, after he had failed to lure into the government any replacements of stature, was he finally forced to turn to Hamilton.

Hamilton could then have felt justified in sulking in his tent; he could have said, "You rebuffed me until you had no other choice. Now you can go fly your kite." He was given further cause to be offended because in several major matters, after Hamilton had labored to draft papers, Washington acted without waiting to receive the drafts. Yet Hamilton served Washington like a loyal minister to a capricious monarch, trying (as in the immense service he did Washington concerning the Farewell Address) to do what was truly best for the reputation of his former chief.

Although Hamilton's motives were certainly not only affection and loyalty — the more he could preserve and use Washington's influence the better for him — yet Washington would have been an insensitive fool not to be conscious of the contrast between Hamilton's behavior towards him and Jefferson's. During the Revolution, when the Continental Congress was indicating distrust of the Continental Army, Washington warned the legislators that the best way to make a man your enemy was to make clear that you considered him as such. Now he was old and his mental balance unsure. He became suspicious of the Republicans' patriotism, and suspected Jefferson (not without some seeming evidence) of an underhand intrigue against him involving an anonymous letter. But even in his last declining years, he fought against as much as he yielded to the influence of Hamilton.

Hamilton (to quote Malone) "focused on the powers of the government and the governors," while Jefferson "emphasized the rights and trustworthiness of the governed."[10] Washington had, after the Revolution, expected that the people would spontaneously work out a government adequate to their needs. He had felt greatly disillusioned — "I am mortified beyond expression!"[11] — when it seemed to him, as well as to most national leaders, that the people were failing to do so. Washington then moved from extreme faith in "mankind when left to themselves" to the belief that the more expert and responsible would have to establish and administer a framework on which a government satisfactory to the people would be maintained. Yet Washington's faith in the people continued to be much greater than Hamilton's. How his later attitude should be defined in relation to the Jeffersonian position depends on how one evaluates agrarian hegemony, states rights, and political parties.

In arguing with Washington, Jefferson excluded from his definition of "the people" men who favored and gained from an urban business economy. That Hamilton's measures profited in the first instance a small minority within the overwhelmingly agrarian population no one could deny. Capitalism requires capitalists. Believing that the land speculators who first explored an area were justified in patenting the best land, Washington saw no reason why innovation should not enrich the innovators. For the capitalists in Congress to concert measures with each other seemed to him no more reprehensible than for the Republicans to do the same. The important matter was that the legislators be elected periodically by the free suffrage of the people. He was thus unmoved when Jefferson — who made no similar suggestion concerning farmers or slaveholders — urged that money men be prevented from voting on bills that served their interests.[12] Washington did not believe that any particular order of men should be discriminated against in government.

Far from agreeing with the rising Jeffersonian contention that the states were the palladium of people's rights, Washington saw organized regionalism as menacing the ability of the federal government to bring together and represent all the people. He was not persuaded that political groups, like the Democratic Societies, were useful in educating the people concerning their rights. The catch was that the "educators" had their own bias for which they were trying to drum up support.

Washington's ideal was to open up communication as direct as possible between the individual voter and the central power. He wished to have the arguments of the most able exponents of the various points of view available to the public in newspapers or widely distributed pamphlets. But he was not in favor of having men whom he regarded as the leaders of factions monopolize the ears of organized followers. He regarded such organizers not as champions of the people but as "demagogues."

Despite the most violent provocations, Washington did not, while he was in power, make or support even the slightest legal or official move towards curtailing the freedom of the press. He consistently urged reduced postal rates that would encourage the flow of news into every hamlet. Although he often excoriated the newspapers for lying and irresponsibility, he could think of no better instrument.

Never supporting any specific candidates, never interposing (while President) in any electoral contests, Washington preferred to limit his appeals to the people to explaining actions and stating principles. For this endeavor, he had particular gifts. Hamilton was glad to feed the people any contention he thought they would swallow. Jefferson often saw two types of arguments: those which appealed to the informed, and more simple considerations that served to sway the people.[13] Washington needed to resort to no such expedients. Seeking before he acted always to bring together the immediate need with basic principles, he reached conclusions that, when presented to the people, revealed a simple profundity that was clear to every thinking mind.* One of the reasons that it is hard for us to appreciate the depth of Washington's intellect is that what he said seems, to historical hindsight, obvious. But to identify, while deep in the trenches of conflict, what the future would consider obvious, is a towering intellectual achievement.

Washington did not believe that it was either possible or practical to

---

* Washington's major failure in this realm was his inability, towards the close of his Presidency, to present the people with a justification that pleased him of the Jay Treaty. However, he did not fudge: he hardly went beyond stating that he had carried out his duty by acting as he considered best for the nation.

supply the people in advance with the information that would enable them to advise wisely before a decision was made. And after the decision, they would first have to be persuaded that the issue was adequately grave to command their deepest attention. Then, so that they would not come up with vaporous ideas, they would have to be made to understand what were the possible alternatives. They would have to be given time to study the matter. If the people then expressed in some finite manner — through a spontaneous flood of mass meetings or through the ballot box — disapproval of the government's actions, it would be "disgraceful" for the government not to follow their lead. "The mass of the citizens," he wrote, "require no more than to understand a question to decide it properly." Even if "we may be a little wrong now and then, we shall return to the right path with more avidity."[14] .

The contest between the Federalists and the Republicans is sometimes thought of as being between those who believed in privilege and those who wished to help the poor. This conception attributes twentieth-century issues to the eighteenth century. The argument was not then basically concerned with the haves and the have-nots: it was between rival economic systems. Those who wished to elevate the poor were in those days called "levellers." Only in the most violent diatribes of his last years, did Washington even hint that the Republicans were "levellers." Because there were levelling components in the Whiskey Rebellion, it was denounced by most of the Republican leadership and also by the influential Philadelphia Democratic Society. In his famous Mazzei letter, Jefferson boasted that "our mass of weight and wealth" was on the Republican side.[15] It was the Jacksonian not the Jeffersonian revolution that brought the common man into the White House.°

The American Revolution was, in the long flow of history, an aspect of the rise of the middle class. Centuries of aristocratic domination having demonstrated that a man who is poor is also helpless, few Americans (except the most impoverished) doubted that "life, liberty, and the pursuit of happiness" were grounded on the sanctity of property. A corollary was that the possession of property made a man more reliable: he had a stake

---

° The "Friends of Jefferson" in radical western Pennsylvania described themselves (1796) in the following statement that avoided all levelling overtones: "Decided republicans, respectable yeomen, opposers of perverse systems of finance, enemies of monarchical trumpery and parade, enemies of peculation, such as wish to reduce the debts of the nation instead of increasing them, men of science and lovers of literature."[16]

in society which he would not wish to lose. In an environment concerned with material gain, a prosperous man was admired. Experience had backed up Washington's belief that common soldiers were more likely to enlist if they knew that their officers were men of substance. Voters were not inclined to send to Congress a neighbor whose horse was ill fed and whose children were ill clothed. In the sense that the poor generally looked up to the rich (they dreamed that their own families would climb the economic ladder), eighteenth-century America was not equalitarian.° Washington's butler, who was instructed only to admit to the Presidential levees men respectably dressed, probably never needed to apply this rule: no ragged varlet would have presumed to come.

Had a welfare state been given consideration in eighteenth-century America, it would surely have been more sympathetic to Hamilton than Jefferson, since it involved so great an increase in governmental power. Washington saw the two sides of the problem of poverty — how it was created and how it could be alleviated — not in class but in individual terms. Inhabiting a society that offered a plethora of opportunity, in so many directions a self-made man, Washington was unimpressed by the improvident and the incompetent. However, if one came to him for charity, he would not be refused. "Never," Washington admonished his stepson, "let an indigent person ask without receiving *something* if you have the means, always recollecting in what light the widow's mite was viewed."†17

To sufferers whose plaint he considered due to misfortune, Washington was generous, often feeling guilty when he decided that his means would not allow him to help even more. His first responsibility, he felt, was to members of his own family; then to people whom he knew personally or who lived in his neighborhood. Although preferring to operate as man to man, he supported what organized charities there then were, and sought to alleviate the suffering of groups such as the poor who needed wood to keep warm in debtors' prison.18

Washington was, of course, an aggressive and successful amasser of property. It is an amazing indication of his ability and energy that he managed to make himself, as almost a sideline to his public duties (and by his own efforts rather than through employees), so wealthy a man. He engaged in no chicanery but drove as profitable a bargain as he could.

° Thus the more prosperous western Pennsylvanians, when they decided that self-defense required their joining the whiskey rebels, had little difficulty in grasping the leadership of an insurrection that had originally been half-directed at them.

† This is one of the very few biblical references in all Washington's writings.

He made little use of law courts, preferring to take losses rather than "distress others" by prosecuting debtors, yet he was strongly opposed to legislation — debasing the currency, inhibiting the collection of debt, etc. — which assisted the poor as a group by what he considered expropriating the property of the prosperous. His vision of social justice was to keep open the avenues along which men advanced economically. The government could best relieve poverty by preserving peace and fostering prosperity.

Jefferson recorded that Randolph had quoted Washington as stating that, should the union break up between north and south, "he had made up his mind to move and be of the northern."[19] Yet there is no indication that Washington's dreams of retirement took any other form than a return to his Virginia home.

Washington's primary loyalty to Virginia had been unopposed until, at the age of forty-three, he accepted the Revolutionary command which kept him away from home (except during one brief respite) for eight years. During this most educational period, he discovered the need for national unity and the limitations of a purely agrarian society. He also became familiar with an economy not grounded on slavery, intimate with men who regarded human bondage as an evil which could not be palliated.

By the time he had been away from home for five years, two ideas had become linked in his mind: the importance to a powerful nation of financial credit and the possibility of his using the business economy as a personal escape from slaveholding. Although he had not yet reached the point of considering manumission, he wrote his overseer of a passionate desire to get quit of his Negroes. He wished he could, without cruelty and in a good market, sell his slaves and put the money into government securities. This would be both to his advantage and to that of the war effort. Yet he found himself emotionally torn, because a deep-seated loyalty remained to the conceptions with which he had been raised. He wrote his favorite brother, John Augustine Washington: "It ever was my opinion, though candor obliges me to confess it is not consistent with national policy, to have my property as much as possible in lands."[20]

As soon as he could leave the army, Washington returned to his lands and his slaves. Even as he kept embedded in the very center of his often enlarged Mansion House the little farmhouse rooms in which he had played as a child, Washington always wished, while advancing as a leader towards new horizons, to keep contact with his personal past. And the only home that he ever loved was a microcosm of traditional Virginia life.

It was probably natural for a man infinitely more famous than any of his forebears to break with southern traditions by being unconcerned with his ancestry,° yet even his lack of any direct descendants did not prevent him from seeing an intimate connection between family and property. He willed nothing more than mementos to his friends, leaving all his important possessions to innumerable relations, many of whom meant very little to him personally.

Although, between the Revolution and the Presidency, Washington became increasingly uneasy about slavery, he saw at that time no real conflict between the northern and the southern way of life. He imported what laborsaving machinery he could to Mount Vernon, and sought to encourage New England manufacturers by attending his inauguration in a suit of American-spun cloth. The conflict came to him in the form of the Jeffersonian protests against Hamilton's economic measures.

This, the original and surely the basic split in Washington's government, presaged to some extent the split that was, several generations later, to cause the Civil War. True, the emancipation of slaves was not, in Washington's Cabinet, an issue. The issue was whether to encourage or repel an alternate economic system to an agrarianism which was, in the Virginian home base of the Republican party, grounded on slavery.[22] The Jeffersonians tried to make out that the Hamiltonian "monocrats" were attempting to set the clock back to an aristocracy, but this contention never impressed Washington.† He from the first saw the controversy as primarily regional.

When Hamiltonism, far from being suppressed, seemed to triumph, Washington's home state turned against him. Virginians (including former close friends and collaborators) led the party that excoriated Washington's policies and libeled him personally. Finding the stance of the federal government so unsatisfactory, Jefferson moved to a position that enabled him at the time of the Alien and Sedition acts, to promulgate the

---

° Washington did not know the first name of his maternal grandfather, nor did he have any knowledge of the English origins of his family. When queried concerning the Washington line by the British College of Heralds, he tried, as a matter of courtesy, to collect information, adding, "The inquiry is, in my opinion, of little moment."[21]

† Jeffersonian agrarianism was in fact the conservative position. The Hamiltonians were initiating an economic revolution that was, as it created the modern world, fatal to aristocracies.

doctrine — a state had a right to repudiate federal action with which it disagreed — that was used to justify the secession of 1860.[23] Washington, on the other hand, had, in putting down the Whiskey Rebellion, established a precedent for the enforcement of federal law in rebellious regions by military action if necessary.

Washington retired from the Presidency to a personal enclave (unlike most Virginians, his Alexandria neighbors supported his policies) in hostile territory. The man who believed in the importance of neighborhoods but not in the importance of states wrote during 1799, "An absence, with short intervals, of near twenty-five years, with the consequent changes, has in a great measure obliterated my former acquaintance with the people of *this state,* and my knowledge of the rising generation in it (scarcely ever going from home) is very limited indeed."[24]

Personally Washington never did more than dip a reluctant toe in Hamiltonian economic currents, buying bank stock only as a temporary haven for cash not yet expended, borrowing from banks with the utmost trepidation. But he did bring back to his southern plantation a good many Yankee ideas. The maxims he composed for young people in his charge sound much less like the "Rules of Civility" he copied during his own Virginia education than the saws of that New Englander, Franklin.° He dreamed of reforming Washington Custis by sending the lad to Harvard. "The habits of the youth there," he explained, seemed superior to those "at the colleges south of it." [26]

Washington had found himself, as his second term approached its end, driven into trying to dismantle the personal haven which the instinctive part of his being so loved. He made attempts to give up control of most of the Mount Vernon plantation so that he could, without bankrupting himself, free most of his slaves.

He was, of course, far from alone among Virginia leaders in recognizing the evils of slavery. The problem (for all except the very few who made the immediate sacrifice of freeing their blacks) was how best to live with their knowledge of profiting from injustice, their sense, greater or less, of guilt. The Republicans who were supporting states' rights in the name of Virginia institutions, who were putting forward the agrarianism they represented as a way of life so superior that alternatives ought to be suppressed, made the compromise more successfully than Washington

---

° To give two examples: "Rise early that by habit it may become familiar, agreeable, healthy and profitable." "The man who does not estimate *time* as *money* will forever miscalculate."[25]

was able to do.° However much slavery was woven into his training and his needs, Washington could not view Mount Vernon and its way of life as another Eden.

In 1798, he told the actor John Bernard (as Bernard later remembered), "I can clearly foresee that nothing but the rooting out of slavery can perpetuate the existence of our union, by consolidating it in a common bond of principle."[27] Had the civil conflict which he dreaded come in his lifetime, Washington might well have, as Randolph said he stated, moved north. But it would have broken his heart.

° None of the three other Presidents of "the Virginia dynasty," not Jefferson or Madison or Monroe, followed Washington into freeing more than a few especially privileged slaves.

48

George Washington

WASHINGTON, it has been commonly stated, displayed not "genius" but "judgment." When, as the nineteenth century rolled along, "genius" became the watchword for all most valuable in man, "judgment" was sneeringly downgraded to "common sense." Judgment, it was thus implied, characterizes the less highly evolved.* Actually, conversation at a workingman's bar can be as full of fantasy and wild talk as a poet's convention. And surely judgment does not particularly flourish among the dull and uneducated.

Genius and judgment are both, in fact, fundamental characteristics of humanity. In some eras one is more emphasized, in some the other. Washington lived at a moment of transition, when the two great systems of thought — classicism, which most valued judgment, and romanticism, which worshipped genius — were actively warring with each other, both still strongly supported.

The life span of a single individual usually includes a natural movement from reliance on inspiration to reliance on reason. As Wordsworth put it from the romantic point of view, "Shades of the prison-house begin to close upon the growing boy." In Washington's case, this normal flow became a torrent.

Had Washington died in his mid-twenties, he could have been presented truthfully as a romantic, almost a Byronic hero. He suffered from a dark love for his neighbor's wife. Turning his back on civilization, he plunged into wildernesses, braving savage dangers, showing herculean

---

* Before the romantic movement, "genius" was often downgraded to "eccentricity."

strength as he pulled his frozen body out of an ice-filled mountain river. In his pride, he battled during the French and Indian War with his superiors. Although almost too sick to ride, he towered on horseback during a disastrous ambush when almost every other mounted officer fell; he survived to lead the pitiful remnant of a civilized army out of the clutches of savage victors. Finally, he resigned his commission in anger, and, returning to his rural retreat, dramatically turned his back on the military life.

When, years later, Washington returned to warfare as Commander in Chief of the Continental Army, it was a still romantic hero who rode to Cambridge. He sneered at the alien New England troops as Manfred might have sneered, and intended to end the conflict in one tremendous military stroke. Had not a storm swooped down (it could be said miraculously) from the heavens, he might well, in one mad act of aggressive inspiration, have lost most of his army and with it the war.°

Washington did eventually succeed in dislodging the British from Boston, but only to have them reappear, greatly reinforced, in a terrain much better suited to their ends. He stood up to them like David to Goliath, but he might just as well have left his slingshot home. The British pushed him and his army around as if they were a group of overweening boys. Washington did succeed in two rash strokes — at Trenton and at Princeton — yet these triumphs, despite their psychological and strategic effectiveness, did little more than nibble on the edges of British power. Washington undertook one more desperate dash — at Germantown — where, as they reached out for full victory, his troops collapsed into complete rout. Monmouth proved inconclusive, and after that Washington utterly changed his strategy: he never again of his own volition attacked a major British force. The campaign against Yorktown was forced on him by the French and largely won through their assistance.

In 1776 and 1777, Washington's genius was wounded by British gunfire, starved by the Continental Congress, battered by bitter experience. Fallen to the ground, it sprang up again in a new form: judgment.

During the dark years of the Revolution, Washington developed his method of asking advice, balancing what alternatives the situation allowed, announcing his own decision only at the last moment. This technique was tailored to his military needs: the problem he faced was always finite; information from all general officers was valuable since a failure of

---

° See volume II, chapter 8.

any one of them during battle could endanger the whole army; and a last-minute decision reduced the possibility that what was planned would leak to the enemy. To this method, he added what seemed an opposite. Once the balance had, after however long uncertainty, tipped however slightly in its final direction, all hesitation left him: he acted on the conclusion he had so painfully reached with a fire that seemed more suited to a "genius" following a flash of inspiration. He had learned to hesitate in thought, but he never hesitated in execution. He was, in fact, once he moved, completely committed — no time now to set up another mental balance. As Jefferson put it, although he always advanced with "prudence," if something went wrong as he was moving, he was "slow in readjustment."[1]

Balancing to reach a final decision took up on occasion more time than the exigencies of warfare would allow. Washington dawdled disastrously concerning Fort Washington and should probably have struck earlier during the Monmouth campaign. For the Presidency, the method worked better: moving deliberately was often the best tactic since problems, particularly when linked to the kaleidoscope of the European war, had a way of disappearing of themselves. And in those days of slow communication, even the most persistent crises took time to ripen. As Mrs. Liston commented, "Most people say and do too much. Washington . . . never fell into this common error."[2]

His slow method of reaching decisions may well have appealed to Washington because it baffled his natural impetuosity. The dissertations in books on how Washington learned to curb his passions usually point only to the passions linked to rage, but it seems clear that he was laboring with the wide range of characteristics associated with "genius." The mature Washington did not, like Jefferson and Hamilton and Adams, express under the moment's incitation a violent opinion one day that he would contradict the next. Nearly all such fluctuations were absorbed in the private process of laying weights on interior mental balances. Intuition was not allowed to fly free, chanting insights like a nightingale; like one of Washington's majestic jacks, it was tethered to the realities of the subject under consideration. As process determines form, so Washington's method dictated judgment.

Yet this shift to attitudes approved by classicism did not mean that Washington had accepted a classical stance. Classicism looks back to precedent. Washington made precedent. As a soldier, he evolved, to meet unconventional situations, an unconventional type of warfare; as a statesman, he presided over an experimental government that sought new solutions to age-old dilemmas of mankind. He tried, in the manner of modern science, to find the universal not in the empyrean but in the particular. His classicism consisted primarily in his effort not to penetrate the future with the bursts of insight romantics sought, but rather to dig down to the ultimate bedrock on which he felt the structures of novelty must rest. Thus he applied "judgment" to the ends more commonly sought by "genius."

There can be no doubt that in Washington's temperament there was a wide streak of darkness. Although the foundations of his faith were positive, he acted from day to day in a cloud of forebodings and anxieties. His mind, when empty, filled with an almost Byronic gloom. But he did not, like many a romantic, revel in that gloom. He did his best to exorcise it.

The major panacea was physical exercise: by summoning his body, he could sidetrack his mind. He rode endlessly around his farms. When in his later years kept indoors by bad weather, he strode by the hour back and forth on Mount Vernon's long piazza. That exercise was hard to come by when he was President was undoubtedly an important cause of his being so unhappy in office, so eager to escape.

Another panacea, although it was more mixed with tensions, was contact with people. If an occasion — a convivial group, a reunion with an old friend, a chat with an agreeable stranger — offered possibilities of diversion, he grasped it eagerly. Although he rarely threw off sparks, he habitually radiated good humor. He laughed at other men's anecdotes and occasionally essayed his own. Yet those who knew him well felt in him always a fundamental gravity.

When the daughter of one of his estate managers, who seemed to be dying of tuberculosis, had an upturn, Washington wrote the father, with the kindest of intentions, not to give in to hopes that were probably "delusive." It would be "best" for Pearce "to make up your mind of the worst." Washington habitually prepared himself for disappointment by expecting catastrophe.[3] This was most conspicuous during the Revolution when his writings day after day, year after year, communicate that the cause was all but lost. But he did not then, or at any time, despair.

The faith that persisted below his pessimism was religious faith, but not of the churches. He did feel it his duty as President * to appear at divine worship, and, having been as a Virginian raised in the Church of En-

---

* When retired at Mount Vernon he explained that "for want of a place of worship within less than nine miles," he spent Sunday writing letters.[4]

gland (he had served as a vestryman) he usually attended Christ Church. However, he did not feel that his duty extended to kneeling when the rest of the congregation kneeled. After the minister, annoyed that when Martha took communion the President waited in his pew, preached a sermon in Washington's presence concerning the duty of great men to set a good example, Washington never attended that church again.[5]

Washington's religious belief was that of the the enlightenment: deism. He practically never used the word "God," preferring the more impersonal word "Providence." How little he visualized Providence in personal form is shown by the fact that he interchangeably applied to that force all three possible pronouns: he, she, and it. Providence ruled the universe and, since Washington was dedicated to the conceptions both of virtue and progress, he could not but believe that virtue would in the deepest sense be rewarded, that although the means Providence pursued were often past the comprehension of humanity, everything would eventually prove for the best.

Jefferson wrote of Washington, "His heart was not warm in its affections, but he calculated every man's value and give him solid esteem proportioned to it." This was another way of saying that Washington put what he considered the public good ahead of personal indulgences and private affections.

The first President did not, like Lincoln, comfort himself in times of suffering by making exceptions to general rules that delighted weeping mothers who managed to gain access to him. Washington would have regarded this as sentimental violation of evenhanded justice. He leaned over backward not to involve the foreign policy of the United States in the plight of his imprisoned spiritual son, Lafayette. He labored to keep, as Jefferson put it, "motives of interest or consanguinity, of friendship or hatred," from biasing his decisions.[6]

This determination undoubtedly stemmed from his early experiences with the opposite system as practiced by aristocratic Great Britain, where a man climbed not because of merit but through family manipulation. His beloved mentor, William Fairfax, had many a horrific story to tell of how he had been battered by half-indifferent relations until their "interest" had found him a safe harbor in Virginia. As Washington himself had watched, Fairfax's position became again perilous with the arrival in Virginia of his capricious patron, Lord Fairfax. Washington blamed his own inability to secure a commission in the British regular army during the

French and Indian War on his lack of pull in exalted places. He may have realized that a major advantage of the Continental Army was that promotion there had been by merit rather than, as among the British across the battleline, by family connection.

The most conspicuous exception in Washington's record on appointments was his designation of Gouverneur Morris as minister to France, an act which he admitted might be considered "a proof of my friendship if . . . none of my policy or judgment." As he grew older, the rigor of his self-control weakened somewhat, but even in those last years he deeply hurt the feelings of one of his oldest and closest friends, Knox. He explained at that time, "Esteem, love, and friendship can have no influence on my mind" as compared to the public good. This attitude did not encourage long-lasting relationships with ambitious men, a fact which created for Washington emotional problems.[7]

Although his intelligence and strength and will carried him ahead on his own momentum, he always felt the need of at least one companion to run beside him. It is amazing how numerous these companions were and for how short a time most of them lasted. Washington's first reliance during the Revolution, Joseph Reed, became his enemy, as did the first two advisers of the fledgling Commander in Chief, Generals Lee and Gates. During the Presidential period, Madison, Jefferson, and Randolph went over to the opposition. The reader can for himself fill in the long list. Even Hamilton, Washington's most faithful coadjutor during the Presidential years, had exploded against him during the Revolution. Significantly, the only man who accompanied him down the long reaches of his entire career, Dr. Craik, lacked the urge to shine in his own right. The trouble seems to have been Washington's fundamental self-reliance; he moved on his trajectory like a cannon ball. Nothing much clings to a cannon ball.

Washington mourned, as he grew older, his lack of a confidential companion.*[8] Through the crowds of men who surrounded him, Washington moved fundamentally alone. What of women?

"There is no truth more certain," Washington wrote, "than that all our enjoyments fall short of our expectations; and to none does it apply with more force than to the gratifications of the passions."[9] Although he put

---

* Craik was more an ancient and admired friend than a close companion. Lear's position was equivocal: although Washington depended on him, protected him, and was fond of him, although he twice married Washington's relations, his usefulness seems always to have been primarily as a second pair of hands.

passions in the plural, this sentence, written to a step-granddaughter, referred in particular to sexual passion.

Myths concerning Washington's sexuality run to extremes: he was, it is said, known to his friends as "the stallion of the Potomac"; he was, it is said, a eunuch, even a woman in disguise.° The authentic evidence — all that is known — indicates that Washington curbed in his maturity his sexual with his other passions. His early, doomed, and guilty love for Sally Fairfax, which makes evident that he had strong passions to control, must have made manifest to him how destructive such urges could be. There are strong indications that, despite his known denial, Washington was sterile. Since there seems to be no scientific psychiatric literature on the subject, it is impossible to guess what effect any anxiety he felt lest this be the case might have had on his sexuality. There can be do doubt, however, that he was no prude. To his step-granddaughters he denounced coquetry as raising hopes in men which the girls had no intention to realize, but he said no word concerning sexual purity. This could, of course, have been because he assumed no such word was necessary.† Yet in his analyses of candidates for appointment, while he worried about their behavior with liquor, he made not the slightest reference to their behavior with women. When Mrs. Powel accused him of having mislaid some love letters, he made clear that the concern he would have felt, had he had such letters to lose, would not have been that he had been caught in adultery but that he had betrayed the confidence of a lady.

Washington's escape from his traumatic entanglement with Sally had been his marriage with Martha. By wooing, while still in love with Sally, the wealthy (if also charming) widow, he may well have followed the principle he had laid out for his step-granddaughters: pursue judgment rather than passion. If so, the principle was triumphantly endorsed. It brought him the strongest, the longest-lasting, the most buoying relationship of his career.§ He wrote that he considered marriage the most impor-

---

° So distinguished an historian as Arnold Toynbee published the statement that Washington died because of a chill contracted visiting a black beauty in his slave quarters. The rumor that he was really a woman has come to this writer from two unconnected oral informants. It seems to stem from a satire, mocking the Rebel commander, published in New York during the Revolution.

† He would have been wrong in the case of Eliza Law, who, while her husband was abroad, took a lover and was said by gossip to have frequented his barracks dressed in an officer's uniform. But this was after Washington's death.[10]

§ Although Martha had conceived four children in rapid succession during her first marriage, Washington liked to feel that she was somehow responsible for his not having an heir. That this did not sour their relationship is testimony to how strong the other bonds between them were.

tant event of a man's life, and contrasted "the giddy rounds of promiscuous pleasure" unfavorably with "domestic felicity."[11] Domestic felicity! The graduate from an unhappy childhood boasted on more than one occasion that he had achieved in marriage not excitement (of which he had plenty elsewhere) but tranquillity.

Martha's ability to soothe diminished as both partners grew old, but, particularly during Washington's Revolutionary years, it had possessed the potency of a magic spell. She was probably the only human being whom the mature Washington allowed access to his soft, defenseless inner core. Outside observers saw only enough to be amazed at the hero's extreme sensitivity. Jefferson believed that Washington suffered from public attacks "more than any man I ever yet met with."[12] Such sensitivity might seem to go with a romantic genius. However, Washington wished to prevent the world from recognizing and fingering his weaknesses. He shuddered away from the thought of receiving anyone's pity.

Washington's vulnerability certainly impelled him to restraint in social situations. Many observers commented on his ability to be at the same time both affable and shut to familiarity. When Henrietta Liston gaily remarked that his countenance revealed the happiness he foresaw in his retirement, the President departed from his habitual courtesy: "You are wrong! My countenance never yet betrayed my feelings!" Mrs. Liston commented, "This was the only weak or vain thing I ever heard Washington utter." She had seen various emotions trespass on his face.[13]

The aloofness Washington combined with graciousness was also motivated by the necessity imposed on a man in power to keep his future acts from being guessed at; and by his conviction that if a man wished to command he could not permit too great familiarity (i.e., officers might not eat and gamble with their troops).° But there must have been more to it than that. Why was Washington more open to strangers at Mount Vernon than he was in the Presidential Mansions?

Throughout his career, despite the power of his personality and the stupendous success that attended him, Washington was shy. He hated to be stared at, as by portrait painters. This shyness was counteracted by lifelong habitude when he met people according to the traditions of Virginia entertaining: ever since he was conscious of the world, he had seen strangers appear on the doorstep and often be put up for the night. But

---

° The conception that the heads of state should be remote was classical. In the romantic period kings (on their way out) pretended that they were regular fellows, and now Presidents kiss (with whatever distaste) a symbolic baby or two.

he never got really used to the formal entertaining forced on him when he was the social focal point of a government operating in a major city.

Washington's shyness was an aspect of what was the most amazing of all his characteristics: the diffidence that traveled down the years in tandem with his self-confident power. The dichotomy goes as far back in his life as the records go. There could hardly have been a more extreme example of youthful cockiness than the wilderness mission which he undertook without a visible qualm at the age of nineteen, even exceeding his authority by undertaking negotiations with the Indians to which his skill was completely inadequate. But when, a few months later, he was under consideration for the command of Virginia's wilderness forces, he wrote the Governor, "I must be impartial enough to confess it is a charge too great for my youth and inexperience." Years later, when he was at the height of his celebrity, he discouraged, despite his lifelong interest in experimental agriculture, the publication of some letters he had written on that subject lest their appearance over his name should seem "a piece of ostentation."[14]

In modern times Washington is commonly criticized because he was not, in his years of fame, a simple friendly soul like your neighbor who will, in a pinch, come over and sit with the baby. Actually, Washington would have been a confinable idiot had he not recognized and responded to what had happened to him. The decorative arts of Washington's era reveal the hagiolatry with which he was regarded. On almost no kind of object to which his image could be applied do we fail to find it: furniture; fireirons; pitchers and bowls and plates; statues for the drawing room or garden in marble or porcelain or stone; pictures in oil or watercolor, or needlework, or wax; textiles; etc., etc., etc. After his death, "The Apotheosis of Washington" was depicted by amateurs and professionals in innumerable media with an elaboration and seriousness to modern eyes often comic.

Adulation accompanied with power tends so mightily to corrupt that it is startling Washington was so little corrupted. He could be, particularly towards the end of his life, self-righteous and stuffy, a tendency encouraged by his need to find protection for his sensitivity from the barbs of his political enemies. ("Conscious rectitude," he would write, "deprives their sting of its poison.")[15] His disapproval of divisive attacks on the administration surely comprised a belief that he knew what was best for the nation. If he sometimes confused his own person with the government, a multitude of the citizenry harbored the same confusion. If he kept a wall between himself and most of his fellow men, he threw almost no thunderbolts at his enemies from the top of that wall.

Washington described himself as "a mind who always walked on a straight line and endeavored, as far as human frailties and perhaps strong passions would enable him, to discharge the relative duties to his Maker and fellow men without seeking any indirect or left-handed attempts to acquire popularity."[16]

Washington never nurtured close contacts, as did Jefferson and Hamilton, with a partially subsidized press: he had no ministry of propaganda, not even a part-time press secretary. However much he may have used, during the Revolution, deception to bolster the record and the presumed strength of the Continental Army, during his Presidency, he never lied to the public. And he did always travel in a remarkably consistent line. From his earliest recorded acts to his senility, the parabola of his career rises from point to point with almost no wobbling. To an extent open to very few men in power, he was able to go his own way — and he had an overriding sense of direction.

Even when a very young man, Washington operated as an individual. His trip through the wilderness was, although on official business, primarily a personal adventure. He led the Virginia Regiment much as he pleased. And when he disagreed with the British higher command, he behaved publicly in a manner they considered insubordinate. Disassociating himself at last from an army where he was not listened to, he set up at Mount Vernon as a private operator. He was successful enough to have to bow to no creditors; he was never caught up in any of the shifts forced on those financially ateeter. In the Virginia House of Burgesses, he voted his own convictions, neither a leader or a follower.

The great break came, of course, when he stepped onto a truly large stage as Commander in Chief. Now he was in a position where a man may well lose much individual initiative. There is firstly the matter of getting the job. Almost all leaders, in amassing the support that puts them in office, incur obligations. Washington, his diffidence coming to the top, had tried to avoid being made Commander in Chief. Although Adams was to claim credit for manipulating the election, he did whatever he did do without Washington's connivance. The General assumed his command devoid of personal obligations. His allegiance was to Congress not as a group of politicians who had voted for him but as an entity representing the people.

As Commander in Chief Washington applied from the first his continuing method of combining cooperation with personal consistency. He had come to know his temperament well enough to realize that in relation to the exertion of power, he had no intermediate speed: he must either ignore or control. The solution was for him to stake out his own ground — in this situation the main Continental Army — and make no effort to dominate other centers of power. He allowed almost complete autonomy to commanders so far away that detailed orders would be crippling. Although he sent recommendations, often reiterated and passionately phrased, to the Continental Congress, he did not pull political strings or use the threat of military pressure to enforce his way. Woe, however, to anyone who, once Congress had ruled, tried to interfere with how Washington applied the decision within his own stamping ground!

In addition to suiting his temperament, Washington's subservience to Congress suited his ideals: at heart a citizen, not a soldier, he believed that, even in a military emergency, the ultimate power should remain with the representatives of the people. He gave a noble example of a general faithful to republican principles. Furthermore — whether or not this ever entered his conscious calculations — he thus passed the buck. There were circumstances often beyond anyone's control that prevented the raising of a stronger army, the amelioration of misery, the more rapid winning of the war. The onus, which human nature had to put somewhere, fell on Congress not on Washington.

And so there was further encouraged a phenomenon which filled Adams and his friends with apprehension and horror. Washington became in his own person the standard of the cause, so powerful with the people that no one could be certain that there were any bounds to how far he could, if he wished, carry his individual will. (The one major effort to displace him from his command, the Conway Cabal, collapsed as soon as the maneuver became public knowledge.) Washington upon occasion complained bitterly that he was an enslaved servant to his "masters," the people.[17] Yet his curtailment of his will became increasingly not a matter of necessity but of restraint. He was still consistently following his own star.

As he envisioned retirement, Washington gleefully foresaw that he would no longer have to take orders from anyone. Once he was back at Mount Vernon he became his own complete master. He so enjoyed this freedom, linked as it was with other pleasures, that his return to public life via the Constitutional Convention was, at least to his conscious mind, a source of deep regret. He achieved the Presidency by the negative act of saying nothing. He traveled to New York not as the captain of an embattled team which had won a tug-of-war with its opponents, but as the pillar around which the government would form itself. Madison wrote that Washington was the only part of the new political dispensation that really appealed to the people.[18] Again Washington owed his eminence to no specific group of men, to no man outside his own skin. Again he was free and again he acted with great restraint.

The separation of powers that had been defined by the Constitutional Convention, over which Washington had presided, was perfectly suited to his temperament, and, indeed, stated the method of handling himself he had applied during the Revolution. He enforced, as President, complete personal control in the executive, and with equal rigor, kept his hands off the other departments. He explained, "As the Constitution of the United States and the laws made under it [by the legislature, of course] mark the line of my official conduct, I could not justify taking a single step in any matter which appeared to me to require their agency, without its being obtained."[19]

In pursuance of the ideal of a recessive executive and a dominant legislature, President Jefferson was to gain his ends of manipulating the legislature. Washington would have considered this a violation of the separation of powers. John Adams remembered, "During President Washington's whole administration of eight years his authority in the Senate [where Adams presided] was extremely weak." This did not mean that he intended to be a doormat for the legislature: he put down with hammer blows the effort of the House to encroach on his prerogatives. The national capital which bears his name still enshrines in its geography his political theories. To keep congressmen out of the executive offices, he grouped the offices around the President's Mansion at a distance from the capitol which it then took some time to traverse.[20]

Only after a bill had been passed by the legislature and laid on his desk for approval or veto did he (in obedience to the Constitution) act. "From motives of respect to the legislature (and I might add from my interpretation of the Constitution) I give my signature to many bills with which my judgment is at variance." [21] He believed, indeed, that the prime purpose of the veto was to enable the President to negate acts that were unconstitutional.

For the President reasonably to carry out this function, he had to be above party. When the President became a party leader, the Supreme Court stepped into the breach. This was in itself a great Constitutional change, since a Presidential veto was not like a Supreme Court decision an ultimate fiat: it could be overruled by two thirds of Congress.

Such matters are obscured by the fact that Washington is not uncommonly described as a Federalist President presiding over a Federalist government. That this fallacy is so rife shows how hard it has become to think of politics apart from party. Even modern dictatorships are called "one-party governments." Dictators are hoisted into power by organized henchmen who then help them rule. Washington had disbanded his organized support when he had sent his army home. Not only did he not secure or maintain his power through the cooperation of any specific group,* but he cannot even be correctly styled as the leader of a coalition government. Such figures rely for their basic mandate on one of the participating parties. Far from being (until after his official career had ended) either a Federalist or a Republican, Washington disapproved of both "factions." He was, as a practical leader, able to do this because he commanded in his own person greater support than either faction could muster. The Republicans, as Jefferson and Madison and Monroe admitted ruefully, were helpless when Washington opposed them in the arenas of public opinion.[22] The Federalists did not bring Washington power but tried to gain it from him; they did their best to huddle in Washington's shadow.

One of Jefferson's main anguishes as Secretary of State was that, by taking the necessary steps to enforce the unavoidable Neutrality Proclamation, he was eroding his political support. Many of the twists engaged in by Jefferson and Madison were required by their need not to lose their power base in Virginia. Hamilton, never himself a popular figure, had to drop plums to supporters. But Washington was free to act as he pleased.

In his youth or early young manhood, Washington had been deeply impressed by Stoic philosophy as it was interpreted in eighteenth-century England primarily through Addison's *Cato*. At first the conceptions seem

---

* The one group that could conceivably be pointed to, the Society of the Cincinnati, was at the polls a feeble force.

to have lain fallow — Washington was anything but a Cato during the French and Indian War — but after his retirement, when he placed behind him the exotic ambition to be a professional in the British army, the Stoic tenets rose to occupy a central place in his mind. He accepted as guiding lights the "Roman virtues" of lofty patriotism, love of freedom, unselfish service to the state, and a self-mastery that excluded all but the most magnanimous emotions.

He had found a persuasive formula for self-regulation, but it did not define effective principles of government. These Washington had to seek in more modern sources. The Americans, he wrote, were lucky to be living in times when the science of government was so much better understood than formerly. However, Washington almost never made specific references to the political theorists who were influencing world thought. The two publications which seem to have moved him most were both written in America: Paine's *Common Sense* and *The Federalist*.[23] More steadily, he was instructed by the thoughts in the minds of the people he met, the aspirations in their hearts.

Many of the philosophical conceptions Washington acted out had originated in France, yet France nurtured in her revolution not another Washington but Robespierre and Napoleon. He relied on British traditions concerning individual liberty, but the British, who had followed Cromwell, were now ruled by George III. Among historians there is a perennial argument over whether the American Revolution was a reaction to British mismanagement of colonial policy, or was inevitable because the new continent had in fact produced a new kind of man: a man who, shaped by a new environment, was more receptive than the French to French libertarian philosophy, more determined than the British concerning individual rights. Washington's career is an argument for the second of these conceptions, all the more because his own contacts with Europe were tenuous compared to his experiences in the American wilderness.

Even as the shaping of Washington was an American achievement, so was the recognition that a giant was being shaped. In another nation and time, the call that sounded would have been a different call, elevating a different kind of man. Yet the fact remains that, after he had achieved his power, there opened to Washington roads other than the elevated path, pursuing the noblest American conceptions, which he followed.

Almost every revolution except the American has eventuated in a dictatorship that extinguishes liberty and human rights. For this there are profound reasons. Existing institutions are destroyed and all is turmoil.

But the time comes when new institutions must grow rather than be instantly cut off at the roots. Then, a strong man puts one faction in power and forces with the sword unity on the nation.

The American Revolution, being in so great a part a foreign war, was less socially destructive within the nation than many another. However, the strain and damage had been great and, as victory began to dawn, the future was murky. No one knew how order could finally be restored, in what way the alliance of thirteen semi-independent states might be continued, how the huge, diverse, incoherent area that was the United States should and could be governed. Washington's successful pursuit during the war of the widest possible support gave additional strength to the universal tendency of men to seek escape from confusion and anguish by following a messiah. Down the centuries almost every man placed by his efforts and his good fortune in the position Washington now occupied has made use of his transcendent power to trample on the rights of others. Having been demonstrated (so it seemed to them) supermen, they have followed their super wills.

Could Washington, had he so wished, have made himself dictator or king? The tempters were there: the army had real grievances and seemed more eager than not to march on the civilian governments: financiers were anxious to put up funds; the field seemed clear; it needed only a nod from Washington. In some of his manifestations the American man would surely have resisted, but that man had still only partially emerged from the older forms, was still not sure that the republicanism to which his instincts pointed could actually be achieved. If the leader so revered, so trusted, so conspicuous as the standard of the patriot cause, had veered from the republican path, how many Americans would have followed? Perhaps enough to crush all opposition to His Royal Highness George I or George Washington, Lord Protector of the United States. Surely enough so that fire would have had to be fought with fire in a way that would have brought republican institutions down in ashes. Before he broke with Washington, Jefferson wrote, "The moderation and virtue of a single character probably prevented this revolution from being closed, as most others have been, by a subversion of that liberty it was intended to establish."[24]

Washington returned to his farm, hoping that the people would work their own way to the creation of national institutions. When the opposite seemed the case, he accepted the necessity of a Constitutional Convention. There have not been lacking historians who viewed the convention as a right-wing plot to put shackles on the people. If so, it was amazingly mild compared to the efforts in other lands to build structure out of post-revolutionary confusion. For his part, Washington saw it as an effort to bring all the people together under a government as satisfactory to variant interests as possible.

While President, Washington continued to see his task as the creation and perpetuation of national unity. However, he was charged with desiring what he had, at a more favorable time, repudiated: he was charged with trying to establish an American aristocracy with himself at the head. Thus menaced by sledgehammer blows of slander, Washington fought back only once — in his attack on the Democratic Societies. His elevation did not encourage him to pounce on his enemies: he seems rather to have been frightened of his power to destroy. His detractors ran around at will, screaming as loudly as they pleased. Jefferson pursued his road to the Presidency without ever being publicly criticized by Washington. The only defense Washington raised against his enemies was a wall of silence. As he retired of his own volition, he made no effort to influence the selection of a successor. He left the field wide open to his foes.

To dig for the ultimate motivation for Washington's behavior, is to unearth a conception mocked at and distrusted in the 1970's as this passage is being written: political virtue. Washington shared, with the rest of the world's great movers, a taste for power and a hunger for fame. The difference lay in his desire to apply that power for the betterment of his fellow men, his belief that his fame would be longer lasting if he did not engage in the dark passions and lust for conquest of his fellow rulers, but led mankind (once the necessary liberating war had been won) towards peace, self-determination for all nations, universal self-rule.

In comparing Napoleon and Washington, the French statesman-author François René de Chateaubriand wrote that Napoleon seemed to exceed to a much greater extent "the ordinary stature of mankind." Yet the empire Napoleon created vanished while Washington's republic remained: "Search the unknown forests where glistened the sword of Washington. What will you find there? Graves? No, a world!"

Washington, so the French writer continued, "seconded instead of thwarting the movement of the mind; he aimed at that which it was his duty to aim at; hence the coherence and perpetuity of his work. The man, who appears not very striking because he is natural and in his just proportions, blended his existence with that of his country. His glory is the common patrimony of growing civilization. His renown towers like one of those sanctuaries whence flows an inexhaustible spring of the people."[25]

After Washington had been long buried, Jefferson wrote of the man with whom he had once wrestled, "His was the singular destiny and merit of leading the armies of his country successfully through an arduous war for the establishment of its independence, of conducting its councils through the birth of a government, new in its forms and principles, until it settled down into a quiet and orderly train; and of scrupulously obeying the laws through the whole of his career, civil and military, of which the history of the world furnishes no other example."[26]

The most famous summary of Washington's career was spoken by Henry Lee in a memorial address delivered at the request of Congress two days after the ex-President died: "First in war, first in peace, first in the hearts of his countrymen."[27] Although efforts have subsequently been made to smudge the record, Washington was, indeed, first in war and first in peace. The third of Lee's contentions — "first in the hearts of his countrymen" — was also true when Lee spoke. However, as generations move by, old hearts give way to new.

When an old man smarting under the lashes of his detractors, Washington comforted himself with the thought that "by the records of my administration and not the voice of faction I expect to be acquitted or condemned hereafter."[28] His hope has been disappointed. Although the Washington who lived and was buried did leave solid records behind him, ghostly imposters, each wearing his face and costume, have walked hardly hindered in the American imagination. Generation after generation, he has been re-envisioned in a kaleidoscope of spurious guises. His memory has been pelted and revered. Politicians, fanatics, heroes, villains, prejudiced historians, superpatriots, inconoclasts, greedy hacks and self-enchanted clowns, sanctimonious simpletons, octogenarians in their wheelchairs and children escaping from their nurseries have all unloaded on his image their psychic wounds, their preconceptions, hungers, hopes, ideals, hates, and fears.

Let us turn away from this hurly-burly which has become almost completely irrelevant to the Washington who really lived; let us descend the bluff on the banks of the Potomac to the little dell which George Washington in his last years selected for his tomb. There is no pomp here, just a small vault embedded in a hillside and preceded by two hideous Victorian shafts raised to later inhabitants of Mount Vernon. Bugles and drums may come here sometimes but they are out of place. Here lies greatness without ostentation, the dust of a man who denied the temptations of power as few other men in history have ever done. A man who desired from his fellow men not awe, not obedience, but love.

Acknowledgments
Bibliography
Source References

Acknowledgments

D URING the many years, now more than a third of a century, that I have been writing books on the American past, I have always been a parasite on libraries. The warmth and courtesy with which I have been almost universally received, the efficiency and understanding with which I have been assisted, are among the most heartwarming memories of my life.

In the preparation of this volume, as was the case with its predecessors on George Washington, I have greatly profited from the assistance of three major institutions. The New York Public Library, which has permitted me to use its Frederick Lewis Allen Room, and the New-York Historical Society, have alternately (and sometimes simultaneously) given me hospitality. And the Mount Vernon Ladies' Association of the Union have opened to me their invaluable collections. Few privileges I have ever enjoyed have equaled that of being allowed to wander Washington's acres, to sit on the majestic portico he designed, enjoying in solitude, as he himself had often done, the light of evening as it waned over his vast Potomac vista.

Among other institutions that have been helpful to me are the library of the Century Association, the Free Library of Cornwall, Connecticut, the Library of Congress, the Frick Art Reference Library, and the New York Society Library.

My wife, Beatrice Hudson Flexner, and my daughter, Helen Hudson Flexner, have helped in many ways. My editor, Llewellyn Howland III, has often put his shoulder to the wheel, helping to pull my project out of the mire. Donald Jackson, editor of The George Washington Papers, on whose advisory committee I serve, has graciously and effectively answered queries. Ellen B. Lorch and Elsie Augenblick have re-created my tangled copy in elegantly typed form.

I am also grateful to Julian P. Boyd, Lyman Butterfield, Manning J. Dauer, John A. Castellani, James Gregory, James J. Heslin, Mary-Jo Kline, Harold C. Syrett, Dumas Malone, Christine Meadows, Henry Allen Moe, Richard B. Morris, Frank E. Morse, and Charles C. Wall.

Bibliography

IN each of the previous volumes of this work, I opened the Bibliography with a general discussion of sources and methods. There is little to add here (except on the matter of slavery), especially since Washington's second term presented to research much the same problems as his first. However, the most important principles I have abided by should perhaps be recapitulated for readers who are beginning the series with this book.

Happenings have been of importance to my labors in exact proportion to how greatly they impinged on Washington, how greatly Washington impinged on them. The nature of his career makes the canvas a very broad one, yet there are many aspects of events and personalities that lie beyond its edges.

Not attempting to summarize the lives or traits of men like Jefferson and Hamilton, I have tried to show Washington's coadjutors only as they acted in relation to him during the years when their careers were closely interwoven with his. This has not kept them from appearing very frequently on these pages. I was, indeed, surprised, when preparing the Source References, to recognize how often I quoted Jefferson. Being less reticent than Washington and Hamilton, Jefferson copiously recorded events and his own reactions. The picture here presented of Jefferson in relation to Washington is, if unconventional, primarily based on Jefferson's own words.

My efforts have brought home to me how grievously the history of the blacks in the United States has been, until recently, neglected. In the two-volume index to Fitzpatrick's edition of Washington's writings — 746 closely printed pages — almost everything is itemized except the names of slaves. Freeman turned his back on the problems raised by Washington

[509]

and slavery; the successors, who wrote the last volume of his series, ignored significant documents. Except for the examinations undertaken by the staff at Mount Vernon for their own purposes of accurate reconstruction, the archives concerning slavery on Washington's plantations — said to be the fullest preserved from eighteenth-century Virginia — have lain fallow. The many mentions of slavery in Washington's correspondence have been largely overlooked. Thus, my determination to do as much as in an all-over biography I reasonably could with Washington and slavery carried me into virgin fields of research. The reward in exciting discoveries was considerably greater than I had anticipated.

I have tried, as far as possible, to consult and quote, concerning the central aspects of my subject, original documents. In finding those documents, and also in filling in the extensive backgrounds against which my action lay, I have been helped by innumerable historical editors and writers.° An attempt to cite all the publications I have consulted would create a list both impractical to use and out of reasonable proportion to my text. In my first volume I included an essay on earlier biographies of Washington which it seems unnecessary to repeat. For a general survey of the period, the reader is referred to the excellent annotated bibliography appended to John C. Miller's *The Federalist Era*. A longer list, filling sixty-five pages, will be found in the sixth volume of Freeman's *Washington*.

The following Bibliography is not intended as evidence that I have studied my subject. Critics can make up their minds on that matter from the text. The Bibliography is aimed at a specific and pragmatic goal: to make it possible, by presenting an alphabetical list of the titles cited, to use abbreviations in the Source References.

Adams, Henry, *Life of Albert Gallatin* (Philadelphia and London, 1880).
Adams-Jefferson Letters, ed. Lester J. Capron (Chapel Hill, 1959).
Adams, John, *Letters of John Adams Addressed to his Wife*, vol. II (Boston, 1841).
—— *Works*, ed. Charles Francis Adams, 10 vols. (Boston, 1850–1856); referred to in Source References as "AA."

° In my previous volumes, I have acknowledged a great obligation to the many-volume life of Washington by Douglas Southhall Freeman, which, as it followed Washington's career from day to day, was as close to a primary source as any such book can be. Freeman, alas, died before he could draw conclusions in the summary of Washington's career that he intended, and also before he could carry his work to the period covered by my present volume. I have found the continuation by his successors, comprising volume VII of the work, also useful, although the incisive judgment of the original author is often lacking.

Addison, Alexander, *Causes and Error of Complaints and Jealousy of the Administration of the Government* (Philadelphia, 1797).
—— *On the Alien Act: A Charge to the Grand Juries* (Washington, Penna., 1799).
Adet, Pierre Auguste, *Notes Addressées par le Citoyen Adet . . . au Secrétaire d'État des États Unis* (Philadelphia, 1796).
Alberts, Robert C., *The Golden Voyage: The Life and Times of William Bingham* (Boston, 1969).
American State Papers, Foreign Relations, vol. I (Washington, D.C., 1832), *Miscellaneous*, vol. I (Washington, 1834).
Ames, Fisher, *Works*, ed. Seth Ames, 2 vols. (Boston, 1854).
Ammon, Henry, *James Monroe* (New York, 1971).
Annals of Congress, First to Fourth Congress, 6 vols. (Washington, D.C., 1834–1849).
Asbury, Francis, *Journal*, vol. I (New York, 1821).
Bacon-Foster, Cora, *Early Chapters in the Development of the Potomac Route to the West* (Washington, D.C., 1912).
Baker, William S., *Character Portraits of Washington* (Philadelphia, 1887).
—— *Washington After the Revolution* (Philadelphia, 1898).
Baldwin, Leland D., *Whiskey Rebels* (Pittsburgh, 1929).
Bathe, Greville, *Citizen Genêt, Diplomat and Inventor* (Philadelphia, 1946).
Bathe, Greville, and Bathe, Dorothy, *Oliver Evans* (Philadelphia, 1935).
Bemis, Samuel Flagg, *A Diplomatic History of the United States* (New York, 1955).
—— *Jay's Treaty*, revised edition (New Haven, 1962).
—— *Pinckney's Treaty* (New Haven, 1960).
—— ed., *American Secretaries of State and their Diplomacy*, vols. I–II (New York, 1917).
Bernard, John, *Retrospections of America* (New York, 1887).
Beveridge, Albert J., *Life of John Marshall*, 4 vols. (Boston, 1916–1919).
Bond, Beverley W., Jr., *The Monroe Mission to France* (Baltimore, 1907).
Bowen, Clarence W., *The History of the Centennial Celebration of the Inauguration of George Washington* (New York, 1892).
Bowers, Claude G., *Jefferson and Hamilton* (Boston, 1926).
Brackenridge, Hugh H., *Incidents of the Insurrection in the Western Parts of Pennsylvania in the Year 1794*, 3 vols. in 1 (Philadelphia, 1795).
Brant, Irving, "Edmund Randolph, Not Guilty," *William and Mary Quarterly*, 3rd ser., VII (1950), 180–198.
—— *James Madison*, 5 vols. (Indianapolis, 1948–1956).
Brooks, Joshua, "A Dinner at Mount Vernon, 1799," *New-York Historical Society Quarterly*, XXXI (1947), 72–85.
Brooks, Noah, *Henry Knox* (New York, 1900).
Bryan, Wilhelmus Bogart, *A History of the National Capital*, vol. I (New York, 1914).
Cary, Thomas G., *Memoir of Thomas Handasyd Perkins, containing Extracts from his Diaries and Letters* (Boston, 1856).
Clark, Allen C., *Greenleaf and Law in the Federal City* (Washington, D.C., 1901).
Cobbett, William, *Porcupine's Political Censor* (Philadelphia, 1796).
Cohen, William, "Thomas Jefferson and the Problem of Slavery," *Journal of American History*, LVI (1969), 503–526.
Coke, Thomas, *Extracts of the Journals of the Rev. Dr. Coke's Five Visits to America* (London, 1793).
Combs, Jerald A., *The Jay Treaty* (Berkeley, 1970).
Conway, Moncure D., *George Washington at Mount Vernon* (Brooklyn, N.Y., 1889).
—— *Omitted Chapters of History Disclosed in the Life and Papers of Edmund Randolph* (New York, 1888).
Cook, Roy Bird, *Washington's Western Lands* (Strasburg, Va., 1930).
"Correspondence of the French Ministers to the United States, 1791–1797," ed. Frederick J. Turner, *Annual Report of the American Historical Association for the Year 1903*, II (Washington, D.C., 1904).

Crawford, M. Macdermot, *Madame de Lafayette and her Family* (New York, 1907).

Cresson, William Penn, *James Monroe* (Chapel Hill, 1946).

Cunliffe, Marcus, *George Washington, Man and Monument* (Boston, 1958).

Cunningham, Noble E., Jr., *The Jeffersonian Republicans* (Chapel Hill, 1957).

Custis, Eliza, "Self-portrait," *Virginia Magazine*, LIII (1945), 89–100.

Custis, George Washington Parke, *Recollections and Private Memoirs of Washington* (Philadelphia, 1860); referred to in Source References as "GWPC."

—— "Letters from . . . to George Washington, 1797–1798," *Virginia Magazine*, XX (1912), 296–311.

Dallas, George Mifflin, *Life and Writings of Alexander James Dallas* (Philadelphia, 1871).

Dauer, Manning J., "The Two John Nicholases," *American Historical Review*, XLV (1940), 338–353.

Davis, David Brian, *Problems of Slavery in Western Culture* (Ithaca, N.Y., 1966).

Decatur, Stephen, Jr., *Private Affairs of George Washington from the Records and Accounts of Tobias Lear* (Boston, 1933).

De Conde, Alexander, *Entangling Alliances, Politics and Diplomacy under George Washington* (Durham, N.C., 1958).

—— *History of American Foreign Policy* (New York, 1961).

Delaplaine, Edward S., *Life of Thomas Johnson* (New York, 1927).

Drake, Francis S., *Life and Correspondence of Henry Knox* (Boston, 1873).

[Duane, William], *A Letter to George Washington . . . containing Strictures on his Address . . . by Jasper Dwight of Vermont* (Philadelphia, 1796).

Dunlap, William, *A History of the Rise and Progress of the Arts of Design in the United States*, 2 vols. in 3 (New York, 1969).

Dwight, Jasper, see Duane, William.

Farrand, Max, *Records of the Federal Convention of 1787*, 4 vols. (New Haven, 1937).

Fauchet, Jean, *A Sketch of the Present State of our Political Relations with the United States of America* (Philadelphia, 1797).

Fielding, Mantle, *Gilbert Stuart's Portraits of Washington* (Philadelphia, 1933).

Findley, William, *History of the Insurrection in the Four Western Counties of Pennsylvania* (Philadelphia, 1796).

Fitzpatrick, John C., *The Last Will and Testament of George Washington* (Mount Vernon, 1939).

Flexner, James Thomas, *America's Old Masters* (New York, 1939).

—— *Doctors on Horseback* (New York, 1937).

—— *George Washington*, vols. I–III (Boston, 1965, 1968, 1970); referred to in Source of References as "Fl, W."

—— *Gilbert Stuart* (New York, 1955).

—— *Steamboats Come True* (New York, 1944).

Floyd, William Barrow, "The Portraits and Paintings at Mount Vernon," *Antiques*, C (1971), 768–774, 894–899.

Ford, David, "Journal of an Expedition in the Autumn of 1794," *New Jersey Historical Society Proceedings*, 1st ser., VIII (1856–1859), 75–88.

Ford, Paul Leicester, *The True George Washington* (Philadelphia, 1898).

Ford, Worthington C., "Edmund Randolph and the British Treaty, 1795," *American Historical Review*, XII (1906–1907), 587–599.

—— *The Spurious Letters Attributed to Washington* (Brooklyn, N.Y., 1889).

—— *Washington as an Employer and Importer of Labor* (Brooklyn, N.Y., 1889).

Freehling, William W., "The Founding Fathers and Slavery," *American Historical Review*, LXXVII (1972), 81–91.

Freeman, Douglas Southhall, *George Washington, a Biography*, completed by J. A. Carroll and M. W. Ashworth, 7 vols. (New York, 1948–1957); referred to in Source References as "F."

Freneau, Philip, *Prose*, selected by Philip M. Marsh (Brunswick, N.J., 1953).

Garrard, Lewis H., *Memoir of Charlotte Chambers* (Philadelphia, 1856).

Genêt, Edmond Charles, "Correspondence," *American Historical Association Annual Report for 1903*, II (Washington, D.C., 1904), 201–286.

Gould, William, "Journal of the New Jersey Infantry during the Expedition into Pennsylvania in 1794," *New Jersey Historical Society Proceedings*, 1st ser., III (1848–1849), 173–191.

Griswold, Rufus W., *The Republican Court* (New York, 1856).

Hamilton, Alexander, *Papers*, ed. Harold C. Syrett, vols. I–XV (New York, 1961–1969); referred to in Source References as "HS."

—— *Works*, ed. John C. Hamilton, 7 vols. (New York, 1850–1851); referred to in Source References as "HH."

—— *Works*, ed. Henry Cabot Lodge, 12 vols. (New York, 1904).

Hiltzheimer, Jacob, *Extracts from the Diary of* . . . (Philadelphia, 1893).

Hough, Franklin B., *Washingtoniana, or Memorials of the Death of George Washington*, 2 vols. (Roxbury, Mass., 1865).

Howard, John Tasker, *Our American Music* (New York, 1954).

Humphreys, David, *A Poem on the Happiness of America* (London, 1786).

—— "The Life of George Washington," ms. Rosenbach Foundation, Philadelphia.

Hunt, Gaillard, *Calendar of Applications and Recommendations for Office during the Presidency of George Washington* (Washington, D.C., 1893).

Hunter, Robert, *Quebec to Carolina in 1785–1786*, ed. Louis B. Wright and Marion Tinling (San Marino, Cal., 1943).

James, Alfred P., "A Political Interpretation of the Whiskey Rebellion," *Western Pennsylvania Historical Magazine*, XXXII (1949), 90–101.

Jay, John, *Correspondence and Public Papers*, ed. Henry P. Johnston, 4 vols. (New York, 1890–1893); referred to in Source References as "JJ."

Jay, William, *Life of John Jay*, 2 vols. (New York, 1833).

Jefferson, Thomas, *Papers*, ed. Julian P. Boyd, vols. VI–XVIII (Princeton, 1952–1971).

—— *Writings*, ed. Paul Leicester Ford, 10 vols. (New York, 1892–1899); referred to in Source References as "JF."

—— *Writings*, ed. A. A. Lipscomb and A. E. Berg, 20 vols. (Washington, D.C., 1903).

Jenkins, Charles Francis, *Washington in Germantown* (Philadelphia, 1905).

Jordan, Winthrop D., *White over Black* (Baltimore, 1969).

Journal of the Executive Proceedings of the Senate of the United States, 3 vols. (Washington, D.C., 1828).

Journal of the House of Representatives of the United States, 9 vols. (Philadelphia, 1826).

Journal of the Senate of the United States, 5 vols. (Philadelphia, 1820).

Kaplan, Lawrence S., *Jefferson and France* (New Haven, 1967).

Kaufman, Burton Ira, *Washington's Farewell Address: the View from the Twentieth Century* (Chicago, 1969).

King, Rufus, *Life and Correspondence*, ed. Charles R. King, 6 vols. (New York, 1895).

Knopf, R. C., *Anthony Wayne* . . . *The Wayne-Knox-Pickering-McHenry Correspondence* (Pittsburgh, 1960).

Koch, Adrienne, *Jefferson and Madison* (New York, 1950).

Lafayette, Marquis de, *Letters of Lafayette to Washington*, ed. Louis Gottschalk (New York, 1944).

Latrobe, Benjamin Henry, *Journal* (New York, 1905).

Laurens, John, *Army Correspondence* (New York, 1867).

Lear, Tobias, *Letters from George Washington to Tobias Lear* . . . , privately printed from originals in the collection of William K. Bixley (Rochester, N.Y., 1905).

—— *Letters and Recollections of Washington* . . . *with a Diary of Washington's Last Days* (New York, 1906).

Leary, Lewis, *That Rascal Freneau* (New Brunswick, N.J., 1941).

Link, Eugene Perry, *Democratic-Republican Societies* (New York, 1942).

Liston, Henrietta, "A Diplomat's Wife in Philadelphia: Letters of Henrietta Liston, 1796–1800," ed. Bradford Perkins, *William and Mary Quarterly*, 3rd ser., XI (1954), 592–632.

—— "Journal of Washington's Resignation, Retirement, and Death," ed. James C. Nicholls, *Pennsylvania Magazine*, XCVI (1971), 511–520.

Lodge, Henry Cabot, *George Washington*, 2 vols. (Boston, 1899).

Logan, Deborah Norris, *Memoir of Dr. George Logan* (Philadelphia, 1899).

Luetscher, George D., *Early Political Machinery in the United States* (Philadelphia, 1903).

Lynd, Staughton, *Class Conflict, Slavery, and the United States Constitution* (Indianapolis, 1968).

Macon, Althea Jane, *Gideon Macon of Virginia and Some of his Descendants* (Macon, Ga., 1956).

Madison, James, "Autobiography," ed. Douglas Adair, *William and Mary Quarterly*, 3rd ser., II (1945), 191–209.

—— *Writings*, ed. Gaillard Hunt, 9 vols. (New York, 1900–1910); referred to in Source References as "MH."

Malone, Dumas, *Jefferson and His Time*, 4 vols. (Boston, 1948–1970); referred to in Source References as "M."

Marshall, John, *George Washington*, 5 vols. (Fredericksburg, Va., 1926).

Mason, George, *Papers*, ed. Robert A. Rutland, 3 vols. (Chapel Hill, 1970).

Mazyck, Walter H., *George Washington and the Negro* (Washington, D.C., 1932).

McColley, Robert, *Slavery in Jeffersonian Virginia* (Urbana, 1964).

McMaster, John B., *A History of the People of the United States*, vol. II (New York, 1885).

Miller, John C., *Alexander Hamilton* (New York, 1952).

——, *The Federalist Era* (New York, 1960).

Minnigerode, Meade, *Jefferson, Friend of France, 1793: the Career of Edmond Charles Genêt* (New York, 1928).

—— *Lives and Times* (New York, 1925).

Mitchell, Broadus, *Alexander Hamilton*, 2 vols. (New York, 1957, 1962).

Monaghan, Frank, *John Jay* (New York, 1935).

Monroe, James, *Autobiography*, ed. Stuart Gerry Brown and Donald G. Baker (Syracuse, 1959).

—— *Papers . . . Listed in Chronological Order from the Original Manuscripts in the Library of Congress*, ed. Worthington Chauncey Ford (Washington, D.C., 1904).

—— *Writings*, ed. Stanislaus Murray Hamilton, 7 vols. (New York, 1898–1903); listed in Source References as "MoH."

—— *View of the Conduct of the Executive of the United States* (Philadelphia, 1797).

Morgan, John Hill, and Fielding, Mantle, *Life Portraits of Washington and their Replicas* (Philadelphia, 1931).

Morris, Gouverneur, *Diary and Letters*, ed. Anne C. Morris, 2 vols. (New York, 1888).

Morris, Richard B., *John Jay, the Nation and the Court* (Boston, 1967).

—— "Washington and Hamilton, A Great Collaboration," *Proceedings of the American Philosophical Society*, CII (1958), 107–116.

Morse, Frank E., "About General Washington's Freed Negroes," typescript (Mount Vernon, 1968).

Mount Vernon, *Inventory of the Contents of Mount Vernon, Privately Printed from the Manuscript Copy owned by W. K. Bixley* (New York, 1909).

Mount Vernon Ladies' Association, *Annual Report, 1944–1970* (Mount Vernon, 1945–1971).

Niemcewicz, Julian Ursyn, *Under Their Vine and Fig Tree: Travels through America*, translated by Metchie J. E. Budka (Elizabeth, N.J., 1965).

Paine, Thomas, *Letter to George Washington, President of the United States of America* (Philadelphia, 1796).

—— *Writings*, edited by Moncure D. Conway, vol. III (New York, 1895).

Palmer, Robert R., *Age of Democratic Revolution*.

Paltsits, Victor Hugo, *Washington's Farewell Address* (New York, 1935).

Park, Lawrence, *Gilbert Stuart*, 4 vols. (New York, 1926).

Parkinson, Richard, *George Washington: Statement of Richard Parkinson* (Baltimore, 1909).
—— *A Tour in America*, 2 vols. (London, 1805).
Paulding, James K., *Life of Washington* 2 vols. (New York, 1835).
Pennsylvania Archives, 2nd ser., IV (Harrisburg, 1896). Various copies of this volume have different pagination. The copy here referred to is in the New York Public Library.
Perkins, Bradford, *The First Rapproachement: England and the United States, 1795–1805* (Philadelphia, 1955).
Peterson, Merrill D., *Thomas Jefferson and the New Nation* (New York, 1970).
Pickering, Octavius, *Life of Timothy Pickering*, 4 vols. (Boston, 1867–1873); referred to in Source References as "PP."
Pleasants, J. Hall, *Four Late Eighteenth Century Anglo-American Landscape Painters* (Worcester, Mass., 1943).
Powell, J. H., *Bring Out Your Dead: The Great Plague of Yellow Fever in Philadelphia in 1793* (Philadelphia, 1949).
Prussing, Eugene E., *The Estate of George Washington, Deceased* (Boston, 1927).
Quincy, Eliza S. M., *Memoir* (Boston, 1861).
Randolph, Edmund, *A Vindication of Mr. Randolph's Resignation* (Philadelphia, 1795). The pagination in the Source References refers to a more easily procurable edition, *A Vindication of Edmund Randolph* (Richmond, Va., 1855).
Richardson, James D., ed., *A Compilation of the Messages and Papers of the Presidents*, vol. I (Washington, 1896).
Ritcheson, Charles R., *Aftermath of the Revolution: British Policy towards the United States, 1783–1795* (Dallas, 1969).
Robinson, Donald L., *Slavery in the Structure of American Politics* (New York, 1971).
Rowland, Kate Mason, *Life of George Mason* (New York, 1892).
Rush, Benjamin, *Letters*, ed. Lyman H. Butterfield, 2 vols. (Princeton, 1948).
Rush, Richard, *Occasional Productions* (Philadelphia, 1860).
Schachner, Nathan, *Thomas Jefferson*, 2 vols. (New York, 1951).
Scharf, John Thomas, and Wescott, Thompson, *History of Philadelphia: 1609–1884*, 3 vols. (Philadelphia, 1884).
Sears, Louis Martin, *George Washington in the French Revolution* (Detroit, 1960).
Sellers, Charles Coleman, *Portraits and Miniatures by Charles Willson Peale* (Philadelphia, 1952).
Smith, Page, *John Adams*, 2 vols. (Garden City, N.Y., 1962).
Sparks, Jared, ed., *Correspondence of the American Revolution, Being Letters of Eminent Men to George Washington*, vol. IV (Boston, 1853); referred to in Source References as "S, C."
Steiner, Bernard C., *The Life and Correspondence of James McHenry* (Cleveland, 1907).
Thomas, Charles Marion, *American Neutrality in 1793* (New York, 1931).
Thomas, Lawrence Buckley, *The Thomas Book* (New York, 1896).
Turner, Frederick Jackson, ed., "Correspondence of the French Ministers to the United States, 1791–1797," *American Historical Association Annual Report for 1903* (Washington, D.C., 1904), 43–1009.
Wall, Charles C., "Housing and Family Life of the Mount Vernon Negro," typescript at Mount Vernon (1962).
Walters, Raymond, *Albert Gallatin* (New York, 1957).
Warren, Charles, *The Supreme Court in United States History*, vol. I (Boston, 1923).
Washington, George, *Calendar of the Washington Manuscripts in the Library of Congress*, ed. Herbert Friedenwald (Washington, D.C., 1901).
—— *Diaries*, ed. John C. Fitzpatrick, 4 vols. (Boston and New York, 1925); referred to in Source References as "GW, D."
—— (forgery) *Epistles Domestic, Confidential, and Official from General Washington, Written about the Commencement of the American Contest* (New York, 1796).
—— *The George Washington Atlas*, ed. Lawrence Martin (Washington, D.C., 1932).

—— *Last Will and Testament,* ed. John C. Fitzpatrick (Mount Vernon, 1939).
—— *Letters of His Excellency, George Washington . . . to Sir John Sinclair, Bart., on Agricultural and other Interesting Topics* (London, 1800).
—— *Presidential Papers Microfilm, George Washington Papers* (Washington, D.C., 1965); referred to in Source References as "LC."
—— "Washington's Household Account Book," *Pennsylvania Magazine,* XXIX–XXXI (1905–1907). See indexes.
—— *The Will of General Washington to which is Annexed a Schedule of his Property Directed to be Sold* (Alexandria, Va., 1800).
—— *Writings,* ed. Jared Sparks, 12 vols. (Boston, 1834–1837); referred to in Source References as "S, W."
—— *Writings,* ed. Worthington Chauncey Ford, 14 vols. (New York and London, 1889–1893).
—— *Writings,* ed. John C. Fitzpatrick, 39 vols. (Washington, D.C., 1931–1944); referred to in Source References as "GW."
Weld, Isaac, *Travels through the States of North America,* vol. I (London, 1807).
Whitaker, Arthur Preston, *The Spanish-American Frontier, 1783–1795* (Boston, 1927).
White, Leonard D., *The Federalists: A Study in Administrative History* (New York, 1948).
Whitlock, Brand, *La Fayette,* 2 vols. (New York, 1929).
Wilson, Bird, *Memoir of . . . William White, D. D.* (Philadelphia, 1839).
[Wolcott, Oliver], *Memoirs of the Administrations of Washington and John Adams,* ed. George Gibbs, 2 vols. (New York, 1846); referred to in Source References as "WG."

Source References

T HE effort is made in these source references to be as succinct as utility allows. Had I noted all the passages in which Washington or his contemporaries mentioned matters discussed in my text, or the many excellent publications dealing in general with the historical background, I would have created an underpinning considerably more extensive than the superstructure. References are commonly to passages from which specific quotations have been taken.

Since the Bibliography gives fuller citations, the source references have been kept as brief as seems clear. When a title is repeated in the notes to one chapter, I have in the later references omitted, as superfluous, the form "*op. cit.*" Manuscript and newspaper dates are eighteenth century unless otherwise specified. The sources most often repeated are referred to by the following abbreviations:

ASP: *American State Papers, Foreign Relations,* I (Washington, D.C., 1832), *Miscellaneous,* I (Washington, D.C., 1834).

AA: Adams, John, *Works,* ed. Charles Francis Adams, 10 vols. (Boston, 1850–1856).

F: Freeman, Douglas Southhall, *George Washington: A Biography,* 7 vols. (New York, 1948–1957). The seventh volume, the one most cited here, was written after Freeman's death by J. A. Carroll and M. W. Ashworth.

Fl, W: Flexner, James Thomas, *George Washington,* vols. I–III (Boston, 1965, 1968, 1970).

GW: Washington, George, *Writings,* ed. John E. Fitzpatrick, 39 vols. (Washington, D.C., 1931–1944).

GW, D: Washington, George, *Diaries,* ed. John C. Fitzpatrick, 4 vols. (Boston and New York, 1925).

GWPC: Custis, George Washington Parke, *Recollections and Private Memoirs of Washington* (New York, 1860).

HH: Hamilton, Alexander, *Works*, ed. John C. Hamilton, 7 vols. (New York, 1851).

HS: Hamilton, Alexander, *Papers*, ed. Harold C. Syrett, vols. I–XV, all that have been published (New York, 1961–1969).

JF: Jefferson, Thomas, *Writings*, ed. Paul Leicester Ford, 10 vols. (New York, 1892–1899).

JJ: Jay, John, *The Correspondence and Public Papers of John Jay*, ed. Henry P. Johnston, 4 vols. (New York, 1890–1893).

LC: Library of Congress, Washington, D.C.

M: Malone, Dumas, *Jefferson and His Time*, 4 vols. (Boston, 1951–1970).

MH: Madison, James, *Writings*, ed. Gaillard Hunt, 9 vols. (New York, 1900–1910).

MoH: Monroe, James, *Writings*, ed. Stanislaus Murray Hamilton, 7 vols. (New York, 1898–1899).

MtV: Mount Vernon Ladies' Association of the Union, Mount Vernon, Va.

PP: [Pickering, Timothy] Pickering, Octavius, *The Life of Timothy Pickering*, 4 vols. (Boston, 1867–1873).

S, C: Sparks, Jared, ed., *Correspondence of the American Revolution; Being Letters of Eminent Men to George Washington*, vol. IV (Boston, 1853).

S, W: Sparks, Jared, ed., *Writings of George Washington*, 12 vols., (Boston, 1834–1837).

WG: [Wolcott, Oliver], ed. Gibbs, George, *Memoirs of the Administrations of Washington and John Adams, edited from the papers of Oliver Wolcott*, 2 vols. (New York, 1846).

1: AN ANGRY INAUGURATION

1. *Gazette of the United States*, Philadelphia, 2/27/93, p. 311.
2. GWPC, 364–365.
3. Howard, *Music*, 107.
4. Fl, *W*, III, 23; Niemcewicz, *Vine*, 85.
5. *National Gazette*, Philadelphia, 3/2/93.
6. GW, XXXI, 54.
7. Ford, *True*, 175; GW, XXXIII, 39.
8. F, VI, 412; GW, XXXII, 400.
9. JF, I, 221–222; GW, XXXII, 361, 361n–362n.
10. GW, XXXII, 374–375.
11. Baker, *After*, 271–272; *Federal Gazette*, Philadelphia, 3/6/93; *Gazette of the United States*, 3/6/93; *National Gazette*, 3/6/93.
12. Miller, *Hamilton*, 363.

13. HS, XIV, 371; JF, VI,˄326.
14. F, VII, 34; JF, VI, 192–193.
15. F, VII, 27–28; JF, VI, 199–201; S, C, IV, 421–423.
16. Marie Adrienne Lafayette to GW, 10/8/92, LC; GW, XXXII, 386.
17. GW, XXXII, 385, 389–390.
18. GW, XXXII, 447–448.
19. Bowers, *Jefferson*, 219.
20. F, VII, 145; GW, XXXIII, 352–353, 482–483.
21. James Craik to GW, 6/13/93, Historical Society of Pennsylvania; Tobias Lear to GW, 6/17/93, 6/24/93, LC; GW, XXXII, 201, 345, 381ff.
22. Fl, W, I, 240, II, 255; GW, XXXII, 494.
23. GW, XXXII, 385.
24. GW, XXXII, 475–476.
25. GW, XXXII, 398–399.
26. F, VII, 37.
27. F, VII, 40; HS, XIV, 291, 295–296; JF, VI, 212.
28. GW, XXXII, 415–417.

2: THE NEUTRALITY PROCLAMATION

1. GW, XXX, 496.
2. GW, XXXII, 448–449.
3. Bemis, *Jay's*, 104 ff.
4. HS, XIV, 297, 299–300.
5. M, III, 68; Thomas, *Neutrality*, 62.
6. HS, XIV, 307–310.
7. JF, VI, 192.
8. JF, VI, 212–213, 263.
9. M, III, 80, 98.
10. GW, XXXII, 419–420; HS, XIV, 308–310; JF, I, 226; Thomas, 27–32.
11. GW, XXXII, 419; JF, I, 226–227, VI, 315–316.
12. GW, XXXII, 419–420; HS, XIV, 328, 367ff; JF, I, 227, VI, 219, 222, 232, 238–239, 327.
13. F, VII, 54.
14. GW, XXXII, 430–431.
15. HS, XIV, 367–396; JF, VI, 218–231.
16. JF, I, 227.
17. JF, I, 224.
18. F, VII, 64; HS, XIV, 412–414; JF, I, 227–228, VI, 239, 250, 260.
19. GW, XXXII, 451.
20. JF, VI, 238.
21. F, VII, 53n; MH, VI, 127, 130–131.
22. JF, VI, 239, 250, 315–316, 328, 368.
23. Fl, W, I, 192.
24. JF, VI, 239.
25. F, VII, 78; JF, I, 231.
26. JF, I, 232–233, VI, 251.
27. GW, XXXII, 449–450.
28. GW, XXXII, 490.

3: CITIZEN GENÊT

1. Bathe, *Genêt*; Miller, *Hamilton*, 372; Minnigerode, *Jefferson*; Minnigerode, *Lives*.
2. *Dunlap's Daily American Advertiser*, 4/22/93; F, VII, 64ff; Thomas, *Neutrality*, 77ff; etc., etc.
3. M, III, 96.
4. Fl, W, II, 327.
5. *ASP, Foreign*, I, 173, 354–355; JF, I, 224n; Miller, 372; S, W, X, 542.

6. *Dunlap's,* 5/6/93.
7. JF, VI, 238, 241.
8. F, VII, 62; HS, XIV, 451ff; JF, VI, 236.
9. F, VII, 62.
10. F, VII, 65–66.
11. F, VII, 67; JF, VI, 253.
12. JF, I, 230.
13. JF, VI, 232; M, III, 134.
14. *Dunlap's,* 5/20/93.
15. GW, XXXII, 460–461; M, III, 93.
16. ASP, 354–355; Morris, G., *Diary,* II, 18, 25, 38.
17. JF, VI, 260–261.
18. ASP, 173; Genêt, *Correspondence,* 217–218, 245, 260.
19. F, VII, 76–77; Minnigerode, *Jefferson,* 69.

4: A DARKLING PLAIN

1. GW, XXXII, 422–423, 434.
2. GW, XXXII, 438–439.
3. JF, VI, 291–293.
4. JF, I, 246; M, III, 103; Minnigerode, *Jefferson,* 212.
5. JF, VI, 323.
6. *Ibid.*
7. F, VII, 82–84.
8. JF, I, 218–219.
9. JF, I, 219–220.
10. GW, XXXII, 449.
11. JF, VI, 116, 269, 278.
12. Thomas, *Neutrality,* 132.
13. JF, VI, 247, 300, 316, 333–334, 337; G, XXXII, 507.
14. JF, I, 235–236.
15. Genêt, *Correspondence,* XXX, 221–222; M, III, 107, 109; Thomas, 184.
16. JF, VI, 316; M, III, 109.
17. *ASP, Foreign,* I, 455.
18. GW, XXXII, 501–502.
19. GW, XXXII, 488–489, 506.
20. M, III, 11, 448–449.
21. HS, XV, 50–51, 621.
22. HS, XV, 13.
23. JF, I, 256.
24. Martha Washington to Fanny Bassett, 6/2/93, MtV; JF, VI, 16; GW, XXXII, 512.

5: THE LITTLE SARAH

1. GW, XXXII, 513.
2. GW, XXXIII, 4.
3. JF, I, 237–241.
4. GW, XXXIII, 4.
5. JF, I, 241.
6. GW, XXXIII, 4.
7. JF, VI, 340n–341n.
8. JF, I, 242, IV, 430–431.
9. HS, XV, 240; JF, VI, 339–344.
10. F, VII, 103–105; JF, I, 241–243.
11. *ASP, Foreign,* I, 163; F, VII, 102.
12. Minnigerode, *Jefferson,* 420.
13. Minnigerode, 420–421.

6. THE GENÊT HARVEST

1. JF, VI, 338–339.
2. GW, XXXIII, 24; JF, I, 253; Miller, *Hamilton*, 377.
3. Bowers, *Jefferson*, 221–222.
4. AA, X, 47–48.
5. GW, XXXIII, 23–24.
6. GW, XXXIII, 476.
7. GW, XXXIII, 15–19; Thomas, *Neutrality*, 145ff.
8. GW, XXXIII, 15–19; JJ., III, 487–489; Thomas, 150–151; Warren, *Supreme*, I, 105–115.
9. JF, I, 254–255; Thomas, 145–151.
10. *ASP, Foreign*, I, 155–156.
11. JF, I, 243, VI, 349; M, III, 376.
12. JF, I, 247–248.
13. GW, XXXIII, 28–29, 34; JF, I, 252–253.
14. JF, I, 253–254.
15. JF, I, 254n.
16. JF, VI, 292.
17. GW, XIV, 267.
18. Flexner, *Steamboats*, 84–86.
19. GWPC, 408n–409n.
20. GW, XXXIII, 354.
21. HS, XV, 33–43, 55–63, 65–69, 82–86, 90–95, 100–106, 130–135.
22. JF, VI, 338, 361.
23. HS, XV, 233–235.
24. F, VII, 116.
25. GW, XXXIII, 38.
26. HS, XV, 233; *New York Daily Advertiser*, 8/12/93.
27. HS, XV, 234.
28. Fl, W, II, 264.
29. HS, XV, 317–318.
30. HS, XV, 233–239.

7: JEFFERSON SEEKS ESCAPE

1. *Dunlap's Daily American Advertiser*, Philadelphia, 7/6/93; JF, I, 244–245.
2. JF, VI, 360–361.
3. M, III, 132.
4. JF, I, 256–259.
5. JF, I, 235, 245–246; Schachner, *Jefferson*, I, 504–506.
6. MH, VI, 194; MoH, I, 275.
7. JF, VI, 430–431.
8. JF, VI, 366–367.
9. GW, XXXIII, 45.

8: A ROCKY ROAD

1. F, VII, 117; M, III, 139; MH, VI, 194; MoH, I, 275.
2. GW, XXXIII, 79.
3. Citizens of Caroline County, Va., to GW, 10/11/93, LC; GW, XXXIII, 91–92.
4. Edmund Pendleton to GW, 10/11/93, LC.
5. GW, XXXIII, 94–96.
6. GW, XXXIII, 58n; JF, I, 259–261; M, III, 128.
7. JF, VI, 362.
8. F, VII, 114; HS, XV, 194–195; JF, I, 256, VI, 362; Thomas, *Neutrality*, 171.
9. Flexner, *Doctors*, 93ff; GW, XXXIII, 66; Powell, *Bring*.

10. GW, XXXIII, 83–84.
11. GW, XXXIII, 86.
12. GW, XXXIII, 104–105.
13. Powell, 107.
14. GW, XXXIII, 104–105.
15. Eliza Powel to GW, 8/9/90, MtV.
16. GW, XXXIII, 86–87.

9: AN ANXIOUS HOLIDAY

1. Bryan, *Capital*, I, 212ff, 273; Delaplaine, *Johnson*, 485.
2. Fl, *W*, III, chap. 26.
3. GW, XXXII, 511–512, XXXIII, 29–30.
4. GW, XXXIII, 104.
5. Ford, *True*, 135.
6. GW, XXXIII, 293.
7. GW, XXXIII, 57–58.
8. Bryan, I, 215; Clark, *Greenleaf*, 67ff; GW, XXXIII, 105.
9. Tobias Lear to David Humphreys, 4/18/93, Rosenbach Foundation, Philadelphia; GW, XXXIII, 104.
10. GW, XXXIII, 76–79, 152.
11. GW, XXXIII, 381.
12. GW, XXXIII, 336–337.
13. GW, XXXIII, 132–133.
14. William Pearce to GW, 10/30/93, LC; GW, XXXIII, 26, 68–70, 273.
15. GW, XXXIII, 97–101, 112.
16. GW, XXXIII, 146.
17. GW, XXXIII, 124–125.
18. GW, XXXIII, 101–102.
19. GW, XXXIII, 102, 125, 130; Powell, *Bring*, 260.
20. GW, XXXIII, 125.

10: FIRST RECKONING

1. F, VII, 132; GW, XXXIII, 102, 107–109, 113, 122n, 126, 177.
2. GW, XXXIII, 107–109, 151.
3. JF, VI, 430–431, 437; M, III, 146.
4. Jenkins, *Germantown*, 97–98, 100–101.
5. Jenkins, 112, 117.
6. Jenkins, 106–107.
7. Jenkins, 119–121.
8. GW, XXXIII, 151, 157; Jenkins, 110–111, 172–173.
9. GW, XXXIII, 173n; M., III, 142.
10. Eliza Powel to GW, 8/9/93, MtV; Alberts, *Bingham*, 247, 490; Rush, *Letters*, II, 635–636; WG, I, 113.
11. JF, VI, 440; Thomas, *Neutrality*, 110–111.
12. JF, I, 265–268.
13. JF, I, 252; GW, XXXIII, 58n, 171.
14. F, VII, 138; GW, XXXIII, 172; JF, I, 271–272.
15. JF, I, 268–269.
16. GW, XXXIII, 164–165.
17. GW, XXXIII, 165–166; JF, I, 270.
18. GW, XXXIII, 167–168.
19. GW, XXXIII, 169.
20. *Federal Gazette*, Philadelphia, 12/4/93; *General Advertiser*, Philadelphia, 12/6/93; GW, XXXIII, 163.

11: EXIT JEFFERSON

1. HS, XV, 621.
2. HS, XV, 13.
3. Delaplaine, *Johnson*, 495; JF, I, 258, VI, 439.
4. Conway, *Randolph*, 24.
5. Conway, 38.
6. Conway, 60; GW, XXVIII, 110.
7. Conway,'57.
8. F, VII, 146n.
9. HS, XIV, 278–279; JF, I, 258.
10. GW, XXXIII, 410.
11. F, VII, 146n; GW, XXXIII, 216.
12. *Ibid.*
13. JF, VI, 496–497.
14. GW, XXXIII, 231.
15. M, III, 11, 448–449.
16. GW, XXXV, 119; JF, VII, 43.
17. HS, VI, 108n; JF, I, 199.
18. JF, I, 168.
19. JF, I, 228–229, 247, 265–267; Schachner, *Jefferson*, I, 504–506.
20. Tobias Lear to David Humphreys, 4/18/93, Rosenbach Foundation, Philadelphia.

12: WASHINGTON AND SLAVERY

1. GW, XXXIII, 78–79, 174–183.
2. GW, XXXIII, 358.
3. GW, XXXIII, 358n.
4. Fl, W, I, 13–19, 114, 286; GW, D, III, 15n.
5. Fl, W, I, 275–276; GW, II, 437.
6. Fl, W, I, 322; GW, III, 242.
7. Davis, *Slavery.*
8. McColley, *Slavery*, 167–168.
9. Mazyck, *Negro*, 35ff.
10. Mazyck, 42.
11. GW, XIX, 93.
12. Fl, W, II, 63; GW, IV, 323, 360–361.
13. Washington, *Writings* (Ford), VI, 349.
14. Fl, W, II, 341n; Laurens, *Correspondence*, 117–118.
15. Mazyck, 70–71.
16. Fl, W, II, 341n; GW, XIV, 267.
17. GW, XXIV, 4, 88n, 421.
18. Fl, W, II, 341; GW, XII, 327, XXVIII, 408.
19. Fl, W, II, 341–342; GW, XIV, 147–148, 338.
20. Lafayette, *To Washington*, 260.
21. GW, XXXVI, 300.
22. Asbury, *Journal*, I, 385; Coke, *Journals*, 45.
23. McColley, 152.
24. GW, XXVII, 424.
25. Fl, W, III, 106–108.
26. GW, XXVII, 407–408.
27. David Humphreys, "The Life of General Washington," ms. Rosenbach Foundation, Philadelphia.
28. JF, II, 228–229; Jordan, *White*, 325ff; Mazyck, 114.
29. GW, XXXI, 30, 522, XXXII, 6.
30. GW, XXXI, 573–574.
31. GW, XXXIV, 21.

32. McColley, 25.
33. John Chew Thomas, Manumission papers and correspondence in possession of the author; Thomas, *Thomas*, 41.
34. Bernard, *Retrospections*, 91; Humphreys.
35. JF, X, 362; McColley, 2–3, 125.
36. GW, XXVIII, 453.

13: THE FRENCH MENACE FADES

1. F, VII, 15, 155.
2. GW, XXXIII, 234, 245–246; HH, IV, 496.
3. F, VII, 156; GW, XXXIII, 304–305.
4. *ASP, Misc.*, I, 929–930.
5. Henry Lee to GW, 9/17/93, 10/7/93, LC; GW, XXXIII, 133.
6. Minnigerode, *Lives*, 207; MtV, *Annual Report*, 1950, 36.
7. Bathe, *Genêt*; F, VII, 154.
8. Baker, *After*, 271–272; F, VII, 154n–155n.

14: RUMBLINGS OF WAR WITH BRITAIN

1. GW, XXXIII, 355.
2. *ASP, Foreign*, I, 428–429; Bemis, *Jay's*, 215–216.
3. Bemis, 236–240.
4. F, VII, 159n–161n; King, *Life*, I, 517.
5. GW, XXXIII, 310–314.
6. Bemis, 261–262.
7. Bemis, 264.
8. HH, IV, 506–508.
9. GW, XXXIII, 306–308.
10. MoH, I, 286–288.
11. MH, VI, 209–210.
12. Bemis, 264.
13. GW, XXXIII, 382–383.
14. GW, XXXIII, 332.
15. Bemis, *Foreign*, II, 112.
16. King, I, 517–518.
17. MH, VI, 208.
18. King, I, 518–519.
19. King, I, 519–520; MH, VI, 394; MoH, I, 291–292.
20. GW, XXXIII, 320–321; MoH, I, 291n–292n.
21. MH, VII, 211–212.
22. King, I, 520–521.
23. JJ, IV, 213; King, I, 520–521.
24. HH, IV, 519–532.
25. GW, XXXIII, 329–330.

15: TWO ENVOYS

1. Bemis, *Jay's*; JJ; Jay, *Life*; Monaghan, *Jay*; Morris, *Jay*.
2. Portraits of Jay by Gilbert Stuart, Joseph Wright, etc.
3. GW, XXX, 432.
4. GW, XV, 38.
5. Bemis, *Jay's*, 282.
6. King, *Life*, I, 520–521.
7. GW, XXXIII, 329, 332–333.
8. Conway, *Randolph*, 22; King, 521–522.
9. GW, XXXIII, 345–346; JJ, IV, 9–10.
10. JF, I, 217.

11. Bemis, *Jay's*, 289ff; JJ, IV, 12ff.
12. Bemis, *Secretaries*, 117ff; Conway, 220–221; GW, XXXVI, 196.
13. Bemis, *Jay's*, 246–247; Conway, 221; Miller, *Hamilton*, 420.
14. Bemis, *Jay's*, 291.
15. *ASP, Foreign*, I, 577.
16. Robert R. Livingston to GW, 5/10/94, 5/15/94, New-York Historical Society; GW, XXXIII, 346, 364.
17. Ammon, *Monroe*, 113–115; MoH, I, 296, 298–301.
18. Ammon; Cresson, *Monroe*.
19. GW, XV, 198.
20. Portraits by Gilbert Stuart, Charles Willson Peale, Asher B. Durand, etc.; Sellers, *Peale*, 144.
21. MoH, I, 300.
22. MoH, I, 386.
23. Bond, *Monroe*, 11; GW, XXXVI, 195; MoH, I, 301–303; Monroe, *View*, IV.
24. Bemis, *Jay's*, 296–297; JJ, IV, 30; King, 521–523.
25. Bemis, *Jay's*, 273–277; HH, IV, 565; Miller, 418–419.
26. GW, XXXIII, 414.

16: EXTREME SENSIBILITY

1. Martha Washington to Fanny Bassett, 10/3/94, MtV; same to same, 11/11/94, Huntington Library; GW, XXXIV, 125, XXXV, 513.
2. Baker, *After*, 277.
3. JF, VI, 503–504.
4. JF, VI, 502–503, 507.
5. GW, XXXIII, 338–339.
6. GW, XXXIII, 414.
7. GW, XXXIII, 356–357, 374.
8. F, VII, 171n.
9. MH, VI, 216–217; MoH, I, 297–298.
10. HH, IV, 495.
11. GW, XXXI, 285–286; HS, VIII, 277–278.
12. Conway, *Randolph*, 216–217.
13. HH, IV, 510, 512–515.
14. GW, XXXIII, 318.
15. HH, IV, 516–519.
16. M, III, 181.
17. Conway, 218.
18. M, III, 181.
19. JF, I, 216–218; GW, XXXIII, 414.
20. GW, XXXIII, 338–342; HH, IV, 533–535, 544–546.
21. HH, IV, 561.
22. GW, XXXIII, 386.
23. GW, XXXIII, 402–403.
24. GW, XXXIII, 411–412, 418.
25. GW, XXXIII, 429, 487.
26. GW, XXXIII, 406, 427.
27. Fl, *W*, III, 58; GW, XXXIII, 406, XXXIV, 89.
28. GW, XXXIII, 412, 418, 424.
29. *ASP, Misc.*, I, 930–931.
30. F, VII, 179n.
31. Henry Lee to GW, 8/17/94, LC.
32. GW, XXXIII, 476–479.
33. Conway, 223–224.
34. F, VII, 180n; JF, VI, 512; M, III, 187.

17: THE WHISKEY REBELLION

1. Fl, *W*, III, see index.
2. Fl, *W*, III, 278.
3. Fl, *W*, III, 290; GW, XXXIII, 523.
4. Baldwin, *Whiskey*, *passim*.
5. Fl, *W*, III, 290; GW, XXXI, 319.
6. Fl, *W*, III, 295; HH, IV, 584.
7. Fl, *W*, III, 370–371; HH, IV, 586–587.
8. GW, XXXII, 208–209.
9. Baldwin, 109; Link, *Democratic*, 145.
10. GW, XXXII, 387.
11. Baldwin, 30.
12. Baldwin, 76; GW, XXXIII, 405–409.
13. Baldwin, 134, 138.
14. Fl, *W*, III, 103; GW, XXXIII, 465.
15. GW, XXXIII, 464.
16. GW, XXXIII, 475–476.
17. Fl, *W*, III, 102.
18. Baldwin, 74.
19. GW, XXXIII, 475–476.
20. *Pennsylvania Archives*, 2nd ser., IV (1896), 122 ff.
21. F, VII, 190; *Pennsylvania*, 103.
22. *Pennsylvania*, 116–118.
23. *Pennsylvania*, 103.
24. GW, XXXIII, 457–461.
25. *Pennsylvania*, 104–105.
26. Baldwin, 183–190; F, VII, 192; GW, XXXIII, 461–462.
27. Baldwin, 98, 139, 198ff, 210.
28. Baldwin, 215.
29. GW, XXXIII, 509; *Pennsylvania*, 267–268.
30. GW, XXXIII, 463, 474–475, XXXIV, 17; Miller, *Federalist*, 158.
31. GW, XXXIV, 34.
32. Bowers, *Jefferson*, 253; Schachner, *Jefferson*, II, 566.
33. HH, V, 30–31, VI, 79–80; Randolph, *Vindication*, 71.

18: THE WHISKEY CAMPAIGN

1. GW, *D*, IV, 209–210; Jenkins, *Germantown*, 276.
2. GW, XXXIII, 513, XXXIV, 11.
3. Gould, "Journal," 179; GW, *D*, IV, 211, 218.
4. Ford, "Journal," 85; GW, XXXIII, 520.
5. Baldwin, *Whiskey*, 228; GW, *D*, IV, 212.
6. Findley, *History*, 172 ff; GW, *D*, IV, 212–216.
7. *Pennsylvania Archives*, 2nd ser., IV, 105.
8. Dallas, *Dallas*, 34.
9. Edmund Randolph to GW, 10/6/94, LC; GW, XXXIII, 521.
10. GW, XXXIII, 520, 522–523, XXXIV, 3.
11. Bartholomew Dandridge to GW, 10/9/94, LC.
12. GW, *D*, IV, 217–219.
13. GW, *D*, IV, 220–221.
14. GW, XXXIV, 2–3; GW, *D*, IV, 221.
15. GW, *D*, IV, 221–222.
16. GW, XXXIV, 7.
17. GW, XXXIV, 7–8, 20.
18. Brackenridge, *Incidents*, 144–145; Findley, 189; Miller, *Hamilton*, 409ff.
19. GW, XXXIV, 62.

20. GW, XXXIV, 34.
21. GW, XXXIV, 98.
22. Bemis, *Jay's,* 25.
23. GW, XXXIV, 35; MH, VI, 221–224.

19: THE DEMOCRATIC SOCIETIES

1. GW, XXXIV, 3–4, 17.
2. Conway, *Randolph,* 194–195.
3. GW, XXXIV, 3.
4. GW, XXXIV, 3–4.
5. Edmund Randolph to GW, 10/22/94, LC; F, VII, 218 n.
6. GW, XXXIV, 16–18.
7. GW, XXXIV, 28–37.
8. GW, XXXV, 325–326.
9. F, VII, 220n.
10. *Annals of the Third Congress,* 794–795.
11. Miller, *Hamilton,* 412.
12. JF, VI, 516, 518, VII, 16; M, III, 188.
13. Baldwin, *Whiskey,* 259; Link, *Democratic,* 14–15.
14. Luetscher, *Early,* 60; Link, 206.
15. GW, XXIX, 22–23.
16. *Annals,* 744–745.
17. GW, XXXIV, 16.
18. GW, XXXIII, 507.
19. GW, XXXIII, 506–507.
20. JF, I, 253.
21. HH, VI, 221–224.
22. JF, VI, 516–517; M, III, 190.
23. JF, VI, 517.
24. F, VII, 391.

20: WEATHERBREEDER

1. Adams *To Wife,* II, 176.
2. Miller, *Hamilton,* 440.
3. Miller, 435–437.
4. HH, V, 75.
5. GW, XXXIV, 109–110.
6. HH, V, 67–69, 77–79.
7. F, VII, 229n.
8. Baker, *After,* 270.
9. Garrard, *Chambers,* 14–15.
10. Adams, II, 176; Baker, 277.
11. Custis, "Self-portrait," 94, 100; Quincy, *Memoir,* 139.
12. GW, XXXIII, 500–501.
13. Clark, *Greenleaf;* Park, *Stuart,* I, 463–464, III, 233–234.
14. Thomas Law to GW, 12/22/97, LC; GW, XXXVI, 115.
15. GW, XXXIV, 457–459.
16. GW, XXXIV, 92–94.
17. GW, XXXV, 14, 17.
18. GW, XXXIV, 142, 176.
19. GW, XXXIV, 87, 207.
20. GW, XXXIV, 124, 207–208, 210.
21. GW, XXXIV, 60n, XXXV, 199–200.
22. Fl, W, III, 75–76; GW, XXXIV, 59n–60n.
23. GW, XXXIV, 59n–60n.
24. GW, XXXV, 316–317.

25. GW, XXXIV, 23.
26. GW, XXXIV, 59–60, 106–107.
27. S, C, IV, 464–469.
28. GW, XXXIV, 147–149.
29. GW, Deed of gift to Washington Academy, 12/7/98, Washington and Lee University; GW, XXXIV, 149–150.
30. GW, XXXIV, 98, 157–158.

21: THE JAY TREATY ARRIVES

1. GW, XXXIII, 483–485; JJ, IV, 26–28.
2. *ASP, Foreign*, I, 673–675.
3. GW, XXXIV, 61; JJ, IV, 58.
4. Conway, *Randolph*, 251–252.
5. F, VII, 233.
6. F, VII, 236.
7. GW, XXXIV, 131.
8. *ASP*, I, 503ff; Conway, 234; F, VII, 237.
9. GW, XXXIV, 244.
10. *ASP*, I, 520–525.
11. GW, XXXIV, 238; Randolph, *Vindication*, 18.
12. Bemis, *Jay's*, 153–154.
13. JF, VII, 65–66.
14. Fl, W, III, 166.
15. Bemis, *Jay,s*, 152ff; Bemis, *Secretaries*, 136ff; De Conde, *Entangling*, 108ff; Sears, *Washington*, 230ff; Marshall, *Washington*, V, 267ff.
16. GW, XXXIV, 227, 340.
17. GW, XXX, 414; Randolph, 18.
18. Bond, *Monroe*, 33.
19. GW, XXXIV, 340.
20. GW, XXXIV, 175.
21. Conway, 234–235; GW, XXXIV, 226; JJ, IV, 177.
22. WG, I, 219.
23. GW, XXXIV, 212–213.
24. F, VII, 250n.
25. Randolph, 18–19.
26. F, VII, 254–256.
27. F, VII, 257; GW, XXXIV, 224–225.
28. *Aurora*, Philadelphia, 6/1/95; Randolph, 19.
29. Conway, 254.
30. GW, XXXIV, 226–228.
31. Hamilton, *Works* (Lodge), IV, 322–363.
32. *ASP*, I, 500–521; GW, XXXIV, 237–240.
33. Ford, *Randolph*, 596 ff.
34. F, VII, 260.

22: TEMPEST STRIKES

1. GW, XXXIV, 295–296; WG, I, 243.
2. Randolph, *Vindication*, 20–22.
3. GW, XXXIV, 255n.
4. GW, XXXIV, 236, 242.
5. GW, XXXIV, 241–242, 248.
6. Boston Selectmen to GW, 7/13/95, LC; GW, XXXIV, 243; GW, *D*, IV, 234; Hiltzheimer, *Diary*, 215.
7. GW, XXXIV, 244.
8. *Ibid.*
9. GW, XXXIV, 257.

10. F, VII, 270n.
11. F, VII, 268.
12. Edmund Randolph to GW, 8/29/95, LC; GW, XXXIV, 251, 265.
13. GW, XXXIV, 263; JF, VII, 27.
14. Peterson, *Jefferson*, 545; Sears, *Washington*, 232.
15. Paltsits, *Farewell*, 171.
16. *ASP, Foreign*, I, 577; HH, VI, 198.
17. Bemis, *Secretaries*, 144; GW, XXXIV, 245 n.
18. GW, XXXIV, 256.
19. GW, XXXIV, 262–263.
20. GW, XXXIV, 255, 266–267.
21. GW, XXXIV, 265.
22. GW, XXXIV, 264, 266.
23. GW, XXXIV, 268.
24. Conway, *Randolph*, 269; PP, III, 188–189.
25. GW, XXXIV, 270–271; GW, *D*, IV, 237.
26. PP, III, 217.

23: THE CRY OF TREASON

1. Schachner, *Jefferson*, I, 505–506.
2. WG, I, 220.
3. WG, I, 218–219.
4. *Ibid.*
5. WG, I, 219–220.
6. F, VII, 279n.
7. WG, I, 232–233.
8. Randolph, *Vindication*, 14, 37, 74; WG, I, 243.
9. PP, III, 217–218.
10. Conway, *Randolph*, 272–281; Randolph, 29–36.
11. Randolph, 29.
12. Randolph, 32.
13. Randolph, 33.
14. *Ibid.*
15. Conway, 265–267.
16. GW, XXXIV, 280; Randolph, 40, WG, I, 243.
17. Conway, 230–231.
18. GW, XXXIII, 424.
19. GW, XXXIV, 266.
20. Randolph, 28.
21. Conway, 268–269; WG, I, 219–220.
22. GW, XXXVI, 195.
23. Randolph, 74.
24. GW, XXXIV, 262; Marshall, *Washington*, V, 226.
25. WG, I, 243.

24: OH, WHAT A FALL

1. PP, III, 189–190, 218; Randolph, *Vindication*, 40–41; WG, I, 225.
2. Conway, *Randolph*, 253–254; F, VII, 288–289; Randolph, 27–28.
3. Randolph, 37.
4. WG, I, 244.
5. Randolph, 37.
6. Conway, 284; GW, XXXIV, 275, 345; WG, I, 244.
7. Brant, "Not Guilty"; PP, III, 218; Randolph, 1–3, 45; WG, I, 244–245, 265.
8. GW, XXXIV, 345.

25: WAR WITH AN OLD FRIEND

1. Randolph, 3–4.
2. GW, XXXIV, 276.
3. GW, XXXIV, 277.
4. Brant, 197; GW, XXXIV, 316–317.
5. Conway, 360–361; F, VII, 315, 332; GW, 339–341; Randolph, 15, 17–18, 40; WG, I, 246–248.
6. GW, XXXIV, 277, 343–345.
7. GW, XXXIII, 343–346; Randolph, 15.
8. GW, XXXIV, 339–342.
9. GW, XXXIV, 343–345; Randolph, 17–18.
10. GW, XXXIV, 321.
11. Conway, 346–347.
12. Randolph, 10–11.
13. Randolph, 11–12.
14. Brant, 188; Randolph, 9–10.
15. Conway, 346; F, VII, 336.
16. Randolph, 37, 39.
17. Randolph, 37.
18. Randolph, 45, 75.

26: BETTER HIS HAND HAD BEEN CUT OFF

1. F, VII, 302–303.
2. F, VII, 320–321.
3. Aurora, Philadelphia, 10/2/95; F, VII, 319; McMaster, History, II, 250–251.
4. Ford, Spurious; New York Daily Gazette, 10/17/95.
5. Aurora, 10/23, 27, 28/95; F, VII, 320; WG, I, 257–258.
6. WG, I, 257–263.
7. F, VI, 301; GW, XXXIV, 293, 295, 302, 306, 330.
8. GW, XXXIV, 311, 315.
9. GW, XXXIV, 280, 310.
10. GW, XXXIV, 284.
11. GW, XXXIV, 284–287, 348.
12. F, VII, 322.
13. GW, XXXIV, 331–335.
14. GW, XXXIV, 348; HH, VI, 61, 63.

27: A BRILLIANT STROKE

1. HH, VI, 61, 63, 67–69; PP, III, 251–252.
2. F, VII, 326, 339–340; GW, XXXV, 365–366.
3. GW, XXXIV, 365, 405, 428, 431; JF, VII, 36n–37n; Steiner, McHenry, 162.
4. Adams, To Wife, II, 195; GW, XXXIV, 447–448, XXXVI, 394.
5. GW, XXXIV, 350; HH, VI, 63.
6. GW, XXXIV, 362, 377; Hamilton, Works (Lodge), V, 12–17.
7. F, VII, 326.
8. Baker, After, 334.
9. GW, XXXIV, 386–393.
10. F, VII, 327n.
11. F, VII, 328.
12. JF, VII, 41–43.
13. GW, XXXIV, 397.
14. JF, VII, 32.
15. GW, XXXIV, 449.
16. GW, XXXIV, 407, 483–484.
17. F, VII, 337.

18. *Annals of the Fourth Congress,* I, 196–198; Baker, 317; F, VII, 337.
19. GW, XXXIV, 413–414.
20. F, VII, 338.
21. GW, XXXIV, 401.
22. Gouverneur Morris to GW, 7/3/95, LC; GW, 187–188, 209–210.
23. GW, XXXIV, 398–403.

28: SWORDS WITH TWO EDGES

1. JF, VII, 27, 33.
2. GW, XXXIV, 433–447, 451, 459ff, 464.
3. Felix Frestel to GW, 8/31/95, LC; George W. M. Lafayette to GW, 8/31/95, LC; Crawford, *Madame de Lafayette,* 118; GW, XXXV, 145; Whitlock, *La Fayette,* I, 298, II, 58.
4. GW, XXXIV, 299–301.
5. HH, VI, 47–48.
6. GW, XXXIV, 346.
7. HH, VI, 61–63; GW, XXXIV, 362, 364.
8. HH, VI, 70–71.
9. GW, XXXIV, 367–368.
10. GW, XXXIV, 374–376.
11. GW, XXXIV, 404.
12. Frestel to GW, 12/25/95, LC; Lafayette to GW, 12/25/95, LC; GW, XXXIV, 404n.
13. GW, XXXIV, 424–425, 478, 485n, XXXV, 8, 21.
14. F, VII, 343; GW, XXXIV, 477n.
15. F, VII, 345n–346n; Bemis, *Pinckney's;* Whitaker, *Spanish-American.*
16. GW, XXXIV, 477.
17. F, VII, 344; GW, XXXIV, 499–500.
18. GW, XXXIV, 481; Marshall, *Washington,* V, 242–243.
19. *Annals of the Fourth Congress,* I, 400–401; F, VII, 348.
20. GW, XXXIV, 505n.

29: THE BRINK OF A PRECIPICE

1. Farrand, *Convention,* III, 372; Marshall, *Washington,* V, 245.
2. GW, XXXV, 29–30; JF, VII, 68.
3. GW, XXXV, 253.
4. JF, I, 189–190; HH, VI, 347.
5. HH, VI, 95–96.
6. JF, I, 141.
7. GW, XXXIII, 414–415, 420–422; HH, VI, 569–570.
8. F, VII, 234, 240–241; GW, XXXIV, 140, 218.
9. GW, XXXV, 32.
10. *Ibid.*
11. GW, XXXV, 34.
12. Adams, *To Wife,* II, 214; JJ, IV, 208–209.
13. Marshall, V, 395.
14. GW, XXXV, 37.
15. Fl, *W,* III, chap. 9.
16. GW, XXXV, 53.
17. GW, XXXV, 30, 32.
18. GW, XXXV, 6–8; Hamilton, *Works* (Lodge), VIII, 385–389.
19. GW, XXXV, 2–5.
20. F, VII, 355; Farrand, III, 372, 374.
21. Adams, II, 217; GW, XXXV, 9.
22. F, VII, 358–359; GW, XXXIV, 498.

23. GW, XXXV, 62.
24. F, VII, 362; JF, VII, 40.
25. JF, VII, 40.
26. *Annals of the Fourth Congress*, I, 1173–1183.
27. *Annals*, 1239–1263; F, VII, 373–374.
28. GW, XXXV, 71–72.
29. GW, XXXV, 62.
30. F, VII, 376; JF, VII, 80.

30: FINIS WITH JEFFERSON

1. Marshall, *Washington*, V, 251–252.
2. Duane, *Letter*.
3. Adams, *To Wife*, II, 206.
4. GW, XXXV, 91–92.
5. JF, VII, 81–85.
6. GW, XXXIV, 325.
7. JF, VII, 81–85.
8. JF, VII, 101–102.
9. GW, XXXV, 118–119.

31: THUNDER ON THE LEFT

1. GW, XXXV, 18–19.
2. Liston, "Journal"; Liston, "Letters"; Park, *Stuart*, I, 478–480.
3. Liston, "Journal," 514–515.
4. Liston, "Journal," 515–516.
5. Lesage, Alain-René, *Histoire de Gil Blas de Santillane*, chaps. III–IV.
6. Baker, *After*, 343; Liston, "Journal," 516.
7. GW, XXXV, 99, 104n; Paltsits, *Farewell*, 30.
8. GW, XXXV, 50.
9. GW, XXXV, 103.
10. Bond, *Monroe*, 32ff.
11. Paine, *Writings*, III, 239.
12. Bond, 36.
13. *ASP, Foreign*, I, 732–741.
14. Gouverneur Morris to GW, 3/4/96, LC; MoH, I, 455, 457.
15. GW, XXXV, 38–41.
16. F, VII, 379n.
17. GW, XXXV, 39, 190.
18. Bond, 46.
19. MoH, II, 402–404.
20. MoH, III, 6–7; WG, I, 367.
21. WG, I, 354–355; *William & Mary Quarterly*, 3rd ser., IV (1952), 512–520.
22. WG, I, 350–351, 367.
23. GW, XXXV, 126, 147–148; WG, I, 365–366.
24. GW, XXXV, 95–97, 101, 103.
25. GW, XXXV, 40, 102–103.
26. GW, XXXV, 153–154; MoH, III, 455–458.
27. *ASP, Foreign*, I, 737–738; GW, XXXV, 150–155.
28. GW, XXXV, 126; WG, I, 366.
29. F, VII, 380; GW, XXXV, 50, 62; Paltsits, 240.
30. GW, XXXV, 130; JF, V, 376.
31. James Maury to GW, 12/26/95, MtV; GW, XXXV, 63, 121.
32. GW, XXXV, 174.
33. GW, XXXV, 144–145, 174.

32: WASHINGTON'S FAREWELL ADDRESS

1. GW, XXXV, 190–193.
2. GW, XXXV, 48–51.
3. GW, XXXV, 51–61.
4. GW, XXXV, 48–51.
5. Paltsits, *Farewell*, 247–249.
6. Paltsits, 249–250.
7. *Ibid.*
8. Paltsits, 250.
9. Paltsits, 200–208.
10. Paltsits, 251.
11. GW, XXXV, 190.
12. GW, XXXV, 191, 199–201, 204–205; Paltsits, 256.
13. Paltsits, 257.
14. GW, XXXV, 217.
15. GW XXXV, 217n.
16. GW, XXXV, 218–225.
17. GW, XXXV, 225–226.
18. GW, XXXV, 226–228.
19. GW, XXXV, 226n–227n, 228–229.
20. GW, XXXV, 229–230; Paltsits, 192.
21. GW, XXXV, 230n; Paltsits, 193.
22. GW, XXXV, 234.
23. GW, XXXV, 233–234; Paltsits, 196.
24. GW, XXXV, 235.
25. GW, XXXV, 236–237.
26. GW, XXXV, 238.
27. GW, XXXV, 191.
28. GW, XXXV, 259; Paltsits, 51.
29. GW, XXXV, 192.
30. Paltsits, 288–291.
31. GW, XXXV, 215n.
32. *Claypoole's American Daily Advertiser*, Philadelphia, 10/19/96.
33. Paltsits, 67.
34. Paltsits, 261–262.
35. Duane, *Letter*.
36. Paltsits, 75–94.

33: FALSE TEETH AND STUART'S WASHINGTON

1. Fielding, *Stuart;* Flexner, *Stuart,* 122–138; Morgan, *Portraits,* 211–361.
2. GW, XXXV, 370–371, 374–375, XXXVII, 28–29.
3. GW, XXXVI, 29n.
4. Flexner, 101.
5. Flexner, 122.
6. Flexner, 124–125.
7. Flexner, 125–126.
8. Flexner, 123, 142.
9. Fielding, 77; Weld, *Travels,* 105.
10. Flexner, 124.
11. Flexner, 128–130.
12. Flexner, 141–142.

34: DARKNESS ON THE OCEAN

1. GW, XXXIV, 398–403, XXXV, 187.
2. F, VII, 410n.

3. GW, XXXV, 244–245.
4. *ASP, Foreign*, I, 576–577; F, VII, 413.
5. GW, XXXV, 251–255.
6. HH, VI, 162.
7. F, VII, 415n; GW, XXXV, 255–256; HH, VI, 163, 168.
8. *ASP*, I, 578.
9. GW, XXXIV, 339–343, XXXV, 237n.
10. Adet, *Notes*.
11. M, III, 249–250, 284–285; Marshall, *Washington*, V, 307.
12. Adet, 53.
13. Adet, 57.
14. *Porcupine's Political Censor*, Philadelphia, November 1796, 61.
15. Bond, *Monroe*, 207; Paine, *Writings*, III, 212–252; Sears, *Washington*, 246.
16. GW, XXXV, 300, 358–359.
17. *Connecticut Courant*, Hartford, 3/20/97; Ford, *Spurious*; GW, XXXV, 364, 414–415; *Western Telegraph and Washington Advertiser*, Washington, Pa., 3/4/97.
18. Eliza Powel to GW, 12/7/96, MtV.
19. Liston, "Journal," 516; Liston, "Letters," 606.
20. Fl, W, III, 308–309; GW, XXXV, 310–320; HH, VI, 167.

35: YOU'RE IN AND I'M OUT

1. GW, XXXV, 320, 358–360.
2. GW, XXXV, 352.
3. GW, XXXV, 360–361.
4. GW, XXXV, 372–373.
5. GW, XXXV, 373, 383; HH, VI, 195; Smith, *Adams*, II, 925.
6. GW, XXXV, 403, 413–414.
7. Adams, *Gallatin*, 182; F, VII, 430–431; GW, XXXV, 302n; GW, D, IV, 248.
8. Baker, *After*, 314.
9. *Claypoole's American Daily Advertiser*, Philadelphia, 2/23/97; F, VII, 431–432.
10. GW, XXXV, 409.
11. GW, XXXV, 385–386.
12. Adams, *To Wife*, II, 244–247.
13. Baker, 343–345; F, VII, 436–437.
14. *Herald*, New York, 3/11/97; Scharf and Westcott, *Philadelphia*, I, 488.

36: FRIENDS AND STRANGERS

1. GW, Memorandum, "Household Furniture," containing two columns, one headed "furnished by the United States," the other, "purchased by George Washington" [1797], LC; Smith, *Adams*, II, 923.
2. GW, Memorandum, "Articles in the Green Drawing Room which *will* be sold" [1797], LC.
3. Adams, *To Wife*, II, 235–236; GW, XXXV, 428–429.
4. Eliza Powell to GW, 2/6/97, MtV.
5. Eliza Powell to GW, 2/8/97, MtV.
6. Tobias Lear to GW, 3/9/97, Historical Society of Pennsylvania; Lear to GW, 3/5/97, LC.
7. Lear to GW, 3/20/97, MtV.
8. Invoice signed Joshua Elkins, 5/14/97, LC; Lear to GW, 3/20/97, MtV.
9. Lear to GW, 3/17/97, LC; GW, XXXVII, 577.
10. Baker, *After*, 320; GW, XXXV, 423.
11. GW, XXXV, 471, XXXVI, 65.
12. Fl, W, I, 199.
13. GW, XXXV, 424–425, XXXVI, 85, 314.
14. GW, XXXV, 430–431, XXXVI, 49, 53.

15. GW, XXXV, 455.
16. GW, XXXIV, 488, XXXV, 489, XXXVI, 25.
17. Martha Washington to Eliza Powel, 12/17/97, Rosenbach Foundation; GW, XXXVI, 109n.
18. GW to Powel, 3/6/97, MtV.
19. Powel to GW, 3/11/97, MtV.
20. GW to Powel, 3/26/97, MtV.
21. Fl, W, I, 197–198.
22. F, VII, 469; Charles Hamilton, *Catalogue*, 12/13/1967, 90.
23. Liston, "Journal," 519.
24. GW, XXXVI, 62–63.
25. David Humphreys to GW, 1/1/97, 2/18/97, LC; Ford, *True*, 111; GW, XXXV, 92, 480–481.
26. Lawrence Lewis to GW, 7/24/97, Morristown (N.J.) Historical Society; GW, XXVI, 2–3.
27. Latrobe, *Journal*, 57–58.
28. Correspondence between Nelly Custis and Elizabeth Bordley, MtV; GW, XXXVI, 56.
29. GWPC, 41.
30. Clark, *Greenleaf*, 233ff; GW, XXXVII, 64; GW, *Writings* (Ford), XIII, 501.
31. Custis, *Letters;* GW, XXXIV, 44, XXXV, 284–286, XXXVI, 117–118, 169, 181.
32. GW, XXXVI, 118, 135–137.
33. GW, XXXVI, 136.
34. GW, XXXVI, 181, 421; GWPC, 106ff.
35. GW, XXXVI, 105; Latrobe, 58; Liston, "Letters," 603.
36. G. W. M. Lafayette to GW, 9/23/97, Historical Society of Pennsylvania; same to same, 10/21–22/97, LC; GW, XXXV, 169, XXXVI, 39, 105, 121; GW, D, IV, 261.
37. Cary, *Perkins*, 199.
38. Latrobe, 50–63.
39. Arnariah Frost, Account of Visit to Mount Vernon, MtV.
40. GWPC, 7–8.
41. Washington, *Writings* (Ford), XIII, 500–501; GW, XXXVI, 266.
42. GW, XXXVI, 262–264.

37: GEORGE WASHINGTON, ART COLLECTOR

1. The basic listings of the pictures Washington owned are as follows: "List of landscape prints in the possession of Mount Vernon which are duplicate editions of landscape prints in the mansion during George Washington's residence," n.d., MtV; "Original landscape prints in the Mount Vernon collection," n.d., MtV; George Washington, Household Account Book, Historical Society of Pennsylvania; Washington, "Size of the impression," two mss. identically headed, LC; Mount Vernon *Inventory;* GW, XXXV, 454–455.
2. GW, II, 333–334.
3. The exact provenance of these prints is not known.
4. Fl, W, III, 25–26; GW, XXVIII, 504.
5. John Trumbull to GW, 3/24/79, MtV; GW, XXXI, 425–426, XXXIV, 411, XXXVI, 367, XXXVII, 124, 150, 247–248, 382–383, 426.
6. Floyd, "Portraits," 773; GW, XXIX, 70, XXXVI, 321.
7. GW, XXXVII, 78–79.
8. GW, XXX, 24–25.
9. GW, XXXI, 426.
10. Floyd; Hunter, *Quebec*, 197.
11. GW, XXXVII, 290.
12. GW, XXXV, 442.
13. Fl, W, III, chap. XXVI.

14. Floyd, 770; GW, II, 23.
15. Dunlap, *History*, I, 394–395; Pleasants, *Four*, 117–140.
16. Washington, Account Book, 4/16/93.
17. Pleasants, 119.
18. GW, XXXIII, 83.
19. Washington, Account Book, 4/28/94.
20. Washington, Account Book, 1/30/97.
21. Pleasants, 11–30; *Portfolio*, 3rd ser., II (1813), 117–122.
22. GW, XXXVII, 338.
23. GW, XXXV, 441–442, 438.
24. Lear to GW, 3/15/97, LC.
25. GW, XXXIV, 138.

38: INCOME IN RETIREMENT

1. Fl, W, III, 158.
2. GW, XXXVII, 369.
3. Clark, *Greenleaf*, 27; GW, XXXVI, 256–257.
4. GW, XXXV, 457, XXXVI, 76–77, 121.
5. GW, XXXVI, 121, 141–142.
6. GW, XXXVI, 256–257.
7. GW, XXXVI, 256–257, 295–300.
8. GW, XXXV, 507, XXXVI, 67.
9. Receipt, Bartholomew Dandridge to Robert Lewis, 9/9/95, MtV.
10. GW, XXXVII, 211.
11. GW, XXXVI, 391.
12. GW, XXXVI, 82–84, etc., XXXVII, 176–177, 215, etc.; Prussing, *Estate*, 464ff.
13. GW, XXXVII, 170–171.
14. GW, XXXV, 497.
15. GW, XXXVI, 146–147.
16. Bacon-Foster, *Potomac*, 95ff; GW, XXXVII, 330; Niemcewicz, *Under*, 102.
17. GW, XXXVI, 264, 276, 381; GW, D, IV, 270n.
18. Bryan, *Capital*, I, 216ff; Clark, *Greenleaf*, 114–115; GW, XXXIV, 247.
19. Bryan, 236.
20. Bryan, 264, 267–268; GW, XXXV, 309–310.
21. GW, XXXVI, 437, XXXVII, 149, 336–337, 342–345, 376; Niemcewicz, 86.
22. Clark, 255.
23. GW, XXXVII, 72, 387.
24. GW, XXXVI, 257, XXXVII, 430.
25. GW, XXXVII, 251–252, 351–352; Prussing, *Estate*, 101–103.
26. GW, XXXVII, 439.

39: THE RETIRED LION ROARS

1. GW, XXXV, 440, 446–447, 471.
2. GW, XXXV, 430, 446–447; WG, I, 495–496.
3. Smith, *Adams*, II, 930.
4. F, VII, 462; GW, XXXV, 456–457.
5. GW, XXXV, 457, 490.
6. GW, XXXV, 453.
7. GW, XXXV, 490.
8. GW, XXXV, 164.
9. GW, XXXV, 469; XXXVI, 89; GW, D, IV, 283.
10. GW, XXXVI, 28, 89, 94.
11. GW, XXXV, 475, XXXVI, 90.
12. GW, XXXV, 488.
13. M, III, 267–268, 302, 306.
14. JF, X, 311–312.

15. GW, XXXVI, 156.
16. GW, XXXVI, 183–184, 194–237; Monroe, *View*.
17. JF, VIII, 183, 190.
18. GW, XXXVI, 156, 175–176.
19. S, W, XI, 501–502.
20. GW, XXXVI, 52–53, 82.
21. Dauer, "Nicholases," 348–349.
22. GW, XXXVI, 81–82.
23. Dauer, 349–350.
24. Dauer, 351–352.
25. GW, XXXVI, 185.
26. GW, XXXVI, 182–184.
27. Bushrod Washington to GW, 3/13/98, MtV; *Virginia Gazette and General Advertiser*, Richmond, 7/3/98, 7/24/98.
28. Bushrod Washington to GW, 8/7/98, transcript, MtV.
29. GW, XXXVI, 408–409.
30. Bushrod Washington to GW, 8/28/98, MtV; GW, XXXVI, 419–420, XXXVII, 81.
31. Dauer, 349; M, III, 309.
32. GW, XXXVI, 69.

40: A NEW CALL TO ARMS

1. GWPC, 171; GW, XXXVI, 179.
2. GW, XXXVI, 248, 254, 272.
3. GW, XXXVI, 15, 39–40, XXXVII, 132.
4. HH, VI, 289–290.
5. GW, XXXVI, 271–274.
6. HH, VI, 293–294.
7. GW, XXXVII, 291.
8. AA, VIII, 572–573.
9. James McHenry to GW, 3/26/98, LC; Steiner, *McHenry*, 307.
10. GW, XXXVI, 312.
11. GW, XXXVI, 457–458.
12. GW, XXXVI, 304–312.
13. GW, XXXVI, 318–320.
14. Smith, *Adams*, II, 972.
15. GW, XXXVI, 396, XXXVII, 99.
16. GW, XXXVI, 396; Steiner, 308.
17. GW, XXXVI, 323, 329; PP, III, 419.
18. GW, XXXVI, 323–327.
19. AA, VIII, 573–574.
20. AA, VIII, 575.
21. HH, VI, 316–317.
22. GW, XXXVI, 328–329.
23. GW, XXXVI, 332, 339, 477–478; S, W, XI, 533–544.
24. GW, XXXVI, 331, 398–399.
25. GW, XXXVI, 332.
26. GW, XXXVI, 310, 333–334.
27. GW, XXXVI, 335.
28. GW, XXXVI, 329–332.
29. GW, XXXVI, 345–347.
30. S, W, XI, 542.

41: A SAD AFFAIR

1. GW, XXXVI, 386.
2. GW, XXXVI, 341.

3. GW, XXXVI, 390.
4. Fl, *W*, II, 518.
5. GW, XXXVI, 339–341, 356–357, 433.
6. GW, XXXVI, 375.
7. GW, XXXVI, 30–31, 45, 299–300, 361.
8. GW, XXXVI, 361–362, 381, 434.
9. GW, XXXVI, 347n–349n, 396; S, *W*, XI, 534–537.
10. HH, VI, 331.
11. GW, XXXVI, 393–401.
12. GW, XXXVI, 402–403.
13. GW, XXXVI, 420, 423, 435, 444, 446; GW, *D*, IV, 283n.
14. S, *W*, XI, 540–541.
15. GW, XXXVI, 432.
16. GW, XXXVI, 441–443; Steiner, *McHenry,* 337.
17. AA, VIII, 587–588; GW, XXXVI, 442.
18. James McHenry to GW, 10/10/98, LC; GW, XXXVI, 452; Steiner, 337.
19. McHenry to GW, 10/10/98.
20. GW, XXXVI, 463; Smith, *Adams,* II, 982.
21. GW, XXXVI, 452.
22. GW, XXXVI, 453–462.
23. GW, XXXVI, 474.
24. GW, XXXVI, 476–477.
25. AA, VIII, 600–601.
26. GW, XXXVI, 502.
27. GW, XXXVI, 501.

42: PLATEAUS ON A DESCENDING PATH

1. GW, XXXVII, 24.
2. GW, XXXVII, 13, 25, 60; GW, *D*, IV, 237.
3. GW to Eliza Powel, 12/9/98, MtV.
4. GW, XXXVI, 505, XXXVII, 14ff.
5. GW, *D*, IV, 288–290.
6. GW to Powel, 11/7/98, 12/1/98, 4/9/98; Eliza Powel to GW, 12/7/98, all MtV.
7. GW, XXXVI, 407; Logan, *Logan,* 86.
8. GW, XXXVII, 18–20.
9. GW, XXXVII, 16–17, 51.
10. GW, XXXVII, 32–58.
11. GW, XXXVII, 60–61, 409.
12. GW, XXXVII, 59, 77.
13. GW, XXXVII, 163; GWPC, 51–52.
14. Eliza Powel to Bushrod Washington, 4/28/99; file of correspondence between Nelly Custis and Elizabeth Bordley, MtV; GW, XXXVII, 169.
15. GW, XXXVII, 108–109.
16. GWPC, 450.
17. GW, XXXVII, 109–112, 127–129.
18. GW, XXXVI, 304 (misdated); GW, *D*, IV, 298–299.
19. James McAlpin to GW, 2/15/99, LC; Eliza Powel to GW, 4/28/99, MtV; GW, XXXVII, 152.
20. GW, XXXVII, 206, 230–231, 254.
21. McAlpin to GW, 6/24/99, 6/27/99, LC; GW, XXXVII, 304.

43: A PASSENGER ONLY

1. GW, XXXV, 238, 325–326.
2. GW, XXXII, 189.
3. Alexander Spotswood, Jr., to GW, 12/9/98, MtV; GW, XXXVII, 23–24, 89.

4. GW, XXXVII, 72.
5. GW, XXXVII, 323, 328.
6. GW, XXXVII, 326.
7. Beveridge, *Marshall*, II, 376–378; GW, XXXVI, 420; *Lippincott's Magazine*, II (1868), 623–626; Paulding, *Washington*, II, 191–192.
8. Patrick Henry to GW, 2/12/99, Historical Society of Pennsylvania; GW, XXXVII, 87–90.
9. F, VII, 493; Smith, *Adams*, II, 950.
10. GW, XXXVI, 368.
11. Baker, *After*, 340; *Claypoole's American Daily Advertiser*, Philadelphia, 11/6/98, 11/14/98.
12. HH, VI, 395–396.
13. GW, XXXVII, 137–138.
14. GW, XXXVII, 157–161.
15. GW, XXXVI, 373, 381.
16. GW, XXXVI, 254n.
17. S, W, XI, 560–563.
18. GW, XXXVII, 119–120.
19. AA, VIII, 624–626.
20. Timothy Pickering to GW, 2/21/99, LC.
21. GW, XXXVII, 126n, 132; PP, III, 387–388.
22. GW, XXXVII, 141–143.
23. GW, XXXVII, 143–144.
24. GW, XXXVII, 325–329.
25. F, VII, 595–596; GW, XXXVII, 312; WG, 243, 245–246.
26. GW, XXXVII, 312–314.
27. Jonathan Trumbull to GW, 7/29/99, 8/10/99, MtV.
28. GW, XXXVII, 349.
29. GW, XXXVII, 399.
30. GW, XXXVII, 409–410, 418.
31. GW, XXXVII, 428–429.

44: BLACK MOUNT VERNON

1. GW to James McAlpin, 5/7/97, 6/3/97, photostats at the New-York Historical Society from originals owned in February 1941 by Pelham Hardy; McAlpin to GW, 5/15/97, LC; GW, XXXV, 462, 484.
2. Martha Washington to Eliza Powel, 5/1/97, photostat, MtV; GW, XXXVI, 63, 70, 123–124, 140, 146–149, XXXVII, 578.
3. GW, XXXV, 201–202.
4. GW to Burwell Bassett, 8/11/96, MtV; Joseph Whipple to Oliver Wolcott, 10/10/96, 11/4/96, LC.
5. GW, XXXV, 296–298.
6. Whipple to GW, 12/22/96, LC.
7. GW, XXXV, 297.
8. GW, XXXIV, 293, XXXV, 34–35.
9. GW, XXXVIII, 268.
10. Liston, "Journal," 515.
11. Fl, W, III, 204; GW, XXXI, 160n.
12. GW, XXXVI, 186–187, XXXVII, 581; GW, D, IV, 262n.
13. GW, XXXVII, 367–368.
14. GW, XXXIV, 108, 135, 154, 171, 476.
15. GW, XXXVI, 444–445.
16. GW, XXXVII, 268.
17. GW, XXXII, 454; Mazyck, *Negro*, 8, 14.
18. GW, XXXIV, 145.
19. GW, XXXII, 66.

20. Tobias Lear to William Prescott, 3/4/88, Massachusetts Historical Society; GW, XXXII, 365–366, XXXIII, 277.
21. GW, XXXIII, 204–205; Wall, "Negro," 20–21.
22. GW, XXXIII, 184, 287, XXXIV, 231.
23. GW, XXXII, 184, 196–197, XXXIII, 242.
24. GW, XXXVII, 124.
25. GW, XXX, 175n; Wall, 21.
26. GW, XXXII, 100; Mazyck, 125.
27. GW, XXXIII, 203–204, XXXVII, 11.
28. GW, XXXII, 65, XXXIII, 134, 394–395.
29. GW, XXXI, 186–189, XXXII, 65–66.
30. Wall, 23–24.
31. Niemcewicz, Vine, 100–101.
32. GW, XXXVII, 256–258; GW, D, III, 15–22.
33. GW, XXXIV, 427, 448, 452.
34. Parkinson, Tour, II, 448; Wall, 23.
35. Wall, 25.
36. GW, XXIX, 154, 199, XXX, 400.
37. Lewis, Robert, "Diary of his trip to New York with Martha Washington, May, 1789," LC; Humphreys, Poem, 10.
38. GW, XXXI, 375ff.
39. Fl, W, III, 45.
40. Jordan, Black, 238ff.
41. GW, XXII, 65–66, XXXVII, 256–268; GW, D, III, 15–22.
42. GW, XXXIV, 501–503, XXXVII, 307, 338–339.
43. GW, XXXVII, 276–278.
44. Abigail Adams to sister, 12/21/1800, Massachusetts Historical Society.
45. GWPC, 12; Prussing, Estate, chap. XIII.
46. GW, XXXIV, 47.
47. Freehling, "Slavery," 86; McColley, Slavery, 21, 71.
48. Cohen, "Jefferson"; Freehling, 90; Jordan, 429–481; M, IV, 494–498.

45: FARMER WASHINGTON

1. GWPC, 168–169.
2. GW, XXXIII, 155, XXXV, 356–357, XXXVII, 194–195.
3. GW, XXXVI, 240, XXXVII, 16–17, 246, 372.
4. GW, XXXV, 501–502.
5. GW, XXXVI, 286.
6. James Anderson to GW, 5/22/98, LC; GW, XXXVI, 110–113, 266.
7. GW, XXXVI, 267.
8. GW, XXXV, 352, XXXVI, 141, 172, 277, XXXVII, 216; Niemcewicz, Vine, 100.
9. GW, XXXVI, 269, 277, 283–287.
10. Richard Parkinson to GW, 8/28/98, LC; GW, XXXVI, 80, 106, 167, XXXVII, 4, 6–8, 24.
11. Parkinson, Tour, I, 3, 6–9, 48–63.
12. GW, XXXVII, 354, 357–358, 368–370.
13. GW, XXXVII, 376–378, 383, 386, 413.
14. GW, XXXVII, 463–472.
15. Fitzpatrick, Will; GW, XXXVII, 275–303; Prussing, Estate.

46: DEATH OF A HERO

1. GW, D, IV, 320.
2. Tobias Lear to mother, 12/16/99, MtV.
3. GW, Writings (Ford), XIV, 425.
4. GW, D, IV, 320.

5. The account of Washington's final illness weaves together the following sources:
(a) Tobias Lear's diary note, 1/14/99. This exists in two slightly variant versions.
One is published in Lear, *Letters*, 129–136, and S, *W*, I, 255–260. The other appears in Washington, *Writings* (Ford), XIV, 245–255. (b) Lear to his mother,
1/16/99, copy at MtV. (c) James Craik and Elisha D. Dick, "Particular Account
of the Late Illness and Death of George Washington," 12/21/99, quoted (with
other Lear letters) in Washington, *Writings* (Ford), XIV, 255–259. These accounts
bear the marks of complete authenticity. Tampering would most obviously have
attributed to Washington Christian sentiments which are completely absent.

47: THE SECOND TERM SURVEYED

1. GW, XXX, 443.
2. GW, XXX, 3–7.
3. M, III, 11.
4. Tobias Lear to David Humphreys, 4/8/93, MtV.
5. HH, VI, 415.
6. HH, VI, 418.
7. Fl, *W*, II, 411–414.
8. HH, IV, 516–519.
9. Conway, *Randolph*, 230.
10. M, IV, 138.
11. Fl, *W*, III, 100.
12. Fl, *W*, III, 375, 387.
13. JF, VII, 27, 68, etc.
14. GW, XXXV, 412, 453, XXXVI, 93.
15. M, III, 268.
16. *Aurora*, Philadelphia, 11/1/96; M, III, 284.
17. F, VI, 590; GW, XXXV, 283, XXXVII, 11.
18. GW to Rev. Elijah Brainerd, 3/2/99, MtV; Decatur, *Private*, 91, 113; GW,
    XXXVII, 252.
19. Jefferson, Heads of Information given me by E. Randolph, n.d., LC; M, III, 297n.
20. Fl, *W*, II, 341–342; GW, XIX, 135.
21. GW, XXXIII, 372, XXXV, 280–281, XXXVI, 173.
22. McColley, *Slavery*, 4, 53–56.
23. M, III, 401–404.
24. GW, XXXVII, 205, 207.
25. GW, XXXVI, 12, 118
26. GW, XXXVII, 100.
27. Bernard, *Retrospections*, 91.

48: GEORGE WASHINGTON

1. JF, IX, 448.
2. Liston, "Journal," 514.
3. GW, XXXIII, 429, 435, XXXVI, 138.
4. GW, XXXVIII, 187.
5. Wilson, *White*, 189–190, 197.
6. JF, IX, 448.
7. Fl, *W*, III, 356; GW, XXXI, 461.
8. GW, XXXV, 480.
9. GW, XXXIII, 501.
10. Clark, *Greenleaf*, 286.
11. GW, XXXVIII, 514.
12. JF, VI, 293.
13. Liston, 516.
14. Fl, *W*, I, 81; GW, XXX, 153.
15. GW, XXXV, 409.

16. GW, XXXVII, 94–95.
17. GW, XXXIII, 95.
18. Fl, *W*, III, 193.
19. GW, XXXIII, 422.
20. AA, IX, 301; GW, XXXVI, 190.
21. GW, XXXIII, 96.
22. JF, VII, 101–102; MH, VI, 216–217; MoH, I, 297–298.
23. Fl, *W*, II, 67–68, III, 143–145.
24. Jefferson, *Papers* (Boyd), VII, 106.
25. Baker, *Character*, 182–185.
26. JF, IX, 449.
27. Baker, 71.
28. GW, XXXVI, 386.

Index

[545]

One of our foremost men of letters, James Thomas Flexner has written with equal distinction in the fields of American history and American art.

In addition to such books as *Doctors on Horseback, The Traitor and the Spy,* and his biography of Washington now complete in four volumes, he is the author of a history of nineteenth-century American painting, *That Wilder Image,* which was awarded the Parkman Prize in 1963, and *The Pocket History of American Painting,* which has been translated into more than twenty languages.

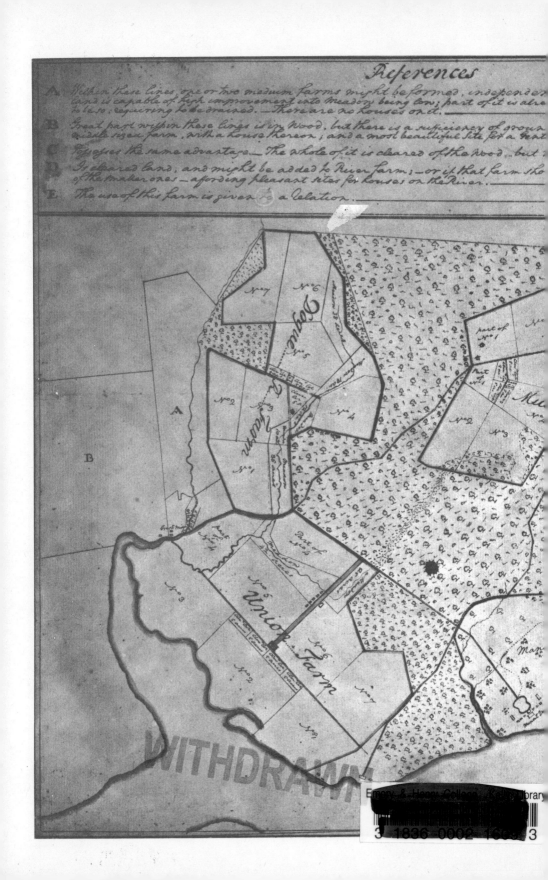